DVD DELIRIUM
VOLUME 4

DVD Delirium Volume 4 first published by FAB Press, August 2010

FAB Press Ltd.
2 Farleigh
Ramsden Road
Godalming
GU7 1QE
England, U.K.

www.fabpress.com

Reviews by
Nathaniel Thompson

A CIP catalogue record for this book is available from the British Library.

ISBN 978-1-903254-62-2

The International Guide to Weird and Wonderful Films on DVD & Blu-ray
Volume 4

reviews by
Nathaniel Thompson

CREDITS

Reviews:
Nathaniel Thompson

Edited by:
Francis Brewster

Design and Layout:
Harvey Fenton

DVD cover designs are copyright © the respective DVD companies,
and the covers are reproduced here in the spirit of publicity.
Picture credits:
101 Films, 4Digital, After Hours, Alternative Cinema, Anchor Bay, Anchor Bay UK,
Arte, Atopia, Barrel, BBC, BFI, Bloody Earth, Blue Underground, BritFilms, Camera
Obscura, Camp, Canvas, Casa Negra, Cecchi Gori, Cinema Abattoir, Cinema Epoch,
Cinema Libre, Code Red, Criterion, Cult Epics, Dark Sky, Dervish Pictures, Dire Wit,
E1, Eros, Eureka, Exploitation Digital, Fantoma, Fox, Halo Park, Impulse, Industrial,
JM Music, Kalashnifilms Atanes, Koch Lorber, Liberation, Lions Gate, Magnolia,
Mars Pictures, Media Blasters, Millennium Storm, Mondo Macabro, Mya, Navarre,
Network, Nucleus, Odeon, Onar, Optimum, Platinum, Polart, Private Screening,
Raincoat Theater, Redemption, Reel, Retro Shock-O-Rama, Retro-Seduction Cinema,
Salvation, Sazuma, Scorpion, Secret Key, Seduction Cinema, Severin, Shameless,
Shock-O-Rama, Shout! Factory, Shriek Show, Silicon Artists, Sony, Sub Rosa,
Subversive, Swinging Axe, Synapse, TLA, Troma, Umbrella, Unearthed, Universal,
Victory Films, Warner.
Any omissions will be corrected in future editions.

INTRODUCTION

How times change! In the four years since *DVD Delirium Vol. 3,* the number of titles on the market has exploded to a level equal to or even beyond the height of the VHS era while a worldwide economic crisis has forced retailers to either shut down or minimise shelf space. As a result, fans of the strange and unusual in cinema must be more resourceful than ever to find their latest fix, with new companies springing up to replace ones that have vanished into the ether and online purchasing now accounting for a larger percentage of sales than ever. Meanwhile studios have tried new formats including digital downloads (sometimes included as bonus discs with DVDs), Blu-rays (which are noted in here where appropriate), and on-demand DVD burning thanks to the experimental Warner Archive program which has unleashed many obscure titles back onto the market. Naturally, you'll read about a few of those long-desired titles within these pages along with the more widely available roster of titles ranging from vintage exploitation to modern horror to far-out art house fare, all of which have many rewards to offer the open-minded.

Each review listing here begins with technical and talent notes to provide some additional information: **"Colour"** or "Black and White" (**"B&W"**), the **year** of film's original release, the running time in minutes (**m.**), the major **director** and **actors**, the name of the DVD company or studio releasing the disc, the video standard (**PAL** or **NTSC**) and region coding ("**R**"), widescreen ("**WS**") format where applicable followed by the aspect ratio (often with **16:9** enhancement, the common industry standard, for higher resolution on widescreen monitor playback), and audio format for multi-channel releases (most often Dolby Digital – "**DD**" – or sometimes "**DTS**"). Multi-region and multi-standard players are also popular in every country, so hopefully this guide will help you determine whether to spend money on an import in preference to your own region's edition.

This fourth edition of *DVD Delirium* can certainly be enjoyed on its own and provides a valuable snapshot of the state of unusual genre entertainment at the close of the format's second decade. If you enjoy it, I would urge you to seek out the previous three volumes, which are also loaded with unique and valuable information about titles you may have missed while perusing your favourite store or online retailer. *DVD Delirium Volume 3* is still in print and available direct from the FAB Press web store (www.fabpress.com), or from all good book retailers. The first two editions are currently out of print, but at the time of writing both are due to be issued as the first ever FAB Press ebooks, so seek them out if you've taken that leap and joined the world of the iPad, Kindle or Sony Reader. Regardless of exactly how you choose to enjoy the *DVD Delirium* series of books, may you have many hours of happy reading and video hunting ahead!

Nathaniel Thompson

THE ALCOVE

Colour, 1984, 91m. / Directed by Joe D'Amato / Starring Lilli Carati, Laura Gemser, Annie Belle, Al Cliver, Roberto Caruso / Severin (US R1 NTSC) / WS (1.78:1) (16:9), X-Rated Kult (Germany R0 PAL) / WS (1.66:1)

 In 1930s Italy at the dawn of the fascist regime, controlling film-maker Elio (*Zombie*'s Al Cliver) comes home from battling on the "dark continent" to find his country estate turning into a hotbed of sexual unrest inflamed by his latest addition to the family, a beautiful and conniving servant named Zerbal (*Black Emanuelle*'s Laura Gemser). Elio's extremely hot-blooded wife, Alessandra (*To Be Twenty*'s Lilli Carati), and her assistant/sometimes lover, Velma (*Laure*'s Annie Belle), are soon drawn into a very hostile, manipulative triangle with Zerbal, which involves lots of girl-on-girl activity. Meanwhile Elio finds his creative impulses (including an unfin-ished manuscript) so stunted he decides instead to mount a homemade stag film involving a domineering nun that goes spectacularly awry, leading to a fiery and deeply ironic finale.

For sleaze fans, *The Alcove* is of primary importance as the initial erotic foray for Joe D'Amato's Filmirage, a company which went on to become an eccentric player in the Eurotrash video market with titles like *Stagefright*, *Ghosthouse*, and softcore films like *11 Days, 11 Nights* and *Blue Angel Café* before morphing into Imperial Entertain-ment. *The Alcove* feels distinctly different from the usual '80s Filmirage fare and more closely resembles Tinto Brass's *The Key* (released a year earlier, not so coincidentally) with its period setting, powdery cinematography, and austere but graphic eroticism, along with a very Brassian prosthetic popping up during the stag film shoot.

Most adventurous D'Amato-philes first encountered this film via its only significant English-language VHS release in the U.K., which was quickly bootlegged all over the grey market. Unfortunately it also lost nearly two minutes of very signif-icant, volatile footage that puts the film into a different realm entirely; while the story still held up fine and established this as one of D'Amato's most accomplished efforts, few people had any idea how far it really went. Import DVDs from the likes of X-Rated Kult eventually popped up, but budget-conscious viewers can finally sample this forbidden fruit in its full-strength form via Severin's DVD, the only anamorphic and complete presentation out there. The 1.78:1 image is slightly more constrained on the top and bottom than the flat 1.66:1 transfers, but nothing seems compositionally affected. Image quality looks fine throughout given the nature of the source, which tends to rely on soft but colourful lensing. The English audio (which, per usual for most '80s Italian films intended for export, is the most legitimate option) sounds fine throughout. Extras include a '90s-era, bizarrely-composed 11-minute video inter-view with D'Amato at a desk talking about his films intercut with a few film clips and the juicy European, English-language theatrical trailer.

ALICE IN WONDERLAND

Colour, 1976, 78m. / Directed by Bud Townsend / Starring Kristine DeBell, Larry Gelman, Bradford Armdexter, Gila Havana, Alan Novak, Bree Anthony, Tony Richards, Juliet Graham, Terri Hall, Jason Williams / Subversive (US R1 NTSC) / WS (1.78:1) (16:9)

Refusing to loosen up and give herself to her gas station attendant boyfriend, buttoned-up librarian Alice (Kristine DeBell) picks up a copy of *Alice in Wonderland* and sings about how she missed out on romantic escapades when she was a kid. Suddenly she's approached by a white rabbit (*The Bob Newhart Show*'s Larry Gelman, hiding out here under the name "Jerry Spelman"), who says he's late for a date with the queen ("a bitch!"). She follows him into a magical world where she gets molested by mischievous animals, attends a tea party with a very forward Mad Hatter (Alan Novak), romps on a hillside with siblings Tweedledum and Tweedledee (Bree Anthony and Tony Richards), and runs up against the Queen of Hearts (Juliet Graham from *Bloodsucking Freaks*) before returning home a little wiser and a lot less inhibited.

After the success of the sci-fi spoof *Flesh Gordon*, enterprising young producer/actor Bill Osco continued mixing juvenile pop culture with smut for an equally ambitious and even curiouser follow-up, a naughty musical version of the children's classic best known to cinephiles as the inspiration for a Disney classic. As with *Flesh*, it was filmed as an effects-laden narrative film with a handful of explicit sequences which never made it into the final product, though in this case a subsequent reissue through Essex Films added back those few minutes of graphic close-ups (some performed by body doubles).

Featuring songs like "What's a Nice Girl Like You Doing on a Knight Like This?", *Alice in Wonderland* is an engagingly sweet and witty film that still holds up as genuine entertainment. Much of its appeal rests with the charming DeBell, a pretty and charismatic actress who had appeared in *Playboy* and went on to a mainstream career in films like *Meatballs* and *The Main Event* as well as lots of television. *Flesh Gordon* star Jason Williams pops up fleetingly as well, while the rest of the cast contains some familiar faces from the naughtier side of the fence, most notably busy X-rated star/dancer Terri Hall, who turns up in numerous roles and shows off her gift for fluid body movement. After the success of this film, Osco, DeBell, and Williams reteamed again three years later for the more mainstream *Cheerleaders' Wild Weekend*, a sex-free drive-in outing also known as *The Great American Girl Robbery*.

Upon its original release, *Alice in Wonderland* carried a self-imposed X rating and was definitely softcore, with much of the dialogue hilariously referring to eye-popping activity that occurred just outside of the frame. Its distribution was handled by several parties over the years (including under the radar handling by 20th Century-Fox!), and its success prompted Osco to reinstate a few seconds of graphic oral DeBell footage as well as some crude insert shots with body doubles (mainly at the end, which seriously hampers the flow of the film); only the added Tweedledum/Tweedledee footage really works at all, and the XXX variant is really a curiosity worth seeing once for novelty value. If you're new to the film, stick with the single-X version (which was later trimmed slightly to gain an R rating by the MPAA) as it really works better with the concept of the film. Both the R-rated and hardcore cuts have been widely available on home video since the dawn of VHS; the soft version in particular turned up at every single mom and pop video shop in the 1980s. The hardcore version popped up on video in a truly sorry transfer from VCX and is best avoided. Fortunately Subversive Cinema has given it a more respectable treatment with its DVD

A

release, which features anamorphic transfers of both versions. Image quality is obviously superior to any video version before (and probably better than any of the ragged remaining theatrical prints); flesh tones look more orange and oversaturated than they should, so prepare to tweak your TV settings a bit. The mono audio on both sounds fine. The general release version opens with a quick, amusing restoration demonstration ("over 500,000 individual corrections!") as well as the General National logo, while the hardcore one begins with a disclaimer about the poor condition of the surviving material (which appears to have been inserted into the body of the other transfer) as well as a scratchy Essex Films logo. Both versions contain the same gag opening credits, complete with "Underwater Nude Volleyball Sequences by Jacques Coote" and "Hawaiian Number Staged by Halelokie Steinberg". The sole extra is a solid featurette, "*Alice in Wonderland*: Back Down the Rabbit Hole", which was shot and edited by maverick Australian director Mark Savage. It features industry vet William Margold, current adult actress Lena Romane, and, believe it or not, Larry Gelman (who doesn't get mentioned on the packaging!) talking about the film and its place in classic adult history. Obviously Gelman talks the most about the production itself ("It was a very strict set; they wouldn't allow me to see what they were doing!"), while the surprisingly intelligent and articulate Romane talks about being a fan of the film and her appreciation for Osco's filmmaking and Margold covers the stories of the various participants and places it in context with the direction the industry has taken since (with a particularly grisly summation at the end involving sex and stomach acid). For some reason the theatrical trailer isn't included, but you can find it on plenty of readily-available compilations.

ALL THE BOYS LOVE MANDY LANE

Colour, 2006, 90m. / Directed by Jonathan Levine / Starring Amber Heard, Michael Welch, Anson Mount, Whitney Able, Aaron Himselstein, Edwin Hodge / Optimum (DVD & Blu-ray, UK R0 PAL/HD) / WS (2.35:1) (16:9) / DD5.1

One of the unluckiest American horror films in many a moon, this better-than-average slasher film from the future director of the critical darling *The Wackness* shifted distributor hands and release dates in its native country for over two years, not even earning a straight-to-DVD release from one-time owners The Weinstein Company despite considerable fan praise at rare screening events. These events conspired to inflate its reputation to cult status in the horror community even among the many who never saw it, making the sole legitimate release in the U.K. (as of this writing) the only, hotly-desired legal viewing option.

Nine months after her onetime best friend Emmet (Michael Welch) goaded a drunk jock into taking a fatal high dive off the roof of a booze-sodden pool party, the recently "hot" Mandy Lane (Amber Heard) has moved on to a different social class at her Texas high school consisting of petty but powerful party animals. She accepts an invitation from the clique's leader, Red (Aaron Himselstein), to spend the weekend with their buddies at a ranch out in the countryside. However, a hood-wearing Emmet decides to crash the party with a shotgun and other deadly implements, ramping up the body count over the course of two days as the survivors scramble for their lives.

Don't worry, the killer's identity isn't even close to a major spoiler as Emmet is clearly unmasked in the most nonchalant fashion possible well before the halfway mark. A certain Columbine-esque unease hangs over much of this film, which takes pains to present more realistic teens than usual with age-appropriate actors who don't necessarily look like they all stepped out of *Gossip Girl*. Of course, it also succumbs to that failing of most '80s slashers, namely offering an entire roster of characters without a single sympathetic personality in sight. Fortunately director Jonathan Levine still keeps viewers sufficiently engaged by tweaking the formula enough to keep them off balance, such as the aforementioned lack of mystery over the assailant, the considerable amount of running time spent in the sun-bleached brightness of daylight, and the unpredictable level of explicitness of the killings with the most notorious and graphic of the bunch involving the butt of a shotgun used in a very inappropriate manner. The sting-in-the-tail ending is also executed with a great deal of verve and sends the film out on a suitably queasy note.

Optimum's release looks quite good considering the extreme colour and light manipulation used throughout the film, ranging from deliberately grainy night scenes to sun-baked day shots with blown-out white levels. The surround audio is mainly limited to the atmospheric music track, while the minimal extras include the U.K. theatrical trailer and a half-hour interview with Heard who talks about the making of the film and the appeal of playing her role.

ALL THE RIGHT NOISES

Colour, 1969, 91m. / Directed by Gerry O'Hara / Starring Tom Bell, Olivia Hussey, Judy Carne, John Standing, Lesley-Anne Down, Edward Higgins / BFI (DVD & Blu-ray, UK R0 PAL/HD) / WS (1.85:1) (16:9)

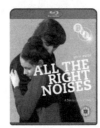

One evening on the metro after a stage rehearsal, theatrical electrician Len Lewin (*The L-Shaped Room*'s Tom Bell) strikes up a flirtatious conversation with pretty young chorus girl Val (*Black Christmas*'s Olivia Hussey) and rapidly plunges into an affair. Len isn't exactly forthcoming that he also happens to be married to Joy (*Rowan & Martin's Laugh-In*'s Judy Carne) and has two small children, but Val has a bigger surprise; when she shows up in her school uniform, Len learns she's still a couple months shy of sixteen, the legal age of consent. As their relationship develops and the wife has to go out of town for a while, the couple must deal with the obvious obstacles while deciding what's best for themselves in the long run.

This surprisingly even-tempered and restrained film was made at the height of Swinging London fever on the big screen, but despite the vivid colour schemes on display, this is definitely a child of the British New Wave with an emphasis on subdued realism and emotional honesty. The film never goes for melodrama, so don't expect any violent deaths or traumatic abortions here. Instead the viewer gets to simply savour three terrific lead performances (Hussey in particular was a hot item fresh off the smash hit *Romeo & Juliet*) while the film also marks a rare directorial effort for Gerry O'Hara, a very busy assistant director on such films as *Tom Jones*, *Exodus* and *Our Man in Havana*; his main directorial career gets quite a bit weirder with credits including the harrowing *The Brute*, the junky *The Mummy Lives*, and one of the trashiest films ever made, *The Bitch*. However, *All the Right Noises* marks one of his few personal efforts and is certainly worthy of rediscovery. His clever eye and impeccable

A

knack for dramatic pacing result in a small, fragile miniature seemingly designed for discovery rather than widespread acclaim, essentially the sort of thing you find flipping channels on a dreary afternoon and can't help but watch.

Held up by distributor 20th Century-Fox for two years in most territories, this film never really found much of an audience but has been given a second lease of life as part of the BFI's superlative Flipside series. The transfer is taken from the best surviving archival print and has been restored to the most pleasing condition possible, but bear in mind this is still obviously below their usual top-notch standards. Detail quality is as good as the source will allow and colours are generally vibrant (though traces of the print's tendency to turn green still remain in a few of the darker moments), and whites are more blown-out than usual. That said, it's still comparable with watching an above-average repertory screening and probably the best it's ever going to look.

The biggest extra on this release is "The Spy's Wife", an amusing 1972 half-hour short with Bell returning as a British secret agent who goes off for a mission while his wife (Dorothy Tutin) dabbles with a Communist spy (*The Apple*'s Vladek Sheybal). It's a fun little diversion with a nice twist in the end, and once again it's nice to see Bell in an all-too-rare leading role. However, the most fascinating bonus here is an unseen, still-raw 17-minute interview with Hussey and co-star Leonard Whiting talking about their recently completed work on *Romeo & Juliet* with Bernard Braden for a projected but never realised TV show called *Now and Then*. The pair (who became an item during filming) discuss their experiences as young performers tackling their first huge lead roles and their living conditions during shooting as well as their aspirations for the future. Hussey is stunning as always, and it's interesting to see the gifted Whiting talk freely about his

love of acting considering he vanished from the screen after 1973's *Frankenstein: The True Story*, leaving many baffled fans in his wake. The thick enclosed booklet contains liner notes by O'Hara, Robert Murphy, pieces on "The Spy's Wife" by Vic Pratt and producer Julian Holloway, notes about the lost interview and two bios.

ALL THE SINS OF SODOM

B&W, 1968, 88m. / Directed by Joseph W. Sarno / Secret Key (US R1 NTSC)

 No other exploitation filmmaker has as many "lost classics" as Joe Sarno, the incredibly prolific softcore pioneer who worked in both the U.S. and Europe and whose past titles have been thoroughly covered here. One of the most tantalising of his early obscurities has been the evocatively-titled *All the Sins of Sodom*, which was prominently featured in the breakthrough *Re: Search* book, *Incredibly Strange Films*. (One of Sarno's other big missing titles, the great *Young Playthings*, now apparently exists only in blurry ancient video masters; a real shame if that remains the case.) Now after decades of only seeing tantalising still photographs, weird cinema fans can finally lay eyes on the real item thanks to Secret Key's DVD release, taken from the recently discovered original negative.

Shot in black and white and considerably moodier than Sarno's earlier films, this film marks something of a turning point to the more psychologically and sexually intense work which lay ahead. The story is mainly a three-person study (none of the actors are credited, but one of them is Peggy Steffans, Sarno's right hand on many of his films as well as his future wife). The centre of the triangle here is

Henning, a (very hairy) fashion photographer with a penchant for draping fabric over his naked models and, in the opening sequence, posing them among lots of string. His agent encourages him to go upscale by using his muse, Leslie, to craft a coffee table book of erotic photography, but things swerve into dark Fassbinder territory when their love nest is upset by the arrival of Joyce, a baby-faced, dark-haired troublemaker who seduces Henning and starts to flush all his ambitions down the toilet. The two women are soon spitting nails at each other (the dialogue here is some of Sarno's nastiest), and of course it's all bound to end in tears.

Not surprisingly, most of the outrageous sins you can think of aren't here – just lots of extramarital sex and some light lesbianism. However, Sarno uses the limited setting (it was shot in a real photography studio in New York for chump change) and occasional wintry exteriors to craft a visually striking, shadow-filled atmosphere of debauchery and doom that rivets the eye from the opening frames. The DVD features an excellent and virtually spotless transfer, easily one of the company's best, along with the usual host of special features. Peggy turns in a solo commentary track this time and recalls this period in her husband's career, when he had returned from Sweden and was given money by a New York distributor to churn out films like this and its closest contemporary, *Vibrations*. Sarno himself can be seen in a new video interview where he talks briefly about making the film and his early relationship with his wife, though no one really sheds light on the actors' real identities. Also included is raw video footage from the film's revival screening in Austin at the Alamo Drafthouse, the usual horde of Sarno trailers (Secret Key's building up quite the respectable library now), and a handy booklet featuring the usual well-researched liner notes by Sarno

biographer Michael J. Bowen, who rattles some nifty facts illustrated with the film's rare poster under its alternative titles, *All the Sins of Satan* (which would have made for quite a different film).

ALTIN COCUK

B&W, 1966, 82m. / Directed by Memduh Ün / Starring Göksel Arsoy, Altan Günbay, Sevda Nur, Reha Yurdakul / Onar (Greece R0 PAL)

The wave of James Bond imitations multiplying across cinema screens in the mid-'60s seemed to come from every direction, and even Turkey got in on the act with a string of spy and action films that emphasised mayhem and titillation to compensate for considerably lower budgets. Among the more memorable of these is *Altin Cocuk* ("Golden Boy"), which feels a bit like a Matt Helm movie filtered through the sensibility of Something Weird Video. Right off the bat you get opening titles unspooling over a dark-haired, buxom beauty gyrating in her underwear in front of a mirror before shaking her goodies in front of our hero, superspy Altin Cocuk (Göksel Arsoy), with whom she hops into bed while a nearby scuba-outfitted villain climbs up the building outside and takes out the stud with a harpoon. "You killed my golden boy!" the woman screams, only for the killer to remove his gear and reveal himself to be... the exact same guy. "He spent five and a half months trying to look like me", he explains, faster than you can say From Russia with Love. "We knew him as 'The Wolf.'" Apparently exerted, he decides to take a vacation and hops a Pan Am flight to London (cue the jazzy travelogue footage with multiple girlfriends), while back in

A

Istanbul, baddies are running rampant shooting people and thwarted secret messages with wild abandon. Turns out this mayhem is all the handiwork of a nefarious, Blofeld-esque bad baddie (Altan Günbay) who enjoys petting a white kitty cat when he isn't plotting to blow up Turkey with an atomic bomb. Can our Golden Boy stop it in time when he isn't distracted by all the belly dancers and extended fist fights? Watch and find out!

The technical calibre of Onar's releases of Turkish cult titles continues to climb pleasingly high with this release, a fast-paced, surprisingly accomplished spy outing that should please any fans of James Bond or his numerous contemporaries. The two leads do a fine job with their comic book-inspired portrayals, and the film doles out kinkiness and violence on a scale that would actually make Ian Fleming proud – particularly a nasty bit involving a near-naked woman hanging in a noose on a fast-melting block of ice, a scenario later repeated more tastelessly with full nudity and piano wire in *Ilsa, She-Wolf of the SS*. You also get the old spikes-through-the-ceiling bit and juicy lines like "I can imagine your screams like a melody", not to mention a few dozen shapely Turkish and European women in bikinis running around. What's not to love? The video transfer is taken from very clean and solid film elements, perhaps the best seen yet for a Turkish film, and apart from some motion blurring during of the action scenes, there's really nothing to quibble about here. The Turkish mono audio sounds fine and brassy, with a non-stop music score including a theme song for our hero and a few incidental bits that will sound more than a tad familiar to fans of *Goldfinger*'s Fort Knox finale.

Along with the welcome nifty insert poster, Onar's DVD contains the usual fun array of extras including a new interview with Günbay, an amiable guy who stayed bald through most of the hundred-plus movies he made over the years and whose contracts even included a "shaved head term". Apparently he wasn't a very good swimmer either. Also present are a filmography of Turkish spy films (including this film's two sequels, which would be great to see as well), a photo gallery, main cast bios, and some tasty Onar trailers both old and new including *Casus Kiran*, *The Serpent's Tale*, the Mancini-flavoured *Rongo Gestapo'ya Karsi*, *Kizil Tug Cengiz Han*, and a fragment of a lost Kilink film without an onscreen title, featuring some more, ahem, "John Barry-esque" music.

AMERICAN PUNKS

Colour, 1997, 91m. / Directed by Michele Pacitto / Starring Mike Passion, Lonnie Jackson, Ron Wicks, Suzanne Labatt / Bloody Earth (US R0 NTSC)

Before directing the by-the-numbers lesbian vampire quickie *Daughter of Dracula*, director Michele Pacitto cut his teeth on this ragged but intriguing indie which features no lesbianism but plenty of gross-out nihilism. Angry punk Bobby (Mike Passion) thinks a snotty yuppie he persecuted earlier is responsible for killing his best friend and embarks on a vicious crime spree to even the score. Unfortunately he seriously miscalculates the full scope of his plan, which leads to a very nasty final showdown.

Set in the backstreets and bars of Detroit, the film is unevenly paced but benefits from Passion's roaring lead performance and some welcome bursts of violence and grotesque comedy which at least come off better than if Troma had been responsible. A number of indie Michigan punk bands contribute to the lively soundtrack, including Shock Therapy, Lab Animals, and Itchy Wiggle Christ. Part of the label's "Generation eXploitation" line of '90s DIY cult films, this release (also available on VHS under the lousy title of *Generation X-tinct*) comes with a Pacitto audio commentary, some casting audition tapes, a particularly foul "Alternative Steak Hut Scene", a deleted monologue sequence, and trailers for other shot-on-video releases.

AMOK TRAIN

Colour, 1989, 94m. / Directed by Jeff Kwitny / Starring Mary Kohnert, Bo Svenson, Savina Gersak, Victoria Zinny / Shriek Show (US R1 NTSC) / WS (2.35:1) (16:9) / DD2.0

 As most fans of Euro horror know, it was common practice to retitle films over and over to associate them as closely as possible with other, more famous titles. Thus you wound up with the likes of *Cruel Jaws*, *Alien Contamination*, and in the case of Mario Bava's *Shock*, a completely ridiculous retitling in America as *Beyond the Door II*. One of the last and most absurd entries in this trend was *Amok Train*, a last-gasp Italian horror film from producer Ovidio G. Assonitis who decided to issue it in America as *Beyond the Door III* (from Columbia Pictures, no less!). Unlike the Bava film, at least this one has some sort of Satanic storyline to justify this marketing ploy, and the addition of Yugoslavian and American financing as well as a collection of mostly unknown international actors gallivanting through Serbia results in a very strange but unmistakably unique horror film. While many horror films tend to push any story plausibility to the edge of disbelief, *Amok Train* gleefully charges off the

tracks in its first act and never looks back. The harebrained story begins with seven SoCal teenagers doing a Balkan studies course in Europe, with Beverly (Mary Kohnert) particularly keen to explore her local ancestry. An opportunity arises in the form of mysterious anthropology professor Dr. Andromolek (Bo Svenson), who guides them to a woodland pagan festival that turns out to be the refuge for a Satanic cult. Drugged and nearly killed, all but one of the kids escape with their lives and climb aboard a nearby train. Unfortunately the forces of evil are not as easily discouraged as the train itself, no kidding, becomes possessed by a demonic force which wipes out nearly everyone aboard and takes the kids both on and off the tracks for a hell of a ride. Much dismemberment ensues as Beverly is informed (by the train, natch) that she's actually promised to Satan and is trapped into fulfilling her destiny, even if all her friends are torn to shreds in the process.

Apart from the always entertaining Svenson, *Amok Train* boasts a hilariously under equipped cast (including the apparently sedated Victoria Zinny, who appeared in tons of schlocky Joe D'Amato '80s films) as well as loads of over-the-top gore, much of which was scissored from the domestic VHS releases. Fortunately Shriek Show's release contains the full, plasma-spattered version with lots of latex and plaster heads spewing Kayro across the screen. Perhaps more perturbing for horror fans is the grinding synth score by Carlo Maria Cordio (obviously inspired by his work on *Aenigma*) and the sheer stupidity of the plot (including a train vs. lake scene you won't forget anytime soon), but rest assured, you'll never be bored for a second. Though films like these almost always went straight to video, *Amok Train* was actually shot in scope which meant its surprisingly slick and atmospheric widescreen compositions were diced to ribbons for home

A

A

viewers. The DVD reinstates the original framing which helps immensely on a visual level along with the added unrated footage. (The print still bears the *Beyond the Door III* title which is bound to confuse more than one consumer out there.) The biggest extra here is a half-hour chat with Assonitis who talks about the genesis of the film (basically a favour for some ambitious family friends) and its biggest cinematic influence, *Runaway Train* – something you'll never hear about any other '80s horror film. He also talks about his rationale for the title changes, his experiences just before this film working for the notorious Cannon Films, and his discovery of James Cameron, a topic still mired in more than a bit of controversy. Also included is a much shorter interview with talented cinematographer Adolfo Bartoli, a batch of other Shriek Show trailers, and a promo gallery.

AND THEN THERE WERE NONE

Colour, 1974, 94m. / Directed by Peter Collinson / Starring Oliver Reed, Elke Sommer, Richard Attenborough, Herbert Lom, Stéphane Audran, Gert Fröbe, Adolfo Celi, Maria Rohm, Alberto de Mendoza, Charles Aznavour / Optimum (UK R2 PAL) / WS (1.66:1) (16:9), Artedis (France R2 PAL) / WS (1.78:1) (16:9)

The third big screen outing for Agatha Christie's immortal whodunit construction is perhaps the most misunderstood, relocating the action to a sumptuous desert hotel (actually the Hotel Shah Abbas in Iran) two hundred miles away from civilisation. Flown in by helicopter, ten strangers are brought together for a weekend of murder and mystery as their first night is interrupted by a tape-recorded stranger (voiced by a never-seen Orson Welles) informing the guests that they are all murderers who will now be punished after escaping any legal punishment. One by one they all die via methods accorded to the children's nursery rhyme, "Ten Little Indians", before a final showdown reveals the surprising culprit.

As with the prior two versions, this adaptation uses the tricky happy ending Christie devised for her stage version of the story rather than the merciless finale from her original novel (which inspired the now senseless title). While Rene Clair's classic 1945 version retained the story's island setting off the British coast, the second 1965 film from producer Harry Alan Towers became more of an all-star showcase located at a Swiss chalet with an eccentric international cast. When *Murder on the Orient Express* proved to be a smash hit in 1974, Towers decided to revive the property again with an even wilder cast; perhaps most interestingly, the passage of time between versions had also seen European cinemas filled with stylish *gialli*, Claude Chabrol thrillers, and Jess Franco exploitation films. The influence of these is unmistakable here as we get Chabrol's leading lady (Stéphane Audran), Franco's frequent starlet (Maria Rohm) and composer (Bruno Nicolai, providing a very lush and memorable score), and a string of murders featuring abrasive experimental music and visual nods to Dario Argento, particularly an outdoor strangulation straight out of *The Cat o' Nine Tails*.

The straightforward but sometimes stylish direction comes courtesy of Peter Collinson, who became one of the U.K.'s most promising filmmakers in the '60s with *The Italian Job*, *The Penthouse*, and *Up the Junction* before stumbling a bit in the '70s with erratic international assignments, though he did still have another masterpiece up his sleeve with the merciless survival classic, *Open Season*. His fondness for unusual camera angles and wide, expansive compositions is well in abundance here but didn't sit well with Christie traditionalists who prefer the more confined, genteel setting of the original story. However, if you have a fondness for '70s European hodgepodges, this film has plenty of pleasures to offer including a very solid lead performance from Oliver Reed, a small but delicious role for French crooner Charles Aznavour (whose piano rendition of "The Old-Fashioned Way" to a beaming Audran is the highlight of the film), and the opportunity to see two James Bond villains (Adolfo Celi and Gert Fröbe, both still dubbed as usual) shuffling among the cast. Though nowhere close to a classic, it's still miles ahead of Collinson's next remake (a muddled rehash of *The Spiral Staircase*) and Towers's next stab at the same material, 1989's *Ten Little Indians*, which moved the location yet again to an African safari during the Cannon Films era.

Optimum's U.K. release (bearing the onscreen title of *Ten Little Indians*) is by far the best presentation of this film ever available; in the U.S. both the theatrical prints and home video releases were misframed and tinged with an ugly brownish hue, while the French DVD release crops down the 1.66:1 compositions with claustrophobic results. The UK disc (licensed through Studio Canal) is perfectly framed and features excellent, vivid colours and detail. Supposedly a slightly longer, padded version with scenes at the beginning showing the cast embarking on the helicopter was shown in some territories to fulfil some international casting obligations, but this has proven elusive so far on DVD and doesn't sound like much of a loss. The Optimum disc also includes the terrific European theatrical trailer that reinforces the *giallo* connection even further, playing almost like a Mario Bava horror film instead.

ANIMALADA

Colour, 2001, 92m. / Directed by Sergio Bizzio / Starring Carlos Roffé, Christina Banegas, Carolina Fal, Walter Quiroz / Synapse (US R1 NTSC) / WS (1.78:1) (16:9) / DD2.0

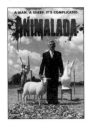

You know what's even sleazier than a New York photographer? A guy having sex with a sheep, which brings us to *Animalada*, an Argentinean black comedy that essentially spins that unforgettable Gene Wilder episode from *Everything You Always Wanted to Know About Sex* into a murder-packed, feature-length oddity. Long-married businessman Alberto (Carlos Roffé) becomes entranced with a newly-arrived sheep at his vacation ranch, and after naming the newcomer Fanny, he decides she's much more appealing than his wife (Christina Banegas), who's been around for decades and no longer interests him. However, when the handyman expresses a little too much interest in Fanny as well, Alberto takes matters into his own hands – which is witnessed by his wife, whose protestations fall on deaf ears and lead her to a sorry, undeserved fate. Then things get even stranger...

The idea of a couple sent to hell by bestiality has certainly been explored before (most notably in *Max Mon Amour* and Bigas Luna's truly astonishing *Poodle*), but *Animalada* puts a new spin on the theme by accentuating the horror as much as the laughs. (Don't worry, the relationship between Alberto and Fanny isn't graphically depicted, which is more than you could say if Joe D'Amato directed this.) Of course, whether you find this funny at all will depend on how pitch-black your sense of humour goes, as this film gets odder and bleaker as it goes along with the expected

A

finale in which no one really comes out very well, with an amusingly twisted sting in the tale. It's definitely unique and probably the perfect second bill to *Zoo*. Synapse's no-frills DVD sports a very attractive anamorphic 1.78:1 transfer, which serves the film well given its visuals are courtesy of first-time director Sergio Bizzio, a novelist and playwright who still pens a lot of scripts for Argentinean TV. However, it's unlikely he's ever conjured up something for the small screen as outrageous as this.

ANITA

Colour, 1973, 95m. / Directed by Torgny Wickman / Starring Christina Lindberg, Stellan Skarsgård, Danièle Vlaminck, Michel David / Impulse (US R0 NTSC) / WS (1.66:1) (16:9)

This vehicle for a young-looking Christina Lindberg is, as with most Swedish erotic films of the early '70s, very serious and dramatic with a few skin shots thrown in for maximum export value. It's actually a pretty solid film, sexploitation or not, and Lindberg gives an admirable performance in a difficult role. It doesn't hurt that her co-star is a young, pimply Stellan Skarsgård, years before Lars von Trier films and *Exorcist* sequels.

Christina plays the title nymphet, whose parental neglect and sexual traumas have turned her into a slut on wheels and a fascinating psychological case study. Naturally, college psychology student Erik takes an interest in her and decides to unblock her sexual pathologies by introducing her to a commune where she might become socially acceptable. Unfortunately her behaviour is still seen as a threat, and Erik decides that she must learn to experience true, fulfilling, orgasmic sex to become a more balanced human being.

The 16x9 transfer on this no-frills disc (framed at 1.66:1) is taken from a 35mm print and looks a bit the worse for wear, but considering the rarity of the film, it's nice to see in any condition. Don't expect a demo piece by any means, but check it out for the quality of the feature. Only the Swedish language track is included with optional English subtitles; unfortunately quite a few steamy bits of additional footage were present in some export prints but are absent here, a correction which will hopefully rectified with another release in the future.

ANNA TO THE INFINITE POWER

Colour, 1983, 101m. / Directed by Robert Wierner / Starring Dina Merrill, Martha Byrne, Mark Patton, Donna Mitchell, Jack Ryland, Loretta Devine, Jack Gilford / Scorpion (US R0 NTSC)

Brilliant pre-teen Anna Hart (Martha Byrne) dreams of becoming a physicist and excels at her gifted school, but her petulant attitude and bouts of kleptomania have her parents and teachers concerned. After a dream about a plane crash, she sees news of the same event the following day with one of the survivors, a young girl, looking exactly like her – and bearing the same name. Anna and her brother (Mark Patton) confront their mother, Sarah (Dina Merrill), who reveals that Anna was in fact born as a clone of Anna Zimmerman, a gifted scientist who died before finishing her revolutionary work that could solve world hunger through manipulation of the earth's elements. However, Anna's continued aversion to flashing lights and piano playing turn out to be symptoms of a much stranger past involving a concentration camp, and a strange medical research institute.

Ostensibly made for a younger audience, this science fiction melodrama begins with a concept almost identical to *The Boys from Brazil* (albeit with a female and much more sympathetic test subject) but soon develops a personality all its own. The first 20 minutes or so don't seem promising thanks to some stilting acting and flat, TV-style direction, but once the real investigation into Anna's past begins, this morphs into a fascinating, atmospheric and rather haunting study in identity, scientific responsibility, and familial bonding. Future soap actress Byrne does a solid job as Anna, transforming from an unsympathetic brat into a more self-aware, compassionate heroine whose plight becomes quite suspenseful in the second half. Best known to horror fans as Jesse in *A Nightmare on Elm Street 2: Freddy's Revenge*, Patton also overcomes his awkward initial impression as a brother who discovers loyalties he never imagined. Frequent TV actress Merrill gets top billing but has the toughest role to play as an extremely stupid mother trying improbably to conceal a hefty secret, but co-star and fellow TV character actor Donna Mitchell fares better as the mysterious piano teacher who awakens some of Anna's more latent, admirable qualities. TV director Robert Wierner doesn't do much more than keep things moving efficiently but, apart from a couple of utterly disposable chase scenes, he handles the tricky plot and emotional gradations with enough skill to leave a lasting impression.

Unreleased in theatres, this independent production became a TV and VHS staple in the mid-'80s but then vanished without a trace for over a decade. Scorpion's DVD release marks a welcome revival for fans of more challenging "family" films that tend to leave a little bit of trauma along with their life lessons, though the film still shows its age thanks to a somewhat dated video transfer. The full frame presentation doesn't  seem to be missing much significant information (it looks almost open matte and plays well about 90% of the time matted off on a widescreen TV), but the mediocre colour and detail rendition don't come close to knockout material. However, it's much better than the terrible '80s video masters and at least brings the film back into public circulation. The disc contains two hefty extras; first up is a 37-minute interview with the still-lovely Byrne, who talks about her entire acting career, her role in this film, her memories of her co-workers, and the much darker ending of the source novel. She's still very proud of the film and enthusiastic about her career, making this a breezy and entertaining watch. The elusive Patton, who paints and now runs an art gallery in Mexico, makes a rare audio appearance here chatting by phone about his first film role moving from Broadway to Robert Altman's *Come Back to the 5 & Dime, Jimmy Dean, Jimmy Dean*, and how he was hired for this film through a recommendation from Merrill, along with other topics like his violin playing in the film.

ANTI-CLOCK

Colour, 1980, 107m. / Directed by Jane Arden & Jack Bond / Starring Sebastian Saville, Suzan Cameron, Liz Saville, Louise Temple / BFI (DVD & Blu-ray, UK R0 PAL/HD)

At first glance, the entire concept of preserving *Anti-Clock* in a high-definition transfer seems like a perverse joke as the opening half hour consists of bluish, often abstract video footage akin to watching the '80s version of a kinescope.

You can almost hear home theatre owners screaming in horror and reaching for their eject buttons. Have no fear, though; the film then switches over to beautiful (albeit still very blue) 35mm film for the bulk of the remaining running time, and the film itself is a tantalising science fiction art film that anticipates the New Wave/punk sci-fi trend of the early '80s which produced such films as *Liquid Sky* and *Repo Man*.

The subject matter here is certainly more commercial and "normal" than Jane Arden and Jack Bond's previous two films (*Separation* and *The Other Side of Underneath*), but the execution is still wildly unconventional and challenging as it charts the psychological state of Joseph Sapha (played by Arden's son, Sebastian Saville, who now runs a prominent addiction outreach organisation), a self-destructive young man cursed with the ability to receive constant visions of the future with no understanding of his present state. Unable to deal with his "memories", he can only relate to a professor (also Saville) attempting to reprogram and unravel these complex thought processes.

Like the prior Arden/Bond films, *Anti-Clock* disappeared from view almost immediately after release, this time primarily because of Arden's suicide which spurred Bond to remove it from public exhibition. Extremely strange and often hypnotically beautiful, this might be the best place to start for newcomers and rewards patience with many provocative ideas about the nature of the human mind, political freedom, and aesthetic perception, which is mirrored in the alternating video and film presentation which veers between jagged, distorted TV screens to lucid, neon-drenched film tableaux. There's certainly never been anything else like it.

The BFI release contains the aforementioned HD restoration of the film itself (which looks exactly as it should, for better and for worse). Extras this time out include a 37-minute experimental, very abstract Super-8 Arden/Bond short called "Vibration", the theatrical trailer, a bonus DVD containing Jack Bond's shorter, more streamlined 2005 recut of the film (paring it down to under 90 minutes), and the usual illustrated booklet, this time with liner notes by actress Penny Slinger, Bond, and Chris Darke, as well as vintage remarks from Jack Kroll and Michael Brook.

AQUARIUM

Colour, 2004, 67m. / Directed by Frédéric Grousset / Starring Karen Bruere, Abel Divol, Capucine Mandeau, Julien Masdoua, Michel Robin / Redemption (UK R0 PAL, US R0 NTSC) / WS (1.85:1) / DD2.0

 Released in France the same year as the original *Saw*, the oddball "six characters in search of an exit" horror film *Aquarium* is at least a huge improvement over their previous "hip" French outing, *The Witching Hour*. The packaging touts this as a sadistic mixture of the *Saw* series and *Big Brother*, though of course anyone familiar with *Cube*, *My Little Eye* and even '70s offerings like *Chosen Survivors* should be able to pinpoint its real predecessors rather quickly.

The premise finds six strangers of various social strata awakening to find themselves in a glaringly white room with no visible windows or exits. A sinister disembodied spectator watching them via camera informs them that they must all perform in a variety of tests which will require teamwork and moral resolve, while anyone who fails to cooperate gets snuffed. Though the constant blinding white of the interiors may give viewers a severe case of eyestrain, it's a stylish and interesting film that wraps up its mysteries with an audacious bit of soapbox moralising that will either have you chuckling or hurling foodstuffs at the TV. In any case it's a fun and tight ride clocking in just under 70 minutes. The non-anamorphic transfer is a letdown (as well as way behind the curve on what's acceptable for commercial DVD releases), but the film itself is worth a look as long as you're not expecting much of a workout for your home theatre setup. Extras include a surprisingly ponderous making-of documentary that seems to overestimate the film's importance quite a bit, as well as stills and behind the scenes galleries, a trailer, the usual Redemption cross-promotional stuff, and most rewardingly, two of the director's earlier short films, "Emergency Stop" and "Shit", both of which also look very, very bleached-out and revolve around people's bathroom functions.

ARABIAN NIGHTS

Colour, 1974, 131m. / Directed by Pier Paolo Pasolini / Starring Franco Merli, Franco Citti, Ninetto Davoli, Tessa Bouché, Ines Pellegrini, Margareth Clémenti, Luigina Rocchi, Salvatore Sapienza / BFI (DVD & Blu-ray, UK R2 PAL/HD) / WS (1.85:1) (16:9), Image (US R1 NTSC) / WS (1.85:1)

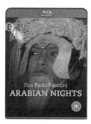

While being sold at a slave market, the feisty Zumurrud (*Eyeball*'s Ines Pellegrini) opts to become the property of a young, financially-lacking prince, Nur Ed Din (Franco Merli, the future poster boy of *Salò*). The two immediately form a youthful bond, but she's abducted by one of her jilted would-be buyers, with her new master in pursuit. During their journey, Zumurrud must escape disguised as a man and is declared a king in another region, while her suitor

becomes the love toy of three beautiful women where the main storytelling aspect comes into play (there's no Shahrazad in sight here, folks). The first major tale follows Aziz (Ninetto Davoli), who rejects his fiancée when he falls in love with another woman but finds the heart's demands more treacherous than he imagined; a prince follows some criminals into an underground lair where he finds a beautiful girl at the nocturnal mercy of a red-haired demon (Franco Citti) who makes some highly unusual demands; and naked royal Yunan (Salvatore Sapienza) abandons ship and washes up on an island where a young boy lives in fear of being murdered. Other characters and fragments interact with the main story, which also involves a fantastical encounter with a lion and more than a few stunning vistas on display.

Regarded as the high point of Pier Paolo Pasolini's controversial, literary "Trilogy of Life" by a wide margin, *Arabian Nights* is certainly the most ambitious and visually impressive. Most of the same crew remained as Pasolini trotted his camera to Africa, Iran, India, and Nepal for a phantasmagorical journey through one of the most famous story collections of all time, and everyone outdoes themselves with a visual feast that ranks as the director's most optimistic achievement. Though much of the trademark eroticism and offbeat comedy remains here, the film is so much more than that and also features a strong linking narrative to pull it all together.

The occasional primitive special effects (including a brief flying scene with the demon) are hardly the focus here, as the natural locations and amateur actors give an entirely different take on this well-worn material which already inspired countless Sinbad and Aladdin movies. This is far removed from such family fare, restoring the original adult tone and sense of peril for what amounts to a celebration of the basics of humanity. While a handful of jolting moments of brutality (dismemberment, a stabbing and a brief but heart-stopping castration) foreshadow the terminal anguish of *Salò*, the tone here is dreamlike and affectionate, while the virtual abandonment of familiar actors results in an undeniable freshness and vitality. Also of note is the beautiful, diverse score by Ennio Morricone, who worked on the previous two films mainly adapting traditional music but gets to really shine here with a full score loaded with exotic, fascinating instrumentation.

Plagued by shoddy transfers through much of the video era, *Arabian Nights* finally soars in the BFI edition which looks light years better. Gone are the ugly brown and orange colour schemes which made all the actors appear to be covered in dirt; the film now looks fresh, colourful and vivid, and the information culled from the transfer from the original negative results in countless new details in every shot invisible even in theatrical screenings. Some noise reduction was apparently applied to overcome damage to the element, but there's enough natural film grain here to still give the impression of watching a top-drawer theatrical screening. If you've ever tried to suffer through any of the other disc editions of this film, the BFI DVD and Blu-ray will feel like a breath of fresh air from the first shot. This version also addresses an issue which has plagued the film since its release: the running time. A screening of Pasolini's first cut at Cannes was 155 minutes, but producer Alberto Grimaldi persuaded him to trim it down by 25 minutes. A reel of deleted footage clocking in at 21 minutes was subsequently issued on a French DVD, but it's presented here in HD as well with Morricone's score filling in for the lost audio. The film's overlapping structure (which led to frequent comparisons to *The Saragossa Manuscript*)

dictated that a story couldn't be simply chopped out; instead, the majority of the cut footage is parallel action during the Princess Dunya segment (the penultimate story) which then continues with an imprisoned Prince Tagi escaping into a small but interesting battle scene in the mountains and encountering his beloved again in drag. It's obvious why this was cut as it could be seen as redundant in the scheme of the entire film (we've already spent plenty of time with the whole king-in-disguise story thread), but at least some of the scenes should have been left to close out the Dunya story more smoothly than its abrupt finish in the final cut. In any case, it's great to finally have this footage back in any form; the remaining time discrepancy may also be due to the original intermission (which came right after the aforementioned castration scene, ensuring some more sensitive viewers may have opted to not return for the rest of the film); the break is missing here but can be seen on the old Water Bearer transfer if you're curious.

As for the language aspect, the Italian track has been the most widely-heard for years and is usually regarded as the most legitimate one, even if only a handful of the performers were actually speaking it. Everyone else is speaking English or something else entirely with post-production looping creating the entire soundtrack no matter how you watch it. The alternative English version here synchs up about as often as the Italian one, but the subtitled version feels more poetic and organic to the film as a whole. Completists may want to check out both, but newcomers should definitely experience it in Italian first. Given the length of the film and high bit rate it occupies on the disc, the only extra here besides the deleted scenes (admittedly one heck of a deal sweetener) is the original theatrical trailer, which again pushes the salacious sequences ahead of the artistic ones.

THE ART OF LOVE

Colour, 1983, 96m. / Directed by Walerian Borowczyk / Starring Marina Pierro, Michele Placido, Massimo Girotti, Laura Betti, Milena Vukotic, Philippe Taccini / Severin (US R1 NTSC) / WS (1.78:1) (16:9), Donut (Holland R2 PAL) / WS (1.66:1)

 In ancient Rome, poet and philosopher Ovid (Massimo Girotti) lectures to a colourful gallery of students whose lives intertwine with the local military. One of these is Claudia (Marina Pierro), a beautiful woman who enjoys rolling around naked in a glass tub while her officer husband, Macarius (Michele Placido), is often away. Ovid's teachings about the "art of love", from initial courtship to seduction regardless of the social boundaries of marriage, encourage handsome young student Cornelius (Philippe Taccini) to make advances towards Claudia to which she proves receptive. Meanwhile Claudia's guardian in her husband's absence, her mother-in-law Clio (Laura Betti), has carnal issues of her own which prove to be her downfall. In between hallucinatory erotic fantasies (including a bizarre sequence involving Pierro inside a hollow cow mounted by a man in a bull outfit and naughty orgy footage pilfered from *Caligula: The Untold Story*), the love triangle builds to a violent resolution and a hugely destructive finale before a surprising, time-tripping twist ending.

Shuffled into production after the international attention given to *Caligula* and its successors, this peculiar sexual fantasy was Borowczyk's follow-up to the considerably more savage and explicit *Dr. Jekyll and His Women*, though there's still a hefty amount of skin and mayhem once you get past the relatively listless opening half hour. Pierro is magnetic and stunningly beautiful as always, while the Italian financing means a surprisingly prestigious cast including pros like Girotti (*Last Tango in Paris*), Betti (*Teorema*), and Placido (*Plot of Fear*) along with the usual cast of undraped Borowczyk extras. This certainly isn't the best place for newcomers to start, but his admirers will find plenty to enjoy in the director's idiosyncratic portrayal of Roman sexual manners. As this is an Italian production, dialogue tracks were assembled in post-production and don't really synch up in any existing version; you can forget the more subtle and witty French tracks found in Borowczyk's other major films. The English dub here is often awkward and unconvincing, but anyone familiar with '80s cult films from Italy will recognise a lot of the voices heard here. Severin's disc is anamorphic and uncut but was probably taken straight from the master the licensor provided, which means it's a bit soft and dated looking (with the director's penchant for hazy lighting not helping things much). The 1.66:1 compositions are also slightly trimmed at the top and bottom, though this only proves destructive in a handful of shots. The only extra is an Italian theatrical trailer which naturally focuses on Pierro's memorable opening credits bathing sequence as its central visual motif. A much more difficult to find Region 2 Dutch release from Donut Media features a non-anamorphic transfer (in English with optional Dutch subtitles) with a bit more vertical information visible thanks to its 1.66:1 framing; extras include the same trailer, a slideshow of frame grabs, a Borowczyk bio, and additional promos for Tinto Brass's *Private* and *Cheeky*.

ATTRACTION (NEROSUBIANCO)

Colour, 1969, 80m. / Directed by Tinto Brass / Starring Anita Sanders, Terry Carter, Nino Segurini, Umberto Di Grazia / Cult Epics (US R0 NTSC) / WS (1.78:1) (16:9)

Tinto Brass's final film of the 1960s is a whirlwind pop art phantasmagoria perfectly situated between his two other free-associative master-pieces, *Deadly Sweet* and *The Howl*. Like the former film, this one hurls its protagonist through Swinging London but makes even less of an attempt at a cohesive structure. Slapped with an X rating and released in America by Radley Metzger's Audubon Films, this originally played in Europe under the title *Nerosubianco* (a triple entendre title literally translated as *Black on White*) but made the rounds under many retitlings in an attempt to find an audience including *Attraction*, *Barbara the Yes Girl* and most absurd of all, *The Artful Penetration of Barbara*. The release from Cult Epics hedges its bets by including both the *Attraction* and *Nerosubianco* titles prominently on the packaging, hoping to snag viewers interested in a heady art film or just a simple heavy-breathing slice of '60s European erotica.

As you've probably gathered, the main character here is Barbara, played by Monica Vitti imitator Anita Sanders (who mostly went on to obscurity after another major role in *La donna invisibile*). She gets dumped in the middle of afternoon shopping time in London by her businessman husband Paolo (*Beyond the Door*'s Nino Segurini). During her wanderings she catches the eye of a handsome black man (Terry Carter, the original Colonel Tigh from *Battlestar Gallactica*), and the two begin an extended dance of flirtation, sexual fantasy and flat-out psychedelia over the course of the day while a persistent rock band (Freedom, consisting of members from the recently disbanded Procol Harum) pops up at every turn to accompany the action.

That description probably sounds a lot more linear than the way this film actually plays as it intersperses Barbara's fantasies and the numerous rock numbers with a pre-music video editing scheme that incorporates pretty much every wild idea that crosses Brass's head. Cow-headed beauty shop clients, vampires, brightly-painted sex clubs and other unexpected elements sideswipe the viewer at every turn, and by the end you're less interested in whether the couple will actually hook up than what delirious concept Brass will hurl at the screen next.

Another early Brass film nearly lost due to a dissolved original distributor and utter disinterest, *Nerosubianco* has been salvaged for its official DVD debut courtesy of a 16mm print in Metzger's collection reflecting the original English language release before it was cut and recut for reissues. Thankfully the quality here is better than you'd expect and the strongest of the Cult Epics trio of pre-*Caligula* Brass releases. Colours have thankfully stayed strong, and while the detail is obviously sacrificed by the source element, it's quite watchable and film-like. Hopefully someone in Italy will salvage the negative someday from the scrapheap to which it's apparently been consigned, but this is a more than satisfactory way for viewers to discover this wild, wild surprise. Speaking of which, it's worth noting that the Italian version (which was released on VHS at one point) reflects a different, longer edit of the film before Audubon retooled it for American consumption; basically several scenes play out slightly longer, and a few of the montages have some extra beats here and there. A composite version with both language options would be interesting at some point, but it's no wonder someone hasn't gotten around to such a daunting task yet. You don't get a Tinto commentary on this one, but the frenzied *Artful Penetration* trailer is here along with a promo for *Deadly Sweet* and a lobby card gallery.

BACTERIUM

Colour, 2006, 87m. / Directed by Brett Piper / Starring Alison Whitney, Benjamin Kanes, Miya Sagara, Andrew Kranz / Shock-O-Rama (US R0 NTSC) / WS (1.78:1) (16:9) / DD2.0

This goofy monsterfest has a surprising PG-13 rating ("for sci-fi horror violence and gore, some partial nudity and language") in the U.S., which might be the most shocking thing about it. The story is your average '50s monster yarn redressed in contemporary threads as a bunch of brainless, paintball-happy youths happen upon a desolate scientific lab in the wilderness where biological weapons experiments have resulted in a slithering, oozing menace which will consume the planet in two days if it isn't stopped. The military shows up, scientific jargon gets bandied around, the girls take showers and parade in skimpy clothes (with one quick frontal pushing that rating right to the breaking point), and lots of green goop splatters across the screen.

Shock-O-Rama's disc includes a passable transfer of a film apparently shot on 16mm but finished on video. Extras include making-of featurette (mostly FX-oriented, of course), commentary with Brett Piper and producer Michael Raso, and the usual trailers and promos. At least more fun than your average Sci-Fi Channel programmer, it's worth checking out on a slow evening.

BAD BIOLOGY

Colour, 2008, 85m. / Directed by Frank Henenlotter / Starring Charlee Danielson, Anthony Sneed, Mark Wilson, R.A. the Rugged Man, Remedy, Tina Krause / Shriek Show (US R0 NTSC), Revolver (UK R2 PAL), Swift (France R2 PAL) / WS (1.78:1) (16:9) / DD5.1

In the 1981 classic *Body Heat*, Kathleen Turner explains herself early on by saying, "My temperature runs a couple of degrees high, around a hundred. I don't mind. It's the engine or something." On the other hand, in *Bad Biology*, the long-awaited directorial return of Frank Henenlotter (*Basket Case*) after a sixteen-year hiatus, the female protagonist Jennifer (Charlee Danielson) runs somewhere around three hundred. See, she's an aspiring, seemingly demure photographer who immediately informs us in voiceover that she's equipped with seven clitorises. Even worse, as we see soon after, she's easily prone to overexcitement and tends to literally bang her lovers to death (which she captures in photos), followed by a quickly-produced mutant offspring she dispenses into the trash. Of course, the film's tagline that this is a "godawful love story" means we have to have another person in the mix, and here it's the unlucky Batz (Anthony Sneed), a young man who copes with a nasty surgical mishap during his birth by abusing steroids and other drastic measures (including a gigantic homemade jerk-off machine) to enhance his reattached manhood. Unfortunately said genitalia develops a mind of its own and lurches out of control inside his pants, a trait noticed by Jennifer when the two finally happen to be in the same room during a bizarre photo shoot for a rap artist. After seeing his monster unsheathed for a few seconds, Jennifer determines that Batz's "gift" is her destiny... but things don't go quite according to plan.

No one familiar with Henenlotter's career could possibly predict where each new project would take him as he lurched from the Times Square griminess of *Basket Case* to the psychedelic smut-horrors of

Brain Damage and the Shapiro/ Glickenhaus era Day-Glo horror cartoons of *Frankenhooker* and the two *Basket Case* sequels. While the outrageous affinity for exaggerated sexuality and body horror are still well in place here, his aesthetic has definitely changed to more of a clean, spare, brightly-lit approach that will disorient more than a few fans, not to mention the expected seasoning of hip-hop music on the soundtrack. Fortunately he still has his mojo, delivering a string of frenzied set pieces worthy of his legacy and a few artsy touches you might not expect. The mostly new actors are definitely troopers, especially the compelling Danielson whose physical energy and go-for-broke attitude far exceed her sometimes unsteady line readings. Die-hards will also be amused by some sly nods to his Something Weird connection, including a few well-placed VHS titles and an unexpected vintage cameo by Uschi Digard. Even by Henenlotter standards, you've never seen anything quite like this... and be sure to stick around through the end credits.

A low-budget indie film, *Bad Biology* made the rounds at various film festivals and one-off screenings while navigating the nightmarish terrain of modern film distribution. The first DVD on the market came in the U.K. from Revolver as a Region 2 release without any extras (and ditto for the French release under the title *Sex Addict!*), but fortunately fans can get much more bang for their buck with the American disc from Shriek Show which features a superior anamorphic transfer (no iffy PAL conversion like the Revolver disc) and a strong Dolby Digital 2.0 mix. (Both discs also contain a very processed, unappetising 5.1 mix that's best ignored.) The Shriek Show extras live up to the expected Henenlotter standard with his usual supplemental sidekick, rapper R.A. the Rugged Man (a major financier of this production most infamous for the location doc on the *Basket Case* disc), joining him for a lively commentary track. You'll learn which cast member was recently released from jail before shooting, how the cameo from *Basket Case* alum Beverly Bonner came off, the digestive difficulties of Sneed during his first day of nude shooting, and the real identities of many of Jennifer's unfortunate victims. Clay Patrick McBride, the hip-hop photographer responsible for the very striking photo souvenirs of Jennifer's victims at the moment of climax and death, gets the spotlight for a funny video featurette showing him, Danielson, and Henenlotter coaching a string of male victims through their paces, and you get a very explicit Henenlotter music video for R.A.'s "I Should'a Never" complete with a sex scene covered in spaghetti, a rifle barrel popping from a woman's crotch, and R.A. yanking his brain from his skull and smashing it to pieces on the floor. Also included is McBride's promo for R.A.'s "Legendary Classics Volume 1", the original trailer, a slew of production stills and promotional artwork, and bonus Shriek Show trailers for *Late Fee*, *Psychos in Love*, *Scream* and *Smash Cut*.

BAD GIRLS DORMITORY

Colour, 1985, 95m. / Directed by Tim Kincaid / Starring Carey Zuris, Jennifer Delora, Rick Gianasi, Teresa Farley, Natalie O'Connell / Exploitation Digital (US R1 NTSC) / WS (1.85:1) (16:9), Westlake (US R0 NTSC)

While most '80s movie audiences got their women-in-prison groove on with *Chained Heat* and *Reform School Girls*, discerning trashophiles in 1985 were discovering the wonders of *Bad Girls' Dormitory*, a particularly seedy but sometimes unexpectedly stylish offering from director Tim Kincaid (*Breeders*, *Riot on 42nd St.*), better known in porn circles as director Joe Gage. Shot in the Big Apple and upstate New York, the film follows the usual routine about a women's prison where the inmates are subjected to the perverse whims of the warden and guards until they're driven to the brink and decide to stage a breakout. They also squabble a lot in the mess hall, get frequent conjugal visits from their boyfriends, and take long, hot, soapy showers. The Times Square opening is priceless, too, as a snapshot of the area before Disney swallowed it whole.

You won't see any big names from the genre like Sybil Danning popping up, but the cast does fine with the ridiculous material; the most familiar faces are regular Kincaid actors Rick Gianasi (the lead in the mind-boggling *Fatal Frames*) and Jennifer Delora (who played Angel in *Frankenhooker*). A terrible quality edition of the film was released several years ago from Westlake and geared for the bargain bins, but the only really viewable option is Exploitation Digital's special edition, which features a much better anamorphic transfer. The film was obviously shot on a low budget and features some odd, rough edits in a couple of spots, but overall it looks just fine. Extras include a photo gallery, the Spanish(!) theatrical trailer, and a long, extremely lively video interview with Delora, who talks about how she lost a pageant crown over the film, her memories of the film (including her nude scene and her very memorable demise), and how the rest of her fan-friendly career has gone in the ensuing years. The featurette is inventively intercut with a B&W "security cam" motif that actually adds tremendously to the enjoyment factor. Delora also appears straddling her motorcycle for a quick intro to the main feature.

BAD RONALD

Colour, 1974, 74m. / Directed by Buzz Kulik / Starring Scott Jacoby, Pippa Scott, John Larch, Dabney Coleman, Kim Hunter / Warner Archive (US R0 NTSC)

Living at home along with his ailing mother (Kim Hunter), lonely high schooler Ronald (Scott Jacoby) overreacts to a young neighbourhood girl's taunts and accidentally kills her. Rather than turn him over to the police, his mom decides to hide him inside their house by creating a secret, walled-over chamber in which he can hide from the cops and prying outsiders. Unfortunately she dies soon after at the hospital, and when a new family moves in with attractive young daughters, no one has any awareness of the secret, increasingly insane young man residing within their walls.

One of the most effective and fondly-remembered of the many 1970s made-for-television horror movies that traumatised young viewers, *Bad Ronald* was based on a thriller novel targeted for young adults by John Holbrook Vance. However, the end result is a harrowing study in psychopathic chills definitely not for impressionable young viewers, and the climax in particular packs a powerful jolt. Jacoby perfectly captures the balance of sympathy and unease as his character gradually descends into insanity, convinced he's a knight in shining armour within his own private kingdom intent on winning the fair maiden in the bedroom only a thin layer of drywall away. Veteran composer Fred Karlin contributes a solid music score that also adds to the viewer's unease, and the solid cast includes a young Dabney Coleman as the patriarch of the innocent new family.

Bad Ronald was a sought-after title for years following a fleeting VHS release, and fans scarred by it finally had their prayers answered when Warner announced it as part of their delivery-on-demand DVD program. The image quality is passable if unspectacular, roughly on par with what the original broadcast would have resembled and at least superior to the tape. Colours are subdued and on the drab side, but the clarity is decent enough and the mono audio sounds fine. No extras of course, but the film comes highly recommended all the same.

BASKET CASE 2

Colour, 1990, 90m. / Directed by Frank Henenlotter / Starring Kevin Van Hentenryck, Annie Ross, Kathryn Meisle, Heather Rattray, Jason Evers, Ted Sorel, David Emge / Synapse (US R1 NTSC) / WS (1.85:1) (16:9), Synergy (UK R2 PAL), Legend (Germany R2 PAL) / DD2.0

 As the 1980s closed out, horror movies found themselves in a very weird place. The slasher craze had run itself into the ground with self-parodies of characters like Freddy and Jason, and the MPAA began cracking down harder than ever before to aid the growing power of big studios at the multiplex. Red-soaked, monster-friendly outings were soon sequelized and given a heavy injection of goofiness, as witnessed with wildly varying degrees of success in the follow-ups to *The Evil Dead*, *Re-Animator*, *Return of the Living Dead*, *Child's Play*, and so on, with even all-new efforts like *Society* and *Dr. Caligari* drenching their stories in weird, Day-Glo late '80s satire. Perhaps the wildest of them all, the two *Basket Case* sequels arrived eight years after the original with director Frank Henenlotter shooting them back-to-back (along with

Frankenhooker), replacing the gritty, comic gore of the 1982 classic with broad, cartoonish freak show visuals and rib-tickling humour straight from the consciousness of a caffeine-addled junior high monster fanatic. *Basket Case 2* will completely baffle anyone who doesn't remember the dawn of straight-to-video mainstream horror, but it's a unique, highly eccentric entry in the horror sequel sweepstakes all the same.

Our story picks up with the closing moments of the original *Basket Case* as Duane (Kevin Van Hentenryck) and his deformed, separated Siamese twin brother, Belial, plunge from the neon-accented awning of their seedy New York hotel. The ensuing media frenzy reveals their grisly secret life to the public, so their protective aunt, "freak's rights" activist and writer Granny Ruth (Annie Ross), spirits them away to her remote mansion where she houses a wild menagerie of freaks. Belial soon falls for Eve, a similar oddity (with whom he couples in a scene unlikely to leave viewers' memories for weeks), while Duane becomes apprehensive about his status as the only "normal" person around except for Granny's daughter, Susan (Heather Rattray). Meanwhile a snooping tabloid reporter (Kathryn Meisle) follows the brothers' journey and tries to infiltrate the haven, with notably grotesque results.

Fast-paced and utterly strange, *Basket Case 2* veers way over the top early on with Ross's impassioned speeches while dressed in quasi-religious white gowns, surrounded by mutated inhabitants with faces resembling moons and tree stumps. The influence of Jerry Springer tabloid culture is unmistakable here and gives the film a nice twist; while the gore is kept to a surprising minimum (this time out the MPAA easily gave it an R rating), the barrage of outrageous make-up effects keeps viewers off balance from start to finish. Van Hentenryck gives an assured comic performance (even doubling as Belial's face in some shots this time out), and Henenlotter follows up his psychedelic *Brain Damage* by getting even more stylised and extreme with his lighting and camera angles. Top it off with a catchy score by Joe Renzetti (*Dead & Buried*) that can only be filed under "quirky" and a memorably sick little ending, and you've got an instant cult favourite.

Ushered to video by Shapiro Glickenhaus back in the early '90s after a handful of token theatrical screenings, *Basket Case 2* disappeared from view for nearly a decade afterwards when the DVD era hit (though a mediocre-looking U.K. release popped up pairing it with the even more absurd third instalment). Synapse's DVD restores much of the brightly-coloured lustre to the film that couldn't be appreciated on a home screen before; the wild colour schemes really pop here like never before, and the anamorphic presentation looks terrific. Also, the stereo soundtrack is more spacious than expected with the music rising up quite effectively during the opening clips from the mono, flatly-recorded original. FX artist Gabe Bartalos hosts the biggest extra, a 20-minute featurette entitled "Behind the Wicker". Packed with camcorder footage of the creation of Belial and the other freaks, it's a fun, low-tech short with Bartalos (who has to be subtitled on occasion due to the loud industrial setting) showing off the production locations, sharing a chatty walk with Henenlotter while talking about the shooting, and turning the camera over for a reminiscence with Henenlotter and Jim Glickenhaus. *Dawn of the Dead*'s David Emge pops up for the second featurette, a five-minute quickie called "The Man in the Moon Mask", in which he talks about how he landed up appearing in his memorable and completely unrecognisable role as "Half-Moon".

BATBABE: THE DARK NIGHTIE

Colour, 2009, 86m. / Directed by John Bacchus / Starring Darian Caine, Robert Mandara, Molly Heartbreaker, Jackie Stevens / Seduction Cinema (US R1 NTSC) / WS (1.78:1) (16:9)

After targeting such successful franchises as *The Lord of the Rings* in their ongoing string of softcore spoofs, it was a given that the lesbo-loving folks at Seduction Cinema would eventually set their sights on *Batman* with *Batbabe: The Dark Nightie*. Of course, the saviour of Gotham has certainly inspired naughty parodies before, most notoriously with the cheapjack '70s porno oddity and current cult favourite *Bat Pussy*, next to which this 2009 offering looks like a mega-million production in comparison.

Spewing out enough groan-worthy puns to put the '60s TV series to shame, this superhero smut fest features Seduction staple Darian Caine as wealthy strip club maven and performer Wendy Wane, who takes time out from loving the ladies to fight crime as Batbabe, a nocturnal avenger whose current foe is The Jerker (a scenery-swallowing Robert Mandara), the self-abusing psychopath who swipes the entire city's porn stash. Batbabe is enlisted by Commissioner Boredom to save Bacchum City to find the hideout of this loony, who also terrorises the city in a helicopter shaped like a giant phallus. Really.

As you can tell, this isn't exactly Mel Brooks humour here, but for dopey comedy with a huge helping of cable-friendly sex scenes, this one fits the bill just fine. Even regular Seduction host 42nd Street Pete pops up as a henchman in an uncredited, semi-disguised bit part. A few scenes actually come off as rather energetic and clever, such as an early police interrogation-turned-sex scene loaded with a hilarious overdose of "hide the salami"-style metaphors. The DVD transfer looks okay given this was shot on video (it's presented at 1.78:1 and 16x9 enhanced, as usual for Seduction) and augmented with a few disposable deleted scenes, audio commentary with "producer and historian Ed Grant" (who essentially runs down the various inspirations for the film and what it took to get all the ladies in the right spirit of the project) moderated by Michael Raso, and a batch of the company's other spoofs like *Kinky Kong*. Some "erotic short films" are also promised on the packaging but are nowhere to be found on the disc itself.

BAVARIAN SEX COMEDY COLLECTION:
I LIKE THE GIRLS WHO DO
Colour, 1973, 80m. / Directed by Hans Billian / Starring Günther Ziegler, Alena Penz, Franziska Stömmer, Robby Murr
BOTTOMS UP
Colour, 1974, 81m. / Directed by Frank Josef Gottlieb / Starring Alena Penz, Alexander Grill, Rinaldo Talamonti
HOUSE OF 1000 SINS
Colour, 1975, 78m. / Directed by Kurt Nachmann / Starring Peter Hamm, Margaret Rose Keil, Gisela Krauss, Eva Gross
RUN, VIRGIN, RUN
Colour, 1970, 95m. / Directed by Hans Billian / Starring Joav Jasinski, Maria Brockerhoff, Helga Tölle / Secret Key (US R0 NTSC)

One of the most spat-upon exploitation genres during its first-run theatre days, the German sex comedy has undergone something of a reappraisal in recent years with people pining nostalgically for those secretive late-night TV airings and beloved, long-gone Private Screenings VHS tapes. However, you can relive those days for a really cheap price with a quartet of amusing slices of '70s skin-coms gathered by Secret Key under the name of the *Bavarian Sex Comedy Collection.* 75% of the films have been available before in various other editions (some now going for stupid amounts of money online), but this is a much handier and more wallet-friendly option. First up is one of the best of the bunch, *I Like the Girls Who Do* (aka *Liebesjagd durch 7 Betten*), a surprisingly funny, imaginative, and genuinely sexy concoction about strapping young Thomas (Austrian-born Günther Ziegler, now toiling away in really awful Ulli Lommel movies), who learns he's the heir of his recently-deceased uncle. However, the old man's will states that, in order to claim the jackpot, the lad has to collect and assemble amulets from all seven of the uncle's sexy, hot-to-trot mistresses. Of course, this also means Thomas gets way more than he bargained for as the lusty lasses entangle him in various embarrassing mishaps involving a department store bed, peeping tom construction workers, a very exhibitionistic dinner theatre, and much, much more. Nicely shot, paced, directed and performed by a more talented and attractive-than-usual cast, this is a real diamond in the rough worth seeking out.

Less impressive but mildly diverting is the following year's *Bottoms Up* (the one new-to-DVD title in the set), originally released as *Auf der Alm, da gibt's koa Sünd*, which was reputedly a big hit in Europe. The English dub track isn't that great and the print's seen better days, but there are still a few chuckles to be had in the tale of a small town turned upside down by the discovery of a process that turns cow dung into gasoline. Industrial spies and lots of drunk, horny German villagers clash as the story gets more convoluted by the minute.

Things perk up again considerably with the second real winner in the batch, *House of 1000 Sins* (*Ein echter Hausfrauenfreund*), whose sleazy-sounding title disguises another surprisingly ambitious and oddly innovative, time-jumping story about Albert (*Bibi*'s Peter Hamm), a gigolo kept on at a hotel where he's expected to honour the whims of all the voluptuous female guests while juggling the demands of his wife at home. Once again this delivers far more complexity, humour and unabashed skin exposure than comparable American and British sex comedies of the time, and it still holds up as a good-natured trifle just about anyone of either gender can enjoy. Last up is the frothy and fun *Run, Virgin, Run*, which was reviewed in *DVD Delirium Vol. 3* as the co-feature of *2069: A Sex Odyssey*. All of the transfers are full frame (the films were either shot open matte or 1.66:1, so not much image loss to comment on here) and look like older masters prepared for home video or cable broadcast, but they're watchable enough. The only really noteworthy extra is a nicely-written four-page booklet by Michael Bowen detailing the films' participants and the basic appeal of these compelling, carnal curiosities.

THE BEAST IN SPACE

Colour, 1980, 91m. / Directed by Al Bradley (Alfonso Brescia) / Starring Sirpa Lane, Vassili Karis, Lucio Rosato, Robert Hundar, Venantino Venantini / Severin (US R0 NTSC), Shameless (UK R0 PAL) / WS (1.85:1) (16:9)

 Wow. High up there on the list of rip-off hybrids that just absolutely, should not exist in this universe, the sci-fi/ softcore pastiche *The Beast in Space* is one of those titles that's been

gracing psychotronic reference books for years with only a few lucky souls actually setting eyes on the thing. This strange celluloid mongrel was the brainchild of the late "Al Bradley", aka Alfonso Brescia, who had already turned out a stultifying string of bargain basement *Star Wars* imitations like *War of the Robots*, *Star Odyssey*, *War of the Planets* and *War in Space* (see a trend here?) along with the occasional head-scratching entry like *Super Stooges vs. the Wonder Women*. With a distinct fondness for very leisurely pacing and droning, sleep-inducing music scores, Bradley never earned much of a cult following like his peers, but there's no mistaking his work when you stumble across it. Of course, it goes without saying that there's nothing else in his skewed filmography that even comes close to the amazing *The Beast in Space*.

Our interstellar saga begins when studly Captain Larry Madison (*Giallo in Venice*'s Vassili Karis) decides to hit on sexy space chick Sondra (Sirpa Lane) while chugging, ahem, "Uranus Milk" at the ship's bar. Another guy, Juan (Venantino Venantini), has eyes for her, too, but Larry wins out and takes her home for the night, only to learn that his competitor had a valuable container of a space mineral that the rest of the fleet could really, really use. Sondra's experiencing some strange dreams about a country house and a hairy, beast-like guy running through the woods, so when she and Larry wind up assigned to a team sent to explore a nearby planet for more minerals, she's more than a little surprised to see the setting from her dreams entering into reality. Oh, and the female crew members are also driven to horny distraction when they spy some space horses copulating nearby. Soon the real space-sex-beast shows up in a frisky mood, and Larry and his crew find themselves battling a bunch of laser-happy space robots. Can they all get back to their ship in one piece?

B

As art-trash film fans may have already gathered, the second half of this film decides rather arbitrarily to inject elements of Walerian Borowczyk's *The Beast* into the storyline, and it shouldn't come as much of a surprise that a big, hairy, hilariously-endowed forest beast doesn't sit very comfortably among all the laser zaps and marauding robots. The fact that the film was obviously shot with leftover props and costumes from Bradley's previous space operas just adds to the weird atmosphere, giving it the feel of a cheapie kiddie matinee movie gone very, very, very wrong. Of course, casting the tragic Finnish actress Lane (who figured prominently in the Borowczyk film's most notorious sequence) was clearly meant to provide some legitimacy, though one can only wonder how far her career had fallen by this point. The Tangerine Dream-lite music by electronic noodler Marcello Giombini (who also drove viewers insane with his plonking around on such films as *Waves of Lust* and Joe D'Amato's '80s cannibal cycle) sounds almost exactly like his other Bradley sci-fi scores, which he did hiding under the name "Pluto Kennedy". Contributing even more to the overall weirdness, cinematographer Silvi Fraschetti (*Alien 2: On Earth*) never seems to be filming anything from the right angles, instead conveying the impression of a constant stream of outtakes that somehow stumbled over into a completed feature.

As if one legit DVD release weren't enough, *The Beast in Space* actually comes in no less than two different variants. The first version available from most retailers offers the standard theatrical cut with plenty of softcore groping and topless nudity amid the bouncing spaceships on strings. It's transferred from the original negative and looks great considering the dodgy nature of the manner in which this film was originally shot (what with the horse-breeding stock footage and ultra-

dark FX space scenes). The Italian language track is ably accompanied by optional English subtitles. Too bad an English dub wasn't ever commissioned as it would've been hilarious. The soft version includes the original Italian trailer and a lengthy interview with Juan himself, Venantino Venantini, who's evidently now a painter. The onetime star of *Black Emanuelle* and *Contraband* talks at length about his career and his memories of working with Bradley, who apparently had gusto even when budgets weren't accommodating.

Even weirder, Severin also managed to uncover a previously buried hardcore cut of the film which adds in a few minutes of unsimulated grinding from some anonymous body doubles and, more importantly, some hysterical prosthetic nastiness with the beast, whose monstrous appendage manages to stop the film cold for about five minutes. The transfer is a bit more erratic as the nasty stuff had to be spliced in from the uncovered print from some Italian porn theatre, but hey, how else are you gonna see it? The interview isn't carried over here, but you do get a different XXX theatrical trailer and a very funny reel of deleted footage, including a ridiculous "beast climax" bit of business obviously intend to outshock the Borowczyk original. Hey, it's different... A subsequent R0 PAL release from Shameless in the U.K. features a hybrid version of the film which essentially adheres to the softcore version but features shots of the beast's formidable endowment from the more explicit cut, thus giving viewers the best of both worlds.

BEAUTY QUEEN BUTCHER
Colour, 1991, 118m. / Directed by Jill Zurborg / Starring Rhona Brody, Jim Boggess, Ryan Martin Dwyer, Steve Kollin / Bloody Earth (US R0 NTSC)

Put-upon, dumpy Phyllis Loden (Rhona Brody) is selected by four snotty beauty pageant entrants to take the slot of "last place" so they all can avoid humiliation. When the prank works, they rub it in even further, sealing their doom as the crown for "Miss Slough" becomes a bloody battleground.

This early '90s shot-on-video curio is distinguished by its female pedigree. Helmed by one-shot wonder Jill Zurborg and with a cast dominated by women (and, uh, one really ugly guy in drag), it's a virtually gore-free but amusingly sick little item made years before *Drop Dead Gorgeous*. It's worth checking out if you want to see a campy horror outing made on a high school budget. Be warned that the pacing goes slack a few times, and for better or worse, it indulges in '80s stereotypical shorthand, like a "nerd" wearing ridiculous big-rimmed plastic glasses. The biggest asset (sorry) is Rhona Brody, who gives an appealing, committed and sympathetic performance as Phyllis that has you rooting for her even when she's knocking off the cast in a hockey mask. The only notable extra here is a vintage, crappy-looking VHS making-of promo from the time of the film's release, mainly showing the cast getting made up and clowning around. Too bad the director and cast have disappeared, as the stories behind the making of this girls' look at the slasher formula would have been very interesting to hear.

THE BED SITTING ROOM

Colour, 1969, 90m. / Directed by Richard Lester / Starring Ralph Richardson, Peter Cook, Dudley Moore, Spike Milligan, Rita Tushingham, Marty Feldman, Michael Hordern, Roy Kinnear, Frank Thornton, Mona Washbourne / BFI (DVD & Blu-ray, UK R2 PAL/HD) / WS (1.85:1) (16:9)

B

After England has been decimated by a nuclear war, twenty survivors mill about the desolate, debris-strewn wasteland performing twisted variations on their normal daily rituals. The BBC still exists thanks to a newscaster (Frank Thornton) who stands in front of a blown-out TV set offering background exposition, and many of the survivors are either mutating into furniture or animals or being told they're dead even when they clearly aren't. Among these lost souls going mad are a pregnant teen (Rita Tushingham) endlessly riding an underground train with her family, a lunatic nurse (Marty Feldman), a lord afraid he's transforming into the titular bed sitting room (Ralph Richardson), two airborne police officers (Dudley Moore and Peter Cook), and a lone mailman (Spike Milligan, who co-authored the source play with John Antrobus). Their fates intertwine in a series of darkly comic sketches which pile on top of each other in front of increasingly surreal vistas, including a mostly submerged cathedral and the climactic transformations of several key characters.

It's a shame midnight movies didn't really catch on until the early '70s, as Richard Lester's absurdly ahead-of-its-time *The Bed Sitting Room* seems perfectly pitched for late night audiences. Absurdist humour with a pitch-black complexion rules this post-nuclear gallery of characters, featuring a host of terrific British performers. Critics at the time were confounded and hardly amused by this depiction of a fallout-laden society where mutation and death linger in many of the punch lines, an approach later picked up to much greater acclaim in the U.S. with *A Boy and His Dog*. Unfortunately Lester, a hot property at the time thanks to *A Hard Day's Night* and *The Knack*, suffered a serious

B

career setback from which he didn't recover until years later with *The Three Musketeers* and the underrated *Juggernaut*.

Incredibly shot by the talented David Watkin (who used a similar visual approach later on Ken Russell's *The Devils*), this film will be a severe eye-opener for fans of another expatriate American director, Terry Gilliam, whose *Brazil* and *Time Bandits* owe a particular debt to the aesthetic approach of this film. Its status as a forerunner to Monty Python is valid as well, particularly the random, "realistic" absurdity of *Monty Python and the Holy Grail*, while the presence of *Beyond the Fringe* vets Cook and Moore (the hottest comedy duo in the U.K. at the time, fresh off of Stanley Donen's classic *Bedazzled*) forms a nice link between two generations of comedy as well. As the liner notes point out, the fact that virtually all of the lead players have died (even the younger ones) adds to the eerie, detached feeling of the film, which would play much better on a double bill with something by Jodorowsky or Lynch than a "traditional" British comedy.

Thanks to its failure at the box office, *The Bed Sitting Room* did not receive an official video release for thirty years and had to earn its reputation through word of mouth and fleeting late-night TV screenings, not to mention the deep underground bootleg videos. For reasons best known only to the movie gods, an HD master was created by MGM and broadcast internationally on a handful of HD channels, despite the fact that they had never released it on video in any format. Thankfully the BFI then picked up the ball with a release using the same master with some additional damage clean-up, and the results are incredibly impressive. The picture quality is pin-sharp (check out the early shot of Michael Hordern atop a mountain of shoes), doing full justice to the ambitious, texture-laden compositions, and from start to finish it's a wonderfully immersive, film-like presentation that surpasses the

hi-def airing by a surprising margin. (For one thing, it's no longer interlaced.) This also marks an early entry in the company's promising Flipside series, which is dedicated to obscure and neglected cult items from Britain's filmic history. If this is any indication of what to expect, collectors have quite a few treats in store. Optional English subtitles are also included, which is helpful for some of the more rapid-fire dialogue. (As with some other BFI releases, the Blu-ray is Region B encoded, so American consumers should find this a prime reason to invest in an all-region player since the odds of MGM ever doing this themselves on BD are very slim indeed.) As for extras, you get the original theatrical trailer and three 1967 interviews from Bernard Braden's *Then and Now* program with Lester (promoting *How I Won the War*), Milligan, and Cook, the last of whom unsurprisingly gets most of the highlights. A hefty booklet also contains liner notes by Michael Brooke, a Russell Campbell review from 1970, and a Lester bio by Neil Sinyard.

THE BERMUDA DEPTHS

Colour, 1978, 98m. / Directed by Tom Kotani / Starring Leigh McCloskey, Carl Weathers, Connie Sellecca, Burl Ives, Julie Woodson / Warner Archive (US R0 NTSC)

 A beguiling mixture of fantasy, horror and doomed romance, *The Bermuda Depths* is the dreamlike tale of Magnus (*Inferno*'s Leigh McCloskey), a distraught young man who returns to the oceanic Bermuda town where his father died in a mysterious storm years before and, as a child, he fell in love with a young girl named Jennie who disappeared into the sea with a hatched turtle they found on the beach. Now he helps his friend

Eric (Carl Weathers) and scientist Dr. Paulis (Burl Ives) explore unusual, often gigantic aquatic life in the area, but things get strange again when he encounters the now-adult Jennie (Connie Sellecca) who, according to local legend, is actually a century-old woman who sold her soul for eternal life.

Surprisingly lyrical and surreal for a made-for-television feature, this production from Rankin/Bass (the team normally responsible for animated holiday fare) was their second foray into live action after *The Last Dinosaur*. The melancholy tone of this film (complete with a haunting theme song) makes it one of their more mature achieve-ments, culminating in a shockingly downbeat finale whose bittersweet memory lingers after the credits like a strange perfume. Many viewers fell in love with this film despite its obvious flaws (some ham-fisted dialogue, highly uneven perform-ances, dubious special effects using uncon-vincing models), as its strengths more than make the journey worthwhile. At the risk of spoiling some of the surprise, the narrative even makes an unexpected detour into monster territory with a climax that wouldn't be out of place in a Gamera film.

Another TV movie long collecting dust on Warner's shelf, *The Bermuda Depths* was revived as part of the company's DVD-on-demand Archive program and looks surprisingly good; in fact, it's safe to say that this is one of the best-looking '70s made-for-TV movies available on DVD, far superior to some of its contemporaries like *Bad Ronald* made available around the same time. Colours look robust and vivid without any unnatural tweaking, and the level of detail is impressive with only some very minor compression issues. Indicating this was intended for theatrical screenings in some markets, the 1.33:1 aspect ratio can also be matted off on widescreen monitors to 1.78:1, which actually improves the visual compositions tremendously.

BETWEEN THE COVERS

Colour, 1973, 82m. / Directed by Ralf Gregan / Starring Heidi Kappler, Heidrun Hankammer, Michael Büttner

SWINGING WIVES

Colour, 1971, 97m. / Directed by Ernst Hofbauer / Starring Astrid Frank, Eva Garden, Karin Götz, Elfi Helfrich / Mars Pictures, distributed by BCI (US R0 NTSC) / WS (1.78:1) (16:9)

This pair of German sex comedies filtered via *Schoolgirl Report*-style reporting deserves a better fate on DVD. The gist here is that all those sweater-wearing *frau-leins* and *hausfraus* are really just craving sex all day long, which should come as no surprise to anyone who's ever watched a cable channel after 10pm. The whole "report" format with a documen-tarian interviewing women on the street is largely disposable here, with both films offering a string of mildly sexy skits. The first film, *Between the Covers* (*Liebe zwischen Tür und Angel*), is one of the more obscure of its ilk with a strange, not-very-tantalising hook in the form of a shapely businesswoman named Nina (Heidi Kappler) involved in a magazine sales meeting where all the men recount the stories of the hard, hard work they had to go through for each sale. You can fill in the blanks from there.

The far more widely seen second feature (which was omnipresent on VHS thanks to its unforgettable sweater-lifting poster art and hot, hot, hot Gert Wilden soundtrack) is *Swinging Wives* (*Der neue heiße Sex-Report – Was Männer nicht für möglich halten*), a slice of average late-night fare consisting of "man on the street" interviews with married women who reveal all the filthy stuff they get up to when their husbands are away from home and failing to attend to their needs. Both films are horrendously dubbed with extremely poor audio fidelity here, but even worse, the films (which appear to have been lensed somewhere around 1.66:1) have been taken from obviously cropped one-inch tape masters which have then been further masked off to create fake 16x9 versions, which means big slices of picture information (including much of the credits and, in many scenes, the top halves of the actors' heads as well as some T&A footage) is completely cropped off screen. Not an optimum presentation by any means, but if you're a German sex comedy fanatic, it may still be worth the investment just for the rarity of *Between the Covers* if you can find it for a very low price.

BEYOND THE DOOR

Colour, 1974, 109m. / Directed by Ovidio G. Assonitis and Robert Barrett / Starring Juliet Mills, Gabriele Lavia, Richard Johnson, Barbara Fiorini, Elizabeth Turner, David Colin Jr. / Code Red (US R0 NTSC) / WS (1.85:1) (16:9), JVD (Japan R2 NTSC) / WS (1.85:1)

 One of the more unlikely box office smashes of the 1970s, this nutty Italian horror film partially shot in San Francisco gained immediate notoriety as the first and most blatant imitator of *The Exorcist*, laced with a heavy dose of *Rosemary's Baby* and seasoned with plenty of Eurosleaze elements for good measure. Though Warner Brothers tried to suppress the film in court, the distributor successfully fought back and kept it in circulation, a fortunate outcome not shared by the same year's blaxploitation variant, *Abby*, which still languishes in MGM's vaults. While *Beyond the Door* fared well enough on VHS (from Media), it eventually dropped out of circulation and took over a decade of DVD's lifespan before finally coming out in the U.S.

The very fragmented storyline begins with a bizarre prologue involving a Satanic ceremony featuring a naked woman on an altar and lots of candles. One of the participants, Jessica (Juliet Mills, formerly a TV darling from *Nanny and the Professor*), elects to leave the sect and abandon her lover, Dimitri (*Zombie*'s Richard Johnson). Much of this is actually conveyed through voiceover from Satan himself, which is a bit unorthodox, but then we flash forward to a funk music recording session presided over by Jessica's jackass husband, Robert (*Deep Red*'s Gabriele Lavia), a music producer who chastises his soulful jam artists by telling them they "have as much balls as a castrated jellyfish". Robert and Jessica have a happy home life with their two kids, Gail (Barbara Fiorini), a foul-mouthed brat who keeps reading multiple copies of *Love Story* all day, and Ken (David Colin Jr. from Mario Bava's *Shock*, also released as a fake sequel to this film), who doesn't do much besides playing with toy cars. When Jessica finds out she's pregnant, at first everyone is overjoyed... but soon her personality begins to change. Meanwhile Dimitri (who's died in a car crash but now returned at Satan's whim, or something like that) stalks the couple around San Francisco as part of a deal with the devil to deliver a new hellish spawn on earth. Jessica quickly spirals out of control, smashing open her husband's fish aquarium, puking green bile and spinning her head backwards just like you-know-who. Will Dimitri let this evil plan come to fruition, or does the devil have an even nastier twist in mind?

Watching *Beyond the Door* as a linear narrative is a frustrating experience as the various story threads (including a very oblique double-twist ending) only bind together if you really, really pay attention. However, the film is a huge amount of fun as a simple spook show experience, with some

B

truly skin-crawling sound experiments and more than a handful of unforgettably grotesque images. Much of the dialogue is ridiculous (especially Lavia's), but Mills's intense dedication to her part still results in a harrowing third act when her full possession kicks in. The amazing funk score by the great Franco Micalizzi adds to the strange brew, with crazy saxophones and soul music mashing together in one of the weirdest horror soundtracks ever produced. Of course, this film is also notable for really kicking off the career of Egyptian-born producer and occasional director Ovidio Assonitis, who had earlier put his name on such films as *Who Saw Her Die?*, *Man from Deep River* and the insane *Labyrinth of Sex*. However, here he really found his niche by taking successful elements from U.S. hits and mashing them into something berserk and unique, a formula he put to even more bizarre use in *Laure*, *Tentacles* and his cracked masterpiece, *The Visitor*. If you're looking for an introduction to his derivative but fascinating style, look no further.

Released in America running barely over 90 minutes, *Beyond the Door* also circulated in a longer, 109-minute edition entitled *The Devil Within Her* which appeared on U.K. videotape and eventually as a non-anamorphic Japanese DVD. Code Red's American release easily bests all prior editions with a colourful anamorphic transfer accurately replicating the dark but effective photography, and it's the complete European print under the *Devil* title. For the record, the extra footage consists mainly of the original opening title sequence (involving the aforementioned funk performance of "Bargain with the Devil"), additional dialogue, and some especially weird footage of oddball San Francisco residents on the street. The disc also comes with a rich bounty of extras explaining exactly how this film came to be. The first audio commentary features a cheerful Mills and *Intruder* director Scott Spiegel chatting about the film with modera-

tors Darren Gross and Lee Christian, who cover not only her work on this film but the rest of her career and her memories about shooting in the American-to-Italian locations. Next up is a commentary with Assonitis (moderated by Christian and this writer) who offers a detailed story about working with (and "firing") James Cameron on *Piranha II: The Spawning* which is worth a listen all unto itself. On the video side, the biggest extra is a 20-minute featurette, "*Beyond the Door*: 35 Years Later", which features Mills, Assonitis, Richard Johnson, and co-writer Alex Rebar (best known for playing *The Incredible Melting Man*) continuing their reminiscences about the creation of the film and its unusual but successful release history which paved the way for a flood of possession films well into the early 1980s. Last up, you get an additional brief featurette with Johnson ("An Englishman in Italy") talking about some of his other Italian films (mainly *Zombie*), a gallery packed with lobby cards, stills, posters and VHS art, and (along with other Code Red promos) the U.S. trailer and TV spot. An exclusive Best Buy two-disc edition adds a bonus disc containing the shorter American cut and some outtakes from Mills's interview if you're so inclined to seek it out.

BILL DOUGLAS TRILOGY: MY CHILDHOOD

B&W, 1972, 46m. / Directed by Bill Douglas / Starring Stephen Archibald, Karl Fieseler, Hughie Restorick, Jean Taylor Smith, Helena Gloag

MY AIN FOLK

B&W, 1973, 55m. / Directed by Bill Douglas / Starring Stephen Archibald, Hughie Restorick, Paul Kermack

MY WAY HOME

B&W, 1978, 71m. / Directed by Bill Douglas / Starring Stephen Archibald, Hughie Restorick, Joseph Blatchley / BFI (DVD & Blu-ray, UK R0 PAL/HD), Facets (US R0 NTSC)

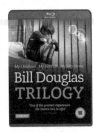

The *bildungsroman*, or coming-of-age novel, has been a staple of literature for centuries, but its importance in filmmaking has been more minimal. Nevertheless, a few film-makers made their careers by finding young actors capable of carrying their visions of growing up onscreen through one film or, in lucky cases, an entire series, most famously with François Truffaut's Antoine Doinel cycle (beginning with *The 400 Blows*) and Sanjit Ray's Apu trilogy. Only in recent years has Scotland's most important contribution to this cycle from director Bill Douglas been truly appreciated; his first three films – referred to in their home video incarnations as the Bill Douglas Trilogy – are stark and sometimes harrowing autobiographical tales, with lead actor Stephen Archibald playing his stand-in Jamie with a power beyond his years. Sadly Douglas completed only one more feature film, *Comrades*, before becoming a film professor and then passing away in 1991.

Funded by the British Film Institute, *My Childhood* became a critical favourite as it depicted the impoverished upbringing of Jamie and his brother, Tommy (Hughie Restorick), while living with their grandmother in a post-World War II mining town as their mother has been committed to an asylum and their father is away for work. A chance encounter with a displaced German soldier forces Jamie to confront his situation without a real parental force in his life, which directly leads into the next film, *My Ain Folk*. Here the brothers are split apart by the death of their grandmother, with Jamie going to live with his father and another, far less welcoming grandmother; meanwhile Tommy's miserable stint in a children's home forces him to reconsider his destiny as well. Finally the boys enter maturity with *My Way Home*, as a homeless Jamie enlists with the

RAF and is inspired to seek a more artistic direction in his life thanks to the influence of a fellow officer. Best viewed as a continuous experience, the three films are not traditional "feel-good" movies, but Douglas's considerable visual gifts and ability to convey his story with only a few quick strokes of dialogue makes these intensely filmic productions well worth discovering.

An American edition of the trilogy appeared from Facets in a soft-looking DVD edition, but the BFI version (on DVD and Blu-ray) transferred from the original vault negatives is really the only way to appreciate all three of these films. Obviously the first film (shot in 16mm) is limited by its low budget and the nature of the film stock, but it still looks quite impressive in the street and landscape shots which deliver a surprising amount of detail. The other two look quite excellent throughout with pin-sharp imagery and very clean presentations making them an utter joy to watch. Optional English subtitles are also provided, which can be quite handy for some of the accents.

The BFI edition also contains a bonus DVD of supplements including the one-hour "Bill Douglas: Intent on Getting the Image" documentary from 2006, a 1970 Douglas student short entitled "Come Dancing", a brief four-minute interview with the director from the BFI vaults, and a 32-page illustrated booklet containing notes by Peter Jewell, John Caughie, Matthew Flanagan, Louis C. Milne, and Sean Martin.

BLACK EMANUELLE'S BOX VOLUME 1: EMANUELLE AROUND THE WORLD

Colour, 1977, 102m. / Directed by Joe D'Amato / Starring Laura Gemser, Ivan Rassimov, Karin Schubert, Maria Luigia, Stefania Pecce, George Eastman, Paul Thomas / Severin (US R1 NTSC), CP Digital (Russia R0 NTSC) / WS (1.85:1) (16:9)

EMANUELLE IN BANGKOK

Colour, 1976, 92m. / Directed by Joe D'Amato / Starring Laura Gemser, Gabriele Tinti, Ely Galleani, Ivan Rassimov, Venantino Venantini, Giacomo Rossi-Stuart, Debra Berger / Severin (US R1 NTSC), Optimum (UK R2 PAL) / WS (1.85:1) (16:9)

SISTER EMANUELLE

Colour, 1977, 92m. / Directed by Giuseppe Vari / Starring Laura Gemser, Monica Zanchi, Gabriele Tinti, Vinja Locatelli, Pia Velsi / Severin (US R1 NTSC), Another World (Denmark R2 PAL) / WS (1.85:1) (16:9), X-Rated Kult (Germany R2 PAL) / WS (1.66:1)

After the smash success of *Black Emanuelle* in 1975, softcore screen siren Laura Gemser worked at a furious schedule on numerous follow-ups over the next three years. The most memorable of these instalments were easily her collaborations with director Joe D'Amato which culminated with the extreme hardcore-and-snuff depravities of *Emanuelle in America*. However, a sure contender for the second most outrageous entry is easily *Emanuelle Around the World*, a flagship title in *Black Emanuelle's Box*, the marvellously titled collection from Severin Films. The original Italian title of this particular 1977 film is *Emanuelle – Perché violenza alle donne?* (or "Why Is There Violence Towards Women?"), which pretty much encapsulates the entire focus of the story. Once again a globe-hopping photographer, pretty and curious Emanuelle (Gemser, of course) is first seen tumbling around naked in the back of a truck in New York with her latest conquest, played (uncredited) by porn actor Paul Thomas (most notorious for starting his film career in the G-rated *Jesus Christ Superstar*).

When she gets wind of an international human slavery ring that preys on nubile women, she decides to recruit her blonde friend, European activist Cora (a pre-porn Karin Schubert), for an expedition into the darker side of human nature. Their exploits range from a visit to an Indian orgy orchestrated by a sex guru (*Anthropophagus* himself, George Eastman), an all-girl sex school equipped with giant phalluses, and the notorious finale beneath the Brooklyn Bridge in which a bunch of drunken senators decide to gang rape Miss Ohio. PC it ain't, but that's the '70s for you.

A perfect tour of all things wonderful about the Emanuelle series, *Around the World* features perhaps the finest score of the series by regular composer Nico Fidenco, with an ABBA-esque theme song you'll be humming for days. Fidenco also finally speaks on the boxed set DVD about his career, how he got into film scoring, and the differences between scoring sex scenes and horror movies. (He also holds up some very tasty-looking vinyl soundtracks of his scores.) The DVD itself is quite fine; apart from some print damage in the opening shots and somewhat hazy credits, the quality is very nice with rich colours that blow away all those miserable VHS bootlegs. The film can be played either in Italian or English (with optional English subtitles translated from the Italian track); it's dubbed either way, and personally the English track feels a bit more in keeping with the tone of the film, but opinions may vary. Along with the Fidenco interview the disc also includes a blurry-looking, non-anamorphic U.S. trailer (with that great Jerry Gross Organization tag) under the same title.

Apart from the boxed set, *Around the World* is also available separately in a rarely-seen, alternative "XXX European Version" (no extras) containing some hardcore footage obviously shot during filming. The sex guru scene is considerably more explicit and marks a rare occasion in which Eastman is clearly seen in the same frame with actors having unsimulated sex; Gemser still refrains from going all the way, of course (apart from an obvious, much paler body double), but there's enough grinding and pumping on display from everyone else to ensure this version will never pop up on TV, not to mention some shots in the bestiality sequence that will certainly keep this off the shelves of your local retailer. In either incarnation, this entry represents the best of what the spin-off Emanuelle series has to offer; it's fast-paced, aware of its own absurdity, and still just socially acceptable enough (i.e., no fake snuff footage). The softcore version was also released on a Russian DVD (with a simulated 5.1 English mix) from CP Digital, featuring R5 coding inside Russia or no region coding for everyone else.

Shot in '76 but released in many territories either simultaneously with *Around the World* or even after it (with *America* falling in between), *Emanuelle in Bangkok* is a slightly more traditional outing for Emmy as she hits the Far East in search of her latest interview conquest, the King of Bangkok, who proves to be elusive enough to justify a feature-length running time. Hot-to-trot masseuses, loudmouthed tourists, and horny politicians soon enter the mix, along with some out-of-left-field mondo footage of a mongoose ripping a snake to shreds in a cage. Oh, and in a nod to the original Just Jaeckin film's notorious "cigarette act", lucky viewers get a naughty nightclub routine involving female privates and ping-pong balls. Once again D'Amato manages to keep the proceedings unpredictable and spicy (note the early piston-pumping sex scene on a ship), with the obligatory sexual assault detour sure to tick off any *Ms.* readers; on the other hand, it provides a surprisingly progressive depiction of a lesbian relationship in the second half, which of course also still functions as a

good excuse for male viewers to simply enjoy watching Gemser and another woman getting it on. As usual Gemser gets to enjoy some screen time with her spouse, the late Gabriele Tinti, who went on to appear with her in many, many exploitation films over the next decade.

Severin's DVD of *Emanuelle in Bangkok* kicks off on a distressing note with video-generated French credits obviously lifted from an old videotape, but after this sequence the film thankfully shifts to a vastly superior, fresh new transfer from film that kills all those old VHS editions. (The brief closing titles are also sourced from the same tape but are less intrusive.) Again the English and Italian audio options are presented with optional English subtitles; this time the English track is really the way to go as the Italian version feels rather forced and artificial, not to mention wildly out of synch. Fidenco's romantic score (with a solid theme song, "Sweet Living Thing") comes through just fine either way and enhances the mood quite nicely. Extras include a Joe D'Amato interview video-taped at a 1995 UK Eurofest convention (in which he talks a bit about his most popular leading lady and his softcore work), with a few glimpses of other Italian-related guest appearances at the show; you also get a non-anamorphic trailer sourced from tape but looking quite watchable all the same. A much less potent, edited version of *Emanuelle in Bangkok* was released by Optimum in the U.K. after losing four and a half minutes of footage involving sexual assault, two animal fight scenes and close-ups of the ping pong ball scene (for obvious reasons).

Finally, Gemser dons a habit for some mild nunsploitation in *Sister Emanuelle*, the only film in the set not helmed by D'Amato (and reviewed more extensively in *DVD Delirium Vol. 3*). Here Gemser mostly takes a backseat to the antics of pretty blonde

Monica Zanchi (her co-star from *Emanuelle and the Last Cannibals*), here playing wanton young teen Monica, whose propensity for luring young boys into public group sex lands her in a convent. Monica tries her best to break Sister Emanuelle, who quickly winds up in hot water with the Mother Superior for exposing her decidedly verboten garters and silky undies during a catfight. Pretty soon Monica's watching over a hunky convict hiding on the premises and luring Emanuelle into sins of the flesh which may force her to break her vows forever. Complete with a Stelvio Cipriani score that huffs and puffs to duplicate that Fidenco sound, this would-be Emanuelle entry has little to do with the rest of the series (heck, Gemser isn't even a reporter this time, for obvious reasons), but the leading ladies still make it a worthwhile outing. D'Amato's outrageous sensibilities would have no doubt resulted in a more fascinating product (as he demonstrated with his own nunsploitation outing, *Images in a Convent*), but at least Vari has the good sense to just strip everyone down whenever the plot threatens to grind to a halt. The barn love scene in the third act is the obvious highlight, with Gemser finally giving in and doffing her habit to do what she does best; it's also one of her more interesting performances, as Gemser is forced to convey a broader spectrum of emotions than usual. Severin's disc presents a beautiful transfer, the all-around best of the set, which easily outclasses the murkier previous DVD editions. The English dub is quite well done and works best here again; extras include the theatrical trailer and several bits of alternative and deleted footage from the Italian VHS, including some awkward hardcore insert footage that was wisely left out of the main feature. For completists, an extended version of the teasing barnyard sex scene which was present on the VHS version and included as an extra on Severin's disc also pops up cut back into the film for the

"X-rated" extended cut present as a non-anamorphic (1.66:1) alternative on the Danish DVD from Another World (English language only with optional subs in Danish, Finnish, Norwegian and Swedish).

A fourth disc included with the box set is a very special goodie that almost merits the entire price tag by itself, a CD entitled "Getting Down with Black Emanuelle". A fantastic companion piece to the essential *Black Emanuelle's Groove* compilation, this disc contains the majority of Nico Fidenco tracks from the soundtracks for the original *Black Emanuelle* (a film still being held hostage by Studio Canal, unfortunately), *Emanuelle Around the World* and *Emanuelle in Bangkok*; between the two CDs you can pretty much assemble the complete scores for the three films and not worry about having to pay stupid amounts of money for the long-discontinued Japanese CD editions.

BLACK EMANUELLE'S BOX VOLUME 2: BLACK EMANUELLE 2

Colour, 1976, 92m. / Directed by Albert Thomas (Bitto Albertini) / Starring Angelo Infanti, Sharon Lesley (Shulamith Lasri), Don Powell, Dagmar Lassander / Severin (US R1 NTSC, UK R2 PAL) / WS (1.85:1) (16:9)

BLACK EMMANUELLE/WHITE EMMANUELLE

Colour, 1976, 94m. / Directed by Brunello Rondi / Starring Laura Gemser, Annie Belle, Gabriele Tinti, Al Cliver, Susan Scott / Severin (US R1 NTSC) / WS (2.35:1) (16:9)

EMANUELLE AND THE WHITE SLAVE TRADE

Colour, 1978, 89m. / Directed by Joe D'Amato / Starring Laura Gemser, Ely Galleani, Gabriele Tinti, Venantino Venantini / Severin (US R1 NTSC) / WS (1.85:1) (16:9)

Another triple helping of exotic Italian smut, Severin's *Black Emanuelle's Box Volume 2* carries on the unabashed tradition of its predecessor with three of the most eccentric entries in the ebony goddess's cinematic cycle. After the success of the original *Black Emanuelle* in 1975 with Laura Gemser, the filmmakers decided to churn out a quick follow-up – but without their leading lady. Instead they found a new "star", one-hit sexploitation star Shulamith Lasri (christened onscreen as "Sharon Lesley"), who, to state the obvious, is no Laura Gemser. Fortunately the sequel offers a string of other insane ingredients to compensate, starting with an opening montage showing our new Emanuelle in a variety of ridiculous degradation scenarios ranging from a police state inquisition to a southern plantation. It turns out these scenarios are all part of the warped psyche of our title character, who's suffering from a series of sexual neuroses and acute amnesia at a posh mental clinic. Her doctor, Paul (Angelo Infanti), tries to get to the bottom of her problems, which cause her to hit on anything in pants but then go batty when things get physical. Through a series of flashbacks (starting in Beirut!) she uncovers her traumas, which include a New Orleans jazz musician father (played by Don Powell, who also composed the eccentric music score), who apparently spent his time puking in the gutter. Of course, when dad really shows up, it turns out she made the whole thing up. Oh, and you also get a hot and heavy session with a basketball player, not to mention some gratuitous nudity from slumming guest star Dagmar Lassander in one of her last real sexpot roles.

Black Emanuelle 2 comes packed with lots of fake-Freudian gibberish including this priceless opening title card: "The sicke-ness that disturb me most is myself – Sigmund Freud" [sic, obviously]. As a result, the frequent chit chat sessions about Emanuelle's uneasy state of mind result in some priceless hilarity, with the hefty amounts of nudity (Ms. Lesley spends at least half of her screen time disrobed) to keep everyone distracted from the fact that nothing's really happening. Viewers probably didn't care, though some of the more sadistic moments wound up getting excised from many TV and video prints. Fortunately Severin's disc appears to be complete, and while the feel is very, very different from the Laura Gemser cycle and often feels more akin to a sexy blaxploitation outing translated by a lunatic Italian, trash fans should find plenty to enjoy. The anamorphic transfer looks fine given the source (don't be alarmed by the scratchy opening logo), though the photography is pretty much confined to bland medium shots. The audio is dubbed English only which is fine given that no one seems to be speaking the same language anyway. Extras include the English theatrical trailer ("Love and cruelty can unite in the strangest of human needs!"), which packs in as much skin as possible for three and a half minutes, and "Diva 70", a very interesting 15-minute Nocturno video interview with the chain-smoking Lassander who talks about her career, her middle class husband's hot-and-cold relationship with her work, being five months pregnant and still acting, doing club appearances, acting for Mario Bava and Lucio Fulci, and the reasons she appeared in this film (her agent told her to do lots of cameos). The same cut of the film subsequently appeared from Severin in the U.K. as well with the same extras.

Of course, Gemser's box office power was soon recognised when she was recruited to appear in a string of additional Emanuelle films; in fact, the same year *Black Emanuelle 2* was released, Gemser appeared in no less than three projects all marketed as unofficial sequels in some form or another: *Emanuelle in Bangkok*, *Black Cobra* and *Black Emmanuelle/White Emmanuelle* (better known to VHS fans under such titles as *Black Velvet* and *Emmanuelle in Egypt*), which teamed her up with *Laure* starlet Annie Belle. Though no character in the film is actually named Emmanuelle, director Brunello Rondi (best known for writing many of Fellini's films) keeps things well within the series template by including lots of travelogue footage interspersed with plenty of softcore sex scenes. The real curio factor here is the fact that Gemser and Belle happen to be teamed up with their real-life boyfriends at the time, Gabriele Tinti and Al Cliver respectively, though oddly enough their screen time together ranges from bland to flat-out unpleasant. There's very little plot here (surprise!), as model Laura (Gemser) and her pal Pina (Belle) go to Egypt for some photo spreads in the desert with a jackass photographer (Tinti) who enjoys degrading Laura in front of the camera and eventually forcing himself on her. They also spend some time with new age mystic Horatio (Cliver), who expands his spiritual horizons by having public three-ways in an Egyptian temple, and Laura and Pina make out here and there. Other miscellaneous supporting characters including breast implant queen Susan Scott drift in and out, usually without even getting character names, and... well, that's pretty much it. Apart from the Tinti-led photo sessions in which he forces a topless Gemser to pose with a worm-ridden jackal carcass and a big pile of camel dung, the weirdest highlight of the film is easily a druggy sequence in which Gemser attends a cult ceremony where she chugs goat's blood, hallucinates an attack by her evil doppelganger, and gets molested by a bunch of priests.

Usually circulated in drastically edited prints which excise most of the good stuff,

the film was also one of the few Gemser vehicles shot in scope and has naturally suffered terribly via lousy pan and scan transfers for years. Severin's disc offers a much-needed restoration of the original framing as well as all of the steamy footage including an unexpected close-up of Cliver's genitalia guaranteed to perturb Lucio Fulci fans. The image quality ranges from scene to scene depending on the film stock and lighting conditions, but the transfer itself looks fine (albeit interlaced for some reason). Surprisingly, the disc includes both the familiar English dub (which isn't bad) and the Italian dub track as well, with optional English subtitles. Both ways work fine, though the latter feels a bit classier with better-matched voices. Bonus features include the Italian trailer (under the title *Velluto nero*) and an interesting if somewhat disjointed 18-minute featurette, "Black Velvet", which features an on-camera Cliver intercut with audio interviews with Gemser and Belle as they discuss the making of the film, the director, Cliver's role in Visconti's *The Damned*, the ramshackle production's impact on parallel Joe D'Amato projects, and Gemser's illness going in and out of the Morocco shoot.

Finally we reach the big prize of the set, *Emanuelle and the White Slave Trade*, the last and rarest of the Gemser/D'Amato *Black Emanuelle* films. Originally released as *La via della prostituzione*, the film once again features Gemser as the titular photojournalist who bounces from one locale to another, this time driven by an episodic plot straight out of a '60s *Olga* roughie. While doing research for a story on organised crime, the nosy Emanuelle hooks up with her modelling buddy Susan (*Five Dolls for an August Moon*'s Ely Galleani). "You still go in for a lot of lovemaking?" asks Emmy, which nympho Susan answers by pulling over into a garage, flashing her undies, and nailing the mechanic. Then they head to the airport where the women spy a wheelchair-bound young woman traded off for a big wad of cash by a suspicious lothario (Tinti), but they're too busy posing as a couple of stewardesses and eyeballing a wealthy polygamist Arab to do much about it. Then they go off to a plantation where they take a steamy shower together. For vague reasons they decide to hop on a plane to Africa where they get involved with fashion shoots, bed down with more guys, and notice Tinti and the same sold woman. Emanuelle follows them and witnesses a boardroom sales session in which young women are trotted out and stripped in front of decadent European buyers, all involved in a white slavery ring. Further snooping brings her face to face with Tinti, lots of open hotel doors with naked women getting felt up inside, the usual implied gang rape scene, a lesbian nurse, and an authoritative transvestite who partakes in the wildest bowling alley fistfight ever committed to film.

Roughly even with the other D'Amato/Gemser titles in terms of outrageousness and quality (except for the wild card *Emanuelle in America*, of course), *Emanuelle and the White Slave Trade* inexplicably became very difficult to see after its initial release, circulating mostly to die-hard collectors in a terrible Greek VHS transfer. D'Amato keeps things moving fast and hilariously throughout, and the dubbing is even more absurd than usual with the quick-to-peel Galleani saddled with one of the goofiest British accents you'll ever hear. Nico Fidenco's score is easily his most disco-influenced, dropping the familiar "Black Emanuelle" theme in favour of a bouncy, wildly overplayed ditty entitled "Run Cheetah Run". Interestingly, the brutal violence which had slowly infiltrated the series (most obviously found in *Emanuelle in*

America and *Emanuelle and the Last Cannibals*) is pulled back here, with only the bloody but cartoonish bowling alley scene reminding viewers how over-the-top these films can become. Gemser and Tinti have even less interaction than usual, mostly observing each other covertly or from afar and sharing an occasional drink here and there; luckily the story itself is so lunatic that most viewers won't even notice. Severin's disc doesn't really have much competition on the home video market, but the anamorphic transfer is a godsend for fans tired of squinting through shoddy bootlegs. It's uncut and anamorphic, the English dub sounds fine, and apart from the obvious and beloved grain present in the recycled travel footage, there's nothing wrong with the film elements. Extras include the lively Italian trailer and "After Hours with Joe D'Amato", a '90s video interview in which the late director enjoys a dinner table conversation about his softcore career.

As with the previous set, customers who purchase the box instead of the individual films are also treated to a bonus CD containing the bulk of three Fidenco scores. The biggest prize here is what appears to be the full soundtrack for *White Slave Trade*, which has never been available before in any format; the "Run Cheetah Run" melody gets a solid workout, but the highlight is easily the slow and sexy vocal piece, "Too Much Again!", which manages to make Barry White sound like Marie Osmond. Also included is a sampling of the monothematic score from *Emanuelle and the Last Cannibals* (previously available as a long-defunct release from Lucertola) and eight tracks from *Emanuelle in America*, which is especially welcome since it contains the first pristine, complete, stereo version of the great theme song, "I'm Your King", inexplicably missing from the earlier vinyl and Japanese CD releases.

BLACK NIGHT

Colour, 2005, 90m. / Directed by Olivier Smolders / Starring Fabrice Rodriguez, Philippe Corbisier, Iris De Busschere, Yves-Marie Gnahoua / Cult Epics (US R1 NTSC), Imagine (Holland R2 PAL) / WS (1.85:1) (16:9) / DD5.1

Unknown outside of die hard art house circles, Belgian director Olivier Smolders has been turning out surreal, often inscrutable short films since the mid-1980s. His work teems with imagery involving human skin, religious iconography, and reptiles and insects, while his formal aesthetic style immediately invites comparisons with other European (or Euro-friendly) directors, most obviously Peter Greenaway (whose *A Zed and Two Noughts* is a clear influence), Terry Gilliam, François Ozon, and Luis Buñuel. Eventually he completed a feature-length film, shot on DV but manipulated to look for all the world like a moody 35mm film, entitled *Black Night* (*Nuit noire*), and its release has allowed his entire body of work to finally gain some appreciation. More a dreamlike experimental experience than a coherent narrative, *Black Night* begins with a pair of old men unveiling a small snowbound stage with two child puppets. Intercut with random shots of insects, the story focuses in on the two children, now real, a brother and sister. After the death of the young girl, the boy, Oscar (Fabrice Rodriguez), grows up to take over as an animal conservator at his father's Natural Sciences Museum, while the world has been consumed entirely in darkness except for a few fleeting seconds of sunlight each day (a device mirrored by the symbolic image of stage curtains opening and closing). One day he finds one of his co-workers, an African woman, ailing in his bed, and she and Oscar copulate (or do they?) before she dies. Then things get really strange, as his bed is taken over by a giant cocoon...

B

Though some critics may be tempted to find some deeper underlying meaning in all of the fragmented images of *Black Night*, the film really works best as a string of visually stunning scenes in which mankind and Mother Nature commingle in some sort of deeply uneasy symbiosis. The actors mainly function as additional visual objects, though Rodriguez does well in a leading role which requires him to devolve from a stoic, buttoned-up mannequin to a sweaty, frenzied wreck. Of course, this being an art film there's a lot of female nudity, though it's rendered in a very anthropological fashion.

The DVD from Cult Epics presents the film in an impressive anamorphic transfer which belies its digital video origins; the saturated colours and omnipresent black shadows come across just fine, and the French stereo soundtrack (with optional English subtitles) sounds clear throughout with a highly atmospheric and unnerving music score. Extras include a 17-minute reel of deleted scenes (nothing too remarkable, but a lot more bug footage), an amusing behind the scenes featurette that culminates on a remarkably naked and slimy note, an interview with Smolders about his maiden feature film voyage, an alternative festival version of his "Spiritual Exercises" short (the original appears on the short film collection of the same title from Cult Epics), and easily the most bizarre of all, a segment entitled "About Black Night" with a French narrator rattling off a string of various symbolic associations tied to the film's recurring visual images (a sample: "An abyss, a hole, a natural orifice, a star, fear of the void, of being devoured, a white series: white particles, snow, spermatozoa, Japanese cherry trees, mother of pearl in a shell..."). A PAL release with the same extras later appeared from Holland on the Imagine label under the title *Nuit noire*, with subtitles in Dutch and English.

THE BLACK PIT OF DR. M

B&W, 1959, 82m. / Directed by Fernando Méndez / Starring Gastón Santos, Rafael Bertrand, Antonio Raxel, Mapita Cortés / Casa Negra (US R1 NTSC)

At a remote and utterly creepy mental hospital, Doctors Mazali (Rafael Bertrand) and Aldama (Antonio Raxel) agree to a wager that whoever dies first will come back from the afterlife to tell the other about what lies in store on "the other side". When the latter passes on (with convenient speed), a séance reveals that Mazali will indeed learn the truth about the netherworld very shortly, while the late doctor's daughter Patricia (Mapita Cortés) is lured to the asylum by her father's spirit. Soon all hell breaks loose thanks to one particularly agitated female inmate, a handy vial of acid, plentiful murder accusations, and a series of supernatural shenanigans that leave the poor surviving doctor sorry he ever entered the deal in the first place.

A film known more by reputation than actual screenings for several decades, *The Black Pit of Dr. M* (shown here under its more appropriate Spanish title, *Misterios de ultratumba*) went straight to American television in a dubbed, heavily butchered edition courtesy of K. Gordon Murray. While this variant has since become extinct, the intact Mexican original proudly stands as one of the best of its country's ilk, a delicious headlong collision between the hoary monster-on-the-loose antics of Universal horror and the bold, stylistic flourishes which became the trademarks of '60s horror cinema (especially in Europe). Though this still has numerous talky passages in keeping with the Mexican horror tradition, director Fernando Méndez (*The Vampire*) keeps even the most static scenes alive by lighting the frame with constant sources of texture like flickering candles, fires, billowing mist, and moving shadows, creating a visually beguiling work that explodes in a few jolting terror set pieces. The sets are also a bit more ambitious than usual, with some wonderfully creepy exteriors that would be right at home in Hammer's *Brides of Dracula* one year later. The influence on Italian horror is obvious as well, considering that bandwagon only began a year later, too; though it can't claim any European pedigree, this film could easily go on the shortlist with Georges Franju's *Eyes Without a Face* as one of the first truly "modern" horror films. Of course, the constraints of Mexican filmmaking at the time prevent Méndez's film from reaching the artistic heights of its more famous counterparts; the actors are competent but rarely hit the delirious heights one might expect with the material, and the overwriting of several scenes will no doubt cause some new viewers to roll their eyes once or twice. However, for anyone accustomed to these films, the much-needed restoration of this crucial title puts back an important piece in the puzzle of assembling a genuine, more respectable view of the golden age of Mexican horror.

Casa Negra provides a wonderfully clean transfer for such an obscure title. Unlike some earlier films, the framing (presented completely open matte here) appears designed to be composed with matting to 1.85:1 or so in mind; there's plenty of dead space at the top and bottom, so viewers with widescreen monitors (who don't mind cropping off the subtitles, unless they have a zoom-friendly DVD player) can actually increase their enjoyment by doing a manual widescreen presentation. Black levels are a bit on the pale side during several scenes (especially the first reel), but this may have been a deliberate photographic choice given the wild visual manipulation on display throughout the film. The mono Spanish audio with optional English subtitles sounds fine throughout. Mexican horror enthusiast and expert (and rocker) Frank Coleman chips in with the most notable extra, a feature-length audio commentary track in which he covers the stories of the various participants in front of and behind the camera, plus a sketch of the film's odd distribution history which left it far more obscure than, say, *Brainiac*. Coleman also appears as part of "21st Century Art" for a '90s homemade music video using clips from the film, sort of in the same spirit as the Argento "Demonia" tributes. Other extras include a director bio, a step-through essay on K. Gordon Murray, the 1961 English script (about as close to that dub as you're likely to get), the Mexican theatrical trailer, and a poster and stills gallery. Unfortunately Casa Negra (a division of Panik House) became defunct shortly after its inception, making this an instant collector's item well worth tracking down.

BLACK ROSES

Colour, 1988, 84m. / Directed by John Fasano / Starring Carmine Appice, Jesse D'Angelo, Julie Adams, Frank Dietz, Vincent Pastore, John Martin, Carla Ferrigno / Synapse (US R0 NTSC) / WS (1.78:1) (16:9) / DD2.0

After the "success" of *Rock 'n' Roll Nightmare*, horror fans were assaulted the following year with another, even more elaborate take on heavy metal horror which received plenty of coverage in *Fangoria* and lured in lots of video customers with its eye-catching embossed cover art. As a horror film the end result is utterly ineffective, but as a time capsule of hair-metal monster mayhem, this

is sheer perfection. After a puzzling prologue with a band of demons rocking out on a small city stage, the story proper begins in Mill Basin, a quiet town chosen to be the kick-off venue for a reclusive but popular metal band, Black Roses. The burly, moustachioed English teacher, Mr. Moorhouse (John Martin), can't understand why the kids would be more fascinated with head-banging than Walt Whitman. (How this band could be so popular without ever performing live is never really explained, oddly enough.) The alarmed parents show up for a demo performance in which the head-rocking band turns out to be more like Chicago-lite, but that's all a clever ruse; before long the kids are exposed to subliminal demonic messages from the monstrous band members whose true nature has yet to emerge. Soon it's up to the stalwart English teacher to stop the escalating chain of youthful misbehaviour consuming the town before the Black Roses give their final, apocalyptic performance.

Needless to say, this film sends out some drastic mixed messages by appealing to metal-loving horror fans while telling them that, well, it really is the devil's music and elders really do know what's best for them. Hopefully the double standard was intentional, though it's difficult to tell for sure even with the DVD supplements. For maximum enjoyment it's best to just shut your brain off and enjoy such sights as Vincent Pastore (*The Sopranos'* ill-fated Big Pussy) getting offed by a *Videodrome*-inspired melting vinyl record and a malicious speaker. Since this is a Shapiro Glickenhaus film that also means lots of rubbery monsters, utterly gratuitous bare boob shots, and a cheerful disregard for narrative logic, all on a budget that wouldn't fund a single episode of *Survivor*. The soundtrack actually got distributed more widely than the film, and since it features such names as Lizzy Borden and King Kobra, that's hardly surprising.

Almost everyone who's seen *Black Roses* encountered it solely through the chalky-looking, pink-hued VHS release back in the '80s, so it shouldn't come as a shock that Synapse's DVD marks a gargantuan leap in quality for this title. It looks like an entirely different film, with bright red-oriented colour schemes and much better black levels. A handful of night scenes come off rather poorly (due to a switch in cinematographers during filming, which is understandable given some weird day-for-night efforts and some truly oddball framing), but 95% of the film looks terrific. Apart from the obviously essential hi-def release someday, it's hard to imagine this looking any better. The Dolby stereo soundtrack doesn't do much with directional effects, but it sounds fine; basically it's your typical low-budget '80s horror sound mix, which means loud music with little bass and lots of flatly recorded dialogue. While most '80s cult items get the bare bones treatment now, *Black Roses* benefits from an all-out deluxe treatment highlighted by an amusing commentary track with the director John Fasano, writer Cindy Sorrell (who cameos in the film as a concerned mom), and actors Carla Ferrigno, John Kody Fasano and Lucia Fasano. They cover all the bases on the film ranging from Glickenhaus's demands for more monsters and breasts to John Martin's funny side careers, as well as the director's erroneous crush on *Creature from the Black Lagoon*'s Julie Adams which got her a small part in the film. They also reveal the goofy reason behind Pastore's odd lack of audible screaming during his death scene and seem to place way too much stock in the main singer's character name, Damian. Also included are a dupey-looking and very long promo trailer, a slightly different Cannes promo reel, and a series of Damian audition tapes packed with a nightmare-inducing amount of fluffy hairstyles. Grab it now and just tell friends the devil made you do it.

BLACK TEST CAR

B&W, 1962, 95m. / Directed by Yasuzo Masumura / Starring Jiro Tamiya, Junko Kano, Eiji Funakoshi, Hideo Takamatsu / Fantoma (US R1 NTSC) / WS (2.35:1) (16:9)

After the snappy corporate satire of *Giants and Toys*, genre-hopping director Yasuzo Masumura returned to the boardrooms again in the '60s for a much darker take on capitalism run amuck with *Black Test Car*. Not surprisingly, this tale of two warring auto companies trying to outdo each other in the quest for the brass ring hasn't dated much over the decades, and in fact its morally bankrupt universe looks almost quaint in a post-Enron and Halliburton world. The madness begins when the Tiger Corporation sends out its newest star, the Pioneer, for a test drive with plenty of execs and experts riding alongside. Unfortunately the new flagship car goes down in flames, literally, while spying shutterbugs from the rival Yamato Corporation capture the whole disaster on film for a front-page news item. Company head Onoda (Hideo Takamatsu) recruits one of his top men, Asahina (Jiro Tamiya), to return the favour by disseminating false information and setting up an internal team to not only get the Pioneer out on the market without a hitch, but to undo the rival company and its ruthless spies as well. Soon Asahina finds his own moral compass going wildly askew as he uses everyone in sight, including his pretty girlfriend (Junko Kano), to achieve his goals at any cost.

Though the back cover tags this as a dark comedy, *Black Test Car* is quite a different animal from the farcical *Giants and Toys* and will probably only be funny to those who think Todd Solondz makes romantic comedies. Once again Masumura's scope framing is dead on, yielding one striking image after another in beautiful monochrome. (Oddly enough, the sleek title vehicle itself gets almost no screen time!) All of the performances are committed and intense, teetering on the edge of melodrama without quite slipping over the edge, even during the bordering-on-preachy finale. According to the solid liner notes by Chuck Stephens, the film's success influenced further "black" studies in financial malfeasance, reflecting a growing dread at the rise of corporate strongholds over post-WWII society. While it would certainly be fascinating to see where else these films went, it's likely that Masumura's take would be hard to top. Fantoma's disc brings this key entry in the director's filmography to DVD in a sparkling anamorphic transfer that's just as enjoyable as the rare repertory theatrical screenings. The optional English subtitles are clear and easy to read, and the Japanese mono audio sounds fine. No complaints here at all. Extras are sparse, consisting of the aforementioned booklet, cast and crew filmographies, and the very dramatic theatrical trailer.

BLACK VENUS

Colour, 1983, 95m. / Directed by Claude Mulot / Starring Josephine J. Jones, José Antonio Ceinos, Florence Guérin, Karin Schubert, Emiliano Redondo / Private Screening (US R0 NTSC), MediumRare (UK R2 PAL)

During the early 1980s with the rise of home video and late night TV, erotic cinema experi-enced a shift from grindhouses and occas-ional arty imports like *Emmanuelle* to premium channel showings. Containing a roster of "tastefully" sexy films primarily from America, Britain, France, and Australia, this fertile period for the softcore fanatic was helped along by Playboy Enterprises, who co-funded a string of European productions often in collaboration with infamous producer Harry Alan Towers.

One of the most widely-shown titles from this golden age was 1983's *Black Venus*, whose effective mixture of elegant period decor, full frontal nudity, and oddball plotting managed to draw in both TV viewers and, believe it or not, video renters courtesy of its release from MGM!

Perfectly in line with the usual Victorian erotica, the plot follows the diffi-cult passion which erupts between 19th-Century sculptor Armand (José Antonio Ceinos) and exotic beauty Venus (Miss Bahamas Josephine J. Jones) after they're brought together by an aging art big-wig, Jacques (Emiliano Redondo). Unfortu-nately, the frequent demands on Venus's time as she supports her lover and ignites the lust in everyone around her eventually tear them apart, and Armand's ultimate masterpiece, a replica of his true love, only provides temporary solace. Will they get together again, or will Venus be consumed in a lifestyle of freewheeling, wanton sex? Beautifully shot by hardcore director Claude Mulot (*Pussy Talk*), this top-drawer slice of erotica still holds up quite well today and features a few memorable set pieces including that reliable standby, the "let's walk through a whorehouse and watch the kinky customers" routine already estab-lished in such films as *Taste the Blood of Dracula*. Jones is hot stuff and has no problem showing off her body (aided by luscious Euro starlets Florence Guérin and on-the-cusp-of-porn Karin Schubert), while the love story carries just enough weight to keep the viewer engaged all the way to the satisfying end. Private Screening's release is certainly an improvement over the hopelessly blurry old MGM version, but don't expect a knockout transfer; it still looks like an average, somewhat dated broadcast master, albeit with better sharpness and colour than you'd expect. The compositions crop off quite well to 1.78:1 framing on widescreen TVs, indicating this could have been shown theatrically with no problems. A U.K. release shortly thereafter from MediumRare features a transfer from the same outdated source material but loses points even further thanks to the BBFC-mandated removal of two minutes from a fairly tame sequence of non-consensual sex.

BLOOD AND SEX NIGHTMARE

Colour, 2008, 81m. / Directed by Joseph R. Kolbek / Starring Julia Morizawa, Andy McGuinness, Dan Petit, Niki Notarile, Anthony Navarino, Tina Krause / Bloody Earth (US R0 NTSC) / DD2.0

A clear winner for truth in advertising, *Blood and Sex Nightmare*, a particularly foul cheapie from Bloody Earth, offers enough "did I just see that?" moments to jar the most seasoned trash fanatics. The (intentionally?) hilarious setup is this: after returning from Japan, Amy (Julia Morizawa) finds that her boyfriend, Nick (Andy McGuinness), isn't happy with her lack of interest in sex. Rather than, oh, seeing a therapist, he whines until she agrees to go with him to the Pleasant Mountain Adult Retreat, where people go to hang out in the woods and then retire to their cabins at night for some mattress bouncing. How this differs from any other wilderness retreat is never explained, but never mind. Crazy, creepy old handyman Walter leers at them, and soon the kinksters in the cabin next door

are murdered (in a distinctly perverse fashion) by a rampaging maniac. Could it have some connection to the infamous serial killer and sex maniac who killed himself in the woods four decades earlier? And who's that spooky face Amy keeps seeing in the mirror? And how will any of this help our heroine's libido? Stick around for the unbelievably tasteless climax to find out!

Shot for the price of a fast food meal on digital video, this offering from Joseph R. Kolbek is at least more interesting than your average DIY video affair and delivers both gore and nudity in bucket loads. Oh, and indie smut regular Tina Krause pops up here to supply some skin as well. The transfer looks dull and smeary for the most part, which appears to be a failing of the original production; for a slasher redo of *Porno Holocaust* on a student-level budget, you can't get much better than this. The disc also comes with two of the filmmaker's incredibly stupid short films, "Chef Boyardemon" and "The Roarin' 20s", which are only worth watching if you're very, very, very curious. (Even the director opines, "They suck.") Don't say you weren't warned. Also included is a rap music video Devils Everywhere (by EYEZ The Filmmaker Emcee who's also a victim in one of the film's most unbelievable scenes), as well as a liner notes booklet with filmmaker recollections (a sample: the filming location was really a gay and lesbian retreat with free condoms in the lobby) as well as a closing tribute to the recently departed John Polonia, a hero to camcorder-toting horror fans everywhere.

THE BLOOD ROSE

Colour, 1969, 92m. / Directed by Claude Mulot / Starring Philippe Lemaire, Anny Duperey, Howard Vernon, Olivia Robin, Elizabeth Teissier / Mondo Macabro (US R1 NTSC) / WS (1.66:1) (16:9)

Billed in France as "the first sex-horror film" (a dubious claim for anyone familiar with the works of Jess Franco), *The Blood Rose* is a title more often written about than seen outside Europe; as such, it now possesses something of a cult mystique among the numerous "rich guy goes nuts and kills to restore a disfigured woman's face" tales released in the wake of *Eyes Without a Face*. This time the perpetrator is Frédéric Lansac (Philippe Lemaire, fresh off Roger Vadim's episode of *Spirits of the Dead*), a well-to-do painter living in a castle who loses his sanity after his new wife plunges face-first into a bonfire during a late night party. Faster than you can say *Circus of Horrors*, he blackmails a discredited plastic surgeon into helping him abduct and kill young maidens for their flesh to restore his beloved's beauty, with the expected disastrous results.

Though heavily indebted in both plot and execution to such past films as *The Awful Dr. Orlof* and *Blood and Roses*, this often striking bit of erotic gothic horror features more than its share of surprising touches such as a pair of cackling dwarf assistants, borderline necrophilic love scenes, and a truly oddball finale best experienced without prior warning. The "sex-horror" tag mostly means that lots of women get their shirts torn open; the lack of much genuinely erotic interplay is surprising considering director Claude Mulot later appropriated the lead character's name for his nom de porn for a series of groundbreaking French hardcore films such as the influential *Pussy Talk* and the superior *La femme object*. Mulot displays a sure sense of colour here with plenty of vivid blues and reds highlighting the deliberately ornate and antiquated costumes with occasional, startling bits of mod architecture. Franco

regular Howard Vernon (the original Dr. Orlof) has another juicy villainous role here, most memorably teaming up with Lemaire for a brutal attack scene in a lake.

Though it's barely been circulated on video both under its original title and the English export title of *Ravaged*, *The Blood Rose* finally gets the real red carpet treatment courtesy of Mondo Macabro's DVD release. The transfer from the original negative looks excellent; though the film stock shows its limitations in a few of the night scenes, the colours and detail are top notch. The mono audio can be played in French or dubbed English, with optional English subtitles provided. (The French version is much better, but the typically awkward dub has its pulpy charms, too.) As usual the extras provide some much-needed context for this film, with Pete Tombs providing a succinct but informative survey of erotic French horror, plus well-written bios for Mulot, Lemaire, and actresses Anny Duperey and Elizabeth Teissier. Other extras include a stills gallery, an updated Mondo Macabro promo reel, and the most substantial goodie, an interview with Didier Philippe-Gerard, his friend and brother-in-law who co-wrote the film and also went on to a porn career as "Michel Barny". The genial, moustachioed fellow speaks fondly of his comrade and offers a satisfying sketch of independent art/exploitation films in France during the 1970s and 1980s, a golden period whose like we shall not see again. All in all, a terrific and fascinating example of a previously neglected gem of sexy European blood and thunder.

BLOODBATH AT THE HOUSE OF DEATH

Colour, 1983, 88m. / Directed by Ray Cameron / Starring Kenny Everett, Pamela Stephenson, Vincent Price, Gareth Hunt, Don Warrington / Nucleus (UK R0 PAL) / WS (1.78:1) (16:9) / DD5.1

Even in the early 1980s, the booming horror cycle had already churned out its share of silly (and often very troubled) parodies like *Student Bodies*, *Pandemonium* and *Wacko*. At the same time Britain turned out its own goofy gore spoof, the aptly-titled *Bloodbath at the House of Death*, which barely made a blip in theatres but earned a decent cult following on home video. American horror kids in particular were drawn in by the promotion of Vincent Price (who basically has a glorified cameo) on the cover of every single VHS release which became a mainstay in mom-and-pop video shops for years. Thankfully time has been kind to the film, which veers from one target to the next with head-spinning speed but scores a surprising number of hits along the way. It also features some hilariously over-the-top gore which is always a good thing.

In a very memorable prologue, the residents and guests at remote Headstone Manor are all slaughtered one night by a bunch of red-cloaked cult members who leave a mountain of body parts in their wake. The police are unable to solve the crime, and years later, a sextet of investigators led by Dr. Lukas Mandeville (late UK TV comedy staple Kenny Everett) infiltrate the house after tangling with the superstitious locals and uncover a variety of threats involving Satanists, ghosts, psycho killers, and... well, something else in the last scene that won't be ruined here, but Peter Jackson must have been more than a tad inspired by this before making *Bad Taste*.

Most British comedies relying heavily on pop culture gags never travelled far out of their native homeland, making *Bloodbath* one of the few happy exceptions. Some of the jokes are still a little too inside to work for many modern viewers, but the tried-and-true horror gags (especially a wild, gory flashback involving a surgery gone horribly wrong) still make this a top-notch cult item. Everett's hit-and-miss performance is a rather iffy way to ground a film but he's carried along by a stellar supporting cast including the always-funny Pamela Stephenson (another TV comedy vet who was also one of the very few good things in *Superman III*) and Gareth Hunt from *The New Avengers*, who plays one-half of a gay paranormal-investigating couple. The effects are surprisingly good for the most part, ranging from some Savini-worthy blood gags to ambitious visuals involving a feisty poltergeist, and the imaginative music score by Mike Moran and songwriter Mark London is dead-on brilliant. Of course, the biggest ace in the hole here is the presence of Price as "the Sinister Man", making the most of his limited screen time with some delicious speeches and wonderful nudgings at his classic AIP horror days. The whole thing's more than a bit disjointed and will never be mistaken for high art, but as a late night party selection, it fits the bill just fine. The packaging touts this as the predecessor to *Scary Movie*, though in the end it's more of an inspiration to more modern and better-regarded British TV horror spoofs like *Dr. Terrible's House of Horrible* and especially the brilliant *Garth Marenghi's Darkplace*.

Considering this film has languished far out of the public eye since the 1980s, it's quite miraculous that Nucleus Films managed to wring a very respectable special edition from it including a much-needed new transfer from the original negative. No one should be surprised that this easily blows away any other editions around, and it even boasts a newly-mixed 5.1 audio version in addition to the original and far more naturalistic mono track, but home theatre buffs should enjoy it either way). You also get optional English subtitles, which, even if you aren't deaf, help catch quite a few lines which zing by too quickly. The biggest new extra here is "Running the Bloodbath", a new 22-minute documentary featuring exec producers Stuart Donaldson and Laurence Myers talking about the making of the film, mixed with archival Australian premiere footage of Everett doing press interviews. Also included are the similar U.K. and U.S. theatrical trailers (with only the latter capitalising on Price) and a pdf of the original script.

BLOODSUCKERS FROM OUTER SPACE

Colour, 1984, 79m. / Directed by Glen Coburn / Starring Thom Meyers, Laura Ellis, Glen Coburn, Robert Bradeen, Kris Nicolau-Sharpley / Shriek Show (US R1 NTSC)

A film that baffled more than a handful of horror video hounds in 1984, *Bloodsuckers from Outer Space* has gained a bit of a cult following over the years by those who share its goofball wavelength. Shot in Texas for chump change, it manages to beat the odds thanks to an unexpectedly clever and witty script which pokes fun at zombie and alien movies without being either condescending or cartoonish. Perhaps it's the Southern humour at work or just the sincerity of everyone involved, but it's an always engaging and strangely loveable gorefest that's thankfully survived long after many of its peers have perished. And hey, *The Return of the Living Dead* even swiped its ending one year later!

An alien contamination becomes adrift on the wind through a series of small towns, wreaking havoc and turning the townspeople into flesh-munching ghouls (though some still retain their manners).

Photojournalist Jeff (*The Nail Gun Massacre*'s Thom Meyers) picks up a pretty hitchhiker, Julie (Laura Ellis), on the way to see the relatives who are pressuring him to return home to run the farm, but upon arriving they find themselves fleeing across the backgrounds to get away from the encroaching zombie menace. Meanwhile the dubious scientists at a nearby research facility perform tests on the undead to figure out exactly what the heck's going on, but their boozing and carelessness don't inspire much confidence either.

While some of the gags threaten to stray into *Attack of the Killer Tomatoes* territory, this is thankfully a much more consistent and entertaining film thanks to its cheap but effective gore FX, some great deadpan delivery, and of course some T&A thrown in for good measure. Or maybe the whole thing's just a happy accident that happened to turn out highly entertaining while fulfilling the requirements of a "good" bad movie, as many of the performers are clearly inexperienced or flat-out awful; the extras here allow interpretation to go either way. Director Glen Coburn (who also plays one of the stoner scientists) prepared a special edition DVD he sold directly on the web, but Shriek Show has repurposed it for mass consumption with the same loving care. The transfer looks about as good as could be expected and is full frame, which is just as it should be. (Don't try zooming it, whatever you do.) Extras include a loving audio commentary with Coburn and a "Bloodsucker Reunion" half-hour featurette, with the director and most of the cast and crew appearing to talk about the making of the film. (For some reason, the male participants far outweigh the female.) Everyone seems to have a solid grasp of this film's minor place in the cult movie pantheon, while many of the anecdotes are often hilarious, especially when discussing the odd cop sex scene and subsequent shower attack.

BLOODY MOON

Colour, 1981, 91m. / Directed by Jess Franco / Starring Olivia Pascal, Christoph Moosbrugger, Nadja Gerganoff, Alexander Waechter, Jasmin Losensky / Severin (US R0 NTSC, UK R0 NTSC) / WS (1.85:1) (16:9), Italian Shock (Holland R0 PAL)

 If Jess Franco's name weren't listed in the credits of this notorious German slasher film, you might be hard pressed at first to guess its director based on the evidence at hand. Once banned in Britain as a video nasty and barely shown in theatres anywhere, *Bloody Moon* would make a perfect companion film to other early '80s outrages like *Pieces* or *Nightmare* thanks to its unrelenting onslaught of gratuitous T&A, inventive bloodshed, and inscrutable plotting. In the *Halloween*-inspired opening, facially-scarred Miguel (Alexander Waechter) lurks around a nocturnal party where the pretty object of his affections spurns him for another guy. Naturally he decides to come on to her anyway wearing a Mickey Mouse mask, but when she realises who's in her bed, Miguel offs her with a pair of scissors. Flash forward a bit to the International Youth Club Boarding School for Languages, where bikini-clad babes spend their time playing tennis, lounging around the pool, and occasionally taking Spanish lessons. Miguel's been released from a mental institution and placed in the care of his sister, Manuela (Nadja Gerganoff), with whom he tends to get a little too intimate for comfort. Unfortunately their presence at the school becomes a problem when various topless students start turning up knifed and scissored and stashed in cupboards, with pretty Angela (Olivia Pascal, the most recognisable name from *Vanessa* and *Behind Convent Walls*) feeling uncomfortable about Miguel's past and the fact that her friends keep disappearing. But is our freed lunatic really the culprit, or is someone else entirely pulling the strings behind these brutal slayings?

Completely ludicrous and entertaining from start to finish, *Bloody Moon* may resemble an '80s slasher film in construction but is a wholly unique experience in practice. Franco's beloved zoom lens and proclivity for wholly inappropriate nudity betrays the man behind the camera from time to time, but who knew he could pull off a body count film with such zeal? The real showstopper here is easily a mid-film set piece in which one unlucky lass gets trussed up on a big chunk of stone and slowly sent gliding into the path of a gargantuan circular saw, with a spying little boy racing against time to save her. It's easily a shoo-in for any Franco highlight reel (not surprisingly, Pedro Almodóvar used it for his opening gore montage in *Matador*) and demonstrates that he can pull off both suspense and gut-wrenching splatter when he really puts his effort into it. Other delights include the piecemeal music score composed of spooky stock music and catchy instrumental Europop (credited to softcore composer Gerhard Heinz but obviously the work of many library sources) and some wonderfully nutty dialogue, particularly whenever Angela and Miguel open their mouths. On the downside, the story only barely makes sense, and for some reason a snake gets beheaded with some shears on camera, a nasty little moment that could have easily been left out.

The video history of *Bloody Moon* winds through a number of different international companies since the early '80s, and finding a decent, uncut copy has been nearly impossible. The best option for years was the scarce Canadian VHS release from CIC, which was intact and obviously squeezed rather than cropped to keep the entire image intact (which became quite handy with the advent of 16x9 TVs). In Britain it appeared fleetingly uncut but cropped, but its banned status ensured highly incomplete releases well into the DVD age courtesy of VIPCO. The Dutch DVD from Italian Shock turned out to be a major missed opportunity, with several missing seconds of gore and a terrible pan-and-scan job that rendered it essentially worthless. Thankfully, after a decade of DVD mistreatment Severin's U.S. release corrects all these problems. The transfer from the long-buried original negative (bearing the original German title, *Die Säge des Todes*) blows away any competitors, with perfect framing and punchy, vivid colours throughout. The only audio option is the original English mono track, which is as legitimate as any other given the variety of languages spoken by the different actors on the set. The international trailer is also included and contains a few interesting alternative snippets of footage, including the saw sequence. Of course, this being a Severin release, it would easily be worth buying just for another one of their devilishly entertaining Jess Franco interviews, this time entitled "Franco Moon". The featurette kicks off with Lina Romay bustling in the background as the chain-smoking auteur lights up another cig, then proceeds to talk about how the producers wanted a movie "with 50 horror spotlights" and had no idea how to prepare the project. He also reveals the identity of enigmatic one-off screenwriter "Rayo Casablanca", the intention to use Pink Floyd for the soundtrack, his comedic subversion during filming, the original Spanish title of *Raped College Girl*(!), and much, much more. Ah, Jess – how dull DVDs would be without him. The same Severin edition later appeared in the U.K., a historically significant moment as it marked the film's first uncut release since the '80s Video Nasties heyday.

BOARDINGHOUSE

Colour, 1982, 98m. / Directed by John Wintergate / Starring John Wintergate, Kalassu, Alexandra Day, Joel Riordan, Brian Bruderlin / Code Red (US R0 NTSC)

Earning a dubious distinction in the horror history books as the first (and for a while, only) shot-on-video gore film with a theatrical release, this ultra-cheap labour of love managed to spawn decades of do-it-yourself camcorder curios ranging from early adopters like *The Ripper* (anybody remember that one?) and *Video Violence* all the way to today's straight-to-video gorefests. Is it actually any good? No, not really, but its impoverished execution can be endearing if you're not expecting anything even remotely close to a genuine horror film. Trying to form a coherent synopsis for *BoardingHouse* is quite impossible, but for the record, it starts off with a rambling back story rolling across the screen apparently shot off the screen of an Apple IIe. The blood-slowing terror kicks off at the titular house which is apparently being menaced by a dark, evil force (i.e., a very funny video superimposition) that kills people, usually when they're near the kitchen or anything watery like a swimming pool or shower. (The beginning of the movie also warns us, William Castle style, that a spooky noise or visual will announce any upcoming traumatic scenes, but this gets abandoned very early on.) Enter Jim Royce (played by director John Wintergate), a telekinetic, womanising playboy who inherits the house and decides to open it up to any nearby homeless California women with big breasts. Some of the women have horrible hallucinations, and one by one they die when they're not busy getting it on with their landlord.

Complete with unconvincing demons, a bizarre dual role for its leading man, and the most pandering T&A and "gore" effects ever inflicted on an audience, *BoardingHouse* certainly can't be called dull even if its artistic abilities never rise above public access levels. Nobody involved went on to anything else of note but at least their film managed to squeak out into theatres at the height of the slasher craze and thoroughly confuse viewers who were absorbing a diet of Lucio Fulci imports. The basement band synth score and inscrutable videography also contribute to the air of an early '80s home movie shot in some jabbering, mystical parallel universe. Don't say you weren't warned.

Briefly released on tape from Paragon back in the early '80s, *BoardingHouse* went out of commission for many years (and according to the filmmakers, they got screwed over on the theatrical distribution while the VHS edition was unauthorised). The feature looks about as good as could be expected; for what it's worth, this is much sharper and cleaner than the old tape version, but that basically just means you can make out some facial features this time around. Ditto for the mono audio which is about what you would expect from a video camera. While the film was matted off for its theatrical exhibition, the DVD is appropriately presented in full frame as originally shot.

No one seemed to know anything about this film when it came out or in the ensuing years, so Code Red's DVD finally answers the question, "Just who the heck are these people, anyway?" Apparent fans of mysticism and definitely not familiar with the horror genre as a whole, Wintergate and wife/co-star Kalassu turn up for a "spooky" video intro, a commentary track (moderated by Lee Christian and Jeff McKay), and a video interview. Among the titbits provided, you'll learn

that the film was originally shot as a horror spoof but was considerably reworked once it was picked up for distribution (a sense of humour certainly would have helped), a script has been written for *BoardingHouse 2* (the mind boggles, though it would probably come out looking a lot like Ted V. Mikels's last two features), what they've been doing since they finished the film and took off from California, and how much they enjoyed seeing it on a theatrical double bill with *Jaws* (though given its vintage, it was more likely screening with one of the sequels). Other extras include two suitably ratty TV spots and some more Code Red release trailers including *Nightmare, Can I Do It... Til I Need Glasses?, The Dead Pit, The Chilling* and *Sole Survivor*.

THE BODYGUARD

Colour, 1976, 87m. / Directed by Simon Nuchtern / Starring Sonny Chiba, Etsuko Shihomi, Judy Lee

SISTER STREET FIGHTER

Colour, 1974, 86m. / Directed by Kazuhiko Yamaguchi / Starring Etsuko Shihomi, Sonny Chiba, Emi Hayakawa, Sanae Ôhori / Navarre (US R1 NTSC) / WS (2.35:1) (16:9)

Navarre's now-defunct exploitation line, Deimos, unleashed this double-feature Sonny Chiba disc as part of their "Welcome to the Grindhouse" series (eventually changed to "Exploitation Cinema" double features after The Weinstein Company balked), and both should bring a huge smile to the face of any Asian action fans with a tolerance for English dubbing. First up is *The Bodyguard (Karate Kiba)*, a popular Chiba home video and TV item widely circulated in terrible pan-and-scan prints since the '80s, now finally presented in a sterling 16x9 scope transfer (still in its American-ized cut with a different opening, but currently the Japanese cut still hasn't popped up anywhere). Chiba portrays a badass who, after taking out a group of terrorists on a plane, publicly hires himself out as a bodyguard and uses the opportu-nity to sort out a ruthless bunch of gangsters while his client has other schemes going behind his back. The plot's not too important, though; mainly it's an excuse for lots and lots of violence, all over the top and delivered for maximum audience enjoyment. The English dub track is great fun and makes one less sorry for the absence of a Japanese language track.

Its co-feature in this set is the fourth film in the popular *Street Fighter* series, *Sister Street Fighter*, which has also been around for ages in less-than-optimum condition. Again, it looks terrific here in a brand-spanking-new scope transfer with all of the violence trimmed by New Line for its initial American run. Actually Sonny makes only a token appearance here despite his star billing, stepping aside to introduce the butt-kicking Etsuko "Sue" Shihomi, a Chiba disciple who was still a teen when this was filmed. She holds the screen just fine as she tries to find her missing brother, an undercover detective who ran afoul of some nasty drug lords. She arrives, she snoops, she kicks and punches out lots of bad guys, and Sonny helps out. Who could ask for anything more? Note that this is again the English-dubbed version, though completists can snag both language tracks as part of the *Sister Street Fighter Collection*. Both films can be watched separately or as part of the "Grindhouse Experience", which sprinkles in trailers for Crown International titles like *Ninja War*, *Burnout*, *Killpoint* and *Kidnapping of the President*.

THE BOLLYWOOD HORROR COLLECTION VOLUME 1: BANDH DARWAZA

B

Colour, 1990, 147m. / Directed by Shyam & Tulsi Ramsay / Starring Anirudh Agarwal, Vijayendra Ghatge, Hashmat Khan, Manjeet Kullar

PURANA MANDIR

Colour, 1984, 146m. / Directed by Shyam & Tulsi Ramsay / Starring Anirudh Agarwal, Mohnish Bahl, Aarti Gupta, Puneet Issar / Mondo Macabro (US R0 NTSC)

Though the Bollywood industry has only recently embraced out-right horror films in the past few years with s o n g - a n d - d a n c e screamers riffing on the likes of *I Know What You Did Last Summer*, the country's horror heritage secretly stretches back several decades, largely thanks to the efforts of two men: Shyam and Tulsi Ramsay. Packing their movies with wild monsters, screaming damsels, gothic castles, hefty doses of gore, and colourful lighting, they stunned Indian audiences with films like these two wild outings, presented to English-speaking audiences for the first time. Cult film fans have been salivating for Ramsay releases on DVD since reading about them in Pete Tombs's indispensable *Mondo Macabro* book, and this double-dose should make a welcome appetiser for Western viewers.

The more famous of the two, *Bandh Darwaza* ("Closed Door") is a colourful, deliberately kitschy, violent vampire saga, with bloodsucker Neola entering an unholy pact with an expecting mother who promises her newborn if it's a female. Not surpris-ingly, mom has second thoughts and sends her husband to dispatch her partner in evil; however, faster than you can say *Dracula, Prince of Darkness*, the vampire is resur-rected eighteen years later to continue his quest for the promised maiden. Not surprisingly, she isn't too thrilled with the prospect of becoming a bride of the undead, and her suitors and friends are packing up their gear for some rough-and-tumble monster hunting.

Though made in 1990, *Bandh Darwaza* feels very much like the Ramsays' more frequent early '80s outings and would play well with the likes of *Fright Night* (itself also remade into a Bollywood film). The ridiculous production design and feisty performances make it great fun to watch, and the Ramsays wisely throw in some action footage every time the plot threatens to lag. The obligatory songs are extremely brief and delivered in an offhand fashion by India's standards, leaving plenty of room for monster mayhem – particularly Anirudh Agarwal's knockout, truly monstrous lead performance, complete with fiery eyes and gnashing teeth. From the profuse fog machines to the bat-themed decor and even some not-too-subtle musical lifts from American horror films, this is about as close to pure drive-in Indian cinema as you can get.

One of the Ramsays' most financially successful films was the earlier *Purana Mandir*, again featuring Agarwal as a vicious monster – in this case, Saamri, a baby-eating, tourist-slashing fiend who gets rounded up and beheaded by angry villagers. Two centuries later, the youngest male descendant (Mohnish Bahl) of the beheaders has a sexy young girlfriend (Aarti Gupta) and a nasty curse hanging over his head; namely, all the women in his family turn into demons after giving birth. With his head and body soon reattached, Saamri is back in business terrorising the countryside, with the naive young couple fighting for their lives to undo the sins of their fathers.

A bit more in line with the usual Bollywood formula, *Purana Mandir* ("Mansion of Evil") spends more time on character development and romantic subplots than the average Ramsay fare but

still delivers where it counts, particularly in the rousing final third when Saamri really cuts loose on the entire cast. Once again the Western influence is evident from the '80s horror-style soundtrack to the heavy doses of neon-coloured stage blood, and the colourless lead characters don't have a chance compared to the flamboyant villain.

Evaluating the condition of these films is a bit tricky, as anyone familiar with most Indian DVDs is well aware that (a) most films aren't well preserved if they even manage to survive at all, and (b) most transfers of anything older than five years or so tends to be plagued by rampant compression artefacts and inconsistent black levels. *Bandh Darwaza* looks surprisingly nice overall – not spectacular by the usual DVD standards, but the colours and sharpness are impressive enough. *Purana Mandir* is taken from the best surviving video master which still looks rather soft and dated – but it's nice we have it at all. Both come with optional English subtitles, and the full frame compositions appear to be accurate. As usual the Mondo Macabro extras offer a solid primer on the country and context for the films, beginning with a nifty featurette, "Freddie, Jason and... Saamri: The Ramsays and the Birth of Bollywood Horror", which covers the Ramsays' pre-'90s horror career (mostly focusing on *Purana Mandir*). The Mondo Macabro episode on "South Asian Horror" broadens the territory a bit with a half-hour overview of unique Eastern terror from India, Pakistan and surrounding countries, with loads of poster art, stills and clips. Additional text extras ("About Bollywood Horror" and "Ramsay Family Values") provide additional details beyond the featurettes, written in MM's usual insightful style. Finally, you get an updated version of that delicious MM promo reel. Very highly recommended all around, and a refreshing demonstration that Bollywood horror goes far, far beyond the musical lite-slashers from the past few years.

THE BOLLYWOOD HORROR COLLECTION VOLUME 2: VEERANA

Colour, 1988, 134m. / Directed by Shyam & Tulsi Ramsay / Starring Jasmin, Hemant Birje, Sahila Chaddha

PURANI HAVELI

Colour, 1989, 139m. / Directed by Shyam & Tulsi Ramsay / Starring Deepak Parashar, Amita Nangia, Sikander / Mondo Macabro (US R0 NTSC)

Bigger and better than its previous volume, Mondo Macabro's second pairing of titles from the shameless Ramsay family features two of their most effective and successful releases, both transferred from negative elements vastly superior to any prior Bollywood horror films out on the market. First up is *Veerana*, a powerhouse Indian riff on the old "witch-demon returns from the dead after being executed" trope that's been around since *Black Sunday*. However, this time the presence of screen siren Jasmin really kicks the proceedings into high gear as she seduces men willy-nilly and occasionally turns into a creepy bug-eyed wraith. In this case she's possessed by the spirit of the original, foxy witch whose disciples decide it would be a great cosmic joke to place her soul into the body of the local *thakur* responsible for the inquisition, using locks of the innocent girl's hair. As she reaches maturity, no one seems to be the wiser as the possessed girl goes about her grim business, picking off locals in cobweb-shrouded palaces. (The character's name is Jasmin, too, which probably resulted in a lot less confusion on the set.) Usually the routine seems to involve her seducing a man while surrounded by candelabra, only to turn into the gross-looking witch monster who likes to suck blood out of the guys' wrists. Meanwhile the disciples stay busy praying to a giant, flame-adorned demon in a nearby cellar before the townspeople gradually wake up and realise what's going on for the big action showdown.

If that doesn't sound wild enough, *Veerana* (which has zilch to do with vampires despite its cover title translation as "Vengeance of the Vampire", a bit of bloodsucking aside) also tosses in a hammy horror writer (whose latest book instigates a "huh?" clip from the 1978 *Invasion of the Body Snatchers*), a possessed TV set, an overactive fog machine, a funk-scored spear fight with a bunch of monks, and lots of fluffy '80s hairstyles. How could you possibly resist? Though Indian films still prohibit actual kissing or overt nudity, this is much sexier than the usual Ramsay offering thanks to the premise, which often feels closer to an Italian gothic in flavour. Obviously, you won't be bored for a minute.

The Ramsays were really known for their wild haunted house films populated with vengeful demons, and *Purana Haveli* on the second disc of this collection is a representative example in line with their other hits like *Purana Mandir*, *Darwaza* and the great *Hotel* (which would make a killer future title for the Mondo Macabro folks). The film kicks off with a monstrous scream in a spooky cemetery (complete with the obligatory thunder and lightning), followed by more screaming, a ticking grandfather clock, and a slow tracking shot through a haunted mansion. That pretty much sets the tone for this film, which also unspools its disco-scored opening credits over paintings of the final days of Jesus Christ (for reasons never really explained). Our tale opens with a horny young couple in a broken-down car forced to spend the night in the spooky ruins only to fall afoul of a hairy monstrosity tucked away in one of the tombs, but the menace is caged in a

B

handy iron-barred basement by a passing priest wielding a crucifix. Cut to our main story as pretty young Anita inherits the estate and decides to check it out, unaware that the drunken groundskeeper and two appraisers have just become the latest victims of dark forces lurking inside. After a baffling but very entertaining action scene with some menacing locals on a bridge, she and her buddies (who all enjoy bursting out in musical numbers, of course) go to check it out, while her scheming uncle (who occasionally disguises himself in drag) tries to figure out how to swipe everything away from her. This sets the stage for pure, demonic evil to be unleashed, with a horned statue kicking things off in high style by perforating one of the guests. Lots of fun in a gory but strangely innocent fashion, *Purani Haveli* is very entertaining and ridiculously stylish, clearly influenced by everything from Edgar Wallace thrillers to... well, whatever you want to call a fat guy stripping down to his knickers while belting Donna Summer's "Love to Love You, Baby".

Given the very dodgy history of Ramsay movies on home video, it's miraculous how good these two titles look on DVD. The previous volume did its best with flawed video masters, but the transfers here look fresh and very crisp, easily outclassing many of India's own digital releases. Some very minor speckles are evident here and there, but that's very negligible quibbling compared to the classiness of the presentation here. As usual, the full frame transfer looks accurate, and the optional English subtitles are just fine throughout. Also as usual, the mono soundtracks can get very loud and shrill sometimes, so be sure to think about the neighbours while you're watching these. Extras are fairly minimal this time out, limited to theatrical trailers for both titles and the usual thorough, well-written text extras for the cast and crew.

THE BOLLYWOOD HORROR COLLECTION VOLUME 3: MAHAKAAL

Colour, 1993, 132m. / Directed by Shyam & Tulsi Ramsay / Starring Karan Shah, Archana Puran Singh, Mayur, Johnny Lever

TAHKHANA

Colour, 1986, 117m. / Directed by Shyam & Tulsi Ramsay / Starring Hemant Birje, Aarti Gupta, Sheetal / Mondo Macabro (US R0 NTSC)

You know what was wrong with *A Nightmare on Elm Street*? It didn't have any Michael Jackson impersonators. Thankfully that oversight is corrected with *Mahakaal*, the headlining entry in Mondo Macabro's *Bollywood Horror Collection Volume 3*. The opening sequence of this unabashed imitation of the Wes Craven classic kicks off with a young college student, Seema, stalked through a creepy, chain-filled subterranean room by a disfigured maniac wielding a nasty, razor-fingered glove, only to wake up in her bed and find scratches on her nightgown and arm. The next day we meet our heroine, Anita, who hangs pictures and makes out with her boyfriend, Prakash, when not prancing around with him engaging in random musical numbers. Meanwhile a tough guy named The Boss and his posse have their eye on Anita, who also hangs out at a cafeteria run by Canteen, a flamboyant Michael Jackson wannabe who prances around in front of a big *Bad* poster, kisses his male clientele on the lips, and brags about getting a part in the new Ramsay Brothers movie (hey, maybe Wes ripped this off for *Scream*!). Turns out Seema is Anita's best friend and tells her about this Freddy wannabe (who looks the same except he has a mullet instead of a big hat), and soon Anita's having similar nightmares about a spooky little girl in a white dress and Hindi-Freddy chasing her while his face melts off. The next morning The Boss and his boys try to gang rape Anita in broad daylight on campus by, uh, spraying her with a garden hose until Prakash shows up to kickbox the stuffing out of them. To get over the trauma, Anita and her pals (including Canteen, of course) decide to head out for a picnic ("where we can sing, dance and have a good time!"), where they perform a big musical number about – what else? – picnics. Unfortunately their car breaks down, so the fun-loving kids have to stay overnight at a weird hotel run by a goofy manager with a Hitler moustache who enjoys peeping in on his guests while they paint their toenails. That night, faster than you can say "Tina, come to Freddy", Seema is butchered in her sleep by dozens of claw-gloved hands bursting through the carpet as her boyfriend watches. Soon Anita's having horrible daydreams about a white-eyed Seema following her in a body bag, Canteen has a daydream where he turns into a Paul Naschy look-alike named Shahenshah (with his own theme song), and Anita's parents reveal the horrible truth about Shakaal, "a foul stain on the human race" who killed children to increase his black magic powers. Turns out they killed him after he murdered Anita's older sister (in a very stylish, very Ramsay flashback), and everyone must race against time before Anita becomes the demon's next victim.

Though the plot itself is more than a bit familiar, the colourful *Mahakaal* is filled with bizarre touches including a big snake attack in a jail cell, an atmospheric night-mare sequence in a labyrinthine aquarium, a nifty spin on the waterbed scene from the fourth *Elm Street* film, and a fluffy-haired mystic guru straight out of an Alejandro Jodorowsky epic. The 132-minute running time zips by surprisingly quickly thanks to the brisk pacing and whiplash switches in tone, though this being a Bollywood film,

the story is more conservative than its model; both of Anita's parents are alive and morally absolved from any wrongdoing, Seema "asks for it" by having sex with her boyfriend and even sabotaging the group's car to isolate them at the hotel, and the family unit is ultimately held as the greatest good above all. Had the Ramsays decided to follow this up with their own version of *A Nightmare on Elm Street Part 2: Freddy's Revenge*, the results would have been really, really interesting. (This film does include some fleeting nods to the other films in the series, but for 99% of the time, it's really all about the first one.) Hilariously, the score also cribs from Charles Bernstein and Christopher Young's music for the first two *Elm Street* films, with Depeche Mode's instrumental "PIMPF" even making an unexpected cameo! As for the obligatory songs, they're all very upbeat and generally catchy, with one third-act disco nightclub number ("Hey Baby, Baby") coming completely out of left field. For some reason the title is translated as "The Monster" on the DVD packaging, but the dialogue instead translates it quite clearly as "The Time of Death".

Now on to disc two in this collection, an earlier and more traditional Ramsay offering entitled *Tahkhana* (or "The Dungeon") is another giddy haunted house with monsters yarn about two Singh sisters, Sapna and Aarti, whose black magician uncle Durjan tried to sacrifice them to a demonic god as children before he was imprisoned for eternity in his dungeon lair. They were separated during the ordeal and possess two pieces of a necklace which leads to a treasure within the cursed estate. Now their wizened evil uncle has managed to finally revive his dark lord, and when word gets out about the hidden fortune which must be secured with the aid of the missing sister, some shady family members come out of the woodwork. Meanwhile Sapna is now an unemployed vixen in a tight leather miniskirt who runs afoul of the scummy Shakhal, coincidentally her cousin, who tries to "ravage" her and in the process comes into possession of her locket. A wild goose chase ensues as he sends everyone else after the wrong treasure while looking for the real loot himself, but in the process the excavation lands everyone face to face with the very angry blood demon now looking to avenge the master whose soul provides its sustenance.

Packed with thunder, lightning, cobwebs, vultures, pounding synth music, and ooga booga beasties, *Tahkhana* is a solid, representative example of Ramsay horror with an original if somewhat convoluted story and the usual creepy-crawly atmospherics. Though you get plenty of shots of the monster's red eyes and scowling face, most of the real mayhem is packed together in the brisk final half hour which finally lets the demon loose with a host of amusing death scenes, most memorably a pick-axe impalement and a bizarre attack scene in a haystack. Made in the prime of the Ramsays' horror stride during the mid-'80s, this isn't the most inventive entry but it's perhaps the most representative and a pretty solid introduction for those who like a bit more plot and music than usual to temper their ghoulish antics.

Both features are presented on separate discs and look vastly superior to the blurry, unsubtitled tape editions fans have had to hunt down over the years. Colour and detail are both very satisfying while the elements look clean and solid throughout. Some ghosting is evident during scenes with heavy motion, indicating this was probably sourced from a PAL master, but it's so gratifying to see these looking good it's a very minor sacrifice. The optional English subtitles are also lots of fun and well-written. Extras here are the usual Mondo Macabro "about" text extras and the Bollywood/Lollywood episode of the Mondo Macabro TV show, featuring coverage of the Ramsays and their

successors with footage from plenty of wild-looking titles like *Ammoru* (which really, really needs a DVD release). As with their other Bollywood horror double bills, this delivers way more bang for your buck than any other collections out there.

THE BOOBY HATCH

Colour, 1976, 86m. / Directed by Rudy Ricci & John Russo / Starring Sharon Joy Miller, Rudy Ricci, Doug Sortino, David Emge, John Upson / Synapse (US R1 NTSC) / WS (1.66:1) (16:9)

If you prefer your '70s drive-in sexploitation with a heavy dose of polyester pants, shaggy hairdos, and S&M monkey suits, then feast your eyes on *The Booby Hatch*, a very silly 1976 nudie comedy written and co-directed by John Russo, the writer of the original *Night of the Living Dead* (with future *Dawn of the Dead* star David Emge popping up for another Romero connection). Kicking off with a sex toy commercial plugging the "XX20 Ultra Vibrator", the entire story revolves around the goofy antics at Joyful Novelties, a "pleasure" manufacturer, and two of its product testers, blonde nymphet Cherry Jankowski (Sharon Joy Miller) and schlubby Marcello (co-director Rudy Ricci). As the company tries out a string of its new products on an increasingly oddball set of characters, Cherry begins to wonder where she'll find true satisfaction (mainly since her boyfriend is secretly pining for a sex change) while Marcello becomes desperate at his ability to fly his flag on a regular basis.

Drawing inspiration from "dirty" mainstream skit comedies like *The Groove Tube*, the film barely holds together as a coherent narrative but works well enough as a string of *Laugh-In*-style gags, laced with topless shots every few minutes to keep the audience happy. This long-lost piece of filmic history (previously available only in a dire VHS release from Super Video) comes to DVD for the first time in an exhaustive special edition from Synapse, who appropriately kicked off the cult movie restoration craze back in the laserdisc days with *Night of the Living Dead.* Here they present two cuts of the film, the original *Booby Hatch* (looking fine enough for a low budget, super-grainy '70s feature with an anamorphic 1.66:1 transfer) and an alternative cut (in much rougher shape) entitled *The Liberation of Cherry Jankowski,* which shuffles several scenes in a different order and concludes with a more blatantly pro-terrorist finale. Extras include theatrical trailers for both versions, a new Emge interview called "A Flyboy in Earth Shoes" mainly focused on the actor's Pittsburgh-oriented acting career (and his odd turn here doing a Humphrey Bogart impression as Marcello's Italian cop brother), and an audio commentary with Russo, Ricci, and fellow *Night* alumnus Russell Streiner, who served as co-producer here. They cover a number of targets including building scouting, the sex revolution targets, and even a quick anecdote about porn actress Georgina Spelvin.

BORN OF FIRE

Colour, 1983, 84m. / Directed by Jamil Dehlavi / Starring Peter Firth, Suzan Crowley, Stefan Kalipha, Oh-Tee, Nabil Shaban / Mondo Macabro (US R0 NTSC) / WS (1.85:1) (16:9)

When violent solar activity including what appears to be a skull-like eclipse causes strange eruptions and nightmarish visions in targeted locations on Earth, a nameless female astronomer (*The Draughtsman's Contract*'s Suzan Crowley) takes her findings to a tormented flutist, Paul (Peter Firth), whose own nightmares appear to be related to his father, who died before his son's birth while seeking an enigmatic, possibly malefic Eastern entity known as the Master Musician (Oh-Tee). Together in Turkey they experience increasingly bizarre encounters involving djinns, dervishes, and the birth of a giant, slimy insect-like beast by our heroine.

Along with *Eyes of Fire*, this oddball British film is one of the most baffling features released in the '80s home video horror wave. It was originally shot in 1983 but treated like a bastard stepchild in its native country while in America it received a token minor theatrical release and confused lots of customers on VHS through Vidmark. However, it must be stressed that *Born of Fire* can't be watched as a traditional horror film; it's more of a dark fantasy based on Eastern mythology and Islamic lore with occasional macabre flourishes. The increased commercial exposure of artists like Jodorowsky and Arrabal should make this much easier to digest now, and it's certainly among the classiest and most visually ravishing films released by Mondo Macabro in their quest to bring the world's most mind-bending titles to a wider audience. Among the biggest surprises here is the participation of Firth, an actor riding high at the time after Broadway successes like *Amadeus* and *Equus* (and more recently a longstanding regular on the excellent *Spooks*). Fortunately he contributes a fascinating video interview on the DVD to explain a bit about his career choices at the time (he turned down a lot of Hollywood projects, a decision about which he now feels conflicted) and his interest in the source material and director Jamil Dehlavi, who largely improvised the film around a framework of concepts to which he'd been exposed since childhood. These influences are explained further in an interview with the director, who admits in retrospect he might have been better following his true love of painting and expounds upon some of the magical ideas he wanted to explore with this film. The challenges of shooting in Turkey (particularly the covert filming of some of the more unclothed sequences) also provides several anecdotal highlights. Last up is actor Nabil Shaban (who plays "The Silent One", a mysterious dervish) who talks more about his career and the basic outline of the plot as it was originally presented. Pete Tombs contributes another outstanding, illuminating set of notes about the film (you really might want to read them before viewing the feature) and a dupey '80s Vidmark trailer used to promote the tape release. As for the transfer of the film itself, it's a sensational upgrade from the scarce prior releases and finally does justice to the rich, often startling visuals, ranging from arid mountains and richly-textured caves to glistening ice formations. Even if you've tried to approach this film in the past and found it daunting, this DVD finally offers a chance to experience it the way it was meant to be seen.

BRAINIAC

B&W, 1962, 77m. / Directed by Chano Urueta / Starring Abel Salazar, Luis Aragon, Ruben Rojo, Rosa Maria Gallardo, David Silva, René Cardona / Casa Negra (US R1 NTSC)

In 1661, the merciless robed initiates of the Mexican inquisition persecute suspicious Baron Vitelius (Mexican horror regular Abel Salazar) for his reputed dealings with Lucifer, an accusation to which he responds by inflicting a curse upon all the descendants of his accusers. Centuries later in 1961, the appearance of a strange comet in the sky portends the much-delayed arrival of this curse by crashing to earth and disgorging a hirsute, big-headed mutation of Vitelius with an insatiable appetite for brains. Disguised as a human nobleman, the Baron throws swanky dinner parties for his potential victims, occasionally reverting into his monstrous state in private to suck out their grey matter with his fork-shaped, skull-puncturing tongue, with leftovers stashed away for late night snacks. Though the police prove to be of little help, harebrained Professor Millan (Luis Aragon), plucky Ronald (Ruben Rojo) and sexy Vicky (Rosa Maria Gallardo) try to solve the mystery of the supernatural murders before they wind up next on the Baron's dinner list.

Drawing obvious inspiration from Universal monster movies and the burgeoning Italian gothic craze (particularly Mario Bava's *Black Sunday*), this jaw-dropping granddaddy of the Mexican horror cycle quickly became a late night television staple thanks to its heavy English-language distribution from flashy distributor K. Gordon Murray. The frequent reprinting of grisly stills in publications ranging from *Famous Monsters of Filmland* to *The Psychotronic Encyclopedia of Film* kept generations of young horror fans seeking this one out, usually under the most desperate of circumstances, and it never failed to live up to its reputation. The thick vein of grotesque humour and unexpected surrealist imagery keep the film from becoming dated, and even seasoned trash film viewers can still be thrown by its brutality and odd narrative rhythms. Director Chano Ureta (*The Witch's Mirror*) once again establishes himself as the prime practitioner of Mexican horror's first great wave, with plenty of expert, atmospheric lighting and effectively weird sets keeping even the most mundane dialogue scenes at a disturbing pitch. And of course, the outrageous flame-throwing climax is not to be missed.

Most widely seen in an English-dubbed version ripe with uproarious dialogue, *Brainiac (El barón del terror)* has been a video staple in various murky editions, with an amateurish budget DVD from Beverly Wilshire quickly pulled off the market and a double-bill version from Something Weird announced but never released. Casa Negra's much-needed restoration (quickly a collector's item when the company went under) presents an edition far clearer and cleaner than anyone in America has ever seen, and the original Spanish language track is a bit more urbane and serious than its goofball English counterpart. (Some brief footage trimmed from the U.S. prints is reinstated here in Spanish only with subtitles.) Likewise, the bilingual DVD sleeve can be flipped to either an English or Spanish version. Pulling the maximum amount of extras out of a title with little promotional history, the DVD augments the main feature with an enthusiastic commentary by "Kirb Pheeler" whose "Brainiac Interactive Press Kit" is also present on the disc. His accompaniment is packed with information and odd bits of trivia and humorous anecdotes, mixing the goofy and the scholarly for a solid listening experience that never takes the film too seriously. Casamiro Buenavista offers a more cut-and-dry Mexican appraisal of the film in an essay, while other extras include a gallery of posters and stills, bios for the actors (including future sleaze director René Cardona, who appears in a supporting role here), a double-bill American radio spot, and the usual Casa Negra game card insert.

BUTTERFLY

Colour, 1982, 107m. / Directed by Matt Cimber / Starring Stacy Keach, Pia Zadora, Orson Welles, James Franciscus, Lois Nettleton, Edward Albert, Stuart Whitman, Ed McMahon, June Lockhart, George "Buck" Flower / Industrial (US R1 NTSC) / WS (1.85:1) (16:9)

It may be hard to imagine now, but only in the last few decades has film noir become accepted as a major, significant style of filmmaking; these tough, lurid thrillers from the 1940s and '50s were regarded as disposable programmers in their day, but now you'd be hard pressed to find a more influential force in Hollywood today. What does this have to do with a trashy Pia Zadora movie, you may ask? Well, in 1981, moviegoers were confronted with two very different attempts to revive the noir tradition with modern stars and more explicit sexuality juicing up stories by hardboiled great James M. Cain: Lawrence Kasdan's *Body Heat* (an unofficial redo of *Double Indemnity*), and Bob Rafelson's *The Postman Always Rings Twice*, which one-upped the Lana Turner original by adding Jack Nicholson groping and throttling Jessica Lange on a kitchen table. While the former film was followed by countless copycats (including perhaps the entire modern "erotic thriller" craze of the 1990s), *Postman* didn't inspire much of anything except *Butterfly*, another James M. Cain adaptation with the same dusty, dreary desert atmosphere and slow-boil pacing. Fortunately what *Butterfly* lacks in pop culture relevance it more than makes up for in pure cinematic trash value, as Pia Zadora (who even gets an "introducing" credit, even though she'd already appeared in *Santa Claus Conquers the Martians* as a wee tyke) pouts and gyrates her way through the film in one of the most deliciously nutty femme fatale roles ever conceived. Add to that a whole heap o' sinful shenanigans including Stacy Keach as her presumed father feeling up Pia in a tin bath, Orson Welles as a clucking judge scolding juvenile delinquents, and James

B

Franciscus as a jailbait-chasing scuzzbag, and you've got one seriously warped good time at the movies.

Our tawdry tale begins as Jess Tyler (Keach) mopes around over the failure of his Depression-era silver mine and the struggling town around him. His life is complicated considerably by the arrival of Kady (Zadora), a pubescent bad girl who waltzes in wearing long, flowing Bob Mackie gowns (the same guy who did *Xanadu*) and proclaims she's his long-lost daughter from a former fling. Kady undresses and bathes herself in front of her pa which leads to more than a few deeply uncomfortable moments, and her true motives emerge when she encourages him to get the mine back on its feet so she can get some money to take care of her baby, whose existence already prompted her into a brief stint of prostitution. Kady's behaviour (which includes inciting bar fights nearby) catches the attention of the local populace, with a trial soon dictating whether Jess overstepped the line by getting a little too intimate with someone who might be his offspring. Meanwhile the daddy (Edward Albert) of Kady's baby and a few other lip-smacking financial predators lie in wait, ready to spring...

Even if it weren't a five-course buffet of cinematic soapy indulgence, *Butterfly* would still be worth a look for the weird roster of its cast (Ed McMahon! June Lockhart! James Franciscus! George "Buck" Flower!) and crew, including a breathy, horny score by Ennio Morricone (who reteamed with director Matt Cimber for the equally hilarious *Hundra*). Of course, the main source of its notoriety is Zadora, whose husband, Meshulam Riklis, bankrolled the film and spent an ungodly amount of promotional money to snag her a Golden Globe Award for "New Star of the Year". Hollywood was not amused, unsurprisingly, and she was quickly given a Razzie Award for the same film, which she

promptly followed up by starring in the notorious *The Lonely Lady* and doing a *Penthouse* spread. Of course, Pia went on to redeem herself with a string of surprisingly credible album releases and stage appearances, and like it or not, she's a pop culture figure like no other. While her acting career never recovered from the pummelling she received in the early '80s, it's also worth noting that, while she has more than her share of script howlers here, she isn't really all that terrible; in fact, she seems flat-out accomplished compared to more recent, blank-faced starlets like Jessica Alba and Miley Cyrus, to name only two blatant examples.

While *The Lonely Lady* still languishes in the obscurity of VHS hell, Pia's unforgettable first big leading role is now preserved on DVD for posterity in a decked-out edition that inspires nothing less than pure awe. The presentation is comparable to previous Cimber releases by Subversive Cinema, with an anamorphic transfer ranging from solid and attractive in some scenes to mistimed and kind of funky-looking in others. It's infinitely better than the wretched old Vestron VHS tapes, but there's some odd jitter and instability in many shots while some of the darker scenes could have benefited from a higher bit rate. It's still okay and watchable, but don't expect visual fireworks. Of course, the disc is easily worth the humble price tag simply for the extras, a true trash fanatic's dream come true. Zadora, Cimber, and Riklis team up for a very interesting audio commentary covering the locations, actors, source novel, public reception, and everything else you can imagine; Zadora alternates between cheerful and more than a little snippy, particularly when talking about the bar fight. Then all three turn up again for a great 41-minute documentary and are joined by Keach, who seems very pleasant and realistic about the whole enterprise. Everyone appears to think that this film has a huge camp film following, which it may very well have despite its extreme rarity since the mid-'80s. In any case, if your taste runs towards guilty pleasures with an emphasis on heavy breathing and juicy plot twists involving lots of famous actors who should have known better, *Butterfly* deserves a dark, secret place on your DVD shelf.

CAN I DO IT... TIL I NEED GLASSES?

Colour, 1977, 73m. / Directed by I. Robert Levy / Starring Roger Behr, Joey Camen, Angelyne, Moose Carlson, Robin Williams, Tallie Cochrane, Jeff Doucette, Vic Dunlop, Walter Olkewicz / Code Red (US R0 NTSC) / WS (1.78:1) (16:9)

If someone started grabbing random selections from a '70s edition of *Playboy's Party Jokes* and slapped them into a screenplay, you'd probably wind up with something exactly like *Can I Do It... Til I Need Glasses?*, a low-brow comedy skit film clearly modelled after the success of *Laugh-In* and its dirtier offshoots like *The Groove Tube.* In fact this was part of a two-film project from director I. Robert Levy, along with another similarly-themed film called *If You Don't Stop It, You'll Go Blind*, though self-abuse doesn't play much of a role in either title. Potty humour and occasional full frontal nudity spark up the usual offerings of groaner punch lines and slide whistle music punctuations, but for most viewers the real selling point here is an early appearance by Robin Williams, who pops up in a couple of sketches originally left on the cutting room floor but reinstated after his smash appearances as Mork on *Happy Days*. Robin wasn't too pleased about this

cash-in attempt claiming to be his "movie debut", though as anyone who's suffered through *Patch Adams* or *RV* can attest, this is still a long, long way from the worst film on his résumé.

Obviously there's no way to offer anything resembling a plot synopsis, but for the record, the film stampedes through a number of jokey scenes, most lasting only a minute or two. Some of the targets include nudist camps, dentists, shipwreck survivors, Little Red Riding Hood, courtroom dramas, flashers, and even a male reproductive gag essentially swiped from *Everything You Always Wanted to Know About Sex (But Were Afraid to Ask)*. Is it actually funny? Well, yeah, if you're in the mood for something really stupid and smutty with the attention span of an eight-year-old, which isn't always a bad thing. Break out a few beers and watch it with some buddies late at night on the weekend, and you can't go wrong. Obscure celeb spotters should also watch for a few marginally familiar names like the comedy team Roger & Roger (doing a couple of Lone Ranger skits), TV regulars Jeff Doucette and Walter Olkewicz, *Skatetown USA*'s Vic Dunlop, big-busted L.A. billboard goddess and gubernatorial candidate Angelyne, and purportedly a fleeting Uschi Digart as one of the showgirls.

As stated previously, this is the Robin Williams reissue version which hit theatres after its initial run. The image quality is definitely better than prior home video versions; you can still tell it was shot for little money back in the '70s but the candy-coloured visual scheme looks great including one red-hued fantasy sequence that'll burn your TV tube. Extras include a full frame theatrical trailer (emphasising Robin, of course), a smartass "extra" feature, and bonus trailers for *The Obsessed One, Wacky Taxi, Power Play, Sole Survivor, The Farmer, Beyond the Door* and *The Dead Pit*.

CANNIBAL

Colour, 2005, 89m. / Directed by Marian Dora / Starring Carsten Frank, Victor Brandl / Unearthed (US R1 NTSC)

Despite what exploitation cinema would have you believe, Germany isn't all about oversexed *frauleins* hopping on every guy they see. Apparently some of them eat each other, or at least that's what the news indicated in real life when two German men met up online to indulge in their mutual cannibalism fetish, with one guy willingly surrendering himself to be cooked and eaten by another. And that's the entire story of *Cannibal*, a visually amazing and stomach-churningly vivid depiction of these true events shot with the gloss and artistry of a Just Jaeckin film. Whether that's a good thing will be up to the individual viewer's appetites, of course, but it's certainly compelling.

Unlike the contemporary bestiality scandal depicted in the somewhat similar *Zoo*, this one isn't legally bound to keep its grotesque offences offscreen; instead you get some of the most startling carnage effects ever seen onscreen along with more male nudity than ten Peter Greenaway films put together. Carsten Frank, best known for a handful of later Jess Franco films like *Incubus*, appears as the Internet-savvy flesh eater, with one-shot actor Victor Brandl as his future meal. Their interplay takes up most of the running time, with director Marian Dora doing double duty as cinematographer to capture each detail along the way. The Unearthed DVD (also released through TLA) looks very sharp and colourful considering this appears to be shot on DV, making its visuals all the more impressive. Incidentally, the same story was also filmed as the very different *Grimm Love*.

CANNIBAL CAMPOUT

Colour, 1988, 90m. / Directed by Jon McBride & Tom Fisher / Starring Jon McBride, Amy Chludzinski, Richard Marcus, Gene Robbins / Camp (US R1 NTSC)

Back in the early days of VHS when Mom 'n' Pop stores sprouted up like mushrooms in every community large and small, horror movies became big business and had the big studios quivering with their ability to scare up huge profits with little investment. Soon enterprising filmmakers were making the packaging bigger, brasher, and more gimmicky by the minute, complete with cover boxes sporting loud voices, squishy liquids, and glowing eyeballs. Of course, all this showmanship was meant to camouflage the essential crudeness of the contents within, leaving horror hounds scraping through countless hours of brain-deadening dreck to find the occasional diamond in the rough. One additional advantage of VHS was the opportunity for anyone with a camcorder and rudimentary editing equipment to churn out a quickie splatter film and pass it off alongside those big 35mm slasher epics, a trend kicked off with the infamous *BoardingHouse* and carried through with such eyeball punishments as *Gore-Met Zombie Chef from Hell*, *555*, and the indisputable anti-masterpiece of this sub-sub-subgenre, *Black Devil Doll from Hell* (still inexcusably absent from the DVD marketplace). Why the rambling history lecture, you ask? Well, you need some context to help explain the existence of Camp Video, an indie VHS label specialising in shot-on-video gorefests from the most remote regions of the United States. None of their output could ever come within spitting distance of being called "good", but as a case study in regional horror filmmaking during a unique period in history, they are instructive lessons in do-it-yourself gumption, albeit of wildly varying entertainment levels.

First up and perhaps the most notorious due to its ultra-graphic cover art, *Cannibal Campout* is sort of an even-lower-rent version of *Don't Go in the Woods* by way of *Mother's Day*, focusing on the exploits of a bunch of depraved, forest-dwelling cannibals whose dying promise to their mom to avoid junk food has turned their taste buds towards a bunch of young campers, led by the director himself, Jon McBride. People get hacked up. More people get hacked up. The end.

Shot on weekends in the woods with an amateur cast, *Cannibal Campout* may be the most gruesome home movie ever made. The acting's awful, the photography is on par with work by your drunk uncle, and the production values are zilch, but that's really part of the charm; if Troma feels too slick and glossy by far, this should easily do the trick. As with most cannibal movies this is also a sick comedy, and on that front it works a bit better. McBride is also on hand with this DVD to explain the existence of his film, thanks to a full audio commentary and a half-hour featurette reteaming most of the cast. Everyone seems to remember the experience well enough, and while it didn't launch any big careers (though McBride apparently got some sweet music video gigs), the movie still has a warm place in the hearts of many diseased children of the '80s. Other extras include a trailer, promos from the "Camp Trailer Vault", a few minutes of boring deleted footage, a ridiculous music video, and a stills gallery. For a perfect companion piece, you should also check out Camp's release of McBride's *Wood-chipper Massacre*.

CANNIBAL DOCTOR

Colour, 1999, 56m. / Directed by William Hellfire / Starring Misty Mundae, William Hellfire, Tina Krause

DINNER FOR TWO

Colour, 2000, 60m. / Directed by William Hellfire / Starring Misty Mundae, William Hellfire, Tina Krause / Shock-O-Rama (US R0 NTSC)

The short-lived, New Jersey-based Factory 2000 was an outfit from zero-budget director William Hellfire, responsible for such shot-on-VHS curios as the now-infamous *Vampire Strangler*. Their most famous participant, Misty Mundae, gets the spotlight treatment again for one of their weirdest double features, *Cannibal Doctor / Dinner for Two*, the same exact movie shot twice one year apart with the same cast. Both of them feature Hellfire as Dr. Ben Orange, a physician whose wife (Tina Krause) shares his belief that chomping down on young girls leads to eternal youth. Enter Misty as a naive patient who's examined, rubbed down, and eventually basted in preparation for a (never shown) cannibal feast. Technically the second feature is a "sequel" with Misty playing her character's sister, but otherwise you'd be hard pressed to tell them apart.

If you weren't yet aware that video buyers with a cannibal fetish even existed, count yourself among the majority; it's tough to see the titillation value in watching Misty getting slathered with basting brushes and trussed up like a turkey, but hey, different strokes for different folks. In any case, this would make a killer double (or triple) feature with Jess Franco's *Tender Flesh*. Ed Grant contributes a hefty liner notes booklet entitled "The Art of Fine Dining" which offers another valuable entry in the history of Factory 2000, complete with full descriptions of how the films were funded for about $800 apiece by anonymous fetish customers who supplied checklists of exactly what they wanted depicted onscreen. (In other words, be very, very careful the next time you're visiting New Jersey.) Also included is a 2000 interview with Krause and Mundae talking about their early careers. Bon appétit.

CANNIBAL TERROR

Colour, 1981, 89m. / Directed by Alain Deruelle / Starring Silvia Solar, Antonio Mayans, Burt Altman, Gerard Lemaire, Pamela Stanford, Olivier Mathot / Severin (US R0 NTSC) / WS (1.66:1) (16:9), HardGore (UK R2 PAL) / WS (1.85:1) (16:9)

 In a genre known for its absurdity, few cannibal films can compete with the delirious inanity of *Cannibal Terror*, a, ahem, "minimalist" French/Spanish produc-tion which inexplicably earned a slot on Great Britain's notorious video nasty list. While the Italians were busy churning out high-profile shockfests from directors like Deodato and Lenzi, this one comes straight from the lunatic house of Eurociné, purveyors of the most charming, cheapjack exploitation France had to offer. Direction here is credited to Alain Deruelle, making his sole horror outing amidst a career in hardcore with films like *Pornographie spéciale – Rage Porno*, which should give you some idea of what the filmmaking level is here. However, no one could possibly be ready for the amount of hilarity that lies in store.

The plot... well, there isn't much of that here, but the setup involves a couple of lowlife crooks who decide to kidnap the little daughter of some rich industrialist (or something) and hold her ransom in the jungle, which actually looks more like a forest outside a Spanish town. They decide to hide out with one of the locals, but he gets a little upset when they decide to rape his wife. So back out on the road they go, right into the middle of cannibal cookout central. Said flesh eaters are Caucasians wearing war paint and bad hairstyles, even more ridiculous than the ones in Jess Franco's comparable efforts in the same genre like *Cannibals*. Then there's that beloved Eurociné dubbing, which never comes even remotely close to matching any single language spoken by mankind. The dialogue is easily as hilarious as *Zombie Lake*, while anyone expecting the no-holds-barred experience of *Cannibal Ferox* will be either amused or utterly deflated by watching the "natives" rubbing and smushing lots of animal guts for what seems like minutes on end. The cast only features a small handful of familiar faces, such as Sylvia Solar (*Eyeball*) and Jess Franco regulars Olivier Mathot and the ubiquitous Antonio Mayans (*Sadomania*), but surprisingly, Franco didn't direct this one, apart from some stock footage yanked from *Cannibals*.

Continuing their raid of the Eurociné vaults, Severin has come up with a surpris-ingly nice-looking DVD that wrings much better visuals than you'd expect based on blurry videotape editions. Naturally it still looks like a cheap movie shot near someone's country house, but no one could have ever expected a spotless anamorphic transfer of this one to come along. The packaging claims it was mastered in HD, too, which means the Blu-ray must be right around the corner. Or not. The film was dubbed in every territory in which it was released due to the international cast, so the uproarious English dub (which in classic Lucio Fulci style uses an adult to dub the child lead) is about as legitimate as any. Extras include the bongo-riffic theatrical trailer and a bonus "spicy" scene with *Lorna the Exorcist*'s Pamela Stanford doing a topless striptease, which was removed from the film for reasons only the cult movie gods will ever decipher. The earlier U.K. release by HardGore (see *DVD Delirium Vol. 2*) only included a gallery of four international video sleeves and some cross-promotional trailers.

CANNIBALS

Colour, 1980, 90m. / Directed by Jess Franco / Starring Al Cliver, Sabrina Siani, Lina Romay, Shirley Knight, Antonio Mayans, Anouchka, Olivier Mathot / Blue Underground (US R0 NTSC), HardGore (UK R0 PAL) / WS (1.66:1) (16:9)

 Better known to trash video fanatics under a slew of alternative titles like *White Cannibal Queen* and *Barbarian Goddess* (not to mention *Mondo cannibale*), this ludicrous gutchomper from Jess Franco arrived at the height of the Italian cannibal craze sandwiched between the far more inflammatory *Cannibal Holocaust* and *Cannibal Ferox*. Here we have none of the animal violence (thank goodness) or narrative and moral complexity (alas), with Franco and regular Eurociné producer Daniel Lesoeur instead turning out a bloody and hysterically cheap homage to great white hunter epics with some flesh-eating action thrown in to spice things up, albeit in very, very, very slow motion. While on a scientific jungle expedition with his family, Jeremy Taylor (Al Cliver) loses his wife and his right arm to hungry, suspiciously Anglo-looking cannibals in day-glo face paint who storm his ship and make off with his young

daughter, Lana (played by Lesoeur's real-life daughter, "Anouchka" of *Zombie Lake* fame). Taylor manages to crawl his way back to civilisation and recuperates in New York, where he decides to sit around for ten years with sexy Ana (Lina Romay) before going back into the emerald inferno to retrieve his daughter, who's now a sexy, naked blonde nymphet (played by *Conquest*'s Sabrina Siani). Of course, by the time he and his rescue crew finally reach the cannibal tribe, Lana isn't too eager to leave her tribe where she's worshipped as a G-string goddess.

An inept feast of wooden acting, baffling editing, atrocious dubbing, and unbelievably protracted cannibalism scenes with painted extras gnawing on raw steak, *Cannibals* is nevertheless a lot of fun if you're looking for a fast-paced, goofy distraction. It's nowhere remotely as offensive as most of its ilk, and Franco keeps the laughs coming fast and furious with the least convincing "exotic" natives ever committed to film. Never one of the most charismatic actors, Cliver seems to be staring off into space in every shot but does finally muster up a little energy for the unforgettable climax, which finds him battling the tribe chief in a creek while soaking wet in a T-shirt and trying to hide his "missing" arm underneath a fake stump. Unfortunately Franco seems to run out of inspiration at the same time, delivering a story resolution that feels more like an indifferent shrug. Oddly enough, there's really no sexual content at all in the film (not even from Lina!) unless you count the casual displays of Ms. Siani's body. Meanwhile Roberto Pregadio serves up an inappropriate but amusing music score that could only have been composed in 1980. Low-rent bliss all the way. For some reason the opening credits attribute the film to mondo kingpin Franco Prosperi, but don't believe it.

Though some completists may have picked up the bare bones British release (reviewed in *DVD Delirium Vol. 3*), most people had to endure wretched-looking video transfers of this title for years. Blue Underground's release looks about as good as this film possibly could given that it appears to have been shot on at least four different types of film stock. Some scenes are wonderfully colourful and razor-sharp while others (mainly at the end) look somewhat bleached out, a deficiency present in many Eurociné titles from the period. The presentation itself is terrific, however. Since at least four different languages must have been spoken on-set, the English dub track here is about as genuine as any out there but is still a complete mess, never coming close to matching anyone's lip movements. The best aspect of the disc is easily the new 20-minute video interview, "Franco Holocaust", in which the thick-accented director speaks in English (with much-needed optional subtitles) about his disdain for the Italian cannibal fad, working with Daniel Leseour, his admiration for Cliver's work ethic, and best and most detailed of all, his attitudes about Sabrina Siani ("One of the most stupid people I have ever worked with"), including a priceless demonstration of her inability to look in the proper direction during filming. Oh, and the cannibals were all played by a bunch of Spanish gypsies they rounded up near the set. A French trailer (under the *Mondo cannibal* title) is also included.

THE CANTERBURY TALES

Colour, 1972, 112m. / Directed by Pier Paolo Pasolini / Starring Hugh Griffith, Laura Betti, Ninetto Davoli, Franco Citti, Josephine Chaplin, Pier Paolo Pasolini, Tom Baker, Jenny Runacre, Robin Askwith, Dan Thomas / BFI (DVD & Blu-ray, UK R2 PAL/HD) / WS (1.85:1) (16:9), Image (US R1 NTSC) / WS (1.85:1)

English tossers around the world threw up their hands in disgust with the release of *The Canterbury Tales*, which finds Pier Paolo Pasolini taking the lead of his previous film by selecting eight of the most cinematic tales from Geoffrey Chaucer's familiar tome about pilgrims on the way to Canterbury Cathedral amusing themselves with ribald tales of lust, murder, and comedy. The fact that Pasolini chose to emphasise the earthy, outrageous aspects of these tales (particular "The Miller's Tale", which usually sends young students into a state of shock) made it highly inappropriate as a teaching tool, but the end result is so extreme and deliciously unflinching that one can't help but admire the director's fearlessness. Virtually chucking out the pilgrimage aspect apart from a quick nod at the beginning and end, the film instead features Pasolini as Chaucer amusing himself by writing the stories as told by a colourful cast of characters. A nobleman (Hugh Griffith) is struck blind after taking on a much younger wife (Josephine Chaplin) in "The Merchant's Tale"; the devil (Franco Citti) reveals himself to a debt collector in "The Friar's Tale"; a genial medieval Charlie Chaplin precursor (Ninetto Davoli) winds up in serious hot water in "The Cook's Tale"; a student (Dan Thomas) decides to bed a pretty married woman (Jenny Runacre) while tricking her husband that a flood is coming, but their crude post-coital antics complicate matters in "The Miller's Tale"; the crimson-clad Wife of Bath (Laura Betti) sets her sights on a startled parson (*Doctor Who*'s Tom Baker, doing a nude scene no sane person ever asked for) in hopes he won't die like the rest of her husbands; two students get back at a landowner who tries to rip them off in

"The Reeve's Tale"; three rowdy friends find a treasure after carousing at a whorehouse but learn the hard way that greed is the root of all evil in "The Pardoner's Tale"; and the scatological "The Summoner's Tale" finds a dying man playing a prank on a friar, leading straight into the now-legendary final minutes in Hell, one of the most unforgettable, jaw-dropping scenes ever committed to film.

Critically derided as the weakest entry in the "Triolgy of Life" series, *The Canterbury Tales* suffered most from being seen in agonisingly terrible home video editions and really bottom-drawer prints, with even the Museum of Modern Art's archival edition looking dull, dreary and colourless. The same goes for early home video editions, from the grimy Water Bearer transfer in America to the equally worthless versions issued around the world. As such, BFI's Blu-ray will be the biggest shocker for anyone familiar with the film; to call it an utter revelation is an understatement. The cinematography by Tonino Delli Colli (who also did *The Decameron* but sat out the third part of the "Triolgy of Life", *Arabian Nights*) is remarkably beautiful, with fantastic landscape photography worthy of classic paintings. The vivid colours also bring out the vibrancy and imaginative touches in Danilo Donati's costumes and Dante Ferretti's sets, which were impossible to appreciate before. And of course, the finale is even more over the top thanks to the clarity of high definition. No matter what one thinks of this film, your opinion is bound to improve after seeing such a radical improvement across the board. This disc also addresses the major sticking issue for many viewers, the language track. Many of the primary players are familiar faces from British film and TV, with the hammy Griffith, delicate Chaplin, and cult favourite Runacre (*The Creeping Flesh*) faring best. All of the British actors performed their lines in English and used their own voices for the

dub (including a small role for Robin Askwith in his exploitation prime before his *Confessions* series of sex comedies, here performing perhaps the longest on-camera bladder relief ever captured on film), so for some this is the most legitimate version; however, the stilted delivery of Chaucer's lines from nearly everyone else sounds canned and awkward, robbing the film of much of its spontaneity and warmth. The Italian track has never been released in America and is rarely encountered elsewhere, so its inclusion here is a fascinating option and in many respects makes for a more enjoyable, smooth viewing experience. The Italian voice performances sound more energetic and natural, while the option to read the lines actually helps some of the jokes play better. Also, since in the final tally the two best performances also come from Italians (Betti and Citti), their own Italian vocal tracks can't help but boost the proceedings. Ultimately viewers should sample both options to see which one they prefer, but at least now it's easy to compare in one simple package. Once again the option to play the English version kicks off with the original UA credits and, in a nice touch, alternates to the English-language inserts when Chaucer is seen writing his stories.

The biggest extra here is "Pasolini and the Italian Genre Film", a new featurette by David Gregory and Alberto Farina examining the director's influence on horror, sexploitation and comedy films. This would have probably made more sense on the *Decameron* disc given that film's more prevalent influence, but either way it's nice to have thanks to interviews with writers and producers who worked with Pasolini (and sometimes imitated him) including Gabriele Crisanti, Paolo Bianchini and Alfredo Bini. You also get a very saucy theatrical trailer and a booklet containing liners by the same participants from the prior disc, here making a case for its wholly unique take on English views of sex and the church. Given that this film added a non-Chaucer scene of a gay man unable to buy his way out of condemnation being roasted alive in an outdoor contraption surrounded by leering buffoons, it's safe to say Pasolini was serious in his jabs against organised religion.

CAPTAIN SWING THE FEARLESS

Colour, 1971, 84m. / Directed by Tunç Basaran / Starring Salih Güney, Gülgün Erdem, Süleyman Turan, Ali Sen / Onar (Greece R0 PAL)

Back in the 1960s, Italian comic books (known as *fumetti*) were extremely popular throughout Europe and circulated widely either in multi-story collections or comic strips. Americans felt their impact only indirectly, however, mostly through film adaptations (like *Barbarella* and *Danger: Diabolik*) or the influence of these Italian artists on American ones throughout the 1970s with increasing levels of surrealism and more adult visual content. Of course, the comic influence could also be flat-out silly, which brings us to the Italian comic series *Il Comandante Mark*, which was started in 1966 by Pietro Sartoris. This goofy adventure strip told the continuing adventures of Captain Swing, a Frenchman raised by Native Americans in the wilderness after his family is shipwrecked on the Northern American coast. When his adopted Indian father is captured and hanged by dastardly British Redcoats, he forms a group of North American rebels called Ontario's Wolves to fight back, along with the aid of his sidekicks, Sad Owl and Mister Bluff. Meanwhile he romances pretty Betty, a buxom lass able to see past his really bad Indian hairstyle.

Never a company to put out more of the usual, Onar Films has veered into yet another undiscovered corner of Turkish cinema with this unheralded adaptation, *Captain Swing the Fearless* (*Korkusuz Kaptan Swing*), which sticks to the main comic story with a striking mixture of spaghetti western flavour and broad comedy. The film packs in lots of action and slapstick, with star Salih Güney giving Marty Feldman a run for his money in the camera mugging department as our hapless hero. It's more strange and hallucinatory than genuinely funny, but that tends to be the case when humour hops from one culture to the next. Oh, and the faux Morricone music is a pure blast from start to finish. And for you Turkish trivia fans, director Tunç Basaran is best known to video collectors as the man behind another mind-blowing 1971 film, *Aysecik and the Bewitched Dwarfs in Dreamland*, better known as *The Turkish Wizard of Oz*.

Onar's limited 500-piece pressing of this title is on par with their previous releases, which means the movie itself is just one factor in an educational and fascinating package. The transfer of the film looks soft, a problem inherent with the surviving video master, but colours are rich enough and the print is in decent shape. The Turkish dialogue can be played with optional English or Greek subtitles. You get text bios and filmographies for the director as well as stars Salih Güney and Ali Sen, while comic fans will squeal with the illustrated gallery which features a treasure trove of covers for many, many issues of the original comic, as published in Greece. Also included is a movie gallery (some lobby cards and frame grabs), the original trailer, and bonus trailers for *Casus Kiran 7 Canli Adam* (one of the *Spy Smasher* films), the gothic *Kadin Dusmani*, *Cellat* and *Altin Cocuk*. Last but certainly not least is the second instalment in Onar's "Turkish Fantastic Cinema" documentary, which features participants like Agah Ozguc, Yilmaz Atadeniz, and Giovanni Scognamillo talking about the golden age of Turkish films, with an emphasis here on westerns and outdoor adventure films including tons of wild-looking film clips.

CECILIA

Colour, 1982, 105m. / Directed by Jess Franco / Starring Muriel Montossé, Olivier Mathot, Pierre Taylou, Anthony Foster (Antonio Mayans), Lina Romay / Blue Underground (US R0 NTSC) / WS (1.66:1) (16:9)

A softcore programmer from Jess Franco's latter tenure with Eurociné Films, *Cecilia* is rather perversely one of his most exquisitely-mounted productions of the eighties. The surprisingly straightforward story, which sounds more like something suited for Joe Sarno, follows a haughty upper class wife, Cecilia (Muriel Montossé), who likes to spend her days re-enacting the opening from *The Story of O* by getting nasty in the back seat in the presence of her chauffeur. Unfortunately she pushes her servants too far, and as retribution she winds up being ravaged by the chauffeur's two brothers – which has the unintended effect of rekindling her bedroom relationship with her husband, Andre (Olivier Mathot), who reluctantly joins her for a swinging lifestyle in their chateau.

Featuring a memorable orgy appearance by Lina Romay and enough sex scenes to keep skin fans entertained, *Cecilia* may not win points for narrative originality but easily scores on the level of pure sensory pleasure. The locales, actors and production design are all unusually lush and elegant for Franco, and even the carnal action is shot in a way that veers more towards Radley Metzger territory than the standard spread-and-grind of his usual sex output. Die-hard Franco fans might be tempted to read the film as a fascinating defence of his unorthodox relationship with star/spouse Lina Romay (who certainly spent enough time copulating on-camera in front of her husband), which gives this film (originally titled *Sexual Aberrations of a Housewife*) an even more interesting twist. None of the actors (Lina excepted) have the intense cinematic magnetism of Franco's most familiar stock players, but they all perform capably enough and go through their often unclad paces well enough. The wild, semi-incestuous orgy scene (which teeters close to hardcore at one point) is easily the highlight, with some strange visual flourishes best experienced without warning.

The video transfer of *Cecilia* is a pure knockout with a rapturous transfer packed with gorgeous imagery. Even when nothing much is going on, you'll be entranced by the rich detail evident in every shot; this dynamic transfer looks great on a widescreen set and really pops through if you can upconvert it for HD. The soundtrack is presented in both English and French dubs with optional English subtitles, and both are quite workable for the film with the French option slightly more appropriate to the actors. Franco pops up again for yet another frank and funny interview, "Sexual Aberrations of Cecila", which spends 17 minutes talking about Franco's intentions for the film (he doesn't mention the Lina possibility above), his distaste for Eurociné's original title, and his love for the Portuguese shooting locations. An English trailer is also included.

CELLAT

Colour, 1975, 82m. / Directed by Memduh Ün / Starring Serdar Gökhan, Emel Özden, Melek Ayberk, Reha Yurdakul, Oktar Durukan / Onar (Greece R0 PAL)

A wonderfully foul entry in the Turkish tradition of co-opting Hollywood hits for local consumption, *Cellat* (which means "The Executioner") lifts the basic plot and social stance from Michael Winner's runaway hit *Death Wish* while giving it a distinctive flavour of its own. The story begins with architect Orhan Polat (Serdar Gökhan) vacationing with his wife, Filiz, and his sister Sevgi and her husband Cahit, where they sit around in the woods laughing uproariously about... well, nothing in particular. Orhan is a real softie who uses women's scarves to mend the broken bones of passing dogs, so you just know he'll get his pinko pacifist views challenged by the end of the first reel. Back in Istanbul, crime is running rampant with girls being assaulted and murdered left and right. Of course this is all the handiwork of three wicked, pot-smoking thugs who sit around in the rocks outside of town mocking all the rich people and dreaming of all the ekmek they can eat. They even steal a poor old lady's cabbage and use it to play soccer in the street. Then the goons follow Filiz and Sevgi home from a day of shopping, break into the house by posing as postmen, and rape and brutalise both of them when there isn't enough money in their purses. Filiz dies afterwards in the hospital, while Sevgi is left a traumatised wreck forced to endure shock treatments. The police can find no clues, so Orhan does what any man would do in his situation: fill up a sock with heavy coins and beat the snot out of a hateful pimp who tries to rob him in the street. Then he decides to take shooting lessons from a guy who says things like "A gun is a man's ornament. Look, this is not a gun; it's a poem. Without them, I feel naked." That night Orhan goes out a shoots a creepy guy who's apparently trying to molest a little boy, then comes home and gets physically sick. At his wife's grave he explains, "I'll keep on killing. The more I cleanse society of vermin, the more I'll feel your revenge has been taken." Immediately afterward he guns down two muggers and goes to hang out at "Club Love Story" (which hilariously uses the paperback cover of *Love Story* as its sign) and unknowingly has a drink with his wife's killers, who stupidly give the dead woman's necklace to a hooker. Soon the cops are noticing that all these bullets come from the same gun, but that doesn't stop our hero from taking out the trash on a commuter train (a great standout scene). Wounded in a gunfight, he takes refuge in the hooker's home and discovers the means by which he can finally inflict some justice on those who directly hurt his loved ones.

Brisk, very violent and highly enjoyable, *Cellat* is easily one of the most essential titles in the ongoing Onar Films series of Turkish cult releases. Gökhan is obviously much younger than Charles Bronson and cuts an impressive figure here, more reminiscent in his physicality of great Italian cop film stars like Maurizio Merli and Fabio Testi. Not surprisingly, he found lots of work in tough guy roles including a few *Dirty Harry* knockoffs, of course. Incredibly, this film makes a good effort at outdoing its predecessor with a string of increasingly violent set pieces, including a jaw-dropping impromptu electrocution scene that must be seen to be believed and a painful final fight sequence combining bricks and a criminal's knuckles. The wrap-up is a little abrupt (much more so than the Bronson version), but by then you won't care at all.

Onar's disc claims to be from the last surviving film print and looks okay; the transfer is definitely on the soft side but colours are punchy enough with decent flesh tones. Some outdoor scenes tend to bloom quite a bit, but given the rarity of the title, it's all just quibbling. As usual the Turkish dialogue is subtitled in both English and Greek. Among the extras, the coolest is "Turkish Vendetta", a blood-soaked new 25-minute featurette that's easily one of the most entertaining to date. Gokay Gelgec hosts the proceedings, drawing distinctions between revenge and vigilante stories before a string of clips from titles like *Buyuk Kin*, *Hamal*, *Insan Avcisi* and many more. You also get bios and filmographies for Gökhan and director Memduh Ün, a photo and artwork gallery, a filmography of revenge movies, and the highly caffeinated original theatrical trailer for *Cellat* plus the creepy *Kadin Dusmani* and the swinging thriller *Altin Cocuk*. The disc also comes with a fold-out poster for *Cellat*, perfect for scaring off anyone who tries to break into your house.

THE CENTERFOLD GIRLS

Colour, 1974, 91m. / Directed by John Peyser / Starring Andrew Prine, Tiffany Bolling, Jaime Lyn Bauer, Aldo Ray, Paula Shaw, Jennifer Ashley, Ray Danton, Francine York, Janus Blythe, John Denos, Janet Wood, Anneka Di Lorenzo / Dark Sky (US R1 NTSC) / WS (1.66:1) (16:9)

 Though its title summons visions of 1970s cheesecake films packed with student nurses or beach bunnies, *The Centerfold Girls* is a considerably more grim and unpredictable slice of drive-in fare. The fact that it was distributed by short-lived indie company General Film Corporation should have been a clue, since they already stunned audiences with twist-packed genre-benders like *Bonnie's Kids*, *Sugar Cookies*, *Detroit 9000* and especially *The Candy Snatchers*. Lithe, blonde-maned Tiffany Bolling, one of the company's frequent stars, returns here for one last exploitation hurrah before venturing off into the world of TV parts and supporting studio roles, though the film also boasts a surprisingly array of actors across the board to support its unorthodox structure.

Most likely inspired by the then-waning horror anthology films like *Asylum* popularised by Amicus, this tawdry trip-tych is united only by the presence of drive-in regular Andrew Prine (*Simon, King of the Witches*) as a clodhopper-wearing, bug-eyed psychopath/neat freak named Clement Dunne who spends much of his time poring over filthy girlie magazines and slicing up the centerfolds in disgust. He vents his rage by killing these models, with the first seen during the opening credits as a pretty corpse falling out of a car and getting buried near the ocean. The film then splits into three separate stalker tales for each centerfold, the first and most victimised being Jackie (soap actress Jaime Lyn Bauer), an aspiring nurse who runs afoul of some home intruder hippies with a clown fetish who try to paint and rape her (almost simultaneously). She manages to escape and finds refuge at a shady motel (run by Aldo Ray, an Oscar winner who was seriously slumming at this point in his career, and *Chatterbox*'s Paula Shaw). Unfortunately, Clement is also waiting for her... and the trouble's just beginning. Then we switch gears for part two with Charly (*Chained Heat*'s Jennifer Ashley) joining a troupe of models, an ill-tempered photographer (the late Eurocult vet Ray Danton), and a haughty queen bee (TV regular Francine York) for a weekend at a remote seaside resort where Clement begins picking everyone off one by one over the course of an eventful night. Boasting a hefty body count and some hilariously snippy banter, this portion seems heavily influenced by the great opening act of 1971's *The Return of Count*

Yorga and must have thrown audiences for a loop during its initial play dates. Finally the third story revolves entirely around Vera (Tiffany Bolling), a cranky stewardess who keeps getting threatening phone calls from Clement, who murders her best friend by mistake. Realising something is amiss, she takes off but winds up in the clutches of some lowlife sailors who slip her a roofie at a beach bar. Barely fazed, she winds up in a car with Clement who pits her in a final showdown back on the beach where it all started.

Though shot on the cheap by John Peyser, a director normally associated with routine television product, *The Centerfold Girls* boasts a few indelible sequences in each segment, most notably the first razor throat-slashing (a startling and effectively staged scene worthy of an Italian horror film), the nocturnal stalking portion of story number two, and Bolling's feisty mano-a-mano with Prine which climaxes in some poetic beach shots reminiscent of Jean Rollin. Of course, it's all perfectly functional as drive-in trash, too, with most of the female cast popping their tops at regular intervals, while the cast includes a roster of familiar '70s exploitation faces including brief appearances from *The Hills Have Eyes*'s Janus Blythe, underrated would-be leading man John Denos, *Up!*'s Janet Wood, and even notorious future *Caligula* starlet Anneka Di Lorenzo.

Despite its can't-miss combo of sex and violence, this film essentially disappeared after initial theatrical showings apart from a fleeting release on VHS in the early '80s. Dark Sky's DVD presents the best possible viewing option (especially compared to the few scratchy prints lying around) with a transfer described in the packaging as being taken from the original 16mm camera negatives (the format on which it was originally shot). The 1.66:1 anamorphic presentation looks surprisingly good, and the framing appears accurate while shearing away a small amount of dead space at the top and bottom compared to the tape edition. There's really nothing to complain about here. The mono soundtrack also sounds as good as could be expected and does justice to the surprisingly rich and varied score by mystery man Mark Wolin (in his only film score), which mixes harpsichord and '70s funk, sometimes in the same cue. Optional English subtitles are also included as per the usual, very commendable Dark Sky practice. The biggest extra here is a dense 15-minute featurette, "Making the Cut: A Look Back at *The Centerfold Girls*", which kicks off with Prine talking about his role and then interjecting comments from York, Ashley, and regular GFC director/writer Arthur Marks (*Bonnie's Kids*), who wrote the original story. No one seems to think the film is high art, but they all speak fondly of it and talk about their efforts to elevate it a bit above the usual throwaway fare. Fans of '70s retro-trash and envelope-pushing genre hybrids watching it now will surely agree they succeeded. Also included are the green- and red-band versions of the theatrical trailer (with the latter packing in almost every topless shot from the movie), two TV spots, a radio promo, and most surprisingly, over 20 minutes of the original score (which sounds like all of it) played as a series of individual cues over images from the film. Considering how sparse respectable genre releases have become in the mature age of DVD, a fully decked-out edition for a long-neglected but fascinating experiment in exploitation like this is cause for celebration indeed.

THE CHAIN REACTION

Colour, 1980, 92m. / Directed by Ian Barry / Starring Steve Bisley, Arna-Marie Winchester, Ross Thompson, Hugh Keays-Byrne / Umbrella (Australia R4 PAL) / WS (1.85:1) (16:9)

Shortly after the success of the nuclear scare film *The China Syndrome*, a few other socio-political imitations popped up – but none as drive-in friendly as *The Chain Reaction*, which throws in car chases and stunt work from the guys behind *Mad Max* (including associate producer George Miller) and even an uncredited cameo from Mel Gibson himself. The race-against-time story follows Larry (Steve Bisley, best known as "Goose" from *Mad Max*) and Carmel (Arna-Marie Winchester), a vacationing couple who rescue an injured nuclear waste storage worker, Heinrich (Ross Thompson), who's trying to warn the public about a deadly leak that's going to contaminate everything within miles. His boss is trying to cover the whole thing up by sending his goons out to silence the whistle blower, and the race is on.

Featuring some eye-popping collision scenes, snappy cinematography by Peter Weir lenser Russell Boyd, and some very queasy segments of radioactive terror, this film probably should've been a bigger hit than it was, though it did earn something of a following on tape and has a similar vibe to contemporary thrillers like *Scanners*.

The Region 4 special edition features the expected high-quality transfer along with some nifty extras, which include "Thrills and Spills"(a very revealing half-hour retrospective with the actors and director Ian Barry), and one of the director's earlier shorts entitled "The Sparks Obituary". Also here are some dupey-looking deleted footage, a TV spot and trailer, and photo gallery. Your social consciousness won't be raised much in the end, but as a Down Under chase flick, this is about as fun as it gets.

CHANTAL
Colour, 1969, 60m. / Directed by Nick Phillips
CHANTAL
Colour, 2007, 73m. / Directed by Tony Marsiglia / Starring Misty Mundae, Julian Wells, Darian Caine, Julie Strain / Seduction Cinema (US R0 NTSC) / WS (1.78:1) (16:9)

C

For a brief period, Seduction Cinema dabbled with the interesting experiment of taking vintage '60s softcore titles and presenting them on DVD along with quickie new remakes, such as *Roxanna*. One of the better results of this approach can be found in this double-disc set containing an interesting contrast in softcore styles old and new, now most historically interesting as the last "sexy" outing for Misty Mundae under that screen name. Both films involve vulnerable young women named Chantal who encounter torment and degradation while seeking stardom in Hollywood, but otherwise they're basically different beasts. The original stars an uncredited actress as the titular character, a clueless dolt who passes through a number of scuzzy Hollywood types and wanders around late '60s L.A., which provides some fantastic travelogue footage of an era long passed. The famous Roosevelt Hotel gets a good visual workout, too, before it got made over as a flash-in-the-pan celebrity hangout during the past few years. The usual down-on-her-luck clichés are all here and accounted for, spiced up with some mild T&A. The same story gets another workout in a bonus short, 1956's "These Girls Are Fools", a cautionary tale about stupid girls getting devoured by Tinseltown.

The *Chantal* remake actually has more substance than the usual Phillips redos, with

Mundae offering a committed performance as the suitcase-toting ingénue who strolls down Hollywood Boulevard, runs afoul of unscrupulous hotel managers, auditions for S&M layouts, and mingles with a colourful cast of busty day players like Julie Strain. Perhaps the most fascinating aspect of this set is the trio of commentaries, with Nick Phillips (*Criminally Insane*) offering a rather jaded view of his late '60s softcore efforts, Mundae ruefully reflecting on her retirement from softcore (in which she felt "out of place"), and Tony Marsiglia checking off his filmic influences ranging from *The Outer Limits* to Rinse Dream. You also get the usual liner notes booklet, a making-of featurette and camera test for the new version, and the expected barrage of Mundae-related trailers.

CHEERLEADERS' WILD WEEKEND

Colour, 1979, 87m. / Directed by Jeff Werner / Starring Jason Williams, Kristine DeBell, Lenka Novak, Marilyn Joi, Anthony Lewis, Robert Houston, Courtney Sands, Leon Isaac Kennedy, Janie Squire / Scorpion (US R0 NTSC) / WS (1.78:1) (16:9)

 Well, there certainly are a lot of cheerleaders, and they do spend a wild weekend – by getting kidnapped! A busload of pom-pommers from rival high schools gets hijacked by some male criminals including down-and-out former footballer Wayne (Jason Williams, also the film's co-writer), who strikes up an odd rapport with one of the pluckiest of the cheerleaders, Debbie (Kristine DeBell). The ransom demands from the kidnappers set up an elaborate police plan involving a reluctant DJ named Joyful Jerome (Leon Isaac

Kennedy, using the name "Lee Curtis"). Meanwhile the girls must contend with tensions between themselves and the demands of the kidnappers, who stage a strip beauty contest and find their plan quickly derailing as the cheerleaders figure out how to fight back in ways involving the resourceful use of all the girls' underwear.

A raucous and completely schizoid experience, *Cheerleaders' Wild Weekend* was originally shot under the more appropriate title of *The Great American Girl Robbery* (the title used on the DVD print here) and apparently also circulated as *Bus 17 Is Missing*, though its most catchy, marketable name is the one that stuck. The film fires in numerous directions at commercial targets right from the opening scenes featuring female cast members doing perky glamour poses accompanied by funky main title music, and the plot skids wildly from leering T&A fantasy to broad comedy to violent roughie melodrama, culminating in wild heist antics right out of a '70s Disney caper. Director Jeff Werner (who later helmed the weirdest Robbie Benson vehicle, *Die Laughing*) certainly never allows the pace to flag, but the brutal tonal shifts nearly knock the film off the rails over and over again. What keeps the whole enterprise together is the game cast with the enormously engaging DeBell making a solid female lead and her *Alice in Wonderland* co-star, Williams (fondly remembered from *Flesh Gordon*), holding his own as the most sympathetic of the kidnappers. Also noteworthy is Robert "Bobby" Houston, best known for his whiny turn in Wes Craven's *The Hills Have Eyes* before he turned director with the Americanization of *Shogun Assassin*, ultimately even earning an Oscar for his documentary direction. He also shares one of the most memorable sequences in the film spying on a lesbian bathtub scene. Gorgeous drive-in actress Marilyn Joi also appears here under the name Tracy King as one of the cheerleaders;

best remembered as Cleopatra Schwartz from *Kentucky Fried Movie*, she also enlivened plenty of classic trash films like *Candy Tangerine Man*, *Black Samurai*, and *Nurse Sherri*. Other familiar faces include Lenka Novak (*Vampire Hookers*) and Janie Squire (*Piranha*).

Originally released by Dimension Pictures, this film changed hands many times over the years and was even issued as a Leon Isaac Kennedy vehicle at one point to cash in on the success of *Penitentiary*. It still works pretty well as an exploitation time waster, with enough creative editorial touches and eccentric grace notes to keep viewers on their toes. Scorpion's DVD release is taken from a solid print with a few battered moments, but it's definitely superior to anything ever available before and finally puts the film back in circulation after decades of oblivion. The extensive extras offer a wide range of viewpoints about the film including two audio commentaries. The first features Werner, Joi, editor Greg McClatchy, and Marc Edward Heuck discussing the film along with yours truly (so don't expect an objective appraisal!) along with an uncredited, mid-film appearance by another cast member whose surprise inclusion won't be spoiled here. Oddly enough, no one can seem to shed any light on the identity of Anthony Lewis, an actor playing one of the kidnappers under a fake name. The second commentary is notable for the first special features appearance by DeBell, who is prompted with a series of questions about her career. She doesn't remember a whole lot, but she does explain why she was the only female cast member to stay clothed and offers only a single, fleeting mention of her most infamous film. DeBell also appears for an interesting half-hour video interview in which she discusses most of the rest of her career including roles in *Meatballs*, *The Big Brawl*, *The Main Event* and TV's *Night Court*. The vivacious Joi returns for an interview in which she recollects her very colourful career including memories of working with the likes of Sam Sherman and Al Adamson. Finally Kennedy turns up for a long discussion of his entire career, ranging from this early film (a part he landed because of his real-life DJ experience as "Leon the Lover") to the *Penitentiary* series to the heartbreak of *Knights of the City*, a reportedly excellent genre-breaking musical mangled beyond recognition by New World when they diced out all of the music numbers! Other extras include the original trailer, the reissue title sequence, a hidden bonus interview, and a hefty stills gallery with plenty of salacious and interesting shots including a rape scene cut from the final film for reasons discussed in the first commentary.

THE CHICK'S ABILITY

Colour, 1984, 90m. / Directed by John Doo / Starring Helena Ramos, Romeu de Freitas, Vanessa Alves, André Loureiro / Impulse (US R0 NTSC)

A peculiar cinematic strain only known to die-hard softcore devotees and collectors of arcane video releases, Brazil's *pornochanchada* films (often just called *chada* for short) flourished from the late '70s through the following decade. Unlike most simulated offerings around the world which had begun to just feel like hardcore with the worst shots taken out, these South American fusions of soap operatics and sweaty coupling feel like low budget Pedro Almodóvar movies filtered through the mind of a depraved grindhouse programmer. Skilled actors and convoluted plotlines drive the sex scenes here, which are definitely integral to the film be it comedy, thriller or drama, and even some of the most renowned actors were willing to go much further in front of the camera than most audiences expected. *The Chick's Ability* (*Volúpia de Mulher*) is a fairly serious entry but certainly doesn't skimp on the entertainment value, delivering the huge doses of flesh typical of the genre (which was even dabbling in brief unsimulated scenes at the time, but not in this case – just barely).

The first section of the film unfolds through flashbacks as pretty young Cristina (*Amazon Jail*'s Vanessa Alves) languishes in a hospital while flashbacks explain exactly how she wound up there, namely by losing her virginity to her first boyfriend at an idyllic waterfall only to be discovered by her disapproving parents, who order her to marry him or get out. Cristina chooses the latter and, upon finding herself pregnant, shacks up with a shady string of characters including a hooker and even a sassy crossdresser who helps deliver her child. Unfortunately complications ensue which force the baby to stay under medical care, so her nurse, Laura (Helena Ramos from Coffin Joe's *Hellish Flesh*), arranges to hook her up as a nude model for her painter boyfriend, Marcos (André Loureiro), both of whom are sexually insatiable. Marcos is inspired by Cristina (who moonlights out on the streets to boot) and quickly falls for her, leading to plenty of domestic jealousy.

Featuring a transvestite catfight, three(!) aquatic sex scenes, and a physically stunning cast who spend over half the screen time naked, *The Chick's Ability* is a wonderful exploitation discovery and offers a rare chance to watch one of these efforts in crisp quality with English subtitles, a relief for anyone who's sat through fuzzy '80s copies of any of these films. The only other remotely comparable titles on the current market are *Amazon Jail* and *Bare Behind Bars*; while this film is nearly as explicit, it's a much more overheated and stylised

affair with both of the female leads steaming up the screen. If you were blown away by Something Weird's *Fuego*, this one ramps it all up even further. Impulse's inaugural release in their "Classic Latin Erotica Collection" looks very nice, featuring a full frame transfer that doesn't appear to be missing anything on the sides. The print is in solid shape and is obviously a new transfer, with optional English subtitles for the mono Portuguese soundtrack.

THE CHILLING

Colour, 1989, 90m. / Directed by Deland Nuse & Jack A. Sunseri / Starring Linda Blair, Dan Haggerty, Troy Donahue, Jack De Rieux, Ron Vincent / Shriek Show (US R1 NTSC)

 In this weird late entry in the '80s straight-to-video horror craze, the biggest draw is the cast which features the unbeatable combo of Linda Blair (post-*Savage Streets*), Dan Haggerty (better known to the world as Grizzly Adams), and late teen heartthrob Troy Donahue (post-*Hard Rock Nightmare*). Basically swiping plot elements left and right from *Night of the Creeps* and *The Return of the Living Dead*, the film dares to depict the cutting-edge technology of cryogenics, which freezes rich people in the hopes that they can be revived and cured somewhere down the road by future scientists. The head doctor (Donahue) is basically a corrupt bastard, which becomes all too evident when a power outage and electrical storm turns his upscale cryogenic farm into a big zombie jamboree filled with shambling, freezer-burned flesh eaters. Can plucky medical assistant Linda Blair escape from their icy clutches? For some reason the film flat-out equates cryogenics with the

devil's work, which seems to take that whole "don't go meddling in God's domain" credo a bit far, but that's just the tip of the iceberg of confusion here. None of the actors seem to be performing in the same movie (or from the same script), which adds a ton of entertainment value to what could have otherwise been a throwaway zombie quickie. Then there's the moralistic end credits that outdo the coda from *Beyond the Valley of the Dolls*, but that's really best left experienced without any further warning.

Originally a Code Red acquisition, *The Chilling* is presented in a "director's cut" on DVD from Shriek Show which basically looks like a spritzed-up version of the original straight-to-tape master used back in the old days. It's fine for what it is (and judging by the credits, this was completed on video so a new film transfer ain't gonna happen), but as for how this differs from the original cut, that's anyone's guess. The history of the film is very confusing, with the original director reputedly leaving the project and the rest assembled under less than optimal circumstances. In any case, while this release doesn't do much to shed any light on the production background, it does feature a hefty 20+ minutes of on-set footage, mostly focusing on the zombies and other miscellaneous FX. It's actually more entertaining than the film, which is also easily true of the next extra, a "blooper reel" that ambushes viewers with some incredibly revealing deleted sex scene footage. Also included are a long trailer (which looks more like a pitch reel) and other Shriek Show promos.

CHRISTINA

Colour, 1984, 91m. / Directed by Francisco Lara Polop / Starring Jewel Shepard, Karin Schubert, Josephine Jacqueline Jones, Ian Sera / Private Screening (US R0 NTSC), MediumRare (UK R2 PAL)

One of the least-familiar Private Screening releases, *Christina* is basically a bump-and-grind vehicle for pin-up/ B-movie starlet Jewel Shepard (*Return of the Living Dead*, *Holly-wood Hot Tubs 1 & 2*) who stars as the title character (it's the first adaptation from a popular book series, according to the main titles), a much-desired heiress who seems to spend all of her time nosing around in people's business and getting laid. Soon she's snatched by a renegade group of "sexual terrorists", including Sapphic leader Karin Schubert and *Pieces* star Ian Sera, who initiate her into their radical group via plenty of soapy baths and soft-lit sex scenes.

Yes, 1984's a bit late for another Patty Hearst-inspired sex flick (years after *Tanya* and *Autumn Born*), but Shepard's unabashed performance carries the film over the rough spots and director Francisco Lara Polop (*Murder Mansion*) keeps things moving without much aesthetic fuss and bother.

The full-frame transfer is on par with the label's other titles, though the compositions appear to be a bit cropped on the sides and don't matte off well at all; expect to watch it only at 1.33:1, and some minor squeezing during the credits indicates this was probably originally shot for 1.66:1 projection. As with the other titles in the series, there are no extras at all; considering the relatively high price tag, you may want to rent this first to see if the steak lives up to the sizzle. Not surprisingly, MediumRare's later U.K. DVD release from the same master fell afoul of the BBFC who demanded an 11-second trim to a gruesome encounter between a motorcycle and an unsuspecting horse.

CHRISTMAS EVIL

Colour, 1980, 90m. / Directed by Lewis Jackson / Starring Brandon Maggart, Dianne Hull, Jeffrey DeMunn, Andy Fenwick, Peter Neuman / Synapse (US R0 NTSC) / WS (1.78:1) (16:9), Troma (US R0 NTSC)

 One of the earlier holiday-themed horror films before the infamy of *Silent Night, Deadly Night*, this oddball mixture of whimsy and anti-corporate rage has long been lumped in with other killer Santa films (most of which don't feature a real killer Claus at all). Originally titled *You Better Watch Out* (a name still present on the uncut source print used for Synapse's DVD), the story follows one extremely unfortunate Christmas in the life of Harry (regular TV actor Brandon Maggart), a poor soul whose love for December 25th was forever warped when he injured himself while watching his parents copulating with the aid of a Father Christmas outfit. Now a toy factory employee, Harry is still obsessed with Christmas but has taken it to rather frightening extremes, keeping an eye on his neighbours and compiling his own naughty-or-nice list with rather nasty punishments in mind. No one else around him seems willing to indulge Harry's dearly-kept dream to bring the Christmas spirit alive, and soon our poor anti-hero has snapped, turning his fragile psyche into the instrument for a rampage of yuletide violence with his non-charitable co-workers getting the brunt of his seasonal rage.

A rather interesting and sympathetic descent-into-madness story, *Christmas Evil* has been confounding viewers for decades when they expect to rent another movie with Santa sliding down a chimney and hacking up topless teens with an axe. The on-screen violence is pretty low-key, with director Lewis Jackson instead opting for an off-kilter atmosphere of black comedy and pathos. Even when Harry goes full-tilt nuts at the end, it's hard to avoid feeling for the guy a little bit, especially since most of the other adults are such stern, dishonest lumps of coal. The much-discussed finale (which the director posits as a fantasy) is certainly memorable, ending the film on a note not unlike *Thelma & Louise*. (Really!) It's no wonder John Waters raved up and down about this one in his book *Crackpot*; it's a holiday film truly unlike any other, for better or worse.

Christmas Evil made its first DVD appearance in a dire edition from Troma, whose track record speaks for itself. Luckily you can toss aside that piece of junk in favour of Synapse's far more attractive special edition, which restores some footage deleted from previous video editions (nope, not extra gore – mainly just more of Harry's trials at work, as far as these eyes could tell). The source print looks great, with those all-important reds and greens popping through quite vividly. The mono audio is also a huge step up compared to the muffled, lifeless past versions. Anyone wondering about this film's origins and intentions will find plenty of answers in Jackson's commentary track, which covers everything from the financing to the visual scheme and the wacko distribution history. He also offers his own personal outlook on the story and what he was trying to convey, which is indeed a far cry from your average "slasher Santa" yarn. Far less serious but just as educational in its own right is a second commentary with Jackson and the always-entertaining John Waters, who's obviously in a mood similar to his one on the *Mommie Dearest* DVD. Expect lots of Santa jokes and stories, as well as far more arcane trivia than the first track. A must-hear, obviously. Other extra goodies include nearly half an hour of fascinating VHS audition footage (it's pretty clear why Maggart got the job), some hilarious audience response cards from test screenings (easily the most enjoyable you'll see this side of Criterion's *Videodrome* DVD), three storyboard demonstrations, and some interesting but inessential deleted footage. Stuff this one in yer stockings, kiddies!

CIRCLE OF IRON

Colour, 1978, 97m. / Directed by Richard Moore / Starring David Carradine, Jeff Cooper, Christopher Lee, Roddy McDowall, Erica Creer, Eli Wallach / Blue Underground (DVD & Blu-ray, US R0 NTSC/HD) / WS (1.66:1) (16:9) / DD5.1, DTS5.1

In a time and place "that never was and always will be", fluffy-haired fighter Cord (Jeff Cooper) is disqualified in combat by the righteous White Robe (Roddy McDowall), who hopes to find a fighter skilled enough to face a powerful opposing wizard, Zetan (Christopher Lee), who possesses a sought-after Book of Enlightenment. Cord believes he's still the man for the job and sets off of his own accord, soon running into a colourful cast of characters including a blind mystic who use his flute as a fighting weapon, a moustachioed sheik, the savage Monkey Man, and a black-clad figure (credited as Death), all played by David Carradine. He also takes time out to bed down a beautiful maiden (Erica Creer) before finally reaching his destination, where a very Zen surprise waits in store.

East meets West and comes out very strangely indeed in *Circle of Iron*, referred to by its creators (and the source print used for its current video release) under the more accurate title of *The Silent Flute*. The film has ensured a cult following for decades to come simply on the basis of its genesis as a pet project of Bruce Lee, who originally planned to play four roles in the Zen-oriented narrative with friend James Coburn coming on board as co-writer and star. (Steve McQueen was also approached but bailed before Lee reached superstardom in the early '70s.) Unfortunately Lee didn't live to see his vision come to the screen, but David Carradine acquired the rights and, recognising it as a logical extension of his famous role in TV's *Kung Fu*, finally put it all together in 1978. The result is an odd beast to be sure, mixing hazy fantasy, philosophy, and martial arts showdowns into an oddly compelling stew that riveted the attention of channel surfers and adventurous video nuts for years.

Shot in Israel with a dreamlike atmosphere reminiscent of classic fantasy novels (or maybe Lucio Fulci's *Conquest* with a bigger budget and cleaner camerawork), *Circle of Iron* will seem either deeply profound or utterly silly depending on the viewer's mood (or perhaps a combination of both). Carradine certainly gets to stretch himself beyond his famous *Kung Fu* persona here with his multiple roles, though obviously his flute character is the most interesting and pivotal to the story. Though he only appears for a few minutes of screen time, Lee also offers a nicely judged performance which plays surprisingly against type (for reasons which shouldn't be revealed here, though it's worth mentioning that the final twist was copied wholesale by *Kung Fu Panda*, of all films). However, perhaps the most memorable performance is delivered by Eli Wallach, again in essentially an extended cameo as "Man in Oil", whose plan to achieve a higher state of enlightenment is highly unusual, to say the least. A friend of Carradine's, Cooper suffers in comparison to his co-stars (and his woolly hairdo doesn't do him any favours either); he seems more like a bemused, over-the-hill surfer than a dedicated seeker of truth. However, in an oddball drive-in sort of fashion, his performance works in the same way as other inexplicably modern leading men in films like *The Sword and the Sorcerer*.

Blue Underground has released *Circle of Iron* in two DVD editions, first as a modest single-disc version and then a tricked-out, two-disc special edition. Their subsequent Blu-ray carries over all of the extras apart from a stills gallery and a pdf of the original screenplay by Lee, Coburn and Stirling Silliphant, and the real clincher for the hi-def option is the obvious huge increase in clarity and fidelity in the transfer of the feature itself. While the standard def DVD struggled with the earthy tones of the film and betrayed some signs of edge enhancement to compensate for the tricky visuals, the Blu-ray has no such issues and looks pleasingly film-like. The amount of film grain looks about right, too, appearing just enough in darker scenes and the opticals used for the credits still look like a real movie. Very nice all around. While the DVDs offer the usual DTS and Dolby Digital EX options, the Blu-ray also trumps them with subtle but immersive DTS-HD and Dolby TruHD mixes along with the prior Dolby Digital tracks and optional subtitles in English, Spanish or French. Extras include a delightful video interview ("Playing the Silent Flute") with the late Carradine (who mimics his characters on-camera and offers his memories of the apparently MIA Cooper), a robust audio commentary with director Richard Moore, interviews with co-producer Paul Maslansky and martial arts coordinator Joe Lewis, an audio interview with Silliphant about working with Lee and Coburn, the American and international trailers using both titles, and TV spots. Apart from the Carradine interview, the Moore commentary (moderated by

David Gregory) is the most substantial of the bonuses, talking about the path of the film on its way to completion and the stories behind the extremely colourful cast of players involved. Certainly one of the most unique martial arts films from the genre's initial heyday around the world, *Circle of Iron* offers much more than just mindless fight scenes and holds up as a fascinating mixture of spirituality and body blows.

CLOAK & SHAG HER

Colour, 2008, 83m. / Directed by William Hellfire / Starring Julian Wells, Den Paul, Darian Caine, A.J. Khan / Seduction Cinema (US R0 NTSC)

A lethargic *Austin Powers* parody (if such a thing could exist) several years past its expiration date, *Cloak & Shag Her* is easily the most lightweight offering yet from inconsistent but sometimes talented zero-budget sexploitation director William Hellfire. Not surprisingly, the entire spy parody angle is simply an excuse to show the usual stable of softcore starlets pulling off their clothes, rubbing their mammaries about an inch from the camera, and lip locking each other.

The "plot" follows curvy agent April Flowers (Julian Wells) and her dimwit sidekick, Basil Shagalittle (Den Paul), as they time travel from '69 London to 2019 (why?) to stop a scheming archvillain, Dr. Mean (Darian Caine), who's trying to take over the world by making everyone uncontrollably horny (shades of the much better *Flesh Gordon*). Much lesbianism ensues.

Most of the film is shot in extremely soft focus for some reason, so brace yourself for major eyestrain by the half hour mark; on the other hand, a few of the gags are faintly amusing, and it's hard to totally knock a film that stars "Mike Roszhart as Kung Po the Karate Chimp". The best thing is the funky soundtrack by "Trigger Finger", which sounds like Iron Butterfly mashed up with a blaxploitation score. It's a lot of fun, and thankfully the DVD comes with a bonus disc of the CD soundtrack. Hellfire provides another commentary track that's lively and interesting, offering a primer on how to stage an ambitious, time-hopping sexploitation epic on the budget of a grocery tab. You also get an "extraordinary behind-the-scenes" reel that's much longer than usual, showing how the green screen effects were accomplished and how silly everyone acted on the set.

CODEX ATANICUS: THREE WILD TALES

Colour, 2007, 70m. / Directed by Carlos Atanes / Kalashnifilms Atanes (Spain R0 NTSC) / WS (1.85:1)

This trio of short films hails from Spanish avant garde filmmaker Carlos Atanes, who's been churning out mind-bending shorts since the early 1990s. The first and earliest, "Meta-minds & Metabodies" (1995), is a shot-on-video 20-minute fantasy about a beer hall outside the entrance to Hell, where a group of debauched arrivals live it up and raving women entertain the audience while lashed to the wall. Or something like that. A likely descendant of the Panic Movement which spawned filmmakers like Alejandro Jodorowsky and Fernando Arrabal, it quickly sets the pace for what's to come and, despite the very low technical quality, it's a suitably frenzied intro.

Next up is "Morfing" (1996), essentially a longer expansion on the same theme with Atanes playing "himself" as an unhinged director who wants to off himself while doing a TV pilot, and a girl intervenes to stop him by introducing him to a world of mutated, sexualised grotesqueries that, er, climaxes in a most unforgettable fashion. Oh, and it also features some now-famous Spanish filmmaking personalities, but I don't want to ruin the surprise.

Finally, "Welcome to Spain" (1999) must be the strangest tourist endorsement ever as two visiting guys by a roadside end up tangling with a quartet of psychos thrashing around with a bunch of chickens, coughing up blood, attacking each other, and yanking their pants down in a bright orange stairwell. It's guaranteed to get a reaction even among seasoned experimental film fanatics. The collection is introduced by actress Arantxa Peña, who appears in many of the director's films. Certainly the perfect title for those who think they've seen it all.

THE COMING OF JOACHIM STILLER

Colour, 1976, 153m. / Directed by Harry Kümel / Starring Hugo Metsers, Cox Habbema, Ward de Ravet, Charles Janssens, Peter Strynckx / Canvas (Holland R0 PAL)

Bachelor newspaper editor and part-time novelist Freek (*Blue Movie*'s Hugo Metsers) finds his daily routine in Antwerp, Belgium interrupted by uncanny events – metro trains stopping for unseen passengers, bizarre street accidents and construction blockages, and so on, all of which lead to a mysterious, persistent entity known as Joachim Stiller. Strangest of all, he receives a letter at work from Stiller, addressed to Freek but postmarked twenty years before he was even born. As he also becomes involved in a sexual relationship with pretty young Simone (Cox Habbema), the inexplicable events continue to escalate including an oncoming comet and the strange phone calls and recurring, eerie music flooding the streets at night...

This fascinating, often chilling mixture of fantasy and subtle horror was directed by Belgium's most significant cinematic practitioner of the fantastique, Harry Kümel, shortly after his two most significant films, *Daughters of Darkness* and *Malpertuis*. His keen visual sense is still well in evidence here as he fills this twisty tale (from a novel by noted Flemish fantasy writer Hubert Lampo, who also makes a quick cameo onscreen) with plenty of sumptuous décor and impeccable, deeply spooky compositions. This being a Belgian/Dutch TV production, it's no surprise there's quite a bit of casual nudity along with some sparse but very effective moments of violence.

At one point thought lost after it was hacked down by over 35 minutes for a fleeting Dutch theatrical release, the complete version of *The Coming of Joachim Stiller* was transferred from the sole remaining film elements in the Belgian TV archives for the Canvas DVD release (under the original title of *De komst van Joachim Stiller*). The transfer looks good for the vintage and history of the film; it's quite crisp and looks very rich and film-like. The mono Dutch audio can be played with optional subtitles in English, French or Dutch, along with an audio commentary by the director (in Dutch only). The disc might be a bit difficult to track down in some countries, but it's worth the effort for fans of unusual, chilling European fare with an artistic bent.

COMRADES

Colour, 1986, 182m. / Directed by Bill Douglas / Starring Mark Brown, Arthur Dignam, John Hargreaves, Barbara Windsor, Freddie Jones, Michael Hordern, Vanessa Redgrave, James Fox, Imelda Staunton, Keith Allen, Stephen Bateman / BFI (DVD & Blu-ray, UK R0 PAL/HD) / WS (1.78:1) (16:9)

A visually stunning portrait of true-life social strife and change painted on an extremely large canvas, this three-hour epic from director Bill Douglas marks a surprising change in tack (if not subject matter) for a filmmaker best known for his autobiographical trilogy beginning with *My Childhood*. The action begins in 19th-Century Dorset where six manual labourers (including British film vets James Fox and Freddie Jones), soon to be known to history as the Tolpuddle Martyrs, decide to organise an early form of a union known as the Friendly Society of Agricultural Labourers. Their efforts get them shipped off to Australia by their displeased landowner, and while their new home promises the chance to establish themselves in a different sort of society, injustice and inhumanity still rear their heads regardless of locale.

Though shot with all the visual precision and splendour of more lauded painterly films like *Days of Heaven*, *Comrades* is hardly a series of pretty picture postcards. The incredible ensemble cast and extremely caustic subject matter (which detours briefly into such surprising areas as bestiality and physical torture) make for a unique and richly varied visual experience which never grows dull over the entire running time. The split structure between the U.K. and Australia is unique as it allows not only a variety of landscapes but in actors as well, with familiar faces like John Hargreaves popping up in the second half which steers into some territory lesser known even to historians. It's a shame Douglas had so much difficulty mounting his feature productions as this ambitious achievement demonstrates he certainly had the ability to carry off any project he so desired.

A title long desired by cineastes but difficult to find in any format, *Comrades* has finally been given a respectable presentation by the BFI on DVD and Blu-ray. The results are, to say the least, astounding; this is a top-notch HD transfer that soars with all the beauty of a freshly-struck print. Colours and detail are faultless, while the level of film grain is just rich and healthy enough to maintain a satisfying level of cinematic texture. This is simply a gorgeous presentation and pure demo material all the way.

A second disc contains a host of additional extras including the one-hour "Lanterna Magicka: Bill Douglas & The Secret History of Cinema" (which examines the director's affection for early cinematic techniques and equipment as well as his international influences), "Visions of Comrades" (a re-editing of footage from the Douglas documentary on the BFI *Trilogy* release related solely to this film), a half-hour interview with the director from the late '70s about his powerful first three films (inexplicably broken into two parts), a theatrical trailer and on-set TV report from the location shoot in Dorset, and "Home and Away", a 1974 short by Michael Alexander co-written by Douglas about another young boy coming of age.

CONFESSIONS OF A YOUNG AMERICAN HOUSEWIFE

Colour, 1974, 73m. / Directed by Joseph W. Sarno / Starring Rebecca Brooke (Mary Mendum), Jennifer Welles, Chris Jordan, Eric Edwards, David Hausman / Retro-Seduction Cinema (US R0 NTSC)

Made shortly after pioneering sexploitation director Joe Sarno began dabbling in hardcore, *Confessions of a Young American Housewife* marked a new period in the director's work as he used some of the more talented adult actors in softcore for dramatic roles exploring the evolving attitudes towards everyday sexuality in America. Some of its more notable companion films include *Misty*, the once-lost *Abigail Leslie Is Back in Town*, and *The Switch or How to Alter Your Ego*, but this particular groundbreaker is still often cited as one of his best. The real centrepiece of the film is its premiere "hotcha!" pairing of two Sarno muses, fragile Rebecca Brooke (aka Mary Mendum from Radley Metzger's *The Image*) and sultry, older Jennifer Welles, cast here as a mother and daughter tangling with the swinging lifestyle in upstate New York. You see, Carole (Brooke) and neighbour Anna (Chris Jordan) are conspiring to hook up Carole's husband, Eddie (David Hausman), with another nubile chickie upstairs, much to his surprise. Turns out they're all a bunch of swingers who enjoy getting together on the weekends for orgies in the den. Enter Carole's widowed and still attractive mother, Jennifer (Welles), who is initially confused by this newfound sexual liberation but soon dives in headfirst by dallying with a local delivery boy, joining the girls for a Sapphic therapy session, and even beginning an affair with Eddie who wants to run off with her. How will all these fleshy shenanigans end?

Though the plot is pure soap opera, *Confessions* is actually quite a bit funnier than one might expect. Audio gags abound, and for once Brooke gets to show off her mischievous side right from the beginning as she leads her cohorts down the road to bohemia. The sex scenes aren't terribly explicit (though in regular Sarno style some might well have been unsimulated on the set), and Jordan (*A Touch of Genie*) and her husband,'70s porn vet Eric Edwards, have a lot of fun as the doppelganger neighbour couple in the film. As usual Sarno manages to work wonders with a tiny cast and limited settings, including his trademark autumnal forest wanderings and shots of women analysing themselves alone in their bedrooms. Extra points for the unorthodox music by Jack Justis, who also scored *Misty* and *Abigail* (and whose striking music is thankfully included as a bonus CD disc with this release).

Like most of Sarno's '70s output, *Confessions* had a strange independent release history in a variety of versions, all softcore but some with "hotter" lingering sex scenes than others. Taken from the best surviving print, the DVD looks much better than the old, scarce VHS edition with relatively solid colour and detail, though it still shows signs of wear and tear in many scenes. It also represents a slightly shorter variant than the old tape, so the noteworthy extra footage is included as "deleted scenes". (Honestly, aside from some surprisingly enthusiastic close-ups during the lesbian shaman sequence, none of it is all that graphic or much of a loss.) The "new digital telecine" is presented full frame, apparently open matte as zooming it in to 1.78:1 on a widescreen monitor works just fine as well for most of the shots. Extras include another solid interview with Sarno in which he talks about returning to American filmmaking in the mid-'70s and the close rapport between him, his wife and Brooke, a gallery of rare erotic photographs of Brooke (who is also depicted in a series of very, uh, unabashed photos in the liner notes booklet by Sarno expert Michael J. Bowen), and the usual roster of the label's Sarno trailers.

CONVENT OF SINNERS

Colour, 1986, 88m. / Directed by Joe D'Amato / Starring Eva Grimaldi, Karin Well, Gabriele Gori, Jessica Moore, Gabriele Tinti / Exploitation Digital (US R1 NTSC) / WS (1.85:1) (16:9), X-Rated Kult (Germany R2 PAL) / WS (1.85:1)

 One of the pivotal names in '80s sleaze, Joe D'Amato, was responsible for this esoteric nunsploitation offering which doesn't even try to be as trashy as his earlier *Images in a Convent*. It still delivers the sinful goods with a tawdry tale about young Susanna (*Ratman*'s Eva Grimaldi), who's forcibly shipped off to a habit-house by her mother because her stepfather can't stop molesting her at night. (Great solution, eh?) Since the convent's populated by D'Amato softcore regulars like Jessica Moore and Karin Well, it's not long before there's a steamy lesbian love triangle erupting with everyone jockeying for power both in and out of the bedroom. Susanna wants out, but the nasty Moore and the corrupt cardinal (a quick stint by none other than Gabriele Tinti) soon have her accused of demonic possession.

Nicely shot (by D'Amato, doubling as his cinematographer as usual) and more than competent on a softcore level, this film won't win any awards but should please Eurocult fans who think the erotic well has run dry. Grimaldi manages to carry her role well enough, though as usual Moore is the real showstopper (check out *11 Days, 11 Nights* for her finest showcase). The worthy anamorphic transfer does what it can with the soft-filtered photography, and D'Amato fans will rejoice at the fun featurette, "Sex, Death and Video Tape", a look at the maestro's career during its final period as a glossy purveyor of straight-to-video Italian hardcore. Also included is a king-sized trailer reel of other D'Amato titles, all worth picking up. The X-Rated Kult DVD release (under the title *Kloster der 1000 Todsünden*) features a non-anamorphic letterboxed transfer that's slightly more battered in appearance and features forced English subtitles for the English dialogue.

COP KILLERS

Colour, 1973, 93m. / Directed by Walter R. Cichy / Starring Jason Williams, Bill Osco, James Nite, Diane Keller / Shriek Show (US R1 NTSC) / WS (1.85:1) (16:9)

After his most famous role in *Flesh Gordon*, blond-haired drive-in actor Jason Williams continued to team up with that film's producer, Bill Osco, for a series of drive-in films, occasionally even co-writing or producing them as well. Check out the misleadingly-titled *Cheerleaders' Wild Weekend* for a prime example, or you could take a look at this one, which pairs up Williams and Osco as scruffy-looking criminals riding through the desert in a junky van who run afoul of and shoot holes in a few cops, swipe an ice cream truck, pick up a female hostage, and bicker and whine at each other before running smack into destiny for a violent finale.

Shot dirt cheap in the wilds of Arizona, the film ladles on enough violence and social misbehaviour for the grindhouse crowd, though despite the folks behind and in front of the camera, sexual activity is extremely minimal. Williams clearly seems to savour his villainous role and once again is better than the material, while Osco handles his more ambiguous role well enough. The transfer looks fine given the threadbare nature of the production (light levels never quite seem to be where they should), and Williams pops up for a great

interview featurette in which he discusses his overall exploitation career and the film's "make it up as you go along" shooting. Then Williams contributes an equally valuable commentary track (moderated by Adam Trash) going into more detail about this film as well as the shooting and legal woes of his most famous leading role. He's definitely an interesting figure in '70s exploitation, and finally getting his thoughts down for posterity makes this a must-buy for any self-respecting trash movie fan. For maximum enjoyment, pair it up with Howard Ziehm's indispensable *Flesh Gordon* commentary for a great two-sided view of the Osco era.

THE CRAZIES

Colour, 1973, 103m. / Directed by George A. Romero / Starring Lane Carroll, Will MacMillan, Harold Wayne Jones, Lloyd Hollar, Lynn Lowry, Richard Liberty / Blue Underground (DVD & Blu-ray, US R0 NTSC/HD), Anolis (Germany R2 PAL) / WS (1.66:1) (16:9), Anchor Bay (UK R2 PAL) / WS (1.66:1) (16:9) / DD5.1/DTS

After reinventing the zombie film with *Night of the Living Dead*, George A. Romero made his first belated colour horror film with *The Crazies*, another social commentary cloaked in exploitation trappings about a small Pennsylvania town decimated by the accidental release of a dangerous biochemical weapon (*Code Name: Trixie*, the original title) in the water supply thanks to a crashed truck. The mayhem begins one night when a family gets a fiery surprise in the middle of the night from a decidedly unstable head of the household, and soon the military – clad in menacing white suits – descends on the population to establish quarantine and deal with a citizenry quickly descending into violent insanity. A local nurse (Lane Carroll), her fireman boyfriend (Will McMillan), and three more locals must quickly navigate the nearby woods to escape town, but the encroaching madness and merciless soldiers both threaten to stop them at every turn.

Though not an official part of Romero's ongoing *Dead* series, *The Crazies* still fits in just fine thanks to its depictions of normalcy shredding apart from the inside and a ruthless but incompetent military ultimately driven by self-interest, themes which would reach their most crystallized version in his now-classic *Day of the Dead*. The invocations of Vietnam (particularly a grisly self-immolation scene) might stamp this as a '70s political statement, but on a larger scale it's clear this film is, along with Cronenberg's *Rabid*, an even more direct influence on today's faux-zombie films like the *Dawn of the Dead* remake, *[REC]*, *28 Days Later* and *28 Weeks Later* which depict a rampaging contagion rather than anything actually undead. The extremely low budget hampers the film on occasion, and the acting isn't among Romero's best apart from the always fascinating Lynn Lowry (*I Drink Your Blood*, Radley Metzger's *Score*) and the colourful Richard Liberty, who went on to horror immortality training Bub in *Day of the Dead*. Romero's usual affinity for library music is also present here, using folk protest music effectively at times with generic creepy wallpaper melodies filling in the rest.

Blue Underground's edition of *The Crazies* appeared first on DVD and then as a Blu-ray timed with the release of the solid 2010 remake. Their transfer is as good as one could possibly expect for this film, which is colourful and often sharp-looking but always maintains a gritty, harsh veneer appropriate to the budget, shooting conditions, and time period. The experience here is akin to watching a freshly-minted print of a vintage title, which is definitely preferable in this case to any digital waxing and buffing

to make it look more modern. It's certainly better than the dismal repertory prints in circulation or awful VHS editions that Romero fans had to endure for years. Only the DVD contains a poster and stills gallery, but extras on both editions include a lively, informative Romero commentary track that covers all the bases (location shooting, music tracking, casting, and financial challenges), two trailers and two TV spots, and a magnificent featurette with Lowry contributing a new video interview about her career, interspersed with clips from her films and footage of her contemporary cabaret act in Los Angeles. Some of her recollections about *Score* seem questionable, but she's a great listen in a must-see for fans of '70s drive-in queens. While the Blu-ray may offer the most impressive A/V presentation all around, Romero fans dedicated to standard def may find interest in the U.K. Anchor Bay edition (which carries over the same extras and adds another of their gimmicky DTS mixes, though at least it isn't quite as disastrous as their *Last House on the Left* abortion), and especially a German disc from Anolis which adds on an exclusive Lynn Lowry commentary, intro, and different featurette called "The Mute Hippie Girl on Acid with Rabies!"

CREATURE FROM THE HILLBILLY LAGOON

Colour, 2005, 90m. / Directed by Richard Griffin / Starring Andrew Vellenoweth, Tanith Fiedler, William DeCoff / Shock-O-Rama (US R0 NTSC) / WS (1.78:1) (16:9) / DD2.0

Imagine a Harry Novak '70s sex comedy mashed up with a '50s monster film, and the result you'd get is this super-low-budget mixture of cornball humour and rampaging mutant fish monsters. (For some reason the original shooting title was *Seepage!*) The film was directed by Richard Griffin, a guy who's obviously filled with ambition when you consider this along with other films like an updated version of *Titus Andronicus*(!) and a version of *The Dunwich Horror*. Here he hurls every redneck stereotype at the audience, from *Deliverance*-inspired sodomy gags to Bubba jokes that even Larry the Cable Guy wouldn't touch. The story is the usual nonsense about a bunch of inquisitive big-city college students coming to the boonies to investigate reports of contaminated water, with lots of people getting grabbed while floating in their beloved lagoon. Yes, it's all utterly stupid and socially pointless, but this is a great drinking movie; also, the lensing and acting are a cut above most direct-to-video programmers. Plus, it still treats the monster genre with some affectionate respect and comes off better than smug fare like *The Lost Skeleton of Cadavra*. The film also makes amusing use of comic book-style graphics and transitions at key junctures as well (but a hint for the filmmakers: don't ever, ever show lime green text on a grey background; it doesn't read at all). Extras include a lively Griffin commentary track, a clutch of non-anamorphic deleted scenes (basically excised footage of our host Bubba talking to the camera), and additional Shock-O-Rama trailers for titles like the interesting-looking *Dark Chamber*. The box advertises a behind-the-scenes extra, but it's nowhere to be found. Maybe all the animated fish in the menu screens ate it.

CRIME BUSTERS

Colour, 1977, 115m. / Directed by Enzo Barboni / Starring Terence Hill, Bud Spencer, David Huddleston, Luciano Catenacci, Laura Gemser / Millennium Storm (Italy R2 PAL), e-m-s (Germany R2 PAL), Somerville House (Canada R0 NTSC), Dutch FilmWorks (Holland R2 PAL) / WS (1.85:1) (16:9)

At a dockyard in Miami, the unemployed Matt Kirby (Terence Hill) and Wilbur Walsh (Bud Spencer, wearing a "Jumbo" denim jacket) run afoul of some corrupt labour bosses and each get even by destroying a trio of automobiles. They decide to join forces and pull off a robbery at a nearby grocery store, but instead they end up in a police recruitment office where an overeager officer signs them onto the force. The boys try to wriggle out of their enlistment but wind up going through academy training and onto a beat together where their efforts at incompetence keep resulting in the accidental apprehension of criminals. When the slaying of some Chinese workers ties in with the shady dock bosses from the beginning of the film, they realise their true calling and decide to kick lots of comical ass.

Known in Italian as *I due superpiedi quasi piatti*, this action-comedy stands as one of the strongest non-western outings for frequent acting pair Terence Hill and Bud Spencer, who shot to international fame with the slapstick western *They Call Me Trinity*. Running nearly two hours in length, the film gives plenty of opportunities for both to shine with Spencer in particular delivering some of the funniest glowering and fight scenes of his career; likewise, the easygoing, Venetian-accented Hill makes for an appealing hero and even gets to spend some time on a motorcycle with Laura Gemser, taking a break from softcore films and looking more beautiful than ever. The exterior location shooting in Florida looks more fascinating now than the filmmakers probably intended, capturing a snapshot of Southern '70s culture you won't find in any other feature film; the addition of nonstop fisticuffs and slapstick mayhem just sweetens the deal even more.

The first DVD of this film arrived from Canada in a decent but unspectacular anamorphic transfer, while Germany and Holland soon chipped in with their own compressed-looking but passable versions. The last but best of the bunch is the Millennium Storm release from Italy (who also released English-friendly versions of other key films including the only worthwhile version of *Super Snooper*); this disc features an excellent transfer from the original Italian negative that looks fresh out of the can. The Italian audio is playable either in a 5.1 remix (the repetitive but catchy Guido & Maurizio De Angelis score sounds great) or original mono as well as the original mono English track. The extras are Italian only, consisting of the theatrical trailer, a featurette about the Hill and Spencer cop films, and video interviews with Spencer, the De Angelis brothers, actor/dubbing artist Glauco Onorato and writer Marco Barboni.

CROOKED HOUSE

Colour, 2008, 89m. / Directed by Damon Thomas / Starring Lee Ingleby, Mark Gatiss, Julian Rhind-Tutt, Philip Jackson, Jennifer Higham, Jean Marsh, Samuel Barnett, Ian Hallard, Derren Brown / BBC (UK R2 PAL) / WS (1.78:1) (16:9) / DD5.1

The cursed and now demolished Geap Manor holds many dark secrets, and a few of them have been uncovered by a museum curator (Mark Gatiss) approached by Ben (Lee Ingleby), a history teacher who believes he's discovered a door knocker from the ruins in his own backyard. The curator regales him with two stories of the house's past, whose misfortune stems from its original owner, wealthy black magic practitioner Sir Roger

Widdowson (Derren Brown), who sought unsuccessfully to sire an heir with the aid of a notorious necromancer named Unthank. In the first tale, callous 18th Century financier Joseph Bloxham (Philip Jackson) bilks innocent investors out of their money regardless of the consequences for their families. Instead he's concentrating on renovating the recently purchased Geap Manor – in particular the new woodwork used to create the wainscot decorations, taken from the finest supplies available. Unfortunately the walls are filled with the sound of mysterious scratching at night, and a mysterious stain begins to appear on one of the new walls... In story two, Felix (Ian Hallard), the privileged son of the manor's current owners in the 1920s decides to announce his engagement during a lively evening party to the comparatively lowly Ruth (Jennifer Higham). This turn of events unsettles more than one of the attendees including his own grandmother, Lady Constance (Jean Marsh), who knows all too well the dangers of announcing a wedding on the premises. Meanwhile a mysterious, veiled Victorian bride hovers about the proceedings, ready to strike before the night is over. The third portion picks up with Ben's modern-day story as he leaves the curator and installs the knocker on his own door, with ghastly supernatural consequences as each night he's plagued by mysterious rapping outside and the sudden transformation of his own home into something quite different... and utterly evil.

Conceived as a revival of the BBC's intermittent "Ghost Story for Christmas" tradition which first rose to popularity in the 1970s, this magnificent chiller is the handiwork of writer/co-producer Mark Gatiss, best known as one-third of the League of Gentlemen as well as a cast member of *Nighty Night* and occasional writer for *Doctor Who*. The approach here is like a more straight-up scary variation on the League's much-lauded Christmas special, an anthology movie inspired by the classic Amicus horror films. This time the Amicus influence carries over along with a heavy dash of M.R. James and Charles Dickens, among others, with splendidly spooky results. The period settings are extremely well-executed, and the scares multiply expertly from brief, palpable shudders in the first story to delicious extended chills in the second, only to blossom into pure terror for the grand finale, complete with a diabolical twist ending. Originally aired in December 2008 as a three-part series, *Crooked House* was repurposed for re-airing and home video into an "Omnibus Edition" which combines everything into one feature. (The original connective bits of exposition from the curator are still included as an extra on the DVD, but are not really missed.) In any form, it's well worth discovering.

Along with an extremely impressive transfer and manipulative audio mix, the Region 2 DVD contains a wealth of informative extras including a 45-minute featurette containing interviews with all of the major participants behind and in front of the camera. The actors are mainly still in their costumes while chatting, which makes the anecdotes even stranger and funnier. Gatiss and director Damon Thomas contribute a commentary track in which actors from each of the stories drift in and out; you'll learn everything imaginable about the stories' conception, the methods used to achieve three entirely separate time periods on a minuscule TV budget, and the little details that might otherwise get lost along the way. Also included are some additional featurettes (the cast answering the question "What Scares You?", a nine-minute outtake reel, and a hidden behind-the-scenes reel), a photo gallery, and the original TV promo trailer. An absolutely essential purchase for ghost story fans or anyone just looking for a good, old-fashioned scare.

THE CURIOUS CASE OF THE CAMPUS CORPSE

Colour, 1977, 90m. / Directed by Douglas Curtis / Starring Jeff East, Kelly Moran, Charles Martin Smith, Sandra Vacey, David Hayward, Brad David, Jim Boelsen / Shriek Show (US R1 NTSC) / WS (1.85:1) (16:9)

A movie marketing team's worst nightmare, the oddball late-'70s film *The Curious Case of the Campus Corpse* popped up over and over for about five years under a number of different titles (most famously *The Hazing*), trying to lure viewers in with either the promise of a college slasher film or a fraternity slob comedy. Actually it's neither, basically a ghoulish, mild-mannered look at malicious campus antics with the feel of an *Alfred Hitchcock Presents* episode spun out to feature length – which isn't necessarily a bad thing. When young Craig Lewis (Jeff East) gets an athletic scholarship to a very sunny Midwestern university, he decides to pledge with the Delts, the biggest fraternity on campus. Along with milquetoast Barney (a pre-Hollywood Charles Martin Smith), he's sent out on an afternoon hazing ritual involving the two of them left in the woods in their jockstraps. Unfortunately when Craig goes to get help, he returns to find Barney dead – and the frat brothers aren't too happy about it. Together they hatch an elaborate scheme to avoid trouble by postponing Barney's death for a week and staging an accident that will absolve them from blame, but a few more twists still lie in store for our hero.

The basic plot of *Campus Corpse* had already been run through pretty thoroughly by '77; in fact, the basic set-up is swiped almost wholesale from Patricia Highsmith's classic mystery novel, *Ripley Under Ground*. The film does manage to coast along on the charm of its performances and the sincerity of its execution, which puts it miles ahead of more recent, dispiriting attempts at the same mixture like *The Curve* and the abysmal *Cry_Wolf*. Not surprisingly, Smith gets most of the acting honours here with his limited screen time, and it's fun seeing Brad David from *The Candy Snatchers* popping up as the thuggish frat king. The easygoing '70s vibe is an asset as well, though the soft-vocal music score might send some unprepared viewers lurching for their fast-forward buttons.

Campus Corpse has been MIA on video for a long time since its early days on VHS from Vestron (simply called *The Campus Corpse* with a misleading skull-faced cover), and Shriek Show's release looks considerably better. The feature kicks off with a disclaimer about the print quality, but it's perfectly fine with accurate widescreen framing and just enough natural film grain to avoid any charges of overzealous digital scrubbing. You'll spot some scuffs here and there if you look carefully, but it's nothing a seasoned trash DVD collector won't cherish. Despite the modest nature of the film, this release definitely goes the extra mile in the extras department. This originated as a Code Red release, so you'll find regular commentator Lee Christian helming the fine, informative commentary track with director Douglas Curtis, as well as actors East, David Hayward and Jim Boelsen. Not surprisingly it's very chipper in tone (just like the movie) and a good primer on how to mount a low budget production when you're not even sure what genre the finished product will fall into. The foursome pop up again for "Dissecting the Campus Corpse: A Look Back at *The Hazing*", which covers some of the same information but also injects a bit more anecdotal material about the rest of their careers, while "Campus Corpse: Alive & Well at the Beverly Cinema" spotlights the crew doing a Q&A after a screening at the venerable L.A. revival theatre. Other

extras include the alternative *The Hazing* credit sequence (why it wasn't released on DVD under that more saleable title is anyone's guess), the theatrical trailer, a stills gallery, and promos for other Shriek Show releases. Well worth picking up for the bounty of extras alone, this is another example of a marginally-known title getting a deluxe treatment that puts most studio catalogue releases to shame.

DADDY, DARLING

Colour, 1970, 93m. / Directed by Joseph W. Sarno / Starring Helli Louise, Gio Petré, Ole Wisborg, Lise Henningsen, Søren Strømberg / Retro-Seduction Cinema (US R0 NTSC) / WS (1.85:1) (16:9)

Pouty young Danish teen Katja (Helli Louise) has a really big problem. Her widowed dad Eric (Ole Wisborg) spends too much time away on business, and whenever he gets home, she gets just a little bit too excited to see him. Katja isn't crazy about the idea of having a babysitter, especially if it's his older gal pal in a bad wig, Svea (Gio Petré), whom he's secretly doing on the side. When daddy announces he's getting married, Katja's shaken out of her daily routine of wandering the streets in deep thought and retreats to her art lessons under the guidance of Lena (Lise Henningsen), to forget her troubles. Going to these classes and doing nude studies under the supervision of the strangely mannish female art teacher helps a little bit, but when Katja catches Lena in the sack with one of her models demonstrating the joys of Sapphic love, our heroine just gets more confused. Katja then decides to pick up a boy toy, Lars, and pass him off to everyone in public as her oddly young father. Though Katja and Lars are happy for a while sitting around eating Corn Flakes and listening to LPs all day, her psychological issues eventually force her to find an even more perverse solution to her incestuous problems.

One of the most notorious films in director Joe Sarno's filmography, *Daddy, Darling* is one of the key films from his Scandinavian softcore period and was his first film to get slapped with an X rating (though it's easily within R territory now). The come-on ad campaign highlighting the incest angle really doesn't sell the film well as the subject is actually handled in an unusual and surprising manner with Katja and daddy only hooking up in one oddly compelling fantasy sequence. The direction and acting are all up to Sarno's usual standards, with the fascinating Louise (a cute Ewa Aulin look-alike who reputedly worked in Danish and U.K. stag shorts on the side while building a mainstream career) easily holding the viewer's attention even when she's behaving very, very badly. *Wild Strawberries*'s Petré manages to overcome her ludicrous hairdo and deliver the most accomplished and nuanced performance in the film, and her key role in the finale is very nicely handled. Sarno fans will immediately recognise his trademarks like long pensive shoreline walks and darkly-lit love scenes, but the real standout here is the spectacularly good Tony Hazzard pop score which ranges from percussive bongo beats to smooth beach-friendly grooves.

Though it received better distribution than many Sarno films in the early '70s before hardcore killed off the market, *Daddy, Darling* fell into neglect for years afterwards and was rarely seen. VHS editions from Something Weird, Electric Video and Alpha Blue popped up in the '80s, all severely cropped on all four sides with almost no colour and littered with print debris, but it was better than nothing. The DVD is obviously a huge step up from past versions for a number of reasons, though as the packaging and the disc itself take great pains to point out, pristine elements of this film no longer exist. The transfer here certainly has its share of hairline scratches, but the colour fidelity is far more accurate and satisfying than ever before and the correct framing restores a considerable amount of punch to the film's emotionally resonant compositions. No, it isn't pristine, but fans should be happy at least to finally see a viewable version. The mono audio actually sounds very good, with the all-important music score carrying a surprising amount of oomph throughout. Extras include a very thorough liner notes booklet by Sarno scholar Michael J. Bowen (who covers the ten-day shoot and the sketchy distribution history), a new video interview with Sarno, Peggy Steffans and producer Kenn Collins (covering the Danish shooting and the logistics of the love scenes), and the usual array of Seduction-related Sarno promos and restoration demonstrations.

DARK FORCES

Colour, 1980, 95m. / Directed by Simon Wincer / Starring Robert Powell, David Hemmings, Carmen Duncan, Broderick Crawford / Synapse (US R0 NTSC), Elite (US R1 NTSC), Umbrella (Australia R4 PAL), BritFilms (UK R0 PAL) / WS (2.35:1) (16:9)

A huge improvement over director Simon Wincer's previous *Snapshot*, this strange but effective oddity examines the supernatural consequences when a creepy magician named Gregory Wolfe (played by Ken Russell regular Robert Powell) works his way into the life of big-time politician David Hemmings and forms a bond with the bigwig's ailing son, whom he mysteriously heals.

Basically an FX-laden modern retelling of the story of unkillable political hypnotist Rasputin, it's a surprisingly effective film if you're willing to go along with its peculiar rhythms and the fact that it's a pretty mild PG-rated horror film. Kitsch fans will also have a field day with Powell's outfits, which seem to grow more ridiculous with every scene and wouldn't be out of place at a Vegas show, as well as the *Highlander*-style finale which finds our protagonist shooting lightning all over the screen. Brian May's excellent score is well-served by the DVD, which offers an isolated music track along with a handsomely-rendered scope transfer and an audio commentary with Wincer and producer Antony I. Ginnane. The transfer and contents of both are the same, though the Elite version is now discontinued. Under its original title *Harlequin*, the Australian release adds a batch of Ozploitation trailers but ditches the isolated score track, whilst the U.K. disc is bare bones apart from some unrelated trailers.

A DAY AT THE BEACH

Colour, 1970, 83m. / Directed by Simon Hesera / Starring Mark Burns, Beatrice Edney, Jack MacGowran, Peter Sellers, Graham Stark, Fiona Lewis / Code Red (US R0 NTSC) / WS (1.75:1) (16:9), Odeon (UK R0 PAL)

 A film still completely unknown outside of die-hard film historians and avid fans of obscure '70s cinema, *A Day at the Beach* is usually referred to as a "lost" Roman Polanski film, in the sense that it was both physically lost for over two decades (due to mishandling by its distributor, Paramount) as well as the opportunity missed when Polanski wrote the script but had to bow out of directorial chores when his wife, Sharon Tate, was murdered by the Manson family. Had timing or circumstances been different and Polanski had brought his words to the screen, it would have certainly fit in with the increasingly dark, despairing tone of his early '70s work like *Macbeth* and *Chinatown*. The story is another riff on the journey of an Anglo-Saxon alcoholic lout, a convention that's out of fashion now but which fascinated Hollywood all the way from *Days of Wine and Roses* to *Arthur* to *Leaving Las Vegas*. Here our protagonist lush is Bernie (Mark Burns), a boozer who takes his young, polio-stricken niece, Winnie (Beatrice Edney), out for a drizzly day at the English beachside where they encounter a colourful array of characters. Winnie is all too aware of her uncle's weakness and tries to keep him grounded for the excursion, but as night falls and the bars begin to call, she isn't sure he'll make it till morning.

Featuring delicate, evocative photography by the great Gilbert Taylor (*The Omen*) and some surprising bit parts (most memorably Peter Sellers, billed as "A. Queen", and Graham Stark as a pair of flamboyant beach vendors), *A Day at the Beach* is a fascinating mood piece if ultimately a minor entry in the Polanski filmography. Director Simon Hesera didn't really do much outside of this, so it's especially easy to read into the writer's contribution here along with the presence of two cast members from Polanski's *The Fearless Vampire Killers*, Jack MacGowran (*The Exorcist*) and the gorgeous Fiona Lewis (*The Fury*). Similarities to Polanski's *Cul-de-Sac*, *Knife in the Water* and especially his short films like "Two Men and a Wardrobe" and "The Fat and the Lean" abound with the seaside doubling as a psychological force which drives the characters and threatens to consume some of them, with its changing rhythms during the day affecting the bustling crowd as well as the flow of the story. Considering almost no one saw this film before a print was resuscitated in the 1990s, it's rather miraculous we have *A Day at the Beach* on DVD at all. Code Red's disc is on par with many other Paramount catalogue titles of the period; the film stock has that somewhat gritty look of the time with chilly flesh tones (think *Don't Look Now* or *Let's Scare Jessica to Death*), and the widescreen framing is about right if a tad snug on the bottom during the opening titles. You don't get any extras here apart from the usual Code Red promos (for films like *The Farmer* and *Choke Canyon*), but that's understandable given the fact that the director's unreachable, the main actor's dead, and everyone knows why Polanski can't exactly be flown in for a commentary. The earlier release in the U.K. from Odeon features a full frame open matte transfer along with a "Drama Notes Booklet" and the company's usual Best of British Trailers reel.

A DAY OF VIOLENCE

Colour, 2009, 90m. / Directed by Darren Ward / Starring Nick Rendell, Tina Barnes, Victor D. Thorn, Helena Martin, Harold Gasnier, Giovanni Lombardo Radice / 101 Films (UK R0 PAL) / WS (1.78:1) (16:9) / DD2.0

Eleven years after his hyper action-gore epic *Sudden Fury*, director Darren Ward returns to familiar turf with his follow-up feature film, *A Day of Violence*. While that previous effort owed a pleasant debt to the Italian cop and crime films of the 1980s, this one spins off into decidedly new territory comparable only to what might happen if someone remade *Sexy Beast* on crystal meth with a few dozen gallons of blood. The two leads from his short film "Nightmare", Nick Rendell and Tina Barnes, return here for the story of a tough guy thug named Mitchell Parker who winds up naked and dying on a slab thanks to a violent ambush after making love to his wife, Abbi. How did he wind up here, and how can he survive through the final reel? Maybe his biggest mistake was pocketing a huge chunk of cash during a shady collection assignment, during which he's caught unaware on video while slicing a junkie's throat and making off with a sack of money. Mitchell decides to switch bosses, which doesn't go over too well and sets off a string of gory confrontations involving guns, knives, castration, and a well-employed chisel.

Boasting virtually no sympathetic characters and barely pausing to catch its breath after the opening credits, *A Day of Violence* (which seems like way too much for a 24-hour period, but who's counting?) is a rough, nasty, thoroughly entertaining piece of work and exactly the kind of thing studios would never want to touch now. Rendell manages to anchor the film quite well in the lead role, using his bulky and intimidating frame to good effect while pulling out some welcome moments of vulnerability and flat-out terror. Of course, it's also worth noting the small but pivotal role of Italian trash stalwart Giovanni Lombardo Radice, better known as the oft-abused John Morghen who underwent the most famous genital hacking of all time in *Cannibal Ferox* as well as *City of the Living Dead*'s show-stopping drill scene. Naturally he doesn't get out of this one intact either. While Ward's previous film had no qualms about showering the screen in torrents of plasma, the increased focus here on character development coupled with more sexuality gives it a different, more multi-dimensional flavour. It will definitely be interesting to see where he goes next after this one.

Overall this film (obtained direct from the makers) is quite nicely shot for a low-budget indie U.K. film and looks several steps up from the rough and ragged appearance of *Sudden Fury* (though that could have also been due to the dodgy compression on that film's DVD release). At the time of this writing it has been passed uncut by the BBFC for release by new label 101 Films, so keep your eyes out for this rough and tumble gem of brutality and nonstop cinematic chutzpah.

DEAD OF NIGHT

Colour, 1977, 74m. / Directed by Dan Curtis / Starring Joan Hackett, Patrick Macnee, Anjanette Comer, Lee Montgomery, Ed Begley Jr., Horst Buchholz, Elisha Cook Jr. / Dark Sky (US R1 NTSC)

Though big screen horror anthologies began to wane after the glory days of Amicus (whose *From Beyond the Grave* marked a sort of swan song), the tradition remained alive a bit longer on television. The most famous example by far came in 1975 with *Trilogy of Terror*, an omnibus directed by *Dark Shadows* creator Dan Curtis and written by the legendary Richard Matheson. The first two stories were disposable filler while the last, "Prey" (which featured Karen Black facing off against the scariest doll of all time), ensured instant classic status. The same formula repeats again with *Dead of Night*, as Curtis and Matheson concoct a trio of stories which ultimately pays off in the last 25 minutes, a nerve-shredding achievement that still hasn't received its due.

In "Second Chance", Frank (Ed Begley Jr.) purchases an old car damaged many years ago when it was hit by a train. After restoring the vehicle, he discovers it can go back in time – and create unexpected consequences. A lightweight piece of fantasy adapted from a story by Jack Finney, this is painless but forgettable fluff. In the quirkier "No Such Thing As a Vampire", Dr. Gheria (Patrick Macnee) doesn't believe the claims of his wife (Anjanette Comer) that she's being drained nightly by a vampire. The doctor consults a doctor friend (Horst Buchholz) who helps reveal the macabre truth. Not bad, this tale benefits from great casting and has a nifty sting in the tale. However, the real payoff comes with tale three, "Bobby," as a grieving mother (Joan Hackett) resorts to a black magic ritual to bring back her drowned son (Lee Montgomery), who promptly shows up sopping wet at the front door during a thunderstorm. At first overjoyed, she soon comes to realise to her horror that Bobby isn't quite the same boy anymore.

A pitch-perfect miniature, "Bobby" is a perfect example of how to tighten the screws through skilful performances and taut, imaginative writing. Both Hackett and Montgomery (who reunited with Curtis for *Burnt Offerings*) deliver intense, unforgettable performances, and Curtis's direction was never better as the cat-and-mouse game plays out in a huge, dark house filled with cavernous, shadowy corners and stairways. Regular Curtis composer Robert Cobert really delivers with this one, too, lashing the viewer's nerves with a haunting, propulsive score. Everyone's at the top of their game here, and the story manages to wrap up with the single most terrifying moment ever broadcast on network TV. Buy the DVD and watch the first two stories if you must, but do not miss "Bobby" under any circumstances.

Dark Sky's special edition DVD features an excellent full frame transfer that looks considerably better than any TV broadcast. As with *Trilogy of Terror*, the film also plays perfectly well zoomed in to 1.78:1 on widescreen sets as a possible European theatrical release was always kept in mind. The biggest extra here is another Curtis pilot film, *Dead of Night: Darkness at Blaisedon*, with Kerwin Matthews (*7th Voyage of Sinbad*) heading a team of paranormal investigators looking into a reputed gothic haunted house. It's very talky and reminiscent of *Dark Shadows*, only shot in colour; a separate VHS of this was available years ago from MPI, but it's really just supplement material. Also included is a bit of deleted footage from the second story, some alternative shots and narrator material unused in the final film, and a stills gallery featuring highlights from Cobert's excellent score.

THE DEAD PIT

Colour, 1989, 101m. / Directed by Brett Leonard / Starring Jeremy Slate, Steffen Gregory Foster, Cheryl Lawson, Danny Gochnauer / Code Red (US R0 NTSC) / WS (1.78:1) (16:9), Midnite Movies (UK R0 PAL)

Released at the tail end of the 1980s, this low budget zombie horror film is fondly remembered by many old-school horror fans as one of the final entries in the decade's unmistakable goopy, Day-Glo splatter horror, which happened to coincide with that other short-lived novelty, the gimmicky VHS cover box. (See *Blood Roses* and *Frankenhooker* for other prime examples.) No horror fan who came of age during the Freddy Krueger era could ever forget the *Dead Pit* cover box which featured a creepy-looking zombie in a strait-jacket climbing out of a pit with eyes that glowed on and off in glorious, bright green thanks to real tiny lights embedded in the cardboard. So, did the movie itself live up to the hype? Well, sort of, if you know what to expect.

At the State Institute for the Mentally Insane (how's that for a PC name?), Dr. Ramzi (Danny Gochnauer) is bringing the great mad scientist tradition to the world of psychiatry by subjecting hordes of his inmates to diabolical lobotomy experiments, then chucking their bodies into a huge subterranean pit for disposal. Fortunately one of his colleagues, Dr. Swan (Jeremy Slate), catches on to the plot and dispatches the doctor with a handy bullet, but of course, the terror is just beginning. Flash forward several years as a new, busty amnesiac patient simply christened Jane Doe (Cheryl Lawson) is experiencing visions of the mad doctor, his eyes now glowing red, and suffering from the delusion that her memories have been erased by force. When an earthquake hits, macabre events plague the reopened hospital, and only Jane (usually clad in her skivvies) and Swan can stop the undead doctor from continuing his sadistic mission – with several dozen blood-soaked zombies coming along for the ride.

One of many horror films to run afoul of the American ratings board during the height of the splatter craze, *The Dead Pit* lost a whopping six minutes in the process for its VHS release but is thankfully restored to its full running time on Code Red's DVD. The extra grue certainly helps, of course, as does the restored brain dissection sequence which wouldn't look out of place in a Stuart Gordon movie. The film itself holds up just fine for its era; if you enjoy such thematically and stylistically similar movies as *Bad Dreams* and Renny Harlin's *Prison*, this should certainly do the trick. Lawson doesn't exactly cut it as a first-league scream queen (surprisingly enough, she's now found a solid career as a stuntwoman), but she does eye candy duties well enough in her too-short T-shirt and undies throughout the film. This also marked the directorial debut of Brett Leonard, who went on to score a surprising box office success with *The Lawnmower Man* (which inexplicably has yet to receive a decent uncut DVD release) and mostly hit-and-miss work afterwards with *Virtuosity*, *Hideaway* and *Feed*. His films generally tend to favour visual style over narrative coherence or naturalistic acting, and *The Dead Pit* is no exception. The film tosses in enough spooky scares to keep fans interested throughout, but the final fifteen minutes when Leonard pulls out all the stops with a blood-splashed zombie attack revolving around the titular pit is where it really justifies its existence. Don't expect a masterpiece, but as far as direct-to-video horror goes, this is still one of the stronger efforts around.

Code Red's anamorphic transfer obviously betters the ancient Imperial VHS by a wide margin, even without those beloved blinking zombie eyes on the cover. The cinematography's aforementioned neon colour scheme (with heavy use of lime greens and lavenders) comes through vividly throughout, and while the anamorphic transfer is interlaced, it still looked watchable enough when bumped up to simulated HD playback on a widescreen set. The film itself still has that vaguely soft look common to the era, which is to be expected. Leonard, the now-deceased Slate, Lawson and writer Gimel Everett contribute heavily to the extras, which include two quick video intros to the film, an entertaining audio commentary (which talks about the location shooting, its purported real ghosts, and the distribution snags hit afterwards), and a slightly redundant but enjoyable set of video interviews with all the participants as they talk about their favourite moments and the special FX snafus encountered during the more ambitious sequences. Other extras include the original (spoiler-packed) trailer and additional Code Red trailers. Interestingly, most retailers carry this single-disc edition, while Best Buy

offers an exclusive two-disc set containing an additional short film and a behind-the-scenes photo gallery. An earlier, much less comprehensive release in the U.K. from Midnite Movies features a dated fullscreen transfer and no extras.

DEAD SNOW

Colour, 2008, 88m. / Directed by Tommy Wirkola / Starring Vegar Hoel, Charlotte Frogner, Stig Frode Henriksen, Jeppe Laursen, Lasse Valdal / E1 (DVD & Blu-ray, UK R2 PAL/HD), MPI (DVD & Blu-ray, US R1 NTSC/HD) / WS (1.78:1) (16:9) / DD5.1

 Heading out to the snowy wilderness for a ski lodge vacation, six students find their holiday disrupted when their host and her family have disappeared and a creepy old local man tells them about a horde of sadistic Nazis who terrorised the area in the 1940s. The same prognosticator of doom soon winds up mauled in his tent the same evening, and after uncovering a stash of 1940s German gold underneath the floorboards, the youths are besieged by a seemingly endless squad of bloodthirsty Nazis from beyond the grave.

A sheer blast from start to finish, this gore-splattered treat from Norway dispenses with the sprinting zombies of late and instead goes back to basics with steady, unstoppable legions of the undead only intent on tearing out victims' entrails. On paper the idea sounds like a basic updating of *Shock Waves*, but the film throws in plenty of curveballs and tons of splatstick comedy; it's no wonder the token film geek character sports a *Braindead* T-shirt. The gorgeous, stark locations are extremely well utilised both from a visual standpoint (it's one of the most exquisite-looking horror films in quite a while) and a narrative one, with snow, avalanches, tree branches, and other natural factors figuring in the ever-increasing bloodshed. For the most part the comedy is well-judged and fits perfectly with the larger horror aspects, particularly a standout scene involving an actor dangling from a snowy cliff by a zombie's lower intestine and a wonderful climactic gag involving how to treat yourself after a zombie bite.

E1 Entertainment's release marked the first English-friendly edition of this film (followed by a U.S. disc from MPI), and the transfer is very satisfying. The DVD looks about as good as the format will allow, but the Blu-ray really takes full advantage with eye-poppingly crisp visuals that surpass the look of the theatrical prints. Some reviewers complained about digital noise, but to these eyes it looked terrific apart from a couple of dubious dark scenes, which were problematic even in theatres. Extras include three Norwegian trailers, the U.K. promo, an extensive making-of documentary called "Ein! Zwei! Die!" (running just a few minutes shorter than the feature itself) covering what appears to be the entire shoot (with some hilarious footage of the Nazis romping around on set), featurettes on the special effects and make-up, and a 17-minute look at the film's journey to Sundance as an official selection, believe it or not. All of the extras are as rousing and entertaining as the film itself, making the entire package an easy recommendation. The same material is included in repurposed fashion on the MPI DVD and Blu-ray, which split everything a bit differently under titles like "Madness in the North", "Madness in the West", and "Behind *Dead Snow*". The only other major difference is the fact that the MPI disc adds on a disposable English dub for good measure (in 2.0 only, unlike the 5.1 Norwegian).

DEADLY SWEET

Colour, 1967, 100m. / Directed by Tinto Brass / Starring Jean-Louis Trintignant, Ewa Aulin, Roberto Bisacco, Charles Kohler, Luigi Bellini, Vira Silenti / Cult Epics (US R1 NTSC) / WS (1.78:1) (16:9)

Long before he became one of Europe's most accomplished exporters of playful erotica, Tinto Brass got his start in the 1960s with a string of oddball, genre-tweaking cinematic statements heavily influenced by pop art and the international avant garde. After tackling the spaghetti western (*Yankee*) and even a sci-fi comedy (*The Flying Saucer*), Brass veered into the increasingly popular thriller genre with the unjustly neglected *Col cuore in gola* ("Heart in His Mouth"), released on DVD under its obscure English release title, *Deadly Sweet*. The film marked the first real starring vehicle for Ewa Aulin, a former Miss Teen Sweden who became the centre of a brief publicity whirlwind in 1968 as the lead in the much-discussed *Candy* before turning out a few more oddball European cult films, including the unjustly-ignored *The Double*. Her co-star here is Jean-Louis Trintignant, one of France's most reliable leading men who had just become a hot property as the star of *A Man and a Woman*. He and Aulin reteamed immediately afterward for 1968's *Death Laid an Egg*, an even stranger variation on *giallo* conventions that earned a considerably larger cult following than Brass's quirky effort, which eventually made its long-delayed English-friendly video debut courtesy of the magic of DVD.

After identifying the body of her father at the morgue, pretty Jane (Aulin) and her brother, Jerome (Charles Kohler), and stepmother (Vira Silenti), decide to cope with their loss like any normal family, by blowing off steam at a nightclub. There she catches the eye of Bernard (Trintignant), a romantic soul who doesn't get a chance to talk to her – at least at first. The next time he sees her is shortly afterwards, standing over the dead body of the club owner insisting she didn't do it. Impulsively he agrees to help her flee the building, and together they embark on a wild journey across London crossing paths with the dead man's associates, including a hot-tempered dwarf and a memorable gangster named Jellyroll. Along the way they also indulge in a bizarre homage to *Blow-Up*'s paper orgy and try to find the real killer, with Jane suspecting her brother might be behind it all thanks to an intricate back story involving blackmail and some elusive incriminating photos. Of course, a final surprise is still waiting...

Ostensibly based on a novel by regular Sergio Leone scribe Sergio Donati, *Deadly Sweet* barely tries to hang together as a narrative (at least superficially), instead deriving most of its energy from the free-flowing avalanche of pop culture nods and images patched together with a comic book sensibility extending to colourful panel inserts cut into the frames during moments of violence or heavy action. In a highly unusual move for the time, comic artist Guido Crepax (*Baba Yaga*) was recruited to actually storyboard the film to give it a strong graphic quality, thus making it a legitimate companion piece to such Italian *fumetti* films as *Danger: Diabolik* and the *Kriminal* and *Phenomenal* films. Granted, there aren't any building-scaling super-thieves in this one, but the stylistic relationship is unmistakable. None of the actors are really required to do much beyond serving as eye candy for the most part, but Trintignant does find quite a bit of pathos in his character from time to time, especially the haunting final scene. Another strong component is the wonderful lounge score by Armando Trovajoli, most of which revolves

around a catchy little ditty called "Love Girl". The Antonioni references seem to serve more than one purpose here, as along with the London setting and obvious homages, this film can also be approached from several different angles and enjoyed on multiple levels depending on one's mood and attitude.

As with many Italian productions, *Deadly Sweet* utilised an international cast with most of the principals speaking English on set and the final soundtracks in English, Italian, etc. created during post-production. Numerous variants were then created, and each country wound up getting something slightly different – with two distinct English tracks created, one by the European distributors and another by Paramount for an insignificant American release. A few scarce VHS editions popped up throughout Europe, followed by a pair of DVD releases in Spain and Italy, but none of them were English accessible. The Cult Epics release contains the complete Italian version with optional English subtitles, and while it quite obviously looks like a PAL conversion (with the 16:9 framing slightly cropping in the original 1.66:1 compositions, which muffs a few compositions), this version is by all reports the best as it features more accurate colour grading and corrects some digital chicanery performed on the Italian one. In any case, it's a film well worth discovering for any adventurous fan of international cinema willing to dig a little deeper than the usual thriller offering, and Brass fans should be delighted to see an early example of the audacious experimentation which would soon come into full bloom with *L'urlo* and *Nerosubianco*. The disc's extras include a theatrical trailer (which looks like it was created for this release) and a full audio commentary by Brass, who apparently hasn't seen the film in a while and spends most of the time discussing the locations, shooting schedule, and character motivations. His accent will probably make it tough going for casual viewers, but his comments are always amusing even when they bear little relation to the film at hand. In any case, it's a real gem ripe for discovery after years of neglect.

DEADWOOD PARK

Colour, 2007, 117m. / Directed by Eric Stanze / Starring William Clifton, Lindsey Luscri, Bryan Lane, Jason Allen Wolfe, Ramona Midgett, Emily Haack, Jason Christ / Cinema Epoch (US R1 NTSC) / WS (1.78:1) (16:9) / DD2.0

 A surprising change of pace from the guys at Wicked Pixel (*Ice from the Sun*, *Scrapbook*), this stylish and atmospheric ghost story by its most recognisable director, Eric Stanze, is a far cry from the aggressive and often experimental cult films in his repertoire. This time he tells a carefully controlled, often bone-chilling tale bathed in ominous shadows and murky lantern light, with a surprising twist waiting at the end. In the small town of Eidolon Crossing, fear still lingers decades later after a string of child murders connected to the nearby Dogwood Park, which was shut down and referred to by the locals as Deadwood Park. Few victims from the 1979 ordeal were found, and the brother of one of them, Jake (William Clifton), returns to put the pieces together. With the aid of the sheriff's daughter (Lindsey Luscri) and more than a few ghostly clues, he investigates whether the accused murderer was really responsible... or something more sinister still waits ahead.

Though it features a few sparing dollops of bloodshed during its finale, *Deadwood Park* is easily the most restrained Wicked Pixel film to date and would make a solid intro for those wary of its more difficult entries like *China White Serpentine*. The actors all do a solid job, and the ambitious production also manages to include a few time-skipping flashback sequences and some clever injections of black and white footage. The abandoned park locale forms the basis for a unique visual by itself, while Stanze also makes expert use of dirty basements, darkly lit bathrooms, and clutching hands to induce shivers with seemingly little effort. Don't expect a shock every second, however; this is a slow and steady spooker more in the British tradition (though some might also compare a couple of moments to J-horror) and all the better for it.

Bearing the new credit of "A Motion Picture by Eric Stanze", this project's aesthetic jump is especially obvious in the use of widescreen framing for the first time, and Stanze and company adapt to the change with a great deal of skill. Stylish landscape shots and unorthodox compositions even in the most mundane dialogue scenes make for an engaging viewing experience, and the use of light and shadow is actually more impressive than that in most major studio horror efforts. The extras include a music video, a quick outtake reel, and a typically insightful and enjoyable audio commentary by Stanze covering the production of the film from start to finish, including scouting for the tricky park location and using actors both seasoned and new (including welcome supporting flashback roles for the reliable Emily Haack and Jason Christ).

DEATH JOURNEY

Colour, 1976, 90m. / Directed by Fred Williamson / Starring Fred Williamson, Bernard Kirby, Art Maier, Lou Bedford, D'Urville Martin / Code Red (US R0 NTSC) / WS (2.35:1) (16:9)

Former cop turned private investigator and martial artist Jesse Crowder (Fred Williamson) has his hands full when everyone who could possibly testify against a powerful mobster winds up dead before their court date. The last possible witness, a timid accountant (Bernard Kirby), is entrusted to Crowder's care, but when thugs smash their ride from California, the unlikely pair are forced to use every available means of transportation to safely get to the courthouse before their two days are up.

Basically another riff on *Narrow Margin* but with far more hand-to-hand combat, this brainless, entertaining action thriller was one of the earliest self-financed efforts for action star Williamson, who had made a name for himself with successful early '70s hits like *Black Caesar* and *Hell Up in Harlem*. Here he directs himself as a no nonsense tough guy who enjoys a good cigar and an even better woman, even if he spends much of his time hauling a milquetoast accountant around by the lapels. Despite the effective but repetitive funk score, this isn't really a blaxploitation picture, though efforts have been made to sell it that way over the years; as with Williamson's subsequent films from his Po' Boy production company, this is just a straight-up, bare knuckles chase movie pitting our hero against a lot of thugs from L.A. to New York.

Due to its indie status, *Death Journey* has been bootlegged frequently on DVD in various black action compilations from a number of budget labels. Most of these have been derived from the miserable-looking Unicorn VHS release, which not only hacked the scope compositions into gibberish but was also taken from a censored TV print. Code Red's official release is a different beast entirely and makes for a far more entertaining experience as it restores the original, essential widescreen framing and reinstates a few extra bits of footage. (And yes, Williamson's hilarious, completely gratuitous nude scene is intact.) The image quality is exceptional, making this one of the company's best-looking releases to date. Williamson appears for an enjoyable half-hour video chat in which he talks about the genesis of the film including the controversial basis of the name of his main character, who was resurfaced in future Po' Boy films like *No Way Back*, *The Last Fight*, and the nuttiest entry of them all, *Blind Rage* (about a heist pulled off by the visually impaired), which really merits a DVD release of its own. He also discusses the budget-impaired difficulties with shooting a cross-country chase film and how he got frequent co-star D'Urville Martin to pop by for a quick role. The original theatrical trailer is included along with additional trailers for *Mean Johnny Barrows*, *Brute Corps*, *Choke Canyon*, and *No Way Back*.

DEATH RACE

Colour, 2008, 111m. / Directed by Paul W.S. Anderson / Starring Jason Statham, Joan Allen, Ian McShane, Tyrese Gibson, Natalie Martinez, Max Ryan, Jason Clarke / Universal (DVD & Blu-ray, UK R2 PAL, US R1 NTSC, France R2 PAL, Japan R2 NTSC) / WS (2.35:1) (16:9) / DD5.1

Though marketed as an escapist slice of sci-fi/action mayhem, this remake of the eternally popular '70s drive-classic *Death Race 2000* opens with a text statement, "2012 – The United States economy collapses", bound to induce a shudder in audiences watching it mere months after its Summer 2008 theatrical release. As the set up explains, "Unemployment hits a record high", while skyrocketing prison rates force corporations to turn the institutions into profit-generating machines. Enter the Death Race, a reality Internet broadcast sensation (mmm, sure this is 2012?) in which inmates race and battle each other to the death on Terminal Island, where their jail is located. When its star racer, Frankenstein (a voice cameo by the original's star, David Carradine) is taken out of commission by newer hotshot Machine Gun Joe (Tyrese Gibson), the prison warden, Hennessey (Joan Allen), is forced to find a replacement for her star's Ford Mustang. Enter Jensen Ames (Jason Statham), a laid-off mill worker and former racer accused of murdering his wife. The warden offers him a chance to go free and be reunited with his child if he wins a single death race, and with the aid of Frankenstein's navigator, Case (Natalie Martinez), he embarks on the challenge – only to find that his wife's real killer is closer than he thinks, and the powers that be have no intention of letting him off the island alive.

The most reliable working star in modern drive-in fare, Jason Statham usually guarantees a rousing popcorn experience (*Crank*, *Cellular*, *The Transporter*) and somehow even manages to avoid humiliating himself in his rare turkeys (*War*, *In the Name of the King*). Fortunately *Death Race* barely squeaks through to the former category, most likely because it wisely keeps similarities to the original 1975 Paul Bartel film to a bare minimum. The basic idea is roughly the same (along with the Frankenstein character), but the original's jolting satire (which somehow managed to completely elude Roger Ebert, who also missed the humour in *Piranha* and *Alligator*) has been largely replaced here with basic action movie storytelling, with a visual and narrative approach closer to post-*Death Race* films like John Carpenter's *Escape from New York* and especially Stuart Gordon's *Fortress*, from which this cribs several narrative ideas.

There's still plenty of humour in the tough-guy dialogue, of course, and Allen as always is excellent and relishes her villainous duties in a role that could have easily come off as slumming. Proving yet again that cable TV seems to be nurturing better talent than theatrical features these days, *Death Race* packs in a roster of familiar TV faces including *Brotherhood*'s Jason Clarke, *Deadwood*'s Ian McShane, Natalie Martinez from *Saints & Sinners*, and even that scary-looking bald guy who played Escobar on *Nip/Tuck*. You also get some shout-outs to Universal's *The Fast and the Furious* in the form of Gibson (who was in *2 Fast 2 Furious*) and even an amusing vehicle cameo.

Director Paul W.S. Anderson planned a *Death Race* remake at least back to 2000 when his original plans were scrapped, and while he's never been a critical favourite, he has managed to escape from the "video game director" stigma of early films like *Mortal Kombat* by turning out films like *Resident Evil* (his best to date and much, much better than it had any right to be, unlike its miserable sequels) and visually accomplished but deeply flawed efforts like *Event Horizon* and the initial *Alien vs. Predator*. His style here is surprisingly gritty and spare, with the whole film rendered in dark browns and steely greys; it's actually a shock to see untreated, colourful footage on the set in the making-of extras. The approach works, though, given the grim and perhaps unintentionally timely nature of the story, and the action scenes are well executed and relatively coherent compared to the "mix it in a blender" approach of many action films, though Allen's presence guarantees this isn't entirely free of post-*Bourne Supremacy* blender editing. On the downside, the film is

D

also loaded with basic logical problems (such as the necessity for a navigator when everyone's essentially driving in a huge circle), so prepare to shut your brain off before hitting "play".

Universal's release contains the standard theatrical R-rated cut as well as an unrated version clocking in six minutes longer. Anderson's been vocal in the past about supposedly longer, drastically different pre-release versions of his films (particularly the still-elusive long version of *Event Horizon*), though these unrated versions tend to turn out to be only slightly different. As with most video releases these days, *Death Race* actually gains more in plot and character development in its unrated form (similar to the major narrative improvements in *Hancock*), with only some fleeting, very minimal bits of violent mayhem added in. It's far more coherent and interesting in the longer cut, however, and the pacing feels significantly more natural. Definitely stick with that version if you have a choice. As mentioned before, the colour palette here is extremely limited, but the clarity and naturally cinematic quality of the transfer is satisfying throughout. The audio mix sounds dynamic and very home theatre friendly in all of its incarnations, with Dolby Digital 5.1 for the DVD while Blu-ray owners get the added bonus of English DTS Master Audio 5.1 as well as Spanish and French DTS tracks. English, French and Spanish subtitles are also provided. Lots of things go boom and crash really loud, exactly as you'd expect. Extras include an audio commentary with Anderson and producer Jeremy Bolt, who also do most of the talking for a 19-minute featurette, "Start Your Engines: Making a Death Race", which also features Statham and other cast members briefly chatting about the shoot. Other goodies include a 7-minute stunt featurette ("Behind the Wheel: Dissecting the Stunts"), a "Tech Specs" dossier on the cars and characters,

and a bonus digital copy disc if you feel like watching lots of cars and bullets spraying around while you're at the gym. The Blu-ray adds the bonus of a "Create Your Own Race" feature (similar to the *Men in Black* exercise of assembling your own edit via seamless branching from long takes of raw footage) and a U-Control Picture-in-Picture feature with bonus cast and crew interviews sliding in and out during the feature playback. If you're D-Box Motion enabled at home, you get that added bonus, too; just brace yourself whenever a crash scene comes up or you might get thrown out of a window.

THE DECAMERON

Colour, 1971, 107m. / Directed by Pier Paolo Pasolini / Starring Franco Citti, Ninetto Davoli, Jovan Jovanovic, Vincenzo Amato, Angela Luce, Pier Paolo Pasolini / BFI (DVD & Blu-ray, UK R2 PAL/HD), MGM (US R1 NTSC) / WS (1.85:1) (16:9), Image (US R1 NTSC) / WS (1.85:1)

The first film by revolutionary Italian director Pier Paolo Pasolini to originally hit the DVD market, *The Decameron* is a bawdy adaptation of Boccaccio's famous morality tales and forms the beginning of his lauded "Trilogy of Life", a trio of movies adapted from famous literary anthologies with an emphasis on humour, sexuality, religion, and sometimes pure fantasy. The films (which also included *Arabian Nights* and *The Canterbury Tales*) encountered numerous censorship difficulties upon their release in the early '70s, getting slapped with deserved X ratings in the U.S. and losing footage in some editions in the U.K. The films were also presented in a bewildering variety of language variants which makes their ideal viewing conditions difficult to assess, but more on that in a bit. They also feature many unknown and usually undraped actors, with only a few familiar faces (like Pasolini regular Ninetto Diavoli, who appears in all three) taking on some of the larger roles.

The Decameron comprises of nine complete stories (and fragments of others) cherry-picked from the original collection (which contained 100 tales), with Pasolini himself appearing occasionally as the painter Giotto's pupil as a loose sort of framing device. A young man (Davoli) falls in with a strange family and some grave robbers; a studly groundskeeper poses as a deaf mute and is forced to satisfy a convent of lusty nuns; three brothers lure their sister's boyfriend to his death with unpredictable consequences; two young lovers steal away for a rooftop rendezvous only to be observed by the girl's wily parents; a man returns from the grave to give his friend some unexpected advice; a priest receives a surprising deathbed confession which leads to miraculous results; and much, much more. The rich tapestry of characters and images doesn't strive for a higher meaning per se and in fact the result is the closest Pasolini ever came to a Buñuel film, packing in lots of good-natured pokes at the church and startling audiences with frank sexuality which comes off here as guilt-free and one of life's greatest joys. There's no predictable divine force controlling anything, as people both good and bad are left to fates whose only consistency is irony. From a less artistic standpoint, it's also worth noting that this film was surprisingly popular around the world and inspired a slew of imitations, mostly medieval sexy stories which carried over its carnal frankness but only a small fraction of its wit or joie de vivre. Titles like *The Black Decameron* and *Ubalda, All Naked and Warm* certainly have their scuzzy charms, but Pasolini's film remains far above in a class of its own.

All three films in this series suffered terribly in the early days of home video (and godawful repertory screenings), with the murky, dark, colour-faded transfers prepared by Water Bearer assaulting viewers throughout the VHS and laserdisc eras as well as the early days of DVD. The original U.K. DVD from the British Film Institute back in 2002 only bettered that one thanks to offering optional instead of burned-in subtitles, while salvation eventually arrived with a U.S. reissue from MGM which finally featured a watchable version with decent detail and solid (if overpumped) colours. (This disc quickly went out of print, and apart from a fleeting Brazilian MGM set release, they abandoned any plans to issue the other two films.) In any case, you can set all of those compromised versions aside thanks to the BFI's miraculous new edition, a stunningly beautiful presentation from the original negative that bests any theatrical experience. The colours are now exactly where they should be (especially the greens, which glowed a bit on the MGM disc), and the razor-sharp picture detail reveals layers and layers of information invisible even on the MGM disc. (And yes, it's uncut complete with one very startling shot of perky male genitalia that makes its eventual downgrading to an R rating in America very unusual indeed.) The BFI version contains the option to watch the film in either its Italian or English language version, with seamless branching allowing it to open and close with either sets of credits; the scratchier English opening with the original United Artists logo is a very nice touch. In this case the film was definitely shot all the way through in Italian, so unless you're really nostalgic for the early '70s dubbed experience (which is actually far better than usual), stick with the original one. The mono audio sounds terrific, with the looped dialogue coming through perfectly. (There isn't much in the way of music, so that's not a factor.) The original Italian trailer is included (you can find the American one on the MGM disc) along with Pasolini's rare B&W 1970 documentary, "Appunti per un'Orestiade africana", which surveys African culture in a manner distinctly different from the more familiar Italian mondo approach. You also get a hefty booklet containing liner notes by Roger Clarke, Sam Rohdie, Nigel Andrews, and Geoffrey Nowell-Smith, essentially a mix of bio information, archival reviews, and new comments about the trilogy, which looks fresher now than ever. Top marks all around.

DEEP THROAT SEX COMEDY COLLECTION:
DEEP THROAT PART II

Colour, 1974, 89m. / Directed by Joseph W. Sarno / Starring Harry Reems, Linda Lovelace, Levi Richards, Andrea True, David Davidson, Chris Jordan, Jamie Gillis, Ashley Moore

THE SWITCH, OR HOW TO ALTER YOUR EGO

Colour, 1974, 100m. / Directed by Joseph W. Sarno / Starring Mary Mendum, Eric Edwards, Sonny Landham, Chris Jordan

A TOUCH OF GENIE

Colour, 1974, 83m. / Directed by Joseph W. Sarno / Starring Douglas Stone, Chris Jordan, Tina Russell, Levi Richards / Secret Key (US R0 NTSC)

 While most film scholars would point to *Exorcist II: The Heretic* as the most inscrutable and ridiculous sequel of the 1970s, its status might be challenged if more people were actually familiar with *Deep Throat Part II*, a "what the hell were they thinking?" follow-up with no deep throating. Or sex. Or coherent story. Released in 1974, it marked a misguided shot at respectability for Bryanston Pictures, whose founders (with dubious origins covered well in the *Inside Deep Throat* documentary) decided to bring back stars Linda Lovelace and Harry Reems, only to stick them in an R-rated espionage comedy. Yes, you read that correctly. Sure, Linda struts around buck naked for a few seconds over the opening titles, but after that you get an hour and a half of New York's finest from the adult filmmaking scene mugging for the camera under the guidance of director Joe Sarno (during his weird comedic mid-'70s period between Euro softcore and American hardcore).

So why is this film actually worth watching? Well, check out the cast! Along with Lovelace and Reems, you also get Andrea True, Jamie Gillis, Levi Richards, Chris Jordan, Ashley Moore, Tina Russell, Helen Madigan, Georgina Spelvin, Roger Caine, and tons of others milling around, some in split-second cameos. (Oh yeah, and future comedienne Judy Tenuta pops up for a minute, too.) The plot is some nonsense about KGB and CIA agents tracking nurse Linda because her nerdy patient is developing a talking supercomputer. The end result is basically the adult equivalent of *It's a Mad Mad Mad Mad World*, except they forgot to have the actors do what they were usually paid for. Sound weird? You bet, and since there's really no target audience for a movie like this, it died a quick theatrical death. Some of the lines are actually funny (Gillis and Richards in particular rise well above the material), and the funky soundtrack by Tony Bruno is quite good and merited numerous reissues on vinyl and CD.

Secret Key's DVD marks the first official release of the film's R-rated cut on disc (though a grey market version yanked from VHS is also available from Alpha Blue along with *Linda Lovelace for President*), and it appears to be taken from a full frame video master matted off to simulate a 16x9 presentation. Unfortunately the obviously clipped opening and closing credits give the game away immediately, but as there's no real compositional integrity to maintain here, it still looks okay about 90% of the time (as long as you overlook the dreary video quality, and it's still better than your average videotape). There's also an unexpected and quite cool extra here, an audio commentary with Richard Livermore (Levi Richards's real name) who's joined midstream by Sarno himself. Lots of ground is covered here, including numerous reminiscences about the industry at the time and the shooting history of the film (it was never shot hardcore, but some additional softcore bits have occasionally appeared in international cuts); you also learn that a young Robert Duvall was reportedly the voice of the computer! Sarno also appears for a 10-minute video interview mostly talking about his comedy films and his brief dabbling in hardcore that came right after this film.

Another good reason to pick this up is the second bonus DVD, which justifies the package's header as "Joe Sarno's *Deep Throat Sex Comedy Collection*". The rarest addition here is *The Switch, or How to Alter Your Ego*, his elusive 1974 sex comedy basically designed as a vehicle for Mary Mendum (aka Rebecca Brooke and Veronica Parrish), the fragile muse from Sarno's *Abigail Leslie Is Back in Town* and Radley Metzger's *The Image*. Here she gets to show off her comedic chops as Dr. Shirley Jekyll, a wallflower chemist who cooks up a powerful potion that turns her into a sex machine on legs. Soon she's embarking on multiple partner escapades, all to the consternation of the man who really loves her (played by Sarno regular Landham before he went legit in Hollywood). It's a stylish and amusing little film nearly lost to the ravages of time, presented here full frame from the only video master around (which alas has burned-in Danish subtitles). Still it's a lot of fun to finally see this one, and as usual the

cast includes such other Sarno regulars as Eric Edwards and Chris Jordan. There's also a pretty scorching orgy scene that ranks as one of the most graphic in Sarno's softcore catalogue. Rounding out the package is a softcore edit of Sarno's *A Touch of Genie*, a Borscht-Belt style comedy that actually works almost as well here in its milder variant. You can read more about the original two-disc XXX edition separately later in this book, and some of the extras from that version (a Sarno interview and a mini-documentary) are carried over here as well.

DELIVER US FROM EVIL

Colour, 1975, 98m. / Directed by Horace Jackson / Starring Renny Roker, Marie O'Henry, Kandi Keath, Danny Martin, Cal Haynes, Juanita Moore

THE FOX AFFAIR

Colour, 1978, 88m. / Directed by Fereidun G. Jorjani / Starring Kathryn Dodd, Robert Bosco, Yuri Alexis, Steve Lincoln / Navarre (US R0 NTSC) / WS (1.78:1) (16:9)

According to Howard Hawks, a good movie had to contain three great scenes and no bad ones. In weird cinema terms, that means *Deliver Us from Evil* (originally released under the title *Joey* which remains on most current circulating prints) is a real diamond in the rough as it contains a trio of sequences guaranteed to stop viewers in their tracks, even if the material surrounding it is just average '70s "issues" preachiness.

The first highlight comes right during the wildly expressionistic opening credits as janitor Chris (regular TV actor Renny Roker) reacts to his demanding boss by smashing up a room full of glass shelves and bottles, only to find himself in a straight jacket inside a rainbow-coloured funny farm where he bellows nonstop at his doctor. From there we get about an hour or so of TV-style plotting as our hero goes back out on the streets and is appalled by all of the violence committed by black people against each other, with schoolyards in particular targeted for bullying and bad influences. A pretty young teacher (Marie O'Henry) and a "cute", wise-beyond-his-years kid in a wheelchair named Joey (Danny Martin) are especially put-upon by neighbourhood thugs who show up in the schoolyard where little kids like to get funky and do dance routines during recess. Then at the 70-minute mark, the film drops another bombshell sequence out of nowhere that's so artistically audacious and out of character with everything before it you have to wonder if Luis Buñuel suddenly showed up on the set for one day. The melodrama continues to escalate and appears to build towards a violent conclusion until… the film instead climaxes by having our hero turn directly to the audience and deliver a pissed-off lecture at the camera about the horrible state of today's neighbourhoods.

Almost every scene in this film is scored to a very long, very repetitive song called "Know What We're Doing to Ourselves", which plays at least 15 times in all. That just adds to the weirdness factor of this major oddity, which looks like it was designed as a forerunner to today's gospel plays and their offshoots, Tyler Perry's static movie sermons about why a man in old lady drag knows better than everyone around him. However, the execution contains so many cockeyed touches it would instead make a perfect companion piece to '70s urban "Christsploitation" classics like *The Cross and the Switchblade*. The only really recognisable name here is a negligible role for Juanita Moore, best known as the put-upon maid in Douglas Sirk's version of *Imitation of Life*, while everyone else's acting is either pitched at pure hysteria or the level of an average *CHiPs* episode.

The lineage of this DVD release is a bit tricky to navigate; it originated as a Code Red title, then got picked up by Navarre to continue their line of "Exploitation Cinema" double features after the collapse of BCI – but the packaging bears the label of the film's licensor, Saturn, a name long dormant since the '80s VHS days. In any case, the transfer's a perfectly good one considering this looks like one of the better surviving theatrical prints; colours are very bold and strong, but damage is evident in many scenes, giving it a vintage grindhouse feel. If you don't mind these imperfections, the presentation is perfectly acceptable and comparable to seeing it now in a theatre.

Unfortunately the film's co-feature doesn't fare nearly as well. *The Fox Affair* is a numbingly dull mixture of blaxploitation and espionage thriller that wastes 95% of its running time on people sitting around at tables or in cars talking about fixing up prominent men with sexy women. Unfortunately this activity is rarely shown and basically leads nowhere except to a state of extreme sleepiness in the viewer. Only two brief scenes shake things up enough to raise an eyebrow: one early, wholly inexplicable bit involving a bodybuilder showing off in bikini briefs inside a hot tub while surrounded by cooing, naked women, and the very last scene which tosses in a gratuitous and quite hilarious car explosion. Otherwise it's a complete waste of time and barely warrants a quick skim using the fast-forward button. The transfer's wretched as well, obviously taken from an old '80s full frame master with soft detail and noticeable telecine wobble from start to finish. Just stick with the main feature, which is worth the price tag alone. Extras include a wonderfully overwrought trailer for *Deliver Us from Evil* and additional previews for *Terminal Island*, *Group Marriage*, *Dr. Black & Mr. Hyde*, *Death Force*, *Cheering Section* and *The Working Girls*.

DERBY

Colour, 1971, 93m. / Directed by Robert Kaylor / Starring Mike Snell, Charlie O'Connell, Christina Snell / Code Red (US R0 NTSC)

You couldn't find a film more firmly rooted in its decade than *Derby*, an Ohio-shot documentary made at the height of the gritty doc craze with films like *Grey Gardens*. That's pretty much the same approach here as we witness a truly surprising character study courtesy of Mike Snell, an aspiring roller derby contestant who works at a tyre company when not at home with his wife and child. However, as the film intercuts with the local derby scene and follows Snell's trajectory under what he hopes will be the guidance of San Francisco Bay Bombers star Charlie O'Connell, the layers of his personality are gradually revealed to expose a fascinating portrait of the often destructive means used to achieve personal happiness and the American dream.

Shot long before celebrity culture really got a stranglehold on everyday life, *Derby* paints a vivid portrait of a craze that still lingers in many American cities but really hit its height during the '70s (epitomised by the immortal Raquel Welch film, *Kansas City Bomber*, which is actually not as good as this film). Director Robert Kaylor makes inventive use of mobile camerawork, even capturing some great tracking shots in front of the skaters; after this he went on to direct two fictional films, *Carny* (which is pretty good) and the now-forgotten *Nobody's Perfect*.

One of the more unorthodox in their already diverse line of releases, Code Red's DVD presents the original R-rated director's cut of the film, which contains some salty language toned down for subse-quent theatrical bookings with a PG rating. The full frame transfer replicates the correct presentation as this was originally shot in 16mm and blown up to 35 for the big screen, and not surprisingly it looks like an early '70s documentary – grainy and often dark, but that's exactly how it was filmed. Kaylor is all over the special features here, contributing an audio commentary talking about the film's genesis as a straight-up look at roller derby, the interactions which led it to change focus along the way, and what happened to everyone after it was filmed. Producer William Richert (*Winter Kills*) also appears for a second chat track in which he talks more about the actual mounting of the production and the vagaries of working in the realm of low budget indies. Also included is *Max Out*, Kaylor's first film, a short(ish) look at life in the U.S. penal system as one convicted felon tries to get his life back together only to find the outside world even more imposing than existing behind bars. It's quite good and foreshadows much of the themes and character treatment in his first big feature, with Kaylor contributing another commentary track to this one as well.

THE DESIGNATED VICTIM

Colour, 1971, 105m. / Directed by Maurizio Lucidi / Starring Tomas Milian, Pierre Clémenti, Katia Christine, Marisa Bartoli / Shameless (UK R0 PAL), New Entertainment World (Germany R0 PAL) / WS (2.35:1) (16:9)

Unhappily married Italian fashion designer Stefano (Tomas Milian) longs to run off with his mistress (Katia Christine), but wife Luisa (Marisa Bartoli) refuses to let him cash out of his share of their company. One overcast day in Venice, he crosses paths with the decadent Count Matteo Tiepolo (Pierre Clémenti), and as they swap personal stories, the new acquaintance proposes a solution: they both want someone out of the way, so why not swap murders? When the Count carries through his end of the bargain, Stefano must decide exactly how badly he really wants his freedom.

Suspense fans will immediately recognise the framework of this plot from Patricia Highsmith's classic novel *Strangers on a Train*, most famously filmed by Alfred Hitchcock in 1951. However, what this film may lack in an original concept it more than makes up for in a dense, beautiful Venetian atmosphere, a haunting music score by Luis Bacalov, and most importantly, two impeccable lead performances from pros Milian and Clémenti who play off each other perfectly. It's a gorgeous, haunting film, easily the best thing from usually workmanlike director Maurizio Lucidi (*Stateline Motel*), and well worth discovering for adventurous viewers.

However, *giallo* fans might be confused by the sell job used for Shameless's DVD, which posits this as another sexy, swinging '70s thriller. There's no mad psycho on the loose, no graphic murders, and really not much in the way of sex appeal; however, if you know what you're getting, this disc is highly recommended. An earlier German release from New Entertainment World was the first introduction many viewers had to this barely-released title, but it was significantly trimmed in several key scenes; the Shameless disc thankfully restores the film to its original length and looks quite good, making this one of their most essential releases. The disc includes both the solid English dub track or the Italian version with optional English subtitles, as well as a stills gallery, a small sampling of alternative and deleted footage, a newly-created trailer, and another one of their lively, terrific pop-up subtitle trivia tracks obviously written with a great deal of knowledge about the film's history. The only advantage to the German disc is the inclusion of Bacalov's original soundtrack as a playable supplement extra, though this can also be tracked down on its own as a Japanese CD.

THE DEVIL

Colour, 1972, 119m. / Directed by Andrzej Zulawski / Starring Wojciech Pszoniak, Malgorzata Braunek, Michal Grudzinski, Leszek Teleszynski, Monika Niemczyk / Polart (US R0 NTSC) / WS (1.66:1)

During the brutal Prussian occupation of Poland, a mysterious black-clad, bearded stranger (*The Tin Drum*'s Wojciech Pszoniak) arrives to claim a young prisoner, Jakub (Leszek Teleszynski), only to attempt to set him free once they are out in the barren wilderness. As they cross the landscape with a young blonde nun (Malgorzata Braunek) in tow, Jakub's fractured past is revealed in a series of disturbing vignettes showing how his family has been driven into degradation and desperation.

One of the finest international filmmakers still unrecognised by the general public, Polish director Andrzej Zulawski caused controversy in his native country from the beginning of his career with a manic, revolutionary WWII period piece entitled *The Third Part of Night*. From his first film his artistic trademarks were already in place: breakneck handheld camerawork, volatile political content, brutal violence usually rendered in broad daylight, and histrionic performances pitched to the heavens. His second film, *The Devil*, pushed the period setting back further to 18th-Century Poland while pushing his technique to such extreme lengths that the finished product was banned for decades via an agreement with the Catholic Church and the state government. Interestingly, the film shares many visual and thematic similarities with Alejandro Jodorowsky's near-contemporary *El Topo*, which managed to win over audiences across the globe as Zulawski continued to toil within the communist system.

In typical Zulawski fashion, *The Devil* barely functions as a traditional narrative, even foreshadowing his best-known film, 1981's *Possession* as the story itself begins to break down in a series of gruesome vignettes including an unforgettable attempted rape and, most bizarre of all, a wolfish transformation scene which literalises the monstrosities against which Zulawski's script has been railing. The bursts of violence (including a jolting gunshot to the face) certainly rivet the viewer's attention, but Zulawski's aggressive, dreamlike style remains the main attraction as his camera careens through the stark landscapes and often right into the actors' faces, their make-up literally streaking black across the screen during one particularly intense moment. The brutality (and, marginally in this case, sexuality) functions more as a Kabuki-like manifestation of the inhumanity present in the story and characters, a stark and stylised method of externalising in stark terms how much one man can wound another simply for existing.

The Devil marks the second release from Polart's library through Facets in the United States. The presentation is roughly on par with their first Zulawski release, the remarkable "unfinished" science fiction epic, *On the Silver Globe*; image quality looks a bit dated and haggard in spots, but at least it's far clearer and more film-like than anything available before (which

didn't amount to much at all). The film is presented letterboxed (non-anamorphic) at 1.66:1 with optional English subtitles (which must be switched on manually with the remote – no menu option here). The whole package doesn't really offer much context for this wild and potentially baffling film; extras are limited to a few sparse text filmographies.

DEVIL HUNTER

Colour, 1980, 101m. / Directed by Jess Franco / Starring Ursula Buchfellner, Al Cliver, Robert Foster (Antonio Mayans), Burt Altman, Antonio de Cabo, Gisela Hahn, Werner Pochath / Severin (US R0 NTSC, UK R0 NTSC) / WS (1.85:1) (16:9)

 Sent to the remote island of Puerto Santo to help rescue kidnapped blonde actress Laura Crawford (Ursula Buchfellner), tough guy Peter Weston (Al Cliver) and his pilot sidekick Jack (Antonio Mayans) must contend with a gang of ruthless thugs who don't take too kindly when the ransom drop goes awry. Now Laura's running loose in the jungle straight towards a tribe of cannibals who worship a naked, bug-eyed devil man (Burt Altman) with a penchant for eating the sexiest women within arm's reach. Can the good guys reach Laura in time before she becomes the island god's next meal?

A completely unrepentant piece of trash, this Jess Franco gut-muncher is easily the most notorious result of his early '80s foray into cannibal cinema. Much of its infamy is due to the fact that it's been circulating on video for years under a number of titles (*Mandingo Manhunter* and *Sexo Canibal* being the most memorable), and somehow it even raised the ire of the

British authorities, who must have simply looked at the cover without actually watching the film. The usual Eurociné bugaboos are here: inconsistent lighting conditions from one shot to the next, wildly indifferent dubbing, fragmented plotting that borders on the abstract, and a nonstop avalanche of nudity and gore.

Severin's DVD from the original negative boasts additional, never-before-seen footage of cannibal terror, and indeed this does run several minutes longer than most VHS releases, which usually clocked in around the 90 minute mark. Of course, this isn't exactly the zippiest Franco film thanks to lots of padding involving people wandering around the woods and having flashbacks; on top of that you also get regular POV shots from the island demon, who wears ping pong balls over his eye sockets to give him a weird bug-eyed look. Image quality is great considering the original film was cheap and ragged, with deliberate gauzy visual effects over several scenes and daylight often switching to dusk and then back again for no apparent reason. Audio is available either in French or in English (with one quick restored bit in Spanish) with optional English subtitles. The only extra is another delirious 17-minute interview with Franco who talks about his relationships both good and bad with the actors and his distaste for the cannibal genre which led him to circumvent normal conventions with efforts like this and the utterly hilarious *Cannibals*. Severin released the same version in the U.K. (in NTSC) after the BBFC passed it uncut for the first time since the video nasty era.

THE DEVIL IN MISS JONES

Colour, 1973, 68m. / Directed by Gerard Damiano / Starring Georgina Spelvin, Harry Reems, John Clemens, Marc Stevens, Judith Hamilton, Levi Richards / Raincoat Theatre (US R1 NTSC) / WS (1.66:1) / DD5.1

Though it wasn't the first theatrical hardcore feature, Gerard Damiano's *The Devil in Miss Jones* was undeniably the first to get good reviews and actually receive critical treatment similar to that for any regular mainstream feature. Far from the grungy, goofy bumping and grinding of Damiano's previous *Deep Throat*, this fusion of Ingmar Bergman-style art house philosophy, psychological horror and kinky imagery proved to be another smash hit and revealed a most unlikely sex symbol in its leading lady, part-time exotic dancer Georgina Spelvin. After despairing, lonely spinster Miss Jones slashes her wrists in a bathtub, she arrives in a sunny but eerily empty afterworld where the surveyor, Mr. Abaca (John Clemens), tells her that she's doomed for the decision to take her own life. However, she also has the opportunity to indulge in all of the sensual pleasures she denied herself while alive, a chance she seizes with the aid of a naughty instructor (Harry Reems) and a wide variety of willing participants including various men, women, produce items, and even a snake. However, as the haunting finale proves, this path has its own problems as well.

A far better actress than your average porn starlet, Spelvin manages to carry the film with a strong performance ranging from meek despair to wild, glittering-eyed abandon. The decision to go with an older-than-average female lead instead of the usual fresh-out-of-high-school nymphet was a very smart one, and the rest of the film wisely strives to stay on her level. Spelvin went on to a number of other films (including mainstream ones like *Police Academy*) and always gave it her best; just check out her hilarious turns in films like *The Private Afternoons of Pamela Mann* to see her impressive range. Her co-stars include a roster of familiar '70s faces, amongst whom are frequent lesbian-scene actress Judith Hamilton (as "Clair Lumiere") (whose appearance is usually omitted from prints but has been restored on this release) and busy actors Marc Stevens and Levi Richards, whose three-way scene with Spelvin near the end of the film remains one of the most startling and intense of its kind. Undoubtedly realising he was onto something special, Damiano wisely recruited a real composer, Alden Shuman, to put together a beautiful original score whose essential soundtrack release has almost always stayed in print over the past three decades.

Though it's been a perennial bestseller on home video, *The Devil in Miss Jones* was treated miserably on DVD since the early '80s thanks to murky, often cut presentations and a simply incompetent initial DVD release that encoded each sequence as a separate film, causing the player to pause and often lock up between scenes while the timer restarted. Obviously the release from the Media Blasters sub-label Raincoat Theater (in conjunction with VCX) didn't have to work too hard to outdo its predecessors, but thankfully they've done this film proud with a transfer that's much easier on the eyes than any viewer would expect. The low budget still hampers the visuals somewhat (presumably the cheap film stock couldn't quite cope with the deep levels of black Damiano was going for in some scenes), but detail and colour saturation are much better and more natural here than before. Some damage from the original element flickers through here and there (including a tiny pinhole that pops in and out through a couple of reels), but considering the rarity of any decent elements at all, fans should be very happy indeed. The audio can be played in either a 5.1 remix or the original mono; though the latter is probably best for purists, the 5.1 does a surprisingly solid job of enlarging the soundscape by channelling the music to the rear speakers and keeping the dialogue dead centre. Not bad either way, really. As if the upgraded transfer weren't enough, this release manages to pack in enough extras for a two-disc edition. Disc one houses the main feature with an informative Damiano commentary track moderated by Casey Scott, who certainly knows his way around the block when it comes to drive-in and exploitation films. They cover pretty much everything you could possibly want to know about the making of the film, from the stories behind each of the actors (with emphasis placed on Spelvin, of course) to the identities and back stories of the various participants behind the camera. There's nothing as scary as Damiano's mob-related murmurings in *Inside Deep Throat*; this is strictly historically-based and a much-needed chapter in preserving the history of the golden age of adult cinema. Then Spelvin steps into the spotlight on disc two for a video interview in which the still-cheery actress talks about the making of the film, her initiation into the business, her stripping career, and recollections about her co-stars and director. The second disc is rounded out with a stills gallery, the much-shortened 50-minute(!) cable version (which is still a lot stronger than what you'd expect to see today), and trailers for this film and other Raincoat titles like *Neon Nights* and *Babylon Pink*.

DEVIL TIMES FIVE

Colour, 1974, 88m. / Directed by Sean MacGregor / Starring Sorrell Booke, Gene Evans, Leif Garrett, Taylor Lacher, Joan McCall, Shelley Morrison, Tierre Turner, Tia Thompson, Gail Smale, Dawn Lyn, John Durren, Carolyn Stellar / Code Red (US R0 NTSC) / WS (1.78:1) (16:9)

Taking its cue from '60s shockers like *Village of the Damned* and *The Bad Seed* with a more explicit '70s twist, the cult video favourite *Devil Times Five* charts the havoc unleashed when a small busload of psychologically unbalanced children en route to an institution crashes in the snow, leaving the twisted tots free to roam the countryside at will. Accompanied by a slightly older psycho in nun drag, Hannah (Gail Smale), they find refuge at a nearby cabin where some twisted adults are busy getting drunk and acting out psychosexual parlour games of their own. Soon the kids – including wannabe child actor David (future singer and tabloid fodder Leif Garrett) and firebug Susan (Tia Thompson) – have wormed their way into the grownups' confidence and can murder at will with any tools they find handy, never raising suspicion until it seems too late.

Of course, none of the adults are all that sympathetic. They consist of three couples of varying ages as well as a mentally handicapped handyman, played by John Durren, the film's screenwriter. Since the film never feels compelled to offer any motivation for the kids' behaviour (apart from the obvious – "They're nuts!") or sketch out the adults with any dimension whatsoever, the best way to approach this film is as an extended E.C. Comics story with plenty of nasty violence inflicted on schemers who deserve what they get. Garrett gives the standout performance of the young cast, though his real-life sister (Dawn Lyn, who appeared in the complete *Walking Tall* trilogy) does a fine job as well; their real-life mom, Carolyn Stellar, appears as well, which must have made for an uncomfortable set at times given some of the sleazier moments in the script. The murders are quite brutal and protracted, but more startling is the heavy dose of sex and equal opportunity nudity which is more uncomfortable than titillating. Perhaps most unexpected is the film's odd connection to Spanish director Narciso Ibáñez Serrador, whose *The House That Screamed* gets a nod here with a slow-motion murder sequence similar to that 1969 film; Serrador must have noticed, since his unsettling cult classic, *Who Could Kill a Child?*, was made two years later and acknowledges this film from its basic premise to the very similar ending. While the killer-kids theme is still potent (obviously), one aspect that really makes this film stick in viewers' memories is the isolated, snowy setting, which is effectively used and offers a legitimate excuse for keeping the potential victims from simply running next door to call the police.

As with many independent horror films, the production history for *Devil Times Five* was quite difficult and rocky, almost ridiculously so in this case. Originally titled *People Toys* (or *Peopletoys* – the spelling seems to vary), the film came in at only about half of feature film length in its original version under director Sean MacGregor, who, according to the supplements here, didn't exactly set the producers on fire. David Sheldon was brought in to shoot more footage to beef up the running time under the supervision of producer Michael Blowitz, and both men cover the strenuous production history on their audio commentary with moderator Darren Gross, who as usual does a solid job of keep the conversation fact-filled and quickly paced. Lyn also joins in and offers her own perspective as a child performer drawn in to a most unusual project. All three are joined by Tierre Turner for the other big extra, a featurette that offers even more stories about the shoestring filming in a less-than-optimum setting with enough continuity problems to fuel months of nightmares. Other extras include the theatrical trailer, some additional Easter Eggs involving the interviewees, an alternative opening title sequence, a promotional gallery, and vintage trailers for other Code Red releases. One of the earliest horror films released on VHS back in the ancient days of Meda (later Media) Home Video, *Devil Times Five* went out of circulation for many years and earned an even bigger following by virtue of its unavailability. Code Red's very welcome release features a sharp new anamorphic transfer that obviously blows past versions out of the water; even the occasional 35mm revivals don't look this clean and clear. The film was subsequently reissued via Code Red and BCI without extras in a different transfer as a co-feature with *Mark of the Witch*, which is discussed later in this book.

THE DEVIL'S BLOODY PLAYTHINGS

Colour, 2005, 85m. / Directed by William Hellfire / Starring Ruby Larocca, Zoe Moonshine, Marzie Lane, Shannon Selberg / Alternative Cinema (US R0 NTSC) / DD2.0

 The most successful fusion of sex and horror from erratic but sometimes inspired shot-on-video director William Hellfire is this acidic and unorthodox tale of Polanski-esque dementia. Shot through with a desolate, sleaze-ridden viewpoint reminiscent of Joe Sarno, Doris Wishman and at times even Andy Milligan, it's one of the closest approximations of a genuine grindhouse film in today's direct-to-video culture.

Regular softcore staples Zoe Moonshine (*Flesh for Olivia*) and Ruby Larocca (*Satan's School for Lust*) team up as Christine and Karen, new roommates whose relationship spirals into knife-wielding and dementia thanks to Christine's

indulgence in domination games and shooting her co-habitants in various states of undress. The surreal and totally unexpected final act really pays off, and the whole project is a modest but welcome relief from the usual SOV eyesores. The full frame transfer looks fine given the DV lensing, and the disc comes with a few minimal extras, namely a ten-minute blooper reel (with footage of Hellfire acting out for the performers) and two trailers.

THE DISTRICT!

Colour, 2004, 87m. / Directed by Áron Gauder / Atopia (US R0 NTSC) / WS (1.78:1) (16:9) / DD5.1

 This hyperactive Hungarian animated feature (originally entitled *Nyócker!*) cleaned up at various festivals around the world including Sitges, and fans of adult TV cartoon shows should be the most receptive to this coke-fuelled outing. The basic story's a self-acknowledged riff on *Romeo and Juliet*, but you'd barely guess it as the plot veers between a trashy cast of characters in Budapest, all rendered in a freaky animation style which places captures of real actors' performing heads on jerky, animated 3-D bodies, with the backgrounds rendered in a psychedelic painterly style. The hero, gypsy brat Ritchie, leads a gang of his friends on a bizarre journey wherein they travel through time and arrange to bury a heap of mammoths under the future location of their city, so in the present day they can all strike oil, become rich, and resolve the conflict that keeps him out of the arms of his true love, Julia. Unfortunately their hijinks draw the attention of the world, with George W. Bush, Osama Bin Laden and Tony Blair popping up for cameo appearances. Hookers, bar fights, and

Hungarian rap music add even more weirdness to the mix, all subtitled in a slangy low-rent British style that seems somehow appropriate. You've never seen anything like it, for sure; crank this up along with *Team America* for any friends who can appreciate a completely rude take on current events.

The packaging touts the film's similarity to *South Park*, though the approach is actually a whole lot closer to Ralph Bakshi (*Fritz the Cat*, *Heavy Traffic*) as it hurls ideas and big boobs helter skelter at the viewer with little regard for a coherent structure or point of view. Based on a Hungarian TV skit and expanded with hit-and-miss results to over an hour and a half, *The District!* may aggravate some viewers and can certainly induce headaches but at least looks phenomenal on DVD, with a bold and often eye-searing transfer and room-engulfing 5.1 mix that will amply show off any home theatre system. The optional English subtitles are fine, though the choice of dialect is not the easiest. Extras include some sample clips from the original TV show, a half-hour documentary covering the animation techniques on show here, and a promotional trailer for this film as well as other Atopia titles such as the excellent, highly-recommended *Missing Victor Pellerin*.

DOCTOR DEATH

Colour, 1973, 87m. / Directed by Eddie Saeta / Starring John Considine, Barry Coe, Cheryl Miller, Stewart Moss, Jo Morrow, Moe Howard / Scorpion (US R0 NTSC) / WS (1.78:1) (16:9)

After his dying wife Laura (*3 Worlds of Gulliver*'s Jo Morrow) vows to return from the afterlife following her car accident injuries (and pops up as a skull-faced apparition for the opening credits), dedicated husband Fred (*Jaws 2*'s Barry Coe) decides to find a way to cheat death and speed his beloved back into the realm of the living. After a handful of thwarted attempts involving fake psychics and body snatching, he finds a solid possibility in the form of Dr. Death (TV veteran John Considine), a flamboyant stage performer whose magic-oriented routines include the transplant of souls from one body to another. Dr. Death becomes relentless in his pursuit of bringing back Laura's essence and sets his sights on a candidate, Fred's assistant Sandy (Cheryl Miller), who would make a lovely vessel indeed.

A wild, garish, entertaining collision of drive-in gothic '60s horror and '70s shag carpet sensibilities, *Doctor Death* doles out the bloody goods while keeping its campy theatrics at just the right pitch. Fans of Robert Quarry and Vincent Price's outings from the same era will definitely get a kick out of the bearded Considine's theatrical performance, which is a pretty good indication of how *The Wizard of Gore* might have played with a competent actor in the leading role. (But then again, who wouldn't cherish Ray Sager's performance in that on a slow evening?) One-off director Eddie Saeta (who had done tons of second unit work since the '30s) keeps the plotline chugging along with just enough twists and turns to keep things interesting, with none other than former Stooge Moe Howard popping up in one scene for his final screen appearance! As with many films of the period, there really isn't a sympathetic character in sight (especially Fred, who takes his wife's death a bit harder than any rational human ever should); however, this just adds to the weird, E.C. Comics-inspired fun.

Anyone who ever suffered through the abysmal VHS tape of this title or any of the battered, washed-out repertory prints will have no idea what awaits them with this release. Surprisingly, *Doctor Death* turns out to be crisp, colourful, and stylish, using colourful lighting and costumes to create a surreal, often very potent atmosphere that often feels like a vintage made-for-TV horror movie on acid. A really fantastic presentation all around that shows how a clean HD transfer from a film's negative can change a viewer's entire perception about the feature itself. The extras don't skip out either, with the best being a fun nine-minute video interview ("Doctor Death Commands") with Considine who colourfully talks about his role and his overall career with a lot of gusto. The late Saeta's son, Steve, also appears for a video chat, "Remembering Eddie Saeta", about how the directorial assignment came about, which seems very unlikely for a first feature film effort. Considine also appears for a scattershot commentary track with *Intruder* helmer Scott Spiegel and Scorpion's Walter Olsen that's less lively than usual for the company but still contains a few useful nuggets of info here and there. Other trailers from short-lived '70s company Cinerama include *Girly*, *Goodbye Gemini*, and *The Last Grenade*; ah, and Considine also has an amusing video intro as Doctor Death himself before the feature in which he practices his art on one of his co-moderators, which must surely be a home video first.

DON'T BE AFRAID OF THE DARK

Colour, 1973, 74m. / Directed by John Newland / Starring Kim Darby, Jim Hutton, Barbara Anderson, William Demarest, Pedro Armendariz Jr. / Warner Archive (US R0 NTSC)

Perhaps second only to *Trilogy of Terror*, this is the best-remembered made-for-TV fright feature of the 1970s which ignited an entire generation's worth of potent nightmares. After moving into a large Victorian home, Sally (Kim Darby) and Alex (Jim Hutton) decide to do a little restoration work which involves such minor changes as prying open doors and opening up sealed fireplaces. This naturally proves to be a rather bad idea as the house is inhabited by evil little creatures who only come out in the dark, and while Sally is quick to catch on that something monstrous is loose, Alex refuses to believe her. Armed only with her wits, she must race against time to save herself before their diabolical plan consumes her forever.

Lean and mean, this crackerjack creature feature still has the power to induce goose bumps thanks to Darby's perfectly-pitched performance and a canny exploitation of everyone's primal fear of things that go bump in the night. Each appearance of the wrinkly-faced creatures is a perfectly-timed shock (the best arriving most inconveniently during a dinner party), and the unforgettable climactic showdown between the terrified wife and the tiny inhabitants is truly the stuff of nightmares. Regular TV composer Billy Goldenberg (who usually scored Universal projects like *Night Gallery* and *Duel*) has to get some of the credit as well for his wonderful, spine-tingling score.

For some reason Warner took well over a decade of DVD releases to get around to even acknowledging this film, which often ranked near the top of horror fans' wish lists. (A bootleg Japanese DVD was briefly available as a double feature with *Gargoyles*, but the transfer was yanked directly from a VHS tape.) Their decision to dump this off along with some of their other prime made-for-TV gems as part of the direct-response Warner Archive line is truly puzzling (just think what an incredible DVD box set they could have put together), but at least it's available in some form at all. The transfer quality is a couple of steps above the long-discontinued VHS edition, but it's still nothing to scream about; this definitely looks like a dated video master that was prepared quite a few years ago. However, this genuine horror classic is worth experiencing in any form at all, and at least audiences can finally have the option of adding it to their collections.

DOOM ASYLUM

Colour, 1987, 79m. / Directed by Richard Friedman / Starring Patty Mullen, Kristin Davis, Ruth Collins, Kenny Price, Michael Rogen / Code Red (US R0 NTSC)

 Imagine a zero-budget cross between *Session 9* and *Student Bodies*, and that might give you some idea of the weird, ramshackle charm of *Doom Asylum*, a New Jersey independent splatter film that wound up garnering a small cult following due to its edited VHS release in the late 1980s. As with many of its ilk, some of the cast members eventually went on to some degree of fame, namely Kristin Davis (later to play "good girl" Charlotte on *Sex and the City* and stuck here in spectacles and a blue bathing suit) and *Frankenhooker*/pin-up model Patty Mullen.

The storyline is another riff on the standard slasher formula with a traumatised car crash victim (Michael Rogen) reacting to the death of his fiancée by killing two coroners who have him laid out on a slab and then finding refuge beneath an asylum. A decade later, some vacationing yuppies (including the daughter of the original car crash victim) and sneering punk rockers happen to barge in on the deserted asylum and, when not squabbling with each other, soon grow to regret their choice of locale when the badly disfigured, wisecracking lunatic starts dispatching them in varying degrees of arterial spray.

A fun artefact if nowhere even close to a "good" film, *Doom Asylum* heaps on the gore and cinematic Cheez-Whiz with gleeful abandon from start to finish, making this the goofiest Troma film that company never actually made. Continuity does not even begin to enter the picture (keep an eye on the killer's TV, which is blank in long shots but runs very long Tod Slaughter clips in close-up), and the actors' various Northeastern accents make for a wonderful clash of delivery styles (with a heavy accent on Joisey). Shot on film but completed on video (complete with chintzy electronic credits), *Doom Asylum* never rises above its budget but makes for a fine time-killer and a fine souvenir of an age when anyone with an affinity for flinging red stuff at the camera could have his own shot at the big time.

You might not guess it from the finished product, but director Richard Friedman actually did manage to go on to bigger things; in fact, this was his second film after the sluggish Farley Granger thriller, *Deathmask*. Some of his future work included episodes of *Tales from the Darkside*, a Billy Joel video, and the VHS staple *Phantom of the Mall*. He's represented well on this DVD release, joined by production manager Bill Tasgal for a lively commentary track in which they frankly assess how the film was made and where it succeeds and fails. Too bad screenwriter Rick Marx (who started in porn and went on to several Cannon Films and crime books) isn't around as well since he seems to have dropped off the face of the earth in the past decade. Friedman and Tasgal are joined on-camera by Films Around the World's Alexander W. Kogan Jr. for a video featurette that covers the making of the film from a broader perspective. The transfer itself is about as good as could be expected given the shooting conditions and less-than-prime materials involved; it's certainly sharp enough, and the tacky late-'80s colour schemes don't look compromised. This also represents the unseen longer cut of the film, specifically including one character's digits graphically being removed in a most painful fashion. The disc is rounded out with some appetisingly trashy trailers for other Code Red titles including *BoardingHouse* (which makes this film look like *Silence of the Lambs*), *The Forest*, *Devil Times Five*, *Human Experiments*, *Stingray*, *The Dark Ride*, *Gang Wars*, *Enter the White Dragon*, *Nightmare*, *Love Me Deadly*, *Silent Scream*, *The Redeemer* and *The Farmer*.

DOOR INTO SILENCE

Colour, 1991, 86m. / Directed by Lucio Fulci / Starring John Savage, Sandi Schultz, Richard Castleman, Jennifer Loeb / Severin (US R1 NTSC), Raro (Italy R2 PAL)

While driving through Louisiana, Melvin Devereux (John Savage) passes a funeral where his last name is prominently on display. He becomes more alarmed when he sees that the body bears a striking resemblance to him, and that night he encounters a beautiful but spooky woman (Sandi Schultz) who helps him find an auto repair shop. As he drives further away from the city, he repeatedly becomes involved in a *Duel*-esque game of cat and mouse with a slow-moving hearse whose creepy driver (Richard Castleman, D'Amato's location scout) won't let him get by. A colourful gallery of characters also passes through, including a hot-to-trot teenager trying to get to Memphis for the "Country Music Festival" ("Randy Travis! Tammy Wynette! It's gonna be great!") who offers to sleep with him for fifty bucks. After a particularly nasty phone call involving a tarot reader, Melvin finally reaches his destiny involving the hearse and a particularly fateful sunset.

Suspense and horror directors have a funny way of closing out their careers. Alfred Hitchcock turned out the decidedly family-friendly and bloodless *Family Plot* before his death, and Lucio Fulci, the master of shambling zombies and psychedelic thrillers, bid adieu to his fans with the likewise bloodless and oddly ethereal *Door Into Silence* (with the film's credits listing the director as "H. Simon Kittay" for some reason). The film was financed by Joe D'Amato's short-lived Filmirage, a company better known for *StageFright*, *Witchcraft*, and, uh, *Troll 2*. This film, Fulci's only for the company, came near its final days, when D'Amato was fond of lensing softcore films in New Orleans like *Any Time, Any Play*. Of course, this was also Fulci's old stomping ground from *The Beyond*, and a modest, peculiar supernatural quickie was born.

On the surface this story might sound like yet another predictable knock-off of *Carnival of Souls*, though the script somehow manages to still make it odd and perplexing with an odd ghost story twist at the end which helps the obvious payoff to be a little more interesting. Of course, anyone looking for his trademark splatter antics will be left in the dust; he definitely bid farewell to his gore days with *Cat in the Brain*. However, the comparatively low gore factor in *The Psychic* and *Manhattan Baby* didn't stop them from finding an audience, so his decision to go plasma-free here shouldn't prevent any of his fanatics from seeking this one out. The arty, meandering tone of the story is offset by a strong, paranoid, somewhat Brad Dourif-like performance by the still-busy Savage (definitely the biggest name Fulci had in the second half of his career), and his decision to shoot on the obscure back roads of Louisiana rather than the familiar tourist areas makes for much more visual interest than usual for the area. Of course, this also means some weird, stilted performances by some of the locals who were apparently non-actors recruited on the spot (check out the two cops), and the one-off score by Franco Piana veers wildly from jazz to thunking suspense cues, with some uncredited filler dropped in from the score to *StageFright*. Incredibly, this was the first Fulci score released in its entirely on CD, while the film itself was barely distributed at all, popping up most widely as a Japanese VHS which barely made a blip on the bootleg market.

Like most Filmirage productions, *Door Into Silence* seems designed more for home video than the big screen, so it's not surprising all the masters are full frame. Nothing substantial seems to be missing on the sides, and the 1.33:1 framing actually looks about right. (The same goes for most of D'Amato's films from around the same period.) The transfer used for Severin's DVD, the first release ever in the U.S., is several notches above the mediocre VHS dupes floating around for years; it won't win any AV awards given the nature of the source, but it's surprisingly colourful and clean and still plays well on larger monitors, too. Bear in mind it'll still look like a 1991 low budget production, and the disc comes through just fine. The mono English audio (which uses on-set dialogue recording for all the actors) sounds okay and true to the original sound mix.

The DVD is no frills, containing only chapter stops from the main menu. Someone should get around to asking John Savage about this film one of these days, as his memories of its creation would be quite interesting. An Italian DVD on the Raro label is also available (featuring the same transfer) with the original English track as well as the Italian dub and an interview and commentary with Fulci writer Antonio Tentori (in Italian only), who is joined on the latter by Fabio Giovannini.

DRACULA'S DIRTY DAUGHTER

Colour, 2000, 81m. / Directed by Michele Pacitto / Starring Alysabeth Clements, Gentle Fritz, Thomas Martwick, Justiz Donaldson / Secret Key (US R0 NTSC), Third Millennium (UK R0 PAL)

 It's hard to ignore a movie with cast names like "Gentle Fritz" and "Alysabeth Clements", so anyone with a tolerance for soft-focus lesbian erotica posing as a vampire flick might want to check out this financially-impoverished but skin-rich offering. Apparently this one snuck out on video before under the title *Mistress of Seduction*, where it unsurprisingly went unnoticed.

In any case, the story revolves around, yes that's right, Dracula's daughter, Vampirina (Clements), a bloodsucking lesbian who feeds from town to town with the aid of her Sapphic groupies. When she finds the beer-swilling reincarnation of the vampire hunter (Thomas Martwick) who killed her dad, she decides to throw a little sacrificial ritual in between same-sex sessions with all the nearby women.

While Clements gives a decent lead performance and the story idea is solid enough, the final result is something of a mixed bag, featuring a few too many scenes of people sitting dead still in the middle of the frame yakking or getting it on with each other under bleached-out, soft focus lighting. That said, the vampiric aspects are handled well enough by director Michele "Mike" Pacitto, and the final few minutes feature sufficient kinky mayhem and blood-dribbling to justify a rental. The transfer does what it can considering this was shot on a camcorder, and the audio ranges from adequate to muffled. Extras include a reel of cast auditions (with almost everyone cracking up), some outtake footage (mostly from the sex scenes), and the usual barrage of cross-promotional trailers. The same transfer was released in the U.K. by Third Millennium as a no-frills disc under the slightly altered title of *Dracula's Dirty Daughters*.

DRAGON PRINCESS

Colour, 1976, 90m. / Directed by Yutaka Kohira / Starring Sonny Chiba, Etsuko Shihomi, Yasuaki Kurata

KARATE WARRIORS

Colour, 1976, 89m. / Directed by Kazuhiko Yamaguchi / Starring Sonny Chiba, Akane Kawasaki, Akiko Koyama / Navarre (US R1 NTSC) / WS (2.35:1) (16:9)

 The second Sonny Chiba two-pack in the "Welcome to the Grindhouse" series (following the double bill of *The Bodyguard* and *Sister Street Fighter*) pairs up a couple more video favourites in new scope transfers easily worth the upgrade. *Dragon Princess* (*Hissatsu onna kenshi*) features Chiba as master karate instructor Higaki, who squares off against four thugs intent on taking his title. Blinded in one eye and beaten nearly to death, he moves to New York where he hones his daughter (*Sister Street Fighter*'s Etsuko Shihomi) into a razor-sharp killing machine to avenge him. Obviously this isn't purely a Chiba showcase, but it is a terrifically enjoyable martial arts flick and a good example of funky '70s action filmmaking.

Chiba returns in *Karate Warriors* (*Kozure satsujin ken*) as Chieko, a loner who uses his skills to play two rival gangs off each other. Yes, it's another rehash of Dashiell Hammett's *Red Harvest* (already the subject of unauthorised remakes like *Yojimbo*, *Last Man Standing* and *A Fistful of*

Dollars) and a pretty cracking fun one at that with as much blood and nudity as a restricted rating will allow. Image quality of the anamorphic scope transfers is vastly superior to average martial arts presentations, even if you can only watch them dubbed in English. The films can be played separately or with the "Grindhouse Experience", which tosses in trailers for *The Bodyguard*, *Legend of the Eight Samurai*, *9 Deaths of the Ninja* and *Sister Street Fighter*.

DRAINIAC

Colour, 2000, 81m. / Directed by Brett Piper / Starring Georgia Hatzis, Alexandra Boylan, Ethan Krasnoo / Shock-O-Rama (US R0 NTSC) / WS (1.78:1) (16:9), Lighthouse (UK R0 PAL)

 If you're familiar with the works of shoestring monster auteur Brett Piper, the title *Drainiac* should already give you a very good idea of what to expect – namely an FX-heavy, gooey dive headfirst into B-movie creature feature territory. Easily the most confusing entry in Piper's filmography, the movie first popped up on rental shelves back at the beginning of the '00s in an essentially unauthorised, unfinished state which left many customers utterly confused by what their DVD player was unleashing upon their fragile psyches. The eventual authorised special edition from Shock-O-Rama thus marks a world-wide debut of sorts, touting it as being "fx-enhanced" in a "never-before-seen cut". It will take a hardier soul than I to catalogue all the differences, but the feature itself seems to boast much better colour grading and slicker (and wetter) FX.

As you can no doubt guess, the entire story revolves around the horrors unleashed

when something liquid and very pissed-off terrorises anyone who enters a decrepit old house, all via the plumbing. The sleeve describes it as a "water demon" though that's more specific than what the story itself implies, with a tentacled, shape-shifting villain shimmying up and down the sinks and toilets while taking more than a few cues from the '88 remake of *The Blob*. The victims include a couple of bums in the prologue and other peripheral characters, but most of the focus rests on the usual clutch of twentysomething dim bulbs led by a stable of TV and straight-to-video actors like Alexandra Boylan and Georgia Hatzis. (Who, you ask? Look 'em up on IMDb and find out!) Piper even throws in a exorcist, err, aquacist for the splashy finale.

The DVD sports a very nice transfer, which benefits from the fact that this was shot on film rather than video (Super 16mm, according to the extras) with a decent enough audio track, mostly featuring dead-centre mono dialogue with some occasional channel separation in the music and gurgling sound effects. Piper contributes another breezy commentary track focusing on the production itself (its fate is covering in the liner notes), with Shock-O-Rama head Michael Raso essentially sitting in as moderator. Not a bad package at all if you're hungering for some pre-CGI monster mayhem that will make you think twice before turning on the garbage disposal. An earlier, extras-free release from a more dated fullscreen transfer is also available from Lighthouse in the U.K.

EAGLES OVER LONDON

Colour, 1969, 111m. / Directed by Enzo G. Castellari / Starring Frederick Stafford, Van Johnson, Francisco Rabal, Evelyn Stewart (Ida Galli), Luigi Pistilli / Severin (Blu-ray & DVD) (US R0 HD/NTSC), Optimum (UK R2 PAL) / WS (2.35:1) (16:9)

Following the chaotic military attack at Dunkirk, Captain Stevens (Frederick Stafford from *Topaz*) realises that dead English soldiers are now being impersonated by German spies (led by Francisco Rabal and Luigi Pistilli) and plan to subvert plans for the Battle of Britain by attacking the RAF's radar system. Stevens and his colleague (Van Johnson) – both of whom have eyes for the same woman (Evelyn Stewart) – must put aside their differences and lead the Allies through a series of ground and aerial showdowns leading to a fiery climax in the skies.

After directing a string of accomplished but mostly anonymous spaghetti westerns, action specialist Enzo G. Castellari leaped forward with one of his most ambitious, large-scale efforts, a sprawling World War II adventure designed to compete with popcorn films like *The Dirty Dozen* and *The Great Escape*. Obviously the star power and effects budget are considerably more modest here, but Castellari pulls off a string of impressively massive scenes involving vast military manoeuvres and ambitious split screen effects. Most of the actors walk through their paces professionally enough (only accomplished pros Rabal and Pistilli really get a few moments to shine), but war film fans will enjoy the twisting plot and many combat scenes involving jeeps and dog-fighting planes. Much of the last reel is hampered by reliance on some pretty awful scratchy stock footage, but otherwise it's a solid, efficient, enjoyable film that lays the groundwork for Castellari's more famous '70s spin on WWII, *The Inglorious Bastards*, which also features a militaristic score by Francesco De Masi whose origins can be found here.

Released in Italy as *La battaglia d'Inghliterra*, this was one of numerous films made with assistance from United Artists who had made a cottage industry of bringing Italian genre films to English-speaking audiences, such as Clint Eastwood's spaghetti westerns. For various reasons this film broke very widely outside of Europe, eventually getting dumped in the U.S. by Cineglobe and receiving only a few sparse TV airings. Severin's release on both DVD and Blu-ray offers the first chance many viewers will ever have to see the film outside of a repertory screening, and a fine presentation it is once you take into account the patchwork methods used in its creation. Various scenes involving opticals (the main and closing titles, the split screens, some rear projection) look ragged and a bit grainy, of course, but the vast majority of the film looks just fine and is thankfully accurately presented in its original scope aspect ratio, which is absolutely essential to understanding what's going on in almost every scene. The only option is the original English audio track, which is fine considering that's the only one featuring the real voices of many of the main leads. Of course, the added clarity of the Blu-ray will also drive WWII purists mad as the often incongruous Italian locations, extras and costumes are only more obvious, but for pasta cinema fans, that just adds to the fun. Extras here include the second half of an impassioned discussion between Castellari and a very caffeinated Quentin Tarantino (part one can be found on Severin's *Inglorious Bastards* release), while both men also appear for an in-person Q&A at the Silent Movie Theatre in Los Angeles following a screening of the film. The original theatrical trailer and a short deleted scene from the German print (with subtitles) are also included and, on the Blu-ray, are also retained in full HD. The same transfer was later picked up for U.K. release by Optimum, who also carried over the Tarantino/Castellari interview.

EMBODIMENT OF EVIL

Colour, 2008, 94m. / Directed by José Mojica Marins / Starring José Mojica Marins, Jece Valadão, Milhem Cortaz / Anchor Bay UK (DVD & Blu-ray, UK R0 PAL/HD) / WS (1.78:1) (16:9) / DD5.1

Though his Zé do Caixão character (better known as "Coffin Joe") appeared in some form or another throughout numerous films by flamboyant horror director José Mojica Marins (he of the long black hat and much longer fingernails), only three have focused solely on this character for the entire length of a feature. The first two, *At Midnight I'll Take Your Soul* and *This Night I'll Possess Your Corpse*, depicted his anti-hero as a young, fiery, atheistic agent of anarchy who uses sadism to continue his bloodline with women both willing and coerced. Decades later, Marins returned to the character as an older, greyer, and even creepier figure in *Embodiment of Evil*, which begins with Coffin Joe released from an asylum onto the streets of Brazil. Joined by a hunchback assistant, he resumes his activities by recruiting new followers (each of whom must pass trials by fire involving loaded pistols and flesh removal) and seeking a new female to bear his spawn. However, he also suffers ghostly (and extremely effective) visions of those he killed in the past, while a brutal police officer (whose wife was responsible for freeing Coffin Joe) decides to put this menace back behind bars.

The idea of making a Coffin Joe film in the 21st Century seemed like a foolhardy task in an age of Rob Zombie and *Saw*, but somehow Marins managed to pull it off. Still spouting melodramatic sermons and wielding his corkscrew fingernails, he integrates flashbacks from the first two films into a macabre tapestry of brutality and peculiar beauty, with the usual gallery of oddball actors willing to perform grotesque acts on camera all for the sake of art. Anyone uninitiated into the singular visions of Marins might be put off by the theatricality of his direction and performances, but that's really part of the charm; it's all an extreme but oddly charming act whose artificiality is reinforced by such devices as frequent wipe transitions between scenes and the very clever idea of making the ghostly appearances monochromatic within the film in-camera using clever make-up and lighting.

Anchor Bay U.K.'s release of this film marked the first English-friendly version anywhere in the world and looks fantastic. The HD transfer is pin-sharp and extremely fresh, while the archival clips from the first two films look so good you'll wish they could go back and retransfer those entire features from the negatives in hi-def, too. Audio is presented in robust two-channel stereo as well as a more muted and ultimately ineffectual 5.1 mix (presented as lossless 5.1 on the Blu-ray, but the 2.0 one is still better). Extras include the theatrical trailer and a half-hour featurette with plenty of footage from the set as Marins's son and various crew members talk about the production.

Marilyn Monroe "look-alike" (at least so her press claims) who basically strolls around the Côte d'Azur, hopping in the sack with strangers and doing impromptu striptease routines. Apparently this was released in 1985 (complete with video-generated opening credits), but it looks for all the world like something patched together with bits shot throughout the same early '80s period as another Cannes exploitation item, *The Last Horror Film*. And it has a cameo from Benji, which has to be an exploitation first.

Director Jean-Marie Pallardy specialised in French hardcore, and while some scenes here might have been shot a bit more explicitly than what's in the final version (particularly a ménage a trois halfway through), this is softcore all the way. That makes this a bit of an odd choice for classic porn label Halo Park, who made a detour from vintage hard-X releases to a handful of Pallardy soft titles like this one, which features the most commercial title even if it's the weakest in the batch. The very short film is presented in non-anamorphic widescreen, roughly 1.78:1, and also includes a batch of sanitised trailers for additional, far more graphic titles.

EMMANUELLE GOES TO CANNES

Colour, 1980, 77m. / Directed by Jean-Marie Pallardy / Starring Olinka Hardiman, Zeta Whitehouse, Giorgos Delerno, Glynis Whitman / Halo Park (US R0 NTSC) / WS (1.78:1)

This bewildering mess of a film relies on overuse of random Cannes footage loosely tied together by the presence of sex starlet and future porn veteran Olinka Hardiman, a

AN EROTIC WEREWOLF IN LONDON

Colour, 2008, 69m. / Directed by William Hellfire / Starring Misty Mundae, Anoushka, Darian Caine, Julian Wells / Seduction Cinema (US R0 NTSC)

While Misty Mundae was apparently shooting around 50 films a week during her Seduction Cinema glory days, a few projects somehow managed to slip between the cracks and

never see a release. One very cheap but interesting oddity which reared its furry head long after she went legit is *An Erotic Werewolf in London*. Barely running over an hour and delivering the lycanthropic goods only in the final few minutes, it's another excuse to get Misty unclothed and rolling around in various beds with other girls. The packaging claims this was actually shot in London, though 99% of it takes place in anonymous apartment rooms that could easily be on your street corner. Anoushka co-stars as the queen werewolf who's going around converting other young females into her fold, including Misty of course. The company's other regulars like Darian Caine and Julian Wells also pop up for the obligatory thigh-rubbing and other lipstick lesbian antics. The film was originally made in 2001 by William Hellfire but remained unfinished on the shelf until 2008, a convoluted story covered in the DVD's liner notes by Ed Grant which actually makes for a more compelling work than the main feature. Also included in the two-disc set is a bonus unreleased and evidently incomplete feature, *Night of the Groping Dead*, though in this case it's easy to see why it never saw the light of day as it's really bargain basement and incoherent, worth a look only if you're a really, really avid shot-on-video softcore completist. Extras include the usual trailers, a "Reminiscing with Ruby LaRocca" featurette about shooting the sex scenes, and a commentary with Hellfire and producer Michael Raso which crams about as much information as they can into the very short running time. Mistyphiles should be quite satisfied, while newcomers will have no idea what they're watching.

L' ÉROTISME

Colour, 2000-2007, 88m. / Cinema Abattoir (Canada R0 NTSC) / DD2.0

A helter-skelter mix of experimental short films, *L'érotisme* feels like a grittier, grungier response to erotic anthology films like the infamous *Destricted*, which it nearly matches in terms of explicitness and fortunately exceeds in entertainment value. Neither collection really qualifies as "erotic" (at least for most people), but this has a lot in its favour if you know what you're in for. The first and least interesting short, "Ritualis", is a quick Canadian piece that pretty much feels like a mid-'90s Goth metal video with lots of blown-out contrast, deep reds and browns, and Satanic orgy imagery. The end result is competent but fades from memory as soon as it's over. 2005's "Maldoror: A Pact with Prostitution" comes off like a dirtier-than-usual Guy Maddin short, using faux silent movie techniques for a series of mildly kinky tableaux. The self-explanatory "Ass" from 2001 is, well, nine minutes of a woman assaulting herself through the title orifice, rendered in a strange, hypnotic editing style. The Canadian "KI" depicts a three-minute act of oral pleasure in an abstract, jittery filmic style that pretty much counteracts any possible categorisation as pornography. The Belgian "La fin de notre amour" is basically an ode to self-mutilation as a muse inspires a man to literally open himself up to his writing; it's striking and strange, never wearing out its welcome. The equally anti-erotic "Extase de chair brisée" is another Canadian offering, this time from 2005, as a woman on a country road is roughed up and kicked around by two hooligans in leather, who soon get their just desserts. Shot in very gritty black and white, this wouldn't be out of place in the filmographies of Michael or Roberta Findlay. The equally unsettling but narrative-free "Baby Doll" from 2006 (those Canadians again!) has the title object being subjected to a variety of indignities on camera, while the prize for most disturbing short easily goes to "The Loneliest Little Boy in the World", which spends five unforgettable monochromatic minutes with a woman in black leather dancing in flames and getting down with a severed pig's head. Finally the set winds up on its most blatantly explicit note with "Paranoid", as a woman uses a variety of sex toys to show off while grinding away to a heavy metal song.

A limited edition of 500 units (with 40 copies in even more limited metallic cases), *L'érotisme* is consistent with other short collections as its quality varies according to the source. Some are deliberately grungy, but others are clear and colourful. Aspect ratios shift between full frame to about 1.85:1, and the stereo audio is fine. Extras include two additional shorts, the 13-minute "D'Yeux" (basically a series of erotic art images) and "Imperatrix Cornicula", which spends about ten minutes depicting a woman's feather self-pleasure. Though an interesting package, it's probably not the best viewing option for couples night (unless you're very broad-minded) but certainly worth checking out if you're a fan of Borowczyk, Matthew Barney, Richard Kern or other artists unafraid to fuse sexuality with art.

THE ESCAPEES

Colour, 1981, 102m. / Directed by Jean Rollin / Starring Laurence Dubas, Christiane Coppé, Marianne Valiot, Louise Dhour, Nathalie Perrey, Brigitte Lahaie / Redemption (UK R0 PAL, US R0 NTSC) / WS (1.66:1)

Withdrawn asylum inmate Marie (Christiane Coppé) finds her daily routine of sitting outside in a rocking chair disrupted with the arrival of Michelle (Laurence Dubas), who decides to drag her along on an escape attempt into the woods. In the outside world they hook up with a travelling circus called "Maurice and His Exotic Dancers", become entangled with a gang of bikers, drink wine and have sex with a bunch of social dropouts on a ship, mingle with some lesbian sailors and a lesbian Brigitte Lahaie, and finally meet their violent destiny on a rain-soaked pier. Hey, it could happen to anyone.

As Rollin himself admits in the supplementary interview to this DVD, *The Escapees* (original title: *Les paumées du petit matin*) had few commercial prospects since it's not a horror film and doesn't quite qualify as erotica either. However, it is a Rollin film through and through, which means dreamy pacing, tender and tragic emotional bonds, and frequent imagery involving theatrical performers and the ocean. The film features most of the same technical team from his peak period in the early '80s, and the film definitely shares a similar mood to *The Night of the Hunted* and *Fascination* with regular composer Philippe D'Aram contributing another lyrical electronic-tinged music score. Anyone unfamiliar with the director's work will be completely baffled, but Rollin junkies seeking a fix of his unique poetic style will find plenty to appreciate.

Redemption's release transferred from the original negative is about on par with their prior Rollin releases, presented in a slightly letterboxed, interlaced non-anamorphic transfer that looks a bit dated and rough at times but is certainly watchable. The only really substantial extra here is a new 32-minute Rollin interview in which he discusses the film in depth, saying "enough with the vampire films" at the time as he wanted to do a "real film with a real story". However, he wound up working with two different scripts put together and had to adapt severely along the way during shooting, particularly with the haunting ice rink scene, which was "terrible" on paper but wound up being the best moment in the entire film. A stills gallery and additional, unrelated Redemption trailers fill out the rest of the disc.

EUGENIE DE SADE

Colour, 1970, 91m. / Directed by Jess Franco / Starring Soledad Miranda, Paul Muller, Jess Franco, Alice Arno / Blue Underground (US R0 NTSC) / WS (1.66:1) (16:9), Wild East (US R1 NTSC), Oracle (UK R0 PAL), X-Rated Kult (Germany R0 PAL) / WS (1.66:1)

Not to be confused with several other de Sade-inspired Jess Franco films bearing "Eugenie" in the title, this deeply kinky vehicle for the director's short-lived muse, Soledad Miranda, plays a bit like an incestuous take on *The Honeymoon Killers*. Miranda stars as the title character, a young woman first seen in a dreamy snuff film seducing a woman who winds up murdered by an off-screen assailant. Turns out the culprit is her stepfather, a debauched writer named Albert (Paul Muller), who has been gradually indoctrinating her into a lifestyle of nightclubs, models, seduction, and murder, with the two carrying on a sadistic affair linking all their victims. Unfortunately one male victim threatens to come between their unholy alliance, with a knife blade ultimately determining the fate of all involved.

Boasting another top-notch Bruno Nicolai score (Franco's composer of choice on many of his best films for Harry Allan Towers and Eurociné), *Eugenie de Sade* received little notice upon its release but gradually built up word of mouth through its video incarnations to become one of the director's most fascinating and respected titles. The presence of Miranda certainly doesn't hurt, as this essentially completes a fascinating trilogy with *Vampyros Lesbos* and *She Killed in Ecstasy* demonstrating what an iconic sex-horror figure she could be. (Her other supporting roles for Franco are less substantial but worth seeking out as well.) Muller matches her throughout as the multi-layered older man who has controlled his beautiful charge's destiny since doing away with her parents, and the snowy settings add a unique atmospheric edge different from the usual Franco beachscapes.

Incredibly, this once-neglected gem has now seen no less than four different incarnations on DVD, though only one really does it justice. The first American release from Wild East offered most viewers their first peek at the film, even though the ragged full frame transfer and dismal English dub track couldn't come close to approximating its aesthetic virtues. A subsequent PAL release in the U.K. presented the far superior French track with English subtitles as well as minimally letterboxing it at 1.66:1, but print quality was still way below par; a German variant presented another lacklustre transfer with a German audio track added as well. Blue Underground's much-needed release is culled from the original negative and easily blows other versions out of the water; the gasp-inducing clarity of the opening images carries through the entire feature, with beautiful detail and colour rendition creating a hallucinatory treat rivalling the finest Franco digital releases to date. You really couldn't imagine this film would ever look so good. The disc also contains both audio options, but only masochists would choose to wade through that muddy, poorly-voiced English track again. This transfer also bears a title card reading *Eugenia*, that carries over to the theatrical trailer which is a bit different from past releases (and confusingly scored with Bruno Nicolai's "De Sade 70" cue from *Eugenie... The Story of Her Journey Into Perversion*). The only other extra is "Franco De Sade", a 20-minute featurette with the typically entertaining and heavily-accented director talking about the film, with a particular focus on his paternal relationship with Miranda. For some reason the hilarity of his interviews has a converse relationship with the quality of his films; since this is a great movie, it's more sedate and touching than, say, *Cannibals*, which is a riot from start to finish. A sterling release all around; however, it's worth nothing that while the European DVD editions are now rendered completely obsolete, completists might want to hang on to their Wild East disc since it contains some tantalising fragments from unfinished Franco Eurociné projects which have failed to materialise elsewhere.

EXECUTIVE KOALA

Colour, 2005, 85m. / Directed by Minoru Kawasaki / Starring Hitomi Takashima, Arthur Kuroda, Eiichi Kikuchi / Synapse (US R1 NTSC) / WS (1.85:1) (16:9) / DD2.0

Even by Japan's standards, Minoru Kawasaki has already proven himself as one of the wildest directors around. No, not in a Takashi Miike-esque excessive way, but in a sort of whimsy shot with adrenaline fashion that makes his freaky creature-filled tales unlike anything else around. They don't always work necessarily, but the results are worth checking out if you want to see something really, really different. His *Calamari Wrestler* was released early on in a mediocre DVD edition, but Synapse has definitely given him a bigger push with no less than three titles at once in their

Kawasaki collection. *Executive Koala* is a riveting study of modern psychological disassociation and corporate chicanery. Oh, and the lead is a human-sized koala. With a rabbit for a boss. No other explanation provided. Turns out our koala hero, Tamura, is in hot water when his girlfriend is slain and the cops finger him as the primary suspect, which also causes trouble for his job at the pickle company. Is he responsible on some subconscious level? Why is there a musical number? And then there's the big martial arts finale which finds him swinging away at a kung fu vixen.

At times this almost feels like a Brad Anderson film (especially *The Machinist*) even with the oversized animal heads, and the occasional bursts of bloodshed push it into horror territory from time to time; however, the sheer peculiarity of the treatment could only have come from one director. The more linear and interesting storyline pushes this a notch above the director's *Rug Cop*, and if you're looking for a place to start, this could do the trick. Extras include the trailer and a making-of covering the film's very quick (one week!) shoot.

EXORCISM

Colour, 1975, 89m. / Directed by Juan Bosch / Starring Paul Naschy, Grace Mills, Maria Perschy, Maria Kosti / Victory Films, distributed by BCI Eclipse (US R0 NTSC)

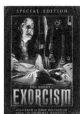

While it spawned a fair share of imitators across the globe, 1973's *The Exorcist* had its most profound cinematic seismic effects in Europe where deep Catholic cultural influences inspired filmmakers to offer their own stories of manly priests facing down plucky possessed adolescents. Though not as well known as its more extravagant Italian cousins, *Exorcism* presents a uniquely Spanish take courtesy of horror legend Paul Naschy in a rare heroic role. The film begins with pretty Leila (Grace Mills) joining her hippie boyfriend for a Satanic ritual out in the middle of nowhere, with plenty of blood spilling into goblets. No sooner than you can mutter "*Dracula A.D. 1972*", she smashes her car on the way home and then becomes possessed by a diabolical force – well, the spirit of her brutish dead father, anyway. Her mom Patricia (Maria Perschy) is none too pleased when Leila (who's also the object of lust for every male employee affiliated with the household) starts disrupting birthday parties and flailing around on the floor, and nasty murders begin occurring nearby. Can burly Father Adrian (Naschy) purge the demon from her body before it's too late?

As with most Spanish horror films of its era, *Exorcism* was prepared in versions tailored to both its puritanical domestic release and saucier markets abroad. Even so, the nudity and bloodshed are mostly confined to the opening and closing sequences with lots of angst-ridden scenes in between as Leila's family squabbles and tears itself apart under the watchful eye of the tobacco-loving priest. Luckily the horror passages are lively enough to ensure a modest cult following, with a particularly amusing German Shepherd bit at the end that predates *Suspiria*. Director Juan Bosch doesn't do much to lend any style or atmosphere (or even give it a coherent ending), but Naschy's committed participation (which extended to writing the screenplay, which he insists predates William Friedkin's film) and the fun Hammond organ-laced score by enigmatic composer Alberto Argudo will bring a smile to the face of any Eurocult devotee. And like most *Exorcist* cash-ins, this one made a mint around the world and proved to be one of Naschy's most commercial outings.

Previously released in a terrible bootleg DVD edition that still litters a few shelves, *Exorcism* gets a much-appreciated revamp courtesy of BCI Eclipse's lovingly-assembled special edition. Though the film has a rather dark and muted mid-'70s look, the picture quality is miles ahead of any other incarnation, video or theatrical. For some inexplicable reason the film is presented completely open matte, though compositions look much better cropped off to around 1.78:1 on widescreen TVs (with the credits obviously framed to be seen in this aspect ratio as well). So if you can zoom in to cut off that empty space at the top and bottom of the screen, do it; the film plays much better like that. Either way the picture quality is fantastic, though. The audio can be played either in the original Spanish (thank God) with optional English subtitles, or the amusingly ham-fisted English dub track. Once again Naschy participates in an interview about his film, and he's informative and engaging throughout as he talks about the place of this film in his body of work, his thoughts on writing it, and the circumstances of horror filmmaking in '70s Europe. He also provides an amusing video intro in which he talks about how the film might be enough to convince him to believe in "dark forces". Other extras include an English-language theatrical trailer (also open matte), alternative "clothed" scenes (which involve sheets and dresses transparent enough to still qualify as nude scenes), stills and promotional galleries, the Spanish-language credit sequences, and more informative, well-written liner notes courtesy of Naschy authority Mirek Lipinski.

EXPOSED

Colour, 1971, 90m. / Directed by Gustav Wiklund / Starring Christina Lindberg, Heinz Hopf, Björn Adelly, Siv Ericks / Synapse (US R0 NTSC) / WS (1.66:1) (16:9), Revelation (UK R2 PAL) / WS (1.66:1)

Still a hot ticket in cult circles mainly thanks to *Thriller: A Cruel Picture*, Swedish sex goddess Christina Lindberg experienced a home video resurgence in the DVD age with many previously undiscovered gems coming to light. However, one of her more widely seen vehicles in theatres around the world took its sweet time to come out digitally, but the wait was worth it. *Exposed*, better known to grindhouse patrons as *The Depraved*, features La Lindberg as Lena, a sweet-looking nymphet who, this being Sweden in 1971, is willing to hop in the sack with anything in or out of pants. She ditches her hot-tempered boyfriend when he doesn't take kindly to her handing out favours to other men, and soon she's crossing the countryside swinging her hair out with her boyfriend and an older, blackmailing suitor hot on her heels. Dirty pictures, dirty deeds, and lots of turtleneck sweaters ensue.

As usual Lindberg manages to elevate the material, another "bad girl in trouble" yarn given an extra boost by her wounded eyes and electric carnal presence – so much so that none of the other cast members have a hope of making an impression. Her surprising third-act bondage scene is likely to win over a few fans, too. Shot with an artistic eye and gift for austere atmosphere by director Gustav Wiklund (who inexplicably did almost nothing afterwards), *Exposed* uses a fragmented structure that makes the tale seem a bit more convoluted and meaningful than it probably is, but the whole thing is still easy enough to follow and quite solid as a slice of vintage Eurosex.

The original Swedish soundtrack is the sole option here with English subtitles on Synapse's DVD release (too bad the English dub couldn't be licensed just for posterity, but that's the breaks), and the anamorphic 1.66:1 transfer looks pretty good considering the film's rarity. Some print damage is evident from time to time and flesh tones tend to veer a bit towards the brownish side (a characteristic common to Swedish titles issued by Impulse, which is also released through Synapse) but that's really the only drawback. The extras are more generous than usual for a title like this, including both the Swedish and American trailers (the latter of which appeared way back on the first *42nd Street Forever* trailer compilation), two great rare vocal tracks recorded by Christina back in her heyday ("Allt Blir Tyst Igen" and "Min Enda Van"), a stills gallery, and definitely the best of all, a great featurette called "Over-Exposed" with Lindberg (who still seems fragile and quite pretty) and Wiklund discussing everything from the making of this film and its worldwide reception to other topics including Lindberg's early career. A non-anamorphic transfer was issued in the U.K. by Revelation as one of the entries in their 3-disc *Swedish Erotica Collection 1* (along with *The Language of Love* and *Anita*) but it lost 12 seconds due to BBFC restrictions concerning the depiction of underage nudity in a magazine picture.

FANTASTIC PLANET

Colour, 1973, 71m. / Directed by René Laloux / Eureka (UK R0 PAL), Accent (US R0 NTSC), GCTHV (France R2 PAL) / WS (1.66:1) (16:9), Anchor Bay (US R0 NTSC), Force (Australia R0 PAL) / WS (1.66:1)

A French companion piece to the rising wave of adult-targeted animated features that would soon become a pop culture mainstay, *Fantastic Planet* marked the feature film debut for French surrealist and animator René Laloux. While animation was on the decline in the United States primarily due to the temporarily aimless state of Disney following its founder's death, Laloux's film injected a surprising dose of oddness and a mature, individual sensibility which immediately marked it as a cult item in the making. The production also boasted reputable credentials, particularly co-writer Roland Topor (a skilled fantasist who collaborated on Laloux's earlier short films and remains best known for *The Tenant*) and music composer Alain Goraguer, a composer and pop music figure who often worked with the legendary Serge Gainsbourg. Presented under the auspices of co-producer Roger Corman's New World Pictures, *Fantastic Planet* surmounted many obstacles (such as relocating its staff from Prague to Paris due to the story's inflammatory anti-communist undercurrents) and managed to take home the 1973 Cannes Film Festival's Grand Prix.

Loosely derived from the Stefan Wul novel *Oms en série*, the barely linear storyline takes place on the planet Ygam, where giant, blue-skinned tyrants called the Draags regard their fellow human-like planet dwellers, the tiny Oms, as trifling creatures not above the level of playthings. One orphaned Om named Terr becomes the pet of a Draag girl and, enlightened by her educational tools, uses his newfound knowledge to aid his brothers in a revolt against the increasingly violent giants.

The basic themes of this film have an obvious kinship with other significant fantastic works like *The Time Machine* and *Yellow Submarine*, but this particular version carries a singularly odd twist at the end and feels like a more heartfelt protest against oppression; in this respect it can also be read as a precursor for the likes of *The Matrix* as well as the anything-goes alien landscapes of subsequent Japanese artists like Hayao Miyazaki. Furthermore,

while the film bore a family-friendly PG rating, its often sensual imagery of female bodies affiliated it squarely with the rising fan base for magazines like *Heavy Metal* and the animations of Ralph Bakshi and his successors. Seen today without any context, *Fantastic Planet* can be a befuddling and often disorienting experience, but viewers willing to open their minds and truly immerse themselves in an alien vision with its own peculiar rhythms and logic will be rewarded.

Laloux's career trajectory shares many parallels with another groundbreaking European surrealist, Alejandro Jodorowsky. Both directors became affiliated with the outlandish Panic Movement, a berserk artistic theatrical association in France and Spain, which had been primarily founded by Topor, and both Laloux and Jodorowsky caused a sensation with their debut features (*Fantastic Planet*, originally entitled *La planète sauvage*, and *El Topo* respectively), only to encounter considerable obstacles which kept their infrequent, subsequent features from reaching the same audiences. The counterculture aspects of *Fantastic Planet* were lost on no one, but children and adults alike were even more entranced with its colourful, often indescribable imagery unlike any other environment captured on film.

Numerous DVD editions of this film have appeared over the years, each quite different from the last. A flat, dated-looking disc from Anchor Bay with burned-in subs quickly went out of print (and was later rehashed for an equally underwhelming Australian release), paving the way for a far more definitive anamorphic edition in the U.K. from Eureka (still the most visually superior of the lot) containing the English and French audio tracks with optional English subtitles as well as extras including two Laloux shorts ("Les escargots" and "Comment Wang-Fo fut sauvé") and a hefty 40-page booklet. (The French release is comparable in quality but features no English language options.) A subsequent U.S. reissue from Accent features a more problematic anamorphic transfer (the PAL conversion didn't quite go flawlessly) and carries over "Les escargots" while adding a nice new half-hour Laloux interview and a Sean Lennon video ("Would I Be the One") inspired by the film. Eureka simultaneously released editions of Laloux's other two feature films, *The Time Masters* (*Les maîtres du temps*) and *Gandahar*, which come recommended as well.

FAST COMPANY

Colour, 1979, 91m. / Directed by David Cronenberg / Starring William Smith, Claudia Jennings, John Saxon, Nicholas Campbell / Blue Underground (DVD & Blu-ray, US R0 NTSC/HD) / WS (1.85:1) (16:9) / DD5.1/DTS 7.1

Years before he melded his body grotesqueries with car collisions in the controversial *Crash*, director David Cronenberg helmed this more straightforward ode to one of his more obscure passions, competitive auto racing. Another tax shelter Canadian project incredibly made back-to-back with the equally personal but far more harrowing *The Brood*, this film offers straight-up drive-in entertainment with a solid cast of B-movie legends.

Facing the end of his run on the drag strip due to approaching middle age, racer Lonnie Johnson (*Grave of the Vampire*'s William Smith), dubbed "Lucky Man" by his fans, is about to lose the sponsorship of the motor oil company with which he's become identified under the rule of a hard-nosed CEO (John Saxon). Aided by his beautiful younger girlfriend, Sammy (Claudia Jennings), he tries to keep up with the accelerating demands of his dangerous profession.

At first you'd be hard pressed to peg this as a Cronenberg film, though the presence of regular collaborators like actor Nicholas Campbell and cinematographer Mark Irwin give it the uniquely '70s Canadian feel also found in his more fantastic projects. You also get an attention-getting scene involving the erotic use of motor oil, which is difficult to forget. However, the actor chemistry is the biggest difference here mainly due to the presence of Saxon, an industry vet from films like *Enter the Dragon* and *Black Christmas*, who really anchors his scenes with great authority. Perhaps even more significant is Jennings, a hugely popular *Playboy* Playmate whose film career had already amassed such credits as *'Gator Bait*, *Deathsport*, *Moonshine County Express* and even a quick bit in *The Man Who Fell to Earth*; unfortunately *Fast Company* would prove to be her cinematic swan song as she died in a car accident shortly after filming, at the age of 29.

Blue Underground's elaborate special edition of this film puts many studio efforts for the director's more prestigious titles to shame with an impressive transfer and a comprehensive roster of extras. Mastered in HD, the film looks terrific and sounds even better with an immersive surround mix. (The original mono is present on the DVD while the Blu-ray ditches it in favour of three similar 7.1 options in Dolby Digital or DTS.) Cronenberg contributes another of his excellent solo commentary tracks and shares many memories of Canadian filmmaking at the time and how his passion for racing fuelled the entire project. Then Smith and Saxon appear for an interview featurette in which they recall how they become involved with the film and the state of their careers at the time, with both coming across as animated and full of enthusiasm. Irwin gets a separate interview discussing his relationship with the director and how they approach the visual scheme for each of their films, and you also get the original theatrical trailer. Both the double-disc limited DVD edition and regular Blu-ray offer the heftiest and more desirable extras: Cronenberg's two most famous early "short" films, *Stereo* (1969) and *Crimes of the Future* (1970), both of which are virtually feature length. The former is an obvious dry run for ideas later explored in *Scanners* and *The Brood* as a psychology researcher at a clinic uses brain surgery to cut off verbal communication from a group of volunteers, but the study begins to go awry as the psychological ramifications begin to manifest themselves. *Crimes* is far less accessible and definitely feels more like an early trial project as a skin doctor named Adrian Tripod (Cronenberg regular Ronald Mlodzik) in a clinical, emotionless future begins to tamper with a contagious version of sexual hysteria, ultimately blurring the lines of gender identity. Both are highly visionary and fascinating films, especially for Cronenberg fans, and are worth the effort to find this release by themselves.

A FEAST OF FLESH

Colour, 2007, 77m. / Directed by Mike Watt / Starring Amy Lynn Best, Stacey Bartlebaugh-Gmys, Sofiya Smirnova, Debbie Rochon, Rachelle Williams, Mike Watt, Zoe Hunter, April Burril / Bloody Earth (US R0 NTSC) / WS (1.78:1) (16:9)

Happy Cloud Pictures, the fellows who gave you such films as *Weregrrl* and *Severe Injuries*, go a bit more ambitious and upscale with this outing, originally announced under

the title *Abattoir*. As far as direct-to-video vampire movies go, it's a lot more complex and thoughtful than most with a twisty story about a gang of horny guys going for a trip to the remote Bathory Brothel and becoming entangled with the disappearance of one guy's girlfriend, who's fallen in with the mysterious ladies of the evening. In this case, that also means they're bloodsuckers. Turns out the brothel and the township have an agreement not to tangle with each other as long as no residents get pilfered, but now the deal's broken and a squad of vampire hunters comes a-calling.

The DVD packaging plays up the "violence, eroticism and throat-ripping bloodlust", though be advised that most of that hits in the second half; the set up is still interesting, though, and worth getting through. Some nice touches abound, including the means used to ward off the vampires (including blessing an Arrowhead bottle), and the lack of budget and hit-and-miss videography still yield a few nice visual effects. And since Dennis Miller isn't around, this is automatically a lot more fun than *Bordello of Blood*. Bloody Earth's DVD features an anamorphic transfer that looks about as good as the uneven source material will allow, and the cast features a few recognisable faces like scream queen Debbie Rochon (*Terror Firmer*) and Chainsaw Sally (aka April Burril) along with the usual Happy Cloud regulars (Amy Lynn Best, director Mike Watt, Zoe Hunter). Extras include a making-of featurette, lighthearted audio commentary with Watt and Best, a five-minute gag reel (mostly hard to hear, unfortunately), additional trailers (*American Punks*, *Blood and Sex Nightmare*, *Killing Machine*), and a pretty nifty 15-minute short film, "A Feast of Souls", about two guys lost in the woods who become entangled in a gory, time-warped nightmare involving slavery and redneck soldiers.

FELICITY

Colour, 1979, 94m. / Directed by John D. Lamond / Starring Glory Annen, Chris Milne, Joni Flynn, Jody Hanson / Severin (US R0 NTSC, UK R0 NTSC), Umbrella (Australia R0 PAL) / WS (1.85:1) (16:9)

 In this successful Australian softcore comedy, the title character, a Catholic schoolgirl, finds her budding sexuality prodding her to go ballistic during a trip to the Far East. Unlike many sex comedies which tend to be rather sexist and sniggering, this one is good-natured and fair to both sexes, with Glory Annen making an attractive and sympathetic lead who never comes off as calculating or stupid. The music is bouncy and enjoyable (with a great theme song), the direction keeps things bopping along nicely, and it doesn't end with any tragedy or moralising, thank goodness.

The DVD edition marks the international debut of the longer director's cut with some additional saucy footage. Director John D. Lamond and Annen turn up on the disc for an entertaining commentary track; both sound quite proud of the film and look back on it with fondness, talking about the location shooting, dealing with the heavy amounts of nudity, and their careers ever since. Other goodies include the theatrical trailer and a stills gallery. A modest but very satisfying little digital treat, lovingly presented all around. The same disc was released uncut in the U.K. by Severin, whilst the Australian edition from Umbrella added an interview with the director and the featurette "Confessions of an R-Rated Movie Maker" (which was also included on their disc of *Pacific Banana*, reviewed later in this book).

FEMALE PRISONER: CAGED!

Colour, 1983, 68m. / Directed by Masaru Konuma / Starring Mina Asami, Shigeru Muroi, Hitomi Yuri / Mondo Macabro (US R0 NTSC) / WS (2.35:1) (16:9)

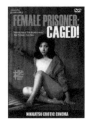 You don't have to be a trash film expert to guess right away that *Female Prisoner: Caged!* (*Joshû Ori*) is a women-in-prison movie, but no one could guess how truly perverse and over-the-top it really is. Complete with kinky wardens, bondage, lesbianism, and one scene of boffing so vigorous and graphic it had to be optically censored on the prints (including this one), this slammer saga is a short and rich feast of drive-in trash, filthy and sweaty and completely devoid of social significance. *Chained Heat* has nothing on this one.

The threadbare story, which might as well star Linda Blair, finds troublesome inmate Masayo (*Dolls of the Shogun's Harem*'s Mina Asami) hauled back to jail after a botched escape attempt, with the warden deciding to not just punish her but make her a case study in how far a prisoner can be degraded. Cat fighting in the jail yard, kinky fetishist male visitors (including some wince-inducing foot worship), and the usual bursts of violence keep things interesting for the quick running time, with our heroine subjected to pretty much every bodily emission imaginable and almost all the inmates participating at some point in this hell behind bars.

Mondo Macabro's disc (a companion release to the slightly less extreme *Sins of Sister Lucia*) features a solid anamorphic transfer of a film made when Nikkatsu was veering away from shooting all of its titles in scope. The informative "Erotic Empire" Roman Porno special prepared for the British *Mondo Macabro* TV show is also added, with participants from the era discussing their memories along with critic Jasper Sharp, who also appears separately for another video discussion solely about this film. The company's co-founder Pete Tombs provides his usual knowledgeable and thorough notes about the production and crew, with a batch of additional Nikkatsu trailers added to lure viewers deeper into these grimy celluloid waters.

THE FERNANDO ARRABAL COLLECTION 2:
CAR CEMETERY
Colour, 1983, 90m. / Directed by Fernando Arrabal / Starring Alain Bashung, Richard Leduc, Juliet Berto, Serge Feuillard, Dominique Pinon
THE EMPEROR OF PERU
Colour, 1982, 81m. / Directed by Fernando Arrabal / Starring Mickey Rooney, Anick, Jonathan Starr, Ky Huot Uk
FAREWELL, BABYLON! / BORGES: A LIFE IN POETRY / ARRABAL, PANIK CINEAST
Colour, 1992-2007, 109m. / Directed by Fernando Arrabal / Cult Epics (US R0 NTSC) / WS (1.66:1) (16:9)

 Most seasoned film fans had little to no familiarity at all with director Fernando Arrabal when Cult Epics unleashed two of his most startling films, *Viva la muerte* and *I Will Walk Like a Crazy Horse*, as standalone DVD editions and then a later box set with another film, *The Guernica Tree*. Surreal, aggressive, smart, and often hysterical, these movies were best received among fans of the director's closest contemporary, fellow Panik Movement innovator Alejandro Jodorowsky, whose own return to prominence on DVD around

the same time signalled an unusual cosmic harmony among the cinematic powers that be. The second batch of Arrabal titles from Cult Epics is definitely not meant to be approached by anyone unfamiliar with at least one or two of his other films, but for those who know what they're getting into, prepare for six hours of mind-spinning madness you'll never forget.

First up is *Car Cemetery* (*Le cimetière des voitures*), a production first shown on French television that plays like *Godspell* staged by New Wave clubbers dropping acid in a junkyard. The plot is essentially a string of vignettes echoing the life of Christ from the Nativity to crucifixion, albeit now populated by a bunch of eccentric characters including thieves, thugs, hookers, and a host of visual surprises like one character turned into a jarred homunculus. The messiah character, Emanou (Alain Bashung), is also something of a musical saviour (not named Tommy, however) whose plans for a grand live finale are thwarted exactly as you might expect. Not surprisingly, this originated as a stage play by Arrabal (which was revived as recently as 2007 onstage in the U.K.), who has written over a hundred works for the theatre, believe it or not. For most this will be the prize of the set as it closely reflects its creator's style and vision, mixing social commentary, dark comedy, and plain weirdness together in a unique setting composed mainly of a nocturnal junkyard filled with dismembered vehicles creating odd and striking visual tableaux. The Cult Epics disc is the first DVD available anywhere in the world; it claims to be a new HD transfer and certainly looks it, with excellent visual details and colour fidelity in evidence throughout. The 1.66:1 framing looks accurate as well; there's really nothing to complain about at all with the presentation here, and the optional English subtitles for the French dialogue are excellent.

F

Next is Arrabal's most atypical film, a delicate family fantasy called *The Emperor of Peru* (also shown as *Treasure Train*). However, if you bear in mind that Jodorowsky went on to make a family-friendly, all-star offering in 1990 with *The Rainbow Thief*, this film doesn't seem quite as odd. The French Canadian funding meant that it was prepared in both French and English versions, with the former presented here on DVD. The charming storyline follows two siblings, Toby (Jonathan Starr) and Liz (Anick) whose family temporarily decides to foster a young Cambodian boy, Hoang (Ky Huot Uk). The three children soon discover a crippled railroad engineer in the woods who sparks a string of fantasies and wild ideas which culminate in their decision to take an abandoned train back to Cambodia to reunite the boy with his family. Though suitable for kids, this film is delight-fully odd and fits in snugly with other nutty Canadian family fantasies from the same era like *The Great Land of Small* and *The Peanut Butter Solution*. Again the transfer is miles ahead of the dire VHS versions, though the low budget conditions are still evident in what is probably the best presen-tation possible for this title at the moment.

The third disc features a hodgepodge of Arrabal-related shorter works including "Farewell Babylon", a 54-minute video piece by Arrabal featuring various clips from films interspersed with 1992 New York footage including appearances from some unexpected participants like Spike Lee. It's a solid if odd bonus for completists, but casual viewers will be more rewarded by "Arrabal, Panik Cineast", a one-hour documentary about the director in which his comments and clips are interspersed with stories about his involvement with the wild Panik theatrical movement, including some great interview footage with Alejandro Jodorowsky as well. Rounding out the disc is the longest and most difficult piece, the 66-minute "Borges: A Life in Poetry",

which covers the famous poet's life in fractured snippets. All three of these appear to be shot on standard def video (even VHS in some cases), so don't expect much in terms of visual quality; however, it's a solid, packed bonus disc whose exclusive presence in the box set makes it a no-brainer for cult film collectors.

FIRE AND ICE

Colour, 1983, 81m. / Directed by Ralph Bakshi / Starring Randy Norton, Cynthia Leake, Maggie Roswell, Susan Tyrrell, Sean Hannon / Blue Underground (DVD & Blu-ray, US R0 NTSC/HD), Optimum (UK R2 PAL) / WS (1.85:1) (16:9) / DD5.1/DTS

Though he established his career with extre-mely stylised, adult fare like *Fritz the Cat* and *Coonskin*, animator Ralph Bakshi began making some important changes to his technique as the 1970s ended. First, he began using rotoscoping (drawing over live action performers) in 1977's *Wizards* and 1981's *American Pop*, while the former film also marked his first significant foray into pure fantasy. He continued to explore both with his controversial adaptation of *The Lord of the Rings* and then took a page from the hit film *Heavy Metal* for his third fantasy, *Fire and Ice*, which added the additional commercial element of plentiful female flesh courtesy of assistance from noted artist Frank Frazetta.

Stripping down the appeal of comic book fantasy to its core elements of scantily clad, buxom women both good and evil as well as plenty of body-smashing action, this film tells the sketchy tale of the land of Firekeep, in which Princess Teegra and her kingdom are under threat from the sinister, rapidly-expanding ice kingdom and its ruthless witch leader Juliana and her barbaric son, Nekron. The only hope for salvation lies with two warriors, Larn and Darkwolf, who must save the princess from constant kidnapping threats as well as hordes of monstrous armies performing Nekron's bidding.

Rated PG and yet far too intense for kids, *Fire and Ice* is targeted squarely at comic book fans who might want to introduce newcomers without swamping them in explicit sex and gore. The plotline itself is as basic and predictable as can be, even more conventional than a random episode of TV's *Dungeons & Dragons*. Instead the appeal lies in the marriage of Bakshi's kinetic style and Frazetta's familiar visual obsessions, with fur-lined flesh and metallic weapons constantly filling the screen. It's all diverting enough considering the short running time and has an understandable fan following, but don't expect a towering animation masterpiece.

Blue Underground's basic DVD and Blu-ray editions contain a colourful transfer that perfectly captures the original look of the film. It is often filled with visible dust and speckles on the frames but otherwise looks terrific. The audio is even better, a powerful mixture of room-shaking bass and powerful music blasting from every speaker. It's definitely demo material for an animated title before the dawn of Pixar.

Extras include an audio commentary with Bakshi and Lance Laspina about the project's entire production process from origins to execution, a vintage 13-minute making-of promotional piece transferred from an archived VHS copy, an 8-minute Bakshi video interview about Frazetta, a theatrical trailer, and a 14-minute piece with voice actor Sean Hannon reading his diary notes from the recording sessions. The British DVD contains no extras but features the same transfer. Blue Underground also released a limited two-disc edition containing an extra bonus available exclu-

sively on the second DVD, the feature-length documentary *Frazetta: Painting with Fire*. Bakshi, *Conan the Barbarian* director John Milius, Bernie Wrightson, Dave Stevens and a host of other talking heads appear along with tons of artwork and demonstrations to carefully chart the course of this influential artist.

FIVE BLOODY GRAVES

Colour, 1970, 88m. / Directed by Al Adamson / Starring Robert Dix, Scott Brady, Jim Davis, John Carradine, John "Bud" Cardos / Shock-O-Rama (US R1 NTSC), Eyecatcher (Germany R0 PAL) / WS (2.35:1) (16:9)

NURSE SHERRI

Colour, 1978, 88m. / Directed by Al Adamson / Starring Jill Jacobson, Geoffrey Land, Marilyn Joi, Mary Kay Pass / Shock-O-Rama (US R1 NTSC)

 One of the most amusing aspects of exploitation filmmaking all the way from the beginning is the old bait and switch, with posters promising lurid sex and violence but delivering something entirely different. (Lest you think this trend is long gone, take a look at the poster for *Primeval*.) That spirit lives on with the double-feature release of these two oddball '70s Al Adamson films; of course, cult film fans worth their salt know that the cover art depicting grinning, misshapen ghouls with bloody knives threatening busty women is just a fake come-on for what's really inside, namely a more-violent-than-average western and a mild blaxploitation-friendly imitation of *The Exorcist*.

For the first film, western actor and occasional Adamson star Robert Dix stars and even chipped in on the screenplay for the story of a loner gunman pitted against a mad scalping Apache named Satago (played by future *Mutant* director John "Bud" Cardos, who also appears in the film as his own do-good brother!). John Carradine and a slew of '50s B-movie actors also turn up to provide local colour and enough body count potential in keeping with the Adamson tradition. Though this is one of the director's more widely-circulated non-horror outings, it has never fared too well on video and doesn't do much better here. The bolted-down framing chops away over half of the original scope compositions (so much for appreciating some early work by Vilmos Zsigmond), making it a real chore to sit through, but at least it looks a few generations above the PD versions that have blighted shelves for years. C'mon, Sam Sherman – grab that negative out of the vaults! Fans eager to see the film in true anamorphic widescreen may want to hunt down the Eyecatcher DVD from Germany (as *5 blutige Gräber*, featuring a trio of alternative covers), but this turns out to be a mixed blessing as seven minutes of footage are missing and included only as full screen extras.

Up next is *Nurse Sherri*, presented on disc one with its video-altered title of *The Possession of Nurse Sherri*. It's an amusing but disposable cash-in of every possession and demonic-related title you can name from the '70s (along with obvious nods to Roger Corman's successful series of nurse drive-in films), as the titular nurse (Jill Jacobson) gets possessed by a big green blob of protoplasm and starts unleashing some telekinetic whoop-ass all over the hospital. Disc two contains the alternative sexy cut of *Nurse Sherri*, which prunes away a lot of PG-rated exposition in favour of cheesecake topless shots and lots of softcore heavy petting. (This version was also available on the previous standalone release and for many viewers plays a lot better.) Extras include the usual Sam Sherman commentaries (with some

additional Dix commentaries thrown in for the first film), a previously unreleased alternative prologue(?) to *Five Bloody Graves* with Dix engaging in a flashback love scene, a video interview with Marilyn Joi, and a drive-in experience option that throws in lots of vintage interstitials and Adamson-related trailers. Finally, the set comes packaged with an amusing liner notes discussion between Chris Poggiali and Adamson biographer David Konow, who point out such titbits as the narrative debt *Five Bloody Graves* owes to *The Seventh Seal*!

FOLLOW ME

Colour, 1969, 75m. / Directed by Gene McCabe / Starring Bob Purvey, Claude Codgen, Mary Lou McGinnis / Scorpion (US R0 NTSC) / WS (1.78:1) (16:9)

"Some people might call this a wild adventure. We call it surfing around the world!" So begins the enthused narration of one of the more blatant *Endless Summer* knockoffs that proliferated throughout the late '60s and early '70s, this time following a merry band of dedicated wave seekers from California and Florida as they travel across the globe. Among the participants are Mary Lou McGinnis (from Redondo Beach, who "looks better than she sews"), Claude Codgen (a Florida native who enjoys reading goofy books like *How to Escape the Portuguese Shark Danger*), and Bob Purvey, our Malibu-based guide first seen dozing on an international flight and eyeballing sexy stewardesses. After watching a short called *California Surfbirds*, they land in Portugal where we get lots of travelogue footage and dreamy shots of our intrepid surfers facing some formidable riptides off the beaches of Guincho, Nazare and Cascais. Then it's off to Morocco (where bystander camels provide comic relief), Ceylon, India, Hong Kong (where they try water skiing behind a fishing junk), a crowded Japan featuring indoor swimming pool surfing, and, of course, the gorgeous Hawaiian Islands where the waves look as big as skyscrapers.

Short, sweet, and summery, *Follow Me* (no relation to the excellent 1972 Carol Reed film of the same title) obviously doesn't try for much of a narrative as it consists of 90% surfing footage. Purvey's narration (actually provided by voice artist and character actor Jerry Dexter of Hanna-Barbera fame) takes a back seat to the real attraction here, an absolutely killer wall-to-wall soundtrack provided by Stu Phillips just before he started work on *Beyond the Valley of the Dolls*. Many sequences sound like a dry run for that Russ Meyer film, particularly when accompanied by the surf pop vocals of Dino, Desi and Billy on catchy songs like "Thru Spray Colored Glasses", "Like the Wind and Sea", and "Just Lookin' for Someone". Hilariously, they even provide the song ostensibly performed by a Japanese pop band surrounded by go-go girls in bikinis. This is ear candy of the best kind, essentially turning this into a string of music videos that will delight anyone with an affinity for surf-oriented pop culture ephemera.

Though it garnered a fairly respectable theatrical release from Cinerama and its soundtrack album has remained a popular collector's item for decades, *Follow Me* has been strangely elusive throughout most of the home video era. Fortunately that oversight is corrected with Scorpion's DVD, which makes the most of the highly variable film stock used throughout the global shoot. The vast majority of the movie looks great, though a handful of early shots have a bluish or greenish tint that appears to be the consequence of inadequate shooting

conditions or really odd lab processing. If you've ever seen any Bruce Brown surfing films, this is about on par in terms of cinematic appearance and the amount of damage on what appears to be a 16mm negative source. The sole extra is the original theatrical trailer.

FOOTSTEPS

Colour, 2006, 79m. / Directed by Gareth Evans / Starring Nichols Bool, Mads Koudal, Jared Morgan / Unearthed (US R0 NTSC) / WS (1.78:1) (16:9) / DD2.0

Footsteps is a moody Welsh cross between a British crime film and a violent study in snuff filmmaking. Talented newcomer and Brad Renfro look-alike Nicholas Bool stars as Andrew, a twentysomething left disoriented by the loss of his parents who becomes entangled with a bunch of counterculture lowlifes headed by Paul (Danish actor Mads Koudal), a bearded sleazebag who, along with his boss and cameraman, has taken the concept of bumfights to the next level by staging real violence and death for commercial profit – all captured on video.

Tightly constructed at less than 80 minutes and very sparing with dialogue, the film is surprisingly restrained given its subject matter (most of the brutality is unleashed in the final few minutes) and for once the whole snuff idea isn't thrown in as a titillating and ill-advised gimmick. The surprisingly solid performances ground what could have been another disposable indie, and while up and coming filmmaker Gareth Evans's visual style wavers a bit from scene to scene, he still achieves some striking moments of kitchen-sink trauma when it's least expected. The fully-packed disc from Unearthed comes with a ton of extras including nearly an hour of interviews with the cast and crew, a quick making-of featurette, additional featurettes devoted to the visual effects, props, dolly rig and music score, some inconsequential deleted footage, a trio of alternative takes for one dialogue scene, a stills gallery, and the original trailer.

FORCED ENTRY

Colour, 1973, 83m. / Directed by Shaun Costello / Starring Harry Reems, Jutta David, Ruby Runhouse / After Hours (US R0 NTSC), Alpha Blue (US R0 NTSC)

One of the darkest, nastiest films ever made, this exercise in sheer, unbridled brutality was marketed as an adult film but features all the titillation value of watching Zapruder's JFK assassination footage. Audiences must have reacted in stunned disbelief when this thing unspooled in theatres, and it's been a forbidden underground video fixture ever since. This was the first directorial outing for exhibitionistic director Shaun Costello, who started out performing in loops and soon began filming himself in a string of grim, better-than-average smut films. However, this will always be his best-known and most controversial title.

After a gut-churning Vietnam atrocities prologue, Harry Reems (looking unsettlingly deranged without his trademark moustache) appears as an unhinged Vietnam vet, now a gas station attendant who's prone to peeping in windows and invading apartments where he attacks women at knifepoint. Reems's hateful speeches in this film really have to be heard to be believed, and the unrelentingly despairing tone puts *Forced Entry* in much

closer company with *Combat Shock* or *In a Glass Cage* than *Deep Throat*. It's also a fascinating snapshot of early '70s New York, with several recognisable locales which still exist to this day.

The transfer is taken from the only located film print around, and it looks fine enough presented in its original 1.33:1 aspect ratio (don't try matting this off on a widescreen TV; the compositions don't work). The picture quality isn't perfect given the nature of the film's history, but it's a lot better than the muddy VHS conversion included in Alpha Blue's Shaun Costello/Avon box set. Also, no After Hours logo appears anywhere on the print – yay! This marks the first instalment in their "Grindhouse Directors" series and remains their most controversial (at least until they get around to a special edition of *Waterpower*). Extras include a knockout set of liner notes written by Costello himself, charting his entry into the industry and his reasons for making this film (the Vietnam footage was included for "social significance", of course). You also get a trio of ragged-looking loops, all under 10 minutes (with Reems and Costello making separate appearances), plus a newly-created trailer. Approach with extreme caution.

THE FOREST

Colour, 1981, 85m. / Directed by Donald Jones / Starring Dean Russell, Gary Kent, Tomi Barrett, John Batis, Ann Wilkinson / Code Red (US R0 NTSC) / WS (1.78:1) (16:9)

One of numerous forest-oriented horror films churned out on home video to capitalise on the slasher craze (see also: *Don't Go in the Woods* and *The Final Terror*, among many others) with a very cheap, convenient location, *The Forest* manages to carve the story down to its bare bones while offering a few novel twists along the way to make it worth a look. In a hook similar to Lucio Fulci's *House by the Cemetery* of the same year, two ghostly children haunt the woods where their still-living father, a cannibal lunatic (Gary Kent) who killed his family, lives in seclusion, offering suspicious sweetmeats to any passing campers who don't immediately fall victim to his hefty blade. Rather than delivering the expected splashy gore and T&A, the film instead takes its time, first with a prologue in which a young couple gets bumped off in the middle of nowhere, and then with the plot proper as two husbands, Steve (Dean Russell) and Charlie (John Batis), and their wives, Sharon (Tomi Barrett) and Teddi (Ann Wilkinson), rendezvous in the same spot (but nobody seems too interested in their spouses, giving this film some peculiar subtext) only to encounter both the maniac and his ghost kids. Much running through the dark woods ensues, and the killer's ghostly wife pops up to shriek a few ill-timed warnings, too.

Though *The Forest* will probably have zero appeal to newer horror fans weaned on the likes of *Saw*, this schlocky little bottom-of-the-barrel number will have plenty of nostalgic value for '80s video hounds who might remember salivating over the eye-catching Prism VHS cover in every single mom-and-pop video store in existence. Featuring the most obnoxious theme song this side of *Silent Running* and an utterly perplexing finale, it certainly doesn't feel like your average slice-and-dicer but doesn't seem too intent on building up the characters enough to make you care, either. Instead it lingers somewhere in between, aiming for atmospheric isolation and natural texture (you get lots of shots of vegetation here) while occasionally remembering to throw in a little screaming or knifing,

mostly in the last 20 minutes or so. Director Donald Jones had already established himself as a worthwhile sleaze auteur with *The Love Butcher* and the very underrated *Let's Play Dead* (aka *Girls in Chains*), while leading man Kent (who gives the best performance in the film by far) had a solid drive-in career stretching back through the '60s with such disparate credits as *The Thrill Killers*, *The Mighty Gorga* and a slew of biker pics. Between them, it's not surprising that Code Red's DVD release is a whole lot more interesting for the extras than the movie itself.

The feature film is presented in anamorphic widescreen from what appears to be a still-decent print that's been through a few projectors in its time. Colour presentation looks okay, but blacks are inconsistent (in what looks more like a flaw with the cinematography); also, something appears wonky with the aspect ratio which looks a little squeezed flat at 1.78:1 but too thin squeezed out to full frame. Maybe this was shot at 1.66:1 and smushed a bit for theatres, or something else went amiss during the telecine process. The mono soundtrack is okay and limited by the threadbare original source. As for extras, the packaging doesn't really list much, but this is a fully-loaded special edition dealing with just about everything you could ever possibly want to know about *The Forest*. Jones and Kent contribute a fact-packed commentary track covering the financing, shooting and casting, and they seem pretty pleased with the results. Then Jones and cinematographer Stuart Asbjornsen join up for a much lesser moderated track that retreads the same material, just a lot slower and less interesting; stick with the director/actor track, which feels much fresher. Then all three men pop up on-camera for a 13-minute featurette that encompasses the film from a broader scope, including some unfortunate fallout for the director afterwards; despite the bleachy, low-grade camcorder lensing, it's entertaining and worth a peek for any aspiring horror filmmakers or actors, especially to learn about pitfalls to avoid. Other bonuses include a stills gallery, a newly-cut promo trailer, and a slew of other Code Red trailers.

42ND STREET FOREVER VOLUME 2: THE DEUCE

Colour, 2006, 121m. / Synapse (US R1 NTSC) / WS (1.78:1) (16:9)

Ready for another two-hour helping of oddball trailers for long-forgotten celluloid curiosities? The *42nd Street Forever* series steps up to bat again with a hit-and-miss collection whose high points make it an easy recommendation for vintage trailer buffs, including a few rarities unavailable elsewhere. First up is the absolutely killer trailer for Abel Ferrara's *Ms.45*, a hypnotic mini-masterpiece inexplicably left off the DVD release (but included on the original unrated laserdisc version), followed by Billy Jack's first cinematic outing, the biker classic *Born Losers*. You get a nice chunk of '70s drive-in fun with the William Devane/Paul Schrader Vietnam vengeance classic *Rolling Thunder*, the Lee Frost moonshine/vigilante feature *Dixie Dynamite*, the biker flick *Hells Angels on Wheels* (with a young Jack Nicholson), MST3000 favourite *The Hellcats*, the '50s JD hot-rodder *Dragstrip Riot*, and the gun-packed '70s speeder, *Stingray*. Take a drag through the Valley with Crown International's *Van Nuys Blvd.*, the proper car racing drama *Burnout*, and the weirder "anything on four wheels" mudfest, *Dirt*. Blaxploitation gets a workout with the tough-to-see *Savage!* and the wild-looking *Kenner*, followed by the southern-fried dramatics of *...Tick...Tick...Tick*, the colour-

blind western *Take a Hard Ride*, the urban action of *Samson* and *The Guy from Harlem*, and of course, that memorable zombies-and-voodoo AIP favourite, *Sugar Hill*.

Head across Europe next for the dopey Italian comedy of the Senta Berger vehicle *When Women Had Tails*, the trendsetting Swede sleaze of *I, a Woman*, the softcore smut of *The Curious Female* and the B&W *The Babysitter*, the colourful *Street Girls* and monochromatic *College Girls*, Crown's randy *The Pom Pom Girls*, the birth-of-a-baby angst of *Helga*, the super-roughie action of *Invitation to Ruin*, the frisky road antics of *Pick-Up*, the cons-and-cuties weirdness of *Delinquent Schoolgirls*, the AIP Filipino explosions of *Savage Sisters*, and for some reason, the B&W Jayne Mansfield vehicle, *Female Jungle*.

Then it's time for gargantuan stars of a different kind with a bunch of '50s monsters both big and average: *Gigantis the Fire Monster* (a retitling of the second Godzilla movie also known as *Godzilla Raids Again*), *The Giant Gila Monster*, *The Hideous Sun Demon*, and the much rarer *The Monster of Piedras Blancas*. The trippy 1970 AIP trailer for *Murders in the Rue Morgue* pops up (looking a tad more ragged than the one on the MGM DVD), followed by the Richard Gordon Brit-horror oddity *The Woman Eater*, the wacko alien-monster thrills of *The Dark*, and an absolutely riotous trailer for the Richard Crenna/Joanna Pettet horror freak show, *The Evil*, that must've packed 'em in back in '78. Then it's back to AIP again for the mostly-forgotten rural terrors of *The Evictors* (featuring the always welcome Jessica Harper), Wes Craven's underrated Hittites-and-spiders mish-mash *Deadly Blessing* (featuring a very young Sharon Stone), and upgraded versions of the two often-seen trailers for *Rabid* and *The Texas Chain Saw Massacre*.

Whew! Yes, there's more, like the long and very freaky, text-heavy promo for *The*

Clones, the '50s sci-fi fun of *Mission Mars* (featuring a disturbingly young Darren McGavin), the silly Terence Hill action of *Mr. Billion*, Brett Halsey and Dana Andrews doing the Eurospy thing in *Spy in Your Eye*, the slapstick stupidity of *The Last of the Secret Agents?*, the what-the-hell shoot-'em-up *Trunk to Cairo*, and the ridiculous James Bond knock-off, *Kiss the Girls and Make Them Die*. Want some peplum? Howzabout *Amazons of Rome* with Louis Jourdan, the wacko muscleman-and-Zorro outing of *Samson and the Slave Queen*, and the decidedly more lavish *Revolt of the Slaves* (with Rhonda Fleming) and *The Revenge of the Gladiators*. Though neither of them are mentioned on the back sleeve, the disc closes out with two of its finest offerings, the reworked Lone Wolf and Cub Americanisation of *Shogun Assassin* and the unique, disco-heavy charms of *Skatetown U.S.A.*, featuring a young, gum-popping Patrick Swayze. After that, your brain will explode.

42ND STREET FOREVER VOLUME 3: EXPLOITATION EXPLOSION

Colour, 2008, 101m. / Synapse (US R1 NTSC) / WS (1.78:1) (16:9)

 After the head-spinning and wildly contrasting first two entries in Synapse's editions of the *42nd Street Forever* series (with an unannounced detour into classic porn), things swerve heavily into '70s and early '80s action territory with this lively entry, a successful stab at a pure party disc which even newcomers can appreciate. The disc opens with a cute cartoon bumper similar to the kitty-car "Restricted" notice and jumps into the explosive trailer for *Sudden Death*

with Robert Conrad, Don Stroud, and lots of punching, shooting, and soul brother karate chopping. Packed with fake Anglo screen names, *The One Armed Executioner* is a particularly berserk martial arts/action epic packed with grenades, helicopter mayhem, and villages exploding all over the place (and narrated by that guy who did most of Russ Meyer's voiceovers). "Martial arts superstar" Joe Lewis stars in *Jaguar Lives*, a mostly forgotten but entertaining piece of drive-in trash starring Barbara Bach, Capucine, Christopher Lee, Donald Pleasence, John Huston and Joseph Wiseman, plus one of the funniest motorcycle gags you'll ever see. Then it's Cannon time with the amazing *Enter the Ninja*, which made Sho Kosugi an '80s action icon and dumped Franco Nero and Susan George into the story of a "white ninja". The Lone Wolf and Cub classic *Lightning Swords of Death* pops up with its original Columbia Pictures trailer; though not as outrageous as the legendary *Shogun Assassin*, it's an interesting example of how this epic series was originally pitched to audiences. The immortal kung fu classic *5 Fingers of Death* (featuring a quick cameo from that familiar "Ironside" theme) makes an inevitable appearance; this one tore up the grindhouse crowds in the '70s and deservedly remains one of the most popular films of its kind. Finally, the martial arts wing of the collection wraps up with Antonio Margheriti's weird spaghetti western chop-socky fusion, *The Stranger and the Gunfighter*, which teams Lee Van Cleef with *5 Fingers* star Lo Lieh and kept circulating for years under a variety of titles like *Blood Money*.

The horror section comes next, carrying over the Italian thread with Ovidio Assonitis's smash *Exorcist* copy, *Beyond the Door*, with a pregnant Juliet Mills rasping, puking, and sending kitchenware all over the screen. A truly great trailer for the truly terrible *Demonoid* somehow manages to make this Samantha Eggar/Stuart Whitman turkey look like a stylish, violent shocker, with a great table-smashing gag really standing out. Then it's back to Italian *Exorcist* territory again with *The Night Child*, a scope trailer (for a non-scope film) featuring Nicoletta Elmi ("Just keep saying to yourself: She's just a child! Just a child!") as another tyke gone bad. And speaking of evil kids, the ridiculously brutal trailer for *Devil Times Five* ("...leaves nobody alive!") features cute little nippers unleashing mantraps and piranhas against a bunch of unsympathetic adults in the woods. Two *Carrie* rip-offs follow with *Patrick* (its American trailer, which is different from the one included on the movie's DVD release) and the ridiculous *Jennifer*, which features Bert Convy and John Gavin in another schoolgirl-gone-evil tale. The excellent *Phase IV* is the sole directorial outing for pioneering credit designer Saul Bass, and the killer trailer on display here is inexplicably absent from the official DVD released by Legend Films. Naturally, you'd have to follow that one with *Bug*, William Castle's memorable nature-amok offering with big hell-beetles munching away at a small desert town. (Its inclusion here should please everyone let down by this feisty trailer's absence on Paramount's DVD release of the film itself.) "The most fiendish, the most fascinating creature of all" attacks next in the British anthology film *The Uncanny*, which recounts three tales of terror instigated by, uh, housecats. The trailer's a riot, though, with Peter Cushing, Donald Pleasence, Samantha Eggar, and Ray Milland all trying to look terrified of hissing kitties. Lest cat lovers be offended, things get remedied next with *The Pack* as Joe Don Baker contends with a rampaging group of bloodthirsty canines on the loose (mostly in slow motion). As the voiceover helpfully intones, "Last summer they were pets; now they are predators!" The familiar trailer for *Alligator* is always a winner; this John Sayles-penned flick still

holds up as a classic of its kind, and the suggestive trailer still works just fine. Things get much junkier with the charmingly stupid *Killer Fish*, Antonio Margheriti's disco-scored rip-off of *Piranha, Earthquake* and *The Deep* starring Lee Majors and Karen Black. Similarly, Cornel Wilde's *Shark's Treasure* features solemn voiceovers trying to grab the *Jaws* crowd while obscuring most of the crime aspects. The movie ain't bad, though. The hilarious *Blood Beach* gets a suitably goofy trailer, featuring perhaps the most bizarre, stoned-out narration ever recorded for a mainstream release. Meanwhile, John Saxon and Burt Young do their best to look serious with lines like "Just when you thought it was safe to go back in the water... you can't get to it!"

The sexploitation section commences with that bubble-headed Cannon ode to the wet T-shirt craze, *Hot T-Shirts*, which basically plays like a long Hooters commercial set to disco music (directed by porn vet Chuck Vincent, no less!). *Cheerleaders' Wild Weekend* tries its best to look like a raucous comedy ("It'll grab you by the pom poms!"), completely obscuring the fact that this Bill Osco drive-in special is really a violent kidnapping crime story, and not a bad one at that. At least *Summer School Teachers* is a genuine trashy sexploitation comedy, with Dick Miller shouting his way through a bevy of nubile cuties in tight shorts and tank tops. One of the best trailers on the disc, *Gorp*, features close-ups of talking mouths to tout this "insulting" and "offensive" film; the movie itself, starring a young Dennis Quaid and Fran Drescher, isn't anything special, but the trailer is a blast. The raunch continues with a terrific trailer for the cinema's most epic ode to flatulence, *King Frat*, another junky "slob" comedy cable classic just screaming out for a DVD release. The 3-D exploiter *Prison Girls* gets pitched with lots of wakka-wakka funk music, while the similar *1000 Convicts and a Woman* uses the women-in-prison template for lots of sexploitation thrills. The more sedate *Chain Gang Women* still looks great with a psychedelic trailer pushing its more delirious moments, even if the actual film is about as interesting as a flat mug of beer.

Another film still woefully missing from DVD, Peter Collinson's *The Penthouse*, is represented with a killer Paramount trailer; you'll want to see the film (starring Suzy Kendall and Tony Beckley), but good luck finding it. Another sleazy sex-and-violence offering, *The House by the Lake*, was originally a Canadian thriller called *Death Weekend* with Brenda Vaccaro but was retitled to cash in on *The Last House on the Left* (with a very similar trailer to match). Roger Corman's *Night Call Nurses* (directed by future mainstream director Jonathan Kaplan) was the second in the successful series of nurse films, with a bit more perversity here than usual thanks to some bloodshed, cop chases and cross-dressing. More TLC turns up with *The Young Nurses*, a reliably typical offering with lots and lots of bare breasts and hot tub action (along with a quick cameo by Samuel Fuller to keep things interesting). Finally the series wraps up with *Candy Stripe Nurses*, which uses cartoons and weird editing to sell what proved to be a rapidly diminishing franchise. The legally-besieged hardcore cash-in, *The Life and Times of Xaviera Hollander*, features a cast of familiar faces walking through the story of the real-life "Happy Hooker", who's also represented in the more mainstream *Happy Hooker Goes Hollywood* with Martine Beswick as the enterprising madam who taps Hollywood (and, ahem, Batman himself, Adam West).

If you're craving munchies by this point, the sleazy Mexican "true life" story of cannibalistic soccer players, Rene Cardona's *Survive*, pops up with its great American trailer packed with lots of voiceover hyperbole and fake snow. (It was later remade as *Alive*, and the Americanised version dubbed and shortened by Paramount has pretty much vanished from sight altogether.) Cardona returns again with another real-life trashfest, *Guyana – Cult of the Damned*, a shameless all-star piece of tabloid cinematic junk with Stuart Whitman and Joseph Cotten in the true story of suicide cult leader Jim Jones. The action ramps up again with Andy Sidaris's second film, *Seven* (a precursor to his seemingly endless string of '80s boobs and boats cable epics), and the generic Stella Stevens action vehicle *Scorchy*, in which the blonde babe tries to look sexy while shooting randomly at lots of props. One of the most memorable '80s drive-in favourites, *Savage Streets*, features New Wave punks, cheerleaders, cat fighting, and a badass Linda Blair; this wonderfully vile gem is out on DVD as an essential item from BCI, if you can still find it. One of Sam Peckinpah's later and least-remembered films, *Convoy*, stars Kris Kristofferson and Ali McGraw in a fun but weirdly impersonal action movie centred around trucker culture. The mostly improvised result was disastrous but rather compelling when experienced without warning on cable. Jerry Reed narrates his way through the trailer for *High Ballin'*, a mostly forgotten AIP trucker film co-starring Peter Fonda and Helen Shaver which barely played anywhere aside from network TV. The stunts look fun, though. Of course, you need a little Charles Bronson in there somewhere, and here he pops up in the peculiar comic western, *From Noon Till Three*, which still seems to pop up on cable TV every other month for some reason. Catch it if you can and stick around for one of the most out-of-left-field downer endings ever sprung on a comedy audience. More typical of big Chucky is the great late '70s Don Siegel thriller *Telefon*, in which he portrays a non-accented Russian teaming up with Lee Remick to stop a series of sleeper agent assassinations triggered by Donald

Pleasence via telephone. Still not on DVD, but well worth catching on TV. The forgotten '80s thriller *Lies* (from the guys who made *Silent Scream*) is worth seeing if you find it on tape, and the trailer's not too shabby either. Anyone who frequented theatres in the early '80s certainly remembers the weird, minimalist trailer for *Tattoo*, a controversial kinky thriller with Bruce Dern and Maude Adams (who later argued in public about the level of non-simulation involved in their love scenes).

Synapse's anamorphic presentation looks about on par with the previous entries; the transfers are fine in terms of colour and clarity, while the source material varies from one trailer to the next. Some scratches and mild wear are evident, but it's entirely appropriate and rarely distracting; all of them are of the same calibre as most vintage trailers on studio releases, in most cases even higher. Only *The Night Child* really looks messy thanks to an avalanche of red speckles. The mono audio for all of the trailers sounds fine throughout; most of them feature bass-heavy, loud voiceovers which come through loud and clear, with no distracting audio splices to pull you away from the fun. Just fine for what it is. The biggest bonus feature by far is an entertaining audio commentary from the first trailer to the last by *Fangoria* editor and *Leeches* scribe Mike Gingold, encyclopaedic film historian Chris Poggiali, and AVManiacs editor Edwin Samuelson, who run through thumbnail histories of each film and offer some great titbits of info, often related to the regional releases of the films during their initial theatrical runs. In another DVD first, you also get to hear the editor of *Fango* utter "the c word", and don't miss the closing line! Also, a perusal of the special features leads to some fun TV spots for *Jaguar Lives*, *Seniors*, *High Ballin'*, *The Last Survivor* (aka *Jungle Holocaust*), the unbelievable *The Jesus Trip* (with nuns on bikes and shotgun crucifix-

ions!), *Naked Angels* ("whether breakin' heads or smokin' pot, they're the cancer of a sick society!"), *Billy Jack*, and yet another kung fu film, *Golden Needles*. Needless to say, you get your money's worth!

42ND STREET FOREVER VOLUME 4

Colour, 2008, 105m. / Synapse (US R1 NTSC) / WS (1.78:1) (16:9)

A more erratic and sometimes puzzling affair than its prior volume, this annual instalment in Synapse's outrageous line of trailer compilations at least starts with a bang with *The Syndicate: A Death in the Family*, the very obscure American release version of a 1969 Italian crime film called *Colpo rovente*. Best known now for its freak-out music score by Piero Piccioni, this psychedelic mob movie is packed with loads of colours swirling all over the screen and screaming women, with those great wash transitions found in other Italian trailers like *Bay of Blood*. Then it's over to America for *Combat Cops*, a hilarious reissue trailer for William Girdler's *The Zebra Killer*, a trashy, PG-rated cash-in on the *Zodiac Killer* story starring Austin Stoker. Continuing the theme of "movies you can't buy legitimately anywhere" is *It Came Without Warning*, the more verbose re-release trailer for *Without Warning*, a nutzoid, gory alien movie from 1980 (now languishing somewhere in the MGM vaults) with very hammy turns from Jack Palance, Cameron Mitchell, Martin Landau, Ralph Meeker, and Larry Storch, as well as a very young David Caruso. Equally tough to see is *No Blade of Grass*, a now-forgotten 1970 dystopian tale from director Cornel Wilde best known for its MPAA-tweaking violence and depictions of sexual assault. Fortunately things lighten up considerably with *Yor: The Hunter from the Future*, everyone's favourite Italian sci-fi/caveman midnight movie with an unforgettable theme song and some truly priceless dialogue ("Damn talking box!"), none of which is indicated by this trailer focused solely on the action and explosion scenes.

Then we move into horror territory, sort of, with *Simon, King of the Witches*, an oddball, blackly comic look at '70s witchcraft with a dynamic star turn from Andrew Prine and loads of LSD-inspired visual effects. It's available on DVD from Dark Sky should you feel inclined to see more. The American trailer for Lucio Fulci's *The Psychic* focuses mainly on the incredible Giger-inspired poster art and a killer voiceover, with the funky Frizzi-Bixio-Tempera music chugging away in the background. A terrific trailer and a great movie, out on DVD from Severin. From there we go to Cannon Films territory with *Schizoid*, one of the earlier slasher offerings with Klaus Kinski and Donna Wilkes headlining the story of a shrink whose female acquaintances are all getting punctured by a maniac with a pair of scissors. Elvira used to show this one on TV a lot in the '80s, but it's tough to see now. Probably the most familiar trailer on the set, *Tender Flesh*, is a cannibal tale best known as the last film of actor Laurence Harvey. The version on this disc is noteworthy, however, as it opens up with some full frontal Meg Foster nudity missing on other trailer comps as well as many prints of the film itself. A drive-in staple that pushed PG horror a bit further than usual, *Die Sister, Die* is a fun trailer for a lacklustre film featuring most of its gory moments (including a wild decapitation). VHS fanatics still hold some affection for it from its days on Gorgon Video, but if you prefer DVD, it's also out from BCI with a far less entertaining cover. A much better film is *Silent Scream*, a brisk

and sometimes jolting boarding house screamer with Yvonne De Carlo and Barbara Steele; too bad its biggest jolt is spoiled here more than once.

Speaking of startling entertainment, you'll get two solid minutes of it with one of the most hilarious horror trailers ever: *New Year's Evil*, another Cannon title shuffled off to Elvira-ville. The movie isn't quite as fun as the trailer, but then, nothing really could be as the killer's voiceover alone makes it an instant classic. Next up is one of the most sought-after trailers, *Let's Scare Jessica to Death*, which was inexplicably left off of Paramount's bare bones DVD release. This preview must have scared the pants off 1971 audiences, and it's still a doozy today. Far less frightening but much schlockier is 1981's *Mortuary*, featuring Christopher George and a boyish Bill Paxton, which became a Vestron VHS favourite in video stores everywhere back in the '80s before disappearing from the face of the earth. This one plays like more of a teaser and works like a charm with some graveyard mayhem under a full moon. A monster movie marketed as a slasher film due to its early '80s vintage, *Humongous* was one of countless indie horrors unleashed on movie theatres everywhere, and the feisty trailer is actually much more powerful than the movie itself. The great long, super-bloody version of the trailer for *The Werewolf vs. the Vampire Woman* is always nice to see again thanks to its funky animated effects and slo-mo bloodsucking, while fans of big stars slumming in utter trash should get a kick out of *Embryo*, a tacky bit of cloning paranoia with Rock Hudson and Barbara Carrera, sold on this promo simply with some creepy graphics and the odd tagline, "Forget the facts of life" (referring to the TV show, perhaps?). *The Boogeyman* still stands as the most popular film by Uli Lommel, who somehow parlayed Ghosthouse's appropriation of his title into a dubious career churning out the most unwatchable films ever released by Lionsgate (and that's really saying something). Easily one of the weirdest splatter movies yet made, it's colourful, nonsensical, and packed with gore, all of which is captured nicely here. Then you get a double header of "true life" horror, first with an atmospheric promo for *The Legend of Boggy Creek* (a quasi-Bigfoot study with an unlikely G rating) and one of the most in-demand "why isn't this on DVD?" titles, *The Town That Dreaded Sundown*, a killer trailer for one of the most memorable drive-in titles from the late '70s.

God only knows why the trailer for *Grayeagle* is on here, but this AIP-released story of Cheyenne warriors battling in the wilderness has some curiosity value for the presence of Ben Johnson and Jack Elam. A more on-target Indian exploitation film is *Shadow of the Hawk*, which has a rousing trailer with Jan-Michael Vincent facing off against a possibly supernatural, knife-wielding killer and one big-ass bear. Hopefully Sony will get off its butt and put this one on DVD some day. The creepiest of all the *Deliverance* imitations, *Rituals* has become quite the fan favourite in recent years with various trailers for its Canadian and American incarnations (sometimes as *The Creeper*) popping up on various comps. The one here under the original title is the nicest-looking and longest of the bunch, which is always enjoyable; the movie's really excellent, too, and worth hunting down.

One of the odder attempts at a star vehicle for a sitcom star, *Americathon* plunks John Ritter in a whiplash-inducing satire of U.S. culture also featuring Harvey Korman, Meat Loaf, Fred Willard, and a ton of great songs never released on CD. The trailer's fantastic and will be a revelation for many, which might prompt a DVD release so people will stop charging so much money for VHS tapes. *Serial* is better, though. Even goofier is *Can I Do It... Til I Need Glasses?*, a gleefully stupid sketch comedy out on

DVD from Code Red (though its sequel still remains MIA). The biggest shocker on this disc is easily *Die Laughing*, the strangest star vehicle for '70s teen heartthrob Robby Benson. Here he plays a cab driver who gets involved in strange shenanigans thanks to a spy monkey, all executed by the director of *Cheerleaders' Wild Weekend*. However, even that's not as weird as *In God We Tru$t*, a frantic religious satire directed by and starring Marty Feldman, playing a monk tangling with Louise Lasser and Andy Kaufman (as "Armageddon T. Thunderbird") with Richard Pryor popping up as, uh, God. A former cable staple now impossible to see, this should jog the memories of lots of viewers who grew up watching HBO in the '80s. Another forgotten comedy, *Undercovers Hero* is the confused American retitling of *Soft Beds, Hard Battles*, a mediocre Roy Boulting comedy from 1973 with Peter Sellers playing six different roles, including Adolf Hitler.

Fans of Jack Hill's *Switchblade Sisters* should get a kick out of the reissue trailer on view here as *The Jezebels*, complete with the infamous roller rink showdown. This one really needs no further explanation; if you haven't seen Hill's drive-in favourite yet, go out and grab the DVD already. One of many vigilante crime films from the '70s, *Breaking Point* is a violent, T&A-laced offering from Bob Clark (in between *Black Christmas* and *Porky's*) with Bo Svenson as an average dad fighting back against the mob, most memorably with a huge bulldozer. In the same vein, *Fighting Mad* has Peter Fonda, the reliably naked Lynn Lowry, and director Jonathan Demme going through the death wish paces as a farmer hits back against the bigwigs trying to take over their farmland. Another mid-'70s actioner, *Moving Violation* ("It wasn't a joyride!"), stars Kay Lenz and Stephen McHattie as two lovers who witness some corrupt cops committing a murder and have to go on the run in what amounts to a 90-

minute chase scene, with one fun truck stunt stealing the show in the trailer. More gun mayhem pops up in *Bonnie's Kids*, one of the most fondly-remembered vehicles for '70s trash cinema queen Tiffany Bolling, who here is part of a criminal sister team on the run causing trouble in Midwest America. Not surprisingly, most of its wildest and nakedest moments get the spotlight. Bo Svenson pops up again in one of his most famous roles as Sheriff Buford Pusser in *Walking Tall Part II*, breaking up a bunch of fascist redneck justice gangs in the Deep South. But that's nothing compared to *The Klansman*, an all-star Southern shocker with Lee Marvin, Richard Burton, Cameron Mitchell, and, uh, O.J. Simpson; tacky and tasteless in the extreme, it's an insane example of how nuts a major studio (in this case Paramount, back to back with *Mandingo*) could go with a few stars and a questionable script.

The trailer for *Monkey Hustle*, a solid blaxploitation comedy with Rudy Ray Moore and Yaphet Kotto, has been around for years on different comps as well as the feature's DVD release, but it's always nice to see again. Returning to action trash but this time in the early '80s, *The Soldier* is a particularly violent offering with Ken Wahl and Klaus Kinski facing off against a bunch of exceptionally nasty terrorists. *Blackout*, a weirdly endearing 1978 thriller, offers a speculative crime story based around New York City's notorious prolonged blackout, which gives a gang of criminals the chance to run wild. Robert Carradine, June Allyson, and Ray Milland are featured in a truly strange aligning of the casting stars. Speaking of weird casts, Lee Marvin and Roger Moore team up with a bunch of Eurosleaze vets for the decidedly non-sleazy *Shout at the Devil*, an action-packed AIP "prestige" film passed off here like some sort of odd period drama about some really violent hunters. Then you get more big-star action, this time out in the desert, with *March*

or Die, featuring Gene Hackman, Catherine Deneuve, Max von Sydow, Terence Hill, and many more wiping the sand out of their eyes among the French Foreign Legion. Next up you get more period mayhem with a slapstick twist courtesy of *The Loves and Times of Scaramouche*, with Ursula Andress and Michael Sarrazin running around surrounded by lots of flying swords and heaving cleavage. Of course, it was directed by Enzo G. Castellari, which is probably the only reason it's on this disc. How about some bikers? Then take a gander at *Hog Wild* and *The Hard Heads*, or put up with Steve Guttenberg for two minutes' worth of the cable classic *The Chicken Chronicles*. A young Richard Hatch appears for the drive-in Crown International obscurity *Best Friends*, followed by the sports triple header of *Our Winning Season*, *Coach* and the Susan Anton oddity *Goldengirl*. Many of the entries in the second half are way too mainstream or slow-paced and cause the collection to sag quite a bit, but the rarities here (especially *Jessica*) definitely make it worth a gander. Once again you get a commentary track by Mike Gingold, Chris Poggiali, and Edwin Samuelson, which helps guide the collection over a few speed bumps and keeps things lively with lots of trivia, much of it hilarious and sometimes utterly foul.

42ND STREET FOREVER VOLUME 5: ALAMO DRAFTHOUSE CINEMA

Colour, 2009, 99m. / Synapse (US R1 NTSC) / WS (1.78:1) (16:9)

If the last four volumes weren't enough 42nd Street mania for you, Synapse throws a curveball with its fifth compilation of rare and wonderfully twisted trailers by collaborating with the folks at Austin, Texas's legendary Alamo Drafthouse Cinema, which has pretty much become the American epicentre of exploitation movies both current and classic as well as the unofficial home of Quentin Tarantino and his coterie of followers. As usual the trailers flow from one to another in something resembling a coherent theme, and all are bound to grab your attention. Each is transferred from the original film reels, which means you get lots of lovely scuffs and scratches to add to the theatrical experience while the actual transfer quality is about as good as you can get with the elements involved. Of course, the material here is so solid it could be projected in Super 8 on a bed sheet and it would still be terrific.

After an amusing PSA with a tennis-playing Charlton Heston explaining the MPAA system, we dive headfirst into *A Life of Ninja*, featuring a Howard Cosell sound-alike droning over insane footage of sword-slicing mayhem in an alley, a shower, and other inappropriate locations. Oh yes, it's got glowing eyes and ridiculous dubbing, too. Then "when there is only torture, only violence, only death", it's time for 1973's *Sting of the Dragon Masters*, another head-splitting kung fu trailer with Angela Mau – inexplicably scored with Bernard Herrmann's music from *North By Northwest*! You can find this one on Hong Kong DVD under the title *When Taekwondo Strikes*, and it's worth the effort of hunting it down. The American trailer for Sonny Chiba's *The Bodyguard* ("Faster than Ali! Meaner than Bruce Lee!") features another goofball voiceover more appropriate to a *Shaft* film, climaxing with lots of voices shouting "Chiba! Chiba!" in unison for no apparent reason. Of course, Shaw Brothers has to come next with one of their wildest and most frequently reissued titles, *Mad Monkey Kung Fu*, which was made immortal by one of Joe Bob Briggs's more memorable reviews. The insane *Wonder Women*, about a female martial arts hit squad, is really a movie you need to see unprepared for maximum impact, but the trailer does a solid job of conveying the wall-to-wall mayhem that populates one of the '70s strangest action films.

Things get decidedly more juvenile with *Lucky Seven*, a kung fu comedy filled with... badass little kids. They sing, too, and there's a bizarre pregnancy fighting gag you won't see anywhere else. You also get to see lots of kids getting hurled through plate glass windows, which is actually rather disturbing. Enzo G. Castellari's *The Shark Hunter* is one of his lesser-known collaborations with Franco Nero, promoted here with plenty of footage of our blond-wigged hero duking it out with man-eaters in the water. For very different animal interactions, *Birds Do It, Bees Do It* is the "intimate story of animal courtship" which will "never be shown on television". Basically it's a nature film of animals copulating in the wild, including, uh, hippos. Human mating habits come next with *Let's Do It!*, a teen T&A favourite from none other than drive-in king Bert I. Gordon. The VHS is now fetching stupid amounts of money online, but the trailer should give you an idea of what to expect from this silly teen farce. Much more unusual is America's answer to *Pussy Talk*, the Candice Rialson singing-vagina favourite *Chatterbox*, with a mugging Rip Taylor and lots of dubbed-in "hoo hoo" effects over any euphemisms for the female anatomy. *Danish Love Acts* ensures this compilation will never get a PG rating as we see lots of naked couples demonstrating softcore, slo-mo sexual positions to a swinging jazz soundtrack, while Stephanie Rothman's *Group Marriage* is a mostly split-screen trailer featuring a bunch of twentysomethings shacking up together in one house. Much less benign is *Violated!* about a "fiendish monster who RAPES and MAIMS and dumps his victims into the gutter!" Naturally, you don't see any actual footage from the film. *Caged Virgins* is the familiar Harry Novak U.S. trailer for Jean Rollin's *Requiem for a Vampire*, recycled here for the hundredth time but still great no matter how you slice it. After an incongruous commercial for BBQ burgers we segue naturally to the 1978 Japanese sci-fi headscratcher, *Message from Space*, featuring Sonny Chiba in a hi-tech fantasy samurai outfit and Vic Morrow as a boozed-up starfighter blessed by magical space walnuts. The cheapo *Doctor Who* knockoff *The Terrornauts* manages to be even more cut-rate, complete with visible strings on ships and fiery miniatures. By comparison, Roger Corman's *Mind Warp* – a retitling of the awesome *Galaxy of Terror* – looks like an FX masterpiece, and having the great trailer here just makes it more irritating how badly this has been treated on video over the years.

Of course, one of the highlights of this compilation is the original U.S. trailer for Hal Needham's career-ending *Megaforce*, which had early '80s kids in a tizzy until they actually saw the finished product, which managed to knock off Barry Bostwick, Michael Beck and Persis Khambatta from major movie screens forever. The "fearless marauders" of *Zebra Force* deliver nonstop gunfire, car chases and action for two frenzied minutes, while *Blazing Battle* nearly tops it with the story of Indonesians battling "Japanese pigs", courtesy of Rapi Films. Super agent flick *James Tont – Operation O.N.E.* is a ridiculous Italian 007 knockoff, whose subtitled trailer features crude cartoon footage and amazingly has an amphibious car years before *The Spy Who Loved Me*. Oh yeah, and James Tont catches bullets with his teeth. *International Secret Police* is a '60s Japanese spy romp with lots of guys chasing around in the desert and looking for diamonds, while the cool John Cassavetes gangster film *Machine Gun McCain* (which still airs on TV occasion-

ally) contains lots of explosions and nice lashings of Ennio Morricone music. The very early Andy Sidaris boobs-and-bullets outing *Stacey* comes packed with cleavage, helicopter chases, and, yes, loads and loads of firing guns. Antonio Margheriti's *Lightning Bolt* is one of the better Italian spy attempts (and can be found in a nice scope print in one of the Media Blasters Rareflix collections), and the Woolner Bros. American trailer seen here is plenty of brisk fun. *Mission Thunderbolt* might sound similar, but it has a lot more chop socky and a hooker slicing her john's throat with a razor between her teeth, not to mention some seriously scary fingernails. *The 3 Supermen in the West* is the obligatory spaghetti slapstick entry, basically a Terence Hill/Bud Spencer imitation without either actor. However, it does have three guys in red tights beating up cowboys, so there you go. The most perplexing film in Roger Vadim's filmography, *Pretty Maids All in a Row*, features Rock Hudson, Telly Savalas and Angie Dickinson in the story of a sexually confused high schooler dealing with a slew of cheerleader murders at his school, accompanied by a hellishly catchy Osmonds theme song. We really need a DVD of this one. Oh, and it was written by Gene Roddenberry. Robert Downey's landmark counterculture study of the advertising world, *Putney Swope*, has a trailer about as wild and irreverent as you might expect, consisting mainly of the film's unforgettable pimple commercial. Things get much pinker with Redd Foxx's only real starring vehicle, *Norman, Is That You?*, an absurdly outdated farce about a dad who finds out his son has "purple drapes" and has become a "tinkerbell". Wayland Flowers and Madame are on hand, too, just so you know exactly where the movie's coming from. One of the coolest finds on this disc, *Redneck County* is one of the many permutations and retitlings of a really nasty, unforgettable little film also released

F

as *Poor Pretty Eddie* and *Heartbreak Hotel*, starring Shelley Winters and a host of other confused-looking guest stars, it's about a black beauty queen who runs afoul of backwater perversion and racism whose severity depends wildly upon which version you see. *Moonrunners*, the now-infamous inspiration for *The Dukes of Hazzard* that caused Warner Brothers a huge heap of legal problems, is represented with a fun trailer loaded with brawls and car chases, all narrated by Waylon Jennings (who went to work on the TV shows as well).

A repellent shrimp roll commercial pops up next, followed by a B&W promo for *The Fabulous World of Jules Verne*, filmed in "Mystimation", which officially kicks off the kiddie segment of the disc. Evidently shot in someone's Florida backyard (featuring a thrilling "runaway lawn mower"), *Magic Christmas Tree* looks like the dreariest kid's film ever made – which of course makes it a must-see. *Pinocchio's Birthday Party* is almost as terrifying, with amateur actors and raggedy puppets cavorting in front of some of the most garish backdrops committed to film. Even odder, some foreign animated fairy tales have been spliced in for "story time" to pad it out, and there's a fairy queen warbling a gooey song about marmalade fountains. It did win a "Best children's Film Award" at the 1974 Atlanta International Film Festival, though, which makes you wonder exactly how fierce the competition was that year. *The Magic Kite* (from Xerox!) is a G-rated fantasy about a kid who goes to China and romps around with some trippy-looking kite creatures, while *The Secret of Magic Island* has a bunch of live farm animals let loose on miniature sets. Where else are you going to see a real duck flying a balloon? *Karzan: Master of the Jungle* is another cheapo Tarzan copy with actors running around in the woods in skimpy outfits, while the infamous AIP bomb *The Norseman* stars Lee Majors as an unlikely horn-helmeted warrior who according to the trailer, discovered America before Columbus. Be sure to watch for this during one of its occasional TV airings, 'cause MGM was far too embarrassed to release it on DVD. The last film by Jack Hill to receive notable theatrical play, New World's *Sorceress* is one of the first and most lurid *Conan* copies and comes packed with nudity and fancy glowing light effects, not to mention a terrifying monkey costume. You can pretty much see where Empire Pictures got all of its ideas by looking at this one. The semi-all-star *Terror in the Wax Museum* is a fun spook show with Ray Milland, Elsa Lanchester, and tons of severed heads, while *The Manson Massacre* is one of the many Charlie cash-ins unleashed in the early '70s in what looks like a quick TV spot. The British *The Devil Within Her* features Joan Collins howling through the *Rosemary's Baby* paces thanks to an evil dwarf; you can catch this one on DVD under the title of *The Monster* or VHS as *I Don't Want to Be Born.* Though it's not credited on the box, the DVD wraps up with a wonderfully lurid trailer for the incredibly hard-to-see *Slaughterhouse Rock*, one of the more memorable rock-monster outings from the late '80s.

As with the last instalment you get a full audio commentary, this time with the Alamo Drafthouse crew including owner Tim League and programmers Lars Nilsen and Zack Carlson. It's a very energetic track packed with trivia and amusing insights, some of which pertain to the films at hand while others verge off on wild tangents while they talk about some of the more memorable fests and related movie events at the Drafthouse. All the partici-pants pop up again for "Remember the Alamo", a half-hour documentary about how the theatre came to be, the most memorable theme nights and film programs from its recent history, and the colourful personalities who have drifted through over the years. A liner notes insert offers more of a thumbnail history of the theatre, illustrated with some tasty poster art from some of the featured films. Obviously worth every single penny, and if you can't plan a trip to Austin anytime soon, this should do nicely as the closest you can come in the privacy of your home theatre.

42ND STREET FOREVER: XXX-TREME SPECIAL EDITION
Colour, 2007, 130m. / Synapse (US R1 NTSC) / WS (1.78:1) (16:9)

The mind-melting trailer series takes a severe left turn with this (unnumbered) entry, a compilation of newly-transferred vintage porn promos covering many of the famous stars and directors from the second half of the porno chic era. Things get hot and heavy right off the bat with *Nasty Girls* as prolific director Henri Pachard (aka Ron Sullivan) gets the spotlight first here with this 1983 episodic romp involving various couplings at a metropolitan singles bar. Of primary interest is the cast, a who's who of performers at the time including Tiffany Clark, Sharon Mitchell, *The Last House on the Left*'s Fred J. Lincoln, Sharon Kane, Robert Kerman, and Ashley Moore. More '80s smut arrives with *Coming Together*, Paul Vatelli's apparently plotless skin-a-thon featuring fan favourites including Sharon Kelly, Kristara Barrington, and the always-busy, inexplicably popular Herschel Savage. Not a particularly interesting movie, but it must have fans since it's been in circulation on video for ages. 1983's *Alexandra* is an okay attempt at a plot-oriented soap opera with sex, featuring Joanna Storm as a woman whose contact with three of her exes has

unusual consequences for everyone involved. Currently available on DVD, it also stars Lauren Wilde, Rachel Ashley, and several familiar faces from above including Robert Kerman, Ashley Moore, and the ever-present Eric Edwards. The trailer pretty much covers all the highlights, so it might save you a rental. Two-hitter G.W. Hunter (*Oriental Jade* – see below) directed *Heart Throbs*, a popular-on-VHS title which features fan favourite Susan Hart, Laurie Smith, and the energetic but physically dubious presence of Ron Jeremy and Harry Reems. The title card is definitely one of the more creatively lewd conceptions of the decade.

One of the best films represented on this collection, Anthony Spinelli's excellent sequel to *Talk Dirty to Me, Nothing to Hide* reteams John Leslie and Richard Pacheco as friends whose contrasting degrees of luck in the sack cause them to establish very different relationships with women, including scene-stealer Holly McCall. Easy to find (cheap!) on DVD and highly recommended. West Coast adult favourite Kelly Nichols (who featured prominently in *The Toolbox Murders*) gets the whole show to herself in *Slip Into Silk*, an *All About Eve*-inspired look at a female radio celebrity who has to turn bi to ward off the scheming of a female newcomer. *Oriental Jade*, the sequel to *Heart Throbs*, features much of the same cast in another Westerners-gettin'-some-in-the-Far-East story, with Kristara Barrington leading a bunch of white girls (with one token Asian) through various sexcapades with, uh, a bunch of white guys. (See *Seven Seductions of Madame Lau* for a more adventurous take on the same idea.)

Kristara pops up again for the choppy but popular sequel *Debbie Does Dallas III*, which at least features a more impressive roster of actors than the original thanks to Joanna Storm and Jerry Butler, as well as original star Bambi Woods (well, sorta). One of porndom's most mysterious cult figures, the beautiful Angel, gets a rare lead role in *Debbie Does 'Em All*, a better-than-average entry in the random series. A former *Seventeen* covergirl, she nabbed a huge fan following in a brief period with her films, and this is one of her best showcases. Also featured are industry stalwarts like Jamie Gillis, Shanna McCullough, Annie Sprinkle and Marc Wallice, but not too many folks noticed.

The late Gary Graver (aka Robert McCallum) was one of the few directors to successfully navigate back and forth between XXX cinema and "legit" B-movies, and *I Want to Be Bad*, his run-of-the-mill entry in the "bad girls" template, is most notable for the presence of the always entertaining Kay Parker, plus pros like Jacqueline Lorians and Paul Thomas. One of the most frequently-compiled adult trailers around, and with good reason, *Sensations* is a chic and stylish piece of promotion which helped catapult erratic but interesting Algerian director Lasse Braun into the porn director elite. Brigitte Maier starts as a nymphet who undergoes a drastic sexual awakening over a 24-hour period, and this beautifully-edited, flashy trailer perfectly captures the elegant but perverse appeal of the film itself, which was reportedly even screened at Cannes!

Then – whoa! The 1984 kinkfest *G-Strings* from Henri Pachard has one of the most frenzied trailers you'll ever see, with Suzy Nero, George Payne, and Kelly Nichols heading a huge cast engaged in, well, everything you can think of. Wild stuff! Totally deranged, and probably the film you'll put on a DVD wish list first after watching this collection. Rick Cassidy features in *For Services Rendered*, a choppy secret agent spoof with Bridgette Monet and Heather Thomas adding some extra spice. "Starring" Ian MacGregor as "James Bomb", tee hee. Originally titled *The Maltese Dildo*, *Blonde Heat* is a brain-dead but moderately interesting spoof of the

Dashiell Hammett classic starring John Leslie as a randy private eye tangling with a colourful cast including Seka, Angel, and none other than the film's producer, exploitation legend David F. Friedman, in the Sidney Greenstreet role. Another one that's been in heavy circulation since the VHS days.

One of the undisputed adult classics and a solid film in its own right, the sexy musical comedy *Blonde Ambition* stars Benny Hill regular Suzy Mandel (with a very unconvincing body double for the hardcore scenes) in the misadventures of a pair of vaudeville sisters as they tangle with a variety of men, a dirty production of *Gone with the Wind*, some frisky neighbours, and a goofy caper that lands them in a transvestite club. A really good movie, with or without the sex. Continuing the vaudeville theme, *Burlexxx* offers a series of stage-bound skits-turned-sex-acts. It's a middle-of-the-road offering more notable for its classic cast including Samantha Fox, Honey Wilder, Jerry Butler, Sharon Kane, and the tireless Gloria Leonard. Fun but disposable. *Showgirls* is no relation to the Paul Verhoeven film, of course; this outing from Gary Graver is, as usual, a professionally-mounted job with Joanna Storm and Nina Hartley and completes the stage-act portion of this DVD, with a bunch of strippers trying to save their place of employment by mounting anything with two legs.

Surrender in Paradise, the companion film to the popular *The Pink Lagoon* (which features most of the same cast), finds Jerry Butler washed up on a tropical island populated by female castaways who... well, you can figure out the rest. Easy to find on video and a good example of '80s porn at its most accessible, with an early memorable performance from Samantha Fox. *Scheherazade: 1001 Erotic Nights* is an early '80s episodic film tied together with Annette Haven as the titular storyteller, teamed up once again with frequent co-star

John Leslie. Pretty soft and forgettable, but the fairly ambitious production values might make this worth a look. Another David F. Friedman special is *Matinee Idol*, this time with Jessie St. James and John Leslie climbing the showbiz ladder while everyone around them takes advantage of the casting couch. It's pretty good as far as these things go, sort of a porned-up twist on Friedman's earlier grindhouse favourite, *Starlet*. A rare attempt to do a '30s art deco period piece, and not a bad one (though you'd never guess it from the wretched-looking DVD available now), *Trashy Lady* stars Harry Reems as a mobster trying to turn a naive working girl into his moll. This would make a great double feature with *The Bite*, another solid XXX stab at the same era. *All American Girls* is an okay, rather popular '82 title with no-names behind the camera and some notable cult names in front of it such as Jacqueline Lorians and the late Shauna Grant. Another episodic outing, *The Ribald Tales of Canterbury* riffs on the Chaucer classic (sometimes with surprising faithfulness) with Hypathia Lee, a bearded Mike Horner, and a very enthusiastic Colleen Brennan making this a lively romp worth checking out, primarily for its marathon-style intercutting of various love scenes throughout the film.

A super-stylish head trip that should have been a midnight movie hit along the lines of *Café Flesh*, the genre-warper *"F"* follows John Leslie who, after leaving his wife, winds up in a spooky house populated by surreal hedonists who get him involved in an eye-popping array of supernatural scenarios. Definitely check it out, and easily one of this disc's brightest moments. An interesting attempt to update the romantic screwball comedy template to '80s smut, *Naked Scents* is an engaging romp that follows Tish Ambrose and Italian horror staple Robert "R. Bolla" Kerman as they try to reconcile their promiscuous natures with promises of fidelity. *Supergirls Do the Navy* has a fun title and a drab trailer; this sex comedy from Henri Pachard is a bit tricky to find now and doesn't look worth the effort, though fans of Raven and Kristara Barrington might find it worth a peek. Then Ron Jeremy and lots of smiling girls star in *Tight & Tender*, an anonymous programmer with no apparent plot.

Things get really, really weird with *Passage Through Pamela*, a porn version of *Dinah East* (sort of) in which the title character (whose real name is never credited) is a supermodel whose quest to complete a sex change operation leads to a number of scorching porn scenes. God only knows who's really responsible, but unprepared viewers will definitely find their attention seized by this one. In *Skintight*, Annette Haven and Paul Thomas team up yet again, and this is one of their strongest outings as they portray the chief therapist and manager of a sanitarium where everyone has an oddball kink of their own. Angel strikes again in *Hot Blooded*, one of her milder vehicles, though the participation of vets like Kay Parker and Harry Reems ensures some classic value. Kay Parker pops up once more in *Desire*, a sultry melodrama about a man trying to uncover his late wife's mysterious past. Also starring William Margold (the closest thing to sandpaper on the eyes in '80s porn), it's easy to find on video if you're so inclined. An anonymous-looking mid-'80s programmer, *Beyond Desire* features appearances by Vanessa Del Rio and Seka. There's not much of a plot or even basic concept in sight except for a discernible lack of lighting.

A bunch of Runaways-style girl rockers tangle with a bunch of frisky New Yorkers in the fun-looking *Hot Lips*, which looks like it could be a cult item if anyone could actually see it. It's also one of the few opportunities you'll get to see late *Sleazoid Express* editor Bill Landis doing hardcore. Despite the generic title, the sci-fi-and-smut title *Aroused* looks interesting enough with Amber Lynn and Ron Jeremy heading a cast assaulted with cheap-looking sex toys and Twiggy-inspired robots. One of the many classics churned out over a brief period by the legendary Chuck Vincent (who directed, produced and/or wrote a staggering number of early '80s gems), *Fascination* stars Ron Jeremy (in one of his earlier lead roles after getting out of the kinkier "hedgehog" period) and the always watchable Candida Royalle.

One of the many attempts to copy the success of *Pretty Peaches*, *Scandalous Simone* is a middling effort from exhibitionistic director Peter Balakoff (who had earlier melded porn with horror for his much more interesting earlier films) doesn't really stick out from the pack here. One of the lightest Jamie Gillis films, *Girls on Fire* was no doubt inspired by *Bosom Buddies* (and thus *Some Like It Hot* by default) with two guys dressing up in drag to elude the mob; also starring eternal fan favourite Ginger Lynn. Speaking of Ms. Lynn, she's featured here far more prominently in one of her better films, *Beverly Hills Cox*, as a private dick (sorry) whose conquests include regular screen partner Jerry Butler. Pure day-glo '80s trash, just the way you remember it. Bonus points for being one of the last trailers hosted by the main star, which always makes it more fun. Another above-average comedic piece of fluff, *Tickled Pink* features ever-busy Eric Edwards and Taija Rae as a couple whose marital problems propel them into the swinger lifestyle; it's especially notable for a prime later appearance by Farrah look-alike Rhonda Jo Petty. *Making It Big* is another one without an apparent plot, but it does feature another name cast including Jacqueline Lorians, Paul Thomas, the controversial Marc Wallice, and Desiree Lane.

One of several vampire spoofs unleashed in the late '70s, *Dracula Exotica* took a backseat in public awareness to the inferior *Dracula Sucks* but is a lot more fun. Jamie Gillis stars as the title bloodsucker, though Vanessa Del Rio really steals the show with her juicy bloodsucking turn. The incredible supporting cast features most of the in-demand performers of the period (Samantha Fox, Randy West, and many, many more); too bad the trailer here looks much better than any existing video transfers of the feature itself! Though it was only marginally noticed upon its release, the delirious sci-fi/hardcore concoction *Ultra Flesh* has amassed a solid cult following in recent years, and with good reason. Seka stars in one of her most appealing roles as a sexy alien trying to cure an outbreak of impotence, but that's just the beginning of what could be the closest thing to a XXX version of *Rocky Horror*. Oh yeah, and Ralphus from *Bloodsucking Freaks* (the late Luis de Jesus) is seen at the height of his porn career mounting Lisa de Leeuw, which is unlike anything else you've ever seen. If you're a fan of the Dark Brothers, they're well-represented with *Devil in Miss Jones III*, the popular sequel to the '70s classic. Their post-*Café Flesh* aesthetic of mixing pitch-black grunge with neon colours is plastered all over the place as various oiled-up bodies pound at each other in the afterlife. The back-to-back sequel, *Devil in Miss Jones 4*, also pops up on the disc for a double dose of Dark depravity. *Supergirls Do General Hospital* is another entry in the Supergirls series, this time with heavyweights Kristara Barrington and Paul Thomas joining in the silliness for an ultra-slight soap parody. While the Dark Brothers would be the most logical place to wrap things up (since they pretty much set the look for years to come), this collection ends instead with *The Oddest Couple*, a kinky comedy about a slutty blonde (Danielle) whose new prudish roommate loosens up under her spell. Another slick-looking offering from Henri Pachard, who opened this entire collection off as well.

DVD DELIRIUM VOLUME 4

The disc is presented at 1.78:1 and enhanced for widescreen televisions; most of the films here were shot open matte to remain TV-friendly but framed for exhibition at around 1.85:1 for theatres. A handful of titles on the DVD are still presented with pillarboxed black bars on the sides to maintain a 1.33:1 aspect ratio, notably *Nothing to Hide*, which could have still been cropped off without doing any damage to the compositions. The film elements look great throughout and have obviously undergone some clean-up, though some of the more cheaply-produced titles will obviously never look pristine. The mono soundtrack is about what you'd expect. Obviously geared for those who came of age to '80s porn before video consumed the industry, this collection is a fun, nostalgic, and utterly randy offering that nicely serves as a companion piece to the vintage '70s trailer comps floating around. Hey, it's packed with big hair, big boobs, and big fun; what more could you want?

FOUR FLIES ON GREY VELVET

Colour, 1971, 101m. / Directed by Dario Argento / Starring Michael Brandon, Mimsy Farmer, Jean-Pierre Marielle, Bud Spencer, Francine Racette / Mya (US R0 NTSC), RetroFilm (Germany R0 PAL) / WS (2.35:1) (16:9)

 One night after finishing a recording session, rock drummer Roberto Tobias (Michael Brandon) confronts and accidentally stabs a mysterious stalker in sunglasses in an abandoned theatre. The slaying is captured on camera by another observer wearing a doll mask, and over the next few days Tobias is tormented by sinister notes and photos

which he keeps secret from his wife (Mimsy Farmer). However, the blackmail soon turns to murder as his extortionist maid winds up murdered in a park, and with the aid of a gay, incompetent private eye (Jean-Pierre Marielle), Tobias tries to uncover the murderer's identity before he winds up next on the list of dead bodies.

This third and least-seen instalment in Dario Argento's initial "Animal Trilogy" of Roman thrillers (along with *The Bird with the Crystal Plumage* and *The Cat o' Nine Tails*) is the most stylistically extreme and eccentric of the three. Once again the plot relies on outlandish gimmicks (in this case, a device capable of capturing the last image on a dead person's retina) and uses detective literature and film noir for frequent inspiration, in this case with a notable debt to Cornell Woolrich's *Black Alibi*. The real fun here lies in the delirious visual details: a whiplash series of pans and cuts following a phone call across town from a blackmailer to a murderer; a potential victim stalked through a nocturnal graveyard surrounded by forbidding stone walls; the opening credits intercutting a pulsing human heart with Brandon attempting to kill a mosquito during a jam session; and the justly celebrated finale, a slow-motion waterfall of shattering glass perfectly timed to Ennio Morricone's sublime score. The script by Argento and Luigi Cozzi seems to go out of its way to make the most passive hero possible out of Brandon's androgynous, victimised character, leaving Farmer wide and clear to steal the film in the third act. The mystery itself should be obvious to most viewers since there's really only one viable suspect, but Argento's masterful hand with individual suspense sequences easily carries the film over any speed bumps and really pays off in the stalking sequence involving Francine Racette, one of the most terrifying highlights in the director's repertoire.

Picked up by Paramount for distribution in most English-speaking areas, *Four Flies* received a substantial theatrical release but promptly disappeared from circulation, only earning a legitimate VHS release in France. As Argento's star rose over the next few decades, fan demand lifted this film to holy grail status among Italian horror buffs who longed to see a decent release better than the miserable bootlegs floating around. A scratchy but watchable transfer of a 35mm film print interspersed with a handful of VHS inserts eventually appeared in Germany, but it was quickly eclipsed by a subsequent U.S. release on the enigmatic Mya Communication label. This DVD was transferred from the original Italian negative (thus the Italian opening credits) and the visual quality is infinitely superior to any other option out there, though the means used to release the film remain mired in controversy. Rumours of legal chicanery and Argento's outrage over the release when he legally owned half of the film began to float around, but most fans were quick to snap up the disc in any case. What is indisputable is that the video presentation is impressive, but the disc drops the ball in other key areas which could have easily been avoided. The English audio track sounds draggy and is pitched much lower than it should be, with Brandon and Farmer's voices in particular sounding as if they're suffering from a bad head cold. The Italian audio track is also included, but in a cheapskate move, no English subtitle option is available which renders it a frustrating bonus at best. Strangest of all, in an anomoly reminiscent of the controversy over *Tenebrae*, some minor slivers of footage are inexplicably missing which drop a few quick lines of dialogue, though some additional (if entirely superfluous) Italian-only dialogue has been restored to the killer's final monologue. This release is still the best way to experience Argento's film so far, but let's

just say there's a reason many resourceful fans have figured out ways to create their own fan versions with audio yanked from other sources. Extras on the Mya disc include the alternative U.S. opening credits (taken from one of the terrible aforementioned bootleg VHS copies), the spectacular and striking Italian theatrical trailer (which is almost worth the price tag alone), a great U.S. TV spot based on the same trailer, and the original, very different U.S. theatrical promo sourced from an old Sinister Cinema VHS trailer compilation. The absence of any substantial extras is unfortunate but understandable given the grey area in which this release operates; anyone looking for loads of worthwhile info should check out Luigi Cozzi's excellent, self-published book about the making of the film, available from his Profondo Rosso shop in Italy.

THE FOX

Colour, 1967, 110m. / Directed by Mark Rydell / Starring Sandy Dennis, Keir Dullea, Anne Heywood / Warner Archive (US R0 NTSC) / WS (1.85:1) (16:9)

At a remote, snowy farmhouse, the comfortable domestic life of Ellen (Anne Heywood) and Jill (Sandy Dennis) is disrupted one day by the arrival of Paul (Keir Dullea), a mysterious and somewhat sinister young man whose grandfather used to own the property. When the women invite him to stay for a short time, he soon drives a wedge between them which results in emotional and ultimately violent consequences.

Based on a celebrated and highly symbolic novella by D.H. Lawrence, this frank and often misunderstood film preceded Ken Russell's more explicit and celebrated Lawrence adaptation, *Women in*

Love, by two years. This three-character chamber drama is certainly more modest in scope, but its sympathetic depiction of lesbianism and bisexuality was certainly ahead of its time; furthermore, while the direction never even attempts the grandiosity of Russell's approach, the actors all do a fine job with their sometimes cryptic characters. The startling, brutal finale was often interpreted as the film's endorsement that lesbians somehow "have it coming" and that it only takes a real man to straighten any woman out, but it's extremely clear from Dullea's first scene that he's the villain of the piece and the outcome is anything but positive. Also effective is the lyrical, haunting score by Lalo Schifrin, whose work at the time was usually in a much groovier mode.

The Fox was originally released with an MPAA "M" rating which was clearly earned by an early scene with a fully nude Heywood pleasuring herself in a front of a mirror and a later, candid love scene between her and Dullea. For reissues the film was slightly trimmed down to a "PG" instead, and this is the version that often appeared on television. The Warner Archive DVD-on-demand release features a satisfying if obviously unrestored anamorphic transfer and thankfully represents the original, uncensored version. The disc also promises a theatrical trailer which instead turns out to simply be the opening two minutes of the film; however, the trailer compilation *Homo Promo* contains the real thing if you're so inclined to seek it out.

FRANKENHOOKER

Colour, 1990, 85m. / Directed by Frank Henenlotter / Starring James Lorinz, Patty Mullen, Louise Lasser, Joseph Gonzalez, Jennifer Delora / Unearthed (US R1 NTSC) / WS (1.85:1) (16:9), Dragon (Germany R0 PAL), Optimum (UK R2 PAL), Simitar (US R1 NTSC) / DD2.0

The last excursion into Upper East Coast depravity from director Frank Henenlotter (*Basket Case*) for the best part of two decades, this whacked-out spoof of *Frankenstein* managed to attract the attention of sleaze gourmets and VHS consumers everywhere with its wild ad campaign including an irresistible video box that, when pressed, literally shouted out, "Wanna date?" Luckily the film lives up to its deranged potential with the story of forlorn Jeffrey Franken (*Street Trash*'s James Lorinz), a drop-out fledgling scientist whose beautiful fiancée, Elizabeth (Patty Mullen), is gruesomely ground into chunks by a new power lawnmower at a birthday party. Luckily Jeffrey's skill with electricity and anatomy (which has already yielded a functioning brain with an eyeball in a jar) comes into play when he keeps Elizabeth's head and concocts a plan to bring her back to life. The first step, of course, involves a journey to Times Square, where Jeffrey rounds up plenty of hookers for potential body parts and gets more than he bargained for when a new, explosive form of crack cocaine sends them flying to bits all over the room. With his beloved finally reassembled, Jeffrey unfortunately realises the error of his ways when his new, neck-bolted creation turns out to be a statuesque killer hooker with an appetite for the blood of johns!

Though some critics railed against *Frankenhooker* for its supposed misogyny and bad taste, the film is far too absurd and playful for these criticisms to hold up. The sight of killer crack blowing up a group of lingerie-clad ladies of the evening in a crackling electrical explosion is one of the most unforgettable moments in the Henenlotter canon (and there's certainly a lot to choose from there), and the table-turning twist ending is an amusing touch obviously designed to ward off any charges of hatred towards women. Lorinz is absolutely perfect as usual, dishing out sardonic one-liners without ever breaking character; likewise, Mullen proves to be a good sport with a role requiring her to go from a victimised, wholesome girl to a shambling, grimacing streetwalker. Joe Renzetti (fresh off the back-to-back production of *Basket Case 2*) turns in an amusing, pitch-perfect score, and the gaudy production design packed with vibrant colours pins this perfectly as a film produced during the waning hours of the 1980s.

Frankenhooker first appeared on video in both R-rated and unrated versions (the former missing quite a bit of exploding hooker footage, for example), with the former only available for years on DVD thanks to a shoddy budget release from Simitar. (The unrated version did turn up on German disc from Dragon and in the U.K. from Optimum, albeit from the same old lacklustre tape master.) Unearthed's much-needed revamp blows away past editions, with rich, deep blacks and perfect detail. The widescreen framing is also a huge improvement over the previous full frame (open matte) editions, which threw all of the compositions out of whack. The stereo audio sounds rich and well-defined throughout. No complaints at all. On the extras side, Henenlotter turns in another jovial, fact-packed commentary track, joined by frequent FX collaborator Gabe Bartalos. (If you're a fan of the *Basket Case* sequels, this would play nicely as a companion to them as well since all were shot closely together.) The various locations, FX necessities, and cast wrangling are covered in fun detail, painting an enjoyable portrait of fast-and-cheap New York filmmaking that doesn't really exist anymore. Though Lorinz is strangely nowhere to be found, Mullen picks up the slack with an entertaining featurette, "A Salad That Was Once Named Elizabeth", in which she reminisces about the casting process, working with Henenlotter, and the nature of her make-up and demanding performance. Co-star Jennifer Delora also appears for "Turning Tricks", offering a somewhat more B-movie-based take on the film with a few memories of her work on other horror and drive-in projects as well; her photo scrapbook is also included as a nice additional supplement. "A Stitch in Time" focuses on the special effects, which are all charmingly latex-based and much more naturalistic than CGI could have provided years later. Finally, you get a hefty helping of production photos, the giddy theatrical promo, and a batch of trailers for other Unearthed releases like *Nails* and *Bone Sickness*.

FROG SONG

Colour, 2005, 65m. / Directed by Shinji Imaoka / Starring Konatsu, Rinako Hirasawa, Takeshi Ito / Redemption (UK R0 PAL, US R0 NTSC) / WS (1.85:1)

 One of the most romantic and – believe it or not – *cutest* pink films around is *Frog Song* (*Enjo-kôsai monogatari: shitagaru onna-tachi*), which comes from the Redemption Films Sacrament line ("Pink Cinema – Erotica for the mind as well as the body"). Akemi (Konatsu), a very young woman, ditches her cheating husband and shacks up with a lesbian comic book artist, Kyoko (Rinako Hirasawa), who subsidises her artistic career by turning tricks. Oh yes, and she likes to dress up in a big fuzzy frog suit. And sometimes they have three-ways.

Needless to say, the crowd of "furries" will find plenty to embrace here, and while there are a few kinky scenes, there's little of the viciousness or ridiculous sadism which characterises much of the later pink titles; instead this one climaxes with a big musical number in a public square. Really! Clocking in at barely over an hour, this could very well be a video cult item in the future. The letterboxed transfer is non-anamorphic, which is typical for lower-end recent pinky films aimed at the home video market; picture quality is soft but watchable, with optional English subtitles. The limited extras include a tiny stills gallery, a completely incoherent and crappy-looking short film by Tobias Tobbell called "Japanese Box", and the usual Salvation crossover items like trailers and book promos.

GHOST STORY

Colour, 1974, 83m. / Directed by Stephen Weeks / Starring Marianne Faithfull, Barbara Shelley, Larry Dann, Murray Melvin, Vivian MacKerrell, Leigh Lawson / Nucleus (UK R0 PAL) / WS (1.66:1) (16:9)

 In a somewhat anachronistic 1930s England, three city men journey to the countryside to spend the weekend at an isolated estate now owned by one of them, the flamboyant McFayden (Murray Melvin from *The Devils*), who, when they aren't all sniping at each other, informs them the place might be haunted. Sure enough, the most sensitive of the group, Talbot (Larry Dann), starts experiencing sightings of a ghost, Sophy (rock legend Marianne Faithfull), whose presence is tied to the property's ignoble past involving a forced stay at a madhouse (run by Hammer Films star Barbara Shelley). The group's ghost hunter (Vivian MacKerrell, the real-life inspiration for *Withnail & I*), snidely dismisses any signs of supernatural activity, but the

influence of the past gradually grows too powerful to ignore. Then there's the creepy porcelain doll that keeps turning up at inopportune moments and seems to be Talbot's escort to the past, or perhaps something much more sinister...

A film apparently designed to be described only by the word "unsettling", *Ghost Story* never tries to outright terrify viewers and only occasionally aims for anything truly shocking or disorienting. Much of the running time simply soaks in the rich period atmosphere and refined performances, which might not sit too well with many horror fans (particularly those who encountered this under its more common home video title, *Madhouse Mansion*). However, the riveting presence of Faithfull and an unusual music score by Pink Floyd collaborator Ron Geesin keep things on track as director Stephen Weeks (in his second and final horror film after Amicus's *I, Monster*) weaves the past and present story threads together into a sly finale. While Shelley has little to do, the rest of the excellent cast acquit themselves well with the male leads in particular getting plenty of juicy dialogue to enjoy as university colleagues not all exactly on the best of terms.

For such an obscure film, Nucleus has gone all out with a laudably extensive special two-disc edition containing everything you could possibly want to know about the production. The transfer is taken from the BBC's master, probably the best one lying around, and is presented moderately widescreen at 1.66:1 (not the 1.85:1 noted on the packaging, which would have been way too severe). The film was shot open matte originally so the ancient VHS actually has a sliver of extraneous information at the top and bottom, but the compositions here look correct. The image quality is definitely a huge step up, obviously, though by current standards it's definitely on the soft side. Fans or even the mildly curious shouldn't have any problem, though. The first disc contains the feature film along with the rarely-seen theatrical trailer and a thorough audio commentary with Weeks and moderator Sam Umland, which covers Weeks's considerable difficulties getting his films off the ground and completed to his satisfaction along with the headaches of dealing with distribution. Disc two features a very extensive new documentary, "Ghost Stories", whose 72-minute running time puts it close to the main feature in terms of value. Weeks, Dann, Melvin, Shelley, and Geesin appear along with Kim Newman for an overview of the entire production, which features some great anecdotes about the vintage costumes (especially poor Dann who had the most unflattering ensemble of the bunch), the ill-fated MacKerrell (who's actually quite good in his only notable film role), Faithfull's severe addiction problems, and the various artistic and period influences on the film. Also included are a host of Weeks short films and commercials including "Owen's War", "Deserted Station", "The Camp" (all 1965), the wonderfully atmospheric "Moods of a Victorian Church" (1967), "Two at Thursday", Tigon's "1917" (both 1968), and the Kenneth Anger-ish "Flesh" (1969), with the last two shorts presented in anamorphic 2.35:1 widescreen (the rest are standard 4:3). Also included are a Weeks commercial for "Chelsea Cobbler", pdfs of the original press book and a making-of overview, the alternative "spooky" opening title sequence created for the *Madhouse Mansion* version, liner notes by Darius Drewe Shimon, and bonus Nucleus trailers for *Death Ship*, *London Voodoo*, *Bloodbath at the House of Death*, *The Ugliest Woman in the World*, *Varietease* and *Teaserama*. The absolute definition of a package that gives you every penny's worth, this is a superlative genre release that pays loving tribute to a film languishing for far too long in the shadows.

GHOUL SCHOOL

Colour, 1990, 87m. / Directed by Timothy O'Rawe / Starring William Friedman, Scott Gordon, Paul Venier, Nancy Sirianni, Joe Franklin, Ed Burrows, Jackie Martling / Camp (US R1 NTSC), HardGore (UK R2 PAL)

The only shot-on-film entry in Camp Video's hideously fascinating Retro 80s Horror Collection, *Ghoul School* is also the closest thing to a "real" movie out of the bunch. Another gory high school zombie film, this one depicts the mayhem that erupts when a school dance featuring the Bloodsucking Ghouls happens to coincide with the arrival of two robbers looking for a stash of money hidden by the school janitor. Soon the crooks accidentally unleash some toxic gas on the entire school and, faster than you can say Linnea Quigley, the students are being turned into blue-skinned fiends out for blood. Can two geeky horror fans save the day? How many zombies in swimsuits can fill up a screen? And why are Joe Franklin and future Howard Stern regular Jackie Martling hanging around for comic relief?

Exactly what you would expect, *Ghoul School* feels for all the world like a Troma film from the rib-nudging jokes to the arch, unconvincing flesh-eating effects. The "postmodern" horror fan twist makes this yet another forerunner to the *Scream* era, which might make it one for the history books along with the likes of *There's Nothing Out There*, and the copious bloodshed at least earns this one a respectable rating on the gore charts. The film's fans (whomever they may be) should be happy with the presentation, which looks fine and comes packed with a ludicrous barrage of extras including three(!) commentary tracks: one with director Timothy O'Rawe, one with cinematographer Michael Raso, and one with associate producer John Paul Fedele and Raso again. If there's anything you wanted to know about this film, it's most certainly included here; good luck spending an entire day with these! An earlier promotional short version of the film is also included (similar to the pitch versions of *Lady in White* and *Street Trash*), with a Raso/Fedele commentary to boot, and it actually benefits from the swifter pacing and more compact presentation. Also included is a making-of featurette with all the commentary participants as well as the FX artists and several actors. You also get a peek at the new photo shoot for the cover, as well as an alternative earlier credit sequence, four very entertaining short films from the same participants (including outtakes from one of the best, "Halloween Tale"), and trailers for other titles in the series like *Video Violence* and *Cannibal Campout*. HardGore's DVD in the U.K., which came out shortly after the Camp release, features the same VHS-style transfer.

GIRLS IN CHAINS

Colour, 1973, 86m. / Directed by Donald M. Jones / Starring Gary Kent, Suzanne Lund, John Stoglin, Greta Gayland, Leah Tate / Exploitation Digital (US R1 NTSC)

 For some reason best left discovered by brave sociologists, movie screens in the early '70s were awash in stories about hapless, freewheeling young women out on their own running afoul of deviant psychopaths either in the woods or lurking in sinister old houses. Thus the box office suddenly exploded with the likes of *The Last House on the Left*, *Deranged*, *House of Whipcord*, *Behind Locked Doors*, *The Sinful Dwarf* and on and on. An obscure but oddly entertaining cheapjack entry in this cycle shuffled into theatres during 1973 under the title of *Schoolgirls in Chains*, though '80s VHS trash addicts will know this one better under its more intriguing alternative title, *Let's Play Dead*. Now it's out on DVD under yet another name, simply *Girls in Chains*, presumably to avoid the wrath of retailers who might think it features some underage bondage. Fortunately the film's opening MPAA R-rating card ensures nothing too unsavoury occurs, but you can't blame the filmmakers for trying.

Gary Kent, a drive-in regular going back to the late '50s in numerous Ray Dennis Steckler and Al Adamson films, is the only major name in the unsavoury story of Johnny and Frank, a pair of brothers devoted to their (offscreen) domineering mother who spend their lonely days swiping passing ladies and subjecting them to a variety of demented games. Sporting really bad teeth and overalls, Johnny has his own unique slant on "playing doctor", while Frank sits around on his piano bench subjecting the girls to his demented monologues and fumbling attempts at straight sex. The surviving captives are kept with chains around their necks, often in the basement with rats crawling around their ankles. However, when the boys decide to pick up the wrong females one day, their peculiar activities are put in danger of discovery.

Though not a title picked up by Something Weird, *Girls in Chains* feels like it should be. Kent and John Stoglin do an efficient job as the wacko siblings, but the rest of the cast is pretty much local theatre quality. Most of the women spend the bulk of the film topless, but their hair and other accoutrements are usually arranged to keep the skin within the limits of that aforementioned R rating. However, that doesn't stop

G

the film from wallowing deep in its sleazy atmosphere, as the protracted scenes of psychological and physical sexual assault ensured this would never, ever become a recommended Oprah movie.

Want to know how this film got made and where everyone is now? Well, guess what – you get three commentary tracks! First up is R.A. the Rugged Man (a rap staple familiar to anyone who's watched Frank Henenlotter DVDs), moderator Lee Christian, and director Don Jones, an amiable guy who also directed the phenomenal *The Love Butcher* as well as *The Forest*. Then Jones returns in two separate chats with Gary Kent and cinematographer Ron Garcia, who went on to shoot *One from the Heart* and win an Emmy for his prolific TV work. All three tracks occasionally lapse into narrating the onscreen action, but for the most part they do a good job of covering the cast's obscure credits, the locations (including the story behind the main house), the doll collection used in the opening credits and throughout the film, and even the great vintage vehicles used in the outdoor shots. The sex scenes provide more than their fair share of funny anecdotes, too, including one actor who kept tossing his leading lady aside after hearing "cut!" For some reason the Kent commentary sounds very hollow and echoey which makes it tough to sit through for more than about half an hour, but die-hards will want to slug it through to the end anyway. Then you get an interview featurette with Jones and Kent talking more about the film (including its original shooting title, *The Black Widow*), the original *Schoolgirls in Chains* trailer (sourced from VHS), a photo gallery, and bonus "Exploitation Digital" trailers (*SS Experiment Love Camp*, *Divine Emanuelle*, *Rica*, *The True Story of the Nun of Monza*). The movie itself looks better than the fuzzy old VHS version, but don't expect fireworks. The full frame transfer presents the entire film information on all four sides,

but there's some obvious damage and colour distortion as well as a gritty visual texture over the entire film. It's watchable but doesn't look especially fresh or exciting. Still, how else are you gonna see it? The disc also contains an option to watch the film matted off to 1.85:1 (anamorphically enhanced), but it's just the same transfer blown up, which you could do automatically on a widescreen TV anyway. This alternative option really isn't at all preferable though as it lops out quite a bit of nudity and doesn't seem to benefit much compositionally either. The beginning of the disc features a crawl explaining that this transfer from 2006 couldn't be redone since the film elements had deteriorated and Jones framed the shots for 1.33:1, so stick with that first option. All three commentaries are available for either version. The main menu screen features the unforgettable theme song, a crooned pseudo-lullaby that adds to the queasiness of the entire experience.

GIRLY

Colour, 1970, 101m. / Directed by Freddie Francis / Starring Vanessa Howard, Michael Bryant, Ursula Howells, Pat Heywood, Howard Trevor, Imogen Hassall, Michael Ripper / Scorpion (US R0 NTSC), Odeon (UK R0 PAL) / WS (1.78:1) (16:9)

In a remote English manor, emotionally stunted Girly (*Corruption*'s Vanessa Howard) and Sonny (Howard Trevor) still frolic around in children's clothing while playing juvenile but often fatal games with strangers they encounter. One afternoon at the zoo they befriend an ill-fated tramp who goes home with them and, distracted by Girly's naughty schoolgirl charms, doesn't realise their role playing might cost him his head. Their antics are overseen by their knitting-happy guardians, Mumsy (Ursula Howells from *Dr. Terror's House of Horrors*) and Nanny (*10 Rillington Place*'s Pat Heywood), who encourage the youngsters to handle any unruly new family members by sending them off to the angels. Enter their latest "New Friend" (*The Stone Tape*'s Michael Bryant), a particularly long-in-the-tooth gigolo whose latest patron (*El Condor*'s Imogen Hassall) runs afoul of Girly and Sonny, leaving the newcomer to upset the homicidal family order when he decides to have Girly to himself.

A peculiar and wildly entertaining horror comedy firmly in the tradition of films like *The Old Dark House* and *Spider Baby*, this parody of traditional English social roles was originally released in its native country as *Mumsy, Nanny, Sonny and Girly*, with the title usually shortened to simply the last word for most export versions (which also lost quite a bit of footage in the process). The film is perhaps most noteworthy to horror fans as a prime offering from director Freddie Francis, one of England's finest cinematographers (*The Innocents, The Elephant Man, Room at the Top*) who branched off into directing with a batch of Hammer horror offerings (*Paranoiac, Nightmare, The Evil of Frankenstein*) before also working for other U.K. horror houses like Amicus (*The Skull, Torture Garden*). Incredibly, *Girly* came out the same year as Francis's most notorious and laughable film, *Trog* (the one with Joan Crawford and a guy in a Neanderthal mask), demonstrating the wild disparity in quality among his films (which subsequently ranged from sublime offerings like *Tales from the Crypt, The Creeping Flesh* and *The Doctor and the Devils* to crud like *The Vampire Happening* and *Son of Dracula*). Thankfully *Girly* plays to most of his strengths, establishing an offbeat atmosphere of meticulous visual detail coupled with a thick vein of sick comedy, here exemplified by the use of traditional children's songs and games like "Oranges and Lemons" and cowboys and Indians as the frameworks for the discreet but grotesque murder sequences. (And just to remind viewers of Francis's Hammer connection, one of the studio's most regular character actors, Michael Ripper, pops up in the opening zoo sequence.) Of course, the real visual hook for the film is the stunning Howard in her best role; often clad in fetching outfits that would be a big hit now with the schoolgirl fetish community, she's always beautiful, compelling, and sinister, making it a real shame she only found limited work afterwards in the underrated *What Became of Jack and Jill?* and the Shane Briant TV version of *The Picture of Dorian Gray*. The other cast members do their duties quite well, with perhaps only one-time performer Trevor showing any weakness in maintaining the tricky tone of the script.

Despite its small but dedicated cult following and prominent availability on home video during the early VHS era, *Girly* sank into oblivion in the late '80s with circulating prints becoming impossible to find and most viewers resorting to dismal bootlegs and online streaming options to see it at all. Fortunately Scorpion's disc is the miracle fans have waited for, a vivid and pin-sharp transfer from the original negative that finally flatters the film's careful cinematography and delicate performances. The result truly feels like a different and significantly better film, and hopefully this twisted treat will be granted a larger audience with this newest edition. Extras include a half-hour interview with screenwriter Brian Comport (who talks about his other films as much as this one and goes into some detail about the film's obscure source play, Maisie Mosco's *The Happy Family*), another half-hour, audio-only interview

G

with the late Francis (who's pretty frank about the state of his career in the '70s and talks about the varying quality of his horror work), the alternative U.S. title card (with the full U.K. title present on the main feature), the American and Spanish theatrical trailers, a TV spot, and an additional grab bag of Cinerama trailers including *Follow Me*, *Fools*, *Goodbye Gemini*, and *The Girl in Blue*. Odeon also slated a U.K. special edition DVD release under the original full title.

GOING UNDER

Colour, 2004, 98m. / Directed by Eric Werthman / Starring Roger Rees, Geno Lechner, Richard Eagan / Blue Underground (US R0 NTSC) / WS (1.85:1) (16:9) / DD2.0

This unusual if not entirely successful little S&M feature merits more than a passing glance. Sort of a updated arty spin on *Maîtresse*, it uses the discipline lifestyle as a backdrop for a fairly conventional relationship drama about married therapist Peter (Roger Rees, from *Cheers*!) and Mistress Diana (Geno Lechner), whose professional domination sessions go a step further when she reveals her real name (Suzanne) and, despite her ongoing relationship with another woman, the two tentatively embark on a love affair that might crash against the rocks.

Well-acted and nicely mounted, the film doesn't really have much of a narrative motor after the initial set up and can make for tough going at times. However, the treatment of its subject matter (which is frank but not salacious and a lot milder than the real thing, as found in the infamous ongoing story of Larry/Lana Wachowski) manages to carry the story over some of its speed bumps. The unrated DVD edition comes in a solid anamorphic transfer that adequately captures the delicate and shadowy lighting scenes, while extras include an informative if occasional space-riddled commentary with Rees and director Eric Werthman. Other extras include "Pushing the Boundaries" (an interview featurette with Rees and Lechner), a fetish featurette entitled "NYC Black & Blue Ball" (ouch), two trailers, and a DVD-Rom text supplement (basically liner notes), "Reflections on *Going Under*".

GOODBYE GEMINI

Colour, 1970, 89m. / Directed by Alan Gibson / Starring Judy Geeson, Martin Potter, Michael Redgrave, Alexis Kanner, Freddie Jones, Mike Pratt / Scorpion (US R0 NTSC), Odeon (UK R0 PAL) / WS (1.78:1) (16:9)

In a swinging London apparently oblivious to the impending death of hippie culture, a pair of wide-eyed blond twins, Julian (Martin Potter) and Jacki (Judy Geeson), arrive at a boarding house along with their tightly-guarded teddy bear, Agamemnon, whose presence at the top of a flight of stairs leads to their landlady's demise. Soon they become embroiled in the local party scene where the pansexual Clive (Alexis Kanner) seems to fancy them both and unleashes a torrent of sexual misadventures, the most unexpected of which involves Julian preyed upon by a pack of drag queens. Blackmail soon enters the game along with a jolting murder involving knives and bed sheets (which logically inspired the film's marketing campaign) as the twins find their lifestyle and possible homicidal impulses to be a very dangerous mix indeed.

Sporting an unusual cast (with Michael Redgrave and Freddie Jones scoring highest as a concerned politician and a very gay dandy, respectively), *Goodbye Gemini* was part of a wave of youth-oriented films with fresh-faced stars greenlit after the success of Franco Zeffirelli's *Romeo and Juliet*, though like another contemporary offering, the wildly underrated *'Tis Pity She's a Whore*, it splashes elements of incestuous longing and horrific violence into the brew for good measure. Based on the novel *Ask Agamemnon* by Jenni Hall (not hard to see why they changed that title), this film is surprisingly stylish and deserves a bit more recognition than the oblivion which largely awaited it. Director Alan Gibson (who mostly toiled in television apart from helming the last two Dracula movies with Christopher Lee for Hammer) delivers some nifty flourishes (especially the central murder scene) when he isn't basking in the gaudy, almost eye-searing art direction. As for the two leads, Potter (fresh from *Fellini Satyricon*) is striking but rather wooden while the charismatic, ridiculously pretty Geeson acts circles around him. Also noteworthy is the catchy, complex music score by Christopher Gunning which has taken on a cult following of its own via a much-delayed soundtrack release. Fans of "mod" cinema will find the depiction here a little different than usual as this feels more like a party with Oscar Wilde and his friends transplanted to the late '60s with the characters spitting out acidic one-liners and eyeing both genders with very questionable thoughts filling their heads. This would definitely make a great double feature with the 1970 Massimo Dallamano version of *Dorian Gray*, with which this shares more than a few creative similarities – but this is definitely the better film of the two.

Though it popped up in the VHS age from Prism under the ridiculous title of *Twinsanity* (complete with a new video-generated title card), *Goodbye Gemini* has been largely unavailable since its release, a fate no doubt attributable to the difficulty in categorizing it. Yes, this could be termed a horror film (definitely so if *The Wicker Man* falls in the same category), but anyone expecting a relentless avalanche of thrills and chills will be confounded by what they get here. However, if you're open to a genre-mashing experiment in melancholy '70s psychological tension with a heavy pop art slant, this should fit the bill just fine. Scorpion's DVD licensed from rights holder Cinerama (who also confounded audiences with *Candy* and a few Amicus offerings) is transferred from the original negative and looks absolutely spectacular. Colours and detail are spot on without any annoying noise reduction or digital fudging, and the entire thing looks so beautiful and clean it could have been shot yesterday. A handful of daytime exterior shots have some odd colour registration issues (mainly some faint red lines around the actors' faces in certain shots) which have always plagued this film, but that's not a fault of the transfer (nor are the occasional artsy soft focus shots, though those are few and far between). The main extra here is an audio commentary with Geeson and producer Peter Snell, moderated by yours truly; obviously I can't evaluate it, but hopefully it makes for an informative listen. Both of them remembered the film well and offer two different perspectives on its creation. Also included are the lurid original theatrical trailer and bonus Cinerama promos. The U.K. release from Odeon ports over the same extras (including two of the bonus trailers) and also adds two tasty new extras: a liner notes booklet by Simon Sheridan and an unreleased featurette consisting of on-set footage from the film shoot at Twickenham Studios, intended but never shown as part of the '70s ITV series *World in Action*. The silent piece is augmented with score selections and Sheridan text commentary.

GRADIVA

Colour, 2006, 118m. / Directed by Alain Robbe-Grillet / Starring James Wilby, Arielle Dombasle, Dany Verissimo, Farid Chopel / Mondo Macabro (US R0 NTSC) / WS (1.85:1) (16:9)

 After the famous but contentious partnership he experienced while writing his most famous screenplay, *Last Year at Marienbad*, French novelist Alain Robbe-Grillet began directing his own material for the screen starting with 1963's *L'immortelle*. Austere, immaculate, precise, and highly erotic, his meditations on time, memory and psychological dislocation are considerably more sophisticated and strategic than your average French erotica, and upon his death in 2008, he left behind a challenging legacy which will continue to be debated for years to come.

Completed two years before his death, Robbe-Grillet's final film, *Gradiva* (full title: *C'est Gradiva qui vous appelle*), works quite nicely as a cinematic swan song, even smoothly integrating startling slices of footage from his past films like *L'éden et après* and *Glissements progressifs du plaisir* (neither of which have received English-friendly releases in any format to date). The film follows the hallucinatory experiences of John Locke (*Howards End*'s James Wilby), who is researching the history of Delacroix paintings in Morocco. A tip on some undiscovered sketches of a mysterious woman results in sightings of the model (Arielle Dombasle) throughout the city; sometimes real and at other times appearing like a ghost, she seems to guide him through a whirlwind of dark and erotic encounters involving a subservient handmaiden (Dany Verissimo), a mysterious S&M-oriented Club of the Golden Triangle, and Gradiva, a woman murdered a century before who seems to be controlling his entire destiny.

Elliptical, sometimes confusing, and always visually ravishing, *Gradiva* features the usual Robbe-Grillet staples like unexplained segues into fantasy sequences and static tableaux of women in bondage (but with nothing resembling a standard sex scene in sight). The film credits its source as the influential 1903 Wilhelm Jensen novel (a psychoanalytical favourite) but is really more of a playground for the director's obsessions and ruminations on aesthetics, which can be frustrating for the uninitiated but fascinating for anyone willing wander through his dark filmic alleys.

For years Robbe-Grillet refused to allow his films to be released on home video, arguing that they could only be appreciated in a cinema. That situation began to change with the official release of his excellent *La belle captive*, and this marks the second sanctioned DVD of one of his titles. Mondo Macabro's gorgeous anamorphic transfer is a stunner from start to finish, filled with burnished gold and brown hues with startling red accents in numerous scenes. It's easily one of the most beautiful discs they've released to date, and the French soundtrack (with optional English subtitles) is pristine as well. Along with a text bio for the director and cast, the disc includes a wonderful half-hour interview with the bearded filmmaker who talks about his work and the often taboo subject matter which landed him in trouble for decades.

GRINDHOUSE TRASH COLLECTION PART 3: HOW TO MAKE A DIRTY MOVIE

Colour, 1968, 60m.

THE ALLEYCAT (HELL'S KITTEN)

Colour, 1972, 78m. / Directed by Otto von Licket / Starring Sandy Dempsey, John Keith, Suzanne Fields, Norman Fields

STAR
(OH! YOU BEAUTIFUL DOLL)
Colour, 1973, 60m. / Directed by Walt
Davis / Starring Cleo O'Hara, Billy Lane,
Sandy Carey, Keith Erickson, Jill Sweete
GO DOWN FOR DOUBLE
Colour, 1972, 65m. / Starring John Holmes
/ Secret Key (US R0 NTSC)

 Easily the most proble-
matic title ever released
by the folks at After
Hours, this quartet of
interesting titles is
rendered nearly useless
by needless censorship.
The previous two
volumes were a great deal of low-rent fun,
and while they weren't perfect, the efforts to
revive truly disreputable multi-feature sets
for the mass population are worthy of
applause. That energy certainly carries over
into the four films selected for this third
collection, which kicks off with the title
feature, *How to Make a Dirty Movie*. This
late '60s softcore quickie features no credits
and a no-name cast in a goofy precursor to
Andy Warhol's *Blue Movie* (and the Terry
Southern book of the same name), basically
offering a self-reflexive look at how the pre-
hardcore skin industry operates. The threadbare story follows an average Joe popping
by his neighbour's house, only to find a
homemade 16mm dirty movie in progress –
with our hero gradually lured into participating. Lots of big, big hair highlights this
fleshy offering which mostly takes place on
a couch and bed under some really heavy
spotlights, giving the whole project a
strange, slightly creepy atmosphere. Not bad
as far as these things go, and the anamorphic
transfer looks just fine apart from the usual
expected scratches and debris.

Next up we have *The Alleycat*, a
retitling of *Hell's Kitten*, a grimy-looking
softcore film with another "I wanna be a
pornstar" story about Chessy (Sandy

Dempsey), who beds everyone in sight
while making her newest opus. The
colourful supporting cast includes plenty of
familiar faces including *Flesh Gordon*
favourite Suzanne Fields as her co-star,
kinda-sorta-hardcore actor John Keith (*The
Pigkeeper's Daughter*) as the film's writer,
and drive-in regular Norman Fields (*Psycho
from Texas*) as the director. The ripe
dialogue and snappy pacing keep this one
entertaining, with the always watchable
Dempsey (*A Touch of Sweden*) holding her
own as the lead.

Disc two begins with the best film of
the set, *Star*, a retitling of *Oh! You Beautiful
Doll*, one of the very few films helmed by
truly fascinating and eccentric sleaze
filmmaker Walt Davis, who shocked even
hardened smut fans with films like *Widow
Blue* and *Evil Come, Evil Go*. Anyone who's
seen Walt's work knows he's not all that
interested in titillating viewers in anything
resembling a traditional sex-and-violence
offering; instead he peppers his features
with snarling line readings, wacko plot
twists, and grotesque imagery. Here he
seems to be mining Paul Morrissey territory
with the sordid antics of Gaye Ramon (*Evil
Come*'s Cleo O'Hara), a faded smut queen
who lolls around her Hollywood mansion
enjoying the occasional piece of boy meat
while not trying on ridiculous wigs and
setting up phoney auditions. Exploitation
regulars Sandy Carey (*Deep Jaws*) and
Keith Erickson (*The Godson*) also appear in
this darkly hilarious treat which really
deserves rediscovery.

Finally we have *Go Down for Double*,
apparently a very, very obscure early John
Holmes (softcore) film about a bunch of
swingers who have sex, have friends over,
then have sex some more. And that's about
it. So, this all sounds great, right? Well,
there's one big, big problem with this
release, and it's a real puzzler. Remember
when Japanese video releases used to have
annoying pixilation over any offending

G

pubic hair onscreen? Well, this DVD does that one better by drenching the screen in huge, annoying digital pixilation boxes every time a naked male appears in both *The Alleycat* and *Star*, which comprises a large percentage of the running time. Even worse, the two films are then re-edited and zoomed in severely to also crop away any visible genitalia, resulting in tons of baffling jump cuts and weird visual inconsistencies, rendering both films unwatchable. A real shame, especially coming from the same company who released *Forced Entry*; since it also involves the two best titles in the set, here's hoping they'll both be reissued at some point in versions that are actually viewable and not ridiculously covered in abstract censorship for nonexistent prudes out there who might be offended.

THE HAIRDRESSER'S HUSBAND

Colour, 1990, 82m. / Directed by Patrice Leconte / Starring Jean Rochefort, Anna Galiena, Roland Bertin, Maurice Chevit / Severin (US R1 NTSC), DVDY (France R2 PAL) / WS (2.35:1) (16:9), Second Sight (UK R0 PAL) / WS (1.78:1) (16:9) (16:9)

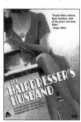 After working as a gun for hire on a string of French comedies, direc-tor Patrice Leconte finally found his real voice during the art house boom of the late 1980s with his short and evocative neo-noir, *Monsieur Hire*, his first title with notable international exposure. A perfect fit for the age of studios like Miramax, he followed up this success with a more benign look at obsession, 1990's *The Hairdresser's Husband* (*Le marie de la coiffeuse*), which was marketed as a sunny, spicy import for romantics. As usual with Leconte, there's quite a bit more here than meets the eye.

Fond of dancing and the ocean where he grew up, Antoine (Jean Rochefort) has always been enamoured with beautiful hairdressers. While some men develop fixations on, say, nurses or cheerleaders, he remains firmly fixed on the idea of marrying a hairdresser and finally finds his dreams coming true when he meets Mathilde (Anna Galiena), who agrees to become his wife. Their idyllic existence consists of Antoine's joy watching his woman at work on her quirky clients, often indulging himself in his little dances or mixing her salon activities with more intimate pleasures. However, Antoine's wide-eyed fixation is about to take a very unexpected turn...

Even shorter than Leconte's previous film, *The Hairdresser's Husband* is an oddly compelling film in that there's very little forward narrative (if you break it down, there's barely more narrative thrust than *My Big Fat Greek Wedding*), yet the wonderful scope photography by Eduardo Serra (*Unbreakable*) and lyrical score by Michael Nyman (with a few Arabic numbers thrown in) creates an intoxicating ambience. Of course, the essential component here is the unlikely but magical chemistry between Rochefort and the stunning Galiena (also seen in much saucier fare like *Jamón Jamón* and Tinto Brass's *Black Angel*), who make a dazzling screen couple. It's difficult to discuss the film more without revealing the surprising ending, a tonal shift that caught many audiences off guard and demands a second viewing to reassess the true emotional nature of everything from the beginning. In any case, it's an essential French film whose disastrous home video history in the U.S. has finally been corrected well into the DVD era.

Initial VHS and laserdisc editions of the film were a complete waste, hacking the compositions into fragments and completely destroying its visual elegance. The first DVD out of the gate came from the U.K., but Second Sight's presentation only letterboxed the film at 1.78:1, barely an improvement and still way too claustrophobic. Still, this version does contain a nice Leconte short film, "La Famille Heureuse", which never surfaced on any of the other discs. The French release restores the original framing but features PAL speed up, which in this case has a detrimental effect on the music score; it also features a different Leconte short ("Le Batteur du Bolero") and a one-hour interview with Leconte and a much shorter piece with Serra, but these are French only with no sub options.

The eventual American DVD from Severin dispenses with the short films but more than makes up for it with the best transfer of the bunch, featuring very rich colours, progressive flagging and perfect framing. It still looks like an early '90s European film and often has a hazy veneer, but that's part of the original aesthetic. All versions indicate a Dolby Stereo soundtrack, but channel separation is extremely minimal. The Severin disc includes a theatrical trailer, a new and very pleasing, tightly-edited 36-minute Leconte interview with English subs covering his career from his early comedies up to this film, and a terrific 17-minute video interview with the still-lovely Galiena, who talks about going after the role thanks to viewing *Monsieur Hire*, her thoughts on eroticism in her film roles, and her prior work with Claude Chabrol. A very solid and worthwhile DVD all around.

THE HANGING WOMAN
Colour, 1973, 95m. / Directed by José Luis Merino / Starring Stelvio Rosi, Maria Pia Conte, Dyanik Zurakowska, Paul Naschy, Gérard Tichy
THE SWEET SOUND OF DEATH
B&W, 1965, 80m. / Directed by Javier Setó / Starring Emilio Gutiérrez Caba, Carlos Lemos, Paco Morán, Tota Alba, Dyanik Zurakowska / Troma (US R0 NTSC)

In a cursed Eastern European village, the death of Count Mihajli unleashes all sorts of pandemonium beginning with the mysterious lynching death of his daughter, *The Hanging Woman*, whose body is discovered by the count's nephew, Serge (Stelvio Rosi), recently arrived for the reading of the will. The count's wife Nadia (Maria Pia Conte) takes him in despite police suspicions that Serge might be the killer, and soon all sorts of suspicious characters begin popping up including a gravedigger named Igor (Paul Naschy) who loves his corpses just a little too much. Mad scientific experiments, a creepy séance climaxing in another murder, and the words "No 37" written in blood on a nightstand soon expose the chilling truth behind this supernatural mystery.

This superior Spanish/Italian horror film boasts a creepy third act filled with zombie mayhem and was one of the most widely-released films of its ilk in the days of VHS, though each version was missing either nudity, violence or significant plot points. Horror fans encountered it under a dizzying variety of titles including *Beyond the Living Dead*, *Return of the Zombies*, *Zombie 3: Return of the Living Dead* and *The Orgy of the Dead*. By any name it's a lot of fun, and while Naschy only has a minor supporting role, he definitely makes a strong impression whenever he's onscreen (with a phenomenally gory final bow you'll never forget). Rosi makes a solid lead in his last film role, though even in period clothes he looks like someone who stumbled out of a spaghetti western. Also noteworthy is the gothic score by Francesco De Masi (spiced up with library tracks from *The Ghost*), and the zombie make-up is surprisingly creepy and effective, paying off with a nifty final scene that delivers a nice, unexpected shudder.

Troma's DVD, an obvious labour of love, assembles all the footage from the various video masters around the work to create the longest version possible, and the results are definitely impressive. The open matte presentation varies depending on the condition of the source used, but the bulk of the film looks fine if not exceptional. Director José Luis Merino (who also helmed the interesting *Blood Castle*) is on hand for both an audio commentary (in Spanish with optional English subtitles) and a video interview in which he clearly recalls everything about the making of the film, from the wide variety of actors used to the demands of Italian co-financing and the necessity for shooting multiple versions of scenes for different markets. Naschy also appears for a new 14-minute interview about his role, which he embellished himself, and the man primarily responsible for dubbing Spanish '70s films, Ben Tatar, gives a fascinating interview about this lost art which could make a great feature-length documentary all on its own. Writer Shane Dallman offers a brisk 10-minute "Paul Naschy 101" overview of the actor/director's unique career, and the disc also includes the original trailer and a lobby card gallery.

That's not all, though; you also get an entire second bonus feature (barely noted on the packaging), 1965's *The Sweet Sound of Death* (aka *La llamada*). A moderately spooky curio, it's essentially an expanded *Twilight Zone* episode in which two lovers, Pablo (Emilio Gutiérrez Caba) and Dominique (Dyanik Zurakowska, also in the main feature), swear that if either of them dies before the other, their ghost will appear to tell them what happens after death. Not surprisingly, tragedy strikes and the pact starts to have some very eerie repercussions. Though low on the terror scale, it's a stylish little programmer with a few notable flourishes that make it worth a watch. The English-dubbed fullscreen transfer looks decent enough for an added bonus feature.

HANNA D.: THE GIRL FROM VONDEL PARK

Colour, 1984, 88m. / Directed by Rino Di Silvestro / Starring Ann-Gisel Glass, Sebastiano Somma, Fausto Lombardi, Karin Schubert / Severin (US R1 NTSC) / WS (1.78:1) (16:9)

Saddled with a drunk, promiscuous single mother (Karin Schubert), pretty Dutch teen Hanna (played by Ann-Gisel Glass) falls in with a bad crowd whose most toxic member, a degenerate playboy (Fausto Lombardi), introduces her to the joys of visiting porn sets, hanging out with streetwalkers in Vondel Park, and pill-popping and heroin use. Soon she's hooked on smack and turning tricks with plans of becoming a stag film actress, but a strait-laced guy named Alex (Sebastiano Somma) spends a passionate night with her and tries to save his beloved from the path to destruction.

The late Rino Di Silvestro had a sparse but memorable career in Italian sleaze, churning out efficient sex-and-violence concoctions like *Women in Cell Block 7*, *Werewolf Woman* and *Deported Women of the SS Special Section*. He brings that same tact into play here, depicting a girl's descent into the hell of addiction with the gusto best described as Lucio Fulci and Jess Franco on a bender. Hysterical anti-drug movies had been common in the mainstream since the days of *The Man with the Golden Arm* and Roger Corman's *The Trip* (or even earlier if you want to go back to the time of marginalized films like *Reefer Madness*), but the subgenre really hit its stride in the '70s and early '80s with fare like *Go Ask Alice* and this film's most obvious antecedent, Uli Edel's *Christiane F.* However, where those films aimed (and sometimes missed widely) at a positive social statement, this one is just ridiculously foul. After getting her start running around naked in David Hamilton's *Premiers désirs*, Glass obviously had no reservations about going to extremes for her craft with this film (an outlook she later proved with the unforgettable *Rats: Night of Terror*) and, aside from shedding her clothes regularly, performs in a number of excessive scenes in which she's either vomiting uncontrollably, having random sex with strangers in unflattering positions, or in the queasiest moment, getting a hit via syringe to the eyelid. The relentless parade of IV drug use and enthusiastic softcore sex scenes really muffle whatever message the film was trying to convey, but it's all so sordid you can't help but enjoy it as a pure guilty pleasure.

Severin's DVD release of this film is a real gem for trash fans, offering a solid anamorphic transfer (which improves substantially after the somewhat rocky opening credits) and a respectable presentation of the English audio track which, in the grand tradition of Italian exploitation, is about as genuine as any other. The early '80s Amsterdam location shooting is a real asset here, offering a glimpse of still-standing landmarks as well as stores and sites now lost in time. The disc includes the original theatrical trailer and, much more importantly, a new 42-minute interview with Di Silvestro (who died shortly before the DVD release) entitled "The Confessions of Rino D". He focuses mainly on the film at hand, calling it a story about an angel's descent into and through hell while eschewing any attempt at stark realism, instead going for an exaggerated depiction of drug addiction. He certainly achieved that, no question. He also talks a bit about his other significant exploitation films, and fans will be happy to note that he often worked (including on this film) with the infamous Bruno Mattei (who edited) and cohorts like composer Luigi Ceccarelli (*Women's Prison Massacre*) and cinematographer Franco Delli Colli (*Strip Nude for Your Killer*).

HARDWARE

Colour, 1990, 93m. / Directed by Richard Stanley / Starring Stacey Travis, Dylan McDermott, John Lynch, William Hootkins, Iggy Pop, Lemmy / Severin (DVD & Blu-ray, US R0 NTSC/HD), Optimum (DVD & Blu-ray, UK R2 PAL/HD) / WS (1.66:1) (16:9), Dragon (Germany R2 PAL)

In a bleak futuristic desert wasteland, military zone patroller Mo (Dylan McDermott) acquires a sack full of mechanical pieces including a fascinating robot head. He decides to offer all of it to his sculptress girlfriend, Jill (Stacey Travis), upon his return along with his mystic, drug-taking cohort, Shades (John Lynch). However, Mo and Jill's reunion lovemaking also triggers a switch in the robot, a military contraption named Mark 13, which assimilates the pieces from Jill's evolving sculpture around it to become a lean, extremely mean killing machine. Meanwhile Jill's activities are being monitored by a creepy, overweight voyeuristic neighbour (William Hootkins), and as Mo begins to realise the full danger of the situation, Jill might be unable to leave her apartment as the technological menace begins its bloody rampage.

Though it won't win points for originality, *Hardware* was never designed to break new narrative ground; even director Richard Stanley (who went on to direct the even more commercially-abused *Dust Devil*) admits the first version of the script was a derivative mess, and even now if you break the story down to its core elements, you've just got Dean Koontz's *Demon Seed* in cyberpunk dressing. What really makes the film is the style; love it or hate it, *Hardware* is a film you'll never forget. Each scene features strong, impressive imagery right from the haunting opening shot of a coated, masked scavenger trudging through the orange sand, and even the soundtrack pulses with a terrific Simon Boswell score and perfect song contributions from Public Image Ltd. and Ministry. Even Iggy Pop and Motörhead's Lemmy pop up, with the former scoring big only as a radio voice. The film also represents a delirious example of how much fun sci-fi could be when it wasn't afraid to splash the screen in blood; while the first half is deliberately paced and the very definition of a slow burner, the payoff is a riotous string of grisly death scenes and wild hallucinogenic sequences that fuse together in the striking finale.

Hardware inaugurated the 1990s on a particularly lurid note as it unspooled in theatres around the world in versions of varying degrees of explicitness. It caused quite a splash in the U.K. and among horror and sci-fi fans, but its wide release from Miramax in the U.S. was plagued with controversy. First the film lost several shots (including arterial spraying in all the major death scenes) in order to avoid a dreaded X rating, and then the studio mounted a lavish but misleading campaign promising a film that would outdo *Alien* and *The Terminator*. Needless to say, many audiences were not amused when they found themselves watching a slow, gory, and sexually perverse art film. Nevertheless a steady cult following evolved, and fans had to scramble to see the uncut version either via a smudgy and barely letterboxed British VHS or a full frame, middling German DVD from Dragon.

Fortunately the frustrating legalities and studio disinterest surrounding the film were eventually resolved, paving the way for a spectacular high-definition presentation that blows away the original theatrical experience. Much of the film was shot in low light with heavy red, orange and blue saturation, making it a nightmare for video technicians and even defeating many projectionists. The version available on DVD and particularly Blu-ray is a revelation, yielding extremely impressive detail and finally showing exactly what's happening in those crimson-hued bedroom scenes. Both the British Optimum release and the American Severin edition are taken from the same HD master, though the former displays quite a bit more cinematic debris during the opening reels for some reason. The audio sounds fine on both, though the Severin edition sweetens the deal with both the original two-channel mix and a 5.1 option, while Optimum only offers the former.

If the technical differences might seem to offer a clear choice between the two, the extras muddy the waters a bit. For the Severin, Stanley contributes a terrific solo audio commentary; as he proved with *Dust Devil*, Stanley's one of the best raconteurs around and delivers a fast-paced if sometimes dark and cautionary chat track loaded with anecdotes about the film. Not surprisingly, his experiences in South Africa and various third world countries had a profound impact on the feature, and he also goes into the visual and narrative influences which informed his first feature and reveals other odd bits of trivia, such as the casting of Sinead O'Connor in Lemmy's small role, which fell through at the last minute. The Optimum version contains a somewhat different track (though with much of the same information) featuring Stanley and producer Paul Trijbits, who also brings his own valuable perspective and often surprises Stanley with sometimes disturbing pieces of new information. Both are great, but either way you'll be happy to spend time hearing from Stanley about the making of the film.

The biggest extra from Severin (but completely missing from the Optimum) is "No Flesh Shall Be Spared: The Making of *Hardware*", a 53-minute retrospective with Stanley, Travis, Lemmy, Trijbits, cinematographer Steven Chivers and prior Stanley cinematographer Greg Copeland, executive producer/Palace founder Stephen Woolley, producer JoAnne Sellar, and conceptual designer (and horror poster artist) Graham Humphreys. It's an excellent piece with everyone painting a thorough picture of the film's genesis; not surprisingly Stanley provides the essential framing device, and you'll hear all about the influences of Dario Argento and Mario Bava, the necessary rewrites when McDermott showed up for shooting far too buff to play the junkie loser Mo as depicted in the script, Travis's reaction to the request to dye her hair red, who came up with the Mark 13 Bible quote, and the convoluted rights and distribution issues which surrounded the film's release and dogged it for much of the video era.

Stanley's shorter work is well represented here on both releases. Sourced from VHS, the 44-minute "Incidents in an Expanding Universe" is a 1985 Super 8 effort about a futuristic bleak society with several elements later to appear in *Hardware* including a lead male character with a robotic hand and lots of Venetian blinds. The earlier "Rites of Passage" from 1982 is a moody 9-minute tale (scored with music from *Cat People* and *The Shining*!) about an immortal South African man dealing with the disillusionment of his condition, while the much more recent Stanley short, 2006's "The Sea of Perdition", is a gorgeous and completely inexplicable scope mood piece about a female astronaut on Mars who stumbles into a watery cave and... well, you'll see for yourself. Music from Paul Williams and *Moonraker* provides a strange accompaniment to this one, which purports to be part seven of a series "to be continued".

A hefty 25-minute offering of deleted and extended footage (sourced from a dropout-riddled VHS tape in Stanley's care) presents some interesting if disposable snippets, including an extended sex scene with some disturbing additional TV footage, a lot of additional chat between the leads, some funny outtakes from one of the key death scenes, and the original footage which eventually made its way into Mo's climactic flashback/hallucination scene. Also included is a 3-minute promo created to sell the film and the original German trailer; for some reason the overplayed Miramax U.S. trailer is absent, but you can watch it online. Exclusive to the Severin (along with the aforementioned doc), Stanley also appears for a 7-minute video interview about the scuttled *Hardware 2* whose script was conceived along with the first film; however, bickering ownership issues prevented it from ever reaching the big screen, and the concept actually sounds quite intriguing. The Optimum disc replaces the absent extras with the Stanley film *Voice of the Moon* which is also available on the Subversive release of *Dust Devil*. Optimum make up some of the ground with nifty limited edition packaging containing the controversial *Shok!* comic strip which provided a partial (legally contentious) basis for the film, notes by Kim Newman, and collectible storybook art cards. However, for the value of the doc alone, Severin's release is the preferable option.

HEADER

Colour, 2006, 89m. / Directed by Archibald Flancranstin / Starring Jake Suffian, Elliot V. Kotek, Dick Mullaney, Tara Brooks / Synapse (US R1 NTSC) / WS (1.85:1) (16:9) / DD2.0

 A shot-on-video taboo-breaker that revels in American gothic grotesquerie solely for its own sake, *Header* charts the hellish trajectory of a disgruntled ATF agent (Jake Suffian) who

takes off from his seemingly happy home life to investigate some illegal liquor-making going on in the backwoods. However, people have been turning up dead with the backs of their skulls hollowed out, and it seems an inbred, psychotic clan at war for ages with its neighbours might be responsible. Exactly what they're doing with those holes in people's heads forms both the meaning of the title and the central shock device that propels its two most "appalling" sequences, though director Archibald Flancranstin never tips over the edge to make it a truly gruelling experience a la *Bride of Frank* or *Bloodsucking Freaks*, which traded in some similarly nasty subject matter.

This deliberate exercise in deviance marks the first adaptation of subterranean extreme horror novelist Edward Lee, who also appears for an interview in the supplements; think of it as a cross between a particularly nasty Jack Ketchum story and *Wrong Turn* and you'll get the idea. Some of the scenes (especially those with crazy Gramps) appear to be half-played for laughs, while most of the moments with Suffian are jittery and dead serious.

The bland DV photography doesn't really do the film any favours (Synapse's disc captures the very limited visual palette about as well as could be expected), but the film tosses in enough curveballs to keep things interesting and really redeems itself with the despairing and poetically sick final ten minutes, which bring the story in an interesting direction that could have inspired a more ambitious sequel away from the usual scary-redneck terrain. The DVD features two trailers and a "making of" featurette sliced into multiple sections, namely separate interviews with the director, Lee, Suffian, and a set-visiting Ketchum, along with a making-of look at the special effects.

HELL'S GROUND

Colour, 2007, 78m. / Directed by Omar Ali Khan / Starring Kunwar Ali Roshan, Rooshanie Ejaz, Rubya Chaudhry, Haider Raza, Rehan, Osman Khalid Butt / TLA (US R1 NTSC) / WS (1.78:1) (16:9)

Touted in its advertising as the first splatter film from Pakistan, *Hell's Ground* (original title: *Zibahkhana*) marks the inaugural feature film effort from the weird worldwide cinema excavators at Mondo Macabro, and as you might expect, it delivers the exploitation goods from the opening scenes with a streamlined narrative owing more than a few nods to '70s drive-in horror. Don't be fooled by the zombie references often tagged with the film, as the undead action is very brief and less relevant than it is in *Lemora*, but backwoods slasher fans should be amused to see a familiar formula trotted out in a very unfamiliar setting. While bopping across the countryside to an underground rock show in their Eastern Mystery Machine van, five plucky teenagers stop off to grab some tea from a sinister geezer named Crazy Ralph – uh, no, make that Deewana (played by *The Living Corpse* star Rehan), who warns them not to drive through the woods known as "Hell's Ground". They do, of course, and soon find themselves contending with an onslaught of horrors ranging from the supernatural (the aforementioned zombies) to the flat-out twisted, namely a creepy old crazy woman and a lunatic slasher running around in a plasma-soaked burqa killing people with a spiky mace on a stick. Before you can say "Who will survive, and what will be left of them?", the body count rises as the woods run red with blood.

Short and slick, *Hell's Ground* was obviously shot on HD but still comes off slicker than many of its predecessors thanks to some colourful, inventive photography and sparing but effective bursts of gore, most notably thanks to that iconic burqa maniac (a very creepy villain who could have used even more screen time). The acting and character development is nothing special, of course, and if this had been in English, you'd be hard pressed to differentiate this from, say, *Wrong Turn*; however, the Pakistan setting makes all the difference here with little touches involving political protests and local mysticism lending the project an air of novelty even if you know where the overall story is going. In one of the most unexpected stylistic flourishes, the film also uses drawn comic book transitions at key junctures (à la *Creepshow*) which has to be a slasher movie first. Oh, and you get a decent amount of songs to keep things lively, too.

Mondo Macabro vet and director Omar Ali Khan contributes an entertaining audio commentary for this DVD release which comes courtesy of TLA's worthwhile and hilariously all-over-the-board Danger After Dark series. He covers pretty much everything you'd want to know ranging from talent scouting to location work and how much the process of mounting a Pakistani film has changed since the heyday of '60s horror. He also appears in a truly unique 12-minute featurette, "Ice Cream Zombieland", which takes you to one of his real ice cream shops (with a striking cinematic visual design) used in the film and how the production fares locally. Other extras include some "LUMS Premiere Footage" with the cast and crew talking about the finished product, a "Zuj Music Video", a softer-looking theatrical trailer, and promos for other titles in the same DVD series. Fans of Pakistani monster films might be a little thrown by the more modern hack-and-slash angle overall, but more open-minded horror fanatics should find plenty of gruesomeness to lap up here.

HEROSTRATUS

Colour, 1967, 143m. / Directed by Don Levy / Starring Michael Gothard, Mona Chin, Peter Stephens, Gabriella Licudi, Helen Mirren / BFI (DVD & Blu-ray, UK R0 PAL/HD) / WS (1.78:1) (16:9)

When he decides to kill himself, despondent poet Max (Michael Gothard) decides to make a grand statement by hiring a publicity firm to ensure the media covers his death, allowing his name to live forever. Max's perception of the world is filled with startling, bizarre visions which can't compare to the horror of what he realises he's created with the media storm swirling out of control around him.

Unseen since its original theatrical release, this stylistically audacious work from one-shot Aussie director/artist/ photographer Don Levy (filmed over a five-year period) is a terrific find from the BFI's Flipside series, a sort of missing antecedent to films like *Performance* and especially *Network*. Interestingly, this opened the same year as another great "lost" British film, Peter Watkins's *Privilege*, and both reflect an increasing paranoia towards the way the media manipulates and often infects people's lives. Needless to say, things have only gotten much more alarming in subsequent decades. The title refers to the Greek man who sought fame by torching the Temple of Artemis at Ephesus, and the concept of seeking fame for its own sake has continued to remain a central concern of society as much as people would like to suppress it. Despite the subject matter, the film is hardly ponderous; in fact, you'd be hard pressed to find a more vibrant, vital, and enthralling visual experience from the same era. Levy makes expert use of colour, editing and framing while integrating fascinating visuals often based on the paintings of Francis Bacon, with Beethoven music even surging on the soundtrack at opportune moments. Also fascinating is the first lead performance from Gothard (who chillingly did commit suicide many years later), who went on to many unforgettable roles including *Scream and Scream Again*, *Lifeforce*, *The Valley*, *Whoever Slew Auntie Roo?*, *For Your Eyes Only* and particularly Ken Russell's *The Devils*.

The BFI release marks the first-ever video release of this title in any format. The transfer from the original 35mm negative is fantastic to behold and was thankfully preserved in HD, with superb colours and excellent detail. The film was shot open aperture at a 1.33:1 aspect ratio but framed to be matted off in theatres, so the BFI release contains both versions for comparison (with the widescreen version occupying the place of honour on disc one). Both are of the same excellent quality, and personal taste will dictate which version takes precedence (though the extra picture information on the 1.33:1 version is quite fascinating and might give it the edge). Extras include a batch of early Levy experimental short films including "Ten Thousand Talents" (1960, featuring voiceover by Peter Cook), "Time Is" (1964) and "Five Films" (1967), plus an interview from 1973 with the director and a 34-page booklet featuring appraisals of the director and stars, info about Levy's short films, and liner notes by film writers Amnon Buchbinder and Henry K. Miller.

HIDEOUT IN THE SUN

Colour, 1960, 70m. / Directed by Doris Wishman / Starring Dolores Carlos, Earl Bauer, Greg Conrad, Richard Falcon, Mary Line / Retro-Seduction Cinema (US R0 NTSC) / WS (1.78:1) (16:9)

Female drive-in pioneer Doris Wishman started off her bizarre, truly unique career with an appropriate project, a mild-mannered but odd nudist camp frolic packed with the all the staples you'd expect: volleyball players with one team wearing pants to obstruct frontal nudity, bare-butt archery, and gals lounging in swimming pools on inflatable rafts with their legs oh-so-strategically placed. Lensed in very bright colour, it's an utterly ridiculous robbery caper shoehorned into a nudie-cutie template as robbers Steve Martin (Doris must've just been watching the original *Godzilla*) and Duke (Greg Conrad) wind up hiding at a Miami naturist resort on their way to Cuba, with a buxom hostage, Dorothy Courtney (Dolores Carlos), in tow. Duke hides out in their bungalow while Steve and Dorothy go *au naturel* to blend in with the locals, and soon their escape plans take a not-too-surprising turn.

It's all rather sweet and innocent, with the heavy amount of bare bosoms and derrieres blending in with the scenery after a few minutes, and Doris's fractured framing is kept to a minimum here. The cast is mostly a bunch of no-names, but nudist movie regular Carlos also popped up in favourites like *Diary of a Nudist*, *Pagan Island*, H.G. Lewis's *A Taste of Blood*, and the immortal *The Beast That Killed Women*. Retro-Seduction Cinema's DVD of this long-lost treasure (thought extinct when the producer died in prison after stashing away all the elements) looks excellent in its digital incarnation; for some reason this open matte (1.33:1) film is presented in both full frame and 16x9 enhanced versions on separate discs. The compositions on the latter look better with all the extraneous headroom lopped away, but it's really a toss-up either way depending on your TV setting. Doris Wishman expert Michael J. Bowen (now the official owner of the film) contributes a full audio commentary in which he talks in detail about Doris's career and the bizarre history of this film, and he also provides liner notes and a text interview with Doris going into some detail about her nudist camp cinematic cycle, which reached its apex with the utterly mad *Nude on the Moon*. The first disc also contains a Wishman interview (excerpted from *Schlock! The Secret History of American Movies*), a 1960 "The Year That Was" newsreel, and a batch of Retro-Seduction trailers, while the second disc adds on a bonus nudie featurette ("Postcards from a Nudist Camp", basically an old European travelogue short) and additional vintage trailers.

HIS LAST REQUEST

B&W, 2005, 27m. / Directed by Simon Birrell / Starring Iris Diaz, Jack Taylor, Carmen Vadillo / Silicon Artists (US R0 NTSC)

A fascinating short film making the rounds as a standalone disc, *His Last Request* (*El último deseo*) feels like an especially arty and perverse offshoot of Jess Franco's recent output, which isn't too surprising given that director Simon Birrell was a co-writer on *Mari-Cookie and the Killer Tarantula* and the star is Franco regular Jack Taylor.

The entire 27-minute short is dialogue-free and accompanied by an oddly hypnotic soft jazz soundtrack, with intertitles (in English or Spanish) covering the actors' lines and important exposition. An ailing father (Taylor) regrets that he never had the chance to pursue any of his erotic fantasies, and when his daughter (Carmen Vadillo) brings home a sexy, dark-haired nurse (Iris Diaz) to tend to his needs, things are, ahem, looking up. However, soon the two girls are getting a little too close for comfort and daddy gets way more than he bargained for in the process. Shot in silky black and white and wisely packing its final moments with unexpectedly hefty doses of blood and eroticism, it's a promising offering from Birrell who will hopefully get a shot at doing an entire feature someday. The DVD also comes with some brief cast and crew bios, stills, and production info.

H

HOME SICK

Colour, 2007, 89m. / Directed by Adam Wingard / Starring Lindley Evans, Bill Moseley, Tiffany Schepis, Forrest Pitts, Tom Towles, Brandon Carroll / Synapse (US R0 NTSC) / WS (1.85:1) (16:9) / DD2.0

A film gorged with enough plasma to fuel a dozen Dimension Extreme releases, *Home Sick* sounds on paper like a horror fan's dream come true. An old-fashioned splatter movie with cast members from *The Texas Chain Saw Massacre* and *Henry: Portrait of a Serial Killer*? Check. A narrative hook that sets up a hefty body count at the hands of a mystery killer? Check. Ridiculous dialogue? Check. So does the end result live up to expectations? Well... not quite. After a puzzling prologue in which a young man winds up filling a bathtub with his blood after a thwarted encounter with a couple of hookers, the film jumps back to the beginning of the story ("earlier that day") as a group of friends in Alabama get together the celebrate the return of one of their friends, Claire (Lindley Evans). All of these twentysomethings are basically abrasive, self-absorbed jackasses, so it's a relief when the tedium is broken with the arrival of a stranger named Mr. Suitcase (Bill Moseley), who uses his case full of razors to slice wounds in himself every time someone answers the question, "Who do you hate?" When the last person jokingly answers that he hates everyone in the room, the suitcase psycho abruptly leaves, and the carnage begins. Realising they're all on a hit list, the friends choose between arming themselves or going to the cops, with everyone stupidly opting for the former courtesy of one guy's creepy uncle (Tom Towles). Not surprisingly, the plan only leads to an expansion of the chopping list before the spatter-soaked finale.

Also featuring a turn from very busy genre vet (and former Troma scream queen) Tiffany Schepis, *Home Sick* starts off like gangbusters with some rapidly-edited kills and a great, energetic turn from Moseley that shoots the film up with a shot of adrenaline it never quite matches. After his extended cameo is over, Towles comes in second best with his over-the-top bumpkin routine and makes an impression, but again he's a small supporting player compared to the rest of the cast. All of this points to the problem with the film, which is alluded to in the special features; namely, the whole thing had to be cobbled together into something remotely coherent in the editing room. The final act in particular shows signs of missing footage (or script pages) and lingers a long, long time on the gory effects to compensate, which actually works less effectively than the initial splattery salvos of the previous scenes. However, if you know this going in and don't expect everything to be tied together with a bow on top at the end, *Home Sick* delivers its share of sick surprises.

Unlike many first-time projects, *Home Sick* was shot on film (16mm, in this case) which puts it a visual cut above the usual DV fare. First-time filmmakers Adam Wingard and producer/writer E.L. Katz do a good job of bathing the screen in vivid, eye-catching colour schemes (but the lighting wanders oddly astray in a few shots), though the aforementioned lopsided editing works overtime to wring some sort of dramatic flow out of several scenes (not helped by a few less than stellar performances in some supporting roles). Synapse's DVD looks solid and is progressive flagged, though the letterboxed transfer is 4:3 (maybe because editing was finished on video, but that's just a guess; a similar thing happened with *Wild Zero*). The whole story about the creation of the film (which finished shooting in 2003 but didn't hit screens until 2007, then DVD the following year) is covered in the two main supplements, a Wingard/Katz commentary track and a featurette, "In a Room Where Darkness Counts", which covers the arduous path of the film from its creation (when the director was only 19) to its eventual completion, as well as the means necessary to obtain the three main stars (with only Schepis having a major role, and of course losing her top for good measure). The commentary's excellent, too, and in many respects is more compelling than the feature itself. You also get three of the duo's short films, "The Girlfriend" (the most interesting of the bunch and clocking in at half an hour), "1,000 Year Sleep", and the perplexing "Laura Panic". Finally you get a 5-minute interview with Moseley about his character and a long deleted opening sequence wisely ditched in favour of the final one.

HORRIBLE

Colour, 1981, 96m. / Directed by Joe D'Amato / Starring George Eastman, Annie Belle, Charles Borromel, Edmund Purdom, Katya Berger, Kasmir Berger / Mya (US R0 NTSC), X-Rated Kult (Germany R2 PAL) / WS (1.66:1)

Primarily because it features hulky, bearded George Eastman as another unstoppable psycho killer, this gory Italian slasher entry is usually categorised as a loose sequel to 1980's *Anthropophagus*, Joe D'Amato's surprise hit also released as *The Grim Reaper*. This one isn't quite so well known and aims for a slightly more traditional storyline as a priest (Edmund Purdom) is hot on the trail of a super-strong, deranged mental patient named Mikos (Eastman) who, after seemingly being mortally injured on a spiked gate, has managed to rejuvenate himself due to a rare genetic condition and is now on a rampage to destroy the entire family of someone who wronged him. After bumping off the babysitter, he's now after two kids left alone to fend off the unstoppable lunatic.

This relentless parade of outrageous gore sequences isn't anything close to a good film, but as a demonstration of '80s Euro-splatter, you can't find a more pure, stripped-down example. Eastman dives into his part with wide-eyed gusto and seems to be having fun in what amounts to an extended, spattered-up homage to the original *Halloween*, with D'Amato going to hilarious lengths to pass off his location and cast as all-American football addicts. Axes, drills, saws, and other handy implements are the real highlights here as Eastman drives them straight through the cast whose most recognisable member is regular sexploitation siren Annie Belle, who gets one of the film's juiciest death scenes.

Available on a bare bones DVD from Mya Communication (with a slightly shorter release out in Germany), this film earned a steady following back in the videotape days under a number of titles like *Monster Hunter* and *Rosso sangue*, even earning infamy as one of the more understandable Video Nasties back in the '80s. None of the violence is imitable, but it certainly is extreme and gratuitous – often outrageously so. The non-anamorphic Mya disc looks passable enough, even blowing up to faux-anamorphic proportions on widescreen monitors. A few slivers of non-violent footage are inserted from an inferior VHS release, but it's a surprisingly minor distraction and doesn't really affect the flow of the film. The dubbed English mono track is considerably shoddier than average for D'Amato, packed with stilted dialogue delivery and some real howlers buried in the script. Naturally, it shouldn't be any other way. An alternative Italian track is included as well but contains no subtitles, rendering it essentially useless for most viewers.

H

HORRORS OF MALFORMED MEN

Colour, 1969, 92m. / Directed by Teruo Ishii / Starring Tatsumi Hijikata, Teruo Yoshida / Synapse (US R1 NTSC) / WS (2.35:1) (16:9)

Banned in Japan for its politically incorrect attitude and still startling for its ferociously grotesque imagery, *Horrors of Malformed Men* has earned a cult reputation since its fleeting domestic release despite the fact that almost no one ever had the chance to see it. In an era marked by the rise of "pinky violence", this contribution to "freak cinema" (paralleled in the West by the offspring of *Freaks* and *Island of Lost Souls* populating drive-ins from the likes of Al Adamson) instead resembles a gothic horror acid trip in a circus tent. Based on an already disturbing novel by Japanese literary maestro Edogawa Rampo entitled

The Strange Tale of Panorama Island, the film charts the surreal journey of medical student Hirosuke Hitomi (Teruo Yoshida), who came of age in a bizarre performing carnival. A knife-throwing mishap and efforts to track down a strange double of himself who died mysteriously lead him to a desolate island overseen by the mad, web-fingered Jogoro Komoda (avant-garde dance innovator Tatsumi Hijikata), who spends his time using his scalpel and chemical knowledge to deform human beings into monstrosities, including the makeshift creation of Siamese "twins". Through monochromatic flashbacks, Hitomi learns about the past of this demented surgeon, who may or may not be his father – with various elements like flesh-consuming crabs, incest, cave-imprisoned women raped by hunchbacks, and devilish, cross-dressing wardens all building to an over-the-top conclusion not easily forgotten.

From the disorienting opening scenes set in a sexually-segregated asylum (which appropriately more closely resembles a performance art routine), it's clear that *Malformed Men* is not going to behave like a normal, linear film. The story veers from one striking scene to the next without any sort of warning, including a striking early scene of semi-clad, painted women being whipped and forced on their knees over a sandy hill, the eerie image of Hitomi stumbling with arms outstretched over the rocky seashore, and the jarring segues to colour-tinted footage for each piece of back story. Director Teruo Ishii (who hit commercial paydirt with such diverse films as Sonny Chiba's *The Executioner*, *The Joy of Torture* and the giddy *Starman* series) pays loving homage to the grotesque theatricality of Rampo throughout the film, including nods to other famous stories (most amusingly "The Human Chair"). However, his literally pyrotechnic finale owes nothing to anyone

and must have certainly influenced the similar visuals in the last scene of Brian De Palma's *The Fury*.

Synapse's lovingly-assembled DVD presents a great deal of context for this film, which will certainly need some explaining for newcomers to Japanese exploitation. The anamorphic transfer looks dazzling, from the split-screen, arachnid-packed opening credits to the wildly colourful lighting effects in nearly every scene, while the mono Japanese audio sounds perfectly clear with solid optional English subtitles. In addition to the theatrical trailer, the disc comes with a full-length audio commentary by critic Mark Schilling (who covers Ishii, the lead actors, the dance troupe, the history of Rampo, and everything in between) and two fascinating featurettes, produced with Outcast Cinema. The first, "Malformed Memories", features Tetsuo director Shinya Tsukamoto and Minoru Kawasaki (*The Calamari Wrestler*) in new video interviews talking about their experiences with Ishii's films (not just limited to *Malformed Men*), often recalling their uproarious reactions to the filmmaker's most audacious flourishes. Ishii (who died in 2005) also appears in snippets of a 2003 video interview talking about his own views as a filmmaker and a few comments related to this title in particular. However, he's more thoroughly represented in "Ishii in Italia", a lengthier session of his comments at the Fear East Film Festival in which he discusses his views on horror and sex cinema, the influence of Rampo, and his affinity for the grotesque. Finally, the disc (which comes packaged in a reversible cover containing both a new cover design and the original Japanese theatrical poster art) has a solid set of liner notes from Jasper Sharp (covering Rampo's cinematic legacy) and Patrick Macias and Tomohiro Machiyama, who cover the film's unfortunate history in its native country and the circumstances which led to even the title itself becoming a cultural taboo.

HOT MOVES

Colour, 1984, 85m. / Directed by Jim Sotos / Starring Michael Zorek, Adam Silbar, Jill Schoelen, Jeff Fishman, Monique Gabrielle / Code Red (US R0 NTSC) / WS (1.85:1) (16:9)

The '80s teen sex comedy has received little critical love even with the added glow of nostalgia, but this an affable entry from the era of *Hardbodies* and *Hot Dog... The Movie*. It has enough worthwhile points mainly courtesy of director Jim Sotos, who also helmed the strange quasi-slasher *Sweet Sixteen*. Though *The Last American Virgin* might be the official Americanisation of the popular Israeli "Lemon Popsicle" films, this one could just as easily fit that description as it follows a quartet of inexperienced Venice Beach teenage boys on their quest to "lose it" before summer's end.

The big draw here for most cult film fans is a leading role for the most appealing scream queen of the '80s, husky-voiced Jill Schoelen (*The Stepfather*, *Popcorn*), who always managed to elevate her material even when it was beneath her. Utterly juvenile and containing the emotional depth of a spit cup, the film still works as a model of cable-friendly pitfalls with a staggering amount of T&A (and more than that in the legendary nude beach voyeurism scene, which seems to last forever). The only other real name here is Michael Zorek, an '80s character actor from *Private School* and TV's *The Facts of Life* who gets the most substantial male role here. The whole film is awash in sort of a post-*Grease*, New Wave-meets-'50s neon hue bound to provoke nostalgic flashbacks in anyone old enough to remember A Flock of Seagulls, and if that's not enough incentive, you also get a small but, well, prominent role by another, more down-market scream queen, one-time *Penthouse* Pet Monique Gabrielle (before she reached immortality in *Amazon Women on the Moon*).

While its contemporaries like *Mischief* languish on DVD in bare-bones editions, *Hot Moves* gets the full-on special edition treatment from Code Red. The anamorphic transfer isn't pristine but works well enough; colours are vibrant and solid, though the whole film has a vaguely soft, gauzy look that may have been intentional. Sotos offers an entertaining commentary track along with co-star Zorek, Adam Silbar, and writer Peter Foldy (but alas, no Schoelen), focusing on the low budget methods needed to compete with the growing teen comedy market and how the film got a bit lost in the wave of competitors. Zorek returns for his own 13-minute video interview in which he talks more about his career in general hopping around between TV and the big screen (as well as what he's been up to since he retired), while a second video featurette has the director, Foldy and Silbar talking much more briefly about their overall experiences with the film. In typical Code Red tradition, you also get a goofy video intro to the movie itself with Zorek clowning around with the disc's moderator and Q&A'er, "Julia". Park this one in your DVD library next to *Losin' It* and your Pac-Man cheat manual.

THE HOWL

Colour, 1970, 93m. / Directed by Tinto Brass / Starring Tina Aumont, Gigi Proietti, Nino Segurini / Cult Epics (US R1 NTSC) / WS (1.85:1) (16:9)

Drawing its title and a dash of inspiration from Allen Ginsberg's famous beatnik classic, *The Howl* (*L'urlo*) is easily the most free-wheeling and unjustly ignored title in the Tinto

Brass canon, with plenty of the auteur's own obsessions and stylistic flourishes congealing into an avant garde snapshot of late '60s global unrest that still resonates today. Mixing anti-war sentiments with a flurry of rapid-fire pop culture references, atrocity footage, abundant nudity, and even oddball comedy, this oft-censored psychedelic madhouse has never before been seen in English and will blow away anyone ready to groove along with its unique, inspirational rhythms.

Torso's Tina Aumont stars as Anita, a lovely young woman escaping the oppression of modern-day society in a globe-hopping travelogue that rivals anything by Alejandro Jodorowsky for sheer mind-melting strangeness. Brass himself admits there wasn't really a script per se, as the film was shot more like a voyage with a vague framework for the actors; thus it's a real "trip" in the truest movie sense, grabbing the viewer by the throat from an opening frames and never letting up for an hour and a half. Basically Aumont is about to marry her conformist fiancé (Nino Segurini) in a bizarre outdoor ceremony, only to take off to escape to a new life. Our runaway bride finds a travelling companion in Coso (Gigi Proietti), a Chaplinesque figure whose smile instigates her rebellion and who accompanies her through picaresque adventures edited like a music video as they tangle with naked hippies, a sex club hotel, bourgeois cannibals, overly enthusiastic soldiers, and other things you don't exactly see every day.

Just why *El Topo* took off as a midnight hit while this languished in obscurity after a few sparse Italian play dates is anyone's guess, but Brass's subsequent career has justifiably spurred interest in his back catalogue before he turned to cheeky erotica. *The Howl* essentially completes a loose trilogy of nearly plotless, experimental cinematic firebombs along with *Deadly Sweet* and *Attraction*, finishing the

cycle on a most extreme, dizzying note. Aumont was already a blossoming starlet with films like Fellini's *Satyricon* and Vadim's *The Game Is Over* under her belt, but she really carries her starring role here incredibly well even when the film makes no sense at all on a rational level. Extraordinarily beautiful and captivating to behold, she only had a middling career later in the '70s (*Salon Kitty* and Fellini's *Casanova* being the high points) but really shone when given the chance. Meanwhile, Brass piles on every cinematic technique in the book, utilising rapid-fire editing in dream sequences, alternating B&W and colour footage, and undercranked slapstick scenes, while semi-regular Brass composer Fiorenzo Carpi accentuates the visuals with an equally wild experimental score. His regular cinematographer, Silvano Ippoliti, also delivers in the visual department, particularly with two memorable sequences involving burning vehicles. You've definitely never seen anything like it.

Finding a decent English-friendly version of *The Howl* has been impossible for decades, with even grey market devotees only turning up awful, dupey copies. It's important to keep its extreme rarity in mind when evaluating the Cult Epics release, which comes from an uncut transfer of a somewhat faded, splice-riddled print reportedly held by Brass himself. The rights history to the film left it essentially an orphan for decades, without usable film elements around to do a proper transfer. The presentation here is definitely better than anything we've had before by a long shot, but don't expect fireworks. The 1.85:1 framing appears to be correct, and all of the sometimes volatile imagery is intact (including nudity that really pushes the envelope way beyond what was accepted in 1970). Brass contributes a commentary track that doesn't even try to offer any sort of linear explanation for the film; instead he mainly focuses on its unorthodox shooting methods, the techniques used to recruit the actors and get them in the right spirit, and his feelings about this extremely fertile period of his career. His accent's still very thick, so prepare to do a bit of rewinding to figure out a few of his observations. Also included are trailers for *Deadly Sweet* and *Attraction* (originally *Nerosubianco*, here under its wildly inappropriate reissue title, *The Artful Penetration of Barbara*). Easily a must-purchase for anyone who wants to see just how far out Italian cinema could really go at its creative pinnacle.

HUNDRA

Colour, 1983, 100m. / Directed by Matt Cimber / Starring Laurene Landon, Cihangir Gaffari, Maria Casal, Ramiro Oliveros / Subversive (US R1 NTSC) / WS (2.35:1) (16:9)

Following the critical disbelief which greeted his bid for mainstream acceptance in 1982 with a pair of Pia Zadora vehicles (including the notorious incest-fest *Butterfly*), drive-in director Matt Cimber reteamed with composer Ennio Morricone for another project the following year. This abrupt change of pace, *Hundra*, is one of many, many *Conan* copies which flooded theatres around the world, though in this case it also predates another Schwarzenegger film as well, *Red Sonja*. One of the more accomplished of its ilk (though certainly not as lunatic as some offerings from the likes of Roger Corman and Lucio Fulci), *Hundra* follows the template of its predecessor fairly closely albeit with a female lead handling the swordplay and tough talk. When her all-female clan is slaughtered by marauders while she's out gathering food, blonde and athletic Hundra is told by a wise old seer

that it is now her destiny to go out into the world and find a way of beginning her bloodline anew. Though she doesn't really know how to interact with men when it doesn't involve bashing them over the head with the brunt of a sword, Hundra decides to make a go of it as she roams through various tribes of midgets, barbarians, and snotty villagers. A potential baby daddy finally appears in the form of Pateray (Ramiro Oliveros), whose roof she falls through in one of the film's goofiest scenes (reproduced again in the menus for good measure). Unfortunately she's a little too scrappy to light his fire, so she decides to improve herself by ingratiating herself with the local prince and his makeover-friendly wife, who further Hundra's quest to create another little fighter for her tribe.

Strangely paced but rarely dull, *Hundra* offers all the usual staples of the genre: flat performances, dusty deserts, lots of costumes assembled from bed sheets and animal pelts, and a boisterous orchestral score. Morricone shines as usual with his musical support (and oddly enough, he'd go on to score *Red Sonja*, too), and Cimber seems to have fun manipulating the action within his scope frame even when cinematographer John Cabrera (fresh off *Hell of the Living Dead*!) doesn't seem quite up to the task; just imagine what Cimber's past cinematographer, Dean Cundey, could have done with this. The film is also far less exploitative than you'd expect; the gore and nudity are kept to a minimum, perhaps in deference to the pro-feminist storyline, but viewers still get lots of rousing action especially in the opening 15 minutes.

Long mangled by unwatchable pan and scan transfers, *Hundra* gallops to DVD with a much-needed restoration of its original anamorphic compositions. The transfer itself is something of a mixed bag; the framing looks right and detail appears sharp enough, but the colours seem a bit unnatural and artificially boosted (while past versions were way too desaturated) Also, while this plays well enough on smaller monitors, sequences packed with movement (especially the opening scene) tend to shimmer and break up on larger widescreen displays. Don't expect a demo piece by any means, but fans of '80s sword and sandal romps should still find this well worth the investment. Subversive has also packed their *Hundra* disc with a worthy selection of supplements, highlighted by the massive 47-minute featurette, "Hunting Hundra". Both Cimber and Laurene Landon appear on-camera to discuss the making of the film, talking about subjects including the feisty actress's performing of her own stunts, the European locations, the nature of independent multi-national financing, and various anecdotes from the set, including the reasons for the obvious visual parallels to *Conan.* Their rapport carries over to the feature-length audio commentary in which both are joined by Subversive's Norm Hill for a fast-paced chat. Landon's deficiencies in the emoting department are largely glossed over, though it's obvious here through inference that Cimber had to work pretty hard with his editors to craft a remotely effective character in the editing room. Other extras include a new promo for *Hundra*, a rather nice colour comic book insert by Phil Avelli with another adventure for the same heroine, additional Subversive promos, and in a welcome gesture for the first few thousand copies, a second disc containing Morricone's original score, which was previously issued several years ago in the U.S. as a budget release from Laserlight.

HURT

Colour, 2006, 107m. / Directed by Scott A. Martin / Starring Scott A. Martin, Ron Burgher, Greg Mason, Jim Meredith / Redemption (UK R0 PAL, US R0 NTSC) / DD2.0

The umpteenth "serial killer confessional" movie released in the last decade, this British horror film is one of the few current-century homegrown offerings from the U.K. horror specialists at Redemption. Presumably aiming for the same audience as films like *Behind the Mask*, *The Ugly* and *Man Bites Dog*, this one falls well short of its predecessors but might be worth a look on a slow evening.

Director Scott A. Martin also assumes star duties as a serial killer who decides to unload about his crimes, which have so far claimed the lives of 47 people. Various flashbacks (in a grating variety of video formats and aspect ratios all the way from full frame to scope) explore his misdeeds, though gorehounds lured in by the creepy cover art may be disappointed that nothing all that harrowing or shocking really happens.

Some of the rough-hewn DIY video techniques are atmospheric and work well, while others are just chintzy and irritating. It would be interesting to see what Martin could accomplish with a stronger script and budget, however. Redemption's disc has the usual cross-promotional trailers, while the sole extra of real note is a commentary track by the filmmaker/star that's actually more engaging than the film itself. He talks about the challenges faced by mounting an indie horror project in the current U.K. market and explains what he wanted throughout, which isn't always clear in the finished product.

HUSH

Colour, 2009, 91m. / Directed by Mark Tonderai / Starring William Ash, Christine Bottomley, Andreas Wisniewski, Clarie Keelan, Stuart McQuarrie / Optimum (DVD & Blu-ray, UK R2 PAL/HD) / WS (2.35:1) (16:9) / DD5.1

While driving along a motorway at night, young couple Zakes (William Ash) and Beth (Christine Bottomley) are on the brink of a breakup due to his inability to finish any of his ambitious projects and her recent, illicit infidelity. While Beth is napping, Zakes nearly sideswipes a truck whose cargo door flies open for a moment, exposing a naked, screaming, caged woman inside. Zakes calls the police but can't make out a discernible tag number, and despite Beth's urging, he decides to let the matter go and continue his job of photographing poster displays in public toilets arranged by his employer. However, the night of terror is just beginning as Beth disappears at a subway stop and Zakes is plunged into a cat-and-mouse game with the ruthless truck driver.

Drawing obvious inspiration from other road peril films like *Duel*, *Joyride* and *Breakdown*, *Hush* (which really could have used a different title since it conjures up memories of a great *Buffy* episode and a not-so-great Jessica Lange film) starts off very weakly by failing to establish any sympathy at all for its two sullen and bickering leads, whom you'll be praying get knocked off in the first five minutes. First-time director Mark Tonderai (a BBC Radio One DJ) also begins on a (literally) shaky visual note by relying on the same unattractive, green-and-yellow digital photography that plagues far too many recent genre films and an overabundance of wobbly, unfocused camerawork that detracts from the narrative focus rather than reinforcing it. Fortunately things improve tremendously after Beth's disappearance as the film finally knuckles down for some solid suspense sequences including a hair-raising men's room stalking and an unexpected third act twist that ups the stakes substantially. It's no minor classic, but *Hush* is worth enduring its unpromising set up for a few decent thrills on a slow evening. Ash manages to turn in a credible leading man performance once the narrative cuts him loose, and though you never actually see his face, Andreas Wisniewski (*Die Hard*, *The Living Daylights*) is quite physically menacing as the main villain. Be sure to sit through the credits for an eerie postscript, too.

Optimum's release features a transfer about as good as could be expected given the erratic source material, which ranges from sharp to murky depending on the scene. The surround mix fares better with the percussive score adding immeasurably to the chase sequences. Extras include a director commentary and two video interviews (all good but featuring a great deal of overlapping info), a video chat with Ash, the theatrical trailer, a making-of documentary split up into five featurettes (mostly EPK-style behind-the-scenes footage and chats), and eight minutes of minor deleted scenes with optional director commentary.

I, A WOMAN, PART II

Colour, 1968, 88m. / Directed by Mac Ahlberg / Starring Gio Petré, Lars Lunøe, Klaus Pagh, Hjördis Petterson

THE DAUGHTER: I, A WOMAN, PART III

Colour, 1970, 83m. / Directed by Mac Ahlberg / Starring Inger Sundh, Gunbritt Öhrström, Klaus Pagh, Tom Scott / After Hours (US R0 NTSC) / WS (1.78:1) (16:9), Something Weird (US R0 NTSC DVD-R)

 As any international sleaze fan worth his salt knows, the whole Eurosex phenomenon really kicked off in Sweden in 1965 with the first big heavy-breathing export, *I, a*

Woman. Not surprisingly, a raft of imitations soon followed, and it wasn't long before two sequels were put into production, both distributed by Chevron (making a short-lived branching out to movies along with peddling gasoline). Our sensual heroine, Siv (here played by Gio Petré from *Wild Strawberries* and *Daddy, Darling*), is now having her adventures in full Technicolor while married to Hans (*The Kingdom*'s Lars Lunøe), a pasty, pervy and well-off furniture dealer who pawns dirty pictures of his wife to his more well-to-do patrons. When he arranges for one of them to tryst with Siv in person, she realises she'd better dump her manipulative spouse in favour of Leo (Klaus Pagh), a nice guy doctor. Her decision becomes even easier when a deep, dark secret from her husband's past is finally revealed.

Only slightly more explicit than its predecessor, *I, a Woman Part II* features a much older heroine and feels like a stab at the more upscale, elegant, continental fantasies found in the films of Radley Metzger (who distributed the original movie, incidentally). The lush decor and decadent aristocratic settings give it a very different feel, and if the main character's name weren't Siv, you'd be hard-pressed to guess this was a sequel. The big reveal at the end is easily the most memorable part of the film, pushing it into seriously twisted territory that will leave more than a few jaws on the floor; let's just say this one predates a very significant and trashy erotic subgenre from Italy by several years. The dreamy soundtrack by Sven Gyldmark (released on an LP, incredibly) is also a solid asset.

Next up is *The Daughter: I, a Woman Part III*, which – you guessed it – follows the escapades of Siv's daughter, Birthe (*The Seduction of Inga*'s Inger Sundh), as the plot is spiced up with plenty of go-go nightclub scenes, interracial sex, lesbianism, and Birthe's troubling, thankfully unrequited attraction to her own mom. Pretty much dispensing with the chi-chi trappings of *Part II*, this outing instead piles on hallucinatory, drug-like stylistics from the protracted opening credits sequence which finds our naked protagonist swirling in snowflakes bathed in lighting out of a Mario Bava film.

The plot itself is pretty dispensable (basically dawdling around while Birthe decides whether she wants to settle down with a black American guy), but the fun all lies in the incidentals cited above. Incredibly, future Stuart Gordon cinematographer Mac Ahlberg directed all three films in the series, though they bear pretty much no stylistic similarities to each other whatsoever.

This double feature DVD from After Hours (under a "Euro Grindhouse" banner) marks the first official U.S. availability of both films, taken from battered but watchable American release prints featuring the original dub tracks and presented in anamorphic 1.78:1 widescreen. *Part II* looks accurately framed for the most part – a little tight (probably shot for 1.66:1), but overall fine. Its companion film is obviously squeezed from a full frame master to fit the frame, meaning the actors' heads look a little squished. (Both titles were also issued earlier on VHS and DVD-R via Something Weird in cleaner but non-anamorphic transfers from the original U.S. negatives, oddly enough.)

The only extra (not counting the usual sexploitation cross-promotion trailers) is a liner notes booklet by Michael J. Bowen, who does an excellent job covering the history of the whole trilogy while rattling off some great facts, such as the presence of Hal Linden as one of the dubbers and the fact that the second film was the first time a sequel ever used "Part II" in its title.

I KNOW WHO KILLED ME

Colour, 2007, 105m. / Directed by Chris Sivertson / Starring Lindsay Lohan, Julia Ormond, Neal McDonough, Garcelle Beauvais / Sony (DVD & Blu-ray, US R1 NTSC, UK R2 PAL, Japan R2 NTSC, France R2 PAL/HD) / WS (2.35:1) (16:9) / DD5.1

Already notorious as one of the past decade's most berserk thrillers, this nail in the cinematic coffin of Lindsay Lohan quickly veers into lunatic territory within the first ten minutes and never looks back on its road to utter oblivion. Lohan stars in two roles (or does she?) as Aubrey Fleming, a pampered high schooler with writing aspirations who gets kidnapped by a sadistic serial killer, and Dakota Moss, a skanky stripper who turns up missing a couple of limbs and who may hold the secret to Aubrey's disappearance. Toss in bionic limbs, a blood-smeared stripper pole, a fairy tale glass coffin, psychic stigmata, and an utterly confused Julia Ormond and Neal McDonough, and you've got one of the weirdest movies to get a major studio release since *Color of Night*.

Though written off as some sort of slasher film/torture porn/erotic thriller, this is anything but. The DVD and Blu-ray versions from Sony look spectacular, making the most of the heaviest blue and red lighting this side of *Suspiria* (albeit with .01% of the artistry) and wonky scope compositions. (The DVD also offers a disastrous full frame alternative if you're feeling masochistic.) Unfortunately the extras don't add much clarity to the film's intentions; you basically get a bunch of deleted footage (with an additional ending suggesting it might all be some weird creative writing exercise), a few bloopers, and some trailers, but a double dip release down the road seems highly unlikely.

IMMORAL WOMEN

Colour, 1979, 93m. / Directed by Walerian Borowczyk / Starring Marina Pierro, Gaëlle Legrand, Pascale Christophe, François Guétary, Jean-Claude Dreyfus, Jean Martinelli / Severin (US R1 NTSC) / WS (1.66:1) (16:9)

Following the success of *Immoral Tales* in the mid-1970s, director Walerian Borowczyk made a belated return to the erotic anthology concept in 1979 with *Les héroïnes du mal* ("Heroines of Evil"), which was titled *Three Immoral Women* for its few English-language appearances and then (wisely) shortened to simply *Immoral Women* for its DVD release. Once again the theme of sex, deception and profit through the ages is prominent here, but this time women gain the upper hand each time through their crafty application of physical attractiveness and emotional manipulation. The always ravishing Marina Pierro (a Borowczyk regular who had just appeared in his *Behind Convent Walls*) stars in the first segment, "Margherita", as a young woman whose passionate relationship with her poor tradesman boyfriend is hampered by their lack of funds. She seizes an opportunity to become the muse and model for a handsome young painter (François Guétary), seducing both him and his unscrupulous patron, Bini (Jean-Claude Dreyfus, best known as the crazed cannibal butcher from *Delicatessen*). How her bed-hopping profits her is, of course, a secret not revealed until the cheeky finale. The second and most notorious episode concerns "Marceline" (Gaëlle Legrand from *Tender Cousins*), a frizzy-haired nymphet who spends her afternoons on the lawn getting a bit more pleasure than is socially acceptable from her fluffy white pet rabbit. Her parents don't approve of her activities and decide to take matters into their own hands, with unbelievably perverse results. The last and shortest story follows the modern day adventures of "Marie" (Pascale Christophe), an unhappily married woman kidnapped by a randy criminal who decides to take advantage of her in his van. With the help of the family pooch, she discovers a way to get rid of all of her problems in one fell swoop, with the expected naughty wink at the end.

Though it doesn't have any casting novelty gimmicks like the preceding *Immoral* film, this is in every way a worthy companion piece and certainly as satisfying a piece of erotica as Borowczyk ever delivered. His wonderfully surreal sense of humour is well in evidence here, with each story taking a number of hilarious and often weird turns with murders often doled out as a matter of course. His anti-clerical jabs are still present as well, with a stern Pope duped by both Margherita and a hilarious Michelangelo who gets away with frolicking with naked boys under the eye of the church. The "immorality" implied by the title is clearly a reference to the women's philosophical choices to achieve their ends rather than a condemnation of their sexuality itself. In purely sensual terms this is also one of Borowczyk's most accomplished films, with Pierro in particular filmed as beautifully as any actress who ever stepped in front of a camera.

Various video editions of this film have circulated on the fan market over the years, usually originating from Greece or Japan. However, many shots were lost depending on the version, with nearly all male frontal nudity and some graphic female close-ups hitting the cutting room floor; one particularly startling visual involving hymeneal blood was always the first to go. Severin's release presents the complete version of the film uncensored, and the image quality is also a considerable improvement; apart from some limitations in the original film itself (a few rough cuts and bits of debris here and there), this is a stunning presentation of a film that's been crying out for an adequate transfer. The soundtrack can be played in the original French with optional subtitles or a not-bad English dub track. Extras include a thorough Borowzcyk bio by Richard Harland Smith and the evocative European theatrical trailer.

IN THE FOLDS OF THE FLESH

Colour, 1970, 87m. / Directed by Sergio Bergonzelli / Starring Pier Angeli, Eleonora Rossi Drago, Fernando Sancho, Luciano Catenacci, Alfredo Mayo / Severin (US R0 NTSC) / WS (1.85:1) (16:9)

Though the *giallo* subgenre of sexy, stylish Italian thrillers was only about seven years old in 1970, it had already neared the self-parody point with the release of *In the Folds of the Flesh*, a lurid, trashy, and appealing slice of opulent excess designed for those who had already become tired of traditional black-gloved killer antics. This time out the obligatory, English-friendly lead actor is Pier Angeli (here billed as Anna Maria Pierangeli), a briefly hot Hollywood starlet from Italy who failed to make it to the big time and retreated home, only to die of a presumably intentional drug overdose in 1971. Here she acquits herself well with a dual (or triple?) role that fits in perfectly with the film's recurring barrage of Freudian quotes and cockeyed psychoanalysis.

The convoluted tale begins when, after a bout of Roger Corman-style swirling psychedelia, escaped prisoner Pascal (spaghetti western regular Fernando Sancho) is apprehended by police right after witnessing a mysterious woman burying a corpse near a lake. Years later he returns to the site, where a bed and breakfast is run by three decidedly unbalanced inhabitants: Lucille (*Camille 2000*'s Eleonora Rossi Drago), her son (Alfredo Mayo), and Falesse (Angeli). However, the buried body turns out to be a dead German Shepherd, strangled for sniffing around the scene of the crime. As it turns out, Lucille was a concentration camp survivor and has been left more than a little disturbed after watching her mother and daughter die in a gas chamber, and she conspires with her two caregivers to off Pascal in an outrageous scene involving a full bathtub, a cuckoo clock, and a couple of cyanide tablets. Then a man shows up claiming to be Lucille's father, and the roster of murderers and dead bodies really starts to pile up.

Though several directors had already become solid *giallo* practitioners by this point (Mario Bava and Umberto Lenzi, most obviously), 1970 marked a period of huge change for the formula with the arrival of Dario Argento (*The Bird with the Crystal Plumage*), Sergio Martino (*The Strange Vice of Mrs. Wardh*), and Mario Bava's game-changing *A Bay of Blood*, but *In the Folds of the Flesh* also breaks new ground by focusing entirely on a lunacy-driven exercise in style and indulgence for its own sake and a focus solely on jolting the viewer with everything from tasteless, black and white Nazi flashbacks to the aforementioned, thankfully simulated doggie killing. Director Sergio Bergonzelli had already cut his teeth on spaghetti westerns for the most part (except for the rarely seen erotic thriller *Libido*), but here he shows an affinity for turning a stagy, limited setting into a cesspool of deviant psyches. Definitely not one for the newcomers, this is one crazy-ass trip for any seasoned Euro-cultist.

Though it never really saw any exhibition in America, *In the Folds of the Flesh* became something of an underground favourite due to its circulation on VHS

swiped from Greece or a short-lived British tape from Redemption. Severin's DVD quickly demonstrates the huge advances in video technology with a greatly improved, uncut presentation, packed with rich colours and dead-on framing. The hilarious, error-packed Freudian intertitles have never looked so vivid, either. Audio is presented in the original English mono, with some of the actors looped afterwards in the usual Italian tradition. The sole extra is the theatrical trailer, which might actually be even more delirious than the main feature.

THE INCONFESSABLE ORGIES OF EMMANUELLE

Colour, 1982, 86m. / Directed by Jess Franco / Starring Vicky Adams (Muriel Montossé), Tony Skios (Antonio Rebollo), Ida Balin (Asunción Calero), Robert Foster (Antonio Mayans), Carmen Carrión / Severin (US R0 NTSC), Anchor Bay (UK R2 PAL) / WS (2.35:1) (16:9)

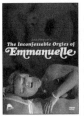

A rather rote skin flick dressed up as an unofficial Emmanuelle film, *The Inconfessable Orgies of Emmanuelle* circulated more widely than most of Jess Franco's other output during his busy return to Spain in the early '80s. Once again the filmmaker's trademark obsessions with seaside locales and cubist decor are in abundance here to offset the frequent writhing naked bodies, though the expected perverse touches are kept to a minimum in favour of a plot straight out of your average cable softcore offering. Occasional Franco collaborator "Vicky Adams", aka French TV personality Muriel Montossé, stars as the title character, who's married to a decidedly piggish macho husband, Tony (Antonio Rebollo), whose past lover is staying nearby. Though they can't keep their hands off each other (even in a wax museum populated by disturbing replicas of Humphrey Bogart and Liza Minnelli in full *Cabaret* gear), they don't seem too disturbed by the idea of dallying around with other vacationers at their hotel resort. Unfortunately the freshly-plucked wife gets a little too out of control, first having a little lesbian action with a burlesque dancer and then initiating a series of extramarital encounters which could destroy the fabric of her marriage forever.

Packed with nudity and attractively shot in scope (an aspect utterly lost in past video versions), Franco's film is a strictly middle-of-the-road affair designed mainly to showcase its cast in as little clothing as possible. The wax museum and climactic sofa-bound orgy are the most memorable sequences, and the thick atmosphere helps carry the film along through its dry stretches. The dreamlike score helps as well (with yet another cameo from that "La vie est une merde" song so prevalent in other Franco films), and the nonlinear device of unfolding the story as a series of recollections through the male lead during an afternoon stroll is certainly an interesting and melancholic one.

Rarely seen in America outside of the usual grey market pipeline, this film gets a shockingly respectable presentation from Severin. The widescreen transfer looks excellent and beautifully film-like, with very minimal flaws and luscious, earthy colour schemes. Both the Spanish and English soundtracks are included, with the former working much better with optional English subtitles; the English dub (particularly the narration) omits several details and simplifies the script far too much, not to mention the damage it inflicts by replacing or submerging most of the music score. The only extra is a typically endearing Franco video interview in which he explains the film's curious title, offers his opinion of the rest of the series, and recalls the shooting

conditions from this curious and rarely-explored period in his filmography. The same uncut transfer and extras were released as part of Anchor Bay U.K.'s "The Jess Franco Collection 2" box set, which also included *Down Town* (open matte 1.33:1), and *Downtown Heat* (1.66:1), along with ports of the Severin versions of *Macumba Sexual*, *Mansion of the Living Dead* and *The Sexual Story of O*, all with AB's usual fake 5.1 treatment.

THE INGLORIOUS BASTARDS

Colour, 1977, 100m. / Directed by Enzo G. Castellari / Starring Bo Svenson, Fred Williamson, Ian Bannen, Michael Pergolani, Peter Hooten, Michel Constantin / Severin (US R1 NTSC) (DVD & Blu-ray), Optimum (UK R2 PAL), DEX (Japan R2 NTSC), Another World (Denmark R2 PAL), Koch (Germany R2 PAL) / WS (1.85:1) (16:9)

 Along with seemingly every other popular genre, the Hollywood war film enjoyed such popularity in Europe that it spawned a stream of imitations designed to cash in on such hits as *The Dirty Dozen* and *The Guns of Navarone*. The 1970s saw these star-studded, action-packed battle epics taking a decidedly weird turn, resulting in such cracked offerings as *The Passage* and *Escape to Athena*. No stranger to war films himself after 1969's *Eagles Over London*, macho director Enzo G. Castellari outdid himself with the supremely entertaining *The Inglorious Bastards*, which also circulated under a few duller but more socially acceptable titles like *Hell's Heroes*, *G.I. Bro* and *Deadly Mission*. Quentin Tarantino's decade-long promise to remake the film caused its legend to grow despite its scarcity

on home video in many territories, while fans had to content themselves with pricey or inadequate import DVDs for the first decade of the format's existence. Fortunately Severin's appropriately excessive American release (available on Blu-ray, a two-disc DVD, and a three-disc "Explosive Edition") rectifies that problem in high style, making it one of the most essential Eurocult titles on the market. Obviously owing more than a nod to *The Dirty Dozen*, our story follows a ragtag gang of World War II soldiers facing court martial whose transport vehicle runs afoul of German forces. The survivors decide to hightail it to Switzerland away from the Axis threat, but the journey is interrupted by such obstacles as machine-gun-toting women skinny dipping in a lake, an attacking force of Nazis who are more than they appear, and ultimately a perilous mission for Resistance forces to ambush a German bomb-hauling train.

While all of the actors create vivid personalities with their roles, this film really belongs to the two American stars, Bo Svenson (fresh off his two *Walking Tall* movies) and Fred Williamson in his cigar-chomping prime about to embark on a career of Italian drive-in films. As with most Castellari films, style isn't really the main concern here as the film does its business without any fancy visuals to get in the way of all the explosions, bullets, and incredibly entertaining tough talk.

The various versions of *The Inglorious Bastards* hailing from Japan and Europe all feature anamorphic transfers, all of them okay but nothing to get too excited about. The U.S. release from Severin looks considerably sharper and fresher, offering the best presentation of this film to date as well as the most substantial extras. The Blu-ray comes with all of the extras and the feature film on one handy disc, and not surprisingly, the 1080p Blu-ray easily wins in the visual department with a surprisingly crisp

and fresh-looking transfer; it's definitely one of the best-looking HD Eurocult presentations around to date. Flesh tones look healthy and vibrant, while on large screens the picture has a very satisfying film-like texture with strong dimensionality. It also bears mentioning that this is one film where the luxury of ultra-clear modern transfer techniques can also be a bit of a curse as well, since the exploding toy trains and railroad miniatures at the finale are even more obvious than ever. Both the BD and DVD editions feature Dolby Digital 2.0 mono options, while the BD also adds a standard Dolby Digital 5.1 track (sorry, no lossless TruHD here, but it's a pretty basic track anyway) which mostly pumps the (very loud) music into the rear channels. The DVD splits the extras onto two discs unlike its BD counterpart; the first disc contains a full-length audio commentary with a heavy-accented Castellari and Severin's David Gregory, covering all the technical bases of mounting the production as well as recollections about the actors and naked female extras. Castellari pops up again on the first disc for a 38-minute chat with Quentin Tarantino, who covers the film from more of a film buff perspective with an emphasis on Williamson and the various genre influences. As long as you can bear listening to Tarantino for that amount of time, it's worth a view but pales in comparison to the mammoth documentary on disc two, "Train Kept-a-Rollin'". Clocking in at over 75 minutes, it features pretty much every living participant (Castellari, Svenson, Williamson, producer Roberto Sbarigia, writers Laura Toscano, Fillipo De Masi (son of the late composer Francesco De Masi), and FX artist Gino De Rossi. Anything you could possibly want to know about the film is accounted for here, including loads of behind the scenes visual material culled from God knows how many archives. Expertly assembled and executed, it's another feather in Severin's special features cap. Last up is a quick but solid featurette showing Castellari returning to the original filming locations as well as the English-language European trailer, which uses stylised graphics similar to those in the memorable opening sequence. Also hidden as an Easter Egg is a VHS-sourced alternative main title sequence from the American reissue as *Deadly Mission*. Exclusive to the DVD is a third disc comprised of a CD with the four extant music cues from the film, previously available as a standalone CD from Dagored (with an extra four concert tracks thrown on, but they're hardly missed here). Completists may want to hang on their Danish Region 2 DVDs for its exclusive interview with Francesco De Masi before he died, but the Severin disc should certainly satisfy the heartiest of cinematic appetites.

INGLOURIOUS BASTERDS

Colour, 2009, 153m. / Directed by Quentin Tarantino / Starring Brad Pitt, Mélanie Laurent, Christoph Waltz, Michael Fassbender, Diane Kruger, Daniel Brühl, Til Schweiger, B.J. Novak, Eli Roth / Universal (DVD & Blu-ray, UK R2 PAL/HD, US R1 NTSC/HD) / WS (2.35:1) (16:9) / DD5.1/DTS5.1

After her family is gunned down in hiding under the authority of Nazi Colonel Hans Landa (Christoph Waltz), dubbed "The Jew Hunter", young Shosanna (Mélanie Laurent) flees to Paris where she assumes a new identity and opens a movie theatre which catches the eye of a publicly lauded military sniper, Private Frederick Zoller (Daniel Brühl), who becomes infatuated with her. In fact, Zoller happens to be playing himself in an upcoming feature film, *Nation's Pride*, and he champions her venue to the Nazis as the best location for the premiere – which might be the perfect place to wipe out quite a few Gestapo officials in attendance. Meanwhile a troop of Jewish-American soldiers recruited by Lieutenant Aldo Raine (Brad Pitt) picks up one ruthless SS-killing German, Hugo Stiglitz (Til Schweiger), and sets about scalping as many Nazis as possible while carving swastikas on the survivors' foreheads. When word of the premiere gets around, Raine becomes involved with a number of collaborators including glamorous German film star/Allied spy Bridget von Hammersmark (Diane Kruger) and German-speaking English officer Lieutenant Archie Hicox (Michael Fassbender) on the road to a literally explosive finale.

Having gotten the controversial distaff meta-cinema study of *Death Proof* out of his system, Quentin Tarantino surprised all of his critics with this film by delivering his most disciplined, refined, and gloriously entertaining movie to date. *Pulp Fiction* will always have the upper hand in the innovation department, but this surprisingly complex and rewarding blend of character study, wish-fulfilment vengeance, and war cinema study thesis might be his most rewatchable work yet. All of the major actors deliver tour de force performances, with Laurent and Waltz anchoring the proceedings as the main forces of nature unleashed in the virtuoso opening twenty minutes. For some reason Tarantino continues to insist on casting buddy Eli Roth onscreen despite his inability to deliver a convincing line reading, but here he's kept mostly silent and does well alternating as comic relief (especially as "Antonio Mar-gher-i-ti") and the screen's most vicious batter. Kruger bounces back from some disappointing Hollywood appearances (including another Pitt film, *Troy*) with her best work so far, and the always excellent Fassbender (*Hunger*) makes a strong impression in what amounts to two long scenes. As for top-billing Pitt, he's much better than the trailers might indicate and in good character actor form here, even if his character is ultimately only slightly necessary to the actual outcome of the plot. The pacing is also excellent and reveals what may be Tarantino's most impressive feat here, delivering a successful popular film consisting of two and a half hours of people sitting at tables talking, usually subtitled, with only a few quick moments of violence peppered in for extra spice. The formula might not have been enough to make a hit out of the shamefully underrated *Jackie Brown*, but it worked like a charm here.

A surprise box office smash that temporarily buoyed the ailing Weinstein Company, *Inglourious Basterds* (no relation whatsoever to the similarly titled Enzo G. Castellari film apart from the World War II setting) comes to DVD and Blu-ray courtesy of Universal in internationally identical editions distinguished only by the far superior U.K. cover art. Both image and sound quality are perfect replications of the vivid theatrical experience; the surround track makes the most of the entirely found music score (whose sources include *White Lightning*, *Revolver*, *The Entity*, and *Cat People*). The most interesting extra is 12 minutes of deleted footage (trimmed from three scenes, presumably the same bits present in the legendary longer Cannes cut), which is most valuable as it expands two of the more intense dialogue sequences, the Goebbels/Landa lunch sequence and the memorable basement bar card game. Tarantino and Elvis Mitchell chat together on camera for a half-hour discussion of the film, and the full six-minute version of *Nation's Pride* (directed by Roth) is included as well. Other extras include a

tribute to the Castellari film (some of whose actors appear fleetingly here), a quick chat with Rod Taylor who is seen in heavy make-up as Winston Churchill for one scene (alongside Mike Myers), a funny look at Tarantino's "camera angel" clapper girl, a string of salutations made for the editing room, an 11-minute overview of the copious poster art visible in the background of several scenes, a poster gallery, a trivia challenge, and four theatrical trailers. The Blu-ray also includes some exclusive additional interactive trivia and BD-Live options as well as bookmarking, but the significantly increased HD resolution should be reason enough to pick up that option for anyone with a BD player.

THE INTERNECINE PROJECT

Colour, 1974, 89m. / Directed by Ken Hughes / Starring James Coburn, Lee Grant, Harry Andrews, Ian Hendry, Michael Jayston, Keenan Wynn, Julian Glover, Christiane Krüger / Scorpion (US R0 NTSC) / WS (1.78:1) (16:9), Fremantle (UK R0 PAL)

 Splitting his time as a financial professor and coordinator for a shady spy ring, Robert Elliot (James Coburn) is offered a powerful new position as the presidential economic advisor. However, at the behest of his rich and corrupt patron, fat cat E.J. Farnsworth (Keenan Wynn), he must first dispatch his four operatives to cover his tracks. The plan to leave no one alive becomes more complicated with the involvement of an intrepid reporter (Lee Grant, shot with more soft filters than Cybill Shepherd) who harbours romantic feelings for Elliot but also wants to bring both him and Farnsworth down. As

plans for the quartet of complicated murders commence by pitting the spies against each other, Elliot must find a way to keep his hands clean at an increasingly high cost.

A fun, gimmicky thriller informed by past modest but efficient narrative clock-works like *The Assassination Bureau* and *Sleuth*, this all-star thriller overcomes its cumbersome title with a can't-miss narrative structure and an impressive international cast who keep the events chugging along at a brisk pace. The twist ending is a kick as well, capping off an exceptionally tight and effective final third on a perfect, unpredictable note that anticipates a similar reveal in Umberto Eco's *The Name of the Rose*. Coburn was in the midst of a real hot streak that didn't become fully appreciated until much later, with work surrounding this including *Pat Garrett & Billy the Kid*, *Bite the Bullet*, *Harry in Your Pocket*, and *Hard Times*. He's quite excellent here as well, holding down the film with a wonderfully villainous lead role that requires a bare minimum of actual physical activity. Also noteworthy is the atmospheric, typically top-drawer score by Roy Budd, who elevated numerous 1970s crime films like *Get Carter* and *The Black Windmill* with his musical gifts. Finally, this movie also serves as a startling reminder of just how different a PG rating could be in the '70s, with a nasty shower sequence that will catch any unprepared viewer quite off guard.

Scorpion's DVD release of this worthy title salvages it from the hell of murky, long-forgotten TV screenings with a solid transfer that makes the most of the movie's uneven 1970s film stock. The interior scenes generally look excellent, while some of the second unit work is more uneven. All in all, it's quite nice bearing in mind the nature of the production. Extras include the original theatrical trailer, a chatty half-hour video interview with screenwriter Jonathan Lynn (who went on to direct *Clue* and *My Cousin Vinny*), a very brief bit of video commentary from Lee Grant, and an audio remembrance from Coburn's daughter, Lisa, along with bonus trailers for the company's other releases including *Silent Scream*, *Skateboard*, *Goodbye Gemini*, and *Voyager*. A much weaker-looking full screen DVD was also released in the U.K. (with no extras) in 2005 from Fremantle.

THE IRON ROSE

Colour, 1973, 86m. / Directed by Jean Rollin / Starring Françoise Pascal, Hugues Quester, Nathalie Perrey, Mireille Dargent / Redemption (UK R0 PAL, US R0 NTSC) / WS (1.66:1) (16:9)

 A fascinating transition film in the career of director Jean Rollin, *La rose de fer* (*The Iron Rose*) arrived after a quartet of colourful, surreal, and highly unrealistic vampire films. Instead of sexualised, comic-inspired tableaux, Rollin switched gears to generate a methodical, eerie film poem about a romance among the damned, a conceit which continued to haunt all of his films to come. The plot is simplicity itself; a young woman (Françoise Pascal) and man (Hugues Quester) meet at a very strange party, where he catches her eye by reciting a morbid poem. The next day they decide to go bicycling together and wind up at a creepy, desolate cemetery, where he encourages her to break in so they can make out in one of the tombs. Unfortunately as night approaches, they find themselves unable to escape...

Though it eschews any obvious monsters, *The Iron Rose* is still usually classified as a horror film due to its overwhelming gothic atmosphere and the morbid nature of its imagery. Imagine the trapped-in-a-cemetery scene from Dario Argento's *Four Flies on Grey Velvet* spun out as an entire film with a little more eroticism, and you'll get the idea. The film's greatest assets are its lilting score by Pierre Raph and the presence of two surprisingly mainstream performers in the leads; Pascal became a reputable TV and international cinema actress, while Quester went on to diverse roles in high-profile art films including *Three Colours: Blue* and, most unforgettably, as Joe Dallesandro's deranged boyfriend in Serge Gainsbourg's *Je t'aime moi non plus*. Frequent Rollin actress Mireille Dargent also pops up as yet another of the director's beloved female clowns.

Rollin's first major financial failure upon its initial release, *The Iron Rose* became nearly impossible to see for decades. When Phil Hardy's influential horror encyclopaedia jump-started worldwide interest in Rollin's films, the tantalising description of this elusive title encouraged eager cultists to seek it out, mostly in vain. Eventually an English-subtitled release turned up in Germany from X-Rated Kult, in a colourful but problematic anamorphic transfer with artificial sharpness, a distracting sackcloth-style texture over the entire image, and woeful motion blurring throughout. Though taken from what appear to be the same film elements (with identical framing), Redemption's release fixes these problems and is much more attractive throughout. (It's still interlaced, though, so set your player accordingly.) The optional English subtitles appear to be a different, more streamlined translation than the PAL release as well. While the German disc only contained a trailer, Redemption's disc piles on some additional extras, most importantly Rollin's 1965 short film, "Les Pays Loins" (also available on the three-disc Dutch DVD of *Les démoniaques*). It's an appropriate companion piece as it follows a young couple during an odd night out on the town, drifting through various nocturnal haunts (most memorably a jazz club). The short is presented in 1.78:1 anamorphic widescreen; the framing looks a bit tight, but it's workable. Unfortunately the video goes to black for the last two minutes, so you'll have to piece it all together through the audio and subtitles (or just watch the import if you can afford it!). Also included is a stills gallery for both the main and short features, additional Redemption trailers, and a promo for the company's FAB Press-published book, *Blood & Dishonour*. Incidentally, this release marked Redemption's opening salvo as an independent into the American DVD market, which explains the peculiar flag-waving imagery of the cover art and opening company logo.

ISLE OF THE DAMNED

Colour, 2008, 85m. / Directed by Mark Colegrove / Starring Larry Gamber, Peter Crates, Patrician Rosa, Dustin Edwards / Dire Wit (US R0 NTSC), Yellow Fever (UK R0 PAL) / WS (1.78:1) (16:9)

 A digital age put-on disguising itself as a long-lost Italian cannibal gore film ("the 1980 cult classic!" that was "banned in 492 countries!"), *Isle of the Damned* is a sophomoric but oddly compelling exercise. As you can probably guess, the main target here is *Make Them Die Slowly*, though an overall familiarity with the works of Ruggero Deodato and Umberto Lenzi will certainly help. Taking a page from *Garth Marenghi's Darkplace*, the whole project sports fake Italian credits ("directed by Antonello Giallo"), though the mastermind was really a fellow named Mark Colegrove at Dire Wit Films.

The nominal hero here is Jack Steele, a degenerate detective hired by some rich fat cats to find the lost treasure of Marco Polo.

He sets off for the expedition with his moronic and sexually-confused adopted son, Billy, who seems to get molested by every old guy he meets including his dad's new boss. While wandering around in the woods we meet a wide variety of colourful characters including a female explorer and the Yamma Yamma tribe, who make a habit of disembowelling and eating anyone who gets on their nerves.

Loaded with gory entrail-pulling and groan-inducing jokes, *Isle of the Damned* is definitely unlike any other movie you've ever seen and often hits its mark, most notably with a deliberately ridiculous scene of cannibal-on-genital trauma, some great ribbing on the "who are the real savages?" gibberish from the Italian originals, and even one character modelled after Maurizio Merli! The whole thing was obviously shot for very little cash but looks surprisingly decent considering it was probably made in the woods behind someone's house, and somehow the fake wigs and costumes just add to the overall weirdness. The only major misstep is the fact that the whole thing is dubbed (by what sounds like the same two or three people), which would be fine except it has no relation at all to what anyone is saying. Anyone who's watched their fair share of Italian gut-munchers knows the real entertainment value is watching actors speak phonetic English only to have it all dubbed afterwards and come out just slightly out of synch; here it's more like an AIP dub of a Japanese monster movie and just feels wrong. Don't let that put you off, though; it's a real kick for Euro horror fans.

Dire Wit's DVD contains a number of extras, some genuine and others utterly ridiculous, including a DVD-Rom function to listen to the entire soundtrack as MP3s (including a few clever nods to Fabio Frizzi), a gag commentary by "The Insultor" (the pseudonymous voice of Jack Steele), a really funny video interview with "family relation" Luigi Giallo (complete with a handsy, black-gloved translator and hilarious voiceover), a "Shameless Art of Self-Promotion" featurette (which looks like it was shot at the Chiller con in Jersey), a batch of trailers (two for this one as well as the "other" Giallo film, *Pleasures of the Damned*, and something called *Post Modern*), and an audio "Message from Prof. Livingstone". If you thought *Cannibal Holocaust* would've been much better with a gay panic joke every two minutes, this is just the movie for you. Lucky U.K. consumers can also take comfort in a DVD release from Northern Ireland-based Yellow Fever Productions.

ITALIAN STALLION

Colour, 1970, 71m. / Directed by Morton Lewis / Starring Sylvester Stallone, Henrietta Holm, Jodi Van Prang, Nicholas Warren, Barbara Strom / Cinema Epoch (US R1 NTSC), Film 2000 (UK R2 PAL), Another World (Denmark R2 PAL)

With all the years of lacklustre celebrity sex-on-camera scandals generated in the wake of Paris Hilton, it's difficult now to appreciate the furore that greeted the 1976 release of *Italian Stallion*, originally a 1970 softcore quickie known as *The Party at Kitty and Stud's*. Though a trailer exists under that original title, no one seems to have actually seen it during its initial run before it was pulled and stuffed away in a vault somewhere. After the success of *Rocky*, somebody noticed that the star of the film was none other than Sylvester Stallone, who spends most of the movie either running around in a ridiculous furry coat or cavorting naked in a house with a bunch of upstate New York actresses. Of course, this was before he started popping up in bit roles in films like *Bananas* and *Klute*, so he looks quite a bit younger here.

The film itself is pretty tame stuff, with lots of groping, up-close flashes of frontal nudity, distorted camerawork in funhouse mirrors, and really, really bad dancing, as well as a brief bit of Michael Findlay-style roughie action with Sly whipping one of his conquests on a bed. There's not much plot per se, except Sly and his girlfriend Kitty (Henrietta Holm) go around picking up other people and having them over to their place, where they get undressed and hop around in a circle and have orgies. The end.

The geniuses at Bryanston Distributing (who released films like *Coonskin* and *Flesh for Frankenstein* while allegedly having more than casual ties to the mob) unleashed a slicked-up edit of this film under its most famous current title, with new credit sequences and a hilarious faux-Bill Conti soundtrack highlighted by an oft-repeated, sub-*Rocky* theme song, "Fly with Me". Best of all, they tried to pass this off as a hardcore porn film by trotting out the new version's editor, XXX "director" Gail Palmer (*The Erotic Adventures of Candy*), to badly read some cue cards for a new prologue in which she tries to drum up as much interest as possible. This hysterical piece of time-padding is missing from some video releases but thankfully remains on Cinema Epoch's officially-sanctioned DVD, transferred from the original negative and looking way, way better than anyone had a right to expect (and certainly better than the cruddy grey market DVD released a couple of years ago). Yes, it still looks like a cheap 1970 New York sex flick shot on 16mm, but the colour and clarity are really very good, equivalent to some of the best Something Weird transfers from the same period. The film's full frame aspect ratio looks correct and thankfully wasn't fake-matted, which would have been disastrous. Also included is the equally amusing trailer,

which finds Ms. Palmer again hyping the film in a deadly monotone while explaining why they can only show audiences two scenes from the film and how Stallone (who was paid two hundred bucks for the part) justified making this film in *Playboy*: "I was hungry". Film 2000 released the same version in the U.K., but gluttons for punishment (or fans of porn inserts) can also experience the alternative German "hardcore" version on Another World's 2-disc Danish release.

JACQUES DEMY: INTÉGRALE: LOLA

B&W, 1961, 90m. / Starring Anouk Aimée, Marc Michel, Jacques Harden, Alan Scott / Arte (France R2 PAL), Koch Lorber (US R1 NTSC) / WS (2.35:1) (16:9)

BAY OF ANGELS
B&W, 1963, 89m. / Starring Jeanne Moreau, Claude Mann, Paul Guers / Arte (France R2 PAL), Koch Lorber (US R1 NTSC) / WS (1.66:1) (16:9)

THE UMBRELLAS OF CHERBOURG
Colour, 1964, 91m. / Starring Catherine Deneuve, Nino Castelnuovo, Anne Vernon, Marc Michel / Arte (France R2 PAL), Koch Lorber (US R1 NTSC), Optimum (UK R2 PAL) / WS (1.66:1 or 1.78:1) (16:9) / DD5.1/4.0/2.0

THE YOUNG GIRLS OF ROCHEFORT
Colour, 1967, 125m. / Starring Catherine Deneuve, George Chakiris, Françoise Dorléac, Gene Kelly, Jacques Perrin, Michel Piccoli, Danielle Darrieux / Arte (France R2 PAL), Miramax (US R1 NTSC), BFI (UK R2 PAL) / WS (2.35:1) (16:9) / DD2.0

MODEL SHOP
Colour, 1969, 91m. / Starring Anouk Aimée, Gary Lockwood, Alexandra Hay / Arte (France R2 PAL), Sony (US R1 NTSC) / WS (1.85:1) (16:9)

DONKEY SKIN

Colour, 1970, 90m. / Starring Catherine Deneuve, Jean Marais, Jacques Perrin, Delphine Seyrig, Micheline Presle / Arte (France R2 PAL), Koch Lorber (US R1 NTSC), Optimum (UK R2 PAL) / WS (1.66:1) (16:9) / DD4.0

THE PIED PIPER

Colour, 1972, 90m. / Starring Donovan, Donald Pleasence, John Hurt, Jack Wild, Diana Dors, Michael Hordern / Arte (France R2 PAL), Legend (US R1 NTSC) / WS (1.66:1) (16:9)

A SLIGHTLY PREGNANT MAN

Colour, 1973, 92m. / Starring Catherine Deneuve, Marcello Mastroianni, Micheline Presle, Mireille Mathieu / Arte (France R2 PAL), Koch Lorber (US R1 NTSC), Optimum (UK R2 PAL) / WS (1.66:1) (16:9)

LADY OSCAR

Colour, 1979, 124m. / Starring Catriona MacColl, Barry Stokes, Christine Böhm, Jonas Bergström, Mark Kingston, Martin Potter, Patsy Kensit / Arte (France R2 PAL), Royal (Japan R2 NTSC), Filmax (Spain R2 PAL) / WS (1.85:1) (16:9)

LA NAISSANCE DU JOUR

Colour, 1980, 90m. / Starring Jean Sorel, Dominique Sanda, Danièle Delorme, Orane Demazis / Arte (France R2 PAL)

A ROOM IN TOWN

Colour, 1982, 90m. / Starring Dominique Sanda, Danielle Darrieux, Richard Berry, Michel Piccoli, Fabienne Guyon / Arte (France R2 PAL) / WS (1.66:1) (16:9) / DD2.0

PARKING

Colour, 1985, 92m. / Starring Francis Huster, Laurent Malet, Keïko Ito, Gérard Klein, Marie-France Pisier, Jean Marais, Hughes Quester / Arte (France R2 PAL) / WS (1.66:1) (16:9)

TROIS PLACES POUR LE 26

Colour, 1988, 106m. / Starring Yves Montand, Mathilda May, Jean-Claude Bouillard, Catriona MacColl, Dominique Varda / Arte (France R2 PAL) / WS (2.35:1) (16:9) / DD2.0

For people who hate musicals because they can't stand the idea of people bursting into song without enough justification from the story, director Jacques Demy is surely their worst nightmare. Still one of the most overlooked and misunderstood directors of the French New Wave, Demy has always been regarded as more artificial and lightweight than many of his contemporaries like Jean-Luc Godard and François Truffaut. Fortunately time has proven his light-as-air, whimsical, and often fantastic universe to be far ahead of its time, perhaps one of the most complete, fascinating cinematic worlds created by one filmmaker. An avid film fanatic from an early age, Demy quickly caused an international splash with his third and most beloved film, *The Umbrellas of Cherbourg*, while most of his other output received only nominal theatrical releases outside France (if at all) and became maddeningly difficult to find even on home video or television. Demy passed away in 1990, and by the end of that decade, his widow and fellow filmmaker, Agnès Varda, undertook the restoration of some of his key films, beginning with a major overhaul and worldwide release of *Cherbourg*. However, even today with occasional retrospectives popping up, his work after 1973 suffered from a lesser reputation and took an insane amount of effort to see, usually in poor copies without any English translation. Fortunately the dream task of compiling all of Demy's films in one handy package with English subtitles was finally undertaken in France by Arte Video, who somehow managed to untangle the endless licensing issues around his later efforts and presented the complete body of work in immaculate transfers as the *Jacques Demy:*

Intégrale box set. And yes, they finally all have English audio and/or subtitles.

His first film, *Lola*, immediately displays many of the themes, characters and visual motifs which would come to define his later work and still stands as an impressive achievement on its own. Fresh off her breakthrough role in Fellini's *La Dolce Vita*, Anouk Aimée dominates the entire film as the title character, a cabaret performer known for singing and gyrating in a top hat and very skimpy outfit. She's also a single mother and finds her life complicated by a chance encounter with Roland Cassard (Marc Michel), a young man with an interest in becoming a diamond smuggler who knew her as an adolescent. Immediately smitten, he determines to win her over despite the fact that many other men are circling around her, including an American sailor on leave, while Lola pines away for the father of her child to return and legitimise her life.

Filmed in Nantes, *Lola* quickly establishes the seaside town setting and iris effects at the beginning and end that would come to reappear in Demy's films, which otherwise grew more stylistically extreme and fantastic in content. Various characters swirl around one another looking for happiness, always idealistic if only rarely connecting at the moments in which they should. Add to that the ravishing mobile scope photography by Raoul Coutard (who went on to shoot all of Godard's most important '60s films) and a gentle, catchy score by frequent Demy collaborator Michel Legrand, and you've got one of the key art house films of the 1960s. *Lola* first appeared on DVD in the U.S. from Fox Lorber (later Koch Lorber) in a transfer of the 2000 film restoration, which was also seen in a few theatrical venues. This disc looks fine if a bit soft and obviously PAL-converted and is now discontinued. The Arte version features better compression and, being in PAL like the original master,

features better motion rendering and is just slightly crisper. Optional English subtitles for both appear to be the same. The French disc also includes (without English subs) the original French theatrical trailer, a poster gallery, a video discussion of the film with critic Benoît Jacquot accompanied by numerous film stills, a verbal appreciation by Mathieu Demy reading a study written by Demy biographer Jean-Pierre Berthomé (a feature repeated for all the subsequent films), and a nifty instalment from the '60s show *Cinéastes de notre temps* with Demy talking about the feature interspersed with home movie footage of the set.

Another flawed woman inhabits the centre of Demy's second film, *Bay of Angels* (*La baie des anges*), on the surface a simpler and slighter tale set among the glittery, treacherous casinos of Nice, another seaside staple of French culture. Here we first iris out in a stunning opening shot on Jackie (Jeanne Moreau), a platinum-haired, cigarette-succoured vamp who trolls the gambling halls in search of her next quick fix. Enter Jean (Claude Mann), a milquetoast young bank clerk lured by a buddy into an afternoon's diversion playing games of chance. After winning a game of roulette, Jean is quickly hooked and becomes entranced with Jackie, whose addiction has robbed her of much of her sense as well as custody of her only child. Their gambling fever soon escalates as their own relationship evolves along lines that could either blossom into romance or push them over into oblivion.

Graced with a dynamic, piano-fuelled Legrand score and a marvellous final visual flourish, *Bay of Angels* feels like it's spinning in circles for much of its time but etches a memorable portrait of two personalities vying for dominance with no idea of how it will end. Screen legend Moreau really controls the entire film with her incomparable presence, turning from a pitiable floozy into a multi-dimensional woman whose actions from one scene to the next remain highly unpredictable. It's simple and much darker and more obsessive than the usual Demy fare, but as a bid to keep step with the growing French New Wave, this is a worthy instalment. *Bay of Angels* was restored and released in tandem with *Lola* both in revival houses and on DVD, likewise going out of print in the U.S. The French DVD also benefits from better encoding and the native PAL presentation, which renders the two biggest tracking shots of the film more smoothly. Extras this time also include further Benoît Jacquot comments, the theatrical trailer, and a poster gallery.

Now we arrive at the film by which all of Demy's others are measured, *The Umbrellas of Cherbourg*. It's difficult to overestimate the impact this film had on popular culture, earning a quick fan following in the U.K. and America while generating two hit singles, revolutionising the use of art direction in film, and making a celebrity out of Michel Legrand with his daring music, which runs nonstop throughout the film as every single line from the actors (no matter how mundane) is sung. The town of Cherbourg was outfitted with building fronts, interiors, bikes, and other accessories to match the colourful scheme of the entire movie, which bursts with unbelievable Technicolor hues in every shot. Incredibly enough, this also happened to be the director's first film shot in colour. For some reason *Cherbourg* is usually thought of as an ode to undying young love, a ridiculous view if you actually watch it all the way through. The bittersweet story starts in 1957 and follows two young lovers, auto shop worker Guy (Nino Castelnuovo from *Camille 2000* and *Strip Nude for Your Killer*) and umbrella store clerk Geneviève (Catherine Deneuve, fresh off her first big starring role in Roger Vadim's *Vice and Virtue*). Their bliss is cut short when Guy is summoned by the

military to serve in Algiers, and they make love before tearfully parting. However, Geneviève soon realises she is pregnant and, at the urging of her mother (*Therese and Isabelle*'s Anne Vernon) when Guy fails to write to her, makes a fateful life choice. To reveal any more would spoil the enjoyment of this film, which somehow manages to mount a wrenching tearjerker plot in the most dazzling fashion imaginable; there isn't a scene that doesn't work perfectly, though Demy outdoes himself with the final moments offering a resolution far closer to what might happen in real life than most viewers probably expected. And a gas station covered in snow at Christmastime has never looked more beautiful. Much has been written about this film over the years, but all you really need to know is that this is simply one of the most intoxicating musicals – or movies, period – you'll ever see. Legrand's score remains timeless, and the use of professional vocalists merges perfectly with the model-perfect actors performing onscreen. While *Cherbourg* works perfectly well on its own, it also gains immensely in emotional resonance on the heels of *Lola* as the character of Roland Cassard returns (again played by Michel), now a diamond jeweller whose back-story contains a reprise of Legrand's original musical theme (and who plays a pivotal role in the second of the film's three acts).

The restoration of this film supervised by Varda is an overwhelming experience on the big screen, and it took a long time before any home video version could come close to approximating the experience. Criterion's U.S. laserdisc (their only stab at a Demy title to date, incredibly enough) was a disaster with murky colours and incorrect framing, a problem carried over to Fox Lorber's miserable, badly-encoded first DVD edition. Meanwhile an anamorphic transfer was released in France that was a huge improvement, even if colours were still on the muted side. Eventually a good, vivid edition came out with Fox Lorber's anamorphic reissue, which was carried over to the double-disc release from Optimum in the U.K. The Arte edition looks closest to these, framed at 1.66:1 with amazing, hypersaturated colours. Extras include the usual verbal appreciations as well as 11 minutes from *Il était une fois... Les paraplouies de Cherbourg*, a documentary by Marie Genin and Serge July about the making of the film with some great new footage of Michel Legrand at the piano. Also included are a poster gallery and the original 1964 trailer, which is sometimes supplanted by the 1999 reissue trailer on other releases, as well as an additional video featurette featuring observations from Virginie Ledoyen, an accomplished musical actress in her own right. Incidentally, the Arte disc features only the uncompressed PCM stereo track for the film, which is still the richest option despite the 5.1 retooling on the American one.

A sequel in spirit if not in story to *Umbrellas* is his next and certainly splashiest film, *The Young Girls of Rochefort*, an unabashed ode to MGM musicals based in the titular city, whose nautical setting this time allows a return of *Lola*'s lovelorn sailors as well as the addition of Demy's first big American star, Gene Kelly, as an American songwriter dreaming of love. Everyone else is either regretting the one that got away or dreaming of a lover who may not exist, which perfectly suits this film's switch from narrative-driven, feature-length singing to an all-out festival of dancing, sweeping camera movements, and numerous characters bouncing around in various configurations before settling into place for the final, perfect shot. Deneuve returns again, this time paired with her real-life sister, Françoise Dorléac (the star of Roman Polanski's *Cul-de-Sac* who

tragically died in a car accident after making her next and final film, Ken Russell's *Billion Dollar Brain*). Not surprisingly, they also play sisters in the film, a pair of music-teaching twins named Delphine and Solange who dream of making the big time in Paris. Then there's Maxence (Jacques Perrin, who went on to a long career as an actor before directing the acclaimed *Winged Migration*), a blond sailor obsessed with his dream girl whom he's captured in a portrait – and who looks strikingly like Deneuve. On top of that you also get another visiting sailor, Etienne (*West Side Story*'s George Chakiris), who wants the twins to help put on a song-and-dance show, as well as shop owner Yvonne (legendary actress Danielle Darrieux, who returned in future Demy films as well as François Ozon's rapturous ode to the director, *8 Women*), who ditched her fiancé (Michel Piccoli) because of his ridiculous last name. How it all turns out isn't really as important as the giddy, silly, and often flamboyant musical numbers, one of which even relates the story of an axe murderer! That's just how love works in Demyville.

Rochefort also received a theatrical reissue, this time from Miramax under the wing of Disney who then issued it as a bare bones DVD. Much more satisfying is the French version, released as a standalone edition and repurposed slightly for the box set. The transfer looks immaculate, and on top of that you get a great retrospective hour-long feature by Varda, "Les demoiselles ont eu 25 ans", which revisits the town 25 years later intercut with terrific footage shot during the making of the original film. Thankfully this bonus is also subtitled in English. Also included are the usual theatrical trailer and poster gallery as well as verbal commentaries (which are exclusive to the box set version). Incidentally, this film was simultaneously shot in an English version which, not surprisingly, was judged inferior and only made a few select TV appearances before disappearing completely; judging from the few surviving audio snippets of this variant, the loss isn't that great. The two-disc set released by the BFI is similar to the separate French release, splitting the feature onto one disc while carrying over Varda's retrospective documentary to disc two along with an excerpt from Deneuve's 2005 Guardian interview at the NFT about Demy and a 1980 audio interview with Kelly about this and many of his other films.

It was just a matter of time before the lure of Hollywood proved too strong for Demy to resist, and that opportunity came in 1969 with *Model Shop* for Columbia Pictures. This time he turns his camera to the dusty, pop culture-drenched landscapes of Los Angeles in a 24-hour period as experienced by George (*2001: A Space Odyssey*'s Gary Lockwood), a young aspiring architect about to be drafted whose apathy extends to spending his money on a car he doesn't need and finding little value in committing to his girlfriend, Gloria (*Skidoo*'s Alexandra Hay). With a payment due to keep his wheels, George trawls across town to find some cash but instead finds himself waylaid by a stop at the Model Shop, where pinup girls pose for clients in revealing lingerie (or less, though we're never shown in detail). There he's captivated by Lola (Aimée again), now living unhappily in L.A., whom he flirted with earlier at a gas station. As the day turns to night, George finds himself returning to the Model Shop again and striking up a rapport with Lola, whose destiny ultimately lies in his hands.

A commercial flop upon its release, *Model Shop* was quickly consigned to the dustbin along with many of its other late '60s/early '70s brethren, with only the occasional unheralded TV screening alerting anyone that it ever existed. However, fan interest grew over the years thanks to its status as a "lost" Demy project

as well as the merits of its soundtrack; for the first time he did not collaborate with Legrand, instead using the rising L.A. band Spirit (who also appear in the film) to provide both the haunting instrumental score and a handful of songs (with some classical selections repeated from *Lola* for good measure). Needless to say, the film is far worthier than its neglect might indicate; the camerawork and art direction are never less than faultless (including another sweeping opening shot that recalls his first two films after the usual iris-in), and the generous footage of L.A. circa '69 is now a treasure trove unto itself. Not surprisingly, scenes from this turned up to great effect in the highly recommended documentary *Los Angeles Plays Itself*, still frustratingly unavailable on home video. For many collectors, this valuable rarity will be reason enough to pick up the box set by itself, and thankfully the anamorphic transfer is a knockout. Colours are extremely rich and vibrant, and apart from some debris printed in during the optical effects of the opening credits, the presentation looks faultless. This was Demy's first film shot in English, and that track is preserved here with optional French subtitles. The disc (a dual-layered one paired up with *Lola* as described above) also includes another Benoît Jacquot commentary, Berthomé's observations about the film, a poster gallery, and a six-minute segment of the B&W show *Chronique cinéma* with Demy talking about the movie. The same transfer is also available as a standalone title in the U.S. which features none of these extras but does add on the original American trailer. Trivia note: Harrison Ford originally auditioned for this feature but lost out to Lockwood.

As Demy's first decade in filmmaking closed, he returned to France and made a startling shift in subject matter that would come to influence all of his subsequent work. Fairy tale aspects had certainly played a role in the stories he chose, but with 1970's *Peau d'âne*, known in English under the less appetising title of *Donkey Skin*, he leaped into outright fantasy with an enchanting ode to filmmaker Jean Cocteau. Based on a story by "Cinderella" author Charles Perrault, the film begins in a kingdom dominated by the colour blue where the King (Cocteau regular Jean Marais) grieves over the death of his beautiful wife, who told him he could only remarry if he found a woman as beautiful as she. Unfortunately the only maiden in the kingdom who fits the bill is his daughter, the Princess (Deneuve), who apparently sits around at her organ outside all day singing about love while banquets are planned around her. When the King demands he marry her, the Princess is shocked and confused; however, a helpful visit from the Lilac Fairy (*Daughters of Darkness*'s Delphine Seyrig) helps straighten things out with a song about why incest is really, really bad. Oh, yes, and the King gets much of his fortune from a magical donkey in his stable that eats straw and poops jewels. To ward off her father's plans, the Princess follows the Fairy's advice and requests a string of seemingly impossible gowns made of the weather, the moon, and the sun, only to have them delivered; ultimately she has no recourse but to flee the kingdom, dressed in the hide of the magical donkey and posing in the nearby red-dominated kingdom as a peasant girl. However, she soon catches the eye of that region's lovesick Prince (Perrin), who devises a plan of his own to win her.

A delightfully odd and visually stunning experience, *Peau d'âne* features the same vivid Demy colours, costumes and Legrand musical numbers, but the sweeping camerawork has been replaced here with a more classical approach, framing almost everything in storybook-style medium shots. The sets are incredibly inventive and rely on charming, old school special effects (just check out the King's big white kitty throne or the delightful bird and cat-themed masked ball), while the finale leaps into flat-out surrealism as the Fairy Queen's ability to travel in time results in a hilariously anachronistic entrance. The film became an instant favourite for viewers of all ages in France where it's regarded as a classic, though it found only sporadic acceptance elsewhere. All of the songs are terrific; as with *Rochefort*, Perrin gets the most haunting and heartfelt melody, while the magic cake-baking number is bound to bring a grin to the face of any viewer. An excellent restoration of the film was conducted by Varda and issued on a double-disc French DVD followed by an American one with essentially the same extras, which include the trailer, a 1908 silent short version of the story, an interview with producer Mag Bodard, "The Illustrated Peau d'Âne" (a look at text versions over the years), an odd video chat with two psychoanalysts, Demy's biographer and a literature professor dissecting the film's unusual themes, a peculiar photo/comic montage, and a cute little short, "Peau d'Âne and the Children", with school kids offering their own versions of the story. For some reason the U.S. disc presents the film with 2.0 and 5.1 audio options while the French one opts for 2.0 and 4.0, but all of them sound rather comparable. The transfer quality is excellent throughout. The single-disc Arte version in the box set is the same apart from the addition of the usual newly-recorded Benoît Jacquot and Mathieu Demy chat tracks. The most sparse offering is Optimum's U.K. release, which features the same transfer and sound mixes but only carries over a trailer for *A Slightly Pregnant Man*.

Apparently reassured by the reception of this lavish fairy tale, Demy decided to take another crack at another children's fantasy – this time in English. *The Pied*

Piper, his adaptation of one of the most disturbing fairy tales, pulls no punches with the source material as it depicts a medieval German town where the plague slowly approaches and rats threaten to invade the city. A travelling troupe of actors arrives at the barricaded town, which allows them in only after one of their party, a vagabond piper (Donovan), revives the mayor's ailing daughter with a song heard through her bedroom window. However, their troubles are only beginning as the snivelling burgomaster (Donald Pleasence) and his corrupt and irresponsible military-aspiring son Franz (John Hurt) perform underhanded deals with the church to establish a papal-sanctioned war and a completely indulgent church based out of the town. On the other side of the moral spectrum, alchemist Melius (Michael Hordern) and his artistic, crippled young assistant, Gavin (Jack Wild), become friendly with the actors. Gavin is nursing a crush on Lisa, who, despite having yet to reach adolescence, is engaged to marry Franz. When Lisa's doomed wedding arrives and the eventual influx of infected rats occurs, the powers that be arrange an unusual bargain with the piper which, as all fairy tale lovers know, is destined to end on a very melancholy note.

Though ostensibly marketed to family audiences with a G rating, *The Pied Piper* is a grim and brutal offering from Goodtimes Enterprises, a UK-based production company during the 1970s whose films like *Performance*, *Lisztomania* and *That'll Be the Day* were largely conceived as star vehicles for music performers. The big name in this particular film is Donovan, a Scottish folk-pop singer best known for 1960s standards like "Hurdy Gurdy Man", "Atlantis", and "Sunshine Superman". His presence in the film is something of a sticking point for many modern viewers, but in fact the small numbers of spare, haunting ditties he performs here work well with the period setting, and while he'll

never be confused with a master thespian, he acquits himself well enough with his one-dimensional role. The real acting demands rest with the British pros like Pleasence, Hurt, and Hordern, who chew into their meaty roles with gusto. The dark undertones of the original story (made famous by the likes of the Brothers Grimm and Robert Browning), essentially a metaphor for the loss of multiple children to a disease epidemic or tragic accident (elaborated upon most tantalisingly in Atom Egoyan's *The Sweet Hereafter*), are certainly not sugarcoated in this version, which presents unflinching depictions of the ravages of the plague, a horrific wedding banquet scene with hordes of rats bursting from a grandiose wedding cake (a moment worthy of Werner Herzog's *Nosferatu*), and a harrowing climactic burning at the stake for one sympathetic character which left many unprepared viewers shell-shocked. The end result would actually make an ideal double bill with Ken Russell's *The Devils* from the previous year, as they share very similar storyline trajectories, visual schemes, and pessimistic views on the poisonous relationship between politics and religion. In fact, this film is a perfect example of the mainstream fallout from the notoriously violent cinematic year of 1971, which found such brutal offerings as *A Clockwork Orange*, *Straw Dogs* and *Macbeth* invading theatres around the world. This one may not be as graphic, but it is easily the grittiest and most brutal "children's" film until it was eventually usurped by *Dragonslayer*.

Though it was widely distributed by Paramount, *The Pied Piper* only did marginal business and disappeared from circulation almost immediately. It rarely appeared on television and became known primarily through word of mouth, and a fleeting Japanese laserdisc release was its only home video edition for three decades. Nevertheless, public curiosity continued to mount for this film. Paramount's aversion to sublicensing its property to other companies eventually took a welcome turn as it began shopping out its back catalogue of unreleased titles, with Legend Films snagging some key cult titles to be issued in brand new anamorphic transfers. Incredibly, *The Pied Piper* was one of the first to make it out of the gate, and the results are quite satisfying all around in terms of the presentation. The DVD itself is bare bones (a shame as Varda and Donovan have both supported the film in recent years), but the transfer looks terrific (though the opening titles have always had a dupey-looking quality – don't let those first three minutes fool you). Decent repertory prints have been difficult to come by, but Paramount finally struck a much-needed new one for limited showings in 2007, which appears to be the same source used here. Demy's trademark aesthetic concerns are still in evidence, from the integration of songs into the narrative to the bittersweet and ultimately unrequited romance at its core which forms the basis of the haunting final shots. The mono soundtrack sounds clear and solid overall, making one also pine for a CD release which sadly never came. Still, as this unexpected and richly rewarding DVD proves, anything is still possible. The same transfer is used for the box set and augmented with a poster gallery, a video commentary featurette with Valentin Vignet (Demy's granddaughter), the alternative French audio track for the curious, and a five-minute B&W sequence from the program *Le journal du cinéma* with Demy discussing the film; it's an essential title in either form. As with his previous English movie, *Model Shop*, Demy did not use Legrand, but the music here is still very potent and deserves a soundtrack release.

Unfortunately *The Pied Piper* proved to be a commercial failure (no wonder considering how many kids it must have trauma-tised), so Demy returned to France again for one of his lightest and most commercial films, the fluffy comedy *A Slightly Pregnant Man* (released in France under the far more cumbersome title of *L'événement le plus important depuis que l'homme a marché sur la lune*, or "The Most Important Event Since Man Walked on the Moon"). Beauty salon worker Irène (Deneuve) is more than a little confused when her driving teacher fiancé, Marco (Marcello Mastroianni, her real-life beau at the time), is told by his physician that he's actually four months pregnant. Paris is thrown into uproar and the scientific community is flipped upside down as Marco contends with his growing celebrity.

Extremely light on plot, this was the first of the odd pregnant man subgenre (followed by uneven efforts like *Rabbit Test* and *Junior*) and, like those followers, it can't quite come up with a satisfactory solution to its provocative story hook; however, Demy manages to casually bat around issues of religion, abortion, feminism, and sexual orientation with ease, and even some musical content slips through with Mireille Mathieu belting out the catchy Legrand-penned theme song a couple of times. Of course, the usual eye-popping colours and wild production design choices (check out that big gold thumb!) are still present throughout. Despite the presence of the stars and a reasonable public reception, the film didn't do much for the director's career. Still it became a video mainstay, usually in a horrendous English-dubbed version on VHS that turned it into a stupid farce. Fortunately the Koch Lorber disc in the U.S. contains the original French language version with optional English subtitles and a serviceable anamorphic transfer; amazingly, this still remains the definitive release as it also contains the English dub as a secondary option and the original trailer. The U.K. Optimum disc has the French track only with burned-in subs and looks far more compressed, while the Arte disc in the box set has the French and English tracks but no subtitles options.

For quite some time Demy had to look outside France to realise more projects, and six years later he finished one of his most mysterious and least-seen films, *Lady Oscar*. This adaptation of *The Rose of Versailles*, a popular manga by Riyoko Ikeda also adapted in the mid-'70s as an anime series, was financed by Japan's Kitty Music, Nippon TV, Shiseido and Toho Companies and was only theatrically released in Japan for legal reasons which still remain muddy. Catriona MacColl (future star of Lucio Fulci's *The Beyond*, *The House by the Cemetery* and *City of the Living Dead*) made her feature film debut in the title role as Oscar, a girl born to a father who wished her to be raised as a boy to serve the French monarchy. She grows up wearing male clothing with only some of those around her recognising her gender-bending nature, while her nanny's grandson, André (*Prey*'s Barry Stokes), becomes her coachman and quietly loves her for years. Oscar becomes captain of the guard for Versailles and closely serves the clueless Marie Antoinette (Christine Böhm) while the royal misuse of state funds slowly boils into a social revolution. Meanwhile lots of duels, lavish balls, and romantic confusions ensue.

Easily the most anonymous of Demy's films, *Lady Oscar* is visually spectacular and was partially shot on the real grounds of Versailles, but even with the participation of Michel Legrand, it's hard to spot his touch here. The film moves very slowly at over two hours, but MacColl does a solid job in the lead and it's fun spotting odd cast members like Martin Potter (*Satyricon*) and a very young Patsy Kensit as the juvenile Oscar. Michel Legrand's score is likewise pretty enough but not terribly committed. That said, the sexual confusion of Demy's previous film carries over interestingly here in quite a few scenes, and the surprisingly tragic finale represents a continuing trend on Demy's part towards downbeat (or at least heavily bittersweet) story resolutions. For years *Lady Oscar* was only available on video in Japan, which was actually fine since it was shot in English anyway. The Japanese DVD features a solid anamorphic transfer, a gallery, and in an exclusive that still makes it desirable for fans, the entirety of Legrand's isolated score as a secondary audio track. The Italian DVD is bare bones and skippable. The Arte disc in the box set features six and a half minutes of home movie footage from the Versailles shoot (with voiceover by Alain Coiffier), a poster gallery, a video commentary featurette by film historian Evelyne Lever, and Mathieu Demy reading more about the film from Berthomé's writings.

The following year Demy returned to France and helmed a much smaller scale but more personal project, a French TV film version of *La naissance du jour* ("Break of Day"), adapted from the often-studied short novel by Colette, itself more or less based on the writer's own autumn years. The meditative film feels a bit like a French *Enchanted April* as Colette (Danièle Delorme) spends her afternoons in the countryside of Saint Tropez writing outside about her transient attempts to find love over the years, only for her romantic yearnings to be awakened by the arrival of the younger Vial (Jean Sorel, star of Buñuel's *Belle de jour* and Fulci's *A Lizard in a Woman's Skin*), who apparently has a severe aversion to shirts. However, the subsequent arrival of Colette's younger, beautiful friend, Hélène (Dominique Sanda, *1900*), threatens to take away her last chance at happiness. Subdued, tender, and interesting, the film moves quickly through its 90-minute running time and is beautifully filmed, with Mendelssohn music coursing delicately through the soundtrack. This rarely seen gem makes its home video debut in Arte's box set and looks fine in this new transfer in the original full frame TV aspect ratio. The same disc also contains Demy's first narrative work, a 1957 half-hour short version of Jean Cocteau's play, *Le bel indifférent*. Reputedly written for Edith Piaf, the spare drama charts the emotional torment of a woman known only as "C" (Jeanne Allard) waiting in a red-saturated hotel room for the arrival of her "indifferent" lover. When he shows up, she doesn't exactly find the happiness she expects. A great find for Cocteau and Demy-philes alike, it's a stylised and striking character study that still plays beautifully. Agnes Varda contributes chats about both of the films on this disc in French only.

Of all the later films ignored outside France, there's really no excuse at all for the mistreatment of his next work, 1982's *Une chambre en ville* (*A Room in Town*). Adopting the same sung-through style of *Umbrellas* with a similarly intimate story, this much, much darker romance takes place in 1955 in the town of Nantes, which is paralysed by labour demonstrations met with brutal police force. One of the strikers, a ship construction worker named François (*La balance*'s Richard Berry), rents a room in the home of Margot Langlois (Darrieux again), a widowed baroness now in decline whose daughter, Edith (Sanda), moved out a month ago to marry an abusive, impotent TV salesman (an unrecognisable Michel Piccoli in a spectacularly fierce performance). François is having a relationship with the sweet Violette (Fabienne Guyon), who takes the relationship more seriously than he. Edith wanders the streets in her fur coat (with nothing on underneath), visiting a tarot reader who instructs her that she will fall in love with a metal worker; soon after that night she and François cross paths and fall for each other immediately, spending a night of passion together. However, their possibly selfish happiness is immediately met with numerous obstacles, leading to a violent finale.

This time out the composer is not Michel Legrand but Michel Colombier (soon bound for more mainstream fare like *Against All Odds* and *Purple Rain*), who contributes a wall-to-wall score often staggering in its intensity and romantic longing. While the worker sequences antic-ipate the smash stage version of *Les Misérables* to come, the characters' individual themes really carry the film (Violette's will stick in your head long afterward) and culminate in third act crescendos worthy of a classical opera. The casual nudity and startling violence (including a jolting throat slashing) are certainly new territory for Demy, but somehow he integrates this imagery into his gorgeous aesthetic without throwing the project out of whack. Fans of *Umbrellas* may be initially put off by characters who are often tense and bitchy, but even from his first film Demy was never afraid to show human behaviour as it really is, not in the idealised Hollywood form of which he was often accused. This unheralded latter-day masterpiece has been infuriatingly hard to see since its fleeting theatrical release in France; it never officially hit home video and finally appears in the DVD box set in a beautiful, colourful anamorphic transfer with an enveloping soundtrack. (The full two-disc CD was finally released in 2007 and also comes highly recommended.) Viewers with even a sketchy knowledge of French may opt to switch off the English subtitles, which tend to simplify many of the poetic verbal flourishes and also obstruct some of the marvellous camera compositions. Extras include two video analyses by producer and critic Gérard Vaugeois, a TV instalment of *Cinéma cinémas* with Demy promoting the film, the theatrical trailer, and a poster gallery.

At this point it's worth noting that, by the mid-'80s, French filmmaking was changing drastically. The old guard of the French New Wave was passing away (literally in Truffaut's case), and game-changing films like Jean-Jacques Beineix's *Diva* and Luc Besson's *Subway* were pushing the stylistic innovations of directors like Demy into new, more Americanised areas of pop culture. This perspective adds an interesting dimension to Demy's next film, 1985's wild and undervalued *Parking*, which found him reuniting with Michel Legrand for a modern, pop-driven version of the Orpheus myth so famously adapted by Jean Cocteau years earlier. Of course, the film also kicks off with a dedication to Cocteau and features that earlier version's star, Jean Marais, as Hades, ruler of the underworld, so that gives a pretty clear indication of where the project is coming from. We first meet our protagonist, pop sensation Orpheus (Francis Huster, star of Andrzej Zulawski's *La femme publique* and *L'amour braque*), serenading and making love to his girlfriend, Eurydice (Keïko Ito), in his remote castle home/recording studio. He then hops on his motorcycle to Paris where he's mounting his latest spectacle at the Bercy theatre. An electrical accident onstage causes him to die for a few minutes, during which time he's escorted by Charon (*La rose de fer*'s Hugues Quester) via car into the underworld, located in the depths of an austere parking deck. In the afterlife (where everything is monochrome except the colour red), Hades decides to let Orpheus return but keeps an eye on him via his ward, Persephone (Marie-France Pisier), who occasionally wanders up to the world of the living. However, Orpheus and Eurydice have difficulty sustaining their relationship, and while he's off scoring a spectacular performance onstage, she takes drastic measures which will send him back to the parking afterlife once again.

Highly imaginative and packed with eccentric touches (like making Orpheus bisexual with a record producer boyfriend or depicting the famous walk back from hell this time with a bright red blindfold),

Parking was decried by critics and audiences upon release, with Legrand griping at the decision to retain Huster's own vocals for the music instead of using a professional singer. Indeed his voice can't grasp all the demands of some of the songs (and you'll really want to tear off his red rope headband after about half an hour), but the music itself is actually very catchy and lots of fun, while the film is never even remotely boring. The transitions in and out of the afterlife are especially effective, with the climax offering a satisfying modern twist that stays faithful to the original. The fairytale approach works well, too, but this one definitely isn't for the kiddies, as the frank nudity from Demy's previous film also turns up here. Once again this largely unseen film makes its mass video debut in the Arte box set and looks terrific; check out the muddy French trailer in the extras for an idea of how bad this must have looked for most audiences. Other extras include the usual critic commentaries, a poster gallery, and another *Cinéma cinémas* snippet with Demy talking about the film on French TV.

Before his death, Demy completed one final film in 1988, *Trois places pour le 26*, an unabashed musical star vehicle for Yves Montand, one of the world's most popular entertainers from the past century. Fresh off the international success of *Jean de Florette* and *Manon of the Spring*, Montand cranks the charm up full force here and clearly relishes the chance to do a splashy, MGM-style song and dance film, which kicks off with a great sequence in which, playing himself, he arrives at his hometown of Marseilles to throngs of twirling reporters. Accompanied by American actress Betty Miller (Catriona MacColl again, showing a very different side of herself here), he's planning to stage a big production, Remembering Montand, which covers his loves and losses with plenty of razzle dazzle. Meanwhile the starstruck young Marion (Mathilda May, everyone's favourite naked vampire from *Lifeforce* – and yes, she disrobes again here) sees him on TV and conspires to get a role in his show, unaware that her baroness mother is his long-lost love from decades ago. Featuring numerous nods to both Montand's and Demy's careers (with one number packed with top hats and tails, multiple Marilyn Monroe look-alikes, and musical quotes from *Some Like It Hot, The Umbrellas of Cherbourg*, and Fred and Ginger), it's a sweet pastry of a film and a loving tip of the hat to the filmmaking legacy that give the star and director so much joy. Legrand's songs mix in some surprising electronic shadings here and there, but for the most part he sticks to old school arrangements which is as it should be. Yet another all-too-rare Demy title, this makes its way overdue debut from Arte with a sharp and very colourful transfer that retains the original clever scope compositions. The closing credits and a few shots here and there look a bit edge enhanced, but there's not much point quibbling when this was impossible to see at all beforehand, let alone with subtitles. Extras include a hefty tag-team video commentary with Agnes Varda, Rosalie Varda and Mathieu Demy, a half-hour '80s TV special on Demy's latter years called "Jacques Demy, ou l'arbre gémeau", a poster gallery, the French trailer, and a 5-minute TV interview with Demy, "Portrait d'invité".

Is that enough yet? No! The box also contains a bonus CD with Demy and Legrand interviews and recording studio chatter (in French only, *naturellement*), a hefty illustrated fold-out booklet, and best of all, another DVD packing in all of his short films. 1950's "Le sabotier du Val de Loire" (23 minutes) is a beautiful character study of a provincial clog maker coming to grips with his post-war life and relationship to the fading world around him; 1959's "Ars" (18 minutes) uses amazing

tracking shots, voiceover, and gothic visuals to tell the story of a rural pastor whose unsparing sermons and self-criticisms left an unusual legacy; 1951's "Les Horizons Morts" (8 mins.) is an overt Cocteau homage with Demy himself heading a story about a young man's surreal self-realisations in the attic bedroom of his home; and a reel of rarities compiles three very short animated pieces, "Le Pont de Mauves", "Attaque Nocturne", and "La Ballerine". Also included is a sort-of short film, "La Luxure", Demy's instalment in an anthology film, *The Seven Deadly Sins* (1962), which also featured contributions from Claude Chabrol, Jean-Luc Godard, Roger Vadim, and others each covering one of the seven deadly sins. This time it's "lust", as seen through the eyes of a young boy who's driven by Bosch's paintings to imagine that dreaming about sexy women leads to fiery hell. It's a visually sumptuous 14-minute treat, shot lovingly in scope and nicely preserved here. Hopefully the whole film will make it to English-friendly DVD at some point. Finally the disc wraps up with even more critic commentaries, a quick vintage TV interview with Demy about "Luxure", and last but certainly not least, *The World of Jacques Demy*, Varda's amazing 90-minute documentary about his entire career, packed with incredible on-set footage. If you ever wanted to see Jim Morrison visiting the set of *Peau d'âne*, this is the place. The doc was issued previously in the U.S. as a standalone title from Koch Lorber and chopped into bits as supplements on many of the individual titles, but the box set is the only way to get it in anamorphic widescreen (1.78:1), with optional English subs, of course. All told, this treasure trove is easily one of the best box sets released in the DVD format's history and is easily worth the cost for any self-respecting fan of world cinema or just pure, energetic moviemaking at its finest.

JUSTINE & JULIETTE

Colour, 1975, 96m. / Directed by Mac Ahlberg / Starring Marie Forså, Anne Bie Warburg. Kate Mundt, Brigitte Maier, Harry Reems, Lisbeth Olsen / Impulse (US R1 NTSC) / WS (1.66:1) (16:9)

 With the sexual liberation of cinema achieved by naughty European imports, the writings of the Marquis de Sade suddenly became a hot property with filmmakers eager to lend a little literary prestige to their tales of carnal yearning. One of his earliest and most scandalous volumes, *Justine, or the Misfortunes of Virtue*, was tackled by everyone from Roger Vadim (the surprisingly timid *Vice and Virtue*) to Jess Franco (the surprisingly ridiculous *Justine*). One of the loosest versions came in 1975 from frequent cinematographer and occasional director Mac Ahlberg, who updated the story (kind of) to the '70s and spiced it up with a bit of hardcore. The basic idea is the same: two sisters, virtuous Justine (Joe Sarno softcore star Marie Forså) and rowdy Juliette (Anne Bie Warburg), find themselves on the road looking for a home and part ways over their very different attitudes to life and sex. While Juliette indulges in wanton behaviour involving rich men and surreal sex clubs, Justine soon finds that the high road doesn't offer much in the way of dividends – which becomes even more apparent when the two reunite, with Juliette having earned a tidy living as a popular hooker in the town's most popular brothel. One of the clients, Robert, talks Justine into bed but has an amateur porn filmmaking ring going on the side; of course, the two eventually intersect, with everyone finally getting it all out in the open at a swanky disco-orgy where one of the wealthiest patrons, a terminally ill millionaire (Harry Reems), beds everyone in sight.

A fascinating if somewhat erratic sample of Swedish sex cinema, *Justine & Juliette* is fairly typical of many of its ilk as the (fairly brief) explicit bits are mostly confined to background players (with an amiably unhinged Reems hogging up the big finale), while the more softcore-friendly stars mainly get naked and gyrate around a lot. What's actually more interesting is Ahlberg's impeccable visual eye as he stages sequences that are far more stylish than they have any right to be. The early sex club scene is a colourful marvel reminiscent of a Mario Bava film, while the eye-catching decor and surprising camerawork keep even the most mundane moments interesting. Forså is mostly confined to standing around looking doe-eyed and nearly being assaulted for most of the running time, but she finally dives in during the last third, which should make her fans happy.

The uncensored DVD features a decent anamorphic presentation that exposes some shortcuts in the source material, namely splicing together some shots that were lensed on varying film stock. Colours look beautiful and are almost blinding in a few scenes, while print damage is at a minimum. The original Swedish audio is presented in mono with optional English subtitles.

JUSTINE DE SADE

Colour, 1972, 115m. / Directed by Claude Pierson / Starring Alice Arno, Diane Lepvrier, Christian Chevreuse, Franco Fantasia / Blue Underground (US R0 NTSC), Oracle (UK R2 PAL) / WS (1.66:1) (16:9)

 This gauzy bit of period French erotica offers another take on the oft-filmed Marquis de Sade story about a virtuous innocent who finds out that only vice and corruption are rewarded

out in the real world. Jess Franco regular Alice Arno is probably the most recognisable name here, but director Claude Pierson opts for a literary and straight-faced approach that generally sticks to the tone of de Sade's writing. Comparisons to Franco's *Justine* (aka *Deadly Sanctuary*) are inevitable, but this version (which also clocks in at just under two hours) notably ramps up the sexual material and makes for a more satisfying viewing experience unto itself. The plot is basically a perverted Disneyland ride through the awakening of young Thérèse, who relates her story through flashbacks as she's being hauled off to prison, and the standout sequence is undeniably one in which she falls afoul of a group of monks who molest her on a table à la *Dracula, Prince of Darkness*.

The film is presented in its longer French cut, so while the French language track (with optional English subtitles, or more accurately dubtitles from the English track) is the more preferable, you can also watch the awkward English dub with a few segments switching to French with subs as well. The anamorphic 1.66:1 transfer looks terrific, with pastel-style colour schemes and rich detail. Extras include an alternative opening, a clothed version of the monk scene, a saucy French trailer, and a strangely horror-slanted English trailer as *The Violation of Justine*. Rather inexplicably, the U.K. disc from Oracle contains a completely different European English dub compared to the Blue Underground version (including different variations among the scenes necessitating subtitles), but unfortunately six minutes of (non-erotic) footage are missing.

KADIN DÜSMANI

B&W, 1967, 89m. / Directed by Ilhan Engin / Starring Ekrem Bora, Sema Ozcan, Gulgun Erdem, Engin Inal / Onar (Greece R0 PAL)

Touted as an early example of a Turkish variation on the popular Italian *giallo*, the atmospheric and wonderfully entertaining *Kadin Düsmani* ("Woman Despiser") in fact betrays a host of influences, such as the popular ooga-booga Edgar Wallace chillers pouring out of Germany and Italian gothic/thriller hybrids around the same time like *The Embalmer*. The film wastes no time at all as it kicks off with two back-to-back stalk and kill scenes, both involving young women who are murdered by a psycho with a penchant for devil or skull Halloween masks and creepy rubber claws. The police opine that the lunatic is a necrophile who rapes his victims after killing them and only goes after women who "seem happy" ("because he doesn't have a lover"). The investigator in charge (Ekrem Bora) deduces that the murderer's methodology is linked by the fact that the victims' first initials are the same as the districts in which they were killed, so he's obviously sending some kind of message. He also strikes up a romance with a beautiful young widow who might be connected to the case (her ridiculously convoluted back story gets rattled off in the first ten minutes), after which they take in a nightclub show where a pre-*Succubus* exotic dancer does a routine with a sword and a mannequin. Pretty much every man connected to the dead women becomes a suspect, including a rich ne'er-do-well and a sinister sculptor, while the percussive music score and increasingly senseless story build up, as these things often do, to a frenzied finale with our heroine pitted against the mask-wearing loony in an abandoned mansion festooned with cobwebs, wrapped up with a flashback-studded explanation of why it all happened. Other peculiar characters are on hand, too, with the detective's scene-stealing sister offering the most eccentric, perverse interlude in the entire film.

Though not as extreme as some of its Italian counterparts like *Blood and Black Lace*, this Turkish competitor does its best to irritate the censors with virtually every female character stripping down to her lingerie (or even further without actually showing much), all tied in directly to brutal murder scenes. There's even a jolting stabbing midway through that anticipates the unicorn killing in *Black Christmas*! Oddly enough, given this approach and the film's title, it's really too exaggerated and lurid to be genuinely offensive, with one delightfully pandering scene after another ensuring that no audience member will dare to even take a bathroom break.

Onar's upward climb in transfer quality continues with this film, possibly their best-looking effort yet. Gone are the days of murky transfers from tape sources; this was lifted from the lone surviving print and, apart from the contrast-pumped opening credits, it's surprisingly good. Yes, there's the usual print damage and miscellaneous debris (this is still an obscure Turkish film, after all), but even viewed on a 65" screen it holds up quite solidly. As usual, subtitles are offered in either English or Greek, and the disc comes in a limited 500-unit run. Of course, it wouldn't be an Onar release without some nice extras, and here you get part three of their "Turkish Fantastic Cinema" series of featurettes, this time focusing on science fiction with a little lip service to horror thrown in for good measure. The usual suspects like the Turkish variations on *Star Trek*, *Young Frankenstein*, *Superman* and *E.T.* are well-represented here, but the real kicker is when Canan Perver, the now-gorgeous actress who played the child lead in *Seytan* (the unbelievable *Exorcist* imitation), shows up near the end with memories of shooting the film. Other goodies include an image gallery, the usual informative bios

for Bora and director Ilhan Engin, and a trailer for the tasty-looking Onar acquisition, *Altin Cocuk*, along with *The Serpent's Tale*, *Casus Kiran* and *Kizil Tug*.

KARAOKE TERROR

Colour, 2003, 112m. / Directed by Tetsuo Shinohara / Starring Masanobu Ando, Arata Furuta, Yoshio Harada, Kanako Higuchi, Fumie Hosokawa, Miwako Ichikawa / Synapse (US R1 NTSC) / WS (1.85:1) (16:9) / DD2.0

A film that truly could have been made only in Japan, *Karaoke Terror* (adapted from a novel by *Audition* author Ryû Murakami) posits a world in which two rival gangs dedicated to escaping reality through stylised Karaoke routines engage in a battle fierce enough to touch off a culture firestorm – literally. The bizarre face-off begins when Sugioka, a member of a young boy gang, murders an older woman who rejects his advances. It turns out she belongs to the Midoris, a rival group of affluent, bored hausfraus who, like the bad lads, are dedicated to performing songs from the Showa pop music era (which lasted until the late 1980s). While not busy staging increasingly surreal musical spectacles, the gangs begin to retaliate against each other in an increasingly brutal fashion, finding some inner vitality in the process.

Though it doesn't aim for the heights of violent satire classics like *Battle Royale*, this film (whose original title, *Shôwa kayô daizenshû*, is translated on the DVD packaging as *The Complete Japanese Showa Songbook*) manages to slip a surprisingly potent amount of social commentary into its succession of gaudy performance art sequences and blood-spewing acts of revenge. The finale may remind more than a few viewers of *Fight Club*, but the film also nods to a number of other influences, most obviously *A Clockwork Orange* as well as the works of Dennis Potter whose juxtaposition of miming pop songs and shocking violence paid huge dividends in *Pennies from Heaven* and, of course, his *Karaoke* miniseries. All of the characters are essentially stylised markers for their gender and class stations, which is as it should be given the nature of the material. Newcomers to Japanese cinema might be completely baffled at times, but when it works, *Karaoke Terror* delivers a solid punch to the chops.

A film festival staple for years, this film finally makes its English-friendly debut courtesy of Synapse's well-appointed special edition which features an immaculate anamorphic transfer and thankfully informative, highly accessible subtitles. Audio this time out is 2.0 stereo, which serves it well enough (though why this film packed with sound effects and music didn't warrant a 5.1 mix is a bit of a mystery). In case anyone is left with lingering questions, the packed liner notes booklet provides a lot of context courtesy of Christine Yano's examination of the songs from the film and Nicholas Rucka's essay about the original source's author. As for video extras, you get the original Japanese trailer (which pretty much blows the finale), a TV spot, and best of all, a half-hour featurette covering the making of the film with the director, author, and most of the cast talking about the experience. Unfortunately a real gang war didn't erupt between the cast members on the set, but that's about the only thing that's missing from this highly recommended release.

KILLER'S DELIGHT

Colour, 1977, 83m. / Directed by Jeremy Hoenack / Starring John Karlen, Joe Ivy, James Luisi, Susan Sullivan / Shriek Show (US R1 NTSC) / WS (1.85:1) (16:9)

Sort of a soft-rock ancestor to the brutal serial killer slashers of the early '80s like *Maniac* and *Nightmare*, the still-unknown *Killer's Delight* (credited as *The Dark Ride* and *The Sport Killer* in many places – including this very same DVD!) is the sort of low-aiming programmer most interesting now for its snapshot of a time long past and a character actor playing way against type. In this case the latter asset is John Karlen, best known to TV fans for his recurring roles on *Dark Shadows* and *Cagney and Lacey* as well as his turn as the belt-wielding male lead in *Daughters of Darkness*. Here he goes all Zodiac on a bunch of pretty young things in San Francisco, all of whom frequent a swimming pool where he hangs out at night scoping for victims. Detective De Carlo (James Luisi) juggles his home life with the investigation, which is complicated by his involvement on the side with a criminologist (Susan Sullivan) a bit too willing to put herself in harm's way and a partner (Joe Ivy) as interested in chasing tail as perpetrators.

Released the same year as John Carpenter's *Halloween*, this is a far more typically '70s exploitation relic filled with gaudy fashions, hairstyles and decor. One-shot director Jeremy Hoenack (who went on to become a busy TV sound man) doesn't make much of a deliberate attempt to generate atmosphere or stylish visuals, though some of the nocturnal pool shots have a weird, desolate quality. Karlen is the real reason to stick around as he chomps up the scenery as a disturbed mama's boy, obsessed with abducting women (who provide the requisite T&A) for regular rounds of cat and mouse. The gore quotient is low, but the sleaze never relents. If you enjoy mid-'70s Harry Novak fare like *Hitchhike to Hell* and *A Scream in the Streets*, this should be just the ticket.

This film straggled onto VHS under its alternative titles for a handful of releases in the U.S. and U.K. without ever building up much of a reputation, so it's quite a shock to see it get such loving treatment here with Shriek Show delivering a solid, colourful anamorphic transfer along with the original trailer under the *Sport Killer* title. Plus you get the always conversant Karlen (who gave good commentary on *Daughters* earlier) providing both a feature-length commentary chat and a video interview along with Hoenack, both of whom are candid and often hilarious in their assessment of mounting a commercially-viable project on a very limited budget. The SF locales and the relation to the real-life serial killer antics of Ted Bundy and his ilk get a lot of the focus here, and true crime buffs should be interested to find out how much of the genuine facts affected the storyline. You also get a batch of press book and still images covering the various promotional tactics, all of them very different. An odd and occasionally fascinating thriller that precedes the modern serial killer film in some interesting ways, *Killer's Delight* is a very modest but worthwhile mixture of grit and unapologetic drive-in grime worth adding to any exploitation DVD library.

KILLER'S MOON

Colour, 1978, 90m. / Directed by Alan Birkinshaw / Starring Anthony Forrest, Tom Marshall, David Jackson, JoAnne Good, Georgina Kean / Redemption (UK R0 PAL, US R0 NTSC) / WS (1.78:1) (16:9)

If you can make it past the first ten minutes of *Killer's Moon* without collapsing in hysterical laughter, then you have no business watching horror movies. Ostensibly a no-budget sex and gore offering in the wake of work from other British exploitation vets like Pete Walker and Norman J. Warren, this cockeyed oddity instead plays like a parody of slasher films before they had even been fully developed (just consider, *Halloween* came out the same year). The entire flick takes place out in the woods somewhere in the wilderness where a camping couple is disrupted in the middle of the night by a three-legged dog wearing a neckerchief. Deducing that the canine's missing appendage couldn't have been caused by an animal trap, they realise that something nasty must be afoot nearby. And indeed there is, as a busload of choirgirls (who spend the trip chanting "Greensleeves") finds out when they break down and have to take refuge at a bed and breakfast which happens to be near a cottage insane asylum where four lunatics have just escaped. But no, it's not enough for them to just be insane; nay, they've been undergoing medical treatment by which the doctors administer LSD and teach them to live their lives as if they're in a dream, which means their actions have no consequences. Exactly why they think this is good therapy is anyone's guess, and the appalled minister of the facility responds quite calmly, "In my dreams, I murder freely, pillage, loot and rape". Yes, of course. Soon a handyman winds up axed, the girls are separated from their chaperones, and the four psychos (in full *Clockwork Orange* regalia) are holding them all hostage when not busy chasing runaways through the woods. Of course, the three-legged dog also gets his revenge in one of the funniest scenes ever committed to film.

As director Alan Birkinshaw and one of the stars helpfully explain on the DVD, this film was originally written and planned as a straight-ahead boobs and blood outing with wooden dialogue and a few kills to keep the crowd happy. However, when some of the character interaction was turned over to sorta-feminist writer Fay Weldon (*The Life and Loves of a She-Devil*), something... changed, obviously. Simply put, forget what Rita Mae Brown did to *The Slumber Party Massacre*; this film takes the cake for the weirdest one-liners in slasherdom. (Most memorably, a choirgirl recovering from a sexual assault on a kitchen table is consoled by her friend as follows: "Look, you were only raped. As long as you don't tell anyone about it, you'll be all right".) If you think the film can't manage to sustain such nuttiness to the end, guess again; the closing shot is a ridiculously perfect summary of the film (be sure to listen to that muffled final line) and encapsulates the berserk appeal of what would surely be a major camp classic if more people had actually seen it. Oh, yes, and there's even an ear-shredding closing theme song.

Though many of Redemption's past releases have been a bit light on the supplements, they've thankfully gone way beyond the call of duty trying to explain how on earth this film ever got out of the gate. The making of *Killer's Moon* is a truly bizarre saga with Birkinshaw and actress JoAnne Good guiding you along a trip via audio commentary and two video interviews through the insanity of finance-famished horror filmmaking in Great Britain during its final days of exploitation glory. Birkinshaw covers his odd first softcore film, *Confessions of a Sex Maniac*, which he reveals was originally entitled *The Tit*(!), and the writing process which turned *Killer's Moon* into the anti-classic we now have with us today. You also get to discover where they found that three-legged dog (who got a bit of media publicity in the process), how the actresses felt about disrobing onscreen, and the reasons for hiring lead actor Anthony Forrest who was supposed to become a big name after his stint on *Star Wars* before his entire part wound up on the cutting room floor. They both seem to feel the film holds up well

enough years later so one can only assume that the bizarre line readings and "dream-like" plotting were intentional. In any case Redemption has done it proud, and the anamorphic transfer is a nice step up from those very rare VHS copies which turned up from time to time. The original blue-heavy colour timing appears to be intact, and apart from some minor print damage here and there, it all looks great. (Yes, it's still interlaced as with every other Redemption title on the market, but that's no surprise.) Along with the aforementioned extras, the disc also contains two U.K. theatrical trailers (one X-rated, the other clean), a stills gallery, and the usual cross-promoting trailers for other Redemption titles.

KILLERS BY NATURE

Colour, 2005, 70m. / Directed by Eric Spudic / Starring Jason Contini, Eric Spudic, William Clifton, Nick Hearne / Sub Rosa (US R0 NTSC)

Bringing the "thrill killers on the loose" subgenre to all-new budgetary depths, the shot-on-camcorder *Killers By Nature* to date marks the sole directorial effort of Eric Spudic, a horror fan who wrote the scripts for such straight-to-video cheapies as *Aquanoids*, *Creepies* and *Deadly Culture* while occasionally popping up on-camera in more high-profile projects like *The Undertow* and *Savage Harvest 2*. This effort actually isn't bad as two put-upon, low-rent buddies, Jeffrey Mordrid (played by Spudic, natch, who kicks off his role by abusing himself in front of a computer screen) and Cory (Jason Contini), sit around getting drunk and rattling off all the people who picked on them in high school. As a gag they decide to pose as homicidal maniacs to terrorise their tormenters, but soon things spiral out of control when a real murder turns them into something more closely resembling the genuine article.

This film strives for shock value with some prolonged violent scenes (sometimes played for laughs) and even a toilet scene that goes right for the gag reflex, which means you won't get bored even if the overall execution falls down in the end due to some really sloppy camerawork (a light meter really would've done wonders) and, you know, an overall lack of funds. Still, it's worth checking out as a lively entry in the always curious DIY horror scene. Sub Rosa's DVD comes with a Spudic audio commentary (in which he doesn't seem embarrassed by the absurd amounts of horror movie posters and T-shirts cluttering up the screen through the entire 70 minutes), a stills gallery, trailers, two bonus videos and, most inventively, a drinking game that will leave even the hardiest wino hammered by the end credits.

KILLING CAR

Colour, 1993, 90m. / Directed by Jean Rollin / Starring Tiki Tsang, Frédérique Haymann, Jean-Jacques Lefeuvre, Karine Swenson / Redemption (UK R0 PAL, US R0 NTSC)

 If you ever wondered what might happen if Jean Rollin decided to make an erotic action film on a budget of about five Euros, *Killing Car*, also known under the far more appropriate title of *La femme dangereuse*, is the baffling answer. Shot on low-grade film sometime in the '80s and evidently finished in post-production on video in 1993, it's a strange, maddening, and sometimes beautiful dream piece revolving around a mostly silent,

alluring female assassin (one-off actress Tiki Tsang), who wanders around the seedy wastelands near Paris killing various people. Along the way she also dances in a small nightclub, stalks her prey through a garden of statues, jaunts off to New York and wafts around a ferryboat, and becomes involved with the modelling industry, all the while observed by a pair of less-than-enthusiastic police officers.

Rollin fans are really the only ones who will find rewards in this little oddity, which trades entirely on the surface appeal of the beautiful and rather captivating Tsang; she can model clothes and slip off sunglasses like nobody's business. Along with the commercially-mandated but rather innocent injections of nudity and blood, Rollin also throws in some amusing nods to his previous films, mainly through prop cameos related to his past vampire projects, and of course the melancholy finale features the heroine crying directly at the camera. Basically a goofy little trifle as far as Rollin films go, it's still unmistakably his work and merits a peek for the Euro-horror completist.

Unfortunately the production history of *Killing Car* means that, barring someone going back to the negative and rebuilding the film from scratch with new edits and credits, there's no way it will ever look better than the video master that's been circulating for the past few years. Redemption's release looks about as dated as you might expect, with burned-in subtitles and very weak contrast. It's still watchable if you don't mind viewing something a step or two above VHS, but don't expect any visual fireworks here. The packaging labels it as Dolby Digital Stereo, but it sounds for all the world like mono to these ears. Rollin fans will certainly be happy to see that this release contains the complete *Eurotika!* U.K. TV episode devoted to him, and for once all the film clips appear to be intact for this video edition. It's a great intro to his work and, in a just world, would be included on all of his releases to lure in the uninitiated.

KIZIL TUG

B&W, 1952, 73m. / Directed by Aydin Arakon / Starring Turan Seyfioglu, Mesiha Yelda, Atif Kaptan, Cahit Irgat / Onar (Greece R0 PAL)

 The most ambitious and epic release to date in the heroic efforts of Onar Films to salvage Turkish fantastic cinema for the DVD market, *Kizil Tug* (whose title is translated as "The Red Banner" on the print and is also referred to as "The Red Plume") bears the packaging subtitle of *Cengiz Han*, or "Genghis Khan", which should give you an idea of what to expect. The disc sleeve refers to this as a previously lost film and "the oldest Turkish Historical Peplum Sword Film surviving" that "precedes the Italian Peplums by many years and puts them to shame", though if you're expecting a Turkish Steve Reeves battling monsters, you've got another thing coming. Instead this is closer in spirit to the lavish, over-the-top action spectacles churned out by Universal starting in the mid-'40s (usually starring Maria Montez) like *Arabian Nights* and *Cobra Woman*. This is every bit as much fun as its American counterparts, and for good measure, it also tosses in plenty of unexpected nods to Sergei Eisenstein, particularly *Ivan the Terrible* and a gory montage finale à la *Battleship Potemkin*!

Three soldiers in the woods (including Genghis Khan and "Gelman the lion slayer") cross paths with a slovenly bum (Turan Seyfioglu) carrying a bloodstained sword. The civilian identifies himself as "Otsukarci" and begins a swordfight with the antagonistic feline hunter, only to be interrupted when another small but violent army shows up. Much clashing of blades ensues, and Otsukarci steps aside only to save Khan's life with a well-timed knife throw. Impressed, the warlord calls off the duel and enlists this new Turkish soldier to retrieve money owed him by another leader holding his brother. Thus begins a string of swordfights, horseback chases, espionage, wine-soaked parties with beautiful women, and a furious battle finale. Extremely fast-paced and without an ounce of fat during its matinee-friendly running time, *Kizil Tug* is a colourful, entertaining adventure with some surprisingly accomplished action scenes and a charismatic central performance by Seyfioglu. It's a far cry from the DIY super-hero Turkish favourite we've all come to know and love, proving the country can turn out rip-roaring fun with the best of them.

Onar's DVD comes from the sole unearthed film print, and considering its history, the presentation is above expectations. The opening credits and final reel display some obvious scratches and other damage, but the bulk of the film is quite watchable with nice contrast levels. Optional subtitles are available in either English or Greek. Even if this film's genre might make you hesitate, Onar's release is still absolutely essential for another reason: the debut of its full-colour, 40-page insert guide to Turkish fantastic cinema, a lovingly-assembled labour of love by Bill Barounis complete with gorgeous ad mats and never-before-seen info and synopses. The guide is divided into horror/mystery, fairy tales/fantasy, karate, historical, western, sci-fi, and superheroes. Prepare to weep with longing for such elusive films as *Sevdalim* (a hardcore *giallo*), *Psycho Woman* ("A sexy psycho slaughters men and women in this sick and bloody obscurity"), and *Vahset Kasirgasi* (a remake of *A Candle for the Devil*!). As for supplements on the DVD itself, you get text bios for Atif Kaptan and Seyfioglu, the first 12-minute instalment from *Turkish Fantastic Cinema* (a 90-minute piece picked up by Onar and turned into an ongoing serial-type supplement, consisting of great interviews with cast members along with rare clips usually pulled from scarce VHS tapes), a photo gallery, and trailers for *Cici Can* (a fun-looking '60s haunted house movie complete with an animated, Casper-type ghost), *Altin Cocuk*, *Kaptan Swing*, and a really crazy-looking action/nudity '60s curio called *Maskeli Ucler*.

LADY LIBERTINE

Colour, 1983, 90m. / Directed by Gérard Kikoine / Starring Jennifer Inch, Sophie Favier, Christopher Pearson / Private Screening (US R0 NTSC)

One of the more obscure and perverse TV collaborations between *Playboy* and veteran trash producer Harry Alan Towers, *Lady Libertine* (originally called *Frank and I*) is basically a fancy-dress sex version of *Victor/Victoria*. A young orphan boy named "Frank" (Jennifer Inch), really a girl on the run dressed up in an unconvincing Little Lord Fauntleroy outfit, is picked up on a desolate road by a wealthy British man, Charles (Christopher Pearson). Failing to see the true gender of his newest acquisition but aroused nonetheless, he takes Frank home and decides to bring him up properly. During a bare-bottom caning, he discovers the deception but keeps it to himself while continuing an affair with his sexy mistress (Sophie Favier). Charles and Frank (really Frances) fool around on the side, but the explanation for the youth's oddball disguise leads them both to a seedy underworld of prostitution that threatens to split them up forever.

Horrendously dubbed and certainly weird, *Lady Libertine* will be something of a tough sell for the average softcore crowd; the odd mix of cross-dressing, S&M, and flat performances make for odd bedfellows, though the minor but often-naked role for French TV presenter Favier gives it a certain curiosity value. Production values are decent enough, and director Gérard Kikoine (who went from hardcore to the wacko *Edge of Sanity*) keeps things slick and glossy even when the film teeters on the brink of sheer stupidity. Transfer quality isn't up to par with other Private Screening releases like *Black Venus* thanks to a much rougher, grittier look and some obvious element damage, but considering its relative rarity, the disc is still watchable enough.

THE LAST HORROR FILM

Colour, 1982, 89m. / Directed by David Winters / Starring Caroline Munro, Joe Spinell, Judd Hamilton, David Winters, Susanne Benton, Mary Spinell / Troma (US R1 NTSC)

A bizarre footnote in early '80s horror history, *The Last Horror Film* was widely-hyped (at least among the *Famous Monsters*-reading fan community), promising to storm theatres during a glut of features starring Jason Voorhees and Michael Myers. Much of the anticipation arose from the reteaming of its stars, Joe Spinell (a character actor from films like *Taxi Driver* and *Cruising*) and scream queen Caroline Munro (*The Golden Voyage of Sinbad*), who worked together in 1980's surprise splatter hit, *Maniac* (not to mention 1979's unsurprising non-hit, *Starcrash*). Their third time out together, shot during the colourful 1981 Cannes Film Festival, promised to be a dizzying meta-horror film that would turn the genre on its head. Then... it pretty much vanished. Yes, it played a couple of token screens (sometimes under the alternative title of *Fanatic*), but the end result proved to be much stranger and certainly goofier than anyone expected, playing more like someone's deranged European vacation sprinkled with a handful of bloody kill scenes and wacko banter between Spinell and his mom. Of course, these oddball qualities are exactly what makes this film so fascinating today and an amusing change of pace from the typical slice-and-dice fare of the period.

Once again playing a sweaty obsessive, Spinell stars as Vinny Durand, a sad-sack cabbie with a deeply questionable crush on horror star Jana Bates (Munro), for whom he's been envisioning a dream project. Undeterred by his kvetching mama, he takes off for France to woo Jana with his movie pitch while she's promoting her latest release. Of course, his efforts to cut through her keepers prove to be more difficult than he anticipated, particularly the strong-arming presence of her boyfriend, Alan (played by Munro's real-life spouse, Judd Hamilton). Soon the men in Jana's life start ending up with their head floating in a hotel bathroom sink or lying in bathtubs with their throat slashed, while Vinny gets closer and closer to the woman of his dreams when not experiencing colourful delusions at local strip clubs.

Unlike *Maniac*, this film tries to pack a sting into its tail (which, now that you know, won't be much of a surprise), but it's still basically a showcase for Spinell to strut his stuff. And strut he does, delivering a scenery-chewing lead performance that manages to almost single-handedly negate the film's multitude of narrative and technical issues. His fantasy scenes are an obvious attempt to riff on the mannequin delusions of *Maniac*, of course, but in this case the idea of a reflexive look at horror idol worship and the superficial allure of moviemaking in general gives it all a distinctly different flavour. Caroline Munro is always worth watching and looks great with her grey-streaked hairstyle, not to mention a show-stopping scene in which she's terrorised and chased from her hotel room in nothing but a towel (which the awaiting press thinks is an elaborate publicity stunt). If that weren't enough, the film is also a delicious early '80s time capsule, kicking off with Depeche Mode's "Photographic" blasting over the opening titles and peppering the entire running time with great on-location Cannes footage promoting the likes of *For Your Eyes Only*, *First Blood*, *Cannibal Holocaust*(!), and Andrzej Zulawski's *Possession*, for which a briefly-glimpsed Isabelle Adjani actually did garner an award for appearing in a horror film. Of course, the obligatory Côte d'Azur topless sunbathing babes are thrown in for good measure, too.

Much of the disjointed feel of *The Last Horror Film* can be attributed to its undisciplined and very messy production history, with director, co-writer and co-star David Winters (a former choreographer and helmer of the patchwork MST3000 favourite *Space Mutiny* as well as some very wild TV specials for Ann-Margret and Raquel Welch) apparently handing many sequences over to Hamilton (who co-wrote and co-produced) and Spinell. At times this nearly rivals *Night Train to Terror* for violent tone shifts, but that also guarantees you won't be bored for a second. You might even say it serves as a sort of forerunner to *Scream* (the name of its movie-within-a-movie, coincidentally) with its house of mirrors approach to horror, refracting each layer upon the other until finally pulling it all away for a truly surreal concluding ten minutes. As if the self-commentary weren't enough, the script also tosses in liberal nods to the wave of early '80s celebrity assassination attempts (especially Hinckley's attempt at Reagan) for reasons which might be considered tasteless if the film didn't have such a scattershot, ultimately light-hearted approach.

The Last Horror Film first popped up on video during the VHS era in its standard R-rated edition from Media in the U.S. and a slightly longer variant in the UK. This extra footage (amounting to barely over a minute, including a noticeably gorier climactic death for the killer) failed to materialise in Troma's first DVD edition under the *Fanatic* title, but their much-needed reissue under the more famous original moniker manages to finally get things right. The extremely obsessed may note that a few frames are still missing from the elements used here (namely a music jump due to the swapped title card and a blood-squirting flash during the first throat-slash murder), but this is still the most exhaustive version of the film ever assembled by a long shot on DVD. The extra footage is integrated back into the film (in what appears to be the exact same transfer), with the new bits being of somewhat lesser quality but quite welcome all the same. The transfer itself isn't the greatest, but it is extremely colourful and clear enough during outdoor scenes. The nocturnal climax looked dark and muddy even in theatrical prints and doesn't fare much better here, so just expect that going in. If the extended running time weren't enough, the special edition sweetens the pot with a number of juicy extras obviously compiled with a degree of care and attention absent from much of the company's self-promoting earlier discs. "My Best Maniac" spends an afternoon trotting around the late Spinell's old haunts with his best friend, Luke Walter, who reels off a string of affectionate anecdotes about his buddy. Walter, who was apparently present for the entire film shoot, also contributes an audio commentary with Evan Husney in which he covers the film from the vantage point of Spinell's contri-butions, which also helps to make sense of

how it all came together and what its star expected to take away from the project. *Maniac* director and Blue Underground founder Bill Lustig also appears for another interview in which he talks about how the film originally came together and the rather immature expectations and circumstances from which it sprang, often chuckling in disbelief at his own memories. "Mr. Robbie" (also pitched as "Maniac 2"), a grim and moody short film by *Combat Shock* director Buddy Giovinazzo, is also presented here in its entirety, a nice prelude to Troma's much-needed special edition of Giovinazzo's nasty little masterpiece. Also included is the usual silly and ultimately head-scratching video intro by Troma founder Lloyd Kaufman, a stills gallery of Spinell images from Walter's archives, a couple of trailers including one under the original title, TV spots as *Fanatic*, and a much more restrained than usual batch of Troma-related promos.

LAST HOUSE ON THE BEACH

Colour, 1978, 86m. / Directed by Franco Prosperi / Starring Florinda Bolkan, Ray Lovelock, Flavio Andreini, Stefano Cedrati, Sherry Buchanan, Laura Trotter / Severin (US R1 NTSC), Sazuma (Austria R2 PAL) / WS (2.35:1) (16:9)

 After the international success of the rape-revenge shocker *The Last House on the Left*, distributors were quick to cash in with plenty of European imports whose connection to the Wes Craven film ranged from uncomfort-ably close (such as a virtual remake, *Night Train Murders*) to utterly laughable (Mario Bava's *A Bay of Blood*, widely retitled as *Last House on the Left Part II*). One of the weirdest offsprings of this craze, *Last*

House on the Beach (originally titled *La settima donna* or "The Seventh Woman" in Italy) managed to inject the scenario with a fresh twist by – get this – mixing in some nunsploitation for good measure. Weird, artsy, unpleasant, and compelling at the same time, it's a fascinating attempt to meld artistry with trash that still hasn't received its due.

Following a deadly bank robbery, three robbers are told by their superiors to hide out and decide to go on the lam in a desolate beachside area. Soon they find refuge at a house where several young girls and their chaperone, Cristina (Florinda Bolkan), are busy rehearsing in surreal animal outfits for a production of *A Midsummer Night's Dream* at an upcoming Shakespeare festival. Soon the females are all held captive both in the house and outside on the beach by the thugs, including leader and professed non-killer Aldo (Ray Lovelock), sex-crazed Walter (Flavio Andreini), and shirt-allergic Nino (Stefano Cedrati). During a bout of verbal taunting, the men discover that Cristina is actually a nun and derive no end of amusement from provoking her, while the girls are subjected to various ordeals culminating in a bizarre sexual assault with Nino dressed in women's make-up. Through various flashbacks and stories the truth about the major players comes to light, and Cristina can only cling on to her holy teachings for so long before eventually exploding in a frenzy of righteous violence.

Though the plot suggests standard exploitation fare, *Last House* rises above the norm primarily thanks to the committed performances by Bolkan and Lovelock (with the latter even warbling a rock tune early on entitled "Place for the Landing"), stylish direction by Franco Prosperi (prior to his outrageous animals-amuck masterpiece, *Wild Beasts*), and a killer score by Roberto Pregadio featuring appropriately lush vocals by the omnipresent Edda Dell'Orso. The scope photography makes

excellent use of the limited locations, often drenching scenes in unearthly blues, and despite the gritty tone of the subject matter, the film manages to evoke its most shocking moments through implication rather than explicit thrills. There are only a few flashes of nudity throughout and the one prolonged rape sequence is rendered almost entirely in the dark, focusing on the participants' faces in slow motion to create a haunting effect. Of course, the movie does slide into the gutter occasionally, mainly due to its obvious delight in placing Bolkan in a nun's habit just so she can be manhandled and persecuted at knifepoint, which is presumably enough justification for her gun-toting revenge. Despite the *Last House* connection, in the end both the plot and treatment more closely resemble the American girls-in-captivity favourite *Cheerleaders' Wild Weekend*, which would make a great double feature.

Though it popped up in an English-language incarnation of varying lengths under its initial export title as well as *Terror*, Prosperi's film has suffered mightily over the years due to brutal pan-and-scan transfers that rendered it completely incoherent. A widescreen Japanese DVD eventually appeared, but the winner in the home video market by far is the essential anamorphic master released by Sazuma and later Severin. The Sazuma packaging only lists audio options in Italian and German, but the English is actually on there as well; Lovelock and some of the supporting performers clearly performed in English, while Bolkan mostly spoke Italian. Both are legitimate, so it's really your call as to which of the two you'd prefer (i.e., the classier Italian track, or the juicy '70s English variant with plenty of the usual suspects from the dubbing community). Subtitles are available in Italian or German. The front of the package credits the film under its original Italian title as well as its German one (*Verflucht zum Toten*) so most dealers may list it that way. Also included on the disc is a lengthy featurette, "Holy Beauty vs. the Evil Beasts", which features Lovelock talking about his career (with some anecdotes carried over from his earlier DVD interviews) as well as his memories of working on the film and his co-stars. He also explains how he got his name despite being Italian, which is an interesting story by itself. Also included are the German and Italian theatrical trailers, the alternative German opening credits, a photo gallery, brief but informative liner notes by Christian Kessler entitled "Of Nuns and Jackals", and a very funny karaoke-style Easter Egg that won't be spoiled here. The niftiest extra by far is a second disc containing the entire CD soundtrack in beautiful, immaculate stereo; Pregadio's score has never been released before in any form (and yes, that song is included as well), so this wonderful bonus is almost worth the entire price by itself.

Following up on the Sazuma release, the American DVD premiere from Severin is virtually identical with the same impressive transfer and Ray Lovelock featurette, as well as the German and Italian trailers. The only difference is that it drops the Italian and German language tracks, the photo gallery, and the Easter Egg (as well as the soundtrack CD, alas), but the lower price tag might make it a more attractive purchase. Either way, it's well worth hunting down and makes for a nice reminder of how politically incorrect international films used to be.

THE LAST HUNTER

Colour, 1980, 96m. / Directed by Antonio Margheriti / Starring David Warbeck, Tisa Farrow, Tony King, Bobby Rhodes, John Steiner, Margit Evelyn Newton, Luciano Pigozzi / Dark Sky (US R1 NTSC) / WS (2.35:1) (16:9), VIPCO (UK R0 PAL) / WS (1.85:1)

British sex comedy and Italian trash cinema regular David Warbeck stars as the title hunter, Captain Henry Morris, first seen during the waning days of the Vietnam War witnessing a high-strung fellow soldier going on a murderous and ultimately suicidal rampage at a whorehouse. Still filled with rage and confusion, he's given the challenging assignment of taking down a local radio outfit broadcasting dangerous propaganda messages, with plucky reporter Jane Foster (Tisa Farrow) accompanying him on an explosion-riddled journey into the heart of the jungle.

A frequent contributor to the Italian practice of tweaking Hollywood blockbusters into eccentric exploitation films, Antonio Margheriti – better known under the directorial screen name of "Anthony M. Dawson" – spent much of the latter portion of his career spawning cash-ins on hits like *Jaws* and *Raiders of the Lost Ark*. Oddly enough, 1980 saw him deliver no less than two spin-offs from *Apocalypse Now*: the Vietnam-vets-turn-flesh-eaters favourite *Cannibal Apocalypse* and, for those with more mainstream tastes, *The Last Hunter*. Featuring an astonishing roster of names at the height of their Italian filmmaking glory, this entry benefits from the feisty performances of Warbeck and Farrow, both of whom achieved immortality in Lucio Fulci films like *Zombie Flesh-Eaters* and *The Beyond*. No less impressive is the supporting cast including John Steiner (fresh from Mario Bava's *Shock* and Tinto Brass's *Caligula*), future *Demons* jive-talker Bobby Rhodes, "Italian Peter Lorre" Luciano Pigozzi, and *Cannibal Apocalypse* actor Tony King. The story itself follows the *Apocalypse Now* template of soldiers embarking on a travelogue-style journey through Vietnam and encountering a variety of eccentric set pieces along the way, but unlike its American counterpart, the film makes no attempts at deep artistic statements, instead using the script by prolific scribe Dardano Sacchetti to pile on the explosions, bloody dismemberments, and nudity (including Ms. Farrow) with no apologies whatsoever. Extra points for a crackerjack surprise ending and the pounding music score by the always fascinating Franco Micalizzi (*Beyond the Door*), who even contributes a dance-worthy theme song.

Not surprisingly, *The Last Hunter* became a popular theatrical and video staple around the world, quickly spawning a lesser Margheriti/Warbeck Vietnam opus (*Tiger Joe*) and providing stock footage for other Italian war films throughout the next decade. Its striking cover box from Vestron Video remained on mom-and-pop rental shelves well into the 1990s, despite the atrocious pan-and-scan transfers which made this a complete eyesore to endure on television. Even the first DVD edition, courtesy of VIPCO, was a half-hearted affair which only letterboxed the image halfway, and was non-anamorphic to boot. Luckily Dark Sky finally got things right (well, mostly) with their special edition, which is presented in the correct 2.35:1 scope aspect ratio, albeit with some slight zoomboxing which crops a few shots a bit too tightly and even crushes in a bit on the main titles. The film elements (taken from a French source, judging by the main titles) are in excellent shape, and otherwise the transfer is quite satisfying. It's certainly more coherent and colourful than any other option around, and the optional English subtitles (a nice Dark Sky feature they still omit from mentioning on their packaging for some reason) come in handy during some of the more chaotic scenes. The film was shot in English with many of the actors looped afterwards, so this is as close to a genuine language track as you'll get. Extras include the action-packed

European theatrical trailer, a stills gallery, and best of all, an interview with Margheriti's son and frequent assistant director, Edoardo, who talks about making the film, his father's career at the time and his own brief role onscreen.

LAURE

Colour, 1976, 95m. / Directed by Emmanuelle Arsan / Starring Annie Belle, Al Cliver, Emmanuelle Arsan, Vicky Asprin, Homer Adams / Severin (US R0 NTSC) / WS (1.85:1) (16:9)

The fine folks at Severin Films have made a specialty of unearthing forgotten classics in pristine new editions, and in this instance, the extras are perhaps even more valuable than the main feature. Better known to softcore junkies as *Forever Emanuelle*, this Philippines-set slice of erotica stars Eurosleaze veteran Annie Belle as the title character who hooks up with bearded anthropology photojournalist Nicolas (a pre-*Zombie* Al Cliver, her real-life beau at the time) for a series of escapades around the exotic East as they seek a mysterious, amnesia-prone tribe. They also rotate through a series of other sexual partners before a climactic jungle journey where Laure gets body-painted silver for a final metaphysical orgy.

The script was penned by "Emmanuelle Arsan", the author of the famous novel, which was actually a real-life husband and wife team. Emmanuelle appears in the film as well (as the shower-loving "Myrte!"), while her husband, Louis Jacques Rollet-Andriane, handled writing and directing chores. Thus, technically this is a film from the "real Emmanuelle" in every possible sense. This cut of the film also runs longer than prior editions, and both of the leads show an unabashed amount of skin in their numerous sex scenes. Technically it's all beautifully shot, but the standout aspect is really the killer score by Franco Micalizzi, who delivers several excellent, memorable themes.

Even if the film itself isn't the most explosive sexploitation title around, the extras make this a must-see all unto themselves. Producer Ovidio Assonitis appears for a terrific interview featurette ("Emmanuelle Revealed") in which he goes into detail about the Emmanuelle identity controversy, the tumultuous making of the film (which originally starred a very uncooperative Linda Lovelace!), and the location shooting, while another featurette, "Laure: A Love Story", features Cliver and a voice-only Belle talking about their relationship and the making of the film, with Belle's sad personal history since the mid-'80s making for some very bittersweet viewing indeed. The 16x9 transfer looks terrific and makes for a welcome upgrade over dreary-looking past editions, and the English dubbing is still a ridiculous mess (a good thing in this case).

THE LEGEND OF BLOOD CASTLE

Colour, 1973, 88m. / Directed by Jorge Grau / Starring Lucia Bosé, Espartaco Santoni, Ewa Aulin, Ana Farra / Mya (US R0 NTSC) / WS (1.66:1)

 One of the most notorious murderous fiends in human history, 17th-Century Hungarian Countess Erzsebet Báthory (Lucia Bosé) discovers to her aston-ishment that the blood of young maidens can restore her youth after accidentally spattering herself while striking the castle maid with a mirror. The dominant personality in the household, she schemes to stage the death of her husband, Karl (Espartaco Santoni), who helps procure more fresh meat for his wife's beauty treatments while also beginning an affair with a sexy local girl (Ewa Aulin). Unsurprisingly, their arrangement is not bound to last for long.

This Italian/Spanish co-production (originally titled *Ceremonia sangrienta*) is of most interest now to fans as the other major horror outing for director Jorge Grau, who crafted one of the decade's best zombie films with *The Living Dead at Manchester Morgue*. He certainly proves his skill with gothic period trappings here and mounts an extremely lush, sometimes surprisingly bloody production, even if it takes its sweet time getting around to the horror material and tends to poke along when it should be galloping at a horrific clip. All of the actors do well with their roles, especially the two villainous leads, but in the end this definitely comes in third behind *Daughters of Darkness* and *Countess Dracula* among the early '70s takes on the Bathory legend.

Mya's overpriced DVD is bound to cause consternation for a number of reasons, chief among them that its feature version is the clothed, watered-down Spanish cut. A more explicit, nudity-filled version circulated throughout Europe, while American audiences saw something in between, also released as *The Female Butcher*. These stronger scenes are presented as a bonus feature from a dupey-looking VHS source if you're interested, but the main transfer is no great shakes either; it's non-anamorphic and very noisy-looking, with loads of shimmering as well as detail and colour definition that could charitably be described as mediocre. The film is definitely screaming out for a better transfer if superior elements are available anywhere. Audio options include the English dub (with subtitled Spanish for some additional dialogue scenes) plus the full Spanish and Italian audio tracks. Also included are some innocuous additional alternative scenes from the Italian version, the Italian and U.S. opening credits, the U.S. closing credits, and a poster gallery.

LEGENDS OF THE POISONOUS SEDUCTRESS 1: FEMALE DEMON OHYAKU

B&W, 1968, 90m. / Directed by Yoshihiro Ishikawa / Starring Junko Miyazono, Tomisaburo Wakayama, Kunio Murai, Hosei Komatsu / Synapse (US R0 NTSC) / WS (2.35:1) (16:9)

 Bearing the intriguing series title of *Legends of the Poisonous Seductress*, Synapse Films in conjunction with defunct Japanese exploitation mavens Panik House released a trio of extreme, eye-catching epics which fuse swordplay with elements of the still-nascent pinky violence genre. The first film, *Female Demon Ohyaku* (*Yôen dokufuden hannya no ohyaku*), is a 1968 black-and-white tale of degradation and vengeance centred around Ohyaku (Junko Miyazono), a circus performer bearing a scar from her mother's ill-fated murder/suicide attempt. A local councilman (Tomisaburo Wakayama) falls for her, and when she spurns his advances, both she and her samurai lover are framed for a gold robbery, with her beau eventually losing his head for his trouble. In prison she's pawned off as a prostitute by the warden, whose wife decides to cover up the inmate's scar with an ornate dragon tattoo – an unintentional symbol of the wrath Ohyaku plans to unleash on those who have mistreated her.

Director Yoshihiro Ishikawa manages to effectively balance clear, powerful storytelling with jolting bursts of bloodshed, as well as some weird kinky touches like the aforementioned lesbian tattooing sessions. As with most Japanese directors, his skilful use of scope adds immeasurably to both the action and atmosphere, and the transfer here brings this previously obscure title to life for what will likely be a most appreciative audience. Expert cinema scholar Chris D. provides a typically informative commentary track, covering the lead actress's career as well as that of formidable co-star Tomisaburo Wakayama (*Lone Wolf and Cub*) while laying out the influences which found their way into this film.

LEGENDS OF THE POISONOUS SEDUCTRESS 2: QUICK-DRAW OKATSU

Colour, 1969, 89m. / Directed by Nobuo Nakagawa / Starring Junko Miyazono, Reiko Ônobuta, Kô Nishimura, Kenji Imai, Tomisaburo Wakayama / Synapse (US R0 NTSC) / WS (2.35:1) (16:9)

 In this second instalment in the loosely connected *Poisonous Seductress* series (under the original title *Yoen dokufuden: Hitokiri okatsu*), Junko Miyazono returns in full-bodied colour as the title character, whose family runs afoul of a corrupt magistrate with an affinity for torture. Teaming up with a pair of swordsmen, she concocts a plan to avenge her father with the obligatory bloody showdown finally tying everything up.

While the storyline may be by the numbers, director Nobuo Nakagawa (*Jigoku*) reveals an engaging comic book sensibility here as he showcases his star in a series of dynamic action scenes, most of

229

them confined to the exciting second half of the film. Arriving one year after the prior instalment, this one already displays a more sadistic bent with such sequences as a bloody man suspended from a ceiling having his feet scorched by candles, and the red stuff spews bright and furiously in several scenes. Once again the scope visuals are top notch, and Miyazono really shows herself coming into her own with this entry. Wakayama returns, too, which can only be considered a good thing. Again Chris D. provides a commentary track, with an understandable emphasis on Nakagawa's career and his own approach to directing this film.

LEGENDS OF THE POISONOUS SEDUCTRESS 3: OKATSU THE FUGITIVE

Colour, 1969, 84m. / Directed by Nobuo Nakagawa / Starring Junko Miyazono, Tatsuo Umemiya , Reiko Ônobuta, Tôru Abe, Kôji Hio / Synapse (US R0 NTSC) / WS (2.35:1) (16:9)

The violent saga wraps up with the only direct sequel in the batch, with Okatsu (Junko Miyazono) and her father (Reiko Ônobuta) attempting to bring to light the corruption which has already scarred their lives. Unfortunately her wedding plans are thwarted when more corrupt officials snatch and kill her parents, while her fiancé (Kôji Hio) turns out to be in collusion with the bad guys. Turning to the only people who will help her, a mysterious swordsman (Tatsuo Umemiya) and some orphaned kids, she once again finds herself pursuing justice against insurmountable odds.

Nobuo Nakagawa's direction again makes the most of the revenge scenario,

amping up the violence to even more exaggerated extremes with some pinky-style sexual assault thrown into the mix. Miyazono runs the show with her iciest performance out of the trilogy, and the film flings as many attackers as possible at her in a series of ever-escalating attack scenes. It's all thrilling to watch and perfectly shot; swordplay fanatics looking for a new heroine should be quite satisfied. Again the scope colour transfer looks immaculate, and the optional English subtitles are literate and well-written. No Chris D. commentary this time around, however, since any relevant territory was pretty much covered in film #2. All three releases include theatrical trailers for the trio of features, an insert booklet with notes by Chris D. about the female swordplay genre, and reversible cover art containing new, shelf-friendly designs as well as the original Japanese posters – a very nice touch.

LET THE RIGHT ONE IN

Colour, 2008, 115m. / Directed by Tomas Alfredson / Starring Kåre Hedebrant, Lina Leandersson, Per Ragnar, Henrik Dahl, Karin Bergquist / Magnolia (DVD & Blu-ray, US R1 NTSC/HD), Momentum (DVD & Blu-Ray, UK R2 PAL/HD), Axis (Singapore R0 NTSC), Living Colour (Holland R2 PAL), Madman (Australia R4 PAL), Sandrew Metronome (Sweden R2 PAL), Vendetta (New Zealand R4 PAL) / WS (2.35:1) (16:9) / DD5.1

In the 1980s Swedish town of Blackeberg, young Oskar (Kåre Hedebrant) lives with his single mother and suffers the taunts of bullies at school. One night outside his apartment building he strikes up a friendship with his new neighbour, a mysterious young girl named Eli (Lina Leandersson) who only comes out after sunset and lives in an apartment with covered-up windows. Meanwhile nearby townspeople begin to turn up exsanguinated and Oskar and Eli's peculiar friendship begins to take some very dark turns.

Each decade sees a revival of interest in vampires, and 2008 marked a major turn in this pop culture fascination with the arrival of offerings both banal (*Twilight*) and pleasurable (TV's *True Blood* and *Being Human*). Easily the best of the lot, *Let the Right One In* (*Låt den rätte komma in*) finds fresh blood in the mythos by combining bloodcurdling chills with a deeply touching and resonant relationship between the main characters. Tomas Alfedson's icily effective direction goes against the grain of modern horror by slowly building the snowy ambience and lingering on the events in carefully composed, lingering scope compositions that allow the viewer to soak in its uncanny atmosphere. The two young leads deserve a huge amount of credit for their spectacular performances, with Leandersson in particular pulling off the difficult trick of conveying both childish curiosity and decades-old weariness and hunger within a single scene. Swedish horror novelist John Ajvide Lindqvist does an efficient job of adapting his breakthrough novel, which was considerably more explicit and perverse than the more suggestive and ambiguous film; most of the queasy paedophilic implications have thankfully been suppressed to the level of slight implication, and Eli's grotesque back story and relationship with her guardian are mercifully left very vague here. Lest one think there's no way the film can maintain its eerie balancing act throughout, the climax manages to top it with an unforgettable swimming pool sequence now justifiably regarded as one of the greatest set pieces in horror cinema.

All of the available video editions of *Let the Right One In* are taken from the same excellent HD-sourced master, which does justice to the delicately-shaded photography. The Swedish audio track sounds excellent with plenty of subtle but immersive surround effects from the soft crackling of snow to the superb music score by Johan Söderqvist whose haunting theme for Eli is not easily forgotten. The two most satisfying English-friendly releases in the U.S. and U.K. feature different extras, but that's not the only difference. Magnolia's American DVD and Blu-ray discs have a simplified and often dumbed-down optional subtitle track that caused an immediate negative fan reaction; the company corrected the subtitles for subsequent pressings (whose tech specs on the back sleeve specify "Subtitles: English (Theatrical)", but incredibly no replacement plan was put into place. The Magnolia release also contains a pointless English dub that's not recommended at all as it features inappropriate voices for the child actors and adds a puzzling amount of vulgarity to the dialogue. Extras include four disposable deleted scenes, a stills gallery, and a behind the scenes featurette with the director discussing his intentions behind the film. The Magnolia Blu-ray does have one advantage as it's the best-sounded release on the market with a spectacularly rich DTS-HD track that's one of the most impressive you'll ever hear. However, the British release (which appeared a few months later) comes out equal and even wins in some respects as it retains the original theatrical subtitles, carries over the deleted scenes, and adds an exclusive, wonderful audio commentary with Alfredson and Lindqvist that's worth the price alone. The British Blu-ray ditches the English dub and only features standard DTS for the Swedish audio, but overall it's quite satisfying and makes a strong case for investing twice in the same title.

LETHAL FORCE

Colour, 2001, 69m. / Directed by Alvin Ecarma / Starring Frank Prather, Cash Flagg Jr., Patricia Williams, Andrew Hewitt / Unearthed (US R0 NTSC)

This obscure frenzy, made long before *Hot Fuzz*, offers an affectionate take on low-budget action films. Mobster Jack's (Frank Prather) family comes under fire from a bunch of thugs who force him to turn on his best friend, Savitch (played by "Cash Flagg, Jr".), an accomplished hit man. Director Alvin Ecarma keeps things moving fast for the extremely compact running time with enough blood, bullets and quips to keep you distracted from trying to follow the plot. (Be warned, though, that slow motion gets done to death very quickly.) Nods to blaxploitation, John Woo, Bollywood, and pretty much every '70s and '80s American action film are cleverly wedged into the script without turning it into a rib-nudging parody.

The 16mm film elements are touch-and-go throughout, but it's certainly watchable. Extras include an Ecarma commentary, some of his short films (with titles like "My Dog Has a Cyst" and "Me!"), a nice production gallery, and a look at some (presumably fake but cool) action figures. Some copies floating around also have a "bootleg" bonus disc included with audition footage and additional short films, so keep your eyes peeled.

A LIZARD IN A WOMAN'S SKIN

Colour, 1971, 103m./98m./96m. / Directed by Lucio Fulci / Starring Florinda Bolkan, Jean Sorel, Stanley Baker, Alberto De Mendoza, Leo Genn, Anita Strindberg, Georges Rigaud / Shriek Show (US R1 NTSC), Federal (Italy R2 PAL), Optimum (UK R2 PAL) / WS (1.85:1) (16:9) / DD5.1

Plagued by unsettling dreams involving an erotic tryst with a spooky blonde woman (Anita Strindberg) and naked copulating people riding public transit, fragile English housewife Carol Hammond (*Flavia the Heretic*'s Florinda Bolkan) reveals her inner anxieties only to her psychiatrist (Georges Rigaud), who theorises it's her subconscious method of acting out against her oppressive marriage to buttoned-down and adulterous Frank (Jean Sorel). However, in the middle of more disturbing visions, Carol also experiences a vivid murder scenario in which she repeatedly stabs the mystery woman in her abdomen with a letter opener. When the identical slaying of her neighbour is reported afterwards, Carol finds herself under scrutiny by a police inspector (Stanley Baker) and the subject of harrowing encounters with a mysterious knife-wielding hippie, bats, and the mysterious devils hidden in her own mind.

Following his audacious *giallo* debut with *Perversion Story*, Lucio Fulci upped the ante to a feverish intensity with his next thriller, *A Lizard in a Woman's Skin*, which reteamed him with star Jean Sorel, cast again as a suspicious husband. This time the film encountered considerable censorship obstacles in nearly every country in which it was released (with the American AIP version, *Schizoid*, suffering the most), and Fulci and FX creator Carlo Rambaldi were even hauled into Italian court over one shocking sequence showing breathing, dissected (but fake) dogs mounted to a wall. Fortunately the film itself proved strong enough to withstand such tinkering, and Fulci felt free to pursue his increasingly extreme visions of violence in the finale of his classic *giallo* trilogy, *Don't Torture a Duckling*.

Best viewed in tandem with Fulci's other efforts in the genre, *Lizard* is in many ways his most outlandish film (at least until *The Beyond*) and finds him refining the techniques established in his previous *giallo*, particularly his ambitious use of split screen and a storytelling method of loading most of the exploitative thrills in the first half with the narrative payoff emerging in the second. Brazilian-born Bolkan, who was already a solid international name thanks to her work in films like *The Last Valley* and *The Anonymous Venetian*, delivers a wonderfully nervous perform-ance that foreshadows her similar, even more impressive turn in the sadly neglected Euro-horror masterpiece, *Footprints*. Sorel isn't given much to do this time, but future Eurosleaze staple Strindberg and her distinctive breast implants make a powerful impression in their brief appearances. Also worthy of note is the dreamy, appropriately spacey score by Ennio Morricone, sadly in his only collaboration with Fulci, and the impressively atmospheric cinematography by the always great Luigi Kuveiller (*Deep Red*). The only real debit is that, from a mystery standpoint, the film cheats a bit by having the guilty parties behave in a manner inconsistent with later revelations, even when they're alone and have no reason to do so (a charge that could also be levelled at *Perversion Story*); much has been made by some critics concerning Fulci's odd treat-ment of hippies, drugs, and homosexuality, which could be read as anything from blindly naive to flat-out ugly and bigoted. However, given the context of the mysteries, they're probably just devices he used to find a way of unwinding the various knots of his narratives while delivering a little sensational juice in the process. Oddly enough, given his supposed conservatism, he clearly gives adultery a free pass in both films, a contradiction very prevalent in Catholic-influenced Italian filmmaking at the time.

The endless censorship which plagued *Lizard* extended well into its first, long-delayed DVD release from Shriek Show, a controversial two-disc platter containing the heavily truncated U.S. version (as *Schizoid*) with an AIP logo in a mostly impressive anamorphic transfer, hampered only by one reel of decidedly lesser and very contrasty quality. The absence of most of the lesbian-related footage and the dog-dissection scene make for a very frustrating experience, and the English track is presented in the original mono and an overly remixed 5.1 track. Also included is a longer Italian version, taken from a bleary-looking full frame print with much cropping on the sides, with optional English subtitles. The biggest extra is a half-hour featurette, "Shedding the Skin", featuring interviews with Bolkan, Sorel, actors Mike Kennedy and Penny Brown, and the FX crew, all of whom speak highly of Fulci and remark on how they partici-pated in the film. Other goodies include the English theatrical trailer, two radio spots, a gallery containing the press book and photos, and bonus Fulci trailers for *Zombi 2*, *City of the Living Dead*, *Touch of Death*, *House of Clocks*, *Sweet House of Horrors* and *Demonia*.

After much fan grumbling following an improved, longer, anamorphic transfer released on DVD in Italy (with no English language options), Shriek Show wisely returned to the well for an additional single-disc edition of the movie containing a much-improved presentation that runs even longer than either version in the prior release, clocking in at a hefty 103 minutes. Apart from some fleeting element damage and a few telltale signs of that one inferior reel, this fascinating and much-needed assemblage of footage from all extant versions is a very satisfying relief for Fulci fans. Judging from the AIP logo at the beginning, some of the AIP negative remains here with the additional footage from the various European editions interpolated back in, without any signs of editing surgery to be found. Bravo!

The soundtrack represents the best of all possible worlds thanks to the original English dub (which generally works best given the presence of English actors in supporting roles and the leads speaking their parts in phonetic English, albeit looped by other voice performers later); however, viewers who bristle at dub tracks may prefer the Italian audio, which features a more aggressive music mix. Also of interest is the "psychedelic" 5.1 mix, which is preferable to the earlier one and does a mostly solid job of spreading the score out to the rear and front channels. Still, audio purists may want to stick with the English mono track for the closest approximation of the film's intentions. However, Euro horror buffs will still want to hang on to the previous release, as this one retains none of its supplements (apart from the bonus Fulci trailers and the alternative Italian credits lifted from the earlier full frame transfer), instead adding two featurettes with Italian writer Paolo Albiero, who talks about Fulci's career in a very thorough and appreciative half-hour overview and then a five-minute explanation of the story behind the film's rocky history with censors in its native country and elsewhere. The U.K. Optimum DVD features more of the English dub track than the American counterparts and also contains some additional slivers of footage as well, augmented with better all-around picture quality (which makes one still wonder where that one reel of the MGM negative vanished to for the second American edition).

LONDON IN THE RAW

Colour, 1964, 77m. / Directed by Arnold L. Miller / BFI (DVD & Blu-ray, UK R0 PAL/HD)

When mondo mania seized the world in the wake of 1962's geek-show documentary *Mondo Cane*, producers across the globe were quick to cash in with salacious looks at the nasty, nasty things crawling around in their own backyards. Italy led the pack for years, of course, often picking up American narrators along the way for the likes of *Ecco* and *Mondo balordo*. Great Britain didn't jump in the mondo pool quite as vigorously at first, but enterprising director Arnold L. Miller (who made his name with nudist camp movies) joined forces with producers Michael Klinger and Tony Tenser (two major figures who also yielded *Repulsion*, *Witchfinder General*, *Frightmare* and *Blood on Satan's Claw*) for one of the first U.K.-based entries, 1964's *London in the Raw*. All the necessary elements are here: the holier-than-thou, faux-American narration (delivered by Canadian TV presenter David Gell), a "socially redeeming" approach to excuse all the burlesque and peek-a-boo topless shots, and hip footage of kids getting down to that crazy rock 'n' roll music.

London in the Raw focuses entirely on the thesis that English culture is primarily dependent on appearances, with substance coming in a distant second. Some fairly innocuous fashion footage kicks things off, but the coverage gets far more interesting as we take a visit to a '60s women's gymnasium (which the narrator regards with a perplexing amount of scorn) and watch such shocking procedures as – wait for it – hair plug treatment and acupuncture. A trip to the city's Whiskey-a-Go-Go provides the requisite footage of youngsters twisting and jiving in their Capri slacks, followed by an "Olde London" fish restaurant called Flanagan's, teenagers sitting around smoking and eating cat food(!), a (ridiculously staged) trendy eatery where patrons can watch or paint a nude model onstage, a performance at the city's only Jewish theatre, a dance bar for German residents and au pairs, and plenty of burlesque and nightclub performances, all capped off with a soul version of the Adam and Eve story and jarring experimental music blasting over a montage of the film's highlights as the narrator warns about London's "cold centre". ("Look, touch, taste and feel; but don't try to break it – it'll break you first!") As with most mondo films, the shock value has been traded out now for fascination with the clothes, attitudes, and practices of a generation on the cusp of major social change. Even the staged scenes reveal much more about the time than what was probably intended (not surprisingly, the Profumo politicians-and-whores scandal is cited right after the opening credits), and at times the narrator and filmmakers seem deeply nostalgic for a time when sex was something naughty kept hidden away from public view. It's a fascinating experience to be sure, and not surprisingly, the crew regrouped the following year for a significantly more outrageous follow-up, *Primitive London* (more on that later in this book). Tossing another curveball to home video enthusiasts, the BFI have unleashed this forgotten curio in both DVD and Blu-ray editions culled from the original negative. To say the least, the results are remarkable and throb with eye-pleasing Technicolor hues that rival the best MGM musicals. Every shot is bursting with candy-coloured images but the real highlights here are the club scenes, featuring bright, vivid outfits and lighting. It's a gorgeous presentation all around, with the Blu-ray delivering a sharper and punchier experience compared to its standard def counterpart. Optional English subtitles are available for the mono soundtrack. As for extras, you get an alternative 45-minute version of the film (which chops out most of the musical interludes and features snippets of alternative footage, including a funny bit with a Siamese kitten); perhaps it was prepared for school exhibition to unprepared youngsters. Also included is the lip-smacking theatrical trailer, and three other mid-'60s short documentaries offering a somewhat different take on London life. "Pub" is a haunting and far more gritty depiction of bar denizens singing and drinking their troubles away, while "Chelsea Bridge Boys" is a half-hour 1965 series of interviews and on-the-fly footage with various biker boys and girls as they speak (often with very thick accents) about their lives and philosophies. It's a bit overlong, but the snapshot depiction of this culture at its height is invaluable. Finally, 1966's "Strip" goes backstage at a burlesque hall where the performers from all walks of life discuss their motivations and dreams. All of the extras helpfully come with optional English subtitles as well, which is especially handy for the second short. The disc comes with a very hefty 40-page illustrated booklet crammed with ads and posters as well as thorough liner notes by Stewart Home (who covers the stories of the major participants quite well), and comments from the short film directors as well.

LOVE CIRCLES

Colour, 1985, 93m. / Directed by Gérard Kikoine / Starring Marie France, Josephine Jacqueline Jones, Sophie Berger / Private Screening (US R0 NTSC), MediumRare (UK R2 PAL)

After the peculiar softcore item *Lady Libertine*, accomplished erotic director Gérard Kikoine reunited with *Playboy* and producer Harry Allen Towers for the more traditional *Love Circles*, yet another version of that old standby, *La Ronde* (also filmed under its original title by Max Ophuls and Roger Vadim). Here sex forms a chain between a group of people in various locales as someone sleeps with someone else who moves onto another person who then jumps off to... well, you get the idea. This time the action moves across the globe from France and Italy to Hong Kong and then both American coasts, including *Black Venus* star Josephine Jacqueline Jones chasing a blond lunk around an apartment before bedding him and straddling him naked in a department store(!). Then there's a sauna orgy, lots of disco dancing, sex on a plane, and so on and so on, with no real plot in sight apart from the same cigarette pack that passes from one hand to the next.

The look of the film is far more in line with Kikoine's '80s output thanks to its gaudy primary colours, with vivid reds often used for accents in the many night scenes. Basically there's lots of dodgy dubbing, tons of sex (including a few shots that verge really, really close to hardcore), and no real characterisation, which makes it either worthless cinema or the perfect party DVD, depending on your mood.

The disc looks exactly the same as the version shown on television, and as usual the full frame presentation is quite workable (better, in fact) matted off on a widescreen set. The same vintage transfer was also issued by MediumRare, uncut, on DVD in the U.K.

THE LOVE STATUE

B&W, 1965, 80m. / Directed by David E. Durston / Starring Peter Ratray, Beti Seay, Gigi Darlene, Hisako "Choko" Tsukuba, Harvey J. Goldenberg, Nancy Norman, Coleman Younger / Secret Key (US R0 NTSC)

Another New York oddity unearthed in the constant stream of exploitation quickies revived on DVD, this grindhouse mixture of mild erotica and drug culture pandering (billed as "The Love Statue LSD Experience" on the packaging) follows the urban misadventures of Tyler (*Young Lady Chatterley*'s Peter Ratray), a struggling bohemian artist with a contentious relationship with his domineering girlfriend, Lisa (Beti Seay). Thanks to the encouragement of a nightclub torch singer (Hisako "Choko" Tsukuba), he decides to find some inspiration by dropping acid. His trip seems to be going fine as he has a heated session with his now-living "love statue" (sexploitation veteran Gigi Darlene), but afterwards there's a dead body in his apartment... and he only has a few hours to unravel what really happened before the police close in.

More of a moody art film than a traditional exploitation experience, *The Love Statue* was one of the earlier efforts from director David E. Durston, who went on to drive-in immortality with the rabid-cannibal-hippie classic *I Drink Your Blood* and the wacko Philip Michael Thomas drug-laced freakout *Stigma*. Narcotics are a continuing theme throughout his work, and on this DVD he even boasts of dropping acid to add some verisimilitude to his direction. The LSD factor is actually pretty marginal in the grand scheme of the film (and contrary to the packaging, it didn't introduce America to acid; that honour goes to William Castle's *The Tingler* six years earlier). However, the wintry footage of Greenwich Village is priceless and lends the film a haunting, gritty ambience that sets it apart from your average studio-bound quickie. The actors are also a bit better than average, and not surprisingly,

Ratray and Seay had continued stage, screen and TV careers.

For its video debut, Secret Key has outfitted this release with a pleasing new transfer from imperfect but certainly acceptable elements and a host of extras. Durston contributes both a commentary and a video interview in which he talks about the project's evolution (it was originally entitled *The Love Drug* and had three now-lost softcore inserts shot without his consent by the distributors). Also included is a second 10-minute video interview with Ratray (who proudly shows off framed photos of the original theatre marquees showing the film), two vintage LSD scare films ("LSD-25" and "Your Amazing Mind"), two alternative scenes, and additional Secret Key trailers.

LUCKER THE NECROPHAGOUS

Colour, 1986, 68m./74m. / Directed by Johann Vandewoestijne / Starring Nick Van Suyt, Helga Vandevelde, Let Jotts, Marie Claes, Carry Van Middel, Martine Scherre / Synapse (US R0 NTSC) / WS (1.78:1) (16:9)

Belgium isn't exactly a country known for its pioneering horror output apart from the occasional stylish one-off like *Daughters of Darkness*. However, in the mid-'80s, even the most impoverished European projects spattered with enough gore could find some willing fans around the world, thanks to pirated VHS editions. One of the first break-through shock indies was Jörg Buttgereit's *Nekromantik*, which proved an artsy foreign-language shocker about corpse-loving could become a notable cult hit. Shortly afterwards, a Belgian straight-to-video outrage called *Lucker the Necro-phagous* began making the rounds, and though it was actually shot a year earlier, it quickly grabbed attention among the same fans. Though its production values are far less artistic, *Lucker* gets by on sheer verve alone, thanks mainly to the potency of its big mid-film set piece... but more on that in a moment.

After a failed suicide attempt and an equally botched effort at murder, serial killer John Lucker (Nick Van Suyt) spends three years languishing in a coma in a mental institution. Upon awakening he conspires an escape and, donning a sinister pair of sunglasses, cuts a bloody swathe across the city as he hunts down the one girl who got away. Along the way he takes time out to stash away some of his female victims' corpses, which he then revisits after an extended period for some romantic downtime. As you may have gathered, *Lucker* exists primarily for the unforgettable sequence in which the title character decides to play bumpy mattresses with a decayed corpse, and unlike *Nekromantik*, this one doesn't lighten the blow with any soft focus shots, sweeping music or optical effects. It's just a long, extended, in-your-face "look at my chewed-up food" sequence, and no horror fan who stumbled across a tape of it has ever forgotten the impact. Van Suyt is actually surprisingly good in the lead role, portraying a menacing, middle-aged, pudgy psychopath who seems a bit too real for comfort, and the self-confessed horror fan director offers a few visual flourishes here and there, mainly an underground pursuit finale and some colourful, Argento-inspired lighting effects. This will still only appeal to very, very specific tastes and ultimately is not a terribly good film, but for anyone hankering for the golden days of '80s extreme cinema, this should be at least a worthwhile curio.

The back story of *Lucker* is extremely complicated, but since it was destined straight for video and didn't offer much in the way of commercial prospects, the producer ditched the original negatives. Most viewers caught this via dupes of a 74-minute English edition with Dutch subtitles, which is also offered on Synapse's disc as an extra. However, the far more viewable option is the newly-assembled "director's cut", which uses the best surviving, non-subtitled video material to create a smoother, cleaner experience that actually clocks in six minutes shorter. Don't worry, all the nasty stuff is still here; the discarded footage basically amounts to some needless padding and awkward bits of, ahem, "Troma-tic" non-acting that inspired unintentional guffaws. The new cut is visibly better, relatively speaking, though it still basically looks sourced from a VHS tape. Don't expect this to come anywhere close to the usual Synapse gold standard of quality, but if you're in a very forgiving mood, it's watchable enough and, for better or worse, the best this title will ever look. The new cut is in English as well and also features newly-created end credits.

The other big extra here is the 36-minute "Lucker: The Story Behind the Film", which finds the director speaking in English (very softly) about the making of his movie and the various permutations it underwent on the way to final cut, including a different and more ambitious plot structure that got lost along the way. It's a fascinating story, in some respects more entertaining than the main feature itself, and well worth viewing. If you've been waiting for a watchable version of *Lucker*, here you go.

MACUMBA SEXUAL

Colour, 1981, 80m. / Directed by Jess Franco / Starring Ajita Wilson, Lina Romay, Robert Foster (Antonio Mayans), Jess Franco / Severin (US R0 NTSC), Anchor Bay (UK R2 PAL) / WS (2.35:1) (16:9)

One of the top "unseeable" Jess Franco titles regularly shown on fan wish lists, *Macumba Sexual* is often regarded as a pinnacle of his cinematic return to post-Franco Spain. Of course, most of the director's fans never had the chance to see it outside murky, cropped bootleg copies in Spanish without subtitles, which says a great deal about the film's sensory power beyond its threadbare plot. Indeed, this is one of his more visually bewitching efforts and arguably his last completely satisfying film, a fusion of sex and horror as only the mad Franco can conjure up. In the middle of the most productive period with husband Franco, Lina Romay stars here (under the name of "Candy Coster" with a surprisingly flattering blonde wig) in one of the strongest of her sexual victim roles (already taken to wonderfully obscene lengths with her playing both sides of the coin in *Doriana Gray*). Here she's Alice, a vacationing wife whose husband (Antonio Mayans) seems to lounge around with her in bed a lot. Unfortunately her idyll is disturbed by recurring visions of Tara (Ajita Wilson), a striking woman leading around two human slaves on leashes by the beach. When she's called in to work on a real estate deal for a mysterious princess, Alice finds the new client to be the literal woman of her dreams, who needs a new vessel to carry on her centuries-old reign of black magic power. Reality and fantasy blur as the couple is initiated into a series of hallucinatory encounters, the most striking of which finds hubby locked up in a remote bamboo oceanside cage.

Complete with a typically amusing and sweaty co-starring appearance by Jess himself, *Macumba Sexual* never flinches from its intense subject matter (including some female probing that could alarm a few viewers) but never feels sleazy or slapdash. The elegant scope framing is constantly flooded with striking sunlight effects, with indoor scenes likewise punctuated by star-like light sources bursting into the corners of the frame at odd moments. Representatives of evil (including the "Bringer of Light" himself, Lucifer) are often associated with bold illumination, and Franco really seems to run with the concept here. Likewise, the segues between dreams and "reality" are beautifully accomplished, with the beguiling image of a scantily clad Wilson splayed on the sand with an ornamental sculpture between her legs offering one of the more indelible moments of '80s Franco cinema. The sparse dialogue never gets in the way here, leaving Romay to exhibit what she does best: carnal abandon and wide-eyed terror, often at the same time.

The revelation of watching this film in its full, widescreen aspect ratio cannot be understated, making Severin's DVD release one of the great salvations of recent European erotic cinema. The transfer looks marvellous throughout, with beautiful colours and no signs of damage. No quibbles at all. The Spanish mono track sounds fine (it was never dubbed into English), with optional English subtitles for those who always wondered what the heck was going on. The only extra, and it's a goodie, is "Voodoo Jess", a choice featurette with Franco and Romay reminiscing about the film (and the purportedly transsexual Wilson in partic- ular) with much explanation about Franco's return to Spain and his outlook on filmmaking at the time.

The same transfer and extras are also available in the U.K. as part of "The Jess Franco Collection 2" box set from Anchor Bay (see *The Inconfessable Orgies of Emmanuelle* review for more details).

MADAME O

Colour/B&W, 1967, 81m. / Directed by Seiichi Fukuda / Starring Michiko Aoyama, Akihiko Kanbara, Yuichi Minato, Naomi Tani / Synapse (US R0 NTSC) / WS (2.35:1) (16:9)

During the 1960s, New York-based Audubon Films made a cottage industry out of picking up a wide variety of erotically-inclined foreign films and streamlining them for American consumption, with Sweden, France and Italy providing the most reliable output of saucy tales ripe for redubbing and recutting. While Japan certainly produced its share of sleazy fare during this period, few of these films (which would go on to officially produce the now-popular "pink" genre and its offshoots) managed to reach U.S. shores. One of the first of these, 1960's *The Weird Lovemakers*, came roaring out of the Audubon gates a few years after its native premiere and shocked viewers with its portrayal of loose, freewheeling teens causing trouble in post-war Japan, but the American distributor largely shied away from anything similar until much later that decade. *Madame O*, a stylish and often savage scope thriller, came from '60s kink- master Seiichi Fukuda (whose final film, the next year's *Boneless*, proved to be his most widely seen) and fits in more snugly with the gaudy, colourful, and sado-erotic aesthetic of its other Audubon cousins like *The Frightened Woman* and *Camille 2000*. However, due to the heavy churning nature of international grindhouse procedures, *Madame O* was quickly forgotten in both Japan and America, with the elements housed by Audubon head Radley Metzger proving to be the only records of its existence. Now that *Madame O* has finally been rescued from a once-presumed "lost

M

film" status, viewers can finally experience a vital missing piece in the development of Eastern roughie cinema.

Our sordid tale begins with our anti-heroine, successful physician Seiko (one-off actress Michiko Aoyama), informing us via voiceover and fragmented flashbacks about her traumatic adolescence, which was completely wrecked by a brutal rape by a trio of boys on the beach which left her both impregnated and saddled with syphilis. Understandably biased now against the opposite sex, she prowls the streets of the city after doing her rounds and often picks off her nightly companions whom she feels are disease-spreading vermin. However, her homicidal urges begin to subside when she settles down with a nice, proper middle-class husband (Akihiko Kanbara), but as it turns out, even nice guys can't always be trusted.

The most obvious stylistic trick of *Madame O* is its random but effective structure in a helter-skelter arrangement of colour and black-and-white footage (Fukuda had obviously seen Claude Lelouch's similar *A Man and a Woman* two years earlier), and in this case the switches to monochrome also give this feature the feeling of a film noir as filtered through the consciousness of a sex maniac. The last third in particular showcases enough double crosses and bizarre twists of fate to put it in good company with a '50s Barbara Stanwyck thriller, but the occasional doses of topless nudity and full-colour blood spraying (including a protracted dismemberment sequence that predates *Ms.45* by twenty years) manage to push it into far more modern territory. The unexpected opening inclusion of real surgical footage (albeit from a tasteful angle) doesn't exactly play by the rules, either. The result is a perfect example of a late '60s film straddling the line between art and trash, and it's a shame Aoyama (who occasionally resembles a Japanese Audrey Campbell)

didn't establish a career well into the next decade. Incidentally, this film's original Japanese title, *Zoku akutokui: Joi-hen* (or, roughly, "Vicious Female Doctor Part 2") makes it a sort of follow-up to Fukuda's prior film, *Akutokui*, which has yet to surface in any form.

Thankfully Audubon has kept the sole surviving version of this film in very good condition, and Synapse's DVD presents it in a terrific DVD edition with a nearly immaculate anamorphic scope transfer. As one would expect for the period, the English dubbing is quite well done and appropriate to the mood of the film. The colour sequences have a beautifully lurid, saturated quality throughout, while the black and white scenes look moody and wonderfully glossy. Extras include the terrific American theatrical trailer (which helped keep this film's reputation alive for decades among collectors) and very informative liner notes by *Midnight Eye*'s Jasper Sharp, who covers the film's difficult history in detail and offers some welcome biographical information about its largely forgotten director.

MADHOUSE

Colour, 1981, 93m. / Directed by Ovidio G. Assonitis / Starring Trish Everly, Michael MacRae, Dennis Robertson, Morgan Hart, Allison Biggers / Dark Sky (US R1 NTSC) / WS (2.35:1) (16:9), Film 2000 (UK R0 PAL) / WS (2.35:1)

One of the many films inexplicably persecuted during the U.K.'s "Video Nasty" panic, this very early offering from the '80s golden era of slasher mayhem comes from an unexpected source, director/co-writer/ producer Ovidio G. Assonitis. Taking a break from his star-studded Italian imitations of American hits, he instead turns out a surprisingly atmospheric and accomplished piece of gory fun originally released as *There Was a Little Girl* (the title retained on the DVD version despite the cover art) and then retitled *Madhouse* for the video market. Lensed in scope and packed with enough jolts and surprises to keep horror fans purring, the film never received much play in the U.S. (with a brief VHS release from the short-lived Virgin label in a godawful cut, pan-and-scan transfer) but is now much easier to appreciate in the digital era.

Haunted by nightmares and memories involving her insane, sadistic twin sister now residing in an asylum, pretty teacher of the deaf Julia Sullivan (Trish Everly) is dreading the impending arrival of her birthday, which her sibling, Mary (Allison Biggers), always celebrated with an extra dose of nastiness. Now suffering from a gruesome skin disease, Mary escapes from the sanitarium and, aided by her trained killer dog, goes on a rampage terrorising everyone around Julia... but a few more surprises still lie in store for our heroine.

Though certainly flawed by the usual oddball Assonitis dialogue and ridiculous bevy of supporting characters, *Madhouse* ultimately comes out ahead of his standard output thanks to a solid scream queen turn from Everly (who disappeared for some reason), excellent scope photography, and a wild score by Italian composer Riz Ortolani, who was doing similar repetitive duties on *Zeder* around the same time. Some critics have pointed out the similarity of the film's climax to *Happy Birthday to Me*, though of course they were shot simultaneously so it's more a coincidence by two different directors going after the holiday-themed slasher box office. And then there's the gore. Remember what it was like watching red syrup and fake guts flying across the screen before CGI came along and ruined everything? Well, this one delivers it in bucket loads, especially in the aforementioned final

act, and of course Ovidio pays homage to *Suspiria* (or maybe the same year's *The Beyond*) by having the big black doggie ripping out some throats in full-blooded detail that gives his Italian brothers a run for their money. If that weren't politically incorrect enough, the film even has the nerve to snuff one of Julia's cute students (offscreen) and that demonic pooch (very much onscreen, but thankfully fake). While '80s slasher fans should get a kick out of this one, it also carries a strong Pete Walker vibe (albeit shot in America) with its strange character relationships and fractured psyches aplenty. As far as vintage horror rediscoveries go on DVD, this is certainly a good choice to kill a free evening. *Madhouse* first appeared on DVD in the U.K. courtesy of Film 2000 in a non-anamorphic transfer with a wretched, unlistenable soundtrack. Fortunately collectors can chuck that one away as Dark Sky presents a much improved, anamorphic presentation that satisfies on all counts. As usual, the disc comes with optional English subtitles, a nice touch especially if you want to share it with any deaf friends who will most likely be appalled by the time it's over. Extras include a hefty stills gallery (including lots of German lobby cards from Warner Bros. with the title, *Party des Schreckens!*) as well as "There Was a Producer", a 13-minute interview with Assonitis in which he briefly recaps his prior efforts like *Beyond the Door* and *Laure* before talking about this film's genesis, the challenges of indie distribution then and now, the Georgia location shooting, and his deep affection for the finished product.

MAID IN SWEDEN

Colour, 1971, 80m. / Directed by Floch Johnson (Dan Wolman) / Starring Christina Lindberg, Monica Ekman, Krister Ekamn, Leif Naeslund / Impulse (US R0 NTSC)

Most significant as the film that introduced world audiences to Christina Lindberg, the vulnerable-looking young woman who quickly became the leading Swedish exploitation pin-up girl, this average sex-lite drama opened the same year as other, more obscure Lindberg titles like *Dog Days* and *Exposed* but benefited from the fact that it was an international, English-friendly production financed by a little fledgling company called Cannon Films. Exactly how this title wound up in the hands of Impulse Pictures is anyone's guess, and presumably the best available elements are now lying around somewhere in the vaults at MGM. In any case, it's nice to finally see this one on DVD, though the end result is something of a mixed bag.

The film itself is set up as a typical young woman's sexual awakening story, with pretty, innocent Inga (Lindberg) heading up from the country to visit her big city sister, Greta (Monica Ekman). Of course, Greta's activities with her randy jackass boyfriend, Carsten (Krister Ekman), set Inga's loins a-burnin' quite quickly. One of Carsten's buddies, Bjorn (Leif Naeslund), sets his sights on the new arrival, but it soon becomes a three-way race as the two men and the bisexual lesbian sister vie to destroy poor Inga's innocence. Of course, all of this is really just an excuse to get Christina naked every few minutes, including a memorable slo-mo shower scene that fuelled much of the ad campaign.

Co-written by exploitation vet George T. Norris (who edited *Lord Shango*, *He Knows You're Alone* and *Exterminator 2*), *Maid in Sweden* should find a happy home in the library of any discerning soft-sex fan; the cherry on top of this particular sundae is a long-desired new video interview with Christina herself, who spends about ten minutes chatting in English about the state of '70s Swedish sex cinema and the genesis of *Maid in Sweden*. The interview could certainly be much longer, but it's nice to finally see the elusive actress on camera after she was conspicuously MIA from the earlier release of her most infamous film, *Thriller: A Cruel Picture*. Unfortunately this release has to make do with a pre-existing full frame master (still bearing the Cannon Films opener), and it definitely shows its age. The cropping isn't too detrimental and even looks completely open matte in certain shots, but the obviously degraded colours, soft English audio track, and wobbly video distortion are unfortunate. Also included is the theatrical trailer (which looks a whole lot fresher) as it appeared on Synapse's earlier *42nd Street Forever Vol. 1* collection. Incidentally, director "Floch Johnson" is really Dan Wolman, who stuck around with Cannon and directed two entries in the cult favourite *Lemon Popsicle* sex comedy series.

MALABIMBA: THE MALICIOUS WHORE

Colour, 1979, 88m. / Directed by Andrea Bianchi / Starring Katell Laennec, Patrizia Webley, Enzo Fisichella, Giuseppe Marrocu, Elisa Mainardi, Mariangelo Giordano / Severin (US R0 NTSC) / WS (1.66:1) (16:9)

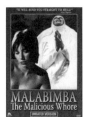

With all the European imitations of *The Exorcist* cranked out on the heels of *Beyond the Door*, filmmakers kept trying to outdo each other on the sleaze scale to make their possession offerings more distinctive and marketable to horror-hungry viewers overseas. However, director Andrea Bianchi (still best known for the outrageous *Burial Ground*) stepped over the line a bit in 1979 with his contribution, *Malabimba: The Malicious Whore*, a supersleazy variation augmented with a bit of nunsploitation and hardcore inserts for good measure. The film apparently did well enough in its native country, but few others got to see it until the grey market VHS era when it finally amassed a reputation as one of the daffiest, most extreme Eurocult offerings around. Fortunately, that's still no exaggeration.

After her mother dies mysteriously during a séance, pretty young Bimba (Katell Laennec) becomes possessed by the woman's spirit and begins engaging in all sorts of misbehaviour like lifting up her skirt at inopportune moments and performing unsolicited, fatal hummers on her bed-ridden old uncle. When her father isn't busy chasing skirt around the family castle, he becomes concerned about her behaviour and enlists the aid of a sexy nun (Mariangelo Giordano) who finds herself exploring Bimba's problems as intimately as possible.

Richly scored and highly atmospheric, *Malabimba* somehow manages to overcome the utter goofiness of its premise (and the tackiness of its brief but distracting hardcore shots) with Giordano and Laennec (who's forced to do some pretty dirty things with her stuffed animals) delivering committed, highly carnal performances; not surprisingly, their unavoidable coupling is wisely positioned as the literal climax of the film. Bianchi will never be mistaken as a major cinematic artiste, but he always delivers the sleazy goods (check out his delightfully absurd *Strip Nude for Your Killer* for further evidence). There's little genuine horror content on display here, but most viewers will be too blindsided to notice.

For decades *Malabimba* was only available in soft, nearly unwatchable dupes from Italian prerecords, with a bootleg DVD release a few years back among the worst offenders. Luckily Severin has given this a much-needed facelift with a sinfully sharp

new transfer with much better widescreen framing. The main feature can be played in its original uncut theatrical version, while 15 short, additional deleted scenes (sourced from a lower-quality Italian tape and sporting such amusing names as "Uncircumcised Shower") can be played either separately or integrated into the main feature. That's enough of an extra by itself, but the disc also comes with a fun new featurette, "Malabimba Uncovered", with Giordano and cinematographer Franco Villa reminiscing about the making of the film. They cover everything from filming in the castle (apparently it was very cold) to those pesky insert shots, which they maintain were done later and without the participants' knowledge. If so, someone went through an unbelievable amount of trouble as the decor and bed sheets still match, and if that's a double for Laennec, it's a very convincing one.

MALPERTUIS

Colour, 1971, 119m./100m. / Directed by Harry Kümel / Starring Orson Welles, Susan Hampshire, Mathieu Carrière, Michel Bouquet, Jean-Pierre Cassel, Daniel Pilon, Sylvie Vartan / Barrel (US R0 NTSC), Royal Belgian Film Archive (Belgium R2 PAL) / WS (1.85:1) (16:9)

Malpertuis seemed like a sure thing during its creation in the early 1970s. Flemish director Harry Kümel was fresh off the international success of his dazzling *Daughters of Darkness*, and an eye-popping international cast headlined by Orson Welles promised plenty of marquee value. Unfortunately the finished product seemed even more cursed than the titular house, as the dream-like and often inscrutable film met with a baffled reaction at Cannes (in a cut the director disavowed) and quickly sank into oblivion. However, students of both horror and art house cinema continued mentioning the film over the next few decades, though few actually had the chance to see it; finally a director's cut was assembled through European funding in the early 2000s and, thanks to repertory screenings, finally restored the reputation of this long-lost Eurocult curio.

Returning from years at sea to the seaside village of his childhood, blond sailor Jan (Mathieu Carrière) finds his old home disappeared and the town populated by eccentrics, one of whom, the giggling Dideloo (Michel Bouquet), follows his every step. At a nearby tavern, he becomes involved in a brawl and is knocked unconscious, only to awake weeks later at Malpertuis, an "evil house" which now serves as the home for his sister, Nancy (former Disney girl Susan Hampshire), as well as his dying patriarch uncle, Cassavius (Welles). All the other residents, a gaggle of oddballs ranging from three prim, knitting sisters to a bearded stranger chained in the basement, eagerly await Cassavius's death so they can hear the reading of his will and finally escape the house that contains them, but Jan soon finds his own fate bound with that of everyone else in the house as the sinister old man's inheritance carries repercussions far more horrific and bizarre than anyone could imagine.

Most reviews of *Malpertuis* casually give away the truly bizarre third-act revelation that explains the true nature of the house and its inhabitants, which is a shame since this is a film best experienced with as little preparation as possible. The unique atmosphere is unlike any other film ever made, veering from humorous fantasy to delicate eroticism to all-out monstrous horror, sometimes all within the same scene. Though his screen time adds up to only a few minutes, Welles makes a strong impression in his key role, while Hampshire shines

in three very different parts (or is it more?) as the pure Nancy, the unearthly red-haired Euryale (who won't look anyone directly in the eye), and one of the prudish sisters. Cinematographer Gerry Fisher (who lensed the great *See No Evil* the same year) helps the director conjure up a wondrous palette of colours throughout, from the blood-red tavern interior to the weird purple, blue and oak-wood hues of Malpertuis, while composer Georges Delerue contributes an enchanting score with a beautifully romantic main theme.

Since it was shot in English (with some actors like Carrière and Bouquet looped by other actors to replace their accents), *Malpertuis* was first shown that way at Cannes in a 100-minute edition which opens with Magritte paintings beneath the opening titles. That version was apparently prepared in haste which might explain the fairly straightforward scene editing and the frequent fades to black which close most of the major scenes. However, it's still an enjoyable experience and offers the wonderful opportunity to hear Welles and Hampshire voicing their own roles. It was later hacked down by as much as ten minutes in various territories, where it was sometimes shown as *The Legend of Doom House*. When Kümel finally assembled his own cut of the film (running just shy of two hours), he drastically altered the entire editing scheme of the film, which still follows the same basic sequence of events but unfolds in a notably different manner. For example, the woodcut main titles are new (with different music), Jan's entrance is presented differently (without mystical overtones), the memorable tavern song by fetching French chanteuse Sylvie Vartan (aunt of Michael Vartan from *Alias*) is chopped up very differently, and Jan's fate when he looks Euryale in the eyes is conveyed only through sound rather than the literal imagery of the Cannes cut. Honestly, both versions are worth watching, and in the end it's hard to say which one is preferable as both have their virtues and faults while offering quite a bit of alternative and exclusive footage; the director's cut is definitely slower and dreamier, while the Cannes version is a more traditional Euro-horror experience. Neither is perfect, particularly since the film chooses to end with one "gotcha!" moment too many that throws many viewers for a loop; still, it's a magnificent achievement and certainly a film whose allure hasn't diminished one bit over the years. The director and subject matter have often landed this one strictly in the horror category, though it's more correctly described as a dark gothic fantasy along the same lines as Mario Bava's near-simultaneous *Lisa and the Devil*, with which is shares a similar air of enchanted decrepitude as well as a virtually identical narrative structure; just check out the opening and closing 15 minutes of each and the parallels are unmistakable.

The restoration of *Malpertuis* first appeared on DVD in Europe courtesy of the Royal Belgian Film Archive (who funded the project in the first place), along with a host of extras. The same materials were used to assemble the American release from Barrel, though their transfer of the long cut, while taken from the same hi-def master, appears quite a bit sharper and more colourful. The mono soundtrack sounds fine, accompanied by optional English subtitles. The English Cannes cut on disc two looks a bit more worn, unfortunately, and some minor vertical cropping on the credits indicates the image could be slightly zoomed in. In any case, the director's cut – which most people will rush to first anyway – is a fantastic presentation and more stunning than the theatrical prints currently in circulation. The Barrel disc also adds on additional material, making this about as comprehensive a release as one could imagine. Kümel appears several times, first with a full audio commentary for the director's cut in which he discusses the source novel, the filming,

the casting, the sad release history, and the intricate symbolism. It's a fascinating chat that barley misses a beat throughout the entire running time. Then he appears on-camera on disc two for "Reflections of Darkness", a lengthy 74-minute video chat with David Del Valle about his entire career in fantastic cinema (making this a fine companion for the special edition of *Daughters of Darkness*). He also shows up for small snippets of two other featurettes, "Orson Welles Uncut" (a 25-minute look at his participation in the film including numerous photos and film outtakes) and "One Actress, Three Parts", a new featurette with Hampshire talking about her role in the film and her approach to the character(s). Other extras include a 7-minute short about the novel's author entitled "Jean Ray/John Flanders", a welcome intro to someone still virtually unknown outside Europe, as well as the original English language theatrical trailer. The two-disc set comes packaged with a booklet containing liner notes by Del Valle and a lengthy history of the film by Ernest Mathijs.

MAN OF VIOLENCE
Colour, 1969, 107m. / Directed by Pete Walker / Starring Michael Latimer, Luan Peters, Derek Aylward, Maurice Kaufmann, Virginia Wetherell
THE BIG SWITCH
Colour, 1968, 76m. / Directed by Pete Walker / Starring Sebastian Breaks, Virginia Wetherell, Jack Allen, Derek Aylward / BFI (DVD & Blu-ray, UK R0 PAL/HD)

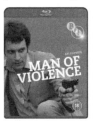

Though best known today for his string of socially savage horror classics like *Frightmare* and *House of Mortal Sin*, director Pete Walker dabbled in multiple genres earlier in his career ranging from sexploitation (*Cool It Carol!*) to these two unheralded gems of British crime cinema. The more ambitious of the two, *Man of Violence*, follows a mercenary named Moon (*Prehistoric Women*'s Michael Latimer) who teams up with two different heavies posing as policemen to steal a huge cache of gold from an Arab country now descending into anarchy. In the tradition of other taboo-bending crime films of the time like *Villain*, Moon also happens to be bisexual and is pursued by a sadistic gay killer, while beautiful actresses like Luan Peters (*Twins of Evil*) and Virginia Wetherell (*Curse of the Crimson Altar*) provide the requisite eye candy. In keeping with the Walker tradition, the narrative takes some surprising twists and turns and concludes on a surprisingly bleak note, and while it may not reach the heights of a bona fide classic like *Get Carter*, this is certainly time well spent for fans of '70s crime cinema.

Paired up with this film on the BFI's release is the slightly earlier *The Big Switch*, another Walker crime outing about a cavalier party animal named John Carter (*The Night Digger*'s Sebastian Breaks) who, apparently having never seen *The 39 Steps*, goes home with a beautiful woman only to find her dead after he slips out for a pack of smokes. He's fired from his job shortly afterwards and becomes entangled with a variety of shady characters and beautiful women (including Wetherell again), ultimately forced into the underworld of pornography where a larger criminal plot is looking to ensnare him. Nudity and exploitation takes a front seat here ahead of the crime elements, but Walker keeps the proceedings clipping along nicely and delivers a solid dockside climax. The Blu-ray version can be viewed in either the U.K. cut (68 minutes) or the longer, saucier export version which adds an additional nine minutes of salacious material. Obviously 99% of consumers will opt for the latter.

Both films are transferred in the 1.33:1 aspect ratio of the original negatives (though they could have probably been matted to 1.66:1 at least without losing anything), and the quality is spectacular. Both look absolutely fresh and vivid with nary a flaw in sight even if the budgets were obviously limited. Optional English subtitles are included and come in quite handy during some of the rougher-sounding passages. Extras include theatrical trailers for both features, an alternative title sequence for *Man of Violence* under the name *Moon*, and a 26-page booklet featuring new essays from Walker himself, Cathi Unsworth, frequent Walker scriptwriter David McGillivray, and Julian Petley.

MAN WITH A MOVIE CAMERA

B&W, 1929, 68m. / Directed by Dziga Vertov / BFI (UK R2 PAL), Arte (France R2 PAL), Absolute (Germany R0 PAL), Kino (US R1 NTSC) / DD2.0

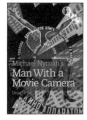

Arguably the high point of the Russian avant garde movement, *Man with a Movie Camera* remains one of the regular staples of film school courses around the world and stands as a perfect distillation of the power of editing and camera movement. With nothing resembling a plot, it simply aims to capture the feeling of a bustling Russian culture solely through the language of film, or as the introduction by the director phrases it, divorced from the separate art forms like literature which rely on more traditional means of communication. Scenes filmed in Moscow, Odessa and Kiev mingle together in a visual symphony conveying a day in the life of a modern industrialised nation where people and machines labour together, mirrored in the relationship between a filmmaker and the camera which captures his visions.

Difficult to describe and wondrous to behold, this frenzied cinematic experiment depends heavily upon the proper presentation for its full impact. As with most silent-era Russian films, prints and video editions vary wildly in quality around the world with one restoration after another announced with very mixed results. The BFI has issued no less than three versions, with the first two consisting of a standard and remastered version of the film with scores by the Alloy Orchestra and In the Nursery, both of which are excellent and exclusive to the Great Britain editions; the reissue contains the same transfer as the remastered one created for the German disc (and a less impressive port onto the French one), which was eventually used for the American Kino version as well. The BFI disc contains a useful commentary by Yuri Tsivian who offers a thorough history of Vertov's techniques and intentions with the film. The German and French discs each contain exclusive documentaries but contain no English-friendly options.

However, the best-looking of them all is the third BFI edition, officially entitled *Michael Nyman's Man with a Movie Camera*, which is part of a trend by which modern composers ranging from James Bernard (*Nosferatu*) to the Pet Shop Boys (*Battleship Potemkin*) provide unique scores for silent movies. Modern classic composer Nyman is definitely in avant garde mode here, appropriately enough, with a pulsating, circuitous work that perfectly accompanies the action, similar to his earlier film scores such as *A Zed and Two Noughts* and *The Draughtsman's Contract*. This DVD contains no extras, but it's a very exciting presentation and obviously a must for Nyman fanatics as the score is available nowhere else.

MANSION OF THE LIVING DEAD

Colour, 1982, 92m. / Directed by Jess Franco / Starring Lina Romay, Robert Foster (Antonio Mayans), Elisa Vela, Eva León / Severin (US R0 NTSC), Anchor Bay (UK R2 PAL) / WS (2.35:1) (16:9)

Often named as an unofficial fifth entry in the Spanish "Blind Dead" series (but with a softcore twist), Jess Franco's *Mansion of the Living Dead* seems to be based on some of the same Templar history and plays with similar imagery; however, if you're looking for eyeless zombies, go back to the de Ossorio series. Four sex-happy German girls arrive at a seaside hotel (the titular "mansion", presumably) next to a desolate church, and decide to play around with each other in the absence of any male guests. Meanwhile the manager (Antonio Mayans) spends his off-time tending to his lunatic, naked wife (Eva León) who's chained to a wall in one of the rooms and displays some especially unpleasant eating habits. When not being menaced on the beach by flying kitchen implements, the girls wander around the hotel, disrobe, and eventually fall one by one into the clutches of a brutal sect at the church whose pasty-faced members subject them to a strange kind of detached gang bang. Luckily for lead girl Candy (Lina Romay), the sect also has a dark secret in which she is deeply involved, leading to an oddly poetic climax.

Alternating between erotic reveries, boneheaded stupidity, and breathtaking gothic lyricism, *Mansion of the Living Dead* is a good litmus test for checking one's Franco boundaries. There's nothing terribly extreme here (apart from the naked groping which won't startle anyone), but the stream-of-consciousness storytelling and eerie locales give the film a distinct flavour not quite like anything else in the Franco canon.

M

Still bearing her wig from *Macumba Sexual*, Romay makes a fine ditzy heroine forced to plumb new emotional depths within herself, and her "possession" in the third act will delight fans. Most of the other actors basically sleepwalk through their roles, which is appropriate given the tone.

Another title rarely seen previously in scope (and never in English), *Mansion of the Living Dead* gets a very respectful treatment from Severin. The dark interior scenes which were completely incoherent and muddy on those old tape editions are now clear and surprisingly beautiful for the most part; the eerie shots of actors wandering down dark corridors with bright lights at the end manage wring some tension out of even the slowest scenes. Optional English subtitles do what they can with the over-the-top Spanish dialogue, which presents its four interloping heroines as slang-talking dingbats eager to shed their tops. Some context (but not much) is offered in another solid new featurette, "The Mansion Jess Built", which dovetails nicely with the similar Franco/Romay interviews on *Macumba Sexual*. Discussing their multiple cinematic identities and the origins of the story (which extend way further back than the de Ossorio films), this irrepressible couple makes for good company and should increase enthusiasm for these previously neglected, personal labours of love and exploitation. The same transfer and extras are also available in the U.K. as part of "The Jess Franco Collection 2" box set from Anchor Bay (see *The Inconfessable Orgies of Emmanuelle* review for more details).

MARK OF THE WITCH

Colour, 1970, 84m. / Directed by Tom Moore / Starring Anitra Walsh, Darryl Wells, Robert Elston, Marie Santell, Gary Brockette, Jack Gardner / Code Red (US R0 NTSC) / WS (1.78:1) (16:9), Retromedia (US R0 NTSC) / WS (1.66:1)

While schlock guru Larry Buchanan was the king of Texas drive-in fare in the 1960s, the following decade saw a significant improvement in the Lone Star State's horror output, most notably with a certain chainsaw-oriented classic by Tobe Hooper. Sandwiched somewhere in between is the mostly forgotten horror oddity *Mark of the Witch*, a Dallas-shot cheapie obviously inspired by *Black Sunday* and *Horror Hotel* – right down to imitating their opening scenes with a nasty witch cursing the descendants of her persecutors, though this time it's the most long-winded and unintentionally hilarious version imaginable. This time the witch is Margery of Jourdemain (Marie Santell), who's apparently a Satanist as well and given to marking the hands of her followers with an occult symbol, and the object of her wrath is Macintyre Stuart (Robert Elston), one of her followers and a town official who turned her in to the hangman's noose. Flash forward centuries later to a college town where perky Jill (Anitra Walsh, who also wrote the interminable main titles ditty) comes across a mysterious red book at a university bookstore. One of the pages in the tome offers instructions on how to summon a witch (involving a bunch of candles, some wine, and rosemary), so she and her pals decide to get together that night and act it out. At first the ritual seems to be a failure, but as Jill quickly reveals to her professor (Elston again), she is now possessed by the wicked Margery and intent on carrying out her supernatural vendetta. Will the Prof and Jill's sweater-wearing boyfriend (Darryl Wells) be able to stop the fiend as she starts bumping off other students in her evil quest?

Originally released with a PG rating in drive-ins around the country (most often in the South), *Mark of the Witch* will never win any awards for acting (the pretty but clearly unqualified Walsh seems to have some trouble keeping her characters straight throughout), but it's a lively and entertaining slice of hokum that really picks up steam in its second half, culminating in a nicely trippy climax with a time-hopping twist ending thrown in for good measure. Director Tom Moore (who went on to make *Return to Boggy Creek* and a long, prolific TV career) pretty much sticks to the H.G. Lewis school of filmmaking, with 90% of the film in static medium shots. However, the punchy colours, '70s art direction, and nutty plot turns still make it a cut above the average supernatural potboiler.

The first DVD of *Mark of the Witch* arrived from Retromedia paired up with the Florida cheapie *The Brides Wore Blood* in its theatrical PG-rated version. The print used was acceptable but incredibly splicy and dirty, though the widescreen 1.66:1 framing looks about right. Most horror collectors obviously assumed that would be the last word for this title in the digital age, but Code Red has resuscitated it in much finer form as part of an "Evil Teen Horror" double feature under the Exploitation Cinema banner once used by the now-defunct BCI. This transfer from the original camera negative is actually the pre-release version slapped with an R rating, mainly for some shots in Walsh's mid-film nocturnal ritual in the woods which now finds her ripping off her top and writhing around on the ground (perhaps a body double, but everyone will pretend it isn't). Image quality is much better all around, with only very minimal damage on display and much richer colours and detail. Just the uncut status alone makes this a substantial double dip, but the added resolution sweetens the deal. The only quibble is the fact that the 1.78:1 framing horizontally squeezes the image slightly to fit the frame (so everyone looks

a tiny bit fatter); if you can adjust the XY scaling on your TV, it comes in very handy here. The Code Red version is double-billed with *Devil Times Five*, a title previously released by Code Red as a stand-alone special edition (full review for that disc also in this book) and which also features prominent plugs for Budweiser Beer, oddly enough. However, the transfer here is completely different (it has the replaced *Devil Times Five* reissue title card instead of the *Horrible House on the Hill* one present on the first release) and presented open matte, which means a lot more, generally extraneous picture information at the top and bottom of the frame. However, picture quality is noticeably inferior (it looks sourced from an older master tape) and the audio is much hissier, so anyone who has the first edition would be well-advised to hang on it and just regard the open matte edition here as an interesting variant. Extras include the trailer for *Mark of the Witch* and additional trailers for other titles including *Caged Men* (under the title *I'm Going to Get You... Elliot Boy*), *The Unseen*, *Beyond the Door*, *Nightmare*, *The Weekend Murders*, and *Dr. Black and Mr. Hyde*.

MARQUIS DE SADE'S PROSPERITIES OF VICE

Colour, 1988, 96m. / Directed by Akio Jissoji / Starring Yasumi Hara, Renji Ishibashi, Seiran Li, Kimiaki Makino / Mondo Macabro (US R0 NTSC) / WS (1.85:1) (16:9)

In 1920s Japan, a debauched count (Yasumi Hara) and his former prostitute wife (Renji Ishibashi) collaborate on staging the works of the Marquis de Sade with the aid of a troupe of performers recruited from the city's criminal element including thieves and whores. The production begins to distort the participants' viewers of reality and morality as the uninhibited fantasies onstage bleed into real life, with often devastating results.

An unusual slice of Japanese erotica, this Nikkatsu production isn't really a traditional Roman Porno film; it's more of a European-styled art movie with a few erotic flourishes and shot with a visual aesthetic similar to Walerian Borowczyk. Every scene is bathed in rich layers of darkness and light with a powder texture over the actors that creates a unique atmosphere, while the stars leap into their roles with a gleeful abandon that culminates in a hallucinogenic finale. In the end this feels more like Japan's answer to *Marat/Sade*, and exactly how this escaped any critical notice since the '80s is perplexing.

Mondo Macabro's English-language debut of this film features a striking anamorphic transfer, and the original Japanese track is presented with optional English subtitles. Extras include their 24-minute "The Erotic Empire" piece about the history of Nikkatsu's erotic movie production featuring historian Jasper Sharp, director Seijun Suzuki, and many more discussing the history of the studio's output which has now finally built up a firm international following.

Also included is the original trailer, a text overview of the studio and the director, and an interview with Sharp about the studio's attempt with films like this to refashion its Roman Porno offerings into the new, artier Ropponica genre. The disc is rounded out with a slew of other Mondo Macabro/Nikkatsu titles like *Watcher in the Attic* and *Assault! Jack the Ripper*. Strikingly beautiful and unique, this is essential viewing for fans of de Sade on film and the outer fringes of Japanese cinema.

MARTYRS

Colour, 2008, 97m. / Directed by Pascal Laugier / Starring Morjana Alaoui, Mylène Jampanoï, Catherine Bégin / Optimum (DVD & Blu-ray, UK R2 PAL/HD), Genius (US R1 NTSC), Wild Side (DVD & Blu-ray, France R2 PAL/HD) / WS (1.85:1) (16:9) / DD5.1

After escaping from a year of imprisonment and torture in a now-abandoned building, young Lucie (Mylène Jampanoï) grows up in a home for abandoned girls and becomes best friends with the more stable Anna (Morjana Alaoui). Years of determination finally bring Lucie to the home of her former captors, with Anna brought along to help clean up once things get very, very messy. However, Lucie continues to be tormented by a monstrous assailant who inflicts savage wounds on her body, and Anna begins to question what Lucie actually endured and what it all really means.

This set-up is just a hint of what lies in store for the viewer with *Martyrs*, the most harrowing entry in the new French wave of horror which ranges from the sublime (*Inside*) to the insipid (*Frontier(s)*). However, none of them have proven as divisive as this film, which pulls off no less than three major shift changes in the narrative and eventually runs the viewer through a gauntlet of torment comparable only to *Irreversible* or *Cannibal Holocaust*. Much of the debate centres around whether this film qualifies as "torture porn" (a vague, somewhat insulting catch-all term), though there's nothing even remotely leering or salacious about the long, gut-churning ordeal undertaken in the third act; while many Abu Ghraib-era horror films do seem to linger on suffering for its own sake, here it has a definite cathartic point and is absolutely necessary to set up the haunting final ten minutes. This leads to the other point of contention, a third act swerve into heady material which some labelled "pretentious" (another overused and nebulous term) as it ties the violence to a philosophical experiment both logical and utterly barbaric. To say more would ruin the experience for new viewers, but while watching the film, bear in the mind the ages of the antagonists and the history of fascism both past and nascent in many European countries. The implications are truly chilling.

As for basic aesthetic qualities, *Martyrs* is exceptionally well-crafted and marks a definite step forward for director Pascal Laugier after his skilful but unremarkable prior effort, *Saint Ange*. Most admirable is the way the film establishes its own internal logic and plays fair by the viewer all the way to the final shot, a quality that cannot be attributed to similar but ultimately dishonest efforts such as *Switchblade Romance* and particularly Michael Haneke's *Funny Games*, both of which seem to feel they are better than their own material and try to make a profound statement about human psychology when in fact they're simply thumping the viewer on the nose. This film is an entirely different beast, an anguished howl from the pit of the soul that tries to find grace at the end of an extremely dark tunnel.

The American DVD of *Martyrs* begins with an apologetic intro from Laugier who admonishes himself for creating a film he himself admits may do some damage, even freely inviting the viewer to hate him. He also appears throughout the extras, which are repurposed somewhat depending on which edition you see. The British release from Optimum contains an 86-minute "Making of *Martyrs*" documentary (also without English subs on the French release) which covers the entire project in depth, with candid and sometimes contentious

comments from the cast and crew along with lots of footage from the shoot with a particular focus on the stunts and special effects. (And no, it doesn't shed any light on the enigmatic whisper at the end of the film.) The same material is refashioned into the 50-minute "Organic Chronicles" documentary on the U.S. disc. Also included on the releases are separate interviews with Laugier (who talks more in depth about the difficult period of his life which spawned the film) and likeable FX supervisor Benoit Lestang, who shockingly died shortly after the completion of the film. The teaser and theatrical trailers are also present on each disc. Image quality is excellent and appears to be from the same master for all editions; the film is shot with an intentionally grey, sometimes desaturated appearance that suits the material well. The surround mix is also excellent and provokes more than its fair share of jolts.

M

MASSACRE MAFIA STYLE

Colour, 1975, 79m. / Directed by Duke Mitchell / Starring Duke Mitchell, Vic Caesar, Lorenzo Dodo, Louis Zito / JM Music (US R0 NTSC)

A *Godfather* imitation gone completely, utterly, and gloriously insane, *Massacre Mafia Style* (better known to VHS junkies via its Video Gems release as *The Executioner*) kicks off in an office building where our two main Mafiosi, Mimi (director/star Duke Mitchell) and Jolly (Vic Caesar), wipe out what seems like an entire office building's worth of victims while performing a hit, allowing only a small kid on an elevator to leave unscathed. However, this title sequence sets up the violently hilarious overkill with which the entire film treats its subject, dabbling in "the Italian-American experience" while delivering pure exploitation sensation on an Ed Wood budget. See, Mimi wants a better life for his family and, after leaving his son back in the old country, finds his violent nature brought out by working for the mob with the blessing of his crime boss dad. Intent on seizing control of the Hollywood underworld from the wet-behind-the-ears new criminals, he and Jolly might have bitten off more than they can chew and have to shoot everything in sight to realise the American dream.

Thanks mainly to its theatrical trailer (essentially the opening scene sans credits), *Massacre Mafia Style* continued to intrigue viewers into the DVD era despite the maddening inability to see it anywhere outside of a die-hard tape collector's library. Fortunately the rest of the film lives up to the promise of its opening with Mitchell delivering an impassioned, eccentric, unpredictable performance unlike anything else ever committed to film. This is definitely one man's vision up onscreen, and considering Mitchell's background (as a nightclub regular and one-time comedy partner with Jerry Lewis imitator Sammy Petrillo, with whom he starred in *Bela Lugosi Meets a Brooklyn Gorilla*), he apparently was more than a little familiar with the real-life interaction of Hollywood glitter and the criminal element. You've certainly never seen another gangster movie like this.

The video history of *Massacre Mafia Style* has been confusing to say the least since VHS rode off into the sunset. Grindhouse Releasing included the trailer on almost all of its output going back to the late '90s, but well over a decade later, their version has yet to surface. Whatever the ownership issues of this film may be, Mitchell's son Jeffrey has put out a privately-distributed, double-disc version (dubbed "The Family Edition") loaded with supplements. On the downside, the transfer is yanked from a VHS tape (you can see some tape tension lines at the bottom of the screen without overscan) and looks exactly like it did in the '80s, all soft and murky, for better or worse. Disc one heaps on three commentaries featuring Jeffrey Mitchell, his dad's writing friend Frankie Ray, and George Jacobs ("Frank Sinatra's assistant and valet", which gets pretty colourful as you might imagine). They don't really address the actual film directly very often, focusing more on Mitchell Sr.'s background and creative endeavours while his son shares a lot of info about himself and his family. You also get the original trailer, a couple of Duke Mitchell-voiced radio spots, and a peek at a Duke Mitchell concert film, "An Impressionistic Tribute to Jimmy Durante", which has apparently been vaulted for decades. You can also find a batch of hidden Easter eggs including Mitchell-performed songs and, of all things, a trailer for *Brooklyn Gorilla!* On to disc two, you get "Like Father, Like Son", an hour-long video piece on Duke Mitchell and his son featuring Jeffrey, Frankie Ray and George Jacobs talking about the career of "the man who was Mimi" interspersed with home movie and nightclub footage. Also included are what appear to be outtake interviews with Ray and Jacobs, a stills gallery of Mitchell's photos throughout his career, audio recordings from one of Mitchell's last live performances, the screenplay in different stages of evolution via DVD-Rom, and three '70s songs by the younger Mitchell ("Jacknife", "Whiskey", "In a Dream"), all packaged with an amusing reproduction of the director's "Italian cheat sheet" used during filming. Definitely an all-but-the-kitchen-sink release, this one loads on the extras and, if you're not expecting anything from the presentation of the main feature, sheds some light on a one-of-a-kind entertainment personality.

MEAN JOHNNY BARROWS

Colour, 1976, 96m. / Directed by Fred
Williamson / Starring Fred Williamson,
Roddy McDowall, Stuart Whitman,
Anthony Caruso, R.G. Armstrong, Elliott
Gould, Mike Henry / Code Red (US R0
NTSC) / WS (2.35:1) (16:9)

 Discharged from the
military after punching
out an abusive superior
officer, Johnny Barrows
(played by Fred Will-
iamson) winds up home-
less when he's robbed
fresh off the bus home to
Los Angeles. His service in Vietnam and
former football glory do little to stop his
downward spiral thanks to repeated police
harassment and low-paying menial gas
station work. However, when the mob ask
him to serve as a hit man for the powerful
Racconi family, it turns out to be an offer he
might not be able to refuse, and soon his
proficiency with weapons proves to be just
the ticket for a whole new life.

Though it starts off like a fairly earnest
social drama, *Mean Johnny Barrows*
eventually explodes into wonderfully entertaining drive-in fare. Williamson's violent
transformation is a wonder to behold, not to
mention the head-spinning cast of buddies
he recruits including a hilarious Roddy
McDowall (as the head of the rival DaVince
family), Stuart Whitman as the Racconi
boss, Elliott Gould in a scene-stealing glorified cameo as a philosophizing barfly,
former screen Tarzan Mike Henry, and even
a bit appearance by Leon Isaac Kennedy.

As with Code Red's edition of *Death
Journey*, this release contains Williamson's
original complete director's cut which
clocks in six minutes longer than the gutted
TV prints included in a number of grey
market releases (which are also brutally
pan and scanned). The restoration of the
original scope framing here is even more
important, finally making this film enjoyable and watchable on a level no one could
have anticipated before. Williamson also
contributes another commentary in which
he talks about making the jump to directing
and starting his own company, as well as
his intentions to diverge from the usual
blaxploitation template of the period. The
menus, which definitely play up the
"Mean" angle, also lead to other extras
including a rough-looking theatrical trailer
and a slew of additional ones for films
like *Stigma*, *Family Honor*, *Changes*,
Challenge of the Dragon, and two more
Williamson films, *Death Journey* and *No
Way Back*.

MERCY

B&W, 2006, 85m. / Directed by Patrick
Roddy / Starring Gary Shannon, Shelly
Farrell, Charles McNeely III, Julie Ann Fay
/ Unearthed (US R1 NTSC) / WS (1.85:1)
(16:9) / DD2.0

 Forever doomed to be
confused with the
sleazy Ellen Barkin
thriller of the same
name, this fascinating
little black and white
indie is a horror film
more in spirit than
execution, with artistic ambitions far more
commendable than your average splatter
effort. The nightmarish journey begins
when convict John Mercy (Gary Shannon)
is released after spending twenty-five years
in jail (exactly why isn't unveiled until later,
of course), only to find that life outside is
hardly less stressful. Besieged by an
unhinged parole officer and stuck in both a
drill-pressing job and a dwelling lorded over
by bullies, he finds solace only in a local
watering hole where he meets Eve (Shelly
Farrell), a friendly blonde aspiring actress.
Mercy dreams of escaping to Montana, a

photo of whose landscape is his one constant souvenir since jail, but when pieces of his body literally start falling apart, he realises that fate is indeed out to get him.

A queasy and undeniably effective mixture of Cronenbergian body horror and good old-fashioned David Lynch surrealism, *Mercy* is an assured debut feature with Patrick Roddy guiding the decomposing protagonist through an unforgettable, noir-tinged world every bit as oppressive as those in such '50s paranoia classics as *Dementia*. Horror fans get a bit to chew on thanks to a few careful dollops of bloodshed and some pretty squishy moments of body violence (the eyeball bit especially), while Shannon never loses sight of the essential, beaten-down humanity in his character. Bear in mind that this is essentially targeted as an art film, so anyone looking for a bare-bones scarefest won't be too nourished; instead, this is more for fans of fare like *The Last Winter* and *The Reflecting Skin* that offer some substance and style with their moments of skin-crawling nastiness.

Unearthed continues its fascinating line of genre-bending releases here in high style, with *Mercy* receiving a solid anamorphic transfer that captures the delicate shadows and greyscales of the cinematography even if it's limited by the budget-constraining limitations of the production itself. Don't expect a slick knockout on the level of such B&W transfers as *Ed Wood*, but it's perfectly fine for what it is. The Dolby Stereo soundtrack does right by the extremely effective sound mix, which uses lots of ambient noises and nerve-jangling bits of period blues music to really get under your skin. (The director previously issued a private edition from a greatly inferior screener source, so even if you've stumbled across an older copy lying around, this is considerably better.) Extras include a "movie comic book" companion to the film, a trailer, and a quick six-minute featurette

covering only the very basics of how the film was made. The rest of the disc is filled out with very contrasting trailers for other Unearthed releases ranging from *Red Room 2* to *Frankenhooker*, so it's probably safe to say that *Mercy* falls somewhere in between the audiences for those two movies.

MESSIAH OF EVIL

Colour, 1973, 91m. / Directed by Willard Huyck / Starring Michael Greer, Marianna Hill, Joy Bang, Anitra Ford, Royal Dano, Elisha Cook Jr., Bennie Robinson, Walter Hill / Code Red (US R0 NTSC) / WS (2.35:1) (16:9)

 In the desolate seaside town of Point Dune, terrible things are happening to the locals. One unlucky resident (young, future director Walter Hill) gets his throat cut in the pre-credits sequence, and the newest visitor, Arletty (Marianna Hill), is trying to find out why her missing father wrote a string of increasingly terrifying letters about impending doom. A trip to a gas station on the way leads her to a creepy albino (Bennie Robinson) and an ill-fated attendant, while the town itself is filled with dead-eyed residents who weep blood and spend their nights on the shore watching the red-tinged moon rise over the water. A local bohemian named Thom (Michael Greer) and his two female companions (Anitra Ford and Joy Bang) fill her in on some of the peculiar local folklore which requires all bodies to be burned upon death, and soon the horrific truth of the town and the malevolent "dark stranger" who cursed it a century before begin to come to light.

The 1970s had no shortage of chilling, groundbreaking horror films, but few were mistreated on the level of *Messiah of Evil*, also known as *Dead People*. One of the decade's most visually audacious and inventive supernatural tales, the film was the brainchild of Willard Huyck and Gloria Katz, the team who often worked with fellow film school alumnus George Lucas and wrote *American Graffiti*, *Indiana Jones and the Temple of Doom*, and, ahem, *Howard the Duck*. Director Huyck reveals a keen visual sense here, unspooling a string of unforgettable, truly harrowing set pieces revolving around such seemingly mundane settings as a brightly-lit supermarket, a movie theatre, the aforementioned gas station, and a striking artist's studio filled with wall-sized, surrealistic creations. The dreamlike, ambiguous nature of the story (which is narrated by Hill in flashback) could have been a frustrating mess, but instead its elliptical mysteries reward repeated viewings while subtle visual details abound. The experimental music score is also a major plus, with discordant synthesizer droning weaving through the night time scenes and greatly enhancing the overall feeling of unease. Indirect references to the Manson Family, the Donner Party, and the still-new modern zombie genre also combine to give it a distinct flavour shared only by some of its immediate companion pieces like *Let's Scare Jessica to Death* and *Lemora*, though a handful of subsequent films like *Dead & Buried* and *Strange Behavior* managed to capture some of the same peculiar magic. It's certainly a film you'll never forget and well worth discovering, preferably late at night with a big bowl of popcorn.

Most of *Messiah of Evil*'s attributes have been completely smothered throughout much of the home video age thanks to unwatchable transfers that made mincemeat of the powerful Techniscope compositions and gorgeous, vivid colour schemes, which betray the obvious influence of Hammer Films and Mario Bava. Anyone who's suffered through any of the public domain cheapie releases might wonder what on earth was going on half the time, as every carefully composed shot was turned into a murky mess. Code Red's officially sanctioned edition marks the first appearance ever on video of the properly framed version of the film, and to say the least, it's a major revelation. Some unavoidable debris is still evident from time to time, but this is such a tremendous leap forward in presentation that any quibbling is swept aside by the powerful experience of simply watching this gem in its first acceptable release. Colours look terrific, with eye-popping reds and blues saturating many scenes and the wild artwork found in the daring set design can finally be appreciated.

The transfer alone would easily place this among the top essential horror releases of recent years, but the deal is sweetened with a host of terrific extras. Huyck and Katz contribute a very informative commentary track moderated by Lee Christian in which they discuss the influence of Polanski and Lovecraft, the segue working from *Graffiti* to this film, the reasons for shooting in scope, their relative ignorance of George Romero, Huyck's early work at AIP, the unwelcome pop song foisted on the film by distributors (which is dropped here in favour of the original director's cut), and the circumstances which prevented the shooting of some crucial footage which would have shed more light on the dark stranger's identity and Hill's ultimate fate. They return for the 22-minute featurette, "Remembering *Messiah of Evil*", along with associate editors Morgan Fisher and Billy Weber and cinematographer Stephen Katz, which covers the making of the film from a more general perspective with a focus on finding the actors and the shooting conditions. Other extras include a phone interview with Joy Bang (who got one of the best scenes in the film), two of the team's early B&W short films (the split-screen "The Bride Stripped Bare", a good companion piece to early De Palma films, and "Down These Mean Streets"), a hidden bonus audio interview for Easter Egg hunters, and the usual reel of Code Red trailers for *The Statue*, *Brute Corps*, *Choke Canyon*, *Night of the Dribbler*, *Rituals*, *Stunt Rock* and *Family Honor*.

THE MIDNIGHT MEAT TRAIN

Colour, 2008, 103m. / Directed by Ryûhei Kitamura / Starring Bradley Cooper, Vinnie Jones, Leslie Bibb, Brooke Shields, Roger Bart, Ted Raimi / Lionsgate (DVD & Blu-ray, US R1 NTSC, UK R2 PAL/HD) / WS (2.35:1) (16:9) / DD5.1

 Clive Barker's ground-breaking *Books of Blood* story collections put him on the horror literary map in the 1980s, and adaptations for the big and small screens have steadily assaulted viewers ever since. One of the most gruesome and beloved of these tales, "The Midnight Meat Train", seemed like a natural cinematic piece, fusing the urban subway dread of *Death Line* with Lovecraftian horrors; however, the adaptation that finally reached screens seemed cursed with an unnatural run of bad luck only partly attributable to the flaws of the film itself.

In an overly art-directed version of New York, aspiring photographer Leon (Bradley Cooper) gets his big break when his girlfriend (Leslie Bibb) arranges a meeting with a prominent gallery curator (Brooke Shields) who sees promise but encourages a more dangerous edge before she will show his work. One night Leon goes snapping shots around the nearby subway station and, along with getting too close to a gang of hoods, takes a photo of a beautiful model who goes missing after stepping on the train. He also shoots a well-dressed, silent brute (Vinnie Jones) carrying a black case who might be connected to the disappearance as well. Encouraged by the positive reception to these shots, he goes back into the subterranean station again only to discover unimaginable horrors when he stops on the last train of the evening.

Though it improves substantially in its second half, *The Midnight Meat Train* doesn't quite work. Director Ryûhei Kitamura (*Versus*, *Godzilla: Final Wars*) creates a cityscape far too stylised and austere to do any justice to a story which would have benefited from a more gritty, naturalistic approach. Also the decision to use rampant CGI in all of the gore scenes is a major misstep, with the train murder of Ted Raimi being the worst offender as digital blood drops and eyeballs fly at the camera via effects that wouldn't pass muster in a decade-old video game. Finally the casting of Cooper is a baffling misstep; though a talented performer, he comes off far too shifty and unstable to convey any of the pathos necessary for the ironic finale to work. On the positive side, Vinnie Jones makes an excellent, physically intimidating villain, and the force of Barker's original narrative still packs enough of a punch for the film to generate occasional stomach-churning chills. Horror fans should find it a worthwhile view, but this isn't close to the gruelling masterpiece it could have been.

Lionsgate originally planned a major international theatrical release, but a regime change coupled with jeering audience reactions to the unfortunate title (which works fine for a story, not so well for a film) left it stranded on a handful of token screens and an early course to video, though at least the latter is completely uncensored. Lionsgate's transfer is extremely impressive regardless of the questionable visual choices in the film itself, and the dynamic surround mix is likewise as excellent as one would expect from a movie of this vintage.

The most interesting extra is a commentary track with Barker and Kitamura which openly trashes the very company releasing the disc; also included is the 15-minute video portrait "The Man Behind the Myth" with Barker talking about his stories and artwork, the quick "Mahogany's Tale" about Jones's character, a 9-minute "Anatomy of a Murder Scene", and the theatrical trailer.

MOONLIGHTING WIVES

Colour, 1966, 86m. / Directed by Joe Sarno / Starring Dianne Vivienne, John Aristedes, June Roberts, Jan Nash / Retro-Seduction Cinema (US R0 NTSC)

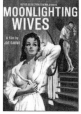 One of the most widely-circulated movies from Joe Sarno's glossy attempts at exposing the seamy side of the American middle class (see *Sin in the Suburbs*, et al), *Moonlighting Wives* is a vaguely tawdry but accessible slice of lounge-era pop culture disguised as a sex film (without much actual sex, but we'll get to that). Joe Sarno and the film's original press materials claim this was based on a real news report of suburban housewives running a prostitution ring out of their houses, eventually evading their arrests by hanging on to dirt about their powerful clients. (The film supplies a more sombre, albeit unrealistic, outcome.) The scandal starts when pouty but determined Joan (Dianne Vivienne) gets sick of her boss's sexual advances and her husband's constant badgering about her spending habits, so she sets up her own stenography business that doubles nicely for selling out sexual favours from her married friends. Pretty soon Joan's schtupping her friend's lover, hubby's off getting intimate with the babysitter, the slow-witted cops are getting suspicious, and everything's gearing up for

a kinky masked orgy in the den that's bound to end in tragedy.

One of Joe Sarno's earlier colour films, *Moonlighting Wives* already shows him at ease with splashing vivid, expressive hues across the screen as he composes each of his characters in a succession of shots right out of a Julie London album cover. The lustrous approach here, coupled with the interesting and unpredictable screenplay, manages to compensate for the lack of skin on display (with some scantily-clad partiers at the end coming closest); it's a perfect textbook example of Sarno's psychological approach to erotica. All of the performers turn in above-average performances, with Vivienne (a.k.a. Tammy Latour from Sarno's *My Body Hungers*) doing an excellent job of portraying a beautiful yet strangely aloof and ultimately ruthless woman. Add a wonderfully randy theme song, and this is pure guilty pleasure territory for anyone with a strong erotic imagination.

Moonlighting Wives circulated for decades on the grindhouse circuit and popped up in the early days of Something Weird in a faded, battered print that did no justice to Sarno's colour schemes. Unfortunately its frequent exhibition meant that most prints were demolished in the process, making this very close to a lost film. This DVD edition presents about as close to a pristine version as possible under the circumstances; as the restoration demonstrates, even the best surviving print had turned red and was littered with damage. Many scratches still remain, but the colour has been returned to its much-needed original intentions. (Unfortunately, that irritating Seduction Cinema logo pops up briefly every fifteen minutes or so; please cut it out, guys!) Sarno pops up for a video interview in which he discusses the making of the film and his career in general at that time; it's pretty brief but interesting (with mention of some unused spicier footage that no one ever saw) and makes a fine companion to his other commentaries and interviews for the company's recommended releases, which are represented here with promos for the likes of *Abigail Leslie Is Back in Town*.

MOTHER OF TEARS

Colour, 2007, 101m. / Directed by Dario Argento / Starring Asia Argento, Cristian Solimeno, Adam James, Philippe Leroy, Daria Nicolodi, Udo Kier, Coralina Cataldi Tassoni / Optimum (UK R2 PAL), Genius (US R1 NTSC), Seven 7 (DVD & Blu-ray, France R2 PAL/HD), Medusa (Italy R2 PAL) / WS (2.35:1) (16:9) / DD5.1

Proof positive that anticipation is more pleasurable than the reward, *Mother of Tears* marked the second time that Dario Argento listened to popular demand (after his poorly-received *Phantom of the Opera*) and embarked on a project that had little chance of satisfying anyone. In this case, he finally decided to shoot a third instalment in the saga begun by *Suspiria* and *Inferno* about a trio of malicious witches who unleash gory pandemonium in New York, Germany and Rome. However, no one could have predicted how sharply this film would diverge from its predecessors or how divisive the final result would be.

While working to restore ancient artefacts in Rome, Sarah Mandy (Asia Argento) is intrigued by a wax-sealed, carved box unearthed from an ancient burial site. She decides to open it with the aid of an ill-fated colleague (*Opera*'s Coralina Cataldi Tassoni) only to release the pitiless Mother of Tears, a robe-clad sorceress whose minions include a bald assassin and a chattering monkey. Sarah runs for her life and seeks help through a number of encounters including her extremely emotional boyfriend (Adam James), the helpful spirit of her white witch mother (*Deep Red*'s Daria Nicolodi), and a knowledgeable priest (*Suspiria*'s Udo Kier), while an inquisitive Roman cop (Cristian Solimeno from *Footballers' Wives*) tries to piece together the brutal murders following in Sarah's wake.

Completely eschewing the vibrant colour palette and flamboyant murder sequences of the first two films, *Mother of Tears* instead features a bright, clinical visual texture and mutilation sequences filled with rubbery special effects and an often unpleasant focus on protracted agony, particularly a reprise of *Tenebrae*'s double-lesbian murder that seems far too vicious for its own good. Even some of Argento's finest films have occasional moments of unintentional hilarity, but this one really goes overboard thanks to that improbably-skilled simian, a truly terrible performance by James, random appearances by Nicolodi who seems to be imitating Casper the Friendly Ghost, a cackling squad of fashion-victim assistant witches (whose first entrance is one of the giddiest moments in the Argento canon), the risible depiction of Rome descending into chaos via some unruly kids attacking an abandoned car, and a topless villainess who represents the nadir of Argento's recent, perplexing obsession with tacky silicone breasts (see also: *Do You Like Hitchcock?*, *Sleepless* and both of his *Masters of Horror* episodes). That said, the film does have its positive attributes: there isn't a single dull moment in the entire running time; Asia has a remarkably poignant moment looking at photographs of her dead mother (played by real-life mom Nicolodi); Claudio Simonetti's score occasionally rouses itself from sub-*Omen* chanting to hearken back to the glory days of the '70s; and the last third delivers a truly marvellous fifteen minutes or so in which Asia discovers the truth from sinister scholar Philippe Leroy, embarks on a nocturnal taxi ride reminiscent of the prior films, and enters another house of the damned in one of the director's elaborate, single-take Steadicam shots. All in all, it's certainly a missed opportunity but mildly entertaining if you keep your expectations way, way below the masterpiece status everyone expected. Plus it's still far better than *Giallo*.

One of the very few Argento films to receive widespread theatrical release since the 1990s, *Mother of Tears* somehow managed to squeak by uncensored in every major country – quite surprising considering the extreme and often highly unpleasant violence on display. The U.K. and U.S. DVDs contain the original English-language track, while the French disc (also available on Region B Blu-ray) adds on an additional French-language track and optional French titles. (The Italian disc has no English-friendly options.) Image quality is comparable on all of them and appears to be taken from the same excellent master, which is actually more vibrant and rich-looking than the depressingly lifeless theatrical prints. The Dolby Digital 5.1 soundtrack is a bit less impressive, offering some surround activity for Simonetti's score but never really delivering a huge aural punch. Apart from the nearly bare bones U.K. disc, extras include the Italian trailer (with the French and U.S. discs adding on their respective country's trailers as well) and a half-hour featurette with Argento and the cast discussing the film interspersed with making-of footage. The French disc also adds a half-hour analysis of the film by critic Vivien Villani (no English), filmographies, and a photo gallery.

MURDER-ROCK

Colour, 1984, 90m. / Directed by Lucio Fulci / Starring Olga Karlatos, Ray Lovelock, Claudio Cassinelli, Cosimo Cinieri / Shriek Show (US R1 NTSC), Cult Cinema International, X-Rated Kult (Germany R0 PAL) / WS (1.66:1) (16:9) / DD2.0

 Apparently, when you are a director like Lucio Fulci, the usual standards of cinema don't apply. You can stage any kind of tasteless atrocity for viewers which involves bodily dismemberment, child endangerment, or sexual mutilation, and the audience will eat it up; however, if you indulge in breakdancing and aerobics outfits, watch out! That's the fate that befell *Murder-Rock*, a pop-horror *giallo* that owes more to music videos than Bava.

At a New York dance academy obviously inspired by a recent viewing of *Fame*, tough-love dance instructor Candice (*Zombie*'s Olga Karlatos) pushes her aerobicising charges to new heights of glory when three spots open up at a prestigious agency. Unfortunately their routines are disrupted when one young lady winds up getting a long metal pin fatally shoved into her breastplate during a nocturnal shower in the locker room, and everyone becomes a suspect. Meanwhile Candice suffers from surreal dreams in which she's chased by a sinister man (Ray Lovelock) whose face happens to pop up on a billboard. A little detective work reveals he's a waning actor with ties to the victim, and soon the body count rises. Who's responsible? And who will live to dance another day?

Fulci got a lot of flack over the years for this one, primarily for its back-to-back opening musical sequences which segue from an ill-advised breakin' routine (intercut with shots of the Big Apple skyline) to a *Flashdance*-inspired class number, both to songs that will linger forever in your memory ("Streets to Blame" and "Tonight Is Your Night", for the record). In the film's defence, it pretty much throws out the whole '80s dance fixation after that and goes into proper thriller mode, complete with the illogical plotting and flat-as-paper characterisations you might expect. The plot is really a thinly-veiled rehash of Fulci's *The New York Ripper* (complete with a similar dream-motivation tactic and red herring ploy), but this time Fulci leaves the gore back in Italy and focuses instead on lots of nudity that can't be classified as gratuitous since, well, the killer likes to poke the dancers in the chest. Prog rocker Keith Emerson returns from *Inferno* for his second Italian horror score, and... well... it's certainly memorable, though no one will ever confuse it with his Argento masterpiece. Easily the most successful aspect of the film is the striking cinematography by Giuseppe Pinori (*Contamination*), who uses strobing lights and filters to a surprisingly rich effect throughout in a manner similar to *The Fifth Cord*.

Fortunately after years of substandard video transfers (and complete dismissal in America after a fleeting theatrical release as *The Demon Is Loose*), *Murder-Rock* looks just fine on Shriek Show's DVD edition. The anamorphic transfer is rich and colourful, with some of that '80s grain still intact where it should be. Note that the opening credits tend to scrape very close to the bottom of the frame, so depending on your set's overscan settings, you might have some issues there. Audio is presented in a fine but dated English stereo mix (canned but appropriate since it matches most of the actors' lip movements) and the original Italian mix, which features much less channel separation and is pretty much indistinguishable from the ancient Domovideo VHS tapes. No English subtitle options are provided, so really the English track is the only way to go.

Shriek Show has somehow managed to bless this unlikely title with a double-disc set, and the results are definitely the equal to their previous double-dip on *A Lizard in a Woman's Skin*. Along with the film itself, the first disc contains an audio commentary with Pinori and writer Federico Caddeo (in Italian with optional subs) that covers the basics of the film's production and memories of working with Fulci. You also get a fake, video-era *Murder-Rock* preview from the European release (too bad as the real Japanese trailer is far superior), plus a fantastic international trailer for *Witchery* and promos for other titles including *The Being*, *Hiroku the Goblin* and *Shadow: Dead Riot*. Disc two features a half-hour tribute video to Fulci entitled "Tempus Fugit", with a variety of luminaries including Dario Argento (via phone), Luigi Cozzi, Claudio Simonetti, Ray Lovelock, writer Antonio Tentori and others sharing their memories of the director, albeit most of them briefly given the compact running time. Lovelock gets more breathing room in a separate 16-minute piece reflecting on his work with the director, and it's a nice companion piece to his appearances on previous Italian genre releases. (Someone should do a comprehensive interview on all of his horror and sexploitation roles, pronto!) Pinori also returns for a video interview, mostly rehashing material from the commentary but also covering his views on the entire industry as a whole during a period when Italian horror was generally considered to be going downhill (and is now unfortunately pretty much extinct). Other extras include a small photo gallery of promotional art and a continuous selection of Fulci trailers. Various editions were put out in Germany by Cult Cinema Intenational and X-Rated Kult, all of which included the same scant few extras, and forced German subtitles on the English and Italian soundtrack options included alongside the German dub version.

THE NAKED BUNYIP

Colour, 1970, 139m. / Directed by John B. Murray / Starring Graeme Blundell, Barry Humphries, Gordon Rumph, Russell Morris / Umbrella (Australia R0 PAL)

It's only fitting that the Australian film industry as we know it began with a sexploitation movie. Other movie-making countries were generating fortunes with pseudo-documentaries about public attitudes towards sex (including popular, unsimulated "demonstrational" documentaries), so a bunch of Aussies got together and decided to lampoon the trend with this goofy outing, which hinges on the fictional framing story of young Graeme Blundell (later a sex comedy star in his own right as *Alvin Purple*) going around Melbourne finding out what the average citizen does between the sheets. Along with familiar faces like Dame Edna, he uncovers the truth about cross-dressing, strippers, lesbianism, swinging, and pretty much everything else you can think of, though it's all depicted in a carefree manner. The running time is way, way too long, but if you want to see a new spin on sex-ed moviemaking, this should be just the ticket.

The full frame DVD preserves the original aspect ratio (it was shot in 16mm, of course) and certainly shows its vintage, but all things considered, it's fine. The region-free disc includes a satisfying slice of extras to put it all in context, including a half-hour featurette called "A Funny Sort of Way" with the cast, director and producer (including a very funny Humphries) talking about the film's censorship history, plus a reel of mild deleted footage, an excruciating single version of the theme song, the trailer, and promotional photos.

An ambitious and unorthodox contemporary offering from Redemption, this British blend of psychological thriller and kinkfest uses a variety of locales and subplots to craft something that feels like a cracked collision of Umberto Eco and Bruno Mattei. The gimmicky plot revolves around a globe-hopping serial killer who's offed ten of the models who sat for a noted painter, and when the artist himself turns up dead, an American investigator (Troy McFadden) and an art expert (Carole Derrien) stumble from France to Thailand into a dark world of depraved sex, dominance, cavalier murder, and sadism.

Surprisingly stylish given the very low budget, the film also sports a strange and sometimes striking score by Siouxsie and the Banshees vet Steven Severin, and director Paul Burrows shows a sure hand dealing with the disparate elements of the story, which culminate in a wild and harrowing final act. The film suffers a bit due to the flat-looking, non-anamorphic transfer, but don't let that scare you away. The stereo audio fares better and extras include a reel of disposable but interesting deleted scenes with an intro and commentary by the director, a trailer, a stills gallery, and a few minutes of inconsequential outtakes, as well as a promo for the soundtrack release. Definitely worth checking out if you like your chills splashed with a dose of erotica and art, and it comes with an enthusiastic printed endorsement from Jess Franco!

NATURE MORTE

Colour, 2006, 89m. / Directed by Paul Burrows / Starring Troy McFadden, Carole Derrien, Laurent Guyon, Jeso Vial / Redemption (UK R0 PAL, US R0 NTSC) / WS (1.85:1) / DD2.0

NECROVILLE

Colour, 2007, 99m. / Directed by Billy Garberina & Richard Griffin / Starring Adam Jarmon Brown, Billy Garberina, Mark Chavez, Brandy Bluejacket / Shock-O-Rama (US R0 NTSC) / WS (1.78:1) (16:9)

The New Mexico-shot *Necroville* does the instant cult thing better than most (read: Troma) in what amounts to a DIY version of *Clerks* crossed with *Buffy the Vampire Slayer*. In the titular town, supernatural beasties like zombies and vampires are running rampant; enter Zom-B-Gone, where two former video clerks, Jack (co-director Billy Garberina) and Alex (Adam Jarmon Brown from *Creature from the Hillbilly Lagoon*), find work dispatching these oversized pests. Meanwhile Jack's unbearable shrew of a girlfriend has them wondering whether she might be involved in these dark proceedings, especially when her sinister ex comes back to town carrying a grisly secret of his own.

Definitely entertaining in an undemanding, beer-chugging sort of way, *Necroville* packs in the monster FX and goop-spewing highlights with utter glee, especially the finale which justifiably receives a mention of its own in the back cover synopsis. It's almost worth a rental just by itself. The two leads tend to mug it up, but considering they all brought this in for a reputed 10 grand, that's a minor complaint. Several of the one-liners are genuinely funny, and some of the set pieces (including one in a sorority house and an inspired bit involving a piano, whose genesis is even explained in the liner notes) are guaranteed to grab the attention of any horror fan.

The Shock-O-Rama DVD comes packed as usual, this time with a commentary by co-director Richard Griffin (who helmed *Splatter Disco* the same year), a batch of bloopers and cut scenes, a goof-off reel with actor Mark Chavez, a featurette on the cheap but often impressive effects, two silly short films from the same crew ("Legend of Aerreus Kane" and "Cumuppance"), bonus horror-related trailers (several from the same crew), and the aforementioned liner notes booklet, which is an amusing read unto itself.

NEXT OF KIN

Colour, 1982, 89m. / Directed by Tony Williams / Starring Jackie Kerin, John Jarratt, Alex Scott / Reel (Australia R0 PAL), X-Rated Kult (Germany R2 PAL) / WS (1.78:1) (16:9) / DD2.0

Reliable Aussie leading man John Jarratt heads up this atmospheric and, in its third act, downright horrifying little gem. The spooky premise places young Linda (Jackie Kerin) in Montclare, a rest home for the elderly she's inherited from her recently deceased mother. While she's busy striking up a romance with local guy Barney, one of the aged residents drowns in his bath, and soon lots of inexplicable events are setting her on edge. When she finds her mother's diary, Linda finds an unnerving parallel between events of decades past and the macabre goings-on in her own life, which finally explode during the blood-spattered climax.

While the opening two-thirds of this film constitute more of a tense psychological thriller than a flat-out horror film, the payoff is worth the wait as all the details culminate in a furious, stylishly-shot riot of violence and mayhem. The plot itself carries a few nifty surprises, too, so be sure to pay attention. Nearly impossible to find now outside its native country, this is well worth seeking out. The DVD edition from Reel offers a very attractive anamorphic transfer but nothing in the way of extras. In lieu of this somewhat difficult to find Australian disc, fans may want to hunt down the X-Rated Kult German release (with two different covers under its original title and

Montclare – Erbe des Grauens) which contains a faux stills gallery (frame grabs), some publicity stills and poster art, a nine-second snippet from the U.S. master missing from the German print, and a newly-created German trailer.

NIGHT OF DEATH!

Colour, 1980, 94m. / Directed by Raphaël Delpard / Starring Isabelle Goguey, Charlotte de Turckheim, Betty Beckers, Michel Debrane, Ernest Menzer, Michel Duchezeau / Synapse (US R1 NTSC) / WS (1.66:1) (16:9)

After a spat with her boyfriend Serge (Michel Duchezeau), pretty young Martine (Isabelle Goguey) takes a job working as the new nurse at Deadlock House, a creepy retirement home with an abnormally high staff turnover. The other nurse, Nicole (Charlotte de Turckheim), seems nice enough, but the head administrator Hélène (Betty Beckers) is more than a little odd, treating her charges sternly while referring to them as "warriors" and continuously playing one song on the piano. One night Nicole is chased down a hallway by the crazed residents who turn out to be quite a bit older than they appear… and they all like to consume human flesh, with Nicole as their latest banquet. However, when one of the cannibals ignores the rules and makes off with the young girl's heart, the group threatens to tear itself apart with feuding… and Martine is running out of time before they choose her as their next meal.

While Jean Rollin was certainly the most important French horror director before the 21st Century, he wasn't the only one. One example is Raphaël Delpard who briefly dabbled behind the camera in the 1980s with a handful of films, most notably

Night of Death! (*La nuit de la mort!*). This one doesn't even try for the poetry or surrealism of Rollin, opting instead for a straightforward gore film with long, static, unsettling camera shots suddenly exploding into creepy chase sequences as young women are pursued up and down hallways and stairways by the leering, middle-aged villains. The real payoff comes in the last fifteen minutes as the majority of the cast is bumped off in an increasingly ridiculous string of bloody attacks that leave hands, heads, and other body parts littering the screen. Unfortunately it also tacks on a completely needless and mean-spirited final shock ripped off from *Castle of Blood*, but otherwise this is good, disreputable, down-and-dirty splatter with a unique French twist.

Though its technical aspirations never rise much above your average Euorciné production, Synapse has treated the first English-friendly release of *Night of Death!* quite nicely with a very solid anamorphic transfer. The mono audio sounds fine, and the creepy soundtrack really gets under the skin enough to merit a separate release on its own someday. Only de Turckheim went on to do much of note, and her scandalously bloody (and extremely naked) early appearance here is totally unlike her more famous respectable fare like Claude Lelouch's *Edith and Marcel* and Volker Schlöndorff's *Swann in Love*. Not surprisingly, it's unlikely she'll ever do a commentary for this film.

NIGHT OF FEAR
Colour, 1972, 58m. / Directed by Terry Bourke / Starring Norman Yemm, Carla Hoogeveen, Mike Dorsey
INN OF THE DAMNED
Colour, 1974, 118m. / Directed by Terry Bourke / Judith Anderson, Alex Cord, Michael Craig, Tony Bonner / Umbrella (Australia R0 PAL) / WS (1.78:1) (16:9)

The name "Terry Bourke" doesn't mean anything to most people, but this obscure filmmaker (who had earlier worked as a production manager on Lindsay Shonteff's *The Million Eyes of Sumuru*) went down in the record books as the first Down Under horror director. *Night of Fear* originally began as the planned pilot episode of a proposed TV series called *Fright*, presumably to compete with the simultaneous (and outstanding) British horror/mystery series, *Thriller*. Needless to say, the harrowing final result proved way too much for the censors. Despite running under an hour, this brutal quickie was shipped off to a few theatres where patrons were left stunned by its unrelenting brutality. With nary a word of dialogue, the film follows the plight of a young woman who wrecks her car out in the middle of nowhere and falls prey to a crazy local, who essentially victimises her for the remainder of the story including a particularly nasty sequence in his basement with lots and lots of rats.

The obvious antecedent to today's "torture porn" craze (as well as the wild backwoods horrors to come throughout the '70s), it's an interesting curio and surprisingly nasty considering its pedigree. *Night of Fear* essentially disappeared after its local release but eventually resurfaced courtesy of a DVD double-bill, looking quite nice with a fresh-looking transfer. Apart from the trailer, the only extra – and it's a good one – is an audio commentary with star Carla Hoogeveen and producer Rod Hay, who talk at length about the furore caused by the film during its difficult initial release.

Best known to moviegoers as the sinister Mrs. Danvers in Alfred Hitchcock's *Rebecca*, stage legend Dame Judith Anderson made her horror debut (and farewell) in this disc's Bourke-helmed co-feature, *Inn of the Damned*, an unlikely hybrid of suspense, sex and spaghetti western, one of the first Aussie shockers to get notable distribution abroad (and even a VHS release from Paragon). The plot follows intrepid hired gun Cal Kincaid (Alex Cord, fresh off *Chosen Survivors* and *The Etruscan Kills Again*) as he investigates a dusty western town where a coachman has a nasty habit of turning his customers over to a pair of homicidal hostel owners (led by Judy) who enjoy killing off their guests. Lots of beautiful scenery, dining, and butt-naked running around pad out the story a bit too much for comfort, but it's certainly a unique attempt at a grisly oater (similar to the much stronger *Cut-Throats Nine*) and worth seeking out for the curious. The Umbrella double feature disc includes a decent audio commentary with actor Tony Bonner and producer Rod Hay, who somehow manage to fill the lengthy running time and talk a lot about the Victorian shooting locations. Again, the anamorphic transfer looks great.

NIGHT OF THE WEREWOLF

Colour, 1980, 92m. / Directed by Paul Naschy (Jacinto Molina) / Starring Paul Naschy, Julia Saly, Silvia Aguilar, Azucena Hernandez / Victory Films, distributed by BCI Eclipse (DVD & Blu-ray, US R0 NTSC/HD) / WS (1.85:1) (16:9) / DD5.1

Unfortunately timed to hit the horror market at the advent of both the slasher boom and the hi-tech werewolf renaissance of *The Howling*, Paul Naschy's inaugural '80s lycanthrope outing,

Night of the Werewolf, was shuffled off to American home video as *The Craving* where it confused countless renters unfamiliar with the history of Naschy's unfortunate shape-shifting hero, Waldemar Daninsky. However, his fans quickly saw through the lousy transfers and haphazard dubbing to recognise one of his finest and most fully-formed efforts, an atmospheric and wonderfully gothic (and thoughtful!) monsterthon that ranks among his finest. In an opening that re-stages the familiar preludes to the likes of *Black Sunday* but this time in broad daylight, bloodthirsty Countess Elizabeth Bathory (Julia Saly) and her lycanthropic servant, Waldemar (Naschy), are sentenced to death by a medieval tribunal who affix a metal mask over the latter's face and a dagger in his heart as additional punishment. Jump forward to the present as thieving interlopers who remove the blade once again free Waldemar to roam the land and watch over the now crumbling area of his grave, awaiting the return of his mistress. Meanwhile three sexy young students arrive, each with different motives; pure-hearted Karen (Azucena Hernandez) once again represents the possible love who could bring an end to Waldemar's monstrous torment, while decadent Erika (Silvia Aguilar) plans to revive Bathory and become her disciple. Before long, the villagers are being attacked by a familiar furry beast, Bathory is slurping down the blood of, uh, non-virgins, and a beastly showdown is quickly brewing.

Aside from utilising much more impressive make-up than usual, Naschy sticks to the tried-and-true Spanish werewolf formula here, approaching his most famous character from the director's chair for the first time as well. He does an excellent job all around, creating a rich and fascinating experience rife with memorable images and a delirious, old-fashioned romanticism. He even gets a mummy in on the action for a handful of brief moments, and the unearthly Saly manages to steal all of her scenes and wipe out any memories of Naschy's past Bathory co-star, Patty Shepard (from *Werewolf Shadow*). As with several other '80s Spanish films, the music consists of a hodgepodge of tracks from the Italian CAM library, with the main titles featuring Stelvio Cipriani's driving, harpsichord-laden theme from 1973's *La polizia sta a guardare* (also recycled in '77 for *Tentacles*).

A gargantuan improvement over all past video versions, BCI's DVD looks radiant throughout with pin-sharp detail and eye-popping colour definition. It's easily one of the most beautiful presentations of a Naschy film on home video to date and most likely better than the few theatrical prints that might be left lying around. Naschy contributes a new, shot-on-video introduction to the film in which he welcomes the viewer and gives a quick bit of context for this release, which is presented in both the (awful) English dub, original Spanish mono with optional English subtitles (the best option), or a re-channelled 5.1 Spanish audio mix which overzealously pumps too much information (including dialogue) into the front and rear channels. The wonderfully ornate menu design also leads you to the rest of the extras including the optional Spanish titles, a long and strangely lethargic European trailer (playable in either Spanish or English), some brief disposable deleted footage from the robber scene, and two mammoth galleries of stills and artwork compiled with the aid of Naschy scholar Mirek Lipinski, who also contributes the stellar liner notes housed within the DVD case. For hi-def fans, this is also available in an even more eye-popping Blu-ray double feature with *Vengeance of the Zombies*, affording you the most crystal-clear Paul Naschy experience possible.

NIGHTHAWKS

Colour, 1978, 113m. / Directed by Ron Peck / Starring Ken Robertson, Tony Westrope, Rachel Nicholas James, Maureen Dolan

STRIP JACK NAKED: NIGHTHAWKS II

Colour, 1991, 91m. / Directed by Ron Peck / BFI (DVD & Blu-ray UK R0 PAL/HD), Water Bearer (US R0 NTSC), Second Sight (UK R0 PAL)

Bearing no relation at all to the Sylvester Stallone action film of the same name, this groundbreaking, atmospheric feature is generally regarded as the first realistic British film to deal with gay life in the 1970s. While 1961's excellent thriller *Victim* played some part in bringing down the U.K.'s criminalisation of homosexuality, the subject itself had largely become the domain of blackly comic farces (*Entertaining Mr. Sloane*) or experimental exercises in surrealism (early Derek Jarman, especially *Sebastian*). Though its importance might seem muted today, *Nighthawks* was startling at the time as a state of the union snapshot for gay culture, showing the status quo and making a jolting third-act argument for progress yet to be undertaken. Lensed under the auspices of the British Film Institute, Ron Peck's film is bathed in an eerie, nocturnal ambience scored with hypnotic electronic music, including a haunting sequence which hones in on the male lead's eyes for several minutes as he stands in a club. This character is Jim (*Flash Gordon*'s Ken Robertson), a schoolteacher forced to hide his sexuality at work who goes out on a few façade-building dates with women while in fact flitting from one frustrating male encounter to another. His frustration builds until he finally unloads his feelings in the classroom, paving the way for an ambiguous conclusion.

Skilfully avoiding the pitfalls of Hollywood films on the same subject, which tend to drown in preachiness (the dire *Philadelphia*) or camp (*Staircase*), Peck's film was surprisingly marketed as a commercial venture instead of a fringe art house release and has actually dated rather well. The simple denim-oriented fashions are a smart choice (often mirrored in the heavy waves of blue light suffusing most of the major scenes), and Robertson holds his own as the lead through a string of difficult dramatic scenes. The film proved influential enough to inspire a whole wave of '80s indie films around the world (including a virtual but more explicit remake, *Taxi zum Klo*, and realistic AIDS-era efforts like *Parting Glances*), even if the careers of everyone involved didn't receive much of a boost from this production.

However, Peck did eventually return to the same territory thirteen years later with an unusual "sequel", *Strip Jack Naked*, a sort of video confessional mixed with a making-of about *Nighthawks* (including outtakes and press snippets). Shot and edited on standard def video, it's a compelling snapshot of British gay life from the '70s to the '90s even if it's wholly reliant on seeing the first film to make any sense out of the proceedings.

Both films have circulated on home video on VHS and DVD in a variety of guises, but the only really satisfactory one comes directly from the BFI, who retransferred the first film directly from the original 16mm negative for DVD and Blu-ray. The results are surprisingly rich and vibrant, leaping ahead of past transfers by leaps and bounds while maintaining the grain and grit of the original photography. The nightclub scenes, which were murky and muted on past editions are now pulsating and crisply detailed, and the dialogue is much sharper and easier to understand. *Strip Jack Naked* is still standard def in both BFI editions given the nature of the source, but that's as it should be.

While Peck doesn't appear on the release himself, the BFI archives have unleashed a nice assortment of his short films including "Its Ugly Head", "On Allotments", "Edward Hopper" (a snapshot of the famous artist), the amusing political jab of "What Can I Do with a Male Nude?", "The Last Biscuit", and "Pilot – Opening Sequence". Peck, James Leggott and Carla Mitchell contribute critical notes and reminiscences to the illustrated 74-page booklet as well; no matter what kind of player you have, this is one of the BFI's most rewarding releases and well worth the investment.

NIGHTMARE CASTLE

B&W, 1965, 104m. / Directed by Mario Caiano / Starring Barbara Steele, Paul Muller, Helga Liné, Lawrence Clift, Rik Battaglia / Severin (US R1 NTSC) / WS (1.66:1) (16:9), Retromedia (US R0 NTSC) / WS (1.66:1), Madacy (US R0 NTSC)

Made at the height of Italy's golden age of gothic horror, *Nightmare Castle* has long been one of the most widely-available titles on home video since the days of VHS, largely thanks to the public domain status of its much-abbreviated American version. Horror fans have long cherished it as perhaps the ultimate visual tribute to its leading lady and Italy's first real scream queen, Barbara Steele, who had already captivated viewers with her sinister, uncanny beauty in films like *Black Sunday*, *The Horrible Dr. Hichcock* and *Castle of Blood*. Add to that some heaping dollops of sadism and you've got an instant drive-in

classic which has nevertheless fared very poorly in every version released on home video... with one huge exception.

The story is extremely basic gothic fare with a bit of E.C. Comics nastiness thrown in, as the opening twenty minutes deftly outlines the final hours of the unhappy marriage between aristocratic scientist Stephen Arrowsmith (Jess Franco regular Paul Muller) and his bitchy, raven-haired wife, Muriel (Steele), who engages in secret trysts with the hunky handyman, David (peplum regular Rik Battaglia). Hubby catches them in the act and, in a string of scenes that push the boundaries of nastiness and kinkiness about as far as '65 cinema would allow, chains them up to a wall, whips them, splashes some well-placed drops of acid, ties Muriel to a bed, electrocutes them both in mid-embrace, and slices out their hearts while burning the rest of them to potted plant ashes. Unfortunately Muriel tells him just before dying that she secretly changed her will and left all of her fortune to her "idiot" stepsister, Jenny. Undeterred, he ignores the attentions of his elderly, evil housekeeper, Solange (Eurosleaze favourite Helga Liné), whom he rejuvenates with some kind of blood experiments, and swiftly marries the nervous, blonde-haired Jenny (also Steele), whom he brings home in lieu of a honeymoon. (The fact that these "stepsisters" look exactly the same is never really addressed by the script, by the way.) Soon Jenny's having bizarre nightmares and wandering around the castle a lot, while the mad scientist's plot to drive her insane is complicated by what might be the ghosts of his recently dispatched victims.

Though shot in black and white and filmed in atmospheric locations, *Nightmare Castle* doesn't even try for the artistic heights of Steele's collaborations with directors like Mario Bava or Riccardo Freda. Instead director Mario Caiano (here using the name "Allan Grünewald") shoots everything in flat medium shots, with a pokey pace probably modelled after Roger Corman's Poe films. Steele's Jenny character is almost hilariously dull (and saddled with a really terrible wig), but thankfully the bad Barbara pops up enough at the beginning and end to keep her fans more than happy. Oddly enough, none other than Ennio Morricone provides the music score (just one year after his breakthrough work on *A Fistful of Dollars*) with organs and tinkling pianos flooding almost every scene, which manages to goose up several stretches in the film's midsection where essentially nothing happens. Old pros Muller and Liné do fine, sinister work all around (at least after the latter ditches her embarrassing "old age" make-up from the first couple of scenes), and the claustrophobic nature of the film (not to mention its incredibly small cast) does set it apart somewhat from its more flamboyant peers. Oddly, this proved to be Steele's last major Italian vehicle to get wide distribution (not counting the weird hybrid *The She Beast* or the barely-seen *An Angel for Satan*), though at least in this case she gets to finally provide her own voice for Jenny's character.

It would take an insane amount of space to recount all of the video incarnations of *Nightmare Castle* over the years, but here's what you really need to know. The film was originally put out in Italy as *Amanti d'oltre-tomba* (or "Lovers from Beyond the Tomb") running 104 minutes, and a full English dub for this edition was created. However, the international distributors mostly went with a drastically shortened version (as *Nightmare Castle*), clocking in well under an hour and a half, which excised many of the film's pregnant pauses and castle wanderings, as well as a few quick seconds of sadism during the opening act. Some U.K. viewers did get to see the longer cut under the title of *The Night of the Doomed*, but for the VHS era almost everyone was stuck with the short version

with really, really hideous video and audio quality. Several PD companies rehashed this version again on DVD, often packed together alongside other vintage horror titles (like Madacy's double bill with *Track of the Vampire*). Retromedia improved things a bit with the first domestic release of the European version under the perplexing title of *The Faceless Monster*, a flat letterboxed edition that would have been great if it weren't for some very distracting compression problems, a distorted running time due to dodgy PAL conversion, a soft and damaged transfer, loads of video crosstalk through the entire picture, and, to copyright it as a "special edition", layers of newly-added sound effects (crickets, wind, howling dogs, etc.) plastered through several scenes.

The odds of an officially sanctioned, top-grade version of this film thus seemed ridiculously unlikely, but Severin has managed to surprise everyone with their release, taken straight from the original Italian negative and looking light years better than it ever has before. Bear in mind this film was never shot with the crystalline intensity of something like *Black Sunday*, but the presentation here is impressive indeed. The blacks are rich and deep, facial details are pin-sharp, and the landscaping around the castle is now clear and free of jittering and distortion. Some fleeting damaged splices appear at a couple of scene transitions (and one notable negative tear at the 58 minute mark), but that's extreme nitpicking in what is otherwise a superlative presentation. Thankfully this transfer was preserved in HD, which means we might even see a Blu-ray of it someday if we're lucky. The audio also runs at the correct speed and sounds clearer than before, though frankly the dub track is still pretty lousy even if the actors were obviously speaking English on the set. That aural disconnect has often been cited by fans as part of its charm, however, so perhaps that's just as well. The Italian credits are also preserved with the original title card.

If the tremendously improved transfer weren't enough of a carrot to get fans moving, the disc also packs in some excellent bonus features. The notoriously supplement-shy Steele has finally started appearing on some of her releases (including the aforementioned *The She Beast* for an amusing commentary track), and here she devotes an entire featurette, "Barbara Steele in Conversation", to an encapsulation of her career from start to finish. It's a dream come true for Steele fans as she discusses her early modelling days, her libertine experiences in boarding school, her miserable experience working for 20th Century-Fox on the Elvis vehicle *Flaming Star*, her big break in Italian films (not just the horror ones), her memories of working with Fellini on *8½* (including a hilarious anecdote about an Antonioni gag left on the cutting room floor), her segue into '70s exploitation immortality working on the first films of Jonathan Demme and David Cronenberg, and finally her unlikely ventures into producing with Dan Curtis and her frustrating recurring roles on the revamp of *Dark Shadows*. Perhaps most valuable of all is her account of shooting scenes as a sexual alchemist for Fellini's *Casanova*, only to have the original footage stolen and the film started over from scratch. The avalanche of rare, priceless Steele images is just icing on the cake, too. You really can't miss this one. Next up is "Black, White and Red", with Caiano appearing in a newly-shot interview along with his very aggressive orange cat for a discussion mostly centred around *Nightmare Castle*, including the explanation behind his perplexing screen credit, his affinity for Poe which exploded throughout the script of this film, and his limited recollections of Steele. Never one of Italy's more distinguished directors, Caiano nevertheless remained busy working on everything from sword and

sandal quickies to spaghetti westerns to oddities like *Nazi Love Camp 27, The Fighting Fists of Shanghai Joe* and *Nosferatu in Venice*, so it's nice to finally get the story behind the career of someone who seems like a good-natured craftsman. Finally you get a pristine U.K. trailer (under the *Night of the Doomed* title) and a much fuzzier U.S. trailer (as *Nightmare Castle*) which is essentially just a chopped-down version of the first one. In short, it's an obvious must for Euro horror fans and especially important for restoring one of the last mistreated titles in the Steele canon. Now if someone could just finally manage to release an uncut, pristine version of *Terror-Creatures from the Grave*...

NIGHTWATCHING

Colour, 2007, 134m. / Directed by Peter Greenaway / Starring Martin Freeman, Jodhi May, Emily Holmes, Michael Teigen, Michael Culkin, Eva Birthistle / E1 (US R1 NTSC), Paradise Digital (Russia R5 NTSC), Axiom (UK R2 PAL) / WS (2.35:1) (16:9) / DD5.1

After the sprawling and mostly ignored indulgences of his still-obscure *Tulse Luper Suitcases* series, director Peter Greenaway thankfully decided to go back to basics with this atmospheric mystery revolving around the creation of one of the world's most famous paintings, Rembrandt's "The Night Watch". As with all of Greenaway's more recent output, this one has had extreme difficulty finding distribution outside the usual festival circuit, but it's easily his most satisfying piece of work of the past decade. In the startling opening sequence, a shadowy group of men waving torches in the darkness assault and temporarily blind

Rembrandt (*The Office*'s Martin Freeman). The story then flashes back to find the bawdy Rembrandt living with his pregnant wife, Saskia (Eva Birthistle). As Holland's most prestigious painter, he's commissioned to create a group portrait of Amsterdam's musketeer militia. When one of the musketeers is killed in a military "accident", the painter suspects foul play and begins to investigate, slipping clues into his painting to create an indictment of the guilty parties. Unfortunately, this tactic exposes more than he expected (including a particularly perverse brothel), and the conspiracy manipulates one of his servants, Geertje (Jodhi May), into contributing to his downfall.

A staggeringly beautiful film, *Nightwatching* wisely drops the hyperactive digital image layering which consumed Greenaway's more recent work. Instead, the narrative (which often deliberately recalls his first feature, the lush art-history thriller *The Draughtsman's Contract*) serves as a more linear structure than usual with a feisty lead performance by Freeman, who imbues the entire project with a welcome amount of lusty humour, energy and soul. Greenaway also includes some welcome elements of other past works (the dark, beautifully-lit stage tableaux from *The Baby of Mâcon*, the Dutch painting obsessions from *A Zed & Two Noughts*, the elaborate and often lewd banquets from *The Cook, the Thief, His Wife and Her Lover*, the birth and creation/destruction motifs of *The Belly of an Architect*), and thankfully Greenaway has finally gone back to using an original score, this time by Wlodek Pawlik with a few potent quotations from Giovanni Solamar. Newcomers probably won't find much to latch onto here, but those lamenting the absence of a really juicy film from the director should find plenty to enjoy. And no one has ever managed to make shots of sweeping torches in the dark look creepier.

Since most viewers will probably never have a chance to see this in a theatre, the DVD releases make for an adequate alternative. The anamorphic transfer used for the releases looks satisfying throughout; some digital distortion is evident in the opening and closing credits, but overall the powerful chiaroscuro lighting effects are captured beautifully. The powerful 5.1 surround mix (in English) is subtle but effective as well, often echoing the unnerving ambient surround effects found in *Cook*. (A 5.1 Russian-dubbed version is also included on the Paradise disc along with optional Russian subtitles). The two-disc U.S. release sweetens the deal with a second DVD containing *Rembrandt's J'accuse*, an ambitious making-of-via-symbolic-rumination on the themes of the film with the director and cast expounding further upon its provocative key ideas. The same two-disc edition was later issued in the U.K. by Axiom Films.

NUDE IN DRACULA'S CASTLE
B&W, 308m. / Secret Key (US R0 NTSC)

A woman does disrobe and a few ghoulish characters do pop up in *Nude in Dracula's Castle*, but anyone expecting a cavalcade of short films combining cheesecake and horror is bound to be confused by this two-disc collection which turns out to be yet another grab bag of random 8mm nudie cutie shorts found in some abandoned theatre basement. All of them appear to be shot sometime between the mid-1950s into the 1960s, though any release years or talent credits will obviously never be confirmed.

The title short starts everything off on a promising note as a sexy young thing goes to spend the night at a creepy old house where she spends the evening running around scantily clad as various blood-suckers and creatures of the night keep popping out to scare her. That's it for the scare quotient though as the subsequent loops just involve smiling women dropping various articles of clothing and shimmying around for the camera, which may be enough for some consumers.

For the record, the remaining titles are "Lynda" (which is surprisingly explicit for its age), "Lusty and Young", "Marty", "Brandi", "Blonde and Spunky", "Red Hot and Ready", "Luscious for You", "Innocent and Willing" (also notably strong), "Groovy for You", "Candy", "Old Fashion", "Spunky and Loving It", "The Smiling Blonde", "Cute and Curly", "Margie", "Sweet and Bored", "Bed Manners", "A Little Tipsy", "More from the Pillow", "Beached Mermaid", "More than a Wink", "The Shave", "Eros POB 813 Copenhagen", "Beauty and the Beach", "Double Your Pleasure", "Cynthia", "Beauties Bathing", "On the Road to You", "Blonde Swinger", "Missy", "Close to You", "Sweet and Anxious" and "Queen for a Night". All are presented full frame and look dingy and scratchy, exactly as you'd expect. The built-in audience for vintage loops like this get exactly what they'd expect.

THE NUDE VAMPIRE

Colour, 1970, 85m. / Directed by Jean Rollin / Starring Olivier Martin, Caroline Cartier, Maurice Lemaitre, Ly Lestrong, Jean Aron / Redemption (UK R0 PAL, US R0 NTSC), Nocturna (Spain R2 PAL) / WS (1.66:1)

Following the nearly plotless black-and-white gothic mayhem of his first film, *The Rape of the Vampire*, director Jean Rollin returned to bloodsuckers again for a far more visually extreme variation that still stands apart from the rest of his filmography. Though his trademark obsessions with beachscapes and aesthetic nudity are still in evidence, the ultra-saturated colour schemes and mad scientist motifs instead feel like some sort of unholy mash-up between *Barbarella* and *The Diabolical Dr. Z* (and almost never like a traditional horror film). The film kicks off with a group of hooded scientists doing something nefarious with their Bunsen burners and brightly-coloured beakers, while others in their cult run around in animal masks and chase passing pedestrians. During all of this mayhem, young Pierre (Olivier Martin) is captivated by a scantily-clad woman (Caroline Cartier) who winds up being apprehended by the sect, which turns out to be a more sinister and deadly group than they first appeared. Visitors commit suicide, blood drinking is involved, and as usual, it all winds up with haunted characters wandering along a beach as their mortality comes back to bite them in the neck.

Though the pacing of *The Nude Vampire* is still recognisably Rollin-esque, this film may prove easier for newcomers to swallow as its story veers from one oddball element to the next. Leopardskin fabrics, party masks, and lots of teasing partial skin shots set this one firmly in 1970, and as a mod French art film gone berserk, it's plenty of fun. Rollin mixes the sci-fi and gothic elements together without really trying to scare anyone, but his poetic touch keeps the entire enterprise from becoming a nasty collision of contrasting styles. The actors aren't required to do much beyond drifting around and acting as clotheshorses, but the limited Martin makes a reasonable enough protagonist whose past causes him to slowly unravel as the film unspools.

Among all of Rollin's horror films on home video, *The Nude Vampire* has easily suffered the rockiest history. Decent video prints have been hellishly difficult to obtain, and even the DVD era has proven wildly erratic. A non-anamorphic Spanish disc contained the dubbed English track (which is a disappointment, but the film only contains about 10-15 minutes of dialogue at the most), and the French-language British edition with English subtitles isn't much of a visual improvement. For some reason, Redemption's North American DVD fudges the release by including only the English dub again, and the transfer's non-anamorphic, which is quite bizarre at this stage in the digital game. (The film's negative was in Redemption's possession, so there has to be more of a story behind this.) That said, colours look bold and bright, and the framing appears accurate enough if you don't mind zooming in a bit on a widescreen TV set. The English dialogue doesn't sound particularly well-mixed, often fluctuating wildly in volume compared to the music and effects track. As far as extras go, you get both the French and English theatrical trailers, a plotless and artsy early short film from Rollin ("Les Amours Jaunes") centred around the beach (of course), stills galleries for the feature and short, and the usual Redemption cross-promoting trailers and book promo.

OASIS OF FEAR

Colour, 1971, 90m. / Directed by Umberto Lenzi / Starring Ray Lovelock, Ornella Muti, Irene Papas, Michel Bardinet / Shameless (UK R0 PAL), Alan Young (Italy R2 PAL) / WS (2.35:1) (16:9)

While traipsing across Italy, young couple Dick (Ray Lovelock) and Ingrid (Ornella Muti) make a little cash by selling naked pictures of the latter and spend their time partying at clubs.

After tangling with some dangerous gypsy bikers, they decide to refuel their car by swiping petrol from the home of a NATO officer but are caught by his wife Barbara (Irene Papas) who nevertheless allows them to stay in the home and puts up with their wild behaviour, even submitting to Dick's scruffy charms. However, the next day reveals a considerably more complicated and deadly plan at work with the roles of victim and predator shifting numerous times.

Also released as *Dirty Pictures* and *An Ideal Place to Kill* (the latter a translation of its Italian title, *Un posto ideale per uccidere*), this extremely entertaining yet very nasty *giallo* is yet another narrative experiment for director Umberto Lenzi, who would also toy extensively with the genre's conventions in such films as *Paranoia* and *Spasmo*. He deftly uses his three leads (all fine performances) to contrast the European attitudes between old and young, rich and "hippie", revealing faults with each and offering a finale whose message is quite open to interpretation. Muti (whose nude scenes use an obvious body double) is captivating in one of her earlier lead roles, while Papas and Lovelock (both on the cusp of recognition in *Don't Torture a Duckling* and *The Living Dead at Manchester Morgue*, respectively) have plenty of moments to shine. A guiltier pleasure is the catchy score by Bruno Lauzi whose infectious theme song, "How Can You Live", gets a thorough workout from start to finish.

While this first appeared on DVD in Italy with no English options, the same base transfer (watchable and with decent colour, but noticeably soft and gritty throughout) was used by Shameless for a more definitive edition containing the English dub track and additional video sources to assemble a longer, more definitive cut of the film. Some Italian-only snippets are reinstated here with English subtitles, and a brief but startling moment with Papas's body double getting intimate with Lovelock has been added as well (all from noticeably inferior sources, as are the English opening credits). However, completists with the old Greek tape may note a handful of alternative and extended (usually not essential) shots exclusive to that version, so a true, 100% integral edition has yet to appear and may not even be possible. Extras on the Shameless disc include an additional subtitle "trivia commentary" track compiled by Kevin and Nicholas Wilson (it's quite funny and interesting), a newly-created trailer, and promos for additional Shameless titles. A hearty recommendation, especially considering the company's thankful consumer-friendly prices.

ÖLÜLER KONUSMAZKI

B&W, 1970, 67m. / Directed by Yavuz Yalinkiliç / Starring Aytekin Akkaya, Oya Evintan, Dogan Tamer, Giray Alpan, Jirayir Çarkçı

ASKA SUSAYANLAR SEKS VE CINAYET

Colour, 1972, 58m. / Directed by Mehmet Aslan / Starring Meral Zeren, Yildirim Gencer, Kadir Inanir, Eva Bender / Onar (Greece R0 PAL)

While Turkish cinema has already gained a wide fan reputation for its wild imitations of popular Hollywood movies, TV shows and comic books, this fascinating double bill sheds some light on their equally colourful appropriations of Italian horror conventions as well. First up is 1970's black and white(!) offering, *Ölüler Konusmazki*, translated as *The Dead Don't Talk*. It's an entertaining approximation of the previous decade's gothic horror offerings, particularly titles like *Castle of Blood*, *The Virgin of Nuremberg* and *Tomb of Torture*. The plot,

such as it is, follows a young couple, Melih (Aytekin Akkaya) and Oya (Oya Evintan), who take shelter at a spooky old house-turned-B&B which they have inherited. Their sinister host (Dogan Tamer) informs them in his bass-heavy voice that they're welcome for the night, but soon they're being assailed by a creepy ghoul who enjoys appearing at windows and cackling or chasing the guests down hallways. Then more visitors arrive, providing even more fodder for a seemingly endless night of terror. Both conventional and yet wholly bizarre, *The Dead Don't Talk* refuses to explain itself and develop any of the characters, instead prowling the camera around to soak up the gothic atmosphere. The monochromatic look pays tribute to everything from Bava to TV's *Thriller* to Hammer Films (and even AIP programmers like *The Headless Ghost*), all on a super-cheap budget. Add some liberal soundtrack sprinklings from then-recent American hits like *2001: A Space Odyssey* and *Rosemary's Baby*, and you've got the recipe for one seriously deranged homegrown offering.

However, the real jackpot here is nothing less than a bona fide Turkish *giallo*, *Aska Susayanlar Seks Ve Cinayet*, or as it's translated on the packaging, *Thirsty for Love, Sex and Murder*. As anyone who's seen the trailer could already tell, this is a close copy of Sergio Martino's 1970 classic, *The Strange Vice of Mrs. Wardh*. Yep, they even manage to find stars who look like Turkish versions of Edwige Fenech and George Hilton! The setup here is almost identical to Martino's, with a married woman (Meral Zeren) fiddling away her time by going to catfight-packed parties, tolerating her dull-as-dirt husband, entertaining a lover on the side (Yildirim Gencer), and quivering in fear from a mysterious sunglasses-wearing stalker. Many highlights from the Martino film are carried over here (including the memorable slo-mo rain assault), but director Mehmet

Aslan (who also helmed the delirious *Tarkan vs. the Vikings*, available from Mondo Macabro) also comes up with a few nifty stylish flourishes of his own, such as a shower stabbing that assaults the camera with a gushing river of water that turns into blood. He also pulls out the stops during a flashy car garage pursuit scene that works quite well given the production's limited means. The entire cast is much more attractive than usual for a Turkish production, which is a good thing given the amount of topless nudity on display. This time the soundtrack samples directly from its sources, with Ennio Morricone getting a thorough workout from start to finish.

Rescuing both films from the brink of extinction (with no surviving film elements and hard-to-find tape masters), Onar gives them a new lease of life with one of the most entertaining and essential world horror releases. Both titles are only as good as the original masters, of course; *The Dead Don't Talk* looks rather soft and drab, but it's watchable enough and better than many other tape-sourced Turkish titles. However, the compression used here is rather unforgiving, as backgrounds tend to look too crunchy for comfort. *Thirsty* fares better, though the original element was obviously damaged by more than a few screenings before its eventual sourcing to tape. Then again, pristine image quality isn't the point here (and never was for Turkish genre releases); you can finally see these ultra-obscure gems with optional English subtitles to boot. Also included are mouth-watering trailers for other Onar releases like *Tarzan Istanbul'da*, *Demir Yumruk Devler Geliyor* and *Superman Donuyor*, plus poster and lobby card galleries and bios for both directors. Leading man Akkaya also appears for a 45-minute video interview in which he discusses the film and his career, which ranges from the instant cult favourite *3 Dev Adam* to a surprising roster of international productions. *Turkish Fantastic Cinema* co-authors Metin

Demirhan and Giovanni Scognamillo appear for separate, shorter interviews (both sporting copious facial hair) to provide an overview of Turkish horror cinema from its early B&W days to the present.

OM SHANTI OM

Colour, 2007, 162m. / Directed by Farah Khan / Starring Shahrukh Khan, Deepika Padukone, Arjun Rampal, Kirron Kher / Eros (DVD & Blu-ray, India R0 NTSC/HD) / WS (2.35:1) (16:9) / DD5.1

 A razzle-dazzle supernatural musical epic, this love letter to Bollywood cinema makes an excellent intro to newcomers and a reference-packed delight for seasoned fans. Following her successful debut feature, *Main Hoon Na*, choreographer-turned-director Farah Khan gets the perfect balance here between a compelling, surprise-filled storyline and a string of eye-popping, extremely catchy musical numbers.

In the 1970s, goofy movie extra Om Prakash Makhija (Shahrukh Khan) dreams of becoming a big star and performing alongside the woman of his dreams, superstar Shanti (Deepika Padukone), who is married to a selfish producer named Mukesh (Arjun Rampal). As the two strike up a rapport, he learns that Shanti is pregnant and her husband isn't exactly thrilled when she pays attention to other men. It's difficult to discuss the film any further without major spoilers, but let's just say that the second half takes place in the present day and involves murder, a tremendous inferno, reincarnation, ghosts both real and fake, and a spectacular finale reminiscent of *The Phantom of the Opera*.

Along with working perfectly well as a romantic fantasy with thriller elements, *Om*

Shanti Om ladles on plenty of references to the industry's biggest stars; one early musical number digitally composites the actors with vintage performers, while the nearly ten-minute title song offers a parade of current Bollywood faces at a party. Also noteworthy is the hilarious and brilliantly-arranged "Dard-E-Disco" number, a visual ode to Khan's abs and a superior editing achievement to any music video out there. Rather remarkably, the pace never flags for a second during the typically lengthy running time as the performers and directors keep the action flying by at a perfectly-judged clip.

Eros Entertainment's edition of this colourful film is simply one of the best Bollywood demo releases on the market along with Sony's opulent *Saawariya*. Each scene is loaded with vivid shades of red, blue and gold that show off any home theatre to its fullest advantage (with the Blu-ray in particular making for a pure visual knockout). The aggressive 5.1 mix is also loaded with dynamic activity in each channel; optional English subtitles are also included. The release includes a host of teasers and trailers, and a fun behind-the-scenes featurette, while the double-disc DVD also adds on a few negligible deleted scenes.

ONE-EYED MONSTER

Colour, 2008, 84m. / Directed by Adam Fields / Starring Amber Benson, Jason Graham, Charles Napier, Ron Jeremy, Veronica Hart, Jeff Denton / Liberation (US R1 NTSC), Metrodome (UK R2 PAL) / WS (1.78:1) (16:9) / DD5.1

No one could have ever expected that a new reunion of '70s legends Ron Jeremy and Veronica Hart could possibly turn out like *One-Eyed Monster*, a comedic, R-rated horror film about the mayhem unleashed around a remote, snowy cabin when a bunch of people gathered to shoot an adult film are terrorised by a ruthless alien – which has inhabited Ron Jeremy's manhood and is wiping everyone out one by one. (Remember, this has an R rating, so you just get hilarious POV shots of the offending interstellar invader.)

Swift, silly, trashy, and entertaining, this resourceful indie has no redeeming social value at all but makes the most of its simple, incredibly dubious concept. While the basic idea of murderous genitalia has been around since the days of *Soul Vengeance*, this is certainly the first time the conceit has been applied to America's hedgehog reality TV star. It's actually quite atmospheric and really funny if you're in the right mood, and director Adam Fields does a good job of keeping things light and interesting even when people are getting their skulls punched open by a rampaging phallus. If that weren't enough, the cast also includes former *Buffy* regular Amber Benson and everyone's favourite '80s drive-in tough guy character actor, Charles Napier (looking incredibly grizzly and easily stealing the movie with an unforgettable monologue).

The U.S. release and its later U.K. counterpart from Metrodome contain the same anamorphic transfer as well as a half-hour video chat with Jeremy and Hart (which finds the pair reminiscing about their '80s heyday) and an amusing six-minute look at the FX "dick wrangler". However, the U.K. disc contains a separate exclusive video chat with Jeremy, while the American one contains four deleted scenes, "More Celebrity Holes" (a lewd outtake), a batch of teasers and trailers, and an audio commentary track with the Fields siblings about their creation of the film over a very long time period with most of the game participants all too eager to jump in when financing was ready.

THE OTHER SIDE OF UNDERNEATH

Colour, 1972, 106m. / Directed by Jane Arden / Starring Susanka Fraey, Sheila Allen, Liz Danciger, Ann Lynn, Jane Arden / BFI (DVD & Blu-ray, UK R0 PAL/HD)

 Apparently deciding that their first filmic collaboration, 1967's fragmented *Separation*, was simply too accessible and cosy, Jane Arden and Jack Bond hurled themselves into one of the most caustic, abrasive, and daunting British films ever made, which was understandably buried upon its release but returns in the digital era to astonish audiences completely unprepared for its full-on insanity.

After being dragged out of a lake, a nameless young woman (Susanka Fraey) finds herself committed to a countryside group therapy session where the main therapist (Arden) – who doesn't seem so stable herself – guides the female patients through a gruelling series of encounters which slip in and out of reality. Hallucinatory and almost completely lacking in any sort of linear storyline, this film was created with the participation of Arden's Holocaust Theatre Company, an avant garde group of players who cut loose here in sequences of mounting hysteria (the most memorable consisting of a half-naked screaming woman crucified and mounted in the air, an image worthy of *The Devils*). The end result plays something like a terrifying, distaff version of a film by Fernando Arrabal or Alejandro Jodorowsky (yes, it's that far out), and the apparent use of illicit substances on the set contributes to the air of improvised chaos. Think of the insane asylum doc *Titicut Follies* under the influence of mescaline, the only way to begin to describe this harrowing experience.

Working from the original 16mm negative, the BFI has done another wondrous job resuscitating a film consigned to oblivion many years ago. The visual scheme is much darker and messier than the previous *Separation*, but the HD transfer looks terrific all the same without any excessive digital noise reduction on display. The DVD and Blu-ray contain the same material, though it's presented a bit differently; on the former, a quartet of long deleted sequences from the work print are included as a supplement, while the Blu-ray integrates them back as an alternative complete work print version of the main feature if you so desire. (As a result, this alternative cut runs well over two hours, which might be too much for most people's sensibilities.)

Actresses Sheila Allen and Natasha Morgan contribute separate video interviews about the project, and they offer incredibly candid and sometimes very negative appraisals of the experience, which apparently claimed the lives of some participants during and after filming. A typically thorough illustrated booklet features liner notes by Sophie Mayer, Susan Croft and Amy Simmons, with additional vintage Arden pieces written for the theatre group and the play *Vagina Rex and the Gas Oven*, bios of the main cast and crew, and a radio transcript from a 1972 David Will piece about the film. Certainly recommended for those who can handle it, but be warned, this film has very sharp teeth.

PACIFIC BANANA

Colour, 1981, 80m. / Directed by John D. Lamond / Starring Graeme Blundell, Robin Stewart, Deborah Gray, Alyson Best, Luan Peters / Umbrella (Australia R0 PAL) / WS (1.78:1) (16:9)

The only film ever made about sneeze-induced erectile dysfunction, *Pacific Banana* is quite possibly the stupidest sex comedy of all time. This T&A-fest from the director of the lacklustre early Aussie slasher film *Stage Fright* became something of a late night TV staple in the mid-'80s but never had much of a home video life before its unlikely special edition DVD courtesy of the lovably deranged folks at Umbrella. *Alvin Purple*'s Graeme Blundell is surrounded by naked women again, this time as a pilot named Martin who's having erectile problems after being accosted by his boss's horny wife. See, every time he gets excited, he sneezes, and, uh, goes limp. Meanwhile his randy co-pilot, Paul (Robin Stewart from *The Legend of the 7 Golden Vampires*), beds everyone in sight, and they spend most of the movie tangling with a bevy of beautiful women in various Polynesian locales, including *Playboy* Playmate Deborah Gray. Blundell spends a lot of time addressing the camera, particularly after his amorous mishaps (which are accompanied by shots of drooping wind sails), and there's even a pompous narrator thrown in for good measure. Yes, it's the usual sniggering sex-com nonsense, but there's something weirdly endearing about this one, particularly its insidiously catchy theme song ("It wants to go up, up, up; it always goes down, down, down…") and the aforementioned wall-to-wall nudity, making this one of the few of its genre to completely deliver on its promises.

Incredibly, the Australian DVD contains not only an immaculate widescreen transfer but a host of extras as well, including *"Pacific Banana* Unpeeled", a very, very piggy half-hour documentary with John D. Lamond and writer Alan Hopgood reminiscing about the film (not always positively), an additional Lamond featurette entitled "Confessions of an R-Rated Movie Maker", a Gray gallery, the original trailer, and a rare pop single by Gray and her co-star Luan Peters called "Trouble".

PAPAYA: LOVE GODDESS OF THE CANNIBALS

Colour, 1978, 89m. / Directed by Joe D'Amato / Starring Melissa, Sirpa Lane, Maurice Poli / Severin (US R1 NTSC) / WS (1.85:1) (16:9), X-Rated Kult (Germany R2 PAL) / WS (1.85:1)

After leaving his mark on '70s skin cinema with his Black Emanuelle movies, director Joe D'Amato decided to explore his tropical side with a string of Caribbean-based exploitation films mixing sex and violence. Well, mostly the sex. The first and most cohesive of these is *Papaya dei Caraibi* (or *Caribbean Papaya*), also released as the more marketable *Papaya: Love Goddess of the Cannibals*. The film didn't travel much outside of Europe but was a solid enough idea to ensure two follow-ups, *Sesso nero* and *Orgasmo nero*, which upped the ante with the inclusion of some brief hardcore footage. Of course this in turn led to his two apocalyptic fusions of horror and porn, *Erotic Nights of the Living Dead* and *Porno Holocaust*, which turned his island settings into the backdrops for far more extreme antics, but that's another story.

Our humid tale begins as shapely island native Papaya (played by short-lived Italian exploitation actress "Melissa", aka Melissa Chimenti) collaborates with two young native boys to arrange the seduction of a visiting businessman whom she beds and then kills in a sequence that puts the opening murder in *Basic Instinct* to shame. Cut to our main couple, visiting white folk Sara (Sirpa Lane) and Vincent (Maurice Poli), who are enjoying a local cockfight while he plans the construction of a nuclear power plant on the island. That night their steamy post-shower antics are interrupted when she finds a charred body in their room which turns out to be the remains of the guy from the opening scene, a fellow employee. Their distress is soon dissipated when they pick up Papaya in their Jeep and give her a few lusty glances; then they spy her again on the town streets and follow her to a remote building where a voodoo priest urges them to drink some blood-like refreshments as the natives disembowel and devour a big hanging pig, followed by a hapless male's nearby body. Of course it's not long before the naive couple is stripped down and partaking in a frenzied blood ritual (aptly described on the packaging as a "Disco Cannibal Blood Orgy") that goes down in the history book of priceless D'Amato moments. Papaya shows up again soon after and initiates a ménage à trois, but of course there's more than meets the eye as a horrified Sara learns about the displacement of the residents' homes for the power plant and Papaya's devious plan begins to fall into place.

Fuelled by an energetic Stelvio Cipriani score and the alluring presence of the late Sirpa Lane (best known for *The Beast*, Roger Vadim's *Charlotte*, and on a different level entirely, *The Beast in Space*), this is actually a solid primer to D'Amato's style of genre-mashing filmmaking with scenes of softcore moaning and groaning giving way to unexpected grace notes of bloodshed and grotesque visuals. Lane and Melissa make for an uninhibited pair to be sure, and it's a bit strange to see an established mainstream actor like Poli (with credits ranging from *The Longest Day* to leading roles in Mario Bava's *Five Dolls for an August Moon* and *Rabid Dogs*) baring as

much as the ladies. As usual for a D'Amato film from this period, the technical aspects range from the oddly slapdash to some breathtakingly beautiful landscape shots, but then again his fans should already know exactly what to expect.

Anyone thorough enough to even be aware of this film's existence has most likely had to suffer through muddy dupes of the old Italian VHS or the slightly better German DVD edition, which still wasn't English friendly. Severin's disc marks the first official release of the English language version; there isn't a huge amount of dialogue but at least now it's clear what's going on in the second half. The image quality is light years beyond past versions and looks very good overall, though the touch-and-go cinematography varies from crystal clear to somewhat gauzy depending on the scene. The mono audio sounds fine and makes one really wish for a full soundtrack release beyond the few scant cues issued on Italian vinyl back in the '70s. The only extra is the original English trailer which packs in as much nudity and sleaze as possible. A must for D'Amato fans, of course, and a good Euro exploitation treat for anyone else if you know what to expect.

PARTY 7

Colour, 2000, 104m. / Directed by Katsuhito Ishii / Starring Masatoshi Nagase, Yoshio Harada, Tadanobu Asano, Keisuke Horibe, Akemi Kobayashi, Yoshinori Okada / Synapse (US R1 NTSC) / WS (1.85:1) (16:9) / DD5.1

A film designed to its core as an international cult hit, *Party 7* tears right out of the gate with colourful splashes of anime mixed with English-friendly credits and whiplash-inducing shifts in plot and characters. Director Katsuhito Ishii cut his teeth on commercials, and the limited attention span shows throughout as he giddily swerves through the dark, dilapidated Hotel New Mexico where a motley assortment of characters indulge in their most extreme, sometimes fetishistic instincts. The catalyst for all this misbehaviour is Miki (*Mystery Train*'s Masatoshi Nagase), a yakuza wannabe who decides to escape his life of crime by hiding out with a stash of his bosses' money. The "7" of the title refers to our hero and other souls who wander into the hotel, which is overseen by the unique Captain Banana (Yoshio Harada), a peeping tom who likes to dress up in costumes and spy on his guests. Also indulging in this pastime is Okita (Tadanobu Asano), who gets an extra charge when Miki's sugar-daddy-marrying, trout-lipped ex-girlfriend Kana (Akemi Kobayashi) turns up to collect on an old debt; toss in a hit man, a mob boss, and lots of surrealism, and you've got a strangely ingratiating entry in the New Japanese cult canon.

If the synopsis above sounds like a Japanese crime take on Paul Bartel's *Private Parts*, that's not too far off the mark though this is actually more daffy and sweet-natured than one might expect. The kinkiness inherent in the premise is played down in favour of a pop-culture cool vibe, with quirky characters and oddball cutting dictating the bizarre flow of the story. All of the actors do well with their parts, and thankfully this doesn't devolve into an in-your-face screaming orgy like many stabs at modern midnight movie fare. The animation and costume designs are also intriguing, and while the visual scheme tends to rely heavily on that murky, green-hued look that's come to plague many Hollywood productions in recent years, Ishii thankfully injects it with a few colourful cutaways and odd bits of visual business, not the least of which is the Captain Banana suit itself. A sweet and tasty party film, this should find a happy home with viewers looking for something a little different.

Synapse's ongoing library of Asian titles has certainly been eclectic during the history of the DVD format, ranging all the way from low-budget zombie chic films like *Stacy* to undiscovered '60s landmarks like *Horrors of Malformed Men*. God only knows exactly where *Party 7* fits into the grand scheme of things, but the company has rolled it out for American viewers with a lot of bells and whistles. The anamorphic transfer looks excellent (not surprising for a film of a relatively recent vintage) and the 5.1 audio pops and zings exactly where it should, while the optional English subtitles seem fine to these eyes, at least. Extras include a 16-minute interview with the director, who chats with one of the film's more memorable props while covering the film's genesis and its placement among his body of work, which also includes other oddities like *The Taste of Tea* and the memorably-titled *Shark Skin Man and Peach-Hip Girl*. A 20-minute making-of featurette is exactly what you'd expect, basically a long press kit-style piece combining on-set interviews with some choice footage of the director shooting a few scenes. Other extras include a brief alternative ending, a complete storyboard version of the film clocking in at over an hour (shades of Peter Jackson) that most viewers won't survive for more than ten minutes, and a slew of promotional material including two trailers, two TV spots, and a teaser.

PATRICK

Colour, 1978, 112m. / Directed by Richard Franklin / Starring Susan Penhaligon, Robert Helpmann, Rod Mullinar, Bruce Barry / Synapse (US R0 NTSC), Umbrella (Australia R0 NTSC), Optimum (UK R2 PAL), Quinto Piano (Italy R0 PAL), Another World (Denmark R2 PAL) / WS (1.85:1) (16:9), Elite (US R1 NTSC) / WS (1.85:1)

Easily the biggest Australian horror export of the '70s, *Patrick* was obviously conceived as a cash-in on the success of *Carrie* with the added twist that the telekinetic main character this time out is actually in a coma. Turns out he became that way after his mother and her boyfriend were mysteriously killed, and now his nurse believes he's sending her thoughts and even toying with her life. Naturally, all hell breaks loose in the hospital for an FX-filled finale.

Today the film is mainly remembered as the big break for late director Richard Franklin, a Hitchcock disciple (and uncredited director of the first *Fantasm* film), who went on to such beloved '80s cable classics as *Psycho II*, *Cloak & Dagger* and *Link*. Oddly, this film was released in a number of permutations including a PG-rated edited version for the U.S. (excising some brief nude scenes and redubbing all the Aussie accents with American ones), a full-strength 112-minute version (the one on DVD), and an Italian-dubbed version with a great Goblin score substituted over the original one by Brian May. (You can hunt down the Goblin score on Cinevox CD, or it's also included with both the Italian and Danish DVDs.) Elite's discontinued disc features a pretty drab 4x3 letterboxed transfer, but at least it's uncensored; the Synapse reissue is significantly nicer-looking and features the original theatrical trailer and an audio commentary with Franklin and writer Everett de Roche. The U.K. edition from Optimum also utilises this improved version, but for the ultimate *Patrick* experience, Umbrella issued an extensive special edition featuring seven minutes of vintage on-set interviews with the cast and crew, an amusing bit on the terrible U.S. dub job, a stills and poster gallery, the U.S. and Aussie trailers, a pdf story outline for the unproduced sequel "The Man Who Wasn't There", bonus Aussie exploitation trailers from the Umbrella catalogue, and "Coffee Break with Antony I. Ginnane", in which the producer talks about the late Franklin and how he got the young Hitchcock-friendly filmmaker his big break in thriller filmmaking.

THE PERFUME OF YVONNE

Colour, 1994, 90m. / Directed by Patrice Leconte / Starring Jean-Pierre Marielle, Hippolyte Girardot, Sandra Majani, Richard Bohringer / Severin (US R1 NTSC), Second Sight (UK R0 PAL) / WS (2.35:1) (16:9)

Between the successes of *The Hairdresser's Husband* and *Ridicule*, director Patrice Leconte hit a bit of a stumbling block with *The Perfume of Yvonne*, essentially a frothy variation on his previous two films which failed to secure any American distribution and was only seen by most English-speaking viewers via a U.K. DVD. Filmed with the director's usual polish and elegance, it's most interesting as something of a transitional title as well as the most overtly sexual of his mid-period work.

Based on the novel *Villa Triste* by Patrick Modiano, the bulk of the story is told in flashback by Victor (Hippolyte Girardot), a young man who passes himself off as a count in Geneva while draft dodging service in the Algerian War. He becomes entangled with Yvonne (one-off performer Sandra Majani), a beautiful actress, by striking up a friendship with her flamboyant travelling companion, Dr. Meinthe (Jean-Pierre Marielle, out-camping his gay detective role in *Four Flies on Grey Velvet*). However, as we already know the outcome is not pretty; their affair is doomed to have a very short shelf life.

In an interesting contrast, *Yvonne* features a much younger male protagonist but feels much more world weary and melancholy; some viewers find this approach thoughtful and poignant, while others just find it aimless. The two romantic leads are definitely among the chilliest in Leconte's repertoire, but the sex scenes (which are among the filmmaker's most revealing) and overwhelming sense of tragedy certainly make it linger in the memory.

Severin's DVD has a superior encoding of the film compared to the U.K. disc; the powdery colour schemes of the flashbacks look terrific, and the scope compositions appear to be accurately rendered. The big extra here is the second half of the Leconte interview (The first part is on Severin's release of *The Hairdresser's Husband*), which picks up with this film and *Tango* and then progressing on to his later films, almost all of which found international favour. Hopefully Severin's two overdue American releases of his films will also encourage film fans to seek out his later films, which include such flat-out masterpieces as *Girl on the Bridge* and *Man on the Train*.

PERMISSIVE

Colour, 1970, 90m. / Directed by Lindsay Shontoff / Starring Maggie Stride, Gay Singleton, Gilbert Wynne, Forever More, Titus Groan, Robert Daubigny, Madeleine Collinson, Mary Collinson / BFI (DVD & Blu-ray, UK R0 PAL/HD)

In a bustling London on the cusp between hippie fallout and '70s decadence, young new girl Suzy (Maggie Stride) finds a pad to crash in and makes friends with auburn-haired vixen Fiona (Gay Singleton), who enjoys long, revealing bathtub soaks when

she isn't knocking boots with the scruffy lead singer of a psych-rock group called Forever More (and sometimes with his band mates as well). However, this freewheeling lifestyle takes a dark turn when Suzy hooks up with a string of ill-advised bedmates including the band's lecherous older manager (*Prime Suspect*'s Gilbert Wynne), a grabby, big-breasted lesbian in a hotel room, and ill-fated loose cannon Pogo (Robert Daubigny). This being the early '70s, it all ends in utter tragedy.

A peculiar and always entertaining mixture of exploitation (including more female nudity than average for the time), post-*Woodstock* artiness, and moral hand-wringing, *Permissive* is obviously a product of the same twelve months that produced the likes of *Groupie Girl*, *Model Shop* and *The People Next Door*, all of which utilised similar rock music to depict the rapidly-changing youth culture that seemed to be speeding in an unknown, possibly terrifying direction. Here the main attraction is the performance footage of Forever More and Titus Groan, intercut with great shots of Suzy wandering the streets of London during its pop culture zenith. It's even more interesting as part of the truly bizarre career of director Lindsay Shonteff, who directed a pair of interesting horrors for Richard Gordon in the '60s (*Devil Doll* and *Curse of the Voodoo*) before swerving into multiple genres including the ridiculous fantasy *The Million Eyes of Sumuru* and the trashy, T&A ripper outing, *Night After Night After Night*. He certainly knew how to construct a marketable piece of drive-in hokum, and in this case he slips in enough sex and turmoil to keep the kids happy (along with a surprise appearance by *Playboy* models and Hammer starlets Madeleine and Mary Collinson as two minor groupies). The strange combination of leering cheesecake imagery and downbeat scolding was hardly new at the time, even affecting most of the sex comedies of the period like *What's Good for*

P

the Goose and on into the '70s with such unlikely variants as *Dracula A.D. 1972.*

This completely forgotten time capsule makes perfect sense as an entry in the British Film Institute's laudable Flipside series, dedicated to reviving forgotten filmic arcana for new generations. Context is everything here as a film lost in the shuffle becomes much more interesting in retrospect, with the raw performance footage jolting things to life every time the story threatens to collapse into pure formula. The transfer is extremely impressive and razor sharp, presented full frame (the correct aspect ratio; don't even bother trying to crop it off on a widescreen TV) with robust hues and only one unavoidable bit of water damage to the negative visible during an early sequence in a nightclub hallway. The optional English subtitles come in handy as well during a few mumbled dialogue exchanges.

The major extra here is *Bread*, a 1971 short feature (68 minutes) primarily dedicated to performance footage of music festival participants Juicy Lucy and Crazy Mabel, loosely held together by a negligible story about a bunch of teens who split their aspirations between throwing a *Woodstock*-style bash after going to the Isle of Wight and making stag films to earn some, yes, bread. The music's great, and many viewers will probably hit the fast forward button a few times to skip over some of the inane connecting tissue to keep the energy level up throughout the film. This transfer has been taken from the only surviving good film elements (most from the incomplete negative) with some additional outtakes also included as a separate extra. The later 1973 short film included here, "'Ave You Got a Male Assistant Please Miss?", is basically a rock-scored educational film about how girls can go about preventing pregnancy before they have to resort to abortion (which leads to a memorable closing piece of onscreen text). The title refers to a suitor's discomfort buying condoms at a pharmacy, a sequence that will no doubt seem a lot funnier to anyone familiar with *Amazon Women on the Moon*. Also included are the original *Permissive* trailer and the usual thick, informative liner notes booklet including overviews of the two features and short by I.Q. Hunter plus comments by members of contemporary band Comus, along with modern-day vocalist Lee Dorrian (from British metal band Cathedral). All told, it's a laudable, rewarding, and fascinating treat for anyone with a love of '70s ephemera.

PERVERSION STORY (ONE ON TOP OF THE OTHER)

Colour, 1969, 103m. / Directed by Lucio Fulci / Starring Marisa Mell, Jean Sorel, Elsa Martinelli, John Ireland, Faith Domergue, Alberto De Mendoza / Severin (US R1 NTSC) / WS (1.85:1) (16:9)

 "Nude is not enough. It needs to be disgusting!" So proclaims a minor character early on in Lucio Fulci's *Una sull'altra*, better known in English as *One on Top of the Other* and christened on DVD under its even more lurid Continental title, *Perversion Story*. Stylish, sexy, and unpredictable, it marked a turning point for the director after churning out a series of comedies and historical dramas. Perhaps inspired by writing a thematically similar Edgar Wallace adaptation, the quasi-*giallo* flick *Double Face* with Klaus Kinski, Fulci begins the film in San Francisco with wealthy Dr. George Dumurrier (Jean Sorel from *Short Night of Glass Dolls*) tending to his ailing asthmatic wife, Susan (*Danger: Diabolik*'s Marisa Mell), whose sleeping and respiratory medications cannot be taken together or else she will – gasp! – expire

horribly. Naturally she drops dead in the first reel, leaving poor George fingered for her possible murder when he winds up inheriting her multi-million dollar insurance policy. As if George's life weren't complicated enough, his partner and brother, Henry (Alberto De Mendoza), is prone to arguing with him about the state of their clinic and their various medical announcements to the press. When George and his unhappily married mistress, Jane (Elsa Martinelli from *Blood and Roses*), decide to get away from it all by visiting an upmarket strip club, he's transfixed by dancer Monica Weston (also Mell), a dead ringer for his wife who does a sultry striptease astride a motorcycle. When he follows Monica to her place, they fall into the sack together... but when he discovers she has the same sleeping medication as his late wife, George becomes suspicious. Unfortunately, the authorities quickly gather enough evidence to land George behind bars in San Quentin, so he and Jane must race against time to unravel the mystery before he winds up in the gas chamber.

A pivotal *giallo* long circulated on the grey market, *Perversion Story* benefits from excellent performances by its cast, with the frequently undraped and multi-wigged Mell especially having a field day in two – or is it three? – roles. Sorel also gets to exercise his thespian skills more than usual as the caddish George, who goes through the wringer during the course of the labyrinthine story. American actors John Ireland and Faith Domergue pop up in minor supporting roles, but it's really the European actors' show all the way. Riz Ortolani also contributes a scorching jazz and lounge score that's been an established Euro soundtrack favourite for years, and Fulci keeps the story moving along and surprising at every turn with some wonderful mod touches thrown in like wild multi-split-screen effects and colourful strip sequences bursting with psychedelic colours.

Anyone who's viewed this film in its past VHS incarnations (or miserable-looking U.S. prints) will be flabbergasted by Severin's DVD transfer, a beautifully pristine presentation that lays waste to every version before it. This edition comes complete with the much snazzier Italian opening titles, which dynamically cut and shift across the screen *Psycho*-style rather than the comparatively drab English credits. This also represents a significantly different edit of the film, clocking in with an extra four minutes of saucy footage missing from prior English releases while excising some driving travelogue bits for some reason. It would be bad form to list the details, but let's just say that Mell and Martinelli fans will be very happy with what they see – and anyone previously annoyed by the film's relative lack of sexiness considering its title will find this release much more satisfying. The familiar English dub track is present here and is serviceable enough despite the flat dubbing of Sorel. (Whoever dubbed Mell certainly jumped in with gusto!) However, the Italian track feels more organic to the film, has more dialogue than the English track, and uses Ortolani's score much more prominently, though the final scene with the radio reporter still plays better in English. (For some reason Mell's first appearance has her clearly speaking in a hallway without any words coming out on both versions, which appears to be sloppy sound editing in the original film.) It's really a toss-up between the two, but newcomers may find the Italian track with its more complete and literate English subtitles the most accessible option. As for extras, you get the very long and spoiler-laden English theatrical trailer (as *One on Top of the Other*), which touts this as the first film to realistically show the incarceration and execution process at San Quentin, and a bonus soundtrack CD containing the full 11-track version of Ortolani's score.

PETS

Colour, 1974, 103m. / Directed by Raphael Nussbaum / Starring Candice Rialson, Teri Guzman, Ed Bishop, Joan Blackman, Bret Parker, Mike Cartel / Code Red (US R0 NTSC) / WS (1.78:1) (16:9)

 On the run from her thug brother (Mike Cartel) who's still in pursuit, pretty young blonde Bonnie (Candice Rialson) descends into the oddball culture of early '70s Los Angeles and teams up with sassy Pat (Teri Guzman) as they hitch a ride with and hold up a middle-aged businessman (Bret Parker) whose house they decide to rob. Then Bonnie gets saved from a misdemeanour rap thanks to possessive lesbian artist Geraldine (Joan Blackman) whose paintings pique the interest of Vincent (Ed Bishop), whose collection of pets consists entirely of females – and these caged subjects extend to people, too.

Though sold as a standard drive-in sexploitation film with poster art promising lots of interracial S&M thrills, *Pets* is something more ambitious and bizarre. It's adapted more or less from a 1969 play by Richard Reich which originally consisted of three separate stories, here fused together into an ode to the late Candice Rialson, a striking California-based actress whose other vehicles include *Chatterbox*, *Candy Stripe Nurses*, *Hollywood Boulevard*, and *Moonshine County Express*. This film marked her first leading role, and she makes the most of it. The mixture of theatrical pretension, T&A, sexual kink, and quirky dialogue gives the film a far different flavour than most films of the period. Director Raphael Nussbaum, who's better known for releasing plenty of drive-in imports and domestic titles through Burbank International Pictures (and other permutations), does a workmanlike job, only showing a few artistic flourishes during the final third when the whole "pets" angle really comes into play and making moderately creative use of cage imagery to dictate his compositions.

Apparently Raphael and his estate didn't take very good care of his titles, as *Pets* has had a very rocky (and until now, quite negligible) history on home video after its days on the drive-in circuit. Rialson fans had to make do with fuzzy PAL-converted copies or cruddy bootlegs for years, and while the sanctioned DVD release marks a bump up in the clarity department, it still suffers obviously from the ravages of time. Apparently this print was the best source available at the time, so be prepared for plenty of emulsion scratches, dirt, and frame damage (with one whole scene so roughed up it's included separately as a bonus feature). Some buzzing about a slightly racier European cut might be true as well, considering the fact that circulating prints appear to have varying degrees of nudity. You'll still see plenty of Candy on display here, so perhaps some intrepid soul will find the time to sit down with every extant celluloid incarnation of this title to work out how this stacks up against other prints. Other extras include the unforgettable theatrical trailer – an understandable mainstay on compilations for years and one of the decade's most potent – along with a handful of promos for the company's other titles. Check it out, but remember... "there's an animal in every woman!"

PLAGUE TOWN

Colour, 2008, 88m. / Directed by David Gregory / Starring Josslyn DeCrosta, Erica Rhodes, James Warke, Lindsay Goranson, David Lombard, Kate Aspinwall / Dark Sky (DVD and Blu-ray, US R1 NTSC/HD) / WS (1.78:1) (16:9) / DD5.1

In an overstuffed world of horror movies crowding the shelves offering the latest belated J-horror imitations or torture fests, it now takes a lot of persistence (or what Stephen King used to refer to as panning for gold) to find something a little different and refreshing. Fortunately the indie *Plague Town* fits the bill and manages to pull off that delicate balancing act between disturbing brutality and delicate lyricism, a quality that was once common back in the '70s with films like *Lemora*, *Messiah of Evil* and *Blood on Satan's Claw*. You might even see a few glimmers of those films with this offering which takes place entirely in a remote Irish village where the houses seem to be miles apart from each other.

After a quick but brutal prologue in which a priest supervising a birth is murdered by a family after he tries to snuff out the new arrival, we pick up in the present day as an American family touring the local ruins passes by for some afternoon sightseeing, only to find their car dead and night quickly approaching. The dad (David Lombard) is the first to go off alone, leaving behind his new girlfriend Annette (Lindsay Goranson) and two bickering daughters, Molly (Josslyn DeCrosta) and Jessica (Erica Rhodes), along with the put-upon punching bag of the film, Robin (James Warke), a British guy Jessica picked up along the way. As it turns out, the unfortunate births from years earlier have now resulted in a cut-off country community filled with depraved, deformed children who play very nasty games with outsiders, which everyone discovers with varying outcomes of survival before morning arrives.

Anyone who has seen a poster or video cover for *Plague Town* is no doubt at least vaguely familiar with its undeniable iconic centrepiece, Rosemary (played rather incredibly by a waifish 13-year-old named Kate Aspinwall), a delicate and deeply creepy killer kid who makes a show-stopping appearance at the start of the third act. Fortunately she's hardly the only ace the film has up its sleeve thanks to a number of compelling and oddly beautiful sequences, including a handful of harrowing moments with groups of kids congregating in the woods to descend upon one of the unlucky travellers. Everything from a tyre hubcap to tree branches is used to vicious effect, but for once the violence here really stings and creates a sense of mounting unease rather than the numbing brutality found in your average *Saw* knockoff.

Plague Town also carries a bit more than the usual genre interest as it marks the debut feature film for David Gregory, a founder of the wonderfully twisted Severin Films and director of two monumental feature-length genre studies, *The Godfathers of Mondo* and *The Spaghetti West*, not to mention a slew of stylish supplementary featurettes. He keeps a firm grip on the film here (including some pretty funny Brit-related jabs) and channels what must be countless hours of movie watching into a lucid understanding of how to wring poetic chills from the most simple of elements. While hordes of horror quickies pound the viewer over the head right from the beginning with flashy cutting and bombastic sound effects, *Plague Town* is more like an icy hand gradually sliding along the back of your neck for 90 minutes. The very deliberate pacing of the opening 40 minutes or so (as well as a few iffy line deliveries during the daylight segment) has confounded more than a few reviewers, but anyone with a reasonable attention span should find the effect more than worth it as the payoff kicks in. The upsetting denouement is also worth noting as it offers a decidedly female-oriented twist ending that will cause more than a few distaff viewers to squirm when they contemplate what's going to happen after the end credits.

In a marked departure from most low budget shoots now done on digital, *Plague Town* was shot on film (16mm, but it looks great) and works all the better for it. The film is available on both DVD and Blu-ray, and while the former looks quite nice, the latter is definitely the way to go if you have the choice. (It's also cheaper at many retailers and comes with more material, but more on that in a minute.) The 1.78:1 transfer features excellent resolution with a fine, film-like texture, and the night scenes (which comprise about 85% of the film) look wonderfully deep and inky without losing any detail. The DVD features a solid 5.1 mix, while the Blu-ray boasts an uncompressed and very immersive DTS 5.1 track that takes full advantage of the diverse soundtrack, which includes a terrific score by Mark Raskin (who really offers some inspired moments in the last half hour) as well as new contributions from Claudio Gizzi (the enigmatic composer of *Blood for Dracula* and *Flesh for Frankenstein*), with a cut from electronic dance gods Ladytron thrown in for good measure.

Both editions contain an audio commentary with Gregory and producer Derek Curl, who fill up every second with loads of details about the production. Everything from the location shooting (in very cold Connecticut) to the effects shooting to the casting is covered in great detail, and it also serves as a pretty good primer on how to shoot a low budget horror feature these days. The first featurette, "A Visit to *Plague Town*", clocks in at almost half an hour with all of the major cast members, Gregory, Curl, and several people from the crew offering a more general overview of the production, augmented with some nifty on-location footage. It's especially fun seeing the younger actors in make-up getting ready for their scenes, which look a lot less intense from a different perspective. Next up is "The Sounds of *Plague Town*", in which Raskin and the sound effects artists talk about the

effective soundscape of the film, with the music and Foley effects often working in tandem during the standout horror sequences. Finally you get the original theatrical trailer, which does an adequate job of conveying the tone but is edited exactly the same as every other cookie-cutter horror trailer you've seen for the last five years. Don't let it put you off; the movie's much better. Anyone who springs for the Blu-ray is also treated to an additional bonus, Gregory's 1995 short film, "Scathed". A truly odd little mood piece, it features Matthew Bell (the narrator of Gregory's *Texas Chain Saw Massacre: The Shocking Truth*) as a guy named Joe who stops off for an afternoon beer at a bar where nudists and weirdoes prowl around outside. There he strikes up a difficult conversation with a beautiful but not-very-conversant young woman in an eye patch who tells him about how she wound up at this hole in the wall, a perverse saga involving an iron-fisted owner named Miss Antonia Curtis (played, believe it or not, by Andy Warhol regular Holly Woodlawn!). From the colourful hand-drawn credits to the Argentoesque, hyper-saturated lighting, it's a peculiar but intriguing calling card with a languorous but disturbing tone that makes it an appropriate companion to the main feature.

PLAYGIRLS OF MUNICH

Colour, 1977, 86m. / Directed by Navred Reef / Starring Roger Caine, Zebedy Colt, Claudia Mehringer, Helga Wild, Christa Abel / After Hours (US R0 NTSC) / WS (1.78:1) (16:9)

If you ever felt an urge to "join in the sexca-pades with dozens of NAUGHTY BAVA-RIAN FRAULEINS" (as the poster subtly puts it), look no further than *Playgirls of Munich*.

This goofy comedy was shot back-to-back in Europe with 1977's *Dutch Treat* (featuring almost the same cast) and follows the sexploits of Chuck (Roger Caine) and Barney (Zebedy Colt), a pair of randy, dimwitted repairmen sent to fix a plane's faulty phone system. Instead they sit around reading a paperback called *Sexy Europe* and wind up stowing away on the aircraft, which dumps them via parachute into the middle of Munich. Immediately they're surrounded by drunk Germans in beer halls, domineering midgets, mobsters, and tons of shapely Alpine vixens including a climactic swimming pool orgy.

As with most of its ilk, this is much more sumptuous, clever, and plot-heavy than your average skin flick, and the interplay of the two recognisable American lead actors (hardcore director/actor and Broadway performer Zebedy Colt and the very busy Roger Caine, who "went straight" briefly in George Romero's *Martin*) is often very funny, particularly when mixed with other bit performers' rude German dialogue complete with English subtitles. The rest of the cast is mostly noname European players, but everyone seems game whether doing comedy or the bump-and-grind. There's even a twist ending, too.

The DVD from After Hours contains a colourful, solid-looking widescreen transfer (and it does look close to the intended aspect ratio) with only a few minor print blemishes to be found. The DVD comes with a mostly disposable bonus disc containing a "raunchy West German loop collection" consisting of some really seedy anonymous quickies of explicit detail and little cinematic value, though curiously Rick Cassidy turns up in one, which makes you wonder how Germanic all these women really are. Stick to the first disc for the best bang for your buck. Also included is a nifty four-page insert containing liner notes by James Hollenbaugh, who talks at length about Colt's very odd career as well as a few trivia titbits about the main feature.

PORN STARS OF THE 80'S

Colour, 2008, 98m. / Starring Al Goldstein, Ron Jeremy, Vanessa Del Rio, Samantha Fox, Nina Hartley, Desiree Cousteau, Paul Thomas, John Leslie, Veronica Hart, Annette Haven

PORN STARS OF THE 90'S

Colour, 2008, 95m. / Starring Al Goldstein, Jeanna Fine, Randy West, Christy Canyon, Ashlyn Gere, Viper, Teri Wiegel, Tom Byron / Blue Underground (US R0 NTSC)

Thematically-related titles on separate discs but essentially inseparable from each other, *Porn Stars of the 80's* and *Porn Stars of the 90's* represent the oddest trashy-but-softcore releases from Midnight Blue, the infamous public access show ramped out onto DVD over a period of years via Blue Underground. Irascible *Screw* editor Al Goldstein guides you through the underbelly of the East and West Coast flesh factories, with the '80s one ultimately coming out a lot more interesting than its companion piece. That's entirely due to the presence of talent involved, including the legendary and apparently very wound-up Vanessa Del Rio ("I don't trust myself!"), a lot of hamming by a young Ron Jeremy (who also demonstrates his dubious stand-up comedy abilities), and lots of facts from the candid (and sometimes undraped) Nina Hartley, an about-to-retire Desiree Cousteau ("I feel overexposed"), Samantha Fox, a very fluffy-haired Paul Thomas, John Leslie, Veronica Hart, and Annette Haven. As you can see, they've got all the heavy hitter bases covered for the era (except for Traci Lords, obviously, but we all know why she isn't there...).

The usual barrage of hilarious and fascinating vintage ads (including escorts and phone sex, not to mention a musical vibrator bit by "Weird Uncle Louie") add more spice to the stew, arguably the most entertaining Midnight Blue title. (The retro menu screen is a nice added touch, too.)

While the '90s era certainly has its fans, the Midnight Blue volume dedicated to it definitely reveals a show on a downswing, losing much of its lo-fi, grubby charm as the business became flooded with a staggering amount of video product, not to mention the dawn of the internet era. The highlight is probably the vivacious Jeanna Fine, one of the most aggressive stars of the decade, who wears a really over-the-top outfit and talks enthusiastically about her work. (Her anecdote about co-star Sikki Nixx is especially surprising.) A leathery Randy West also gets a huge chunk of interview time, and other contributors include Ashlyn Gere, Christy Canyon, Viper, Teri Wiegel, and Tom Byron. Both discs come with an optional "Money Shots" text trivia track that rattles off lots of arcane titbits about each person onscreen, and the '90s DVD piles on a few oddball extras like Al Goldstein cussing out Jenna Jameson, Annie Sprinkle's "Titty Cupcakes", and a Ron Jeremy primer in... well, just watch for yourself.

PORN-O-RAMA

Colour, 1994, 152m. / Directed by Paul Norman / Starring Ron Jeremy, Samantha Strong, Tom Byron / Private Screening (US R0 NTSC), MediumRare (UK R2 PAL)

Best known for reviving scores of forgotten '80s softcore favourites, the folks at Private Screening change tack with this five-part documentary lensed in the early '90s by Paul Norman, the director who crammed the Clinton decade with countless straight and bi titles. Ron Jeremy and Alexis DeVell walk you through a series of interviews with familiar faces from the era along with plenty of backstage footage (nothing explicit, though lots of bare breasts are on display).

There have been plenty of backstage and blooper releases before, but this one is truly exhaustive as it spends two and a half hours in the trenches, asking lots of wildly inappropriate questions and getting answers ranging from the hilarious to the utterly perplexing. Each episode seems to revolve around a basic theme (why they do it, how family and friends react, etc.), though you won't find any major revelations as everyone just seems to be having lots of laughs (not surprising given that this was crafted by the industry itself). Among the subjects here are Samantha Strong, Tom Byron, Jon Dough, Francesca Le, Brittany O'Connell, Nick East, the tragic Cal Jammer, and lots, lots more.

The whole enterprise was shot on a home video camera and definitely looks it, so don't expect any striking home theatre demo material here. As a time capsule, it's pretty fascinating to see a parade of faces like this, especially when many of them are long gone (from the industry or even from this planet). Just don't expect much titillation value, 'cause it ain't there. Oh, and the cover art is supremely disturbing. Also available in an equally uncut U.K. DVD edition from MediumRare.

POULTRYGEIST: NIGHT OF THE CHICKEN DEAD

Colour, 2006, 103m. / Directed by Lloyd Kaufman / Starring Jason Yachanin, Kate Graham, Allyson Sereboff, Robin Watkins, Joshua Olatunde, Caleb Emerson, Rose Ghavami, Khalid Rivera, Ron Jeremy / Troma (Blu-ray & DVD, US R0 NTSC/HD) / WS (1.78:1) (16:9) / DD2.0

While making out in a cemetery which contains the remains of numerous Native Americans, homebound Arbie (Jason Yachanin) and college-bound Wendy (Kate Graham) are interrupted by an axe-wielding peeping tom who drives them off and gets attacked from behind (literally) by a zombie. Soon the cemetery is razed to the ground to make way for the opening of a new fast food restaurant, American Chicken Bunker, whose racist founder, General Lee Roy (Robin Watkins), is about to visit for the grand opening. Unfortunately the celebration is hampered by a horde of protestors including a gang of ticked-off lesbians led by Micki (Allyson Sereboff), who has stolen Wendy away from Arbie – who decides to go work for the chicken chain to get revenge. The franchise owner, Denny (Joshua Olatunde), hires him as a counter girl (with a "Daisy" nametag) to work alongside the burqa-wearing fry cook Humus (Rose Ghavami), closeted Jose Paco Bell (Khalid Rivera) who enjoys adding his own special sauce to the chicken, and animal-loving idiot Carl Jr. (Caleb Emerson). Oh, and they've tossed all the exhumed bodies from the cemetery out back in the dumpster. Soon all the dead chickens and Indians combine to form a supernatural perfect storm in which customers and employees are infected by a monstrous contagion that turns them all into beaked, feathered, flesh-eating zombies intent on inflicting fast food mayhem on the surviving humans. Can Arbie and Wendy fend off the fiends before they become the next meal?

As the low-budget horror landscape has shifted almost entirely to home video, enterprising indie companies have become far more selective about which projects to give a big theatrical push and market as tent pole releases for a wider audience. One of the more prolific companies of the entire video age, Troma has become a good case in point with only a few select titles – usually helmed by company founder Lloyd Kaufman – gracing theatre screens in the past decade, like *Terror Firmer*. Easily the most ambitious and aggressively promoted Troma film in years, *Poultrygeist: Night of the Chicken Dead* had some high expectations to meet among fans, who were promptly dished up a gore-drenched monster comedy featuring Native American chicken zombies, numerous musical numbers, scheming lesbians, a Ron Jeremy cameo, and a possessed gay fast food sandwich. Needless to say, it's a unique experience that covers so many bases you're bound to raise a chuckle and gag at the same time throughout the entire experience. Aggressively gross, stupid, and sophomoric, *Poultrygeist* is also rip-roaring fun if you catch it in the right mood and benefits from setting its sights higher than usual, particularly the big, gore-spraying zombie attack near the one-hour mark that gives George Romero a serious run for his money. The musical numbers range from utterly dispensable (Arbie's duet with Kaufman, both wearing skirts and little else) to surprisingly inspired, such as a topless lesbian sing-along that, judging from the making-of documentary, caused Sereboff more than a little trauma. The usual infantile Troma obsessions are here: jokes about blind people, deliberately offensive jabs at various creeds and sexual orientations, anti-consumerist grandstanding, and explosions of bodily fluids with an emphasis on blood and faeces. However, what makes the difference here is the surprisingly sturdy story structure and some amazingly committed, fearless performances, with Yachanin and the pretty, very game Graham and Sereboff swiping the film as they effortlessly bounce between the numerous tonal shifts. Here's

P

hoping we see much more of all of them in the future. The fast food jabs are surprisingly funny as well (check out the names of all the major characters); in fact, the reincarnation of the dead Jose into a cute, wisdom-spouting chicken sandwich with pimento eyes might be the funniest running gag in the entire Troma library. And at the very least, this does almost as good a job at warding viewers away from junky eating habits as *Food, Inc.* For Troma fans, it's also worth noting that this film closes hilariously with a very familiar car crash that seems oddly perfect.

After a successful limited theatrical run that caused a surprising ruckus in some major cities, *Poultrygeist* made its way to DVD in two versions, a standard two-disc edition and an "Eggs-clusive 3-Disc Collector's Edition" that's frankly not that amazing, as it basically just tacks on Karaoke versions of all the songs along with some random trailers. In any case, the DVD contains an anamorphic transfer that's the best-looking version of any Troma film to date, though it's hampered by some distracting motion blurring, interlacing issues, and way too much compression to fit in on the disc with its horde of extras. Speaking of which, the goodies include an audio commentary by Kaufman and co-writer/editor Gabe Friedman that lays out the basic groundwork of how the film came to be and some of the many, many, many hurdles overcome along the way. You also get a quartet of deleted scenes (none necessary, all somewhat interesting, such as a jettisoned happy ending with Ron Jeremy), a couple of music videos, and a gory extended trailer labelled as outtakes from Bergman's *The Virgin Spring*. Disc two is highlighted by the feature-length (83 min.) "Poultry in Motion", an amazing documentary about the making of the film that covers everything from initial casting to the premiere. You'll see just how much trouble a poverty row budget can cause with a production of this scale, as everything from the effects to the "free talent" causes rifts in filming. You also get smacked early on with some surprisingly explicit nudity during the audition process. The opening cemetery sequence alone was a nightmare to pull off for reasons that will soon become apparent, and it's amazing it still holds together as well as it does. Other extras include footage from the New York premiere with the cast, snippets from a roof re-shoot including an appearance by Debbie Rochon, and additional short featurettes about the effects and sound editing.

However, *Poultrygeist* will also go down in the history books as Troma's first Blu-ray release. Given the company's history of bumping over VHS-era masters through the entire DVD age, fans were justifiably curious about whether Troma would make the leap to HD by bumping up the old version or actually delivering the goods. Fortunately the latter turns out to be the case, as the Blu-ray fixes many of the issues with the DVD; it's much clearer, smoother, and more film-like, with a definite boost in detail (check out the protest signs and flyers) and much better compression. Film grain is light but thankfully still present enough to look like celluloid, even giving away a few scenes where film stock actually switches from shot to shot. Some occasional black flecks appear on the left side of the screen during the first and last reels (a flaw also on the older version), which seems to be an issue with the original source material itself. (Bear in mind also that the opening company logo and much of the cemetery sequence, which was actually shot at night, still look kind of cruddy.) Sound is also punchier and features better separation during the musical numbers. Hi-def junkies still won't do cartwheels given the nature of the film and its scrappy shooting conditions, but all in all it's heartening to finally see a Troma film on home video looking like this. The Blu-ray ports over all the extras from the standard two-disc edition apart from some Troma cross-promotional trailers and the obligatory Kaufman intro, which is replaced here with a new, shot-on-HD skit about the company's move to Blu-ray (dubbed "Brown-Ray" here, of course) complete with a pretty funny demonstration involving a Tromette. However, this release also sweetens the deal by adding a new commentary track with leads Yachanin and Graham that's pretty much worth the upgrade itself as they give an actor's perspective on the shooting and recall some wild stories from the set, with the antics of the cast and crew taking up much of the time along with a few hilarious observations about their unforgettable first scene together.

POWER PLAY

Colour, 1978, 101m. / Directed by Martyn Burke / Starring Peter O'Toole, Donald Pleasence, David Hemmings, Barry Morse, George Touliatos, Alberta Watson / Scorpion (US R0 NTSC) / WS (1.78:1) (16:9)

This modest, entertaining actioner came at the height of a time of international productions awash in intrigue and affordable rosters of familiar actors willing to cash a paycheck while dodging enemy spies and explosions. Anyone old enough to remember seeing fare like *The Wild Geese*, *Escape to Athena*, or *Bear Island* should have a fair idea of what to expect here; the only huge surprise is the fact that Roger Moore wasn't also around for an appearance. The plot basically involves a bunch of disgruntled professionals and military men who decide to get together and form their own militia, way before that kind of activity became a notable, even commonplace presence in America. Disgusted with the

corrupt current regime, Colonel Narriman (David Hemmings) leads the effort along with Dr. Rousseau (Barry Morse) and Colonel Zellar (Peter O'Toole) to acquire enough force, namely tanks, to stage a revolution against their government (which is conveniently never named). When the powers that be get wind of this plot, secret police chief Blair (Donald Pleasence) springs into sadistic action in a testosterone-fuelled face-off involving espionage and violent force.

The idea of men discussing political machinations might not sound like the makings of a great thriller, but *Power Play* comes off far better than it should thanks to a sterling cast who make the most of their material. Hemmings in particular offers another in his roster of excellent, frequently undervalued performances, anchoring the proceedings with a complex mixture of anger, tenacity, frustration, and melancholy. Pleasence comes in a close second as the antagonist of the story, offering a menacing yet fascinating characterisation that makes the stakes mean far more when the action eventually kicks in.

Scorpion's DVD of this seldom-seen political thriller features a solid anamorphic transfer that handily outclasses prior washed-out TV and video editions. The presentation is attractive and film-like throughout with solid colours and enough natural film grain to look like an excellent theatrical print rather than a scrubbed-over digital overhaul. Extras include an interview and audio commentary with director Martyn Burke, an interview with George Touliatos, and the theatrical trailer, along with additional promos including *The Farmer*, *Skateboard*, *The Last Grenade*, *Voyager*, and *The Girl in Blue*.

PRIMITIVE LONDON

Colour, 1965, 87m. / Directed by Arnold L. Miller / BFI (DVD & Blu-ray, UK R0 PAL/HD)

Mods! Rockers! Teddy boys! Beatniks! All these and more are on display in *Primitive London*, the considerably more shocking follow-up to *London in the Raw*, which kicks off with the first birth-of-a-baby footage ever preserved in hi-def. Naturally it's perfect for showing off your home theatre setup to unsuspecting visitors. From there we inexplicably jump to London's youth culture, with the narrator and interviewer confusingly reserving most of their scorn for the coffee shop beatniks (most unemployed poets, apparently) who answer arbitrary sex questions with an amusing look of confusion on their faces. The gym sequence from the first film is topped here by the narrator's insistence that women couldn't possibly take any similar enjoyment from men's bodies, which is then proven by lingering for what seems like hours on the homeliest bodybuilder ever captured on film. This time the film goes for a bit more structure than its predecessor by returning to (staged) footage of an often-botched commercial taping, but the most audacious highlight comes early on when the voiceovers of the film's director and editor start quibbling about artsy nature footage which then switches to a topless bathing suit show. What else do you get? Goldfish surgery! A gory Jack the Ripper re-enactment! A brutal chicken farm! Tattoo parlours! Female martial arts! Turkish baths! Swinging key parties! And a men's hat-measuring shop! The growing preoccupation with strippers also foreshadows the director's following film, *Secrets of a Windmill Girl*, which pushed the showgirl fixation to its logical conclusion.

Faster and nuttier, *Primitive London* never stops to catch its breath as it drags the viewer through a head-spinning array of sights and sounds, all beautifully captured by the BFI's immaculate presentation. The region-free DVD and Blu-ray editions are shockingly colourful and look like a first-night theatrical projection. This time out you also get an alternative French language track and two subtitle options, a literal English one as well as an English translation of the French track (which basically means the slang terms get replaced by more standard, accessible verbiage). The mono soundtrack is also worthy of note, featuring a delightful blend of jazz, early rock by The Zephyrs, and avant garde music by composer Basil Kirchin, who later went on to *The Shuttered Room* and *The Abominable Dr. Phibes*. The most interesting extra this time out is "Carousella", a 26-minute, 1965 early short by John Irvin (who later directed *The Dogs of War* and *Ghost Story*). It's a surprisingly well-made and visually striking look at three strippers' day-to-day lives, edited and shot with an amazing degree of style. A vintage 17-minute interview with Al Burnett covers the illogical and arcane alcohol licensing laws of the day, which are also addressed rather venomously in *London in the Raw*, while stripping turns up again in a 1968 Stuart McCabe interview and a chat with "Shirley" about the rules and regulations which governed the 1960s.

The booklet this time is just as substantial, loaded with great original ad art and liner notes by Ian Sinclair, who takes a more creative approach with the material than the trivia-based *Raw*. He also sheds a bit more light on cinematographer Stanley Long, who went on to become a director in his own right with plenty of '70s sex comedies like *Sex and the Other Woman* and three of the Peter Long *Adventures of...* films. Definitely recommended for reasons far too numerous to count.

PRIVATE COLLECTIONS

Colour, 1979, 102m. / Directed by Just Jaeckin, Shuji Terayama & Walerian Borowczyk / Starring Roland Blanche, Laura Gemser, Juzo Itami, Hiromi Kawai, Marie-Catherine Conti, Yves-Marie Maurin / Severin (US R0 NTSC) / WS (1.66:1) (16:9)

 By the late 1970s the whole "sexy European anthology" idea was largely played out, but that didn't stop French producer Pierre Braunberger from trying to update the formula by bringing together three very different directors for a collection of erotic tales. The most obvious choice of these is Polish filmmaker Walerian Borowczyk who had already made a splash with his "dirty history" collection, *Immoral Tales*, but the other two contributors have plenty to offer as well.

The film begins with its most jolting segment, "L'île aux sirènes", by Just Jaeckin, a fashion photographer-turned-director still hot from *Emmanuelle* and *The Story of O*. Here he teams up with star Laura Gemser, best known as Black Emanuelle in a series of enjoyable Italian knock-offs, and the results are even more perverse than you might imagine. A shipwrecked sailor (*La Femme Nikita*'s Roland Blanche) finds himself on a sunny island where he begins to set up a sustainable lifestyle for himself. However, his routine is distracted by frequent glimpses of a beautiful, naked woman (Laura Gemser) darting around nearby, and soon the two are coupling in the surf. Afterwards she introduces him to the beautiful, equally unclad female members of her tribe nearby, and the sailor thinks he's found paradise as the women give him free sexual license. However, when he begins to weary of the situation, he finds escape might not be as easy as it seems. Beautifully shot and surprisingly gory, this segment – sort of a kinky *Twilight Zone* episode – marks an interesting change of pace for Jaeckin and makes for a fascinating bridge between his dreamy '70s films and the more lurid, pulp-fantasy aspects of his later *Gwendoline*. Gemser is gorgeous and fun to watch as always, while regular Jaeckin composer Pierre Bachelet contributes a memorable electronic-pop score that perfectly suits the frequent sun-drenched love scenes.

Unintentionally continuing a theme, the film then presents a piece by Japanese director Shuji Terayama, who went on to direct the startling sequel to *The Story of O*, 1981's *Fruits of Passion*, but who was barely known outside his native country aside from occasionally-screened future cult items like *Emperor Tomato Ketchup*. "Kusa-Meikyu" is easily the most stylish and extreme entry, focusing on a young peasant boy constantly distracted by the haunting call of a crazy female neighbour, whose house is off-limits. The boy undergoes face-painting and self-induced bondage to resist her, but ultimately the secrets of the mystery woman are revealed in a visual orgy involving talking severed heads, a giant red spider web, lots of sex, and a bunch of crazy demon-people. Featuring the late director Juzo Itami, this will appeal to fans of surreal Japanese cinema as well as "pink" fans looking for a fusion of horror and erotica with a kicky psychedelic twist.

Finally Borowczyk's "L'Armoir", adapted from a more straightforward tale by twist-master Guy de Maupassant, is more of a mood piece than a narrative as it uses an interrupted night between a Parisian prostitute (Marie-Catherine Conti) and her well-to-do client (Yves-Marie Maurin) as a springboard for a series of the director's beloved antiquated images of sexuality, including a carousel filled with call girls in their underwear and various female-and-male combinations in bizarre period dress coupling in doorways. It's all beautifully shot, though the sex content is actually pretty low with very little skin on display; Borowczyk fans will eat it up.

Although two of the directors are deceased, Severin does a commendable job of bringing this rarely-seen but important gem of international erotic cinema to DVD. Image quality varies depending on the shooting styles of the directors; the second looks best thanks to the eye-popping colours and crystal-clear cinematography, while the third features Borowczyk's beloved soft-focus, powdery textures that come across as hazy on video. The 1.66:1 framing features some windowboxing on the sides. Audio can be played either with the original French and Japanese soundtracks with optional English subtitles, or an alternative, partially-English-dubbed soundtrack; stick with the former. Extras include a fantastic theatrical trailer (which makes it amazing this film got such limited cinema play), bios for the directors, and a new video interview with Jaeckin, a fine companion piece to his chat on Anchor Bay's *Emmanuelle* release in which he talks about his career and how he became part of this unusual production, as well as memories of working with the iconic Gemser.

PRIVILEGE

Colour, 1967, 103m. / Directed by Peter Watkins / Starring Paul Jones, Jean Shrimpton, Mark London, William Job, Max Bacon / BFI (UK R2 PAL), New Yorker (US R1 NTSC) / WS (1.85:1) (16:9)

Possibly the best 1960s movie most people haven't seen, Peter Watkins's *Privilege* was the first feature film from the controversial director of *The War Game*, the infamous banned TV post-nuke "documentary". With this feature, Watkins turned his eye to a story of Britain "in the near future" where a pop idol, Steven Shorter (Paul Jones, former lead singer of Manfred Mann), holds a powerful sway over the population thanks to his elaborate stage shows which feature him hauled out of a burlap prisoner's sack and into a cell where stage police beat him savagely while he sings songs pleading for freedom. Naturally, the teenagers eat it all up, much to the delight of his hyper-efficient PR team which has managed to turn his persona into a massive commercial industry manipulated by both church and single-party state. The game starts to change when pretty painter Vanessa (real-life super-model Jean Shrimpton) is brought in to create his portrait only to fall in love with the battered, bruised, manufactured idol, whose misery mounts when his handlers make him the centrepiece of a nocturnal festival honouring a country-wide Christianity week meant to convert all of his susceptible young fans.

As with Watkins's other films, *Privilege* is almost queasily prescient as it looks forward to the media's use of corporate-owned celebrities to push specific political and religious agendas, an aspect many critics at the time found far-fetched. Now that pop culture has been swamped with the bizarre sexualized/conservative mutations of "performers" like Miley Cyrus, the Jonas Brothers, Britney Spears, and dozens of Disney-stamped clones, the music doesn't even matter at all; as *Privilege* proved, it's all about keeping young little consumers in line. Watkins constructs the film as a narrated documentary (which creates a wonderful hall-of-mirrors effect for a story taking place in the future) but also unleashes a number of unforgettable, stylish set pieces, with Shorter's major performances being the standouts along with some hilariously biting television commercials. The two non-actor leads deliver appropriately low-key and sometimes awkward performances which actually work in the film's favour, and surprisingly, the soundtrack features plenty of standout pop tracks that could have been real hit singles with a bit more of a label push. In fact, if there's one quibble with the film, it's the omission of Jones's title song, one of the finest things he ever recorded, which kicks off the soundtrack LP but appears nowhere in the feature itself. Strangely enough, Jones eventually went on to become a born-again entertainer at the urging of Cliff Richard, which adds yet another layer of meaning to a film already operating on many, many levels at once.

Whether due to its indifferent box office reception or potentially incendiary subject matter, *Privilege* became extremely difficult to see with Universal essentially letting it gather dust in the vault for decades along with many of the studio's other forgotten gems of the same period like *Games*. Nevertheless, the film's influence and cult following continued to grow over the years, particularly as subsequent musicals displayed unmistakable nods to this film such as the following year's *Wild in the Streets* (basically a simplified remake) and even Ken Russell's *Tommy*. Of course, one could argue that the real germ of this idea began in 1957 with the classic *A Face in the Crowd*, but that film's unlikely "happy" resolution makes it pale next to this one's far more ambiguous, haunting conclusion. With the DVD market unleashing many of Watkins's films to widespread praise, it was just a matter of time before *Privilege* finally appeared on home video after the studio struck a new print for retrospective screenings. In America the rights were licensed to Project X and distributed through the now-defunct New Yorker Films whose HD-sourced release looks excellent (albeit interlaced) and features some solid extras including "Lonely Boy", a half-hour 1962 documentary about Paul Anka that Watkins referred to heavily in the creation of his screenplay. Other extras include the theatrical trailer, a poster gallery, and a thick booklet containing a fascinating Watkins "self-interview" (shades of David Byrne) and two additional essays about the film.

About a year and a half later, *Privilege* hit DVD in its native country courtesy of the BFI who released it as part of their Flipside series (though given the film's excellence and importance, it could have easily qualified as a standard release from them as well). The transfer appears to be from the same HD source but this one is flagged for progressive scan (unlike the interlaced U.S. disc) with a bit of additional cleanup removing some dirt and debris, and the extras apart from the same trailer are completely different. (The BFI disc includes two excellent Watkins short films, 1959's "The Diary of an Unknown Soldier" (a 17-minute portrait of a WWI fighter preparing to charge into the fray) and 1961's "The Forgotten Faces", an 18-minute look at a major Hungarian public revolt. Both feature glimpses of the genius soon to come with Watkins's first two features and make for an invaluable accompaniment to the main program. Finally the U.K. release contains a different, 28-page booklet featuring essays by film historian Robert Murphy and Watkins expert John Cook, a Watkins overview by William Fowler, a Paul Jones bio by the BFI's Vic Pratt, and a nice smattering of behind-the-scenes photos. For technical quality and overall value the BFI disc comes out ahead, but both releases are highly recommended for a film that should absolutely be seen under any circumstances.

THE PSYCHIC

Colour, 1977, 97m. / Directed by Lucio Fulci / Starring Jennifer O'Neill, Marc Porel, Gabriele Ferzetti, Gianni Garko, Evelyn Stewart (Ida Galli) / Severin (US R1 NTSC), Studio Canal (France R2 PAL) / WS (1.85:1) (16:9)

The final film in Lucio Fulci's '70s *giallo* cycle before he turned to innards-splattering supernatural epics, 1977's underrated *Sette note in nero* (retitled *The Psychic* for its U.S. release) functions as a clever, surprisingly restrained summation of his thriller career to date while anticipating a few ideas yet to surface in the following decade. The film kicks off with an outrageous suicide reprise of the finale from *Don't Torture a Duckling* as a woman hurls herself from a cliff, her face smashing against the rocks on the way down to the sea. The horrific event is telepathically witnessed by her young daughter, Virginia, who grows into an adult (now played by Jennifer O'Neill) happily and wealthily married to Francesco (Gianni Garko). One afternoon while driving through a tunnel, she has another chilling psychic vision involving a dying woman walled up alive, a cigarette, and a magazine cover. When Francesco goes away on business, she decides to surprise him by redecorating his old house – which frighteningly resembles the murder scene in her vision. With a handy pickaxe, she whacks away some drywall to expose a long-decomposed cadaver; not surprisingly, the police quickly arrest her husband upon his return. However, Virginia becomes convinced that portions of her vision have yet to pass and enlists the aid of her therapist, Luca (Marc Porel), to uncover the sinister truth.

Though promoted as a horror film, *The Psychic* is a much trickier beast as it navigates between a genteel drawing room mystery, a pulse-pounding traditional thriller, and Poe-inspired gothic horror. This wasn't the first Italian thriller to lift from Poe's *The Black Cat* (Sergio Martino beat Fulci to the punch by a couple of years), but the narrative gimmick is nicely carried over

here and sets up Fulci's later return to the same story with 1981's *The Black Cat*. Fans of Fulci's *One on Top of the Other* and *A Lizard in a Woman's Skin* will find a few subtle echoes here as well, though the lack of overt sadistic violence or sex has often confounded newcomers expecting another black-gloved special. Instead viewers are given surprisingly rich and committed performances by O'Neill and the late Porel, a knockout music score by the triad of Frizzi/Bixio/Tempera (later reprised prominently in the hospital sequence of *Kill Bill*), a tight and twisty narrative, and a nicely ambiguous resolution. Unfortunately the American ads blatantly gave away the film's big mid-story twist, but it still stands up well even with the key reversal exposed. Many of Fulci's best collaborators are in fine form here, with prolific scribes Dardano Sacchetti and Roberto Gianviti offering a much more coherent and literate script than usual for a late '70s Italian exploitation film and talented cinematographer Sergio Salvati making skilful use of shadows and sparing coloured lighting for maximum dramatic effect.

Many sources claim *The Psychic* was heavily butchered for its U.S. release, though most of the missing running time can be attributed to the fact that the opening titles (complete with a wonderfully kitschy theme song) were hacked away by more than half and the end titles were removed entirely. The bulk of the film remained intact, though the poor prints and absolutely wretched VHS incarnations from Vestron Video did little to win the film over with North Americans. It was one of the first Fulcis to receive a truly prominent stateside release, though, and its great Giger-inspired poster art managed to lure in a few ticket buyers. (Indian filmmakers must have been impressed, too, since they hilariously remade it almost scene-for-scene in the '80s as *100 Days*.) Grey market buyers had to resort to tracking down uncut, widescreen

Japanese dupes (under the wonderful title of *Murder to the Tune of the Seven Black Notes*), and eventually a remastered French DVD (under the title *L'emmurée vivante*) popped up briefly without any English-friendly options.

Severin's American release offers the best of all possible worlds with the original English language track (the preferable one as this was how the film was obviously shot, even though many of the supporting cast were looped by other voice performers later) and a cleaner, more skilfully compressed presentation of what seems to be the same anamorphic transfer (albeit with a different title card). Colour and sharpness look just fine, and the framing appears ideal. (The transfer is interlaced but seems to play just fine even bumped up to HD progressive, for those whose DVD decisions live or die by that.) The disc includes the rarely-seen U.S. trailer, in scratchy but colourful condition, which makes vivid use of the poster art and the Frizzi score, and a half-hour featurette, "Voices from the Black", using audio interviews (with various video clips to cover the footage) with Sacchetti (who has some clearly mixed feelings about his Fulci collaborations), editor Bruno Micheli, and costume designer Massimo Lentini, all of whom share stores about working with one of the grand fathers of Italian horror. Highly recommended, and a solid start for anyone wanting to enter the bloody waters of Lucio Fulci without getting soaked too heavily.

PSYCHO KICKBOXER

Colour, 1997, 90m. / Directed by David Haycox & Mardy South / Starring Curtis Bush, George James, Rick Clark, Kim Reynolds, Tom Story

CANVAS OF BLOOD

Colour, 1997, 89m. / Directed by Joel Denning / Starring Jennifer Hutt, Jack McClernan / Shock-O-Rama (US R0 NTSC)

If you thought Jean-Claude Van Damme movies were made for a bunch of wimps, then check out the 1990s zero-budget drive-in variation *Psycho Kickboxer*, a long out-of-print martial arts/vigilante/neon trash cult item paired up on DVD with the far more obscure *Canvas of Blood*, both from 1997. Real-life kickboxing champ Curtis Bush stars as Alex Hunter, an up-and-coming martial artist whose life is turned upside down when his father and girlfriend are brutally slain and he's beaten within an inch of his life. With the aid of a putty-faced, crusty Vietnam vet, he becomes the Dark Angel (the film's original title), a street-fighting, kickboxing, killing machine in a black body-length disguise which enables him to fight his opponents in Day-Glo surroundings. Blood sprays continuously amid cardboard performances and some of the funniest straight-to-video dialogue ever recorded; you could literally yank almost any scene from this film and make a perfect answering machine message. You really, really need this one in your collection, preferably for viewing late at night with friends and suds.

Far less notorious is its co-feature, a not-disguised-at-all rip-off of *Rolling Thunder* about a Vietnam vet whose daughter gets really bad carpal tunnel syndrome (or something... it's not really very clear) after being attacked by some thugs, so he hooks up a bunch of random sharp instruments to his stumpy arm for an ass-kicking rampage. As far as vigilante films go, this can't hold a dinky birthday candle to the main feature, but it's worth sitting through once your brain has been pulverised by the sheer awesomeness that is Curtis Bush. The Shock-O-Rama disc comes with both features on one disc in decent enough transfers given their direct-to-video origins, plus some great *Psycho Kickboxer* news spots and extraordinarily silly liner notes replicating a column from *Alternative Cinema* magazine.

PSYCHOS IN LOVE

Colour, 1987, 88m. / Directed by Gorman Bechard / Starring Carmine Capobianco, Debi Thibeault, Frank Stewart, Jerry Rakow / Shriek Show (US R1 NTSC)

If your taste in direct-to-video horror leans towards the nostalgic, this low-budget mixture of shocks and belly laughs earned a lot of indie ink in its day. While the title might lead you to expect some sort of '80s update of *The Honeymoon Killers*, this is a much odder beast as it chronicles the warped romantic relationship between two closeted serial killers, Joe (played by co-writer Carmine Capobianco), a lonely guy with a grape phobia, and Kate (Debi Thibeault), who likes to kill people when she isn't doing their nails. Their surprisingly blissful relationship is soon strained by external factors, including a cannibalistic plumber (Frank Stewart) and the competitive natures that arise when couples have similar interests – in this case, committing as much homicide as possible.

As much a comedy as a horror film, this labour of love packs in knowing references to its illustrious predecessors without becoming obnoxious or overdone, and in this case the simplistic, go-for-the-throat '80s aesthetic works in its favour. Chintzy synth music, a topless new wave chick, non sequitur monologues to the camera, even a theme song... If you're in the right frame of mind, it doesn't get better than this. Both leads are quite likeable; it's too bad no one ever made a crossover sequel teaming them up with the Blands from *Eating Raoul*.

After years of video limbo, this lovable sick puppy is finally back in circulation courtesy of Shriek Show, whose lavishly-appointed release comes with two Bechard commentaries (one solo, the other with Capobianco; the first one's better), a montage of making-of photos, the title sequence created for the Wizard Video release, a modest reel of extended footage that completists might enjoy, and weirdest of all, a highlight reel from the stage version mounted in Chicago in 2003! It's up there with the theatrical production of *The Children* seen on Troma's DVD for oddball novelty value. Meatiest of all is a new featurette, "Making *Psychos in Love*", which features just about everyone involved both behind and in front of the camera discussing the making of a movie whose full cult potential has yet to be reached. The new full frame transfer itself looks exactly like what you'd expect for a low budget '87 feature; it won't give Warner Brothers any sleepless nights in the tech department, but it's fine, splashy, and colourful, right up there with the better ones done from 16mm.

PUNK ROCK

Colour, 1977, 96m / Directed by Carter Stevens / Starring Wade Nichols, Robert Kerman, Jean Sanders, Susaye London

PLEASURE PALACE

Colour, 1979, 81m. / Directed by Carter Stevens / Starring Jamie Gillis, Eric Edwards, Serena, Robert Kerman / Secret Key (US R1 NTSC) / WS (1.78:1) (16:9)

One of the strangest phenomena about '70s adult filmmaking was the trend of creating multiple versions at the same time, one for the raincoat crowd as well as a softer cut often

featuring more plot and plenty of alternative footage. One of the most extreme examples of this approach is 1977's *Punk Rock*, also known on video as *Rock Orgy* and *Teenage Runaways*. The film was originally shot as a full-on porno flick starring late switch-hitting soap actor Wade Nichols as Jimmy Dillinger, a private eye combing New York's rock 'n' roll underworld as he follows a Spillane-esque trail after a tycoon's kidnapped daughter with plenty of murder and dope dealing around the corner. Then the producer recruited director Carter Stevens to revisit the film as a much less explicit grindhouse film with its brief bits of new wave performances expanded or replaced to spotlight the burgeoning punk scene, represented here by garage bands like The Stilettos, The Fast, The Squirrels and the Spicy Bits doin' their thing at Max's Kansas City. It's pretty fascinating stuff, and while the hard version has been around on video for ages (most recently in Alpha Blue's Carter Stevens triple bill set), this R-rated 96-minute variant has been incredibly elusive until now. For once it's great to finally see this very different and in some ways far more interesting retooling of one of the decade's most interesting trash cinema hybrids.

Accompanying this DVD release is the significantly less interesting softcore version of *Pleasure Palace*, a crime and sex outing with Eric Edwards and Jamie Gillis about a couple of big city guys who decide to open a whorehouse in the countryside, only to get far more than they bargained for. Serena and Robert Kerman are also on hand in a fairly well-acted but innocuous potboiler whose most intriguing aspect is the fact that, according to the commentary and liners, it was shot in a real brothel. Stevens actually provides full chat tracks for both films and seems to have a good memory for the production of both, talking about his experiences with the actors, the necessities of theatrical

tweaking for films in the '70s, the nature of porn pseudonyms, and much more. Secret Key's release also has a video interview with Stevens (in a funny T-shirt) about his career (including some good memories of Serena), a music video by The Fast for "It's Like Love", and the aforementioned liners, written by Michael J. Bowen. Only the second film is presented in 1.78:1 widescreen, with *Punk Rock* full frame and looking fine if a bit worn and soft and *Pleasure Palace* much more vivid and colourful but more tightly framed.

QUANDO L'AMORE È SENSUALITÀ

Colour, 1973, 89m. / Directed by Vittorio De Sisti / Starring Agostina Belli, Gianni Macchia, Françoise Prévost, Ewa Aulin, Femi Benussi, Umberto Raho / Cecchi Gori (Italy R2 PAL) / WS (1.85:1) (16:9)

Locked into an arranged marriage to chauvinistic meat dealer Antonio (*Emanuelle Around the World*'s Gianni Macchia), pretty young noble-woman Erminia (*The Fifth Cord*'s Agostina Belli) is alarmed when her new husband tries to join her in the bathtub and then attempts to have his way with her on their wedding night. Antonio finds solace by nailing a cheap hooker on a butcher's slab, while the virginal and extremely ill-informed Erminia seeks and fails to obtain advice from her prudish contessa mother (*The Murder Clinic*'s Françoise Prévost) and the prissy local priest (Umberto Raho). Confused, she retreats to stay with her wilder, blonder sister Angela (*Candy*'s Ewa Aulin) who immediately shows her a "great new way to massage your breasts" and plays sexy pranks on the local boys. Meanwhile Antonio brings home a hot-to-trot married woman (*Strip Nude for Your Killer*'s Femi Benussi) who gets heated up watching him chase cattle and asks him to "make me obey you like those cows did" while running around naked except for a wedding veil. All this fornication becomes too much for mama, who soon winds up in the sack with Antonio, too, before Erminia finally comes home and realises it's time to grow up.

A very confused but fascinating mixture of pro-sex education sermonising and Catholic guilt, this sexy potboiler is mainly worth watching for Belli and Benussi, two of the most beautiful '70s Italian starlets who drop their gowns with astonishing frequency here, as well as an excellent and often very groovy Ennio Morricone score. However, acting honours surprisingly go to Aulin, a Swedish sexpot actress who usually played passive, doe-eyed bimbos (and only rarely did real skin scenes, but not in this film); here she gets to cut loose with a third-act tirade that indicates her thespian skills could have been put to much better use by other directors. This being an Italian film, the dense, gold-digging, unfaithful Antonio (who surprisingly bares even more than his female co-stars) is freed from any responsibility for his behaviour, while the script wraps itself in knots to ensure Belli remains a virgin until the end credits, which roll over one of the most unintentionally bleak finales imaginable.

Virtually unknown outside Italy except to rabid Morricone fans, this film was apparently prepared with an English dub but never widely released. The good if imperfect 35mm print used for the Cecchi Gori DVD sports this English track along with English-language opening credits which bear the title *When Love Is Lust*. There's also an Italian language track with optional Italian subtitles. Much of the film is dubbed either way, so the English version is as good as any; Aulin's lines remain in synch, while everyone else seems to drift in and out depending on the scene. Extras are limited to text bios for the director (who mostly did minor sexy dramas and comedies) and major cast members.

QUEEN OF BLACK MAGIC

Colour, 1979, 90m. / Directed by Liliek Sudjio / Starring Suzzanna, W.D. Mochtar, Alan Nuary, Sofia W.D., Teddy Purba / Mondo Macabro (US R0 NTSC) / WS (2.35:1) (16:9)

When international horror first infiltrated the home video market back in the early 1980s, the Indonesian supernatural freak-out *Queen of Black Magic* was many viewers' first taste of low budget but outrageous Eastern filmmaking insanity, albeit in a badly cropped and borderline unwatchable form. Its title, which was often shortened to simply *Black Magic* or some variation thereof, caused it to often become confused with the gross-out Shaw Brothers series from Hong Kong in some reference guides, but this is pure 100% Indonesian insanity. Even if it doesn't quite hit the madcap heights of the legendary *Mystics in Bali* (and what could?), this makes a fine companion feature all the same.

After ditching the sexy Murni (*White Crocodile Queen*'s Suzzanna), young dolt Kohar (Alan Nuary) decides to marry his more traditional fiancée, Beda (Sofia W.D.). However, their wedding day is disrupted when the bride is subjected to traumatic visions which the groom naturally blames on his ex. Naturally, he does what any normal humiliated bridegroom would do – namely, rally up the villagers to burn down her house and chuck her off a cliff. Unfortunately for him, Murni survives and, understandably in a foul mood, enlists the aid of a dark magician hermit (W.D. Mochtar) to get revenge. As she crafts her evil powers in a remote cave, those who wronged her begin to die in outrageously gory sequences with the impulsive groom saved for last on her supernatural hit list.

Featuring one of the most memorable decapitation scenes ever seen and enough bright red plasma to satisfy any country's drive-in audiences, *Queen of Black Magic* still holds up as a raucous, entertaining joyride through the Asian horror catalogue of ghoulish treats and would make a fine introduction for anyone willing to dip their toes into this exotic territory. The more extreme elements of some Asian horror films (bug eating, flying entrails, etc.) hadn't really settled in yet, so even novice horror viewers should find this perfectly accessible. While the gore effects are certainly memorable (including some nasty skin bubbling), the real showstopper here is Suzzanna herself, who manages to ramp up the melodramatic fury to a delicious degree by the end of the film. Whether whirling around practicing her sorcery in front of a full moon or inflicting bloody whoopass in the finale with evil yoga (yes, really), she's always the centre of the film and understandably was a busy actress in the industry. Director Liliek Sudjio only directed a handful of features after this, but he displays a sure command of scope framing and works up a slow, creepy atmosphere of provincial dread punctuated with Grand Guignol insanity.

If ever there were a prototypical Mondo Macabro title, this would be it. Not surprisingly, they've gone all out rescuing it from VHS bootleg hell with a perfect new anamorphic transfer that looks as vivid and colourful as you could ever imagine. Like most Indonesian films, this was primarily made for an export English-speaking audience, so the English dub here is all that seems to be lying around. It's an amusing

but not particularly good track, and the hissy sound quality isn't much of a boost over the old VHS, but it's tolerable enough all the same. Extras include a really dire-looking, VHS-sourced trailer prepared for the home video release, and a great 10-minute "Indonesian Light & Magic: A Tour Around the Studio of SFX Maestro El Badrun", which features the make-up artist goofing around with some of his monstrous creations, demonstrating a few moulding effects, and generally showing off his studio, which looks like a straw shack in the middle of the woods with lots of preteen local boys helping him out. Definitely worth a look, and a far cry from the usual FX featurettes found on Hollywood DVDs. Also included are a typically well-written essay about the film and that beloved Mondo Macabro promo reel.

RAREFLIX TRIPLE FEATURE VOL. 1:
POSED FOR MURDER
Colour, 1989, 90m. / Directed by Brian Thomas Jones / Starring Charlotte J. Helmkamp, Rick Gianasi, Michael Merrins, Herb Farnham, Terri Brennan
DEATH COLLECTOR
Colour, 1988, 92m. / Directed by Tom Garrett / Starring Daniel Chapman, Ruth Collins, Loren Blackwell
THE DISTURBANCE
Colour, 1990, 93m. / Directed by Cliff Guest / Starring Timothy Greeson, Lisa Geoffrion, Ken Ceresne / Media Blasters (US R1 NTSC)

In an interesting bid at capturing viewer interest in straight-to-video obscurities that might have little customer appeal on their own, Media Blasters kicked off a series of

"Rareflix" collections highlighting weird diversions unseen since the vintage VHS days, usually dating from the mid-'80s to '90s. The *Rareflix Triple Feature Vol. 1* set packs together three very different films, all of which are definitely off the radar of all but the most thorough excavator of video store arcana. *Posed for Murder* is essentially an American slasher variation on movies like *Murder-Rock* and *Too Beautiful to Die* courtesy of director Brian Thomas Jones, the guy behind *The Rejuvenator*. Buxom *Playboy* Playmate Charlotte Helmkamp stars as Laura, a pinup model (of course) who's branching out into scream queen roles. Her bodybuilder boyfriend Danny decides he doesn't want all the pervs out in the audience drooling over his girl, so he goes nuts and starts hacking and slashing his way through all the men in her life, perhaps working his way up to the hunk-lunk male cop (*Sgt. Kabukiman*'s Rick Gianasi) assigned to the case. Utterly trashy and oh-so-very 1989 (with that great soft, Day-Glo veneer more commonly found in the Shapiro-Glickenhaus canon), this is delicious cinematic swill.

Up next is *Death Collector*, an odder genre hybrid made one year earlier, in which the America of the future has morphed into some sort of rockabilly western no man's land, where a diabolical insurance company (not called AIG, alas) rules the town of Hartford City. After being set up for his brother's murder, Wade (Daniel Chapman) pops out of prison and, with the aid of two cohorts, embarks on a quest for justice – future style! Dark, stylish and definitely weirder than its generic VHS cover would indicate, this is one odd find to be sure and features a few unexpected faces like female lead Ruth Collins (who appeared in plenty of films for everyone from Roberta Findlay to Joe D'Amato) and even the once-ubiquitous splatterpunk writers Skipp & Spector!

Finally it's back to psycho territory again with *The Disturbance*, probably the most accessible film out of the bunch. Taking a page from the splatter classic *Nightmare*, it's the story of disturbed, frizzy-haired Clay (Timothy Greeson, in his only film role), a schizophrenic dumped out of a mental hospital who tries making a go of getting a girlfriend, but finding his perception of the world around him growing more terrifying by the day as he hallucinates demons in his TV, floating eyeballs in his bathtub, and even his mom coming on to him in the shower (probably the most startling scene in the movie), with disastrous results for the family cat. Meanwhile people are dying off in his vicinity, which isn't exactly an encouraging sign. Featuring show-stopping horror and gore effects by Tom Savini protégé Barry Anderson (*Jeepers Creepers*), this one (also apparently released as *What's Wrong with the Neighbor's Son?*) packs in the shocks and T&A aplenty and makes for a pretty solid portrayal of mental illness as well.

All three titles are presented full frame and are most likely pulled from the original masters used for their VHS releases, though obviously the leaps made in video technology mean these are at least crisper and more stable-looking than their home video ancestors. You get a few trailers with each disc, but the coolest extra is an Easter Egg commentary for each movie, accessible either by clicking on the "Rare" logo in the menu or just switching audio on the fly with your remote. At least two of them were recorded on the same night and feature some audible beer consumption, which is probably a good idea for viewers trying to tackle more than one in a day, too. The commentators here are Media Blasters personnel William Hellfire, Richard York and Dave Beinlich, who generally stick on-topic to the films at hand while rattling off frequently surprising credits for everyone involved. It's also hilarious, too, with perhaps the highlight being Helmkamp's bust described as "full and life-giving".

RAREFLIX TRIPLE FEATURE VOL. 2:
RUN LIKE HELL
Colour, 1995, 78m. / Directed by Eric Brummer / Starring Robert Z'Dar, Elizabeth Lamont

MOLLY AND THE GHOST
Colour, 1991, 87m. / Directed by Donald M. Jones / Starring Lee Darling, Ena Henderson, Daniel Martine, Ron Moriarty

THE KILLER LIKES CANDY
Colour, 1968, 85m. / Directed by Federico Chentrens & Maurice Cloche / Starring Kerwin Mathews, Marilù Tolo, Venantino Venantini, Gordon Mitchell, Umberto Raho, Fabienne Dali / Media Blasters (US R1 NTSC)

Once again this oddball triple bill series sets its sights on wonderful hidden treasures outside the norm for the current DVD market. Basically these are all obscure, often startling films that no sane person would ever expect to see released on any kind of digital format, so let's start off with the looniest and crappiest of the bunch, *Run Like Hell*, which is best described as 78 minutes of shot-on-video drive-in pandemonium. Utterly gratuitous T&A, radioactive zombies, shotgun battles, filthy voyeuristic sex scenes, a monosyllabic pseudo-ninja wielding a sword, a chainsaw duel, depressing desert scenery and lots of bad lighting are just a few of the joys you'll experience here. The sketchy plot takes place in the far-off, desolate future of 2008 (this was shot in '95, after all) in which single women are kept naked except for G-strings at a dusty outpost, where militaristic Robert Z'Dar entertains his men with the occasional prisoner dalliance. Eventually some of the women get out, a bounty hunter is recruited to go after them, and the second half of the film involves random people colliding in the desert and fighting over and over again. It's utterly incompetent on every possible level, which of course makes it perfect late-night viewing, preferably with a little alcohol to make the ride go a little easier.

Up next is the considerably more professional (but less outrageous) *Molly and the Ghost*, an erotic supernatural thriller most interesting for the fact that it was directed by Don Jones, best known for weird exploitation favourites like *Girls in Chains*, *The Forest* and the sadly still-MIA *The Love Butcher*. Molly (Lee Darling) and her sister, Susan (Ena Henderson), don't have the greatest relationship, which is proven when the latter falls in love with Molly's stud-muffin husband and hires a hit man to take Molly out so she can have him all to herself. However, the idiot caps Susan instead, who comes back as a ghost to... uh... really upset everyone around her. Part *Playboy* pictorial, part soap opera, and part ghost/zombie flick, it's a strange outing indeed with a surprisingly attractive and accomplished cast and some nutty plot turns that rapidly head towards a truly whacked-out finale. Imagine a gothic romance novel channelled through Full Moon Pictures, and you'll sort of get the idea.

Last up we hit Eurocult territory with the oldest film of the trio, *The Killer Likes Candy*, a title beloved by anyone who remembers the days of Video Gems VHS tapes (whose release sported a rifle-toting assassin munching on some taffy). The cast here features former Harryhausen heart-throb Kerwin Mathews, "handsome" '70s Euro starlet Marilù Tolo, and peplum favourite Gordon Mitchell, while die-hards will also spot regulars like Umberto Raho and Fabienne Dali in the story of a relentless ex-Nazi contract killer who, yes, likes candy. Apparently nothing calms one's nerves during an assassination like a good piece of taffy. Kerwin's the American agent

R

brought in to protect his latest target, an important Asian ruler, while funky lounge music by Gianni Marchetti blasts away on the soundtrack. The killer's repeated attempts send our hero all over Italy wind up with a nifty showdown in the Roman catacombs. Quite fun actually if you have a taste for '60s Euro-spy antics, and the set's DVD presents the usual English-dubbed version in what at least appears to be a generation or two above the old tape edition. This time just two of the titles feature "hidden" drunken commentaries by DVD Talk writer Ian Jane, who reels off some hilarious observations and obscure trivia that can only enhance these unorthodox viewing experiences.

RAZORBACK

Colour, 1984, 95m. / Directed by Russell Mulcahy / Starring Gregory Harrison, Arkie Whiteley, Bill Kerr, Judy Morris / Umbrella (Australia R0 PAL), Anchor Bay (UK R2 PAL), e-m-s (Germany R2 PAL), Warner Archive (US R0 NTSC) / WS (2.35:1) (16:9)

 Who would've guessed that the biggest Aussie horror hit of the '80s would be about a killer pig? Future *Highlander* director Russell Mulcahy got his start with this unlikely outback fright film, which was also the first leading man vehicle for TV star Gregory Harrison. Something big, hairy and tusky is ripping apart homes and residents in the outback, particularly a small child whose grandfather is blamed for the death. An American TV reporter (Judy Morris) arrives on the scene, and when she also runs afoul of the oversized terror, her husband (Harrison) takes up arms to hunt down the menace.

The smart script features some amusing one-liners, and the film offers plenty of juicy gore scenes while playing around with the template established by *Jaws*. *Razorback* got a hefty international release by Warner Brothers and found plenty of admirers on TV (even with its evocative scope compositions lopped in half). So far the Australian DVD is the best way to go; the film was slightly trimmed of some spewing blood shots in its native country, and while the extra footage slipped into some of the Warner prints, it's missing on the remastered anamorphic version used for the R0 issue as well as the less decked-out Region 2 Anchor Bay U.K. edition and bare bones (not to mention ragged-looking) DVD-on-demand version from Warner Archive.

The cheaper Umbrella disc wins by including the extra shots as bonus material and for also including a new documentary, "Jaws on Trotters", which features pretty much everyone from the film except for Harrison talking about its creation and the elaborate special effects. However, Harrison does pop up along with cinematographer Dean Semler for a few audio recollections about the film, probably recorded via telephone. You also get the trailer and a stills and poster gallery.

The e-m-s release from Germany is essentially the same as the Aussie version, spreading the same transfer and extras onto two discs while adding a batch of animal horror trailers like *Rottweiler*, *Pythons 2*, and *Arachnid* as a minimal extra enticement.

REFINEMENTS IN LOVE

Colour, 1971, 90m. / Directed by Carlos Tobalina / Starring Liz Renay, Rene Bond, Ric Lutze, Ron Darby, William Howard, Brigitte Maier / Impulse (US R0 NTSC) / WS (1.66:1) (16:9)

This sex-ed "documentary" is basically a mondo project spiced up with hardcore vignettes. Credit goes to busy and always intriguing adult director Carlos Tobalina, who even goes post-modern by including references to himself and his films as case studies.

The narrator, Liz Renay (late star of *Desperate Living*), informs us that a new sexual morality has taken hold of the world, a revolutionary freedom which can be found in, well, porn films and San Francisco free love. Some uncredited adult performers strut their stuff (with phoney stories narrated to give them justification), including Rene Bond, her real-life boyfriend Ric Lutze, Brigitte Maier, Ron Darby, and one of the few explicit performances from William Howard, best known for a string of Zoltan G. Spencer softies like *Danish and Blue* and *Terror at Orgy Castle*. (The mysterious identities of both Tobalina and Spencer have spurred theories that they are one and the same.) It's utterly random and unpredictable (with the title card popping up halfway into the film!), creating a disorderly but compelling experience. Anyone expecting a normal adult film will be baffled, but if you're up for some delirious tabloid film-making with whiplash-inducing sex scenes, you can't do much better. The anamorphic transfer looks excellent with only some minor print damage, surprising given the obscurity of this movie, which probably only saw the light of one projector.

Little seen in America, *Rica* was part of Toho's three-film attempt to compete with the growing wave of Pinky Violence movies in Japanese cinemas from studios like Toei. (Trailers for the other two, *Rica: Lonely Wanderer* and *Rica: Juvenile's Lullaby* are included as extras.)

Rika Aoki stars as the title character, the teenaged offspring of a Japanese woman raped by a GI. She's first seen avenging the death of a fellow gang member who's just given birth by demanding the gangster bury his infant, which quickly escalates into violence and lands her in reform school. Soon she breaks out when she learns her gang sisters have been shipped off into Vietnamese sex slavery, and the plot continues to escalate into a breathless series of maimings, go-go strip scenes, sexual assaults, murders, chases... well, you get the idea. Any ten-minute segment of this film would make a priceless drive-in movie by itself, and the entire film barely pauses to catch its breath. The style is gritty and natura-listic overall (with none of the stylisation which tended to creep into many Pinky Violence and Roman Porno films), but it ladles on the sleaze with plenty of topless nudity and a startling arm removal by butcher knife that must be seen to be believed. A great party film, to be sure. The Media Blasters sub-label Exploitation Digital brings this to English-speaking audiences in fine form with a splendid 16x9 scope transfer and a new English subtitle translation.

R

RICA

Colour, 1972, 92m. / Directed by Kô Nakahira / Starring Rika Aoki, Kazuko Nagamoto, Masami Souda, Michi Nono / Exploitation Digital (US R1 NTSC) / WS (2.35:1) (16:9)

RIOT ON 42ND ST.

Colour, 1987, 89m. / Directed by Tim Kincaid / Starring John Hayden, Michael Speero, Jeff Fahey, Kate Collins, Rick Gianasi, Zerocks / Shriek Show (US R1 NTSC)

A latecomer to the grind-house game near the end of the '80s, this ode to the wonderfully sleazy cesspool known as 42nd Street is most valuable now as a snapshot of this extinct terrain before its Disney-led consumerist overhaul. The first twenty minutes is essentially a loving portrait of the area as the camera lingers on trash cinema marquees and hookers who physically assault potential johns who don't want to pony up enough cash. The events are held together by our protagonist, military vet Glen Barnes (John Hayden), who returns to his old stomping grounds fresh from the slammer. His plans to open up an ambitious strip club/gambling joint called The Garage don't sit well with vice baron Farrell (Michael Speero) across the street, who senses competition against his own den of inequity. Their duel comes to a head on opening night when Farrell takes drastic, violent action against his rival, which kicks off the uprising of the title with a brawl erupting out in the streets.

Though it received a nominal VHS release in Asia, this has been a film far more known by hearsay than actual viewing experience thanks to a mysterious lack of distribution in all major English-speaking territories. Perhaps this can be attributed to lousy timing, as the theatrical demand for flicks like this suddenly bottomed out with greater studio control over movie screens as well as a tighter grasp on the video rental market. Of course, the fact that it's a technically inept movie featuring zonked-out performances probably didn't help, but the avalanche of sleaze on display (including the very violent finale) should have ensured at least some commercial prospects. No one seems to quite know how Jeff Fahey managed to land in this film as a detective when his career was otherwise on a roll at the time, but it's hilarious to see him looking confused in the midst of all the mayhem. Director Tim Kincaid (also known as busy gay porn helmer Joe Gage) was in the middle of a weird three-year attempt at "mainstream" filmmaking that also included *Bad Girls Dormitory*, *Robot Holocaust*, *Breeders*, and the misbegotten *She's Back*, which will give you an idea of what to expect here.

Given the extreme rarity of this film before its DVD release courtesy of Shriek Show, most viewers shouldn't be surprised that it appears to be derived from the existing '80s video master (i.e., the one they used to create the VHS version but looking a bit better here). It's doubtful whether any film elements even exist for this thing anymore. In any case, for what it's worth, the presentation is very dated and underwhelming but somehow appropriate given the film itself. Unfortunately the major players don't show up to offer any insight, but you do get an amusing short skit on comedian Zerocks (who has a small role in the film), a brief "Death of the Deuce" piece comparing the locations then and now, a hidden Easter Egg, and trailers for pretty much every Shriek Show grindhouse-related title (23 in all) including *Love Me Deadly*, *Bad Girls Dormitory*, *Burial Ground*, and many, many more.

ROCK 'N' ROLL NIGHTMARE

Colour, 1987, 89m. / Directed by John Fasano / Starring Jon-Mikl Thor, Teresa Simpson, Jesse D'Angelo, Dave Lane, Rusty Hamilton / Synapse (US R0 NTSC) / WS (1.78:1) (16:9) / DD5.1

Ah, heavy metal horror, you are missed. Gone are the days of the late 1980s when intrepid terror fans could enjoy video favourites like *Rocktober Blood* and their theatrical brethren such as *Trick or Treat*, all feature-length fusions of head-banging metal and gore-drenched horror. Key among this subgenre was director John Fasano, who assaulted the world with his astonishing 1987 home video favourite, *Rock 'n' Roll Nightmare*, and its equally worthy successor, *Black Roses*. Starring the unofficial godfather of Viking rock, Jon-Mikl Thor, *Rock 'n' Roll Nightmare* uses that old horror chestnut, a bunch of people going out to an old farmhouse and discovering unrelenting terror, only to break the rules during a climactic showdown that simply must be seen to be believed. Here the potential demon food is an aspiring metal band, the Tritonz, led by blond-maned singer John Triton (Thor), whose choice of a remote farmhouse proves to be unfortunate considering the site consumed its previous residents. Along with some ditzy groupies, the band members talk a lot, eat, and "rock", but something nasty is waiting in the shadows. After a few false scares, the interlopers are picked off by a demonic force until Triton eventually reveals his true persona in the mind-shattering final plot twist, which pits him against Satan himself. No kidding.

This movie is just incredible. Shot in the wild woods of Canada with a menagerie of monsters straight from a deranged kiddie show, *Rock 'n' Roll Nightmare* is a far cry from the usual slasher-choked '80s horror fare. No one can act, but Thor's antics manage to ramp up the entertainment value scene by scene until the final climactic explosion of pure cinematic Limburger. Still a rock/metal personality, Thor (who previously headlined the *MST3000* favourite *Zombie Nightmare*) really chews the scenery here, particularly the iconic climax in which he battles Play-Doh monsters with all the zeal of a professional wrestler. And then of course there's the music, since the film was evidently designed as an extended commercial for his band (and Coca-Cola as

well); by the film's end, you too will be screaming, "We live to rock!"

Salvaged from the refuse of '80s VHS hell, *Rock 'n' Roll Nightmare* is presented in a ridiculously extravagant special edition (under its original title, *The Edge of Hell*), complete with an HD transfer that looks a million times better than you would ever expect. Now every metal stud, coiffed blond hair, and rubbery beast looks crystal clear. Then there's the audio, which comes in the original mono or, far more delightfully, a rousing 5.1 remix guaranteed to make your home theatre system beg for mercy. Want even more? How about an audio commentary by Thor and Fasano, both of whom seem to have a pretty good grasp on the movie's absurdity and relate plenty of stories about the production – identifying friends and relatives, explaining what the hell "Special Appearance by Rusty Hamilton" means, pointing out that none of the band members actually played their instruments, and explaining the role of Cheerios in creating a starfish monster. Thor (in a Synapse T-shirt) also supplies brief opening and closing wraparound comments for the film and gets into the spotlight completely for "Revelations of a Rock 'n' Roll Warrior", a featurette interspersing a new Thor interview with plenty of music bits, film clips, backstage video footage, and other visual ephemera, plus a new performance of "We Live to Rock" over the end credits. The behind-the-scenes featurette "Creating a Child-Wolf" covers the creation of the furry kid-monster via plenty of VHS footage, while "Rock 'n' Shock Memories" features another 21-minute compilation of backstage coverage, mostly focusing on the monsters. Top it all off with newly-created music videos for "Energy" and "We Live to Rock", plus enthusiastic liner notes by Ian Jane from DVD Maniacs, and you've got one seriously essential, certifiably insane release.

ROSARIGASINOS

Colour, 2001, 90m. / Directed by Rodrigo Grande / Starring Federico Luppi, Ulises Dumont, María José Demare, Francisco Puente / Synapse (US R0 NTSC) / WS (1.85:1) (16:9) / DD2.0

This fast-paced and oddly affectionate crime comedy follows the autumn-year antics of two shabby robbers, Tito (Federico Luppi) and Castor (Ulises Dumont), who get released from the slammer after a couple of decades and, as you'd expect, emerge to find their whole environment radically changed. Like a couple of criminal Rip Van Winkles, they do all they can to connect with their old cohorts in crime and find the stolen cash they stashed in a lake, but the plan doesn't remotely go as planned and they must resort to their rusty thieving skills to make it in a much faster lifestyle than the one they knew.

A modest, witty, and sometimes stylish character study, *Rosarigasinos* is well served by a great central performance from Federico Luppi, a very busy actor best known for his stellar work in *Pan's Labyrinth*, *Cronos* and *The Stone Raft*. Synapse's DVD is bare bones but offers a sturdy anamorphic 1.85:1 transfer (albeit with inexplicably severe window-boxing), while the Spanish language track sounds fine and features optional English subtitles.

ROSELYNE AND THE LIONS

Colour, 1989, 175m. / Directed by Jean-Jacques Beineix / Starring Isabelle Pasco, Gérard Sandoz, Gabriel Monnet, Philippe Clévenot / Cinema Libre (US R0 NTSC), M6 (France R2 PAL) / WS (1.85:1) (16:9) / DD2.0

After his two best-known films, *Diva* and *Betty Blue*, director Jean-Jacques Beineix bid adieu to major international releases with this barely-seen but extremely worthwhile romantic fantasy, an ode to circus life, big cats and domination. Isabelle Pasco (*Prospero's Books*) stars as the title character, a beautiful girl first seen taming lions by Thierry (Gérard Sandoz), a rebellious student prone to playing mean-spirited pranks on his instructor. He signs up for lion taming sessions and eventually becomes an assistant, but after being fired he and Roselyne go on the road to find their destiny, ultimately getting their big chance in Germany with a lavish circus where jealousy threatens to tear them apart.

As with the director's previous films, this is a colourful, visually ravishing experience and a tender look at the wondrous mysteries of the human heart. Originally the feature was prepared in a 115-minute cut for international consumption but barely found an audience, so a longer, two-part version was prepared for French television. This same edition forms the basis for the "integrale" cut released on DVD, compiling all the footage from both extant versions, and it's a huge improvement; the restored opening scenes in particular are crucial to establishing the character of Thierry, who otherwise makes no sense at all.

A major international undertaking to restore Beineix's films resulted in two DVD releases, with the American edition from Cinema Libre offering the restored anamorphic transfer, optional English subtitles, and a fascinating 78-minute documentary, "The Grand Circus", with the director and cast shown throughout the filmmaking process and exploring their relationships with the incredible big cats seen onscreen.

Unfortunately it's all shoved onto one DVD which results in some noticeable compression problems; 253 minutes is way too much for comfort on a dual-layered DVD, but the release is recommended nevertheless simply as a way to experience this underrated, extremely rewarding film. The double-disc French release from M6 has no English subtitle options but wisely allows the feature to breathe by itself on the first disc, and the director contributes a French-only commentary track as well. The second disc contains "The Grand Circus" and a host of additional extras including three theatrical trailers, a storyboard comparison, a photo gallery, and an additional 45-minute documentary, "Des fauves et des hommes", about the preparation, filming and aftermath of the production. It's probably not very useful for non-French speakers, but completists may want to check the French release out all the same.

THE RUG COP

Colour, 2006, 85m / Directed by Minoru Kawasaki / Starring Fuyuki Moto, Hitomi Takashima, Yusuke Kirishima / Synapse (US R1 NTSC) / WS (1.85:1) (16:9) / DD2.0

A self-proclaimed spoof of Japanese cop shows, *The Rug Cop* (*Zura Deka*) comes off like it's aspiring to *The Naked Gun* without all the pop culture references. (Or maybe *Hot Fuzz* without the blood.) Our hero, Inspector Genda (Fuyuki Moto), is able to take out criminals with his powerful toupee, which has the Oddjob-like ability to fly through the air and inflict serious bodily harm. Assigned to a new precinct, he finds his skills put to the test when terrorists make off with enough nuclear material to take out the nation's capital. And that's pretty much it.

Goofball director Minoru Kawasaki (*Executive Koala*, *The World Sinks Except Japan*) piles on the visual gags, though the humour here doesn't translate quite as well as most of his other films available with English subtitles. At least Moto makes for an amusingly peculiar leading man, and if you're in an undemanding mood, this could do the trick. Synapse's disc showcases a pleasing-enough anamorphic transfer and includes three making-of featurettes (behind the scenes, cast and crew interviews, and a press conference), plus the trailer. At least it's a lot better than that terrible "Hell Toupee" episode from *Amazing Stories*.

RUNNING HOT

Colour, 1984, 95m. / Directed by Mark Griffiths / Starring Eric Stoltz, Monica Carrico, Stuart Margolin, Virgil Frye / Code Red (US R0 NTSC) / WS (1.85:1) (16:9)

Though it bears a 1984 copyright mark, anyone could be easily forgiven for mistaking the couple-on-the-run saga *Running Hot* for a '70s drive-in movie. Drawing inspiration from the likes of *Dirty Mary Crazy Larry*, *Macon County Line* and *Badlands*, it features a young, pre-*Mask* Eric Stoltz as Danny, a teen falsely accused of murdering his father. Sentenced to death, he manages to escape from prison and goes on the lam with Charlene (Monica Carrico, a good actress who basically vanished), a hooker and exotic dancer whose clients enjoy scenarios like having sex in presidential face masks. Charlene's crush on Danny (including love letters to him in prison) motivates her to help him find the real killer, with a dogged and very brutal cop (Stuart Margolin) closing in fast behind them.

With guns, T&A, skinny dipping and a literally explosive, downbeat finale, *Running Hot* earned only a few appreciative followers during its sparse theatrical run and short VHS life, but it deserves a much wider following now that a watchable version is on DVD. Surprisingly, this was the first feature by Mark Griffiths, who went on to direct both *Hardbodies* films and a slew of made-for-TV features. The fact that he never dabbled in territory like this again is a shame, but at least we can enjoy this one.

Griffiths is all over the DVD, offering a video intro to the film, a lengthy on-camera interview in which he talks about his segue from writer to director mounting a low budget production with a mostly unknown cast, and most detailed of all, an audio commentary with producer David Callaway and moderator Lee Christian. It's a detailed, informative chat that covers the careers of most of the actors along with the shooting locations and the logistics of the sparse but effective action scenes. The transfer looks fine, if a tad soft and slightly horizontally squeezed (which can be fixed on most TV sets). Other extras include a hefty stills gallery (with lots of foreign lobby cards) and an alternative European title sequence.

SACRED FLESH

Colour, 2000, 72m. / Directed by Nigel Wingrove / Starring Sally Tremaine, Moyna Cope, Simon Hill, Kristina Bill, Eileen Daly / Redemption (UK R0 PAL, US R0 NTSC), Heretic (US R0 NTSC) / WS (1.78:1) (16:9) / DD.20

Redemption Films founder Nigel Wingrove takes a stab at reviving nunsploitation with this short and swift tribute to the blasphemous Italian and British sexathons from the '70s.

Interestingly, the film doesn't try to outdo its predecessors for shock value, instead opting for surrealism and post-music-video style to buoy the familiar story of a Mother Superior, Sister Elizabeth (Sally Tremaine), whose own carnal desires and accusations of inappropriate behaviour among her sisters provokes an investigation into her potential possession by the devil. Soon she's experiencing intense visions which bring all of her religious training into doubt and the residents at the Church of the Sacred Heart into sexual turmoil.

Slightly smarter and weightier than one might expect given the subject matter, the film still piles on the gropings and bare flesh enough to satisfy casual drive-in fanatics despite such drawbacks as budgetary restraints, excessive slow motion and some very tacky, anachronistic breast implants. All of the DVD editions (the Heretic one sports the most peculiar menus) present a colourful 16x9 transfer that makes the most of the DV photography. Extras include a somewhat dry feature-length Wingrove commentary, two trailers, storyboards, stills, and a soundtrack promo.

THE SADIST WITH RED TEETH

Colour, 1970, 80m. / Directed by Jean Louis van Belle / Starring Daniel Moosmann, Jane Clayton, Albert Simono

FORBIDDEN PARIS

Colour, 1969, 82m. / Directed by Jean Louis van Belle / Starring Ben Ghou Bey, Gene Fenn, The Cyclamen Angel / Mondo Macabro (US R0 NTSC) / WS (1.66:1) (16:9)

Just when you thought the wildest recesses of vintage French exploitation had been explored, this double bill from Mondo Macabro proves there are plenty of mysterious dark

corners still out there awaiting rediscovery. A name known only to die-hard repertory programmers, Jean Louis van Belle began his career as an assistant director on a handful of unassuming titles but went wild when he got to helm his own projects throughout the 1970s. None of his films were widely seen, but a few intriguing titles popped up in reference books. Chief among these is *The Sadist with Red Teeth* (credited on the print here as *Dents rouges*), a fascinating semi-horror oddity that predates *Martin* and *Vampire's Kiss* as the first psychological portrayal of an unstable, would-be vampire. Our tale begins with graphic artist Daniel (*My New Partner*'s Albert Simono) released from an urban mental hospital despite the fact that he's clearly still unbalanced from a car wreck that left a friend dead with blood splashing onto his mouth. Daniel is now convinced he's a vampire, and his doctors have come up with the theory that he should be encouraged in his delusions so that he can "work through it to the other side" and find sanity. Well, you can obviously see how that plan might go a tad awry. Daniel's girlfriend, Jane (Jane Clayton), obviously has some difficulty figuring out what's wrong with him and why he goes out prowling for prey, and things gradually get more feverish until the grand finale which finds Daniel donning some plastic vampire fangs at a costume ball that quickly turns into a nightmare. On paper, the storyline for *Sadist* sounds fairly straightforward, but van Belle's execution definitely is not. Trippy music, psychedelic opening credits, and regular interjections of stock footage and free-associative cutaways worthy of Nicolas Roeg make this a constantly disorienting experience, more pop-art mash up than horror film. He does include some of the requisite commercial elements like topless nudity and occasional splashes of blood, but the execution is going to sit far better with art house devotees than anyone looking for a Hammer-inspired vampire romp.

Incredibly, things get even nuttier with the DVD's companion feature, *Forbidden Paris*, van Belle's debut feature. This late entry in the mondo craze is one of the most berserk offerings from this often reviled subgenre, with van Belle distressingly claiming that everything in it is real. Once again the colourful, negative-processed opening credits indicate you're in for something special, and soon the standard mondo structure of a narrator unveiling various eccentric practices in a known metropolis gets turned into something bordering on the maniacal. A fakir and his followers jab needles and small blades through various soft areas of their bodies, a group marriage finds all the men and women swapping vows and sloppy kisses with each other, a horse slaughterhouse gets detailed a little too much for comfort, and most horrifically, we get to see a taxidermist specialising in pet preservation tackling his latest project, a cute doggie whose road to immortality is preserved for ten excruciating minutes before its owner sees the finished product and lets out a bark of approval. Ah, and then there's the sequence in which we meet a bunch of Nazi-obsessed fetishists led by an aging Hitler look-alike who induct new members by stripping them and painting their bodies with a yellow Star of David before marching proudly down the Champs-Élysées. A quick look at a real-life Parisian vampire will also look suspiciously familiar to anyone who's seen the first feature, too. Though stylistically more restrained then *Sadist*, this more than equals it in terms of sheer nerve and shock value.

Mondo Macabro continues its unsurpassed track record with absolutely stunning, mint quality HD-sourced transfers of both features that look remarkably fresh and vivid even on large displays. The 1.66:1 framing looks perfect, and the optional English subtitles are well-written and appear to be accurate. As usual the disc provides plenty of bonus material for context because frankly a lot of viewers would just be baffled otherwise. The director provides intros to both features, explaining how they began as commercial projects which morphed to conform to his own artistic sensibilities. His defence of the "realism" of *Forbidden Paris* basically argues that the actors really did these things on camera, thus making it "genuine", but apart from the two scenes involving animal carcasses, this still qualifies it as staged in most people's book. Also included is a longer documentary about van Belle with various film festival programmers, critics, and co-workers offering an appraisal of this unique director whose body of work is ripe for rediscovery. Here's hoping some of his ten other unavailable films make it out of the gate somewhere down the line. Also included are well-written production notes on disc one and, of course, the obligatory Mondo Macabro promo reel.

SALÒ, OR THE 120 DAYS OF SODOM

Colour, 1975, 116m. / Directed by Pier Paolo Pasolini / Starring Paolo Bonacelli, Aldo Valletti, Franco Merli, Hélène Surgère, Elsa De Giorgi / Criterion (US R1 NTSC), BFI (DVD & Blu-ray, UK R2 PAL/HD), Gaumont (DVD & Blu-ray, France R2 PAL/HD) / WS (1.85:1) (16:9)

In 1944 fascist-controlled Italy, a group of debauched, ruthless libertines and their armed cohorts force a group of young teenagers into a nearby palace where an additional quartet of equally degenerate women regales them with stories of sexual depravity, often with musical accompaniment. The tyrants forbid any sexual activity without permission but subject their usually nude prisoners to a series of degrading social experiments involving a grotesque wedding, an even more repellent dinner banquet, a contest to determine the most attractive derriere with the winner threatened at the barrel of a gun, and other constructive pastimes.

Still one of the most incendiary movies ever made, this film was the last for controversial director Pier Paolo Pasolini and, according to many conspiracy theories, was largely responsible for his still-debated murder. Sections of footage were stolen, the Italian government was outraged, and censorship and distribution obstacles plagued the film for years following its release; however, its status as a harsh but essential classic of world cinema has only continued to grow over the years. Certainly the subject matter is stomach-churning and hardly a fun evening at the movies, but the execution is elevated by ravishing cinematography, sparse but intelligent use of music (from Pasolini's regular collaborator Ennio Morricone), and all-too-convincing performances (with many actors reportedly quite jovial on the set and unaware of the tone the finished product would achieve). The finale in particular remains a hot topic of discussion, essentially taking Michael Powell's *Peeping Tom* a step further by staging an entire courtyard full of atrocities through the eyes of various spectators who invert their binoculars and close out the film with a haunting, oddly touching slow dance.

On home video the film has proven no less inflammatory, igniting a much-publicised police bust of an American gay bookstore and also going down in history as the first Criterion DVD to go out of circulation, quickly earning absurd amounts of money from online sellers. The BFI introduced its own version licensed from MGM in the wake of this discontinuation, but both titles were highly problematic due to soft, noticeably cropped non-anamorphic transfers, a lack of any useful supplemental material and, in the case of the Criterion version, the absence of 25 seconds of footage from a Gottfried Benn poem reading at a mock wedding. Both Criterion and the BFI eventually offered their own remastered special editions, each of which was licensed from MGM and transferred from the original Italian negative with somewhat different visual results. The Criterion features more intense colours (possibly artificially enhanced) while the BFI is much, much sharper (definitely artificially enhanced), which makes it look crisper on smaller monitors but causes havoc on large displays with trees and finely detailed clothing suffering from very bright, distracting aliasing. It's still an attractive transfer but definitely a notch or two below the BFI's superlative work on Pasolini's Trilogy of Life. (A simultaneous French release has no English-friendly options and basically uses the same extras as the BFI edition.) Both releases also contain the optional English dub, which isn't bad at all; given the nature of Italian filmmaking at the time, the film was shot without sound and had each language soundtrack created in the studio, with Pasolini personally preferring the French one. In any case, the Italian version is just as dubbed and even less in synch then the English track.

The two-disc BFI and Criterion editions share some common ground in terms of extras: the Italian theatrical trailer and "Fade to Black", a 23-minute featurette with Mark Kermode covering the film's influence via fellow directors like Bernardo Bertolucci, Catherine Breillat and John Maybury along with writer David Forgacs. After that things get trickier as much of the same material is repurposed into different featurettes, though the final impression is roughly the same. Criterion's "Salò: Yesterday and Today" devotes half an hour to the film's legacy with archival Pasolini footage and comments from director Jean-Claude Biette

and actor/former lover Nineto Davoli, the 40-minute "The End of Salò" devoted mainly to the production of the climactic sequence complete with images from scenes deleted from the final film (including the infamous bound girl in a chair attacked by rats), and new video interviews with the film's famous production designer Dante Ferretti and filmmaker Jean-Pierre Gorin, plus a hefty booklet containing essays from many of the same participants along with snippets from an on-set journal by Gideon Bachmann (who shot most of the on-set footage seen in both releases). The BFI condenses this down a bit with a basic 25-minute featurette of behind-the-scenes shots, the additional critical featurettes "Open Your Eyes" and "Walking with Pasolini", the complete one-hour 1981 documentary "Whoever Says the Truth Shall Die" (featuring many regular actors like Laura Betti commenting on the director's working methods along with an in-depth look at the various theories behind his murder), "Ostia" (a very abstract 25-minute 1991 short film starring Derek Jarman about the director's death), a Coil 1987 music video devoted to Pasolini also entitled "Ostia", and a mostly different booklet packed with archival reviews, a rundown of the initial British censorship of the film, on-set photos, a new essay by Pasolini scholar Sam Rohdie, and a different presentation of Bachmann's diary notes. Whichever option you choose, this is not a film – or a supplemental experience – easy to shake off.

SATAN'S BABY DOLL

Colour, 1982, 74m. / Directed by Mario Bianchi / Starring Jacqueline Dupré, Mariangela Giordano, Aldo Sambrell, Marina Hedman, Joe Davers, Giancarlo Del Duca, Alfonso Gaita / Synapse (US R0 NTSC), Shameless (UK R0 PAL) / WS (1.85:1) (16:9), X-Rated Kult (Germany R2 PAL)

After her mother dies during a séance, young Miria (played by Jacqueline Dupré) and her kin are alarmed when the corpse twitches on its slab in the family crypt. The attending physician tells them not to worry, blathering something about it begin part of the mystery of the human body. He ain't kiddin'! Pretty soon Miria is unravelling lots of mysteries within everyone's bodies as dead mom's spirit takes over, leading her to seduce all of her relatives with lots of diabolical results.

If the synopsis sounds familiar, that's because this early '80s Italian exploiter (originally titled *La bimba di Satana*) is pretty much a remake of *Malabimba* made three years later by the unrelated Mario Bianchi. Mariangela Giordano returns this time as a potential saviour figure and once again gets a steamy lesbian scene, but this time the story ramps up the horror quotient considerably (with lots of crypt scenes and even a mummy!). There's no way it could be trashier than the original thanks to the absence of porn inserts this time out, but the filmmakers certainly give it the old college try with lots of T&A, plenty of claustrophobic atmosphere and some truly weird flourishes like the paraplegic uncle (now played by a much younger actor) getting a naked wash down from the nun right in the middle of the family drawing room and the burly family patriarch getting chased fully naked in an open bathrobe to his doom (a scene repeated almost identically with even less appetising results by Frank Langella in *Lolita*). The whole thing runs a very tight 74 minutes, with Mario Bianchi barely pausing to deliver a coherent plot. The strongest aspect, however, is the killer psychedelic score by Nico Catanese (who?), a terrific slice of post-Goblin rock that demands its own soundtrack release.

Pretty much impossible to see at all (let alone in English) since its release, *Satan's Baby Doll* benefits considerably from Severin's sleek digital treatment. The transfer looks very nice indeed, perfectly capturing each crumbling sarcophagus and exposed inch of flesh with clear optional English subtitles. Extras include the rather good Italian theatrical trailer and "Exorcism of Baby Doll", an 18-minute video interview with Bianchi in which he talks about putting his own spin on the story and his rationale for dealing with the heavy amount of coupling in the script. Watch it back to back with *Malabimba* for the maximum damning effect. For die-hard Eurotrash fanatics, there's also an X-Rated Kult DVD from Germany containing an alternative hardcore cut of the film (under the ridiculous title of *Dr. Porno und sein Satanszombie* but credited onscreen as *Orgasmo di Satana*). It's in much rougher shape and has no English-friendly options, as well as completely different opening titles; however, it also has tons of extra sex footage including a lesbian pre-titles routine, some unsimulated oral activity with the paraplegic uncle and Marina Hedman, additional *Hustler*-style solo shots of Giordano, and, of course, some full-on inserts. None of it adds much to the film, really, but it is a curious variation all the same. The much later Shameless British Region 0 release features some of the hotter lesbian footage integrated back into the soft cut of the film, along with some alternative scenes, trailers, and a Giordano bio.

SATAN'S PLAYGROUND

Colour, 2005, 81m. / Directed by Dante Tomaselli / Starring Felissa Rose, Ellen Sandweiss, Edwin Neal, Irma St. Paule, Danny Lopes, Christie Sanford, Salvatore Paul Piro / Anchor Bay (US R0 NTSC) / WS (1.78:1) (16:9) / DD5.1

The third horror offering from New Jersey director Dante Tomaselli, *Satan's Playground* finds him diverging from the free-associative funhouses of his prior work and going for a more linear, traditional scarefest based around one of his stomping ground's most enduring legends, the Jersey Devil. Of course, it helps if you're somewhat familiar with the background of that supernatural entity (which also inspired the wildly erratic but interesting *The Last Broadcast*), as this particular twist essentially offers three different spooky threats to its lead characters but only barely attempts to connect the dots for the unfamiliar.

Drawing '80s horror inspiration right down to its casting, this outing stars Felissa Rose (the notorious "Angela" from *Sleepaway Camp*), who also had a small role in Tomaselli's *Horror*, and *The Evil Dead*'s tree-assaulted Ellen Sandweiss as two members of a family driving through the desolate Pine Barrens along with an autistic teen son (Danny Lopes), and Sandweiss's much older husband (Salvatore Paul Piro), not to mention a little baby for some additional potential trauma. Naturally their car gets stuck in the middle of nowhere, and we know the area's being stalked by some sort of flying, slashing thingy thanks to a prologue involving a hapless traveller getting mauled in the woods. One by one they get separated as they look for help, either running afoul of a nefarious, hooded cult lurking in the hinterlands or the sole residents nearby, a grotesque clan ruled by creepy old Mrs. Leeds (Irma St. Paule) in a ramshackle, spooky old house. Will any of them escape alive, and more importantly, when will that pesky Jersey Devil show up to start slashing a few throats?

Obviously aiming at something more escapist and accessible, *Satan's Playground* looks considerably slicker than his past two films and boasts some fairly strong performances, notably Rose and Sandweiss of course, with Tomaselli regular Christie Sanford scoring the most indelible impression as a hammer-swinging psycho with a highly unusual hairdo. Oddly, the one who fares worst is Lopes, normally the director's leading man, who has no dialogue and basically drools a lot before exiting the film in the most inexplicable of its many death scenes. Also unusual this time out is the stronger injection of black humour, which balances out some of the wilder curlicues of the plot. Along with the casting of its two female leads, Tomaselli makes a few other unexpected nods to classic '70s and '80s horror staples, most obviously *The Evil Dead* (the swooshing Steadicam monster, the spook house cabin, etc.) as well as atmospheric nods to the likes of *The Texas Chain Saw Massacre* and even what looks like a deliciously stylish homage to *Bloody Pit of Horror*. The gore here is fairly restrained, limited to a few cracked noggins and one show stopping climactic bit involving a great throat-splitting effect, but the well-paced jolts generally pay off; the only major misfire, alas, is the final shot, an attempt at a Raimi-esque jolt that lands with a thud. Interestingly, the end result divided the critical and fan community, earning surprising raves from *Variety* and *Slant* while a puzzling war appears to be waged against it at the Internet Movie Database. As usual, the truth is somewhere in between; horror fans willing to overlook budgetary limitations and the occasional narrative stumble should find enough chills here to merit an evening's viewing, while those who chafed at Tomaselli's somewhat oblique directorial choices in the past should find it interesting to see him tackling a more straightforward project with traditional, bare-bones scares.

Anchor Bay's DVD marks a distributor switch for Tomaselli and represents the most thorough treatment of one of his works to date, with more projects in the pipeline. The film looks terrific considering it cost somewhere in the neighbourhood of half a million to shoot, at least according to the supplements. Speaking of which, the disc comes packed with a heavy amount of extras, kicking off with a Tomaselli commentary covering the shoot (it was done on Super 16 and makes the format look as slick as possible), the meagre financing, his relationships with actors both old and new, and his own artistic intentions with this film. Much of this material dovetails with the two featurettes, "The Making of *Satan's Playground*" (basically ten minutes of behind-the-scenes footage) and "Dante Tomaselli and the Jersey Devil", which finds the shades-sporting auteur talking about his personal fascination with the titular demon and how it blossomed out into the full premise of the film. Also included are a teaser and theatrical trailer, a stills gallery, and promo trailers for other low budget Anchor Bay titles like *Hatchet*.

SATANIC SLUTS:
THE BLACK ORDER COMETH
Colour, 2008, 80m. / Directed by Nigel Wingrove / Starring Poisoned Venus, Dischordia, Kerosene / Redemption (US R0 NTSC, UK R0 PAL) / WS (1.78:1) (16:9)

God only knows what's going on with this Redemption in-house effort geared towards folks who really, really dug those Eileen Daly goth-kink intros on their older DVD horror releases. As the sleeve subtly explains it, "Redemption Films presents the Satanic Sluts – Six Women Unleash the Darkness and Lose Their Souls". Yes, that about covers it. Apparently this was cut in the U.K., but lucky Americans can enjoy every second of, to quote the sleeve again, "real bloodletting, Japanese rope bondage, whippings and satanic crucifixions" plus "fantasized sequences involving torture, medical experiments and vampirism".

Well, it's mostly vampirism and looks like the Dark Brothers trying to do a Nine Inch Nails music video, plus about only half of the women are remotely attractive. That said, the nun segment is actually pretty entertaining in a blasphemous, music video sort of way. If stylised goth fantasies are your thing, look no further. The aspect ratio is completely perplexing; everything is encoded as 16x9, but a lot of the footage was clearly prepared as flat 4:3 letterboxed or full frame and then squeezed in or pillar-boxed to fit the frame. As a result, some scenes play out fine while others are squished and distorted. If you have a widescreen monitor, prepare to do a lot of squinting. Extras include an alternative version of the "Gimp" segment, some extended footage cut from the final product, a stills gallery, cross-trailers for other titles like *Hurt* and of course, a promo for the Satanic Sluts book, *Blood & Dishonour*.

SAVAGE SINEMA FROM
DOWN UNDER:
MARAUDERS
Colour, 1987, 74m. / Directed by Mark Savage / Starring Colin Savage, Paul Harrington, Megan Napier, Zero Montana, Richard Wolstencroft / Subversive (US R1 NTSC)

SENSITIVE NEW AGE KILLER
Colour, 2000, 84m. / Directed by Mark Savage / Starring Paul Moder, Carolyn Bock, Kevin Hopkins, Helen Hopkins, Frank Bren / Subversive (US R1 NTSC), 20th Century Fox (Australia R4 PAL) / WS (1.85:1) (16:9) / DD2.0

DEFENCELESS

Colour, 2006, 98m. / Directed by Mark Savage / Starring Susanne Hausschmid, George Gladstone, Erin Walsh, Anthony Thorne, Bethany Fisher / Subversive (US R1 NTSC) / WS (1.85:1) (16:9) / DD2.0

 Following its standout genre entries in the '70s and early '80s, Australia hasn't really become known for its horror and action in recent years. However, a few stalwart heroes are still carrying the torch such as Mark Savage, whose three provocative and very different films have been collected in a box set not for the faint of heart. The first disc in the set (though perhaps not the best introduction to his work) is 1987's *Marauders*, a shot-on-video study of teen violence revolving around two kill-crazy youths, J.D. Kruger (Zero Montana) and crazy-haired Emilio East (Colin Savage), whose recent murderous exploits have left them with hair-trigger tempers. When J.D. is struck by a hit-and-run driver, the duo decides to make the driver, David (Paul Harrington), and his girlfriend Becky (Megan Napier) their next targets. Tracking them to a cabin retreat in the woods, the psycho pair starts a whole new wave of violence when they decide to pick on one of the locals and instigate a full mob retaliation. A solid start to an exploitation career, *Marauders* has a similar feel to some of grittier drive-in films of the late '80s (particularly *Deadbeat at Dawn* and the output of New World Pictures). Though not quite as extreme as its reputation and premise might suggest, the film offers enough decadent pleasures to carry it over some obvious budget deficits. (Whether the hilariously dated hairstyles and clothing are a plus or a minus will be entirely up to the viewer, however.)

The much glossier and more impressive *Sensitive New Age Killer* is next in the set, and this berserk comic-horrific-kinky crime film should make a fine starter for newcomers. Though he's a hit man, Paul (Paul Moder) is, as the title implies, a sensitive guy whose childhood experience watching the handiwork of "The Snake" (Frank Bren) inspired his career choice. Unfortunately none of his assignments seem to be going smoothly, as his unscrupulous and wildly unstable partner George (Kevin Hopkins) is set on getting Paul killed in the line of duty and living out a weird baby fetish with Paul's wife. On top of that, Paul spends his time after hours with Matty (Carolyn Bock), a ruthless cop prone to performing dominatrix duties on her unwilling suspects. Certainly wild and unpredictable, *Sensitive New Age Killer* (or *SNAK* as it's called everywhere on the disc) again isn't terribly explicit (a few bloody squibs here and there and lots of softcore grinding are about as hard as it gets), but the dark, sleazy subject matter still gives the film a raw, transgressive edge, leavened with some very funny black humour. It also offers an amusing take on late-20th Century masculine anxiety with Paul's faulty "gun" and frequent submissive situations at the hands of those around him reflecting the increasingly jittery male egos proliferating around the same time.

Fast forward to 2004 (past two erotic thrillers Savage directed that aren't included here, *Fishnet* and *Trail of Passion*) with the creation of *Defenseless*, a film screened in variant states until its final, completed edit presented on this disc with a 2006 copyright date. Easily the most extreme title here, this grim but beautifully poetic tale (subtitled "A Blood Symphony") features no dialogue as it follows the plight of a married woman (Susanne Hausschmid) whose refusal to submit to a group of vicious land developers puts her friends, her family, and her own life in jeopardy. A series of brutal attacks follow, and... well, it's best to stop here if you want to remain spoiler-free, but since the packaging gives away the mid-story twist, let's continue. After perishing during a violent rape attack by the developers, she's reborn in the foamy sea months later and embarks on a silent, relentless, and curiously child-like quest for revenge. Though the unflinching approach to sexual assault (on both genders) and explicit revenge imagery might put some viewers in mind of *The Last House on the Left*, Savage's lyrical technique instead carries this into the more surprising, fantastic terrain of filmmakers like Jean Rollin, whose similar affinity for quiet, beachside meditations on vengeance is carried over nicely here. There isn't a single line of dialogue in the film, leaving the actors' physical performances and the astounding sound mix to carry the narrative weight. Hausschmid is excellent in the difficult leading role, creating a delirious intensity with the force of her eyes and pulling the viewer's sympathy along even for the harrowing final few scenes, with a thankfully peaceful and haunting coda awaiting her and the audience after their trials.

Anything you could possibly want to know about these films is included on Subversive's exhaustive set, which features booklet inserts with Savage's candid production diaries (with a few names thoughtfully obscured to protect the not-so-innocent) for each title offering a taster of what lies in store. *Marauders* includes a half-hour documentary, "Making Of (Four Friends in Low-Budget Heaven)", with the two Savages, Harrington and Richard Wolstencroft talking about the film production (sometimes in really harsh sunlight) including plenty of anecdotes about the other absent performers. An audio commentary track reunites the quartet to offer their observations in a scene-specific

forum, with lots of detail offered on how to shoot violent scenes with limited funds and a lack of professional talent. *SNAK* includes a slightly longer featurette, "*SNAK*: A Post-Mortem", with the two Savages, Bock, both of the Hopkins, Moder, and others covering the basics of how the film came to be, then embellishing the stories in more detail on the audio commentary track (which, among other subjects, covers the surprisingly ambitious gun battles which had to be executed rather resourcefully). *Defenceless* gets an even longer featurette, the 43-minute "Inside *Defenceless*", in which Savage, Hausschmid, and the supporting cast (Anthony Thorne, Erin Walsh, Bethany Fisher, George Gladstone) discuss the making of the film, including some friction and reservations that arose over the contentious brutality of the storyline; Savage and Hausschmid then return for an audio commentary covering the film from a more technical, production-oriented angle. Each disc features bios for the involved talent and stills galleries, as well as trailers for all three movies and other Subversive releases. *Sensitive New Age Killer* was also put out as a separate DVD in Australia by Fox and later re-issued by Subversive, along with *Defenceless*, as single discs.

A limited edition version of the box set also features a fourth bonus disc containing Savage's most recent completed work, a handful of early 8mm short films and a gruelling half-hour TV film entitled *Stained*, the stark depiction of the violent consequences unleashed when a man searching for his missing child runs into a nasty pair of brothers involved in an international kiddie snuff online community. (Don't worry, the child stuff is never even remotely depicted on-camera.) Fusing together two real-life Australian crime stories, it features Kevin Hopkins, Grant Mouldez, Helen Hopkins, Steve Hutchison, and Jenny Loncaric, all of whom are excellent.

SCHIZO

Colour, 1976, 109m. / Directed by Pete Walker / Starring Lynne Frederick, John Leyton, Stephanie Beacham, John Fraser, Jack Watson / Redemption (US R0 NTSC, UK R0 PAL) / WS (1.85:1) (16:9)

In "North-East England, June 18th", some crazy old guy in a red ski cap is planning to do something really, really nasty. How do we know? Because he lives in a boarding house, makes crazy swirly scratches in the daily newspaper with a ballpoint pen, and packs a machete in his suitcase. Ah, yes, and as the opening title card screams out, he's *SCHIZO*! That's how things appear, anyway, as this released murderer proceeds to stalk pretty ice skater Samantha (played by the late Lynne Frederick, the last and most controversial Mrs. Peter Sellers), who's engaged to be married to the amiable and incredibly dull Alan Falconer (John Leyton) with whom she lives in an apartment serviced by a particularly perverse interior decorator. Her best friend, Beth (Stephanie Beacham), is a happy camper, too, which makes it all the more disturbing when Samantha realises that the crazy *SCHIZO* – who's prone to leaving bloody cutlery next to her wedding cake – is in fact her mother's lunatic lover (John Fraser), sent up the river years ago for brutally hacking up Sam's mom with a knife. Soon the bodies being piling up all around, and when visits to a psychiatrist and a psychic fail to pan out, Samantha must come face to face with her gruesome past and uncover the *SCHIZO* truth.

Devoid of the savage social commentary which characterised Pete Walker's previous horror films, this later shocker instead fits in more snugly with the increasingly bloody and violent British product unleashed in the wake of the *giallo* craze, epitomised by the sleazier (and far less artistic) output of Norman J. Warren. Blood and breasts figure prominently throughout (in some cases at the same time), though that beloved Walker pessimism still manages to rear its head during the nasty (and not terribly persuasive) finale, which of course features a big senseless twist and an ironically downbeat coda. Most critics tend to dismiss this film as a lesser Walker effort, but when taken in the right spirit, it's still a whole lot of fun with a highly non-PC attitude (just check out that opening monologue's definition of schizophrenia). The séance sequence alone is one of the creepiest things Walker ever put on film, and the pulpy thrills come fast and furious from Frederick's naked-in-peril shower scene to a nasty close encounter between a knitting needle and an eye socket. The score by Stanley Myers isn't exactly subtle either as it ladles on the shrieking strings whenever Samantha starts to look a little nervous. Significantly, this marked the last collaboration between Walker and regular screenwriter David McGillivray, who deserves just as much credit for establishing this style of '70s British horror. Both men continued to work on two separate horror projects each before moving off to other areas of interest, leaving behind a bloody legacy that still resonates with audiences today.

Often censored during its theatrical release (with as much as 11 minutes shorn from its running time in some territories), *Schizo* has thankfully appeared in its intact, 109-minute version for most of its various video incarnations over the years, with only the cranky BBFC keeping it scissored down in the U.K. until 2008 when it was finally passed uncut. The first no-frills DVD edition from Image (see *DVD Delirium Vol. 1*) only stayed on the market for a few years and then began demanding stupid amounts of money from online sellers, so the

DVD DELIRIUM VOLUME 4

American reissue courtesy of Redemption can only be considered a good thing. The transfer appears to be from the same source, an uncut British element using the Warner Brothers logo; it's still anamorphically enhanced (with identical framing) and features the same print damage (which is actually fairly minimal, but that was enough to tick off some critics the first time around). For some reason this edition looks a bit darker and softer, particularly during the opening exterior shots; that may or may not be beneficial considering the atmosphere of the film, as it certainly gives it a seedier ambience. The mono audio sounds fine. There still isn't much here extraswise, though you do get a small stills gallery, a Walker filmography, and the usual Redemption promotional spots and book teaser.

SCHOOLGIRL REPORT #1: WHAT PARENTS DON'T THINK IS POSSIBLE

Colour, 1970, 84m. / Directed by Ernst Hofbauer / Starring Günther Kieslich, Wolf Harnisch, Helga Kruck, and "many anonymous parents and students" / Impulse (US R1 NTSC), Kinowelt (Germany R2 PAL) / WS (1.66:1) (16:9)

 Following the success of Italian mondo films which depicted the disturbing "reality" of human life around the globe, some enterprising German producers decided to take it one step further by smashing this template together with the saucy Scandinavian sex films raking in cash thanks to the likes of *I Am Curious (Yellow)*. The result? Instant box office gold with the *Schoolgirl Report* series, a "life on the street" look at all the trouble young nymphets were getting into

around Deutschland, featuring "candid" interviews and various naughty scenarios amply balancing bare flesh with rib-nudging comedy. The first film in the series, 1970's *Schulmädchen-Report: Was Eltern nicht für möglich halten*, was loosely based on a sex report manual by Günther Hunold and quickly inspired 13 official sequels, not to mention plenty of uncredited imitations. Even Jess Franco cashed in on the craze with his *Virgin Report*.

Our story begins when plucky 18-year-old Renate decides to take matters into her own hands on a school field trip and starts making out in the back seat with the bus driver while everyone else is outside. Unfortunately, one of the prudish teachers catches her in the act and drags her into the headmaster's office, where she stands up for herself as simply going about her own business. The obvious solution? Kick her out, of course. However, adolescent psychologist Dr. Bernauer defends her actions as part of the new youth's sexual freedom and promptly gives plenty of examples to back up his thesis. His case studies include plenty of shameless minxes talking dirty to a priest in the confession booth, going at it with each other in the locker room, and showing off in public dressing rooms, all interspersed with off-the-cuff street interviews with various German teens talking about their views on sex.

Though the passage of time has rendered this film's "shocking" depictions of frisky youths rather quaint by today's standards, the first *Schoolgirl Report* still holds up as a solid slice of counterculture pop art erotica. From the fashions and hairstyles to the free-for-all natural nudity (lots of ungroomed pubic hair and not a trace of silicone in sight), it's a refreshing step back to a more innocent time when the mere thought of an unmarried young girl getting it on with someone of her own free will was enough to send the establishment into spasms of moral outrage. Of course, this basically being a European sex comedy at heart, much of the humour just seems flat-out bizarre, such as this early exchange between a young boy and girl at a family barbeque:

"Your sausage is burnt".
"It's my sausage. I can burn it as often as I want. Like our history teacher: black on the outside and brown inside".

Though German audiences recognise that as a dated political joke, for anyone else it's just confounding. Also noteworthy is the fantastically catchy easy listening score by German B-movie legend Gert Wilden, whose work on these films experienced a new lease on life in the 1990s thanks to a hit soundtrack compilation CD à la *Vampyros Lesbos*.

First released in English in an edited, mostly frontal-free version as *The School Girls* (with occasional appearances on VHS under that title), the first *Schoolgirl Report* is presented uncut on Impulse's DVD with the original, vastly superior German language track, with optional English subtitles. The German version has circulated without subs on Japanese and German DVD, but this marks the first English-friendly, complete presentation anywhere. Apart from the ragged-looking main titles, which appear to be spliced in from an inferior, slightly cropped print, the bulk of the transfer looks fantastic and easily eclipses those scratchy old reissue prints and dupey video copies. The luscious colour schemes come out nice and clear, and the deliberately low-tech appearance of the street interviews still has a pleasingly film-like look without breaking up into swarms of grain. No extras, but it took so long to get a good English version of one of these films out to the public, that it's hard to complain. In Germany the full 14-film series is also available in a box set from Kinowelt, but beware that these are all heavily condensed with many key sequences missing.

SCHOOLGIRL REPORT #2: WHAT KEEPS PARENTS AWAKE AT NIGHT

Colour, 1971, 91m. / Directed by Ernst Hofbauer / Impulse (US R1 NTSC), Kinowelt (Germany R2 PAL) / WS (1.66:1) (16:9)

In this entertaining follow-up (*Schulmädchen-Report 2: Was Eltern den Schlaf raubt*), the German pseudo-documentarians set their sights on more illicit activities committed by those scheming, innocent-looking nymphets. As the narrator explains in the opening, "The first *Schoolgirl Report* told you about masturbation, petting, that is, playful intimate contact, deflowering or losing one's virginity, intercourse and same-sex love. So we had to do further studies and reveal the facts that even young people don't talk about!" Well, yes, obviously.

A visiting doctor talks to a classroom of girls about "getting tingly", a girl photographs her best friend getting it on with an older neighbour, a teen loses her virginity in a barn loft, a stupid blond guy in the woods loses his girlfriend to a passing hunter in a ridiculous hat, 16-year-old Tessie ("now beyond the reach of the Protection of Minors Act") turns into an IV drug user and gets gang banged after going to a local pub, and various ladies on the street talk about their own sexual opinions. It all ends, as such things must, with a courtroom showdown and an attempted hanging. Yes, it's just as awesome as it sounds, and the peppy theme song will stick in your head for weeks. Once again this print is in German only with optional English subtitles, as this is the original longer cut with about 20 minutes of footage (including lots of frontal shots) hacked away from the dubbed American prints. Image quality is fine given the scruffy nature of the film; it's anamorphic widescreen (1.66:1) and colours have that slightly washed-out, unnatural early '70s look.

SCHOOLGIRL REPORT #3: WHAT PARENTS FIND UNTHINKABLE

Colour, 1972, 97m. / Directed by Walter Boos & Ernst Hofbauer / Starring Friedrich von Thun, Michael Schreiner, Claudia Höll, Karin Götz / Impulse (US R1 NTSC), Kinowelt (Germany R2 PAL) / WS (1.66:1) (16:9)

 One of the most infamous cult DVD releases immediately upon its release, this third instalment in the comedic docu-sex series (*Schulmädchen-Report 3. Teil – Was Eltern nicht mal ahnen*) ratchets up the shock value considerably after the first two engaging but hardly outrageous instalments. The basic template's the same this time around, as a narrator kicks things off by wondering aloud what could possibly be left to cover in the sordid lives of loose-skirted German schoolgirls after the past two successful films, already "seen by millions". Well, apparently you ain't seen nothin' yet, folks! The first half follows the formula with a few extra dollops of seediness, such as a vignette involving a high schooler who gets lured into a gangbang in the boys' bathroom only to be caught by the school janitor. No one believes she isn't a complete harlot, so she decides to prove them all wrong by, uh, seducing the janitor so he'll back up her story. Turns out he's actually the one who set the whole nasty thing up, and soon things devolve into prostitution, arrests, and tragedy. Other bits involve some boys hiding out a bunch of girls in their dorm room, a nymphet jumping her best friend's dad after

playing tennis, and the typically bizarre "girl on the street" interview segments. But that's nothing compared to what the film has in store halfway through as it plunges into *Maladolescenza* territory with a joltingly graphic sketch involving a frisky girl's decision to get into the pants of a very young boy, whose on-camera enthusiasm pushes the boundaries of any other softcore DVD out on the marketplace.

Not surprisingly, Synapse (who release Impulse's titles in the U.S.) had to pull some distribution plans for this title and sold it only online, so the original edition of this DVD is now very scarce and hard to find. At least they went out of their way to release the longest version of this film available anywhere despite the understandable moral fallout. The transfer itself is definitely a few notches above the past two releases, looking quite a bit crisper and fresher; the optional English subtitles are just fine and often hilarious. For some reason the packaging gives two credits for the fantastic music to prolific series composer Gert Wilden, though this particular entry was actually scored by *St. Pauli Report* composer Siegfried Franz.

SCHOOLGIRL REPORT #4: WHAT DRIVES PARENTS TO DESPAIR

Colour, 1972, 88m. / Directed by Ernst Hofbauer / Starring Christina Lindberg, Wolfgang Scherer, Carmen Jäckel, Anne Graf / Impulse (US R1 NTSC), Kinowelt (Germany R2 PAL) / WS (1.66:1) (16:9)

 It's time for more oversexed Germans, which can only mean *Schoolgirl Report #4: What Drives Parents to Despair* (or in its native tongue, *Schulmädchen-Report 4. Teil – Was*

Eltern oft verzweifeln lässt). This one is nowhere even remotely as scandalous as the third report, but on the other hand, it's got Christina Lindberg, the Swedish softcore vixen who earned a huge following with *Thriller: A Cruel Picture*. The template here is pretty much the same as the other films, with a narrator revealing that there's still so very, very much we all have to learn about what teenage girls really get up to when their parents aren't looking. Namely, they go around chasing older men, have sex in rowboats, and, in Christina's case, fantasise about stripping nuns and firing squads while trying to arouse their sleeping brothers. No, really, it's all true! The actual sex content here is noticeably lower than past instalments, but there's still loads of female nudity on display and some hilariously bizarre dialogue throughout.

As with Impulse's previous DVDs, the anamorphic transfer looks better than those cruddy tape editions but still betrays its vintage, particularly the rough-looking opening credits. Still, it's in its original language with subtitles, has a really swinging Gert Wilden music score, and appears to be complete.

SCREAM

Colour, 1981, 86m. / Directed by Byron Quisenberry / Starring Pepper Martin, Hank Worden, Ethan Wayne, Ann Bronston, Woody Strode, Alvy Moore / Shriek Show (US R1 NTSC) / WS (1.78:1) (16:9)

 For reasons never quite explained, a handful of river rafters decide to head downstream to an isolated Texas ghost town for some rest and relaxation. Soon their rafts have been sabotaged, and one by one they're being picked off by an unseen predator. Could it be the pair of helpful dirt bikers who show up out of nowhere? Or what about Woody Strode popping up on a horse to tell a weird story about sea captains? Or perhaps it's one of the rafters themselves? Your guess is as good as the filmmaker's.

Made at the height of the theatrical slasher boom, this flimsy attempt at a stalk-and-slash film (also known as *The Outing*) somehow became a VHS mainstay despite the absence of any notable gore or, more importantly, a compelling or even coherent storyline. The creators quite obviously fling their hands in the air and give up by the time the film limps to its conclusion, and aside from some mildly atmospheric location shots and a vaguely creepy opening, one-shot director Byron Quisenberry shows little affinity for the horror genre, choosing to let his camera wander around at will while the murders happen mostly off-camera. The major point of interest is the odd cast of character actors including Pepper Martin (*Walking Tall*, *Superman II*, *Return to Horror High*), Hank Worden (*The Ice Pirates*, *Chisum*), a young Ethan Wayne (son of John), and most surprisingly, bit parts for Alvy Moore (*A Boy and His Dog*, *The Witchmaker*) and action/western favourite Woody Strode. That said, there's a certain homegrown charm at work here if you're willing to coast along with the soporific pacing and oddball tangents.

Shriek Show's DVD release retains the eye-catching sickle artwork from the tape cover and might provoke a minor nostalgia rush among horror completists. Not surprisingly, the transfer is a huge improvement over Vestron's typically washed-out, sludgy presentation on tape, with the 16mm photography coming across about as well as it could given the cheap shooting conditions. Former stuntman Quisenberry pops up for the most notable extra here, an audio commentary moderated by Marc Edward Hueck (who can also be heard on *Cheerleaders' Wild Weekend*) and Code

Red's Bill Olsen. It's a fun listen that goes some way to explaining the intentions behind the film, which was meant to be a more suggestive alternative to the boobs-and-blood offerings at the box office. The stories about the director's other careers are much more interesting, though he has a few worthwhile anecdotes about how he roped in some familiar faces for the shoot on such short notice. Other extras include the theatrical trailer and TV spot, a stills gallery, and additional trailers for *Just Before Dawn*, *Killing Birds*, *Cop Killers*, and *Evils of the Night*.

SCREWBALLS

Colour, 1983, 79m. / Directed by Rafal Zielinski / Starring Peter Keleghan, Kent Deuters, Linda Speciale, Alan Deveau, Linda Shayne, Jason Warren, Jim Coburn, Raven De La Croix / Severin (US R0 NTSC) / WS (1.66:1) (16:9), Platinum (UK R0 PAL), Marketing Film (Germany R2 PAL)

Though no one knew it at the time, 1978 saw a major sea change in the way teen movies would be handled for decades to come thanks to two films: *Grease* in America, and *Lemon Popsicle* in Israel. Both were comedies set in high schools between the late 1950s and early 1960s, with smutty jokes and lots of pop culture nostalgia making them palatable to multiple generations. Of course, the Israeli movie was much more explicit than its PG-rated but sniggering counterpart, and the two approaches eventually collided a few years later in the early '80s in Canada, of all places. The result was *Porky's*, Bob Clark's record-smashing hit about horny guys and girls pulling pranks on each other in high school during the early '60s, with

only the mildest lip service paid to the period as the screen was flooded with ridiculous jokes involving characters named Lassie and Cherry Forever. The actors and filmmakers were mostly Canadian, but the film was shot in Florida to ensure broader theatrical play. Not surprisingly, imitations were soon to follow with one of the first out of the gate, *Screwballs*, making even less of an effort to conceal its Great White North origins. It also managed to be even filthier and more ridiculous than its inspiration, which is why its reputation still lingers today.

At T&A High School, five of the male students wind up in detention one day for trickery involving mirrors, posing as doctors, and stripping in a meat freezer. The new transfer student "from Idaho" is unfamiliar with the pretty Purity Busch (Linda Speciale), the sole virginal holdout in the entire school (where freshman girls are apparently snatched as soon as they enter the door). Randy hunk Rick (comedian Peter Keleghan), chubby Melvin (Jason Warren), the newbie Tim (Jim Coburn), and snotty trust fund kid Brent (Kent Deuters) conspire to get a look at exactly what Purity's hiding under her prim and proper sweaters, but their plans tend to go wildly awry until they join forces with the rest of the school for a climactic stars and stripes performance unlike any other.

One relentless sight gag and groan-inducing sex joke after another, *Screwballs* piles on a succession of set pieces designed for very short attention spans with the maximum amount of nudity allowed for an R rating. It's all goofy fun and oddly endearing now, with the unforgettable bowling alley strip-off still ranking as a high point in the teen sex comedy canon. Another scene with the boys all aroused under a library table attempts to outdo the locker room contest from *Lemon Popsicle* (which was not surprisingly remade in '82 by Hollywood as *The Last American Virgin*), and director Rafal Zielinski keeps things lively enough that he returned to the same well for more Canadian imitations like *Loose Screws* and *Recruits*. However, the weirdest *Screwballs* imitator from Canada has to be *Oddballs*, a film that must be seen to be believed.

A glance at the credits for *Screwballs* reveals a few surprises particularly from its co-writers, prolific drive-in director Jim Wynorski (*Chopping Mall*) and Linda Shayne (the director of *Purple People Eater*), who also appears in the film as Bootsie Goodhead. The future director of *The Gate* and *I, Madman*, Tibor Takács, also had one of his first gigs as a production manager. During the sequence in which the boys visit a strip club, that's vivacious Russ Meyer vixen Raven De La Croix (*Up!*) doing the main performance. And strangest of all, this was co-financed by New World Pictures, which explains the unexpected Roger Corman nods flitting by in the background including an inscrutable clip from *The Arena*.

A steady renter on VHS, this film was stuck in various rights issues which prevented a legitimate special edition. That didn't stop mediocre releases from old VHS-era masters popping up in the U.K. and Germany, but Severin's officially-sanctioned DVD and Blu-ray is really the way to go. The film looks about as good as possible given its low budget origins; colours are extremely vibrant and film-like, and the transfer appears faithfully cinematic without any undue digital cleanup. Of course, this isn't exactly artistically accomplished eye candy, but all the T&A shots look crystal clear. Zielsinski pops up twice on the disc, first for an audio commentary with Severin's David Gregory and John Cregan and then for a separate 11-minute video interview. He remembers a great deal about the production and goes into detail about Canadian indie filmmaking at the time, with tax shelter productions turning the country into an exploitation mill until the late '80s. Wynorski and Shayne appear together for another video piece in which they talk about the film's influences, how they met, and where inspiration came from for some of the most memorable set pieces. Deuters and FX artist Gerald Lukaniuk get shorter separate interviews as well, discussing the original casting choices and how some of the ridiculous visuals were achieved (with Lukaniuk perhaps conjuring up more phallic and breast-oriented imagery than any other commercial film from the decade). For some additional context you also get a great piece with Paul Corupe, editor of the essential Canuxploitation.com, who talks about the film's place in the great and majestic tapestry of tax shelter classics, while modern media legend Mr. Skin and his writer, McBeardo, offer an appraisal of '80s sex comedies and how that era could never be duplicated today. Finally you get the surprisingly raunchy theatrical trailer and a handful of deleted and extended footage taken from a dupey-looking Spanish tape, which are interesting alternatives but nothing essential. It's an absurdly comprehensive and wonderfully entertaining release that puts major studios' treatment of other films from the same era to shame.

THE SECOND COMING OF EVA

Colour, 1974, 93m. / Directed by Mac Ahlberg / Starring Teresa Svensson, Kim Frank, Rune Hallberg, Jime Steffe, Brigitte Maier / Impulse (US R0 NTSC), Mike Hunter (Germany R0 PAL) / WS (1.66:1) (16:9)

 After getting caught having a very naughty dream while sleeping naked, young nymphet Eva (Teresa Svensson) gets shipped off to a private boarding school by her outraged yet

suspiciously sexy sister (Kim Frank from *Swedish Wildcats*). Upon arriving, she finds herself surrounded by frumpy, chaste old maids and fat, impotent men. Oh, wait, this is a Swedish sex comedy, so scratch that – everyone there is young, nubile, and prone to dancing around in the lobby and throwing wild orgies at the drop of a hat. Soon it's time for *The Second Coming of Eva* as the entire school (which looks a lot like that elegant estate in Jean Rollin's *Fascination*) is overrun with students and teachers making the beast with two backs outdoors, indoors, and everywhere in between. Then a snooping lawyer investigating claims of sexual misconduct and Eva's own sister shows up, and... well, you can pretty much fill in the blanks from there.

So what makes this sexploitation outing interesting? Well, several things, actually. It looks like the majority of the film was planned as a softcore comedy by director Mac Ahlberg, who was still riding high from his successful *I, a Woman* series, but somewhere along the line a few of the performers crossed over and started doing their love scenes for real. That makes this Ahlberg's first hardcore film, though the film doesn't really expend any effort on capturing the usual clinical close-ups that came to define the genre. Instead it all looks as colourful and aesthetically pleasing as most of Ahlberg's other work (he also went on to shoot such films as *Re-Animator* and *Hell Night*), and he manages to keep the story bouncing along at a rapid clip. Ahlberg later used the same approach in the far more surrealistic *Justine and Juliette* as well as the interesting *Molly* (a much-needed DVD release) and his best-known smut outing, *Bel Ami*. Also, one of the main participants in the full-on footage is none other than Brigitte Maier, a German-born bit player and *Penthouse* and *Playboy* model who used this film as a catapult to porn stardom with the help of boyfriend/director Lasse Braun in flicks like *Sensations*, *How Sweet*

It Is and the unforgettable blaxploitation oddity, *Tongue*. Most English-speaking viewers only got the chance to encounter this one in dubbed form, usually missing 12 minutes of the good stuff (though a harder version did briefly turn up from Cal Vista and a dubious online-only VHS from Excalibur). Well, Impulse's DVD edition is completely uncut and presented with the original Swedish language track, with optional English subtitles. The 1.66:1 anamorphic transfer looks great; along with *Justine*, it's the best-looking feature they've put out so far. Good, clean, nasty fun for all you Swedish movie sexaholics. (If you're really a completist, this is also available on German DVD along with the utterly unrelated *The Starlets* and *Inspirations*).

SECRETS OF SWEET SIXTEEN

Colour, 1973, 74m. / Directed by Ernst Hofbauer / Starring Christina Lindberg, Claudia Fielers, Maja Hoppe, Fernando Gomez

LOOKING GOOD

Colour, 1983, 60m. / Starring Laura Gemser / Mars Pictures, distributed by BCI (US R0 NTSC) / WS (1.78:1) (16:9)

Billed under the bizarre heading of "Lindberg vs. Gemser", this sex bomb double feature from the Burbank Drive-In line pairs up two lesser but distinctly strange entries from both of the screen sirens involved. The first is a typical Swedish sex comedy consisting of a string of vignettes that barely titillate but sometimes enter into the bizarre, such as a tale about Satanist wrestlers looking for a hot teenager to sacrifice or the mayhem unleashed by a sprightly nymphet in a post office. Burdened with an agonisingly slow pace and barely enough wit or T&A to justify its existence, this is really for Lindberg completists only (she figures in just one of the tales); to make matters worse, the film kicks off with a disclaimer, "The following material given to us does not live up to our usual standards. We sincerely apologize." Yep, no kidding. As with Burbank's previous softcore transfers like *Swinging Wives*, this looks like a pre-cropped tape master further cropped on the top and bottom to make it fill a 16:9 TV frame, resulting in a claustrophobic presentation with the actors' heads clipped off in many shots and awkward framing knocking every composition out of whack. The actual image quality isn't bad, surprisingly, if a bit soft. However, colours are stable and certainly better than the earlier DVD-R version available from Something Weird before they eventually cleaned up their house and dropped anything with "teen" in the title, regardless of the fact that everyone appears well over the age of 18. Still, you get to see Lindberg for a bit, and the Herb Alpert-style music score is really catchy.

Now we get to the co-feature, which packs in a whole lot more kitsch value and pretty much justifies the set just for sheer weirdness alone. See, it's an exercise video. With Laura Gemser. Yes, that's right. Clad in an aerobics outfit, Laura leads a quartet of headband-wearing lovelies through a shot-on-video workout routine, narrating the whole thing accompanied by a head-splitting soundtrack of synthetic '80s Euro-pop. Throw this one on late at night after promising a Laura Gemser movie and watch the confusion mount by the second.

SEPARATION

Colour/B&W, 1968, 93m. / Directed by Jack Bond / Starring Jane Arden, David de Keyser, Ann Lynn, Ian Quarrier, Terence de Marney / BFI (DVD & Blu-ray, UK R0 PAL/HD), Microcinema (US R0 NTSC) / WS (1.85:1) (16:9)

A film that should send devotees of feminist literature into ecstasy, *Separation* feels like a lost post-Victorian study of female psychological rupturing mainlined directly into film through the sensibility of a mad filmmaker like Ken Russell. If you're in the right frame of mind, this film – unloved and essentially unseen since its original release – is a tremendously thrilling disc as it now represents something fresh and valuable, a pop-art-inspired gender study worlds away from cinema as we know it today.

First-time director Jack Bond (who went on to direct the bizarre Pet Shop Boys vehicle *It Couldn't Happen Here*) teams up with leading actress Jane Arden (his real-life companion with whom he would collaborate on two more films, *The Other Side of Underneath* and *Anti-Clock* before she took her own life in 1982) for the fragmented and sometimes bewildering story of a woman dealing with the fact that her marriage is essentially over, and the psychological demands of coping with her identity as a female out of her teenage years in mod London threaten to overpower any means of adapting she can find, which include taking a young lover who may be unable to keep her grounded.

This sort of loose, abstract storytelling can test viewers to the limit (some people will most likely be tempted to shut it off half an hour in), but the best way to approach it is either as a nonlinear look at a fracturing personality or an absorbing snapshot of late '60s London culture, complete with a great soundtrack fuelled by Procol Harum music (including a few bits unreleased anywhere else) along with contributions by the still-underrated Stanley Myers, who went on to work regularly with Nicolas Roeg.

S

Though the BFI release of this film (the first on video anywhere in the world) is careful not to oversell the movie, its supplements do their part in offering some context and a solid argument as to why it's worthy of attention. The hi-def transfer itself is a real beauty, with the majority of the film in razor-sharp monochrome interspersed with a few bursts of colour footage, some of which becomes quite psychedelic. (Contrary to the packaging which indicates a full frame presentation, it is indeed anamorphic widescreen.) No complaints whatsoever on the technical side. Optional English subtitles are also included, which can be handy when your eyes are busy being bombarded with the avalanche of imagery throughout the many montage scenes. The biggest extra here is a rich and interesting commentary track with Bond and the BFI's Sam Dunn which covers the entire history of the film, from Arden and Bond's initial working relationship through their intentions and inspirations while mounting this very challenging and unorthodox production. Also included is the abstract short film "Beyond Image" (whose artistic visual effects by Mark Boyle and Joan Hills were used in the colour portions of the main feature) and trailers for this feature as well as *Anti-Clock*. A colour illustrated 36-page booklet also makes a good case for the film in the '60s English cinema canon thanks to essays by Claire Monk, Maria Walsh and Michael Brooke along with vintage press coverage. It's obvious this film's reputation can only increase with this release given its complete neglect for decades, so a hearty pat on the back must go to the BFI for bringing attention to such a challenging but ultimately rewarding undertaking. A later U.S. DVD from Microcinema makes this the only Arden film to hop over the pond, carrying over the same restored transfer, audio commentary, and booklet essays.

THE SERPENT'S TALE

Colour, 1993, 91m. / Directed by Putlog Ataman / Starring Gone Bombay, Metin Outgun, Daniel Chance / Onar (Greece R0 PAL) / WS (1.85:1) / DD2.0

While most international viewers tend to associate Turkish horror and fantasy cinema with cheap, insane knockoffs of box office hits, *The Serpent's Tale* (*Karolin Solar*) offers something a bit different. Part art film, part atmospheric horror, and part mindbender, it's an ambitious if not entirely successful attempt at a literate, distinctive chiller. Shot in a mixture of English and Turkish, it begins in a movie theatre where visiting American Hunter (Daniel Chance) sees a strange young girl lure an older man outside, where he soon turns up dead. A mysterious stranger, Haldun (Metin Outgun), informs him that the girl is a member of supernatural royalty and sends Hunter with an ancient compass to see his mother (Gone Bombay), who informs him that her son died years ago. The engraved compass proves a key to leading both of them to uncover a mystical sect prone to putting on theatrical performances and sacrificing newcomers over ancient texts. Then things get strange.

Sort of an atmospheric cross between *Apartment Zero* and *The Saragossa Manuscript*, this odd and stylish outing doesn't really go for outright scares as much as gothic surrealism, be it a ghostly little girl with sharp choppers or a collected theatre audience (used in the effective bookend sequences) silently weeping at something we never see. The story basically ties itself in knots as it spins from one level to the next, but director Kutlug Ataman still holds interest with a grab bag of visual tricks including vivid colour filters straight out of an Argento film, sparse but surprising bursts of bloodshed, and goofy moments of black comedy. The little girl imagery has been around since the days of Mario Bava, but this film gives the device a novel cinematic spin by keeping the viewer unsure about her true nature and appearance from one scene to the next.

Completely unknown to most English-speaking viewers, *The Serpent's Tale* gets a welcome chance at recognition with Onar's lovingly-assembled DVD. The flat letter-boxed presentation looks very colourful but a bit on the soft side; the occasional burned-in English subtitles are positioned within the film frame, so you can zoom it in on a widescreen TV without losing anything. Labelled as 2.0 on the packaging, the sound-track sounds fine but appears to be mono, which is no problem; it's a fairly quiet, dialogue-centred film anyway. As for extras, you get plenty of context with a 20-minute, English language interview with the director who talks about his aspirations and influences for the movie, a stills gallery, very succinct bios and filmographies, a collection of reviews and articles about the film, the original trailer, and bonus previews for other Onar titles including *Tarzan Istanbul'da*, *Casus Kiran*, *Zorro Kamcili Suvari* and more. As usual it's strictly limited to 1200 numbered copies.

SEX MACHINE
Colour, 2005, 64m. / Directed by Yûji Tajiri / Starring Rinako Hirasawa, Mutsuo Yoshioka / Salvation (US R0 NTSC, UK R0 PAL) / WS (1.85:1)

The strange Japanese pink film/romantic comedy *Sex Machine* (or as the full title apparently reads, *The Strange Saga of Hiroshi the Free-loading Sex Machine*) exists primarily to

deliver acrobatic sex scenes that look like they were designed by Jerry Lewis. It's the undeniably unique story of a single mom/postal worker (Rinako Hirasawa) who hooks up with Hiroshi (Mutsuo Yoshioka), the freeloading sex-robot of the title, who possesses as great a sex drive as she. Unfortunately he's also prone to infidelity and avoiding anything resem-bling real labour, so she also has to contend with the advances of one of the town's most influential men, who controls the local cricket racket. This isn't just British-style cricket, though; it's an amped-up version that has everyone in an uproar.

At times playing like a pink film as envisioned by Stephen Chow (but on a very meagre budget), this is peculiar viewing for sure and peppered with some hilariously nasty bodily function gags for good measure. Salvation's widescreen transfer is comparable to their other Japanese releases, meaning it's a bit soft-looking and non-anamorphic (no surprise since this was intended for the home video market). Audio is presented in Japanese mono with optional English subtitles. Apart from the usual company promos, the only notable extra here is a completely unrelated short film, "Blood", which features plenty of the title fluid spewing all over the place in what amounts to an experimental look at a woman trying to remember how she might have killed a visitor in her apartment. Well, it's different.

SEX ON CAPITOL HILL: PRESIDENTIAL PEEPERS
Colour, 1975, 208m. / Starring Marc Stevens, Tina Russell, Richard M. Dixon, Helen Madigan, Ugly George
ALL THE SENATOR'S GIRLS
Colour, 1977, 62m. / Starring Glenn Swallow / After Hours (US R1 NTSC) / WS (1.78:1) (16:9)

Lurking somewhere in the digital gutter is this '70s retro-smut double feature, which pairs up two politically-themed '70s quickies presumably timed to coincide with the aftermath of the 2008 U.S. presidential election. The big draw here is *Presidential Peepers*, the "lost" Richard Nixon-themed smut flick from '75. Watergate jokes and unsimulated copulation don't really seem like a natural mix, and this one proves it – but boy, is it strange enough to hold your interest. Late sex flick legend Tina Russell (in what is purportedly her last film) gets to act a little more than usual (which isn't necessarily a good thing given her limited skills). There's not much plot here as Tina and two other girls pal around a cheap simulation of the Oval Office with "Richard M. Dixon", a Nixon impersonator whose resemblance to Tricky Dick earned him a string of odd '70s roles like *The Private Files of J. Edgar Hoover* and *Good to See You Again, Alice Cooper*. Here he pretty much sits at his desk and does his Nixon shtick (while keeping his clothes on, thankfully) as everyone else bumps and grinds in what looks suspiciously like spliced-in loops. Russell has two scenes, mostly involving the ubiquitous Marc Stevens (oddly enough, both of them wrote incendiary autobiographies around the same time) as well as short-lived regular Helen Madigan. Manhattan public access smut legend Ugly George (who essentially started the "Girls Gone Wild" template years before it caught on) also pops up near the end as a photographer in an amusing softcore orgy scene. The packaging boasts this transfer is taken from the original 16mm negative, the sole surviving element, and this actually is one of the best-looking releases in their grindhouse line.

Considerably more banged-up and obscure is its co-feature, *All the Senator's Girls*, which features "Glenn Swallow" as a moustachioed politician whose anti-porn crusade doesn't exactly jibe with the fact that he sleeps with anything in a skirt, be it at his desk or on a yacht. Errr... and that's pretty much it. Both films are anamorphically enhanced and actually look okay framed that way; apart from the usual trailers, the big extra here is another set of Michael J. Bowen liner notes with an understandable focus on Ms. Russell covering most of the highlights of her career and the possible cause of her untimely, mysterious death.

THE SEXPERTS

Colour/B&W, 1965, 77m. / Directed by Jerald Intrator / Starring Lana Lynn, Rusty Allen, Ken Naarden, John Lyon, Audrey Campbell / Retro-Seduction Cinema (US R0 NTSC)

This exploitation oddity from infamous showman William Mishkin (best known for his tumultuous distribution history with Andy Milligan) inexplicably never saw the light of home video until this DVD release. A weird mixture of gritty black and white footage and gaudy colour inserts, it tells essentially the same story as the '50s trash classic *The Flesh Merchant* albeit in Greenwich Village, which automatically gives it a very different feel. Two roommates, Liz (Lana Lynn) and Connie (Rusty Allen), discover what it takes to get ahead in New York. Liz takes to opportunism and screwing around like a fish to water, while good girl model Connie isn't too keen on jumping into every orgy she sees. Director "J. Nehemiah" (aka Jerald

Intrator, maker of *Satan in High Heels* and *The Orgy at Lil's Place*) keeps things percolating nicely with lots of vintage '60s sleaze, and best of all, "Olga" herself, Audrey Campbell, pops up near the end for a very special guest appearance. It's not quite deranged enough to be a full-on trash masterpiece, but this should satisfy anyone itching for a dose of vintage T&A with a Big Apple twist.

Image quality looks very clean and sharp, and the mono, narration-heavy audio sounds fine. Incredibly, this film gets the double-disc treatment, with the feature housed on the first disc along with four full-on colour bonus scenes as entertaining as the film itself. Then buckle down for the real coup of the set, a trio of TV commercials featuring Madame Olga pitching floor wax, upholstery, and "Vulcan Waterproofing". Perfect for your next party compilation, of course.

Disc two, which is entitled *Naughty Nudes '65*, offers eleven vintage loops (inexplicably not mentioned anywhere on the packaging) with anonymous girls stripping, bumping and grinding through routines like "Milky Thighs, Bedroom Eyes". As usual, the set also includes a huge helping of trailers from the Retro-Seduction catalogue.

THE SEXPLOITERS

B&W, 1965, 65m. / Directed by Al Ruban / Starring Jackie Miller, Terri Steele, Gigi Darlene, June Roberts / Retro-Seduction Cinema (US R0 NTSC)

On the mean streets of '60s New York, filmmakers were busy cranking out very odd black and white projects which then evolved into full-fledged roughies. An interesting, once-obscure transition film from this period is *The Sexploiters*; as the original poster pitched it, "This picture could not have been made by professionals! Many scenes were originally shot in 8mm home movie film... Now we can show them on a large screen thru a special process developed in Paris!" Yes, and there's this big bridge over there near Brooklyn that's up for sale, too.

The main claim to fame for this one is the fact that it's the sole directorial effort for Al C. Ruban, who produced most of John Cassavetes's groundbreaking early films and got his start under Barry Mahon working on films like *The Beautiful, the Bloody and the Bare*. An interesting precursor to Luis Buñuel's *Belle de Jour* (no, really!), it's the story of married housewife Lynn (Terri Steele) who hooks up with a modelling agency that hires her out as a hooker with a specialty in kinky clients, who enjoy toying with whips and playing dead in coffins. Meanwhile her working colleague Suzy (*Olga* regular Jackie Miller) goes from doing cheesecake boob shots to hooking on the side, and it's not long before reality comes colliding with everyone involved. Featuring gritty monochrome photography (some of it by Doris Wishman's regular cinematographer, C. Davis Smith) and an eye-popping supporting cast (including softie vets like Gigi Darlene and June Roberts, whose footage may have been inserted later), this is great vintage scuzz and a welcome rescue from the depths of cinematic obscurity. Michael Bowen provides some insightful liner notes, while Smith pops up for a rare and interesting commentary track in which he only sparingly talks about this film but gives a fascinating overview of his career at the time toiling in the New York softcore industry. The full frame transfer looks fine given the highly variable nature of the movie itself – and no, none of it actually looks like it was shot on 8mm.

S

SEXUAL FREEDOM IN DENMARK

Colour, 1970, 79m. / Directed by John Lamb / Starring Lizzie Bundgaard, Dorrit Frantzen, Suzanne Fields, Uschi Digard

SEXUAL LIBERTY NOW

Colour, 1971, 80m. / Directed by John Lamb / After Hours (US R0 NTSC)

One of the more unlikely filmmakers revived due to the magic of DVD is John Lamb. Who's that, you may ask? Well, this enterprising photographer and filmmaker never really made much of a name for himself as a visual stylist, but he quietly punctured quite a few taboos with his handful of films, ranging from 1965's *The Raw Ones* (the first nudist camp movie to show "the full monty") to the following year's *Mondo Keyhole* (the first movie to send patrons scrambling to a sanitarium) and finally to the two films under consideration here, a double feature of *Sexual Freedom in Denmark* and *Sexual Liberty Now*. Lamb's earlier fare has already been celebrated via a pair of not terribly well-publicised box sets from VCI, and After Hours steps up to the plate with a set that – "in full color" – "rips aside the curtain of Victorian prudery and openly explores the amazing experiment in Denmark – where there is no adult censorship. Filmed around the world two years in production at last comes the most important statement on human sexuality of our times." Yes, these are the two infamous how-to sex manual films that managed to swerve around censorship guidelines by using on-camera sex in an instructional, "safe" documentary format, which of course was really fooling no one.

So what you get here from Mr. Lamb (under the name "M.C. von Hellen") is lots of narration and peculiar interview footage, usually involving "Danish" girls (who come off more like aspiring L.A. models) sitting around naked talking about how happy and free they are. Most of the first film is pretty tame stuff, covering such topics as strip clubs, sex shops, and beauty pageants, before suddenly swerving into less than arousing territory like venereal diseases and on-camera childbirth, with Suzanne Fields and Uschi Digard popping up for sex position demonstrations.

The film made a boatload of money, so Lamb's second outing ratcheted up the titillation value by dedicating an entire film to the rising forces of sexual freedom being oppressed by nasty prudes in the USA (gosh, thankfully that's all way behind us). Infamous anti-porn advocate-turned-swindler-and-jailbird Charles Keating kicks things off on an appropriately hysterical note, followed by some tumescent footage of John Holmes and lots of action from various couplings, some simulated and others not, with serious, urgent voiceovers intoning the importance of freeing ourselves from the shackles of prurience. The double-disc set comprises of both features in very attractive full frame transfers on disc one, a rather expendable 16x9 enhanced version of the first film on disc two (basically just matted off, which you can do anyway with a "zoom" function on a widescreen TV), and a liner notes booklet by the always interesting Michael J. Bowen. As the poster itself explains, "Here is a staggering undertaking in a deep search for human happiness that will tear asunder puritanical hypocrisy." You bet.

THE SEXUAL STORY OF O

Colour, 1984, 92m. / Directed by Jess Franco / Starring Alicia Príncipe, Carmen Carrión, Daniel Katz, Mauro Ribera, Mamie Kaplan / Severin (US R0 NTSC), Anchor Bay (UK R2 PAL) / WS (2.35:1) (16:9)

After financers imposed a connection to *Emmanuelle* on one of his 1982 films, Jess Franco found himself saddled again with cashing in on a hit Just Jaeckin release two years later with *The Sexual Story of O*, one of the stronger entries in his sex-heavy '80s Spanish cycle. Prone to lounging around in her hotel room naked and reading books, young and nubile Odile (Alicia Príncipe) catches the eye of a frisky couple (Carmen Carrión and Daniel Katz) who watch her while they're getting busy in bed. Unable to resist her, they wander over to her room and introduce themselves, with immediate carnal consequences. However, things get darker when they subsequently introduce Odile to a decadent older couple (Mauro Ribera and Mamie Kaplan) whose S&M proclivities prove to be everyone's undoing.

Though Franco professes his admiration for the original *Story of O* novel by the pseudonymous Pauline Réage, his film is markedly different in tone and intent thanks to its chilling third act developments, which push this into serious horror territory. The druggy fate of our heroine is rendered in one of the director's most potent climaxes, a harrowing assault on both her and the viewer that echoes the finale of *Eugenie* but with an even darker romantic agenda behind it. The final shot, a nice reprise of *A Virgin Among the Living Dead*, will also ring a bell with any Franco disciple, and the score assembled from various Daniel White library tracks is used to marvellous effect. The sexuality is also considerably more erotic and urgent than usual for this Franco period, as well as closer to hardcore than usual (with Katz even visibly, uh, perky during one of the more heated encounters). Franco has few kind words for his leading lady, but she's a beguiling presence

and a more likable heroine than usual for a sado-sexual "exploitation" film.

For its first official presentation in English, *The Sexual Story of O* looks exceptionally good thanks to Severin's immaculate DVD. Though the budget was obviously very limited, Franco makes skilful use of the scope frame, an attribute impossible to appreciate in past, cropped bootleg editions. The nautical locations and startling visual distortion effects look terrific, and colours are nice without being too pumped up. Once again there's a chatty Franco video interview, in which he offers candid assessments of his cast members, casting aspersions against other softcore filmmakers, and generally being his usual, take-no-bull self for a rich and randy 17 minutes. One of the most intoxicating presentations of a Franco film to date, this is a recommended antidote for those who normally shy away from his output after the late 1970s. The same uncut transfer and extras are also available in the U.K. as part of "The Jess Franco Collection 2" box set from Anchor Bay (see *The Inconfessable Orgies of Emmanuelle* review for more details).

SHAUN COSTELLO ONE DAY WONDERS HONEYMOON SUITE GRINDHOUSE TRIPLE FEATURE: HONEYMOON SUITE

Colour, 1973, 58m. / Directed by Shaun Costello / Starring Tina Russell, Marc Stevens, Shaun Costello, Georgina Spelvin, Levi Richards, Valerie Marron

JOE ROCK SUPERSTAR

Colour, 1973, 54m. / Directed by Shaun Costello / Starring Marc Stevens, Ultramax, Jamie Gillis, Tina Russell, Valerie Marron, Ashley Moore

COME AND BE PURIFIED

Colour, 1973, 60m. / Directed by Shaun Costello / Starring Jamie Gillis, Erica Eaton, Shaun Costello, Valerie Marron, Ashley Moore / After Hours (US R1 NTSC)

S

After Hours continues its authorised series of Shaun Costello releases. His grim *Forced Entry* remains one of their standout titles, with this confusingly-titled trio of quickies from the early '70s, and at least two of them are actually pretty big eye-openers. As a way of introduction, these "one day wonders" were essentially films of one hour or so shot quickly with a handy cast, usually confined to one or two rooms with everyone (literally) banging away quickly before their next gig. *Honeymoon Suite* is the most ordinary of the bunch, basically following the escapades of three couples who decide to commit to each other after years of swinging. However, their new exploration of monogamy comes with a few unexpected hitches. The cast is certainly game, but there's nothing on hand that hasn't been done a million times before.

Things get much more interesting with an improved transfer (relatively speaking) of Costello's most widely-circulated quickie, *Joe Rock Superstar*, a pretty stunning mix of glam rock and hardcore featuring Marc Stevens as Joe Cock (hmm, wonder why they changed that for the title?), a glitter-wearing, eyeliner-sporting rock idol who's having trouble keeping it up. Meanwhile everyone around him including his drummer (Jamie Gillis) and guitarist (Costello) gets a different groupie every night. What to do? Well, after performing one song called "My Dick" onstage without pants, he finally finds his libido turbo-charged thanks to... his mom. Pretty wild stuff, and the concert scenes feature Stevens lip-synching while the other actors pretend to play their instruments – and also pop up as audience members at the same time. How very existential.

Then the set reaches its climax in every possible sense with the rarely-screened *Come and Be Purified*, the most audacious and clever of the trio, with Gillis taking centre stage as Father Sexus, a phoney priest who preaches to the newly converted about the spiritual freedom of rampant, indiscriminate coupling. His randy assistant, Brother Francis (Costello, of course), gets to savour the goods, too, along with the fiery Miss Divine (Erica Eaton). The newest members of his little congregation are soon sweet-talked into orgies and other activities, though what con man Sexus is really up to isn't fully revealed until the last scene. Not surprisingly, the image of Gillis in full priest gear getting it on didn't play too well in most parts of America, and the film quickly vanished. Thankfully it's been revived here and definitely cements Costello's status as the adult equivalent of a master storyteller. Costello also provides some great liner notes in which he talks about the four-month period in which he made 32(!) of these puppies and also gives details about the mob connections he discovered behind the whole enterprise. Fascinating stuff, and the transfers are about as good as can be given the scruffy nature of the original productions.

THE SHE BEAST

Colour, 1966, 79m. / Directed by Michael Reeves / Starring Barbara Steele, Ian Ogilvy, Mel Welles, John Karlsen / Dark Sky (US R1 NTSC) / WS (2.35:1) (16:9)

After a prologue modelled after the likes of *Horror Hotel* and *Black Sunday* in which a malignant sorceress is put to slow, agonising death by angry European villagers in the 17th Century, this film follows the grisly misadventures of Philip (Reeves's regular leading man Ian Ogilvy) and Veronica

(Barbara Steele), a married couple exploring the present-day Communist region in their little Volkswagen. Their romantic stay at a small inn is disrupted by the peeping tom innkeeper (Mel Welles), who sends them fleeing in their car, which promptly crashes into the lake where the witch died centuries earlier. Now possessed, Veronica transforms into the ghastly local terror and goes on the loose, with a disbelieving Philip teaming up with local scientist/monster hunter Count von Helsing (John Karlsen) to stop this distaff threat who is, as the posters scream, "Deadlier than Dracula! Wilder than the Werewolf! More frightening than Frankenstein!"

A shaggy horror quickie whose cult longevity depends entirely on the cachet of its star and director, *The She Beast* is one of a slew of international co-productions churned out in Europe during the decade, a breeding ground which cultivated a number of directors ranging from Bernardo Bertolucci to Claude Chabrol. Though short-lived, the career of one of this decade's beneficiaries, Michael Reeves, generated huge amounts of fan discussion and studies thanks to a mere three feature films. After cutting his teeth by jumping in to direct uncredited scenes for the ragged but fascinating Italian/French gothic *Castle of the Living Dead*, Reeves was allowed to go solo by that film's prolific American producer, Paul Maslansky, to shoot his own script for a modest monster movie, with busy Italian scream queen Barbara Steele stepping in for less than 24 hours in the "lead" role. The fact that Reeves managed to create a solid, atmospheric, and sometimes clever creature feature laced with unexpected comedic elements proved impressive enough to land him two more directorial outings, *The Sorcerers* and *Witchfinder General* (aka *The Conqueror Worm*), both of them considerably darker and more pessimistic than this maiden voyage.

Actually, the fear factor in *The She Beast* is extremely low unless you're afraid of mucky witch make-up or bizarre Communist jokes. In fact, for decades this film proved baffling to those trying to tie it to Reeves's more accomplished subsequent films, thanks to its survival primarily in wretched, horrendously-cropped video editions all culled from grainy, blown-up 16mm TV prints. However, as with many of its predecessors granted a second life in the digital era, Dark Sky's much-needed DVD restores the original widescreen scope framing and reveals a surprisingly assured, even sometimes striking effort loaded with gothic landscape shots and quirky framing choices. The extra breathing room does wonders for the actors as well, with the scrawny-looking Ogilvy in particular coming off much better than before with his reaction shots finally back onscreen. Steele fans have often felt short-changed by the film, as the leading lady's brief availability resulted in her presence only for the opening twenty minutes and a quick reappearance at the end. However, given that she spends most of her time either looking fetching in androgynous chic gear (including a man's hat belonging to the producer) or wrapped in a bed sheet, Reeves certainly made the most of his limited time.

The whole film breezes by at just under 80 minutes, so Steele's absence is soon forgotten as the narrative swerves between beastly mayhem, strange Cold War-era gags, and unexpected toying with horror conventions. The main setup feels straight out of Hammer's *Kiss of the Vampire*, but the second and third act become increasingly unpredictable with comic relief provided by the local secret police and the late Welles, best known as flower shop owner Gravis Mushnik in Roger Corman's *The Little Shop of Horrors* as well as the unlikely director of offbeat drive-in fare like *Lady Frankenstein* and *Man Eater of Hydra*. The political humour also becomes more interesting when taken in context with Reeves's *Witchfinder General*, an unforgettable flip side to this approach which depicts fascist rule (enabled by religion in this case rather than communism) as a modern disease impossible to stamp out.

The long wait to get a watchable version of *The She Beast* is more than fulfilled with Dark Sky's release, whose aforementioned widescreen transfer is reason alone to make it essential. The print is vastly superior to any on view before, and apart from the occasional fleeting nick here and there (mainly in the credits), it's a startlingly clean and colourful presentation light years beyond what any horror fan could realistically expect. However, the disc manages to pull out another ace in the form of a very lively and often hilarious commentary track, with Maslansky and the always entertaining Ogilvy (whose chat on *And Now the Screaming Starts!* is also a must) carrying the first chunk of the track along with occasional moderator David Gregory. Steele joins in shortly thereafter and seems in good spirits, with Maslansky's early recollections of their decade-long estrangement over her shooting arrangement apparently having been long forgotten. It's a bit baffling that she'd agree to participate in this disc while declining offers for *Black Sunday* or *8 1/2*, but it's wonderful to have her in any form at all. Obviously Reeves is a frequent topic of conversation, and as Ogilvy in particular was one of his closest collaborators, the recollections on hand are very valuable indeed. Steele's memory seems quite a bit sketchier, but her perspective on this point in her career is also a wonderful addition. The DVD also includes a modest stills and poster gallery, though for some reason the trailer is nowhere in sight. However, die-hards can track it down (under its retitling as *Revenge of the Blood Beast*) in glorious scope as well on Ban 1's original, now

somewhat scarce *42nd Street Forever* trailer DVD collection. In any case, this is one of Dark Sky's most commendable releases to date and a welcome resuscitation of a film whose merits have proven far more considerable than previous stages in the evolution of video have led us to believe.

SHIVER

Colour, 2008, 91m. / Directed by Isidro Ortiz / Starring Junio Valverde, Blanca Suárez, Jimmy Barnatán, Mar Sodupe / Dark Sky (US R1 NTSC) / WS (1.85:1) (16:9) / DD5.1

A minor but occasionally striking entry in the Spanish horror sweepstakes popularised by films like *The Others*, *The Orphanage* and *The Devil's Backbone*, *Shiver* (aka *Eskalofrío*) bears a thematic kinship with those films' examinations of childhood's passage dramatised through the supernatural. In this case, teenager Santi (Junio Valverde) is unable to bear exposure to sunlight, so his mother Angela (Blanca Suárez) trots him off to a remote village in the hills where it's always overcast and shrouded in shadows. Soon both livestock and residents are getting their jugulars torn open by a fanged menace, which Santi believes is related to the mysterious girl who resided in his house before him. Believing she's now living out in the woods, he and some other neighbourhood boys embark on a nocturnal trip amongst the trees they'll never forget.

Director Isidro Ortiz (who helmed the much nuttier *Fausto 5.0*) manages to wring some decent shocks from the material, even if it ultimately winds up hitting a wall in the last ten minutes, and the valley atmosphere is a nice change of pace which results in some arresting visuals. Dark Sky's disc contains an impressive anamorphic transfer of the film (which often uses a chalky, bleached-out colour palette), the original Spanish track in Dolby 5.1 or stereo options (with English subtitles) or a much weaker English dub, and only the theatrical trailer as an extra.

SHOCK-O-RAMA

Colour, 2005, 88m. / Directed by Brett Piper / Starring Misty Mundae, Duane Polcou, Michael R. Thomas, David Fine, Julian Wells / Shock-O-Rama (US R0 NTSC) / WS (1.78:1) (16:9) / DD2.0

The horror swan song for Misty Mundae before she switched names to Erin Brown, *Shock-O-Rama* is an amusingly low-rent Brett Piper monster fest about scream queen Rebecca Raven, who gets tossed aside by her studio and goes off to recover at a remote country house where she's besieged by hungry zombies. Meanwhile execs looking for the next big thing sample two projects, an aliens-on-the-rampage quickie called *Mechanoid* and a sexy mad doctor romp, *Lonely Are the Brain.*

Tremendously ambitious by the standards of the studio which bears the same name, it comes packed with special effects ranging from quaintly tacky to surprisingly twisted, and the high quotient of busty scream queens certainly won't hurt its fan base either. There's way too much talk in a few sequences, but Piper does an adept job of making the 16mm production exceed its limited budget and pulls off the anthology format better than, say, the execrable *Creepshow 3*, displaying a love for the genre that results in a visual assault of aliens, giant robots, ripped-out hearts, flesh-tearing ghouls, and other sundry nastiness. The anamorphic transfer looks great with bright, vivid colours throughout , and the disc also includes a slew of interviews from the cast and crew, a making-of featurette, footage from the New York premiere, and an amusing Piper commentary track in which he expounds upon his love for vintage monster films and gripes about critics who incorrectly fault his effects work.

SICK GIRL

Colour, 2007, 83m. / Directed by Eben McGarr / Starring Leslie Andrews, John McGarr, Charlie Trepany, Stephen Geoffreys, Chris W. King / Synapse (US R1 NTSC) / WS (1.78:1) (16:9) / DD5.1

Bearing no relation to the considerably odder *Masters of Horror* episode of the same name, first-time director Eben McGarr's *Sick Girl*, is a film that will certainly push the buttons of anyone who's squeamish about post-Columbine kid-on-kid violence. Basically a much gorier version of *The Cement Garden*, it's the story of Izzy (Leslie Andrews), an orphaned misfit in high school whom we first see getting on a school bus, beating up one passenger in front of two appalled onlookers, and urinating on her victim (a nun, no less) before waltzing off to calmly kill two gun-toting guys in a field. As it turns out, Izzy is fiercely protective of her younger brother, who is apparently a magnet for bullies, and her ability to calmly inflict sadism on anyone who crosses her leads to some spectacularly grisly set pieces. With her older brother off in Iraq and both parents presumably dead (you get to fill in the blanks there), Izzy pretty much has free reign to splatter the countryside with blood, though her actions prove to have extremely dire consequences by the third act.

Definitely more accomplished and atmospheric than your average low-budget horror quickie, *Sick Girl* will prove to be tough going for some (especially anyone quick to classify fare like this as torture porn, though there's clearly more going on here than suffering for entertainment), while horror fans should enjoy some knowing nods to the genre. Chief among these is the surprising return of Stephen Geoffreys, an '80s cult icon for his idiosyncratic turns in *Fright Night*, *Heaven Help Us* and *976-EVIL* before embarking on some far more unorthodox career choices. It's great to finally have him back here as Izzy's nervous teacher, and he even contributes a fun new video interview to the DVD in which he talks about his memories of creating Evil Ed, a lunchtime tiff he had with Roddy McDowall, his reasons for ducking out of *Fright Night 2*, and his love of working with Robert Englund. You also get an extremely gory outtake reel (set to the song "I Want 'Em Dead"), a sick-joke PSA about bringing babies and cell phones into theatres, a very unusual 11-minute video interview with Andrews, and a teaser and trailer. Video quality is very good per Synapse's usual standards, especially for a shot-on-video title (that looks way, way better than usual for the format), though the overly aggressive sound mix (with music presented about ten times louder than the dialogue) might have you adjusting the volume of your rear speakers.

SILENT SCREAM

Colour, 1980, 87m. / Directed by Denny Harris / Starring Rebecca Balding, Cameron Mitchell, Avery Schreiber, Barbara Steele, Steve Doubet, Brad Rearden, Yvonne De Carlo / Scorpion (US R0 NTSC) / WS (1.85:1) (16:9) / DD5.1

A police call brings two cops (Cameron Mitchell and Avery Schreiber) to the sprawling beachside boarding house of Mrs. Engels (Yvonne De Carlo) and her son Mason (Brad Rearden) where, in slow motion, they make their way to the attic and recoil in horror. What did they find, you may ask? Well, you don't get to find out until the climax as we jump back in time to meet the Engels' newest boarders including perky Scotty (*The Boogens*'s Rebecca Balding, sporting an amusing Debby Boone haircut) who joins three other college students already settling in. While Mrs. Engels tends to disappear upstairs for long stretches, the jittery Mason helps make them at home – at least until one of them ends up knifed on the beach and another in the basement while doing the laundry. The police investigation uncovers some odd mysteries about the old place, and it's only a matter of time before the remaining guests find their names next on the chopping list.

Made during the initial spate of slasher films in the wake of *Halloween*, this independent chiller (billed as *The Silent Scream* on the title card and nowhere else) aims for a combination of modern thrills (including intercutting a knife murder with a sex scene) and tried-and-true old dark house shudders, with the two colliding head on for a memorable climax featuring a mute but quite unforgettable scene-stealing turn by scream queen Barbara Steele. De Carlo is basically wasted in her few minutes of screen time and the extensive cop footage is obviously padding that adds nothing to the story, but the rest of the cast (Balding in particular) does a fine job of creating interesting, sympathetic characters, while the skilful construction pulls off some nifty jolts including one marvellous shock scene unfortunately spoiled in the theatrical trailer. Modern horror fans might not warm up to this one right away, but it's worth the effort on a dark, spooky night and delivers the goods if you're in the right mood.

Eagle-eyed viewers could spot some signs of editing used to spackle over a disjointed production, and the excellent DVD release courtesy of Scorpion finally explains exactly how the whole affair came to pass. One-shot director Denny Harris originally made the film in 1977 with a mostly different cast (including a familiar face from *Jaws* in the Steele role), but most of the footage was scrapped by producing/writing brothers Jim and Ken Wheat (*Pitch Black*, *The Fly II*). After much recasting and the creation of a new set, the story went before the cameras again and emerged as the padded but spookily effective minor gem we now have. The HD transfer is miles and miles ahead of the past video edition from the '80s (first from Media, then a bargain version from the notorious Video Treasures); colours are rich and accurate, while the framing and detail look quite satisfying. Dolby Stereo and 5.1 mixes are offered (the former very close to the original theatrical mono mix). The Wheats and Balding contribute the lion's share of the supplemental material including an audio commentary and a new featurette, "The Scream of Success", which recount the history of both versions of the film, the various locations, and working with the impressive cast of veterans. Shorter separate video pieces discuss the Wheats' other projects (which also include *The Birds II: Lands End* and an Ewok film), Balding's other beloved horror title, and a discussion of the original screenplay, while Harris appears solely in an audio interview via telephone shortly before his death. The effective trailer and TV spots close out the disc, a highly recommended edition of a film that has languished in utter neglect for far too long.

SILIP: DAUGHTERS OF EVE

Colour, 1986, 125m. / Directed by Elwood Perez / Starring Maria Isabel Lopez, Sarsi Emmanuelle, Mark Joseph, Myra Manibog / Mondo Macabro (US R0 NTSC) / WS (1.85:1) (16:9)

 Whoa! Just when you thought you'd seen it all, along comes one of the strangest, sweatiest, sleaziest films ever made. No, seriously; though the packaging likens it to Japanese pink films, a closer description for this Filipino stunner might be an acid-fuelled remake of *Maladolescenza* by Alejandro Jodorowsky with lots of graphic sex and violence. Former Miss Philippines Maria Isabel Lopez was making a name for herself in the '80s thanks to a well-timed erotic acting career during the country's relaxing censorship under the control of Imelda Marcos, who used proceeds from the more expensive "hot" screenings to fund the country's cultural programs. As a result, filmmakers suddenly realised they could churn out whatever extreme visions their hearts desired, resulting in better-known films like *Snake Sisters* and *Scorpio Nights*. But folks, you've never come across anything like this.

In a primitive and conservative salt-making community called Ilongo, a bunch of kids are so distraught over the butchering of their beloved buffalo by town stud Simon (Mark Joseph) that a young girl is induced into her first period. Simon spends his spare time sleeping with Maria (Myra Manibog), but he's also lusted after by hot-to-trot Selda (Sarsi Emmanuelle), who's just come home from the city with an uncouth American boyfriend in tow. Meanwhile her more devout sister, Tonya (Lopez), teaches church lessons to the kids and eases her raging libido but rubbing salt in her crotch.

Pretty soon everyone's lusts are running way out of control, resulting in violent and protracted deaths, incest, and some horrific, misguided village justice.

Though it's over two hours long, *Silip* is certainly never boring and can't really be classified as a straight-up sex film. It's far too surreal and unpredictable for that, which should be obvious from the opening ten minutes that will have any PETA members howling at the screen. (Try eating a burger while you're watching it.) There's only one major gore set piece in the film, but it's a real doozy and kicks off the gripping final act of the film, which really puts the two female leads through their paces. (Apparently they weren't exactly faking their panic during the fiery climax either!) The haunting music score, fetid village atmosphere, and striking photography involving the nearby beachscapes and desert result in a wholly unique and fascinating spectacle impossible to describe.

Languishing in obscurity outside its native country for decades, *Silip* has long suffered from a woeful English dub track which replaces all of the music with bland, Romero-style library tracks. Though that unsatisfying track is present on Mondo Macabro's disc as well, all viewers should instead opt for the original Tagalog audio track with English subtitles, which results in a completely different experience. The anamorphic transfer from the original negative looks terrific; a disclaimer at the beginning warns of some unavoidable damage, but apart from a dupey-looking title card, it's quite clean and clear. Even better, this is a two-disc set which provides some essential context for the film. A Pete Tombs essay covers the basics of Filipino erotica from the early "wet" days of starlets in clingy, soggy see-through dresses to the days of the "soda" girls (all named after soft drinks, though Mountain Dew doesn't seem to have been taken), to this particular film's presence in the "bold" '80s era, which was sometimes referred to as "pene" to suggest actual hardcore in the films. *Silip* doesn't quite get there, but one scene does come very, very close. Other background info provides lots of surprising biographical details about the director and the major leads, all of whom led very eventful lives to say the least. Director Elwood Perez appears on-camera for a lengthy interview (shot in what appears to be a mall food court) in which he discusses his film career and his directorial intentions, covering the details of what directors were allowed to do at the time and how they had to satisfy the foreign market. He's jovial enough and seems to know his stuff, but the real fun can be found in the companion featurette which finds the still-ravishing Lopez talking about the origins of her acting career, her conflicting distrust and admiration for her director, the near-death shooting experiences, the sense of respect her family and children still show for her thanks to her career, and her international roles in films like *Black Cobra 3* and *Dune Warriors*. Easily one of Mondo Macabro's most eye-opening and valuable releases to date.

THE SINFUL DWARF

Colour, 1973, 92m./96m. / Directed by Vidal Raski / Starring Torben Bille, Anne Sparrow, Tony Eades, Clara Keller, Werner Hedman / Severin (US R1 NTSC), Another World (Denmark R2 PAL)

Sporting one of the greatest (and most accurate) titles in sleaze history, *The Sinful Dwarf* has been an underground video mainstay for at least two decades based on sheer curiosity value alone. Fortunately the film itself delivers exactly what you'd expect – namely, a perverted, cackling little person (played by former Danish family TV figure Torben Bille) who lives in a boarding house with his equally demented mother. One by one he stashes female guests up in the attic where he keeps them hooked on junk and available for seedy clients to enjoy. The main, er, thrust of the story concerns the mishaps of a young couple who decide to stay at the house, and by the third act hubby's wondering why his blushing bride seems to have disappeared. Commencing with a disturbing credit sequence designed around mechanical toys and the most abrasive music score this side of *Death Laid an Egg*, this little sickie was unleashed on most viewers by Box Office International guru Harry Novak, who was known to occasionally sideswipe viewers with nasty surprises like this. Though made in Denmark, the film was shot in English with an international (and pretty much unknown) cast, including one-off leading lady Anne Sparrow; the odd mélange of accents just adds to the strangeness of the entire enterprise. Most home video treasure hunters encountered the movie through Something Weird Video, who licensed it as part of the Novak library but had to keep it on the DVD-R circuit when it proved too depraved for their official line of DVDs. Fortunately Severin had no such qualms about releasing it, and their new transfer of the complete export print looks quite satisfactory (with the correct 1.33:1 framing; this one definitely does not matte off well on widescreen TVs). Anyone who ponied up for past versions should find this worth an upgrade. The biggest extra here is a hilarious promo prepared by Severin last year entitled "The Severin Controversy", which features various folks (including staff at the Video Vault) explaining how deeply this film scarred them and why it should never be unleashed upon the viewing public again. Also included are the U.S. theatrical trailer (retitled as *Abducted Bride*) and a pair of salacious radio spots.

Die hard completists may also note than a slightly longer (four minutes), alternative hardcore variant was prepared and released by Severin as a no-frills release, though the extra footage isn't particularly arousing and appears to at least partially consist of body doubles. A Danish two-disc set is also available containing an inferior transfer of the U.S. version as well as the slightly longer edition (in English with burned-in Danish subtitles) of the explicit cut. Certainly either version should satisfy anyone curious about the most amazing dirty dwarf move ever made.

SINS OF SISTER LUCIA

Colour, 1978, 70m. / Directed by Koyu Ohara / Starring Yuki Nohira, Rei Okamoto, Rumi Tama / Mondo Macabro (US R0 NTSC) / WS (2.35:1) (16:9)

 Best known as Japan's oldest studio and the originators of the Roman Porno line, Nikkatsu churned out numerous erotic, shocking films which skipped from one genre to the next. For example, take *Sins of Sister Lucia*, a solid companion piece to the delirious anti-convent epic, *School of the Holy Beast*. Using a similar set up, this outing charts the misadventures of Rumiko (Yuki Nohira), a new entrant into a Japanese abbey after her bigwig dad sends her away after she starts raiding his bribe money and banging her teacher. Behind convent walls, she is rechristened "Lucia" and finds out the nuns are all really a bunch of suppressed perverts whose claims of virtue hide secret needs for bondage and degradation. Numerous perverse set pieces ensue (including a great "spider web" sewing scene), and when Lucia sneaks a couple of criminals onto the premises, things quickly escalate out of

control with one sister trussed up onto a cross while topless for the big finale. Crazy stuff, to say the least!

Mondo Macabro's DVD sports a very colourful and attractive scope transfer (in Japanese with optional English subtitles) and features the "Erotic Empire" Roman Porno special prepared for their self-titled TV show, with commentators ranging from the studio's directors to Western fans like critic Jasper Sharp (who also provides a separate video featurette himself devoted exclusively to the film at hand). It's certainly the only special edition about a director whose titles include *White Rose Campus: Then Everybody Gets Raped.* You also get the usual superlative essays from Pete Tombs and a huge chunk of additional Mondo Macabro/Nikkatsu trailers.

THE SISTER OF URSULA

Colour, 1978, 95m. / Directed by Enzo Milioni / Starring Barbara Magnolfi, Stefania D'Amario, Marc Porel, Yvonne Harlow / Severin (US R1 NTSC) / WS (1.85:1) (16:9)

By the late 1970s, the *giallo* craze in Italy had started to lose some of its lustre thanks to increasingly sleazy cinematic offerings involving nuns, Nazis, and other taboo-bashing staples. Filmmakers eager to stay viable either hopped over into flat-out supernatural offerings (e.g. Dario Argento and Mario Bava) or increased their chances of popularity by injecting their mysteries with heavy doses of kinkiness and sleaze. A perfect example of this latter strategy is *The Sister of Ursula*, an utterly batty shocker that should have earned a hefty cult following by now along with its fellow trashy brethren like *Strip Nude for Your Killer* and *Red Rings of Fear*, though perhaps the unavailability of an English language track may account for its relative obscurity. In any case, it has now been rescued from bootleg oblivion and presented all shiny and digitally-scrubbed to startle a whole new audience.

Two sisters, jittery Ursula (Barbara Magnolfi, best remembered as the scene-stealing bitch Olga in *Suspiria*) and clothing-averse Dagmar (*Nightmare City*'s Stefania D'Amario), arrive at an oceanside resort where they spend their time watching a ridiculous nightclub act by the slutty Stella Shining (Yvonne Harlow) and hobnobbing with her handsome junkie pal (*The Psychic*'s Marc Porel). Meanwhile a sadistic killer is stalking the grounds knocking off women of loose morals with a giant wooden dildo. Yes, that's right, a dildo. First a hooker gets attacked in her room after trysting with a client, and then another couple is attacked after copulating in the cellar when they can't get a hotel room. Even stranger, Ursula experiences premonitions of these slayings and feels they're related to her own traumatic family experiences. Who's responsible, and can they be stopped before one of the sisters is next?

As a mystery *The Sister of Ursula* is really no great shakes, nor does it try to be. The killer's identity should be patently obvious, and first-time filmmaker Enzo Milioni (who assistant-directed the great *Mad Dog Killer* the previous year) seems far more concerned with photographing his gorgeous cast and locations and delivering humid, close-to-hardcore sex scenes. The phallus-inflicted violence is mostly off-camera but enough aftermath is depicted to induce viewer squirming. Far more amusing is the over-the-top lounge music score by the obscure Mimi Uva who shamelessly piles on the breathless vocals and sub-Morricone suspense strings.

An equally interesting but seldom-discussed aspect of the film is the relationship between two of its stars, as Magnolfi and Porel had been married for less than a year when this was shot. A beautiful and extremely magnetic actress who never really received her due, Magnolfi carries most of the dramatic weight of the film (and barely shows any skin in the process) in a rare leading role, while Porel, a more experienced actor from work like Luchino Visconti's *The Innocent* and Ruggero Deodato's *Live Like a Cop, Die Like a Man*, fills in what amounts to a glorified supporting role. Unfortunately he was grappling with a drug problem and had to enter rehab prior to filming, and while he stayed clean for a few years, a trip to Morocco in 1983 hooked him once again. He died there, officially from meningitis but with his friends confirming the death was drug-related. Magnolfi became reclusive and largely refrained from filmmaking afterwards, though she did make sparse supporting appearances in movies like *Cut and Run*. Back to *The Sister of Ursula*, perhaps the creepiest moment of the film is not one of its outrageous murders but rather a scene which finds Porel shooting up on-camera in his hotel room, a ghoulish foreshadowing of events to come.

Certainly not a likely candidate for a first-rate American DVD release, *The Sister of Ursula* has gotten its first respectable video presentation ever courtesy of Severin's recommended disc. The opening titles suffer from erratic contrast levels and some visible damage, but the rest of the feature looks just fine and easily blows away any of the murky-looking copies trickling quietly through the grey market for the past couple of decades. The optional English subtitles are also commendable; most of the actors' lip movements indicate that, per usual Italian filmmaking custom at the time, the major performers were speaking English during filming, though no English track was apparently ever prepared.

The biggest extra here is "The Father of Ursula", a half-hour interview with director Milioni, and as one might expect with a film this juicy, it's a fascinating experience and highly recommended for providing some context for this truly bizarre movie. He talks about how he got into the business, this film's origins as a bet and its unlikely connection to Dirk Bogarde, his friendship with the married lead actors, the drug tragedy, and of course the infamous murder weapon, which he still owns and proudly displays on camera! Incredible stuff, it's also quite stylishly mounted and ranks as one of Severin's best featurettes to date. The only other extra is the amazingly salacious theatrical trailer, which packs about as much nudity as possible into three and a half minutes.

SKIN IN THE FIFTIES

B&W, 1951-1959, 256m. / Starring Virginia Bell, Stacy Farrell

THE FLESH MERCHANT

B&W, 1956, 67m. / Directed by Merle Connell / Starring Joy Reynolds, Geri Moffatt, Marko Perri / Secret Key (US R0 NTSC)

Continuing the ongoing project by Secret Key (aka Seduction Cinema/ ei Cinema / Shock-O-Rama) to document America's sordid cinematic past, *Skin in the Fifties* represents their most "vintage" compilation to date and ends up as something of a mixed bag. On the positive side, it contains two DVDs packed with charmingly naive "nudie cutie" loops, most in scratchy but watchable condition and thankfully presented full frame without any of the phoney matting that's compromised other releases like this in the past. Plenty of familiar faces and figures appear here like Virginia Bell and Stacy Farrell in 23 loops, with titles like "African Frenzy", "Bumper Lil", "Girl in a Cage", "Nudes on a Bed", and so on. Basically it's lots of footage of girls smiling, stripping, and flashing bare breasts here and there; needless to say, the kitsch value far outweighs any erotic potential.

The major promotional gimmick of this release is a "never-before-seen" and "restored" version of *The Flesh Merchant*, a grimy little one-hour 1956 quickie about two girls who wind up getting sucked into the skin trade in the City of Angels, with several moments (especially the climax) which prefigured the roughie movement to come. Also released as *The Wild and the Wicked*, this is vintage '50s trash with plenty of weird mobster characters, teasing almost-nudity, hilarious fashions, and sexy girls who can't act worth a flip. It's been available for ages in various public domain editions, most widely as a terrible cheapo DVD from Alpha Video. On the positive side, the presentation here is mostly taken from film elements and, despite an avalanche of scratches and debris, looks much sharper and fresher than prior versions; unfortunately, a few minutes here and there have been sourced from an obvious VHS tape, and even worse, the result has been "spiced up" by inserting quick nudie "hot shots" from the other loops contained in this set!

The liner notes contend this is in keeping with exploitation practices of the period when producers would randomly insert skin shots to make their pictures more commercial, but in this case the tactic really works against the film and is more of a distraction than anything else. Still, if you can look past the tacky monkeying with the main feature, this set is recommended as a valuable look at America's libido during the atomic decade.

SKIN IN THE SIXTIES: THE MADAM

Colour, 1969, 67m. / Directed by Don Brown / Starring Uschi Digard, Tom Lee, Sue Peters, Jo Little

L'AMOUR DE FEMME

Colour, 1969, 74m. / Directed by Nick Phillips

TAKE THEM AS THEY ARE

Colour, 1968, 67m. / Secret Key (US R0 NTSC) / WS (1.78:1) (16:9)

 No matter how innocuous or even worthless a skin flick might be, buxom Uschi Digard sparks life right into the screen whenever she appears. Case in point: *The Madam*, part of Secret Key's triple-feature collection (which, in a rarity for them, comes on a single disc). There's little plot as Uschi plays a buxom young thing who talks a chopper-riding stud into giving her a lift to her mom's place, which turns out to be a very busy cathouse. John samples the wares, helps out with clients trying to pick a lady for the evening, and finally winds up in bed with Uschi herself. The set pieces are quite gynaecological for a softcore film, but as usual it's Uschi who really makes this worth watching with a final ten-minute sequence guaranteed to steam up a few pairs of glasses.

Next up is another unearthed film from the idiosyncratic Nick Phillips, *L'Amour de Femme*, which not surprisingly smacks viewers across the face with lesbianism left and right in a threadbare story about... well, experienced girls messing around with girls, repressed girls learning to mess around with other girls, and guys turning gay because they're not girls messing around with girls. It's all very colourful and very, very '60s and would make great video wallpaper at a retro party. None of the performers are identified.

Finally the third "feature", *Take Them As They Are*, is understandably treated as a supplement on the disc itself. Basically it's a very ragged-looking collection of sex scenes edited together in a blender, with lots of really ugly people spreading their legs for the camera. Don't watch it before a big meal. Picture quality varies, with the Phillips feature looking quite pristine, the Uschi one passable if a bit worn at times, and the last one... well, just don't say you weren't warned. 42nd Street Pete pops up for a quick video intro about peep loops (for no apparent reason) and then contributes a more relevant set of liner notes about the films, with supplemental comments from a "Dr. Eroticus" covering some of the actors involved.

look at even if the premise wears thin well by the halfway marker. The 100-minute running time feels at least 20 minutes too long, but if you throw this one on as background viewing and just pay attention whenever someone bites the dust, it can be a decent time waster. This first debuted on DVD from MTI but got a recent overhaul from Redemption, who pack the release (featuring an appropriately vivid anamorphic transfer, albeit interlaced) with a fairly amusing Chainsaw Charlie faux-interview, a hefty batch of deleted scenes including some eye-popping bonus gore, and a behind the scenes featurette that serves as an interesting primer on how to keep a film moving along with limited sets and assets.

$LASHER$

Colour, 2001, 100m. / Directed by Maurice Devereaux / Starring Sarah Joslyn Crowder, Tony Curtis Blondell, Kieran Keller, Jerry Sprio / Redemption (UK R0 PAL, US R0 NTSC), MTI (US R1 NTSC) / WS (1.78:1) (16:9)

Sort of a hack-and-slash cross between *Battle Royale* and *The Running Man*, this Canadian-lensed gorefest was originally made in 2001 but, sadly, still feels all too current with the wave of depressing reality shows hogging prime time airwaves. The premise is quite simple, as a smash Japanese game show inaugurates its big Western debut in America by choosing six dopes to compete on air in a scenario that pits them in a game of survival against a trio of over-the-top psychopaths named Chainsaw Charlie, Preacherman and Dr. Ripper.

Bright colours and explosive bouts of bloodshed abound, making this amusing to

SLIME CITY GRINDHOUSE COLLECTION:
SLIME CITY

Colour, 1988, 85m. / Directed by Greg Lamberson / Starring Robert C. Sabin, Mary Huner, T.J. Merrick

UNDYING LOVE

Colour, 1991, 73m. / Directed by Greg Lamberson / Starring Tommy Sweeney, Julie Lynch, Andrew Lee Barrett

NAKED FEAR

Colour, 1999, 79m. / Directed by Greg Lamberson / Starring Robert C. Sabin, Tommy Sweeney, Peggy Crown

JOHNNY GRUESOME

Colour, 2007, 8m. / Directed by Greg Lamberson / Starring Misty Mundae, Ryan O'Connell / Shock-O-Rama (US R1 NTSC)

In what amounts to an entire director's showcase packed into two discs, Shock-O-Rama's *Slime City Grindhouse Collection* offers four works of varying quality (and wildly

varying running times) from New York DIY horror director Greg Lamberson, best known in trash VHS circles for the first feature offered here, *Slime City*. As you might expect, it's a very gooey piece of work from 1988 shot in Brooklyn, Queens and the Bronx to give a gritty quality to this saga of a young couple, Alex and Lori, who find their idyllic existence in their new, modest apartment threatened when Alex takes up a neighbour's offer to consume some funky-looking yogurt and wine. Pretty soon our hero is turning into a slimy mess, and the body count begins to climb. Though touted as a gore film, it's really more squishy and grotesque in a cheaper Brian Yuzna sort of fashion, while the filmmakers genuinely manage to pull out all the stops for the head-spinning finale. Neither of the leads (Robert C. Sabin and Mary Huner) did much beyond a handful of additional no-budget horror titles, but they're surprisingly good with the latter particularly excelling in a role that continues to surprise as it evolves.

Next up is *Undying Love*, which was originally released three years later under the more interesting title of *New York Vampire*. This one tries to go much artier and actually predates other Big Apple bloodsucker mood pieces like Abel Ferrara's *The Addiction* and *Nadja* by a few years. Unfortunately it can't help but feel a bit half-baked and draggy compared to its predecessor, as the story of a failed suicide named Scott hooking up with a hot female vampire carries few surprises and is way, way too chatty for its own good. The pseudo-art house vibe is constantly undercut by the pedestrian camerawork, and the acting isn't remotely as good as the prior film's. Ah, well.

Things perk up on disc two with *Naked Fear*, which concerns a guy named Camden who's afraid to go out of his apartment but has to find a roommate to make ends meet. Obviously having never seen *Apartment Zero*, he settles on the suspicious Randy who, not surprisingly, proves to be a severe impediment to our hero's journey back to mental health. There isn't really anything too naked or fearful on display here, but it's a fun, Polanski-esque little thriller with fairly decent acting considering what appears to be the lowest budget of the three.

Finally we wrap up with the eight-minute "Johnny Gruesome", an adaptation of the director's novel (and tie-in CD!) about a leather-wearing high school rocker who returns from the dead to ride his motorcycle and kill people, not necessarily in that order. Misty Mundae pops up here (as Erin Brown, her working name now even though she's credited as Misty on the packaging) long enough for a minor love scene and plenty of screaming at the camera. It's a diverting, campy little diversion, though what this set really accomplishes is a strong desire for Lamberson to finally get that promised sequel to *Slime City* underway.

The director chips in with commentary tracks for the three main features, covering the long, multi-year process involved in getting his first movie made, the means used to secure the various local shooting spots, and the necessity for low-budget but effective splatter effects. You also get a "Making Slime" featurette on the FX, a "Making Love the Grindhouse Way" featurette, a "Meeting His Maker" peek at the production of *Johnny Gruesome*, and a fold-out poster. Also, *Document of the Dead* helmer Roy Frumkes contributes some extremely solid liner notes which lay out the director's surprising connection to *Street Trash* and *Brain Damage*.

SLOGAN

Colour, 1969, 90m. / Directed by Pierre Grimblat / Starring Serge Gainsbourg, Jane Birkin, Andréa Parisy, Daniel Gélin / Cult Epics (US R0 NTSC) / WS (1.66:1)

A pop art curio barely seen outside of its native country despite a few fleeting subtitled screenings, *Slogan* is best remembered today as the first onscreen pairing of Serge Gainsbourg and Jane Birkin, still regarded as France's first couple of pop music years after Serge's death. The two went on to scandalise the world with their orgasmic hit singles and worked together cinematically again both as an onscreen couple (including an unlikely *giallo* from Antonio Margheriti and the oddball crime film *Cannabis*) and with Serge directing her behind the camera, most outrageously in his rarely-seen ode to sodomy, *Je t'aime moi non plus*. The plot of *Slogan* is so wispy it barely holds the film together, but for the record, Serge stars as, well, Serge, a chain-smoking commercial director with a pregnant wife at home. He's summoned to a big ad agency festival in Venice, and there he becomes entangled with Evelyne (Birkin), a young British girl visiting with her father (*Murmur of the Heart*'s Daniel Gélin). Along the way the film indulges in numerous parties, travelogue scenes in Venice, and strangely hilarious commercial parodies before it all winds up, as all things in '60s France must, with a bittersweet ending.

Presumably modelled after the still-fresh success of 1966's hit French export *A Man and a Woman*, this effort from Pierre Grimblat (better known as a French TV producer) gets by almost completely on the chemistry between its leading actors, who were falling in love off camera as well. An unorthodox beauty previously seen as scantily-clad window dressing in films like *Blow-Up* and *Wonderwall*, Birkin makes the most of her role here with her broken French and slim physique, while Gainsbourg gives one of his most leisurely performances, drifting through Venice looking oh so deep and melancholy. It's all great fun if you're in the right mood, and the mod touches here and there just add to the enjoyment. Of course, the film's other great asset is its Gainsbourg-penned score, which revolves entirely around two insanely catchy themes, the torchy "Slogan" (which also appears in a vocal version) and a sparkling secondary theme called "Evelyne", which accompanies a sexy improvised Birkin dance in one of the movie's best moments.

Considering this film has remained completely under the radar for over three decades, it's remarkable that anyone would think to revive it for DVD while the more familiar *Cannabis* remains MIA. Well, surprise, surprise; it's been unearthed by the fearless folks at Cult Epics, finally with optional English subtitles. The flat letter-boxed (1.66:1) transfer is interlaced and was most likely taken from a PAL source, but it's fine for what it is; nothing too dazzling, but the colour saturation looks decent enough, and it blows up well on 16x9 monitors if you feel so inclined. The only extra is the very sleek original French trailer, a nice bonus indeed. The back sleeve indicates this is suitable for "all ages", which it probably is, though a few dark, diffused glimpses of Birkin's bare derriere might make some more puritanical parents raise their eyebrows. Then again, they probably wouldn't be out there buying Cult Epics titles in the first place. In what must surely be one of the quickest and most startling double-dips in DVD history, a two-disc edition of *Slogan* followed a few months later. The first disc is the same, of course, while the second one heaps on a surprisingly substantial amount of material that became available after the nearly bare-bones version. "Pierre Lescure Interviews Jane Birkin and Pierre Grimblat" features half an hour with Birkin commenting on the director's Bardot obsession and describing her initial impressions of her co-star and future partner as "very Slavic, very sexy, disturbing and magnificent", among many other gems, all sprinkled with vintage interview clips, comic strip art and private photos from Birkin's collection. Grimblat and Lescure go at it again for another half-hour chat in which he talks about indoctrinating the introverted Gainsbourg into acting (with one terrifying surprise), intercut with some of Grimblat's commercial work. Then writer Frédéric Beigbeder offers a 10-minute appraisal of the movie and its importance in depicting the world of advertising and media manipulation, followed by five minutes of vintage Gainsbourg/Birkin TV interviews about the film and a further 12-minute sampling of Grimblat's '60s and '70s TV commercials, including some very quirky and often hilarious spots plugging boat cruises, cars, Colgate toothpaste, Palmolive, Shell, and much more. If you don't have the first DVD version, the deluxe one should be a no-brainer and comes highly recommended; for those considering an upgrade, let's just say that those with a taste for delicious '60s European pop culture should find their money well spent, while more casual fans might have a tougher decision awaiting them.

SNAKE WOMAN'S CURSE

Colour, 1968, 85m. / Directed by Nobuo Nakagawa / Starring Sachiko Kuwahara, Seizaburô Kawazu, Kô Nishimura, Yukie Kagawa / Synapse (US R0 NTSC) / WS (2.35:1) (16:9)

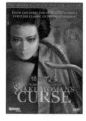 Another Synapse title inherited from the Panik House library of Asian exploitation classics, *Snake Woman's Curse* (*Kaidan hebi-onna*) is essentially a Japanese horror version of *Jean de Florette* (no, really!) courtesy of director Nobuo Nakagawa, whose cult reputation in the West has soared in recent years thanks to the classic *Jigoku*. This ghostly yarn charts the damage, both physical and supernatural, wrought by vicious landowner Chobei (Seizaburô Kawazu), who destroys the life of one of his farmers, Yasuke (Kô Nishimura), whose passing leaves a daughter (Sachiko Kuwahara) to pay off his debt. Chobei has big plans for his family, but the callous killing of a snake opens up the floodgates for a nasty supernatural curse which only amplifies with another death and a series of hauntings.

Impeccably shot and decidedly anti-materialist in the best *kaidan* tradition, the film isn't as audacious as some of its more famous counterparts but is certainly worth a look. Surprisingly, the snake aspect is a fairly minor part of the story for most of its running time, though some of the scaly rascals come in for some physical abuse so prevalent in Eastern cinema at the time. (Don't worry, though – this doesn't come anywhere near *A Calamity of Snakes*.) The provincial atmosphere is beautifully rendered, and the sparse but effective horrific effects during the payback portion of the film are skilfully executed.

The anamorphic transfer is a knockout, with rich colours and beautiful scope framing making this a treat to watch from start to finish. The optional English subtitles are well written and seem to convey the story nicely enough, meaning this is a must for anyone who tried to puzzle it out in the past without the aid of subs. Japanese cinema expert Jonathan M. Hall contributes the biggest extra, a feature-length audio commentary with a focus on the local customs and storytelling conventions which influenced the film and the social mores underpinning its more political twists and turns. Also included are the original Japanese trailer, a Nakagawa poster gallery and bio, and additional facts about the film courtesy of Alexander Jacoby's succinct and informative liner notes.

SNAPSHOT

Colour, 1979, 101m. / Directed by Simon Wincer / Starring Chantal Contouri, Robert Bruning, Sigrid Thornton / Platinum (US R1 NTSC), Elite (US R1 NTSC) / WS (1.85:1) (16:9)

Shamelessly passed off in several countries as *The Day After Hall-oween* (thus a fake sequel to *Halloween*), this mild thriller was the inauspicious feature debut for gifted director Simon Wincer, who went to bigger and better things like *The Lighthorsemen*, the underrated *Quigley Down Under*, and most famously, *Lonesome Dove*. This one feels more like one of Pete Walker's early '70s suspensers as it follows pretty hairdresser Angela (Sigrid Thornton), whose free-spirited behaviour gets her thrown out of her house. She decides to try out some model-ling with the encouragement of super-bitchy buddy Madeline (Chantal Contouri) but gets distracted when her psycho ex-boyfriend starts following her around in an ice cream truck. And that's about it. Paced like molasses, *Snapshot* tries to throw in some skin here and there as well as an ear-shred-ding love ballad, but one can only imagine the riots this caused among audiences expecting a slasher movie.

The budget-priced Platinum DVD actually looks pretty good with a decent enough anamorphic transfer that beats out the old VHS editions (including one from the beloved Magnum Home Video). It was also fleetingly available (with the same transfer) as part of Elite's long-discontinued

"Aussie Horror Collection Vol. 2" along with *The Survivor* and two incredibly dull, obscure oddities, *The Dreaming* and *Voyage Into Fear*.

SO SWEET, SO DEAD

Colour, 1972, 95m. / Directed by Roberto Bianchi Montero / Starring Farley Granger, Sylva Koscina, Silvano Tranquilli, Annabella Incontrera, Chris Avram, Femi Benussi, Susan Scott (Nieves Navarro) / Camera Obscura (Austria R2 PAL) / WS (1.85:1) (16:9)

The throat-slashing murder of a prominent general's unfaithful wife proves to be a challenge for the chief investigator, Insp-ector Capuana (Farley Granger), who is soon ordered by the public and his boss to catch the killer without causing any humiliation to the cuckolded husband or the mystery lover, whose face is scratched out of incriminating photos left at the crime scene. Soon another important man's wife (Femi Benussi) is sliced up on the beach after being photographed in the park with her lover, and Capuana realises he has a serial killer on his hands. However, the black-gloved, black-coated assassin's agenda seems to run deeper than simply punishing women for straying from their spouses, which leads Capuana into very dangerous territory when his own wife (Sylva Koscina) might be one of the next targets.

Despite lifting its killer's appearance straight out of *Blood and Black Lace*, this nasty piece of work clearly belongs to the 1970s as the relaxation of worldwide censorship allowed *gialli* to ramp up the sex and violence to ridiculous extremes. As with the previous year's similar *Black Belly of the Tarantula*, this effort uses a married inspector as the focus of a story that exists primarily to trot out a string of gorgeous female guest stars who disrobe and die horribly. However, this one outdoes its predecessors by unleashing a breast-and-blood quotient that's truly surprising for 1972. Considering the opening pre-credit scene begins with the line "Be sure to get lots of close ups" over the bloody body of a naked woman, it's clear right away where this story is heading. Director Montero (a genre-hopping craftsman who dabbled in every-thing from westerns to action films to hardcore porn) barely tries for cinematic artistry here apart from Benussi's slow-motion beach murder at dusk and the startling final ten minutes, a twisted climax that really sets this apart from its ilk.

Not surprisingly, the original unwieldy Italian title of *Rivelazioni di un maniaco sessuale al capo della squadra mobile* (or "Revelations of a Sex Maniac to the Criminal Investigation Chief") was adapted for English speakers to more grindhouse-friendly options like *The Slasher Is the Sex Maniac!* (shortened to simply *The Slasher* more frequently during the VHS era) and the more appropriate *So Sweet, So Dead* with which it's more commonly associated now. However, its most notorious permutation came in 1976 when American distributor William Mishkin (best known for Euro imports and a string of Andy Milligan films) repur-posed the film by replacing the shutterbug sex scenes with hardcore porn inserts composed of loop footage featuring Harry Reems, Kim Pope, and Marc Stevens. The subsequent patchwork version was reissued on the X-rated market as *Penetration* before being yanked from release (at Granger's behest according to most accounts). Given the Mishkin legacy of trashing most usable film elements, it's no surprise that this variation has yet to resurface anywhere on home video.

The various video editions of *So Sweet, So Dead* have been fairly miserable over the years, with VHS copies from Japan and the U.S. (among many others) all missing various snippets of footage and sporting wildly varying aspect ratios. Camera Obscura's DVD marks the first official digital release and turns out to be quite a firecracker indeed. The transfer from the original Italian negative is an absolute knockout with stunning colour saturation and razor-sharp picture detail; even upscaled on a large monitor, this could almost pass for HD. Two parts (a very enthusiastic sex scene with the typically exhibitionistic Susan Scott and some inter-rogation footage between Granger and one of the victim's spouses) were extended slightly in some non-Italian prints, so that extra shots have been reinstated here from a noticeably inferior tape source. Don't worry though; it's quite a quick interruption, and the attention to detail here is welcome indeed. Mono audio options in Italian and German are included with optional English and German subtitles. The widely bootlegged English dub is absent, but it's not much of a loss; Granger (star of Hitchcock's *Strangers on a Train* and *Rope*) didn't provide his own voice, and everyone else was clearly speaking Italian. Incidentally, Farley was quite busy in the early '70s in Italy appearing in the likes of *They Call Me Trinity*, *Amuck*, *The Red Headed Corpse*, and a puzzling bit part in *What Have They Done to Your Daughters?* Not surprisingly, the film plays much better overall in Italian with English subtitles; the story makes much more sense, and some of its sexual politics are a bit more compli-cated than expected. The biggest extra is a lengthy interview with composer Giorgio Gaslini (who also scored Argento's *Deep Red* before Goblin came aboard and changed the entire musical direction), who certainly seems to appreciate the luxurious perks of his job and talks more about his overall career than this particular title. Christian Kessler and Marcus Stiglegger contribute an enthusiastic commentary track in German with optional English subtitles; they cover Granger's career, the *giallo* conventions of the time, and the histories of the all-star cast of familiar Italian exploitation faces. Kessler also provides the liner notes (in English and German) in a booklet offering a more overall appreciation of the film, while the disc extras finish off with the French photo novel (with optional subs) and a solid gallery of poster, still, and video art.

SOLE SURVIVOR

Colour, 1983, 85m. / Directed by Thom Eberhardt / Starring Anita Skinner, Kurt Johnson, Robin Davidson, Caren L. Larkey, Andrew Boyer, Brinke Stevens / Code Red (US R0 NTSC) / WS (1.85:1) (16:9)

One of those horror films that seemed to be everywhere on VHS in the mid-1980s, *Sole Survivor* is a moody and often surprising twist on the "life after death" scenario. It's impossible to discuss this movie without immediately referencing other related horror titles before and after, especially since the packaging touts its thematic similarities to the *Final Destination* series (which it resembles in concept if not in execution). The initial first half also seems to recall such "Wait, am I still alive?" chestnuts like *Carnival of Souls*, though thankfully the twist ending goes in a very different direction from what most viewers will expect. In short, it's a slick, simple, down and dirty spooker that keeps its ambitions limited and succeeds admirably as a late night diversion.

After ignoring a premonition from her colleague Karla (Caren L. Larkey), Denise Watson (Anita Skinner) goes on a plane flight and finds herself the only survivor after a catastrophic crash. She tries to get her life back together with the aid of her bratty neighbour Kristy (Robin Davidson) and coverboy shrink Brian (*Ghost Story*'s Kurt Johnson, who creepily died soon after this film's release), who offers such encouraging titbits as the fact that most disaster survivors tend to drop dead under mysterious circumstances within 24 months of the initial event. Soon Denise is being followed around by weird-looking stalkers who might be the same people who died in the accident, and even worse, those close to her start dying very mysteriously and very violently...

A film that gains in impact considerably with a little bit of context, *Sole Survivor* comes to DVD with enough participation from co-producers Larkey and Sal Romeo to shed some light on how it was created. Most horror fans know this as the debut effort for director Thom Eberhardt, who followed it up with one of the most endearing cult hits of the '80s, *Night of the Comet*. It's a shame he doesn't seem to participate in DVD releases of his films, but the producers fill in the blanks by going over the entire history of how the film was made, how they shot the atmospheric town scenes for free, and what a mess the film's distribution turned out to be. Interestingly, they spend quite a bit of time lamenting the fact that once the film was sold, it lost about three minutes of comic relief among the characters which would have given it a more varied and distinctive flavour. (However, a longer cut evidently slipped out on VHS in the U.K. years ago, so snap it up if you can find it.) In any case, there's still plenty for horror fans to enjoy here, even if the gore is deliberately kept to a minimum (basically a couple of mildly bloody stabbings, some traumatic post-plane crash footage, and slit wrists). As an added bonus, scream queen Brinke Stevens even turns up in an early role for a quick game of strip poker that finds her providing the film's requisite T&A.

Considering how bad the old tapes of *Sole Survivor* looked, it's a welcome relief to finally see it looking clear and colourful with a new anamorphic transfer. Not many people had the opportunity to see it in the theatre, but this is a good approximation and still has that beloved low budget, rough look found in many horror films from the period; think *My Bloody Valentine* and you'll get the idea. Extras include the aforementioned commentary (which is moderated by enthusiastic *Leatherface* director Jeff Burr and writer Jeff McKay), a fun and pretty ridiculous theatrical trailer (complete with an unrelated slimy demon claw emerging from some dry ice fog), a video intro from Larkey, an on-camera video interview with Larkey and Romeo (who cover some of the same territory as the commentary but offer some additional nuggets about the cast), appreciative liner notes by *Nightmare USA* author and Lucio Fulci expert Stephen Thrower, and trailers for other Code Red titles including *The Unseen*, *The Dead Pit*, *Silent Scream*, *Human Experiments* and the vigilante classic *The Farmer*.

SPIRITUAL EXERCISES

Colour/B&W, 1984-1999, 180m. / Directed by Olivier Smolders / Cult Epics (US R0 NTSC)

 If *Black Night* is the culmination of experimental Smolders's directorial mind to date, this short film collection from Cult Epics shows the foundation being laid with ten films showing his development over a fifteen year period. "Adoration" follows a cannibalistic murderer who uses a camera as a tool in his trade; "Seuls" presents an affecting portrait of autistic children; "Point de fuite" (the funniest of the bunch) is about a math teacher confounded when her entire class shows up nude; "Mort à Vignole" uses monochromatic home movie footage to document a watery tragedy; "L'amateur" features a fledgling filmmaker encountering the female form in all its age-related permutations; "Neuvaine" draws disturbing visual parallels between religious ceremony, drug use and animal slaughter; "La philosophie dans le boudoir" features explicit recitations from the famous Marquis de Sade novel over beautiful black and white portraits and figure studies of various actors (with "Ravissements" offering an alternative version of the same film); "L'art d'aimer" etches a portrait of residents at a nursing home talking about a very violent incident; and "Pensées et visions d'une téte coupée" (the longest of the series) features a strange art gallery guide explicating the meaning of a series of paintings as the visitors become more reflective of their surroundings.

The transfers are taken from a variety of video sources of varying quality as well as different aspect ratios; all are watchable but definitely show their age with the appearance of a video master from at least a decade ago. Still, how else can you see them? The collection comes with a hefty 48-page booklet containing essays and interviews about the films (in both English and French), two "Court Circuit" shorts summarising his strongest images ("Spiritual Exercises" and "Images Enamored of Love and Death"), and a three-minute excerpt from *Black Night*.

SPLATTER BEACH

Colour, 2007, 70m. / Directed by John & Mark Polonia / Starring Erin Brown, Erika Smith, Dave Fife, Brice Kennedy, Ken Van Sant / Camp (US R0 NTSC)

For her first full-length straight (read: non-naked) horror film, Misty-Mundae-turned-Erin-Brown made the odd move of teaming up with the Polonia Brothers, purveyors of bargain basement shockers like *Splatter Farm*, for this cheap-jack remake of *Horror of Party Beach*. Everyone's heart seems to be in the right place, even if the final result is way, way too talky (even by grade-Z drive-in standards) and filmed on what looks like the edge of a small Northeastern lake rather than a full-fledged beach.

Interestingly, this marks the maiden attempt by Camp Motion Pictures (best known for unearthing '80s straight-to-video oddities) to churn out new horror product with the same DIY aesthetics, resulting in a weirdly nostalgic homage to both shot-on-camcorder cheapies and '60s beach horror films. The script is better than it has any right to be, and the film wisely acknowledges its silliness with some surf-rock interludes and unexpected injections of fake drive-in movie footage. The whole thing was shot in three days, so don't expect a masterwork; however, if you're pining for a gorefest put together on the cheap with a seasoned scream queen carrying the thespian weight, this should fit the bill. The full frame video transfer looks decent given the modest origins of the movie itself, and the DVD comes packed with tons of extras including a Polonia commentary track, a music video, a behind-the-scenes featurette with Brown and the directors, a vintage news segment on the enterprising filmmakers, a Q&A with the composer, a bonus soundtrack CD, extra Camp trailers, and most curious of all, a one-hour VHS "bonus feature" entitled *Hallucinations*, which is impossible to describe, riddled with '80s tape distortion, and weirdly compelling at the same time.

SPLATTER DISCO

Colour, 2007, 92m. / Directed by Richard Griffin / Starring Ken Foree, Trent Haaga, Jason McCormick, Debbie Rochon, Lynn Lowry, Sarah Nicklin / Shock-O-Rama (US R0 NTSC) / WS (1.78:1) (16:9) / DD2.0

For evidence the slasher parody is still alive and kicking today, look no further than *Splatter Disco*, "the first slasher musical", whose title is a bit of a cheat as there's nothing even remotely resembling disco music and only a few tiny glimpses of bloodshed. Still, where else can you see *Dawn of the Dead*'s Ken Foree in a dance club wearing a big fuzzy animal outfit?

The story revolves around a hangout called Den O' Iniquity where the patrons can indulge in any of their harmless personal quirks, including an entire musical performance of "Let's Do It" with the cast decked out as furries. (Look that up if you aren't familiar with it.) Unfortunately the mayor and his domineering mom want to shut the place down, and people start dying in the process. Though it features spanking, hangings, and knifings, not to mention a guy who gets his jollies by getting walked on while he's rolled up in a carpet, the film is surprisingly chipper and colourful, with a bouncy attitude and sense of fun that sets it apart from most DV-shot horror films. It's also superior to anything Troma's done in eons, an apt statement considering several former Troma performers pop up here including Debbie Rochon (*Tromeo & Juliet*) and Trent Haaga (*Terror Firmer*). You also get a small but memorable role for Lynn Lowry, thankfully back on the screen again after her glory days of *The Crazies* and *Score*.

Director Richard Griffin (*Creature from the Hillbilly Lagoon*) takes a huge leap forward in terms of visual skill here, handling elaborate musical sequences and stalking scenes alike with skill. The DVD features a solid 16x9 transfer that looks as good as standard digital video possibly can, along with "Inflicting Joy" (a fun behind-the-scenes featurette with the filmmakers and cast), an audio commentary with Griffin, Lowry and other cast members wandering in and out, and some quick alternative versions of the "Let's Do It" number and one suspense sequence.

SPLATTER FARM

Colour, 1987, 70m. / Directed by John & Mark Polonia / Starring Todd Smith, John Polonia, Mark Polonia, Jeff Seddon, Marion Costly / Camp (US R0 NTSC)

 Nothing says do-it-yourself camcorder bloodletting quite like a film by the Polonia Brothers. *Splatter Farm* is one of the gore brothers' first outings, years before they assaulted the world with anti-classics like *Holla If I Kill You* and *Peter Rottentail*. Yes indeed, it's another gem from the golden age of '80s homemade video gore obscurities, sharing shelf space with the likes of *Goremet Zombie Chef from Hell* and *Woodchipper Massacre*. The brothers also star as Alan and Joseph, two siblings holed up for the summer at a farm run by their old Aunt Lacey (Marion Costly), an incestuous, necrophilic biddy whose loco handyman, Jeremy (Todd Smith), gets his kicks by chopping up townspeople and stashing their remains under the house. Then the gore really starts to fly.

Completely amateurish yet strangely compelling, this beloved relic from the VHS era comes to DVD with all of its fuzzy camcorder lensing, dropouts and bad sound intact, which is just as it should be. The liner notes explain that the original VHS version was actually a rough cut shopped around for distribution without any funding provided to finish the actual movie, so this DVD in essence marks the first officially-sanctioned release. The entire disc is basically a Poloniapalooza, complete with a new "Back to the Farm" featurette (with the brothers talking about the making of the movie and its creepy farm location), a hilarious and very self-aware audio commentary pointing out the shortcomings and challenges of the DIY project, and a huge heap of Super 8 splatter shorts (all silent with the brothers' audio commentary), nine in total, including such titles as "GI Joe Versus the Alien", "The Mad Slasher", "A Toast to Death" and "The Killer". Of course, you also get trailers for Camp's other essential '80s cheapo classics like the *Video Violence* and *Zombie Bloodbath* series, all of which would make perfect co-features to the pure genius that is *Splatter Farm*.

THE STARLETS

Colour, 1977, 80m. / Directed by David Summers / Starring Laurien Dominique, Monique Cardin, Candida Royalle, Joey Silvera, Spring Finlay, Desiree West, John Leslie, Ken Scudder

CHASTITY AND THE STARLETS

Colour, 1986, 85m. / Directed by David Summers / Starring Amber Lynn, William Margold, Tom Byron, Taja Rae / After Hours (US R0 NTSC)

 One of the most famous entries from one of the briefest fads in movie history, the 3-D feature-length porno, is *The Starlets*, another entry in the "Grindhouse Directors Series" from

After Hours, this time dedicated to the much more obscure David Summers. Actually 90% of the film makes no use of the 3-D format (here dubbed as Quadravision 4-D, whatever that means), only to throw in some hilarious third-act visuals like flaming sparklers (during an orgasm), clutching disembodied hands, ooga-booga devil masks, and psychedelic skulls. Sound weird? Oh, yes, it is, but that's not surprising given that this was produced by exploitation vet John Lamb (under the name "M.C. von Hellen") whose *Mondo Keyhole* was an obvious influence here. The film itself has virtually no plot, instead revolving around the fleshy shenanigans at the Starlets Club, an exclusive Hollywood organisation where everyone apparently gets together at a mansion and samples a bunch of upscale hookers. The cast includes a lot of familiar faces including Desiree West, Candida Royalle, John Leslie (briefly), Joey Silvera, and Ken Scudder, and Summers does a surprisingly deft job at juggling numerous simultaneous scenes together for the entire running time, creating the impression of forward momentum for the film itself rather than stopping dead for one isolated scene after another.

Summers turns up for the DVD's liner notes booklet and contributes quotes about the film and the challenges of shooting in 3-D as well as its lesser and basically plotless shot-on-video sequel, *Chastity and the Starlets*, whose star, Bill Margold, also pops up for a quick interview about his career and the intimate challenges of shooting sex scenes in a chlorinated swimming pool. Both movies are presented full frame from what appear to be the original elements (great for the first title, but that's not saying much in the case of the second one, which looks like it was shot on VHS); the DVD also includes trailers for both films as well as the usual After Hours cross-promotional hard sell gallery of promos.

STASH

Colour, 2007, 97m. / Directed by Jacob Ennis / Starring Karen Boles, Nathan Day, Stacey T. Gillespie, Kevin Taylor, Debbie Rochon / Bloody Earth (US R0 NTSC) / WS (1.85:1) / DD2.0

Drug-related horror movies tend to be really, really awful and reactionary (e.g. *Shrooms*), but one moderate exception is the unsung *Stash*, probably the best title ever released by Bloody Earth Films. This southern-fried concoction takes place in a Kentucky hemp road hell where two backwoods potheads, Stan and CJ, decide to swipe the stash of Ol' Bud, a local pot dealer. Unfortunately Bud catches them in the act and blackmails them at gunpoint into procuring women he can keep, uh, stashed away in his basement. However, one of their victims of choice, Sarah, is quickly missed by her parents and the local authorities, triggering a race against time as she fends for her life at the hands of this moonshine-swilling psychopath.

Taut, tense, and surprisingly atmospheric despite its admittedly massive technical shortcomings, *Stash* is thankfully more unpredictable than the "torture porn"-style packaging might indicate, with an interesting cast of characters and a refusal to fall back on either cheap drug humour or simple misogyny to keep its audience interested. Apart from a few dubious art direction choices (a big Confederate flag hanging on a wall? Really?), this is definitely better than you'd expect from a shot-on-video recent horror film. The non-anamorphic transfer looks adequate (about as good as you'd expect for something lensed in DV), and extras include a director/producer commentary with Jacob Ennis and Billy and Denise Blackwell, a making-of featurette, a short blooper reel, a video interview with genre vet Debbie Rochon (who appears in a supporting bit as one of Bud's other victims), and a music video for a song called "Still I Bleed".

THE STEPFATHER

Colour, 1987, 89m. / Directed by Joseph Ruben / Starring Terry O'Quinn, Jill Schoelen, Shelley Hack, Charles Lanyer, Stephen Shellen / Shout! Factory (US R1 NTSC), Marketing Film (Germany R2 PAL) / WS (1.85:1) (16:9), Carlton (UK R0 PAL), Umbrella (Australia R4 PAL) / DD2.0

 After murdering his family in a quiet suburban neighbourhood, a serial killer (Terry O'Quinn) with a longing for domestic perfection moves on to a new community by posing as a realtor named Jerry Blake. His latest wife, Susan (Shelley Hack), thinks everything is ideal with the new family unit, but her teenage daughter Stephanie (Jill Schoelen) begins acting up at school in hopes of being sent away from her new stepfather. Things get worse when she spies Jerry having a violent tantrum in the basement, and even with the aid of a school psychologist, she still fears Jerry is much more dangerous than he appears.

A film that seemingly came out of nowhere, *The Stepfather* remains one of the finest and most intelligent horror movies of the 1980s. Superb performances, precise direction by drive-in vet Joseph Ruben (who went from *The Pom Pom Girls* to *Dreamscape* and *Sleeping with the Enemy*), and best of all, a crackerjack script by hardboiled mystery writer Donald E. Westlake, who shares a story writing credit with Brian Garfield (*Death Wish*) and Carolyn Lefcourt. Many critics and viewers were surprised when a film marketed as

another slasher outing turned out be such a superior piece of entertainment with a strong satirical edge, ruthlessly exposing the downside of the American family ideal. The timing of its theatrical release was ironic as well, coming at the end of Reagan's second term just before the mantra of restoring "family values" began to overtake the public consciousness; not surprisingly, viewers creeped out by this conformist chanting found their fears perfectly confirmed by the chilling vision found here. Perhaps its most subversive element might be the subplot involving Ogilvie (Stephen Shellen), the brother of Jerry's previous wife, who spends the film tracking the murderer. The resolution of this narrative thread startled many viewers and remains a jolting twist best left unspoiled.

Thanks to various legal entanglements, *The Stepfather* sat out the first ten years of the DVD era in America but appeared elsewhere in bare-bones editions of varying quality. The German disc features a solid anamorphic transfer, while the British and Australian editions are culled from inferior full frame sources. The much-delayed U.S. edition from Shout! Factory (licensed from ITC once they got the paperwork in order) is easily the best of the lot, featuring a fresh new transfer and a host of exclusive extras. Best of these is "The Stepfather Chronicles", a wonderful half-hour look at the making of the film with Ruben, Garfield, producer Jay Benson, and the still-gorgeous Schoelen (easily the most winning horror actress of her era) discussing the making of the film from story conception to release. Ruben also appears for an audio commentary track with *Fangoria* editor Mike Gingold which focuses more on the production minutiae and offers plenty of info about the actors including O'Quinn and Hack (whose absence on the supplements is regrettable, but you still get more than enough here). Also included is the full frame theatrical trailer and liner notes by Shout! producer Cliff MacMillan.

STEPFATHER II

Colour, 1989, 93m. / Directed by Jeff Burr / Starring Terry O'Quinn, Meg Foster, Caroline Williams, Jonathan Brandis, Henry Brown / Synapse (US R1 NTSC), Buena Vista (US R1 NTSC) / WS (1.85:1) (16:9) / DD2.0, Carlton (UK R2 PAL) / WS (1.78:1)

Despite the fact that he was filled with gaping knife wounds after his last rampage, the serial killer known as Jerry Blake (Terry O'Quinn) has survived and for some reason undergoes rehabilitation in a psychiatric hospital. Not surprisingly, this plan is short-lived as the psycho stepfather knocks off his shrink and a guard for a tidy escape back into the suburbs. Now going under the name Gene Clifford, he sets his sights on another single mom, Carol (Meg Foster), and her son Todd (Jonathan Brandis), with a swift courtship that soon leads to a marriage proposal. Carol's friend Matty (Caroline Williams) harbours some suspicions which put her next in line on the lunatic's hit list and, as the countdown to the wedding day approaches, Carol has only a short amount of time to realise the danger that awaits her.

Since the surprise hit *The Stepfather* proved to be one of the most powerful horror movies of the 1980s, it was only natural that a sequel would be put into production right away. Of course, the fact that the film's very human villain was handily dispatched at the end set up one of many obstacles for the script (an issue solved even less convincingly in the ludicrous *Stepfather 3*), and the decision not to use any of the creative talent behind the first feature means this one can't hope to measure up. However, on its own modest terms, *Stepfather II* offers plenty of entertainment value primarily thanks to the return of O'Quinn, a terrific actor who eventually got the credit he was due on TV's

Lost, Alias and *Millennium*. Spooky-eyed Foster (*They Live*) and the late Brandis (TV's *Seaquest DSV*) have less to do with their sketchy roles, which are completely sabotaged by the script's idiotic assertion that no modern kid would possibly know how to whistle the song "Camptown Races" on his own.

Upon its initial release, *Stepfather II* (sometimes shown under the irritating title of *Stepfather 2: Make Room for Daddy*) had quite a bit of horror community buzz as the first big film for director Jeff Burr, who caused a minor stir with his grisly anthology, *The Offspring* (aka *From a Whisper to a Scream*). Despite the deeply flawed script, he does a fine job here and executes some solid suspense sequences while ratcheting up the brutality as well, particularly the blood-spattered wedding finale. After this he went on to a far more problematic sequel, *Leatherface: Texas Chainsaw Massacre III*, and a couple of *Puppet Master* sequels to boot. For some odd reason Miramax wound up with the rights to this film and tagged it for full-on special edition treatment on DVD, and all of those supplements are carried over along with a new featurette for Synapse's reissue. Burr and producer Darin Scott appear for a good commentary track about the making of the film; Burr in particular is one of the better chatters around for horror commentaries, and his enthusiasm and excellent memory serve him well here. On the video side you get over 30 minutes of deleted footage including some additional gore during the most memorable murder sequence; it's taken from a VHS-sourced work print but its nice to have all the same. The new addition to the Synapse release is "The Stepfather Chronicles: Daddy's New Home", a half-hour featurette prepared at the same time as the supplements for Shout! Factory's release of the first film. It's a very informative and well-constructed piece with Burr, Scott, Williams, writer John

Auerbach, cinematographer Jacek Laskus and editor Pasquale Buba chatting about the making of the film, including its convoluted road from conception to screen and the challenges posed by creating new scenarios for America's most unhinged step dad. Theatrical trailers and a stills gallery round out a very solid presentation. A stripped-down U.K. version (only containing the trailer) was also released by Carlton as part of its "Silver Collection", but as with their treatment of the first feature, the dated transfer is inferior; go for either the Disney or Synapse versions if possible.

THE STRANGENESS

Colour, 1980, 92m. / Directed by David Michael Hillman (Melanie Anne Phillips) / Starring Dan Lunham, Terri Berland, Rolf Theison, Keith Hurt, Chris Huntley, Mark Sawicki / Code Red (US R0 NTSC) / WS (1.85:1) (16:9)

Most people probably aren't aware that there was a small subgenre of mining horror movies in the early 1980s, but sure enough, if you looked around hard enough, you could find plenty of people getting offed by tunnel-dwelling terrors in films like *My Bloody Valentine* and everyone's favourite monster title, *The Boogens*. Far more obscure but just as likeable in its own way is *The Strangeness*, a very low-budget production that shuffled off straight to VHS in the U.K. and America and barely made a blip on the horror fan radar until a lengthy, mouth-watering appraisal finally appeared in Stephen Thrower's essential study of Americana horrors, *Nightmare USA: The Untold Story of the Exploitation Independents*. Of course, the fact that the film was only available in extremely low-grade transfers that made pea

soup out of its dark, source-lit photography didn't help its reputation, but the official DVD release finally allows curious monster fans to see it on its best behaviour.

The story takes place around and almost entirely in the Gold Spike mine, a desolate location haunted by stories of mishaps and disappearances which eventually led to it being shut down for good. Now targeted as a possible location for re-opening, its latest visitors consist of an exploration group headed by engineer Myron (Rolf Theison) and a batch of geological consultants, writers, and curious companions who hope they might strike a little gold along the way. As they delve deeper into the mine accompanied only by a few handy light sources, they begin to realise that the more grotesque rumours about the place are not only possible, but likely to still be around and able to pick them off one by one.

Shot in moody low lighting on an estimated budget of around $20,000, *The Strangeness* is remarkable simply as a group effort that managed to reach completion and turn out as an entertaining, above-average monster flick able to win over a few fans. A far cry from the slick, glossy and often soulless horrors going direct to video now, it's filled with blood, sweat, and lots of affection, particularly when the much-awaited monster finally rears its head in the final reel and turns out to be far wilder than expected thanks to some imaginative lighting and stop-motion animation. The film was shot for many months on available weekends, with FX artists Chris Huntley and Mark Sawicki (who also appear in the film) using limited means to turn out admirably effective results.

Notoriously difficult to see in past video editions (literally, as in you couldn't see what was going on), *The Strangeness* will be a revelation on DVD for anyone who tried to slog through any previous versions. The film has been transferred from the original

16mm negative, and detail and colour accuracy are improved tremendously. The filmmakers hoped for a 35mm blow-up to show theatrically when the movie was originally in the can, but a string of dubious distribution details ensured that would never come to pass; as a result, this marks the first time anyone – including the creators – could see it matted to 1.85:1, and the results are pleasing indeed. Bear in mind that this is still a scrappy production (think *The Deadly Spawn*) with a little unavoidable wear and tear in a few spots, but there's little room for complaint here. The audio also sounds much better and is, according to the commentary, much closer to the original intentions before Trans World mucked around with the music mix and muddied much of the dialogue and sound effects. The commentary (which features Huntley, Sawicki and director Melanie Anne Phillips) is extremely entertaining (apart from the lack of decent recording for moderator Jeff McKay, who seems to be prompting from down inside the mine itself) and comes packed with fun anecdotes, including the resourceful and very cheap means used to secure locations and create the illusion of a mine in various handy California structures. You also get three video interviews with the same participants, who talk more about how they came to the film and the lessons they learned from it, as well as how they originally knew each other from their USC days. Speaking of which, six early USC shorts by Sawicki and Huntley are included: "Origins" (a neat stop-motion look at Darwinism in action), the more modest animated "Eat at Joe's", the mild pseudo-horror "It Stalked the Night", the thrillers "Grave Sight" and "Daddy's Gone A'Hunting", and the apocalyptic animated short, "The End". Other extras include a hefty photo gallery of stills and ad art, a surprise video appearance by the monster and trailers for additional Code Red titles like *Brute Corps*, *The Statue*, *Trapped*, and *The Visitor*.

STUNT ROCK

Colour, 1978, 91m. / Directed by Brian Trenchard-Smith / Starring Grant Page, Monique van de Ven, Margaret Gerard, Sorcery, Richard Blackburn, Phil Hartman / Code Red (US R0 NTSC), Madman (Australia R4 PAL) / WS (2.35:1) (16:9)

Part pseudo-documentary, part rock film, and all kinds of crazy, *Stunt Rock* is essentially a feature-length poem to fearless Aussie stuntman Grant Page from cult director Brian Trenchard-Smith, a man boasting probably the weirdest roster of credits ever for a single filmmaker. At the time he was definitely going through a big action phase in the '70s, starting with the 48-minute doc *The Stuntmen* and then moving to the TV action film *Kung Fu Killers*, the terrific George Lazenby/Wang Yu action classic *The Man from Hong Kong*, and the bizarre, family-friendly stuntapalooza, *Deathcheaters*.

Those last two films introduced the director to Page, and for their third and final collaboration, they pulled out all the stops for this not-quite-real cinematic odyssey which follows our intrepid stunt man from doing dangerous stunts in Australia to working on a TV show in Los Angeles, where he hangs out with his main squeeze (Margaret Gerard, the future Mrs. Trenchard-Smith) and perky Dutch reporter Monique van den Ven (during her big Paul Verhoeven phase). Loads of clips from his most dangerous stunts pad out the running time, and he hangs out with L.A. types who like to do escape artist routines at pool parties. What really sends the film over the top is its "subplot" as Page also serves as a consultant for Sorcery, a rock band who also happen to be magicians. They dress up as Merlin the Magician, Satan, and other fantasy figures doing lots of over-the-top magic acts; basically imagine a cross between Rush and Doug Henning and you'll get the idea.

The frequent intercutting of Sorcery's antics and Page's brushes with death is both rousing and strangely hypnotic, with many vintage stunt clips presented in elaborate split screen sequences (to fill the very wide scope frame) and often slowed down to the accompaniment of a dreamy, experimental music score. The end result is like watching a Werner Herzog film collide headfirst with an MTV music video, and surprisingly, the whole thing actually works if you're in a receptive mood. No one even tries to act, with Page just sitting back and spinning out stories without trying to engage the camera. It's not hard to see the link between this film and the much later *Death Proof* from the vocal Trenchard-Smith admirer Quentin Tarantino, who also designed his entire film around his stuntwoman playing herself. Sharp-eyed viewers should keep a lookout for a very young Phil Hartman in the Los Angeles footage, and even weirder, *Lemora* director Richard Blackburn also pops up in a small role as an agent and worked as an assistant on the film.

Virtually ignored on its theatrical release and initial VHS edition (whose brutal cropping didn't help matters), *Stunt Rock* began causing some ripples when the trailer started to show up at repertory screenings and on compilation DVDs; in fact, if you've seen the trailer, there's no way you can resist the urge to rush out and find the film. However, don't be misled by its tagline promising "*Death Wish* at 120 Decibels", which makes no sense whatsoever. The rise in interest in Aussie exploitation certainly helped, too (not to mention the release of the great doc *Not Quite Hollywood*), with a single-disc Australian DVD finally offering a chance to see the movie in scope. However, Code Red's American release blows it out of the water with a two-disc edition; the anamorphic transfer looks fine and roughly comparable to the theatrical prints making the rounds. The mono audio sounds good and will make many susceptible viewers ache for the soundtrack, which can be purchased directly from Sorcery themselves.

You'd better like to listen to Trenchard-Smith because he's all over this DVD, spinning out hours and hours of stories. Luckily his future career was just as wild, consisting of films like *Escape 2000*, *Dead-End Drive-In*, *BMX Bandits*, *Leprechaun 4: In Space*, *Megiddo: The Omega Code 2* and the very controversial pro-Bush TV movie, *DC/911: Time of Crisis*. He appears here for a video intro, a lengthy new interview, and two commentary tracks, one with actors Page and Gerard and another with Blackburn and producer Marty Fink. You'll hear pretty much everything about the film you could want to know (how Sorcery was hired on a weekend's notice to save the project from collapsing, how the idea of the film originated as a basic, can't-miss prospect for teen audiences, etc.), and luckily Trenchard-Smith also talks about some of his other films, including a justification for working on *DC/911* despite his diametrically-opposed political beliefs. You also get additional video interviews with Blackburn (who also talks more about his career at the time), band member Smokey Huff, and line producer Marty Fink, while Sorcery drummer Perry Morris contributes an audio interview. The first disc is rounded off with the aforementioned trailer, and then on disc two you get *The Stuntmen*, a video Q&A with Trenchard-Smith at the Alamo Drafthouse to accompany a screening of *Stunt Rock*, a dupey-looking Cannes promo reel to drum up distributor interest, and a ton of additional Code Red trailers including *The Internecine Project* and *Brute Corps*. By comparison the Aussie disc simply contains *The Stuntmen*, the first Trenchard-Smith commentary, the Morris interview, and the trailer, so it should be obvious which one is the better buy.

SUCCUBUS: THE DEMON

Colour, 2006, 85m. / Directed by Sami Haavisto / Starring Markus Salo, Pekka Oinonen, Veera Toivanen, Mika Vattulainen / Redemption (US R0 NTSC) / WS (1.85:1) (16:9)

 Finland isn't exactly known for its prolific horror output, but apparently a director named Sami Haavisto has been churning out some straight-to-video titles under the banner of Blood Ceremony, a label whose *Succubus: The Demon* marks their first international release. (Its actual onscreen title is simply *Succubus*, but presumably the subtitle was added in the U.S. to avoid confusion with the Jess Franco film.)

The story's basically a thin framework to use for an artsy, psychological study of Henri (Markus Salo), a stringy-haired, middle-aged salesman thrown into a tailspin when his wife dies from causes her physicians can't pinpoint. Henri turns to a shrink and then to darker territory courtesy of an occultist who points him to some rituals to get in touch with her spirit. However, his dabbling in the dark arts results in a demonic succubus being allowed entry into his life, resulting in bloody consequences for everyone around him.

Alternating between chilly-looking apartment scenes and vivid, hallucinatory netherworld passages, *Succubus* does a decent job of eking an interesting visual style out of its low budget videography and packs in some intriguing Satanic imagery, with the succubus herself making some brief but compelling appearances. Not a masterpiece by any means, it's still an interesting peek at homegrown horror from a country rarely known for blasting plasma all over the screen. Redemption's DVD features an anamorphic transfer that looks faithful to the original 2006 source material, while extras include a "Diaries of a Mad Man" featurette (which explains the no-profit, lobbyist-driven methods at Blood Ceremony), additional "Erotic Nightmares", "Making of Cine Photography" and "Making of Blood FX" featurettes, along with a stills gallery and some Redemption promos.

SUMMER PEOPLE

Colour, 2008, 70m. / Directed by Scott Feinblatt / Starring Neil Kubath, Nyssa Zeona, Kelsey Scheider, Luke Schneider / Dervish Pictures (US R0 NTSC) / WS (1.78:1) (16:9)

 A welcome throwback to the days of scaled-down, DIY shot-on-video horror in the woods like *Savage Harvest*, *Summer People* is that rarity in indie horror, a slow burner that takes its time to build atmosphere, characters, and creeping dread rather than assaulting the viewer from frame one with jackhammer effects and editing.

This debut feature for director Scott Feinblatt follows four kids as they venture out into the boonies to stay at a remote cabin, and the local townspeople don't seem entirely comfortable with these "summer people" stirring up trouble in their neck of the woods. Before you can growl "I'll swallow your soul", the idiots are dabbling around in black magic, unaware that Native American spirits control the land and are still coexisting harmoniously (more or less) with the residents. Freaky little events like rearranging furniture set everyone on edge, and then things... start to turn nasty. Though obviously shot on the cheap (most daylight scenes rely entirely on natural light) and reliant on the most familiar plot in the horror handbook, *Summer People* distinguishes itself with solid perform-ances by the leads (especially Neil Kubath, who could be an indie actor to watch), some surprisingly ambitious shocks in the second half, a creepy downbeat ending, and the aforementioned confidence to rely on story and pacing instead of pure sensa-tionalism. Ah, and there's an animated opening and closing, too!

An on-demand DVD can be purchased from Amazon.com and is presented in anamorphic widescreen, looking about as good as it could. Extras include a handful of deleted (basically just expanded) scenes with some additional exposition, a funny 15-minute collection of behind-the-scenes footage (most memorable for accounts of the director's accidental double entendres and an impromptu trip to WalMart), and galleries of special effects make-up, stills, and storyboards.

SUMMERFIELD

Colour, 1977, 95m. / Directed by Ken Hannam / Starring Nick Tate, John Waters, Elizabeth Alexander / Umbrella (Australia R0 PAL) / WS (1.66:1) (16:9)

This fascinating thriller bears a certain atmos-pheric resemblance to *The Wicker Man* as it treads between eerie provincial mystery and flat-out horror. The twisty story follows new schoolteacher Simon Robinson (TV actor Nick Tate) as he becomes suspicious when he learns that his predecessor, who had stayed in the same boarding house, vanished without a trace. Police don't seem interested, and at work he forms a bond with young student Sally, whom he accidentally knocks from her bike with his car after school. Simon seeks aid and returns Sally to her remote home at a fenced-off community where she lives with her reclusive mother (Elizabeth Alexander) and uncle (John Waters); later he discovers that Sally suffers from a strange, hereditary blood disease, and she and her family figure prominently in the missing prior schoolteacher's belongings. What Simon eventually discovers is not pretty, to say the least.

Since it features the same screenwriter (Cliff Green), producer (Patricia Lovell), and composer (Bruce Smeaton) from the very successful *Picnic at Hanging Rock*, this film had some awfully big shoes to fill. For reasons extrapolated upon in the DVD, its immediate critical and financial reception was quite grim (and virtually nonexistent outside Australia), but it finally built up a following among younger viewers who were haunted by it on television. No wonder, as it's really a terrific genre feature with some absolutely stunning imagery and one of the finest, eeriest music scores ever written. The last 20 minutes is where the film really shines, offering a highly unusual double-twist ending whose final moments quietly but brutally undercut one of the most sacred rules of thriller plotting.

Umbrella's DVD looks outstanding (with a gorgeous transfer that's ironically superior to any version of *Picnic* out there today), and the extras go a long way to explaining how this odd but fascinating movie came about. The 48-minute "Secrets of Summerfield" features Waters, Tate, Alexander, and the crew covering its entire history from conception to troubled release, while a vintage featurette, "A Shattered Silence", is a more traditional EPK-style piece featuring the director, who mostly went on to TV work. Also included is a stills gallery and the usual batch of vintage trailers.

SUPERMEN DÖNÜYOR

Colour, 1979, 80m. / Directed by Kunt Tulgar / Starring Tayfun Demir, Güngör Bayrak, Esref Kolçak

DEMIR YUMRUK: DEVLER GELIYOR

B&W, 1973, 64m. / Directed by Tunç Basaran / Starring Enver Özer, Feri Cansel / Onar (Greece R0 PAL)

Hot on the heels of Richard Donner's smash 1978 superhero film, *Superman: The Movie*, the awkwardly-named and industrious actor-turned-director Kunt Tulgar (best known for *The Deathless Devil*) decided to helm his own version of the Man of Steel saga, apparently on a budget of about five dollars. In this version, our hero (Tayfun Demir) comes from Krypton, represented by Christmas ornaments hanging in front of black cloth (all introduced, naturally, after construction paper credits arranged to a tinny variation on John Williams's familiar theme music). The story follows the established pattern, albeit with a distinct Turkish twist, as Demir passes himself off as a human by posing as a mild-mannered reporter, all to the confusion of pretty Lois Lane – uh, that is, pretty Alev who works in his office. Bad guy Ekrem is devising a way to develop kryptonite, or at least something like it, and Superman fights with lots and lots of people. Furniture gets smashed, firearms get smacked out of villains' flailing hands, and things blow up real small. A blast from start to finish, this is inventive, trademark-smashing fun all the way, right down to the rear-projection doll on a string representing our hero in flight. One of the most often-cited Turkish films (along with its fellow imitations of *Star Wars* and *Star Trek*), this title has been widely available on bootleg video for years but never in anything resembling a watchable form. Onar's version still obviously looks a bit ragged and bleached out but is much better in terms of quality and a thankfully adequate presentation. Presented in full frame and looking fine that way, the film is in Turkish only with optional English or Greek subtitles.

The co-feature offered here has only a marginal Superman connection, but it's still a doozy. *Demir Yumruk: Devler Geliyor* (translated here as *Iron Fist: The Giants Are Coming*) is a madcap and surprisingly perverse superhero outing, with a character named Enver – sort of a Superman/Batman mash-up with fewer abilities than either – squaring off against one of the most memorable villains you'll ever see, a black-haired, cackling, razor-nailed Fu Manchu transvestite in a wheel-chair. There's some story nonsense about finding a sacred dagger that leads to treasure and whatnot, but mostly the film hops from one goofy action sequence to another with some light bondage, laugh-ably artificial fights, and florid dialogue providing tons of entertainment.

Shot in black and white (despite its reputed production year of 1973, it looks like something from the late '60s), this one is taken from a pre-existing video master. Picture quality is okay but on the soft side, at least avoiding the pitfalls of VHS bootlegs from ages past. Once again the Turkish audio can be played with optional English or Greek subtitles. Extras include a new video interview with Tulgar (who seems to fluctuate in his opinion about his contribution to Superman cinema, though he certainly produced a more enduring and intelligent work than *Superman III*), bios and filmographies for the key players, photo galleries, and a slew of Turkish trailers including the Kilink cycle and one-offs featuring interpretations of familiar characters like Zorro and Tarzan.

S

THE SURVIVOR

Colour, 1981, 87m. / Directed by David Hemmings / Starring Robert Powell, Jenny Agutter, Joseph Cotten / BritFilms (UK R2 PAL) / WS (2.35:1) (16:9), Platinum (US R1 NTSC) / WS (2.35:1)

 Though he sold boatloads of horror paperbacks during the '70s and '80s, writer James Herbert has been adapted to the big screen only a handful of times (most recently in 1995's interesting *Haunted*). The first shot at bringing his words to the screen came from much of the same team behind the paranormal oddity *Dark Forces*, albeit with somewhat shuffled roles. This time David Hemmings took over directorial duties, while Robert Powell returns to star as Captain Keller, the lone survivor after a disastrous plane crash. While a sexy psychic (Jenny Agutter) helps him come to grips with the trauma, the ghosts of the victims begin to appear and kill off anyone either responsible for the crash or attempting to exploit the tragedy.

Extremely atmospheric and filled with spooky imagery, the film is a bit of a mess at times thanks to some odd editing choices but is still rewarding; the lead performances are committed (though Joseph Cotten offers little more than a glorified cameo), and the ending is nicely orchestrated. The premise itself is also a great device, similar to the ones later used in *Sole Survivor* and *Final Destination* (and like those, it wisely doesn't go for an "Oh my God, I've been dead the whole time!" cop-out ending). Hemmings keeps the direction spare and simple, but the spectacular scope photography is the film's greatest asset. The U.S. budget edition from the normally dubious Platinum offers a crisp (albeit non-anamorphic) 2.35:1 transfer that nicely captures the original compositions, along with the theatrical trailer. The best-looking option around is actually the U.K. release from BritFilms, which is anamorphic; it also contains the same trailer plus bonus ones for *Malcolm*, *Storm Boy* and *Doing Time for Patsy Cline*.

SUSPECTED DEATH OF A MINOR

Colour, 1975, 100m. / Directed by Sergio Martino / Starring Claudio Cassinelli, Mel Ferrer, Lia Tanzi, Gianfranco Barra, Barbara Magnolfi / Sazuma (Austria R2 PAL) / WS (2.35:1) (16:9)

 This movie is *nuts!* By 1975, director Sergio Martino had obviously had enough of straight *gialli* (his last pure one was really *Torso*), but he sort of dipped his toes in one more time with this half-comedic, all-over-the-map mixture of gory slashings, Italian cop conventions, and the goofiest car chases this side of a '70s Disney film. The structure passing itself off as a plot begins with a frizzy-haired young hooker being stalked during and after a wedding celebration by a sinister man in sunglasses who eventually catches up with her at her apartment, where he slashes her throat. Her presence had been noticed earlier by Inspector Germi (Claudio Cassinelli), a not-by-the-book undercover cop who teams up with a sly thief (Gianfranco Barra) to track down both the vicious murderer and the instigators of a widespread kiddie and drug-dealing ring. When not being lectured by his boss (Mel Ferrer), the unstoppable cop undergoes a series of bizarre adventures including a wild shootout on a kiddie rollercoaster ride, a knife attack in a theatre filled with necking lovers during a screening of Martino's *Your*

Vice Is a Locked Room and Only I Have the Key, two gruesome encounters with subway trains, a fight on the roof over a theatre, and much, much more.

No synopsis can really convey the whiplash tone of this film, which never stops for a minute to rest as it ricochets between gory attack sequences (including one unlucky overweight victim in a towel getting knifed and face-dunked into a glass window), sexy Eurostarlet encounters (with *Suspiria*'s Barbara Magnolfi making a brief but memorable appearance), and "what the hell?" plot twists culminating in a suitably dark, cynical finale. The whole thing is buoyed by Luchiano Michelini's amazing music score (which really, really needs a CD release), an energetic Goblin-style rock symphony similar in tone to *Deep Red* (which came out the same year).

Virtually impossible to see for decades, this film's reputation is bound to improve tremendously for anyone who sets eyes on Sazuma's very welcome DVD edition (under the Italian title, *Morte sospetta di una minorenne*). The anamorphic transfer looks great throughout, and the audio is in Italian mono with optional English, Dutch or German subtitles. (It doesn't appear this was ever released with an English language track, but anything's possible.) In any case, the actors are all clearly speaking Italian which (for once) seems to have been recorded on-set and seems in synch, so that's really the best way to go. Extras include the lively Italian theatrical trailer, a very academic German audio commentary track (with optional English subtitles) by critics Christian Kessler and Robert Zion (who focus on the film's place in the Italian exploitation canon, Martino's directorial history and the clever manipulations of multiple genres), a poster gallery, and a half-hour interview with Martino (who also briefly introduces the film) entitled "Crime Scene Milan", playable in Italian with either English or German subtitles. He talks more

about horror and action filmmaking at the time in general (often bemoaning his own country's lack of appreciation outside its favourite auteurs) and, like many Eurocult interviews these days, frequently invokes the name of Quentin Tarantino. Highly recommended.

SUZIE HEARTLESS
Colour, 2009, 75m. / Directed by Tony Marsiglia / Starring Wendy McColm, Andrea Davis, Ivan Crasci
PHOENIX
B&W, 1995, 90m. / Directed by Tony Marsiglia / Starring Aisha Prigann, Mark Schultz, Sasha DeMarino / Alternative Cinema (US R0 NTSC)

A dialogue-free cinematic howl, *Suzie Heartless* comes from director Tony Marsiglia who presumably alternates his directorial efforts between experimental art films and more accessible softcore horror fare like *Lust for Dracula*. This one's basically a kitchen sink look at the day-to-day existence of the title character, a teen prostitute (Wendy McColm) with a traumatic past who reflects on the circumstances that brought her onto the streets while her life quickly goes swirling down the toilet with the help of a lot of really lowlife johns. Seedy in subject matter but surprisingly austere and artistic in execution, this isn't a pleasant watch by any means but it definitely does make for a gripping artistic statement. Newcomer McColm is surprisingly affecting in the lead, using her often moist and damaged-looking eyes to convey what can't be said (obviously, since there isn't a single spoken line). Marsiglia contributes a commentary for the rather brief feature along with producer Donna Kane, which actually helps explain some of the underlying themes in the film along with the usual production trivia, as well as a good deleted scene.

Surprisingly more enjoyable as far as viewing entertainment goes is the bonus disc, which contains Marsiglia's equally artsy, earlier 1995 effort, *Phoenix* (released on VHS as *Ashes and Flames*), which features some really ambitious and often striking monochromatic photography and a more lively, off-the-cuff editing style. It's sort of a grim character study about a woman who winds up connecting with her dead sister's boyfriend (or something like that), whose own emotional and sexual stunting has caused him no small share of torment. That shred of a story isn't really the point here, though, as the film dollops on the atmosphere and eye-opening visuals in a steady, dreamlike stream that makes it difficult to tear away. In all honesty, newcomers might be better off starting with this disc and then progressing to the newer feature when they feel their constitution can take it. This one also contains a director commentary (way more candid, and you won't believe the hell he went through on this production), along with a making-of featurette and audition footage.

SWEET SIXTEEN

Colour, 1983, 87m. / Directed by Jim Sotos / Starring Bo Hopkins, Susan Strasberg, Patrick Macnee, Don Stroud, Aleisa Shirley, Dana Kimmell, Sharon Farrell, Michael Pataki, Larry Storch / Code Red (US R0 NTSC) / WS (1.85:1) (16:9)

Released at the height of '80s slasher mania, *Sweet Sixteen* was passed off as another teens-in-terror outing and got lost in the avalanche of other copycat films. However, its one-of-a-kind cast of cult actors (some used far better than others) and bizarre narrative tangents earned it a respectable cult following, mainly among those willing to watch it more as an unorthodox murder mystery than a straight-up gorefest. The story primarily revolves around pretty Melissa Morgan (Aleisa Shirley), who's about to turn sixteen in a small Texas town brewing with tension between the hard-drinkin' white folks and nearby Indians. Her archaeologist dad (Patrick Macnee) is too busy rummaging around in Indian burial grounds to notice that guys who come near Melissa are starting to turn up knifed out in the desert, while her mom (Susan Strasberg) is focused on planning the big sweet sixteen party. The local sheriff (Bo Hopkins, of course) tries to piece together the facts and avoid a race riot after the son of the town's biggest barfly jackass (Don Stroud) gets slashed to death, and the sheriff's mystery-loving daughter (Dana Kimmell) gets in on the action by using her friendship with Melissa to do some snooping of her own. Melissa seems to be the obvious suspect, but naturally, there are a few surprises waiting in store.

This storyline sounds like your average TV movie-of-the-week thriller, but director Jim Sotos (whose only previous credit was the bizarre "mainstream" '76 remake of *Forced Entry*) assembles the film in a bizarre, almost non-linear fashion with scenes colliding against each other and actors appearing to improvise their way through conversations that often wander off into nowhere. As a slasher, the film only offers a handful of rote knife murders (shot so darkly you can barely tell what's going on); however, as a drive-in potpourri of sleaze elements and overripe performances, it's hard to beat. The always entertaining Stroud wins the scenery-chewing award as he dials each line reading up to 11, but Kimmell (who got the lead in *Friday the 13th Part 3* on the basis of this film and went on to infamy biting the slasher hand that fed her) delivers the weirdest performance as some sort of closeted lesbian Nancy Drew whose mood shifts from one second to the next. Then there's a treacly theme song, "Melissa", which pops up at least three times for maximum comic relief. The double-twist ending (which cribs shamelessly from *Alice, Sweet Alice*) is lots of fun in a deranged sort of way, and the whole film moves along at a fast clip despite Sotos's inexplicable fondness for long, lab-created slow motion shots.

An independent film released in theatres by the short-lived "Century International", *Sweet Sixteen* became a regular VHS favourite from Vestron but eventually slipped from the shelves, popping up on DVD at first only in an awful grey market dupe of the VHS in one of Brentwood's PD party packs. Code Red's authorised DVD edition proclaims a "director's cut" on the cover and actually offers two versions of the film, both clocking in at 87 minutes but containing some interesting differences. The director's cut opens with the "Melissa" song playing over black opening credits and segues into a slow pan of Melissa's bedroom, past some tarot cards and eventually ogling her fully naked in the shower. The theatrical cut instead starts with a sequence obviously shot after the main production with Kimmel having a gothic nightmare fantasy while reading one of her mystery novels, with a portion of the naked shower footage awkwardly shoehorned in slightly later in the film. The ridiculous theatrical opening is still nice to see, even if it has nothing to do with the rest of the movie, but the director's cut is at least a bit more coherent. Neither of the transfers will win any awards given the lacklustre surviving materials, but it's watchable enough. Both are featured in anamorphic transfers (which thankfully shear off lots of excess headroom compared to the open matte Vestron version), but the

director's cut fares a bit better with a minimum of print damage. Flesh tones look a bit murky and smeary in some scenes, but again, this is all that survives. Theatrical prints are few and far between, and the one used here for the theatrical cut has certainly seen better days with some obvious signs of misuse over the years. Still, it's about the same as what you'd see at a drive-in, and that's satisfactory enough unless someone manages to unearth the negative someday.

The director's cut is preceded by a new, shot-on-video intro featuring Shirley and a very animated Scott Spiegel (director of *Intruder*) horsing around with a fake axe in his horror memorabilia playroom. The main feature contains an audio commentary with Shirley, Sotos, and Spiegel covering the making of the movie (presumably recorded to the theatrical cut given the obvious evident audio edits during the opening scenes), and both the actress and director are enthusiastic and warm in their memories of the famous cast members, Shirley's first-time acting nervousness, the shooting locations, and the challenges of putting the project together without studio financing. For some reason Spiegel's voice sounds warbled and distorted much of the time, but he also has some entertaining observations about a film he clearly admires and enjoys. Next up is a video featurette with a laid-back Hopkins talking about his own memories of the film and its colourful cast, including good buddy Stroud; he's then joined by Shirley and Sotos as they talk about the shoot, including a fun story about Shirley's slow-gestating friendship with the late Strasberg. Hopkins also freely admits he had to ad lib his incoherent, *Psycho*-style explanatory wrap-up in the last scene, which should come as a surprise to no one. Also included is the original trailer, a stills gallery (mostly the press book), and trailers for Code Red titles including *Nightmare*, *Stunt Rock*, the excellent *Rituals*, and as a pure gag, *The Balalaika Conspiracy*.

SWINGING IN THE '70S:
GRINDHOUSE TRIPLE FEATURE:
KEEP THEM HAPPY AT HOME

Colour, 1971, 78m.

HARVEY SWINGS

Colour, 1970, 74m. / Directed by Stu Segall / Starring Suzanne Fields, Jeff Roberts, Donna Nation

YOUR WIFE OR MINE?

Colour, 1971, 81m. / Starring Cleo O'Hara, Keith Erickson, Rene Bond, Ric Lutze / Secret Key (US R0 NTSC) / WS (1.78:1) (16:9)

 In a welcome return to form after their badly botched *Grindhouse Trash Part 3*, Secret Key delivers the unseemly goods with the unofficial fourth entry in their series, which actually shapes up as arguably the most enjoyable entry of them all. This time out the focus is entirely on the wife-swapping phenomenon which turned into a full-blown media fixation in the '70s, long after exploitation filmmakers like Joe Sarno had introduced it to discerning fleapit viewers. All three films are very obscure and date from the early '70s, kicking off with *Keep Them Happy at Home* (shortened to simply *Keep Them Happy* on the title card), a no-star piece of softcore fluff about three enterprising wives who decide the only way to deal with their away-on-business husbands is to rent themselves out to the randy local working men, including the requisite dirty joke bits with a plumber and milkman. Packed with skin and nowhere close to hardcore, it's amusing, fast as a bullet, and paves the way for the more explicit features to come.

That brings us to the slightly later *Harvey Swings*, the most familiar title here thanks to its earlier availability from Something Weird as a "Double Softies" co-feature with *Panty Party*. This odd concoction revolves around two couples, a pair of goofy would-be swingers answering an ad in the paper and the more experienced husband and wife awaiting them. Oh, and then there's the ridiculous gay stereotype butler, who inexplicably goes straight later in the film, along with some lesbian encounters and a comedic failed wrist-slashing(!). The most famous faces here are easily the ubiquitous Suzanne Fields (*Flesh Gordon*), who's already merited a DVD collection of her own, and short-lived softcore leading man Jeff Roberts (*Weekend Convention*).

Easily the best of the three is saved for last with *Your Wife or Mine?*, a funny and genuinely scorching romp featuring an eye-spinning cast of West Coast regulars. Things kick off with the always dynamic Cleo O'Hara getting revenge on her cheating hubby by going out and banging the guy next door, in this case played by busy goofball Keith Erickson. Meanwhile Cleo's hubby Sheldon is off introducing a new couple to swinging by, uh, having a self-abuse contest with the husband and telling the shocking neophyte wife to join them, in what looks an awful lot like a dry run for Radley Metzger's *Score*. Then some blond surfer guy and his petite spouse join the scene with the aid of – who else? – Rene Bond and Ric Lutze, followed by the entire cast getting together for an orgy (mostly offscreen). You've really got to wonder how many more of these undiscovered, grime-encrusted jewels are lying around in basements and vacated movie theatres across the country. Transfer quality on all three titles is better than average with a minimum of print damage, and the anamorphic framing actually looks just about right. The two-disc set comes with the usual trailer reel and a lengthy booklet of liner notes including some nifty newspaper ads.

SYLVIA

Colour, 1977, 92m. / Directed by Peter Savage / Joanna Bell, Peter Savage, Sonny Landham, Helen Madigan, Helen Devine, Marc Stevens, Turk Turpin / After Hours (US R0 NTSC) / WS (1.78:1) (16:9)

 Another entry in the valuable Directors' Series from After Hours (which previously included *Forced Entry* and *A Touch of Genie*), this one's a bit different in that it's already had a prior DVD release from VCX, though that edition was missing some footage of... well, it's best not described here, but most viewers should figure it out pretty quickly. The film started life as sort of a low-budget variation on the hit TV miniseries *Sybil* (with Sally Field morphing through a series of multiple personalities), though the end result turned into something far more interesting and filthy. The versatile Joanna Bell (what ever happened to her?) stars as the title character, a prim and proper suburban resident who's secretly housing a whole slew of deviant inner sluts eager to dabble in every aspect of human excess. She goes to see her shrink (played by the film's director, Peter Savage under the name "Armand Peters", a Jake LaMotta cohort who went on to act in *Taxi Driver* and *Raging Bull*), but that doesn't stop her from going out and getting into trouble, whether waving a cross around like a lunatic, getting into orgies, and most memorably, tangling with a couple of junkies (one of whom is played by future mainstream actor and would-be politician Sonny Landham of *Predator* fame). Many of the actors consist of LaMotta friends and relatives, but connoisseurs should recognise a few of the more explicit performers including Marc Stevens, Helen Madigan, and Turk Turpin.

As the packaging rightly points out, this film is of highest value for the family names behind it and its vivid depiction of gritty late '70s New York filmmaking, with a few startling visuals far removed from your standard skin flick. You might say this movie, like its heroine, is crazy. Surprisingly enough, the DVD contains an incredible audio commentary by none other than Bill Lustig, the founder of Blue Underground and nephew of Jake LaMotta, who also took a brief sojourn into New York's hardcore world as both the director of *Hot Honey* and *The Violation of Claudia* (where's the special edition of that one?) and the assistant director and production manager of *Sylvia*. Moderated by regular After Hours historian Michael Bowen, it's a terrific track covering how this unusual production came about, the various relatives who make fleeting appearances onscreen, and the good and bad side of mounting an indie production, explicit or otherwise, during this unique period in grindhouse history. Surprisingly enough, this also makes a fascinating companion piece (or a prelude, if you will) to his commentaries on his more famous mainstream cult films like *Maniac*, *Vigilante* and *Uncle Sam*. The extras make this a solid purchase anyway, but anyone who's suffered through the fuzzy-looking previous edition should find this worth an upgrade thanks to the improved anamorphic transfer. The print used here is much sharper and more colourful than prior versions, and while there's quite a bit of expected damage visible in spots, it's tough to complain whenever one of these films gets a much-needed makeover.

SYNGENOR

Colour, 1990, 98m. / Directed by George Elanjian Jr. / Starring Starr Andreef, Mitchell Laurance, David Gale, Charles Lucia, Lewis Arquette / Synapse (US R0 NTSC), Elite (US R1 NTSC) / WS (1.85:1) (16:9) / DD5.1, Prism (UK R2 PAL)

A very low budget pastiche of pretty much every Hollywood sci-fi hit from the 1980s, the heavily-hyped and instantly forgotten *Syngenor* assaulted unsuspecting home video viewers in 1990 but feels very much like a product from the decade before. Neon colours, feathered hair, and lots of old-school monster effects highlight this straightforward romp about the havoc unleashed by the Norton Cyberdyne company (hmm, where'd they come up with that one?), which has created a new breed of soldier able to aid the military's efforts in the Middle East. Named Syngenor (an abbreviation from Synthesized Genetic Organism, of course), this creature soon kills its creator and engineer, Ethan (Lewis Arquette), whose niece, Susan (Starr Andreef), teams up with a reporter (Mitchell Laurance) to uncover the truth. Of course, said truth is a little hard to take when you're talking about rampaging genetically engineered mutant bio-lizard men who rip off people's heads and suck the juice out of their nervous systems. Meanwhile the company head (late *Re-Animator* star David Gale) becomes more than a bit monstrous himself as he tries to control the continuously escalating mess around him, namely by shooting himself in the neck with various chemicals and doing unspeakable things with fake bunny ears.

Kind of a sequel to director William Malone's first film, 1981's *Scared to Death*, this guilty pleasure recycles the monster suit and the name of the creature, but little else. The rest is blatantly pilfered from *The Terminator* and *Aliens* (as well as *Contamination* and a slew of others if you're paying attention), with the gaudy visual gloss you usually don't see outside of a Shapiro-Glickenhaus production.

Apart from Gale, everyone seems to be a TV actor cashing in a check, but the script manages a few nice little humorous riffs now and then, particularly during the berserk climax. No, it's not really very good at all, but the entertainment value is definitely there if you're in the right frame of mind.

Syngenor first bowed on DVD courtesy of Elite Entertainment, then went out of print and was subsequently resuscitated by the good folks at Synapse. The transfer looks great considering the movie came out during a period not known for visually sumptuous horror films; the anamorphic widescreen framing looks fine, and those hot neon colours pop right off the screen. You also get a new 5.1 mix along with the original two-channel stereo track known and loved by old-school VHS collectors. Not surprisingly, most of the extras centre on David Gale, who's seen promoting the film in 1990 at the Tokyo Fantastic Film Festival (along with a guy in the Syngenor suit) and even auditioning for the film. You also get a look at the FX shop of creator Doug Beswick, some footage of the movie's publicity photo shoot, and the deliciously dated theatrical trailer. A stripped-down budget version from an older master was released in the U.K. by Prism.

TARZAN ISTANBUL'DA

B&W, 1952, 74m. / Directed by Orhan Atadeniz / Starring Tamer Balci, Hayri Esen, Kunt Tulgar, Necla Aygül / Onar (Greece R0 PAL)

Something of a vintage anomaly from Turkish cinema saviours Onar Films, *Tarzan Istanbul'da* delivers exactly what it advertises, a muscular Turkish vine swinger in the jungle.

Of course you'll have to wade through a lot of plot to get to him, as a journalist (Hayri Esen) on holiday in Africa uncovers an elaborate back-story involving a tribe of vicious natives, an escaped boy who grew up in the jungle (played by young, very busy and regrettably-named Kunt Tulgar), and hidden treasure with a handy map for guidance all the way to "Death Mountain". He eventually runs into the animal-loving Tarzan (now played by Tamer Balci), whose best friends are a chimp and an elephant. Those pesky natives turn up again, and the actors spend lots of time trudging up and down through the jungle and riverbeds. And that's pretty much it.

A standard jungle adventure lensed in black and white (just like the Johnny Weissmuller classics), this Tarzan outing isn't remotely as outrageous as the superhero efforts from the same period but might be worth a look for the curious. As usual Onar has done a fine job of resuscitating a lost Turkish oddity, this time looking very soft and worn but pretty typical for the time considering the few tape sources still surviving. Fortunately it includes optional English (and Greek) subtitles, which are often as bizarre and fascinating as the elaborate (and incredibly racist) native fashions and make-up designs.

This release (numbered to 1200 units) is easily worth picking up for its most significant extra, a half-hour video interview with Tulgar in which he talks about his career at the height of Turkey's most outlandish cash-ins on international cinematic hits. He also gets a text bio and gallery, while other extras include a baffling, silent "lost check scene" (which involves one of the actors, well, signing a check next to a river), plus trailers for other essential Onar titles including *Casus Kiran*, *Zorro Kamcili Suvari*, and *Karanlik Sular*.

TERROR CIRCUS
(BARN OF THE NAKED DEAD)

Colour, 1973, 86m. / Directed by Alan Rudolph / Starring Andrew Prine, Manuela Thiess, Sherry Alberoni, Gyl Roland, Sheila Bromley, Jennifer Ashley / Shriek Show (US R1 NTSC) / WS (1.78:1) (16:9), Legend House (US R1 NTSC) / WS (1.85:1), X-Rated Kult (Germany R2 PAL)

Featuring a similar setup to *The Texas Chain Saw Massacre* with about .0002% of the scare value, 1973's *Terror Circus* has long haunted drive-ins and video shelves under numerous alternative monikers including *Nightmare Circus*, *Caged Women* and, in its most notorious and misleadingly-titled form, *Barn of the Naked Dead*. The film also experienced a spike in interest value thanks to the fact that its director, Robert Altman protégé Alan Rudolph, finally hit the critical big time in the mid-'80s with art house hits like *Choose Me* and *The Moderns*, not to mention some seriously odd side projects like *Roadie*, *Endangered Species* and *Mortal Thoughts*. Rudolph frequently disavowed this film along with its predecessor, his odd debut entitled *Premonition*, with some critics even suggesting they were directed by a different Alan Rudolph entirely. Well, it's the same man all right, though you'd have to be psychic to guess it judging from this stark, desolate, sleazy little curio.

The story's your standard chestnut about three girls driving through the middle of nowhere who wind up in big trouble, and in this case our protagonists are wannabe showgirls named Simone (Manuela Thiess), Sheri (Sherry Alberoni), and Corrine (Gyl Roland). Their trek to Vegas gets waylaid when their car breaks down, leaving them stuck out in the desert. Help arrives in the

T

form of Andre (Andrew Prine), who takes them out to his farm where he keeps a caged cougar around for company. Unfortunately the snooping girls stumble on his big secret, namely a bunch of women chained in his barn for a twisted circus routine with his prisoners as animals. Our three little showgirls wind up becoming the newest main attraction, while their suspicious agent and the local police start searching for the missing ladies. Oh, and there's something very strange, very big, and very ticked off lurking in the nearby outhouse...

Though there isn't much in the way of blatant skin or gore to be found here, fans of degenerate '70s horror should still enjoy the antics of the always watchable Prine, a busy cult favourite who specialised in oddball horror films like *The Centerfold Girls*, *Simon, King of the Witches*, *Grizzly* and *The Town That Dreaded Sundown*. He was already a seasoned TV name (and occasional Disney feature player!) by the time he made this film, but God bless him for having the cojones to play shaggy-haired psychos in movies like this. Whether wrapping a boa constrictor around one of his "animals" or doing his circus routine in a top hat and coat, he's definitely the star here with none of the actresses having a prayer of matching him. On the other hand, Rudolph shows pretty much no affinity for the horror genre at all, preferring instead to let his camera soak up the arid locales and linger on pregnant, meaningful pauses between the actors. These directorial tics served him well enough in "mainstream" fare like *Welcome to L.A.*, but here you'll just be itching for him to get to the good stuff already. On the other hand, it did inspire the title of a rap album, so that's got to count for something.

So many awful-looking copies of this title have appeared on VHS (not to mention a dodgy Legend House release that basically slapped a letterbox matte over one of those blurry, faded old masters) that many have assumed over the years that this movie was simply flat-out ugly from the day it was born. Surprisingly, Shriek Show has produced evidence to the contrary with its authorised release from the original negative (under the *Terror Circus* title), a real stunner that looks like a different film entirely. Incredibly vivid and sharp, the transfer features rich, vibrant colours and looks like it was shot yesterday, with only a few very fleeting glimpses of negative dirt giving the game away. The mono English soundtrack is a huge step up as well. Given Rudolph's refusal to acknowledge this film, it's up to the rest of the talent to provide the extras here. Special effects artists Douglas White and Byrd Holland carry a feature-length commentary by themselves, chatting a lot about the director and leading man along with details about the various make-up FX (with the biggest one saved for the grand finale, of course, in which we finally meet Andre's radiation-damaged daddy). Also included is a 24-minute featurette, "Barn Again: Returning to the *Terror Circus*", in which both gentlemen return for a more generic overview of the film, interspersed with comments from costumer Allan Apone (whose work must have been pretty easy given the limited number of performers), *Centerfold Girls* co-star Jennifer Ashley (who has a small role here), and audio snippets from the associate producer, Marvin Almeas. You also get the alternative *Barn* opening title sequence, a promotional art gallery, a *Terror Circus* theatrical trailer apparently pulled from a negative with missing audio (so music from the feature itself fills in the silence), and additional Shriek Show trailers for equally disreputable releases like *Blood Shack*, *Love Me Deadly* and *Psychos in Love*. Who would've thought a movie this grimy could end up looking so sparkling clean? Also available in Germany from X-Rated Kult under the *Barn* title, but this is taken from another ancient VHS-intended master and is best avoided.

TERROR EXPRESS

Colour, 1979, 82m. / Directed by Ferdinando Baldi / Starring Silvia Dionisio, Werner Pochath, Zora Kerova, Gianluigi Chirizzi, Carlo De Mejo, Fausto Lombardi, Giancarlo Maestri / Camera Obscura (Austria R2 PAL) / WS (1.66:1) (16:9)

 On an overnight train ride going out of the country, three unruly passengers – David (Werner Pochath from *The Cat o' Nine Tails*), Ernie (*The Gates of Hell*'s Carlo De Mejo) and Philip (*Hanna D.*'s Fausto Lombardi) – decide to rudely persecute the other travellers in the dining car. Among the potential victims are a pretty upper-class prostitute named Giulia (Silvia Dionisio) who gets clients sent to her room by the conductor, a cop (Giancarlo Maestri) trans-porting good-hearted felon Pierre (*Burial Ground*'s Gianluigi Chirizzi) back to jail, a bickering and ailing elderly couple, and frustrated married woman Anna (*The New York Ripper*'s Zora Kerova), who initially defends the trio's behaviour only to get gang raped in a bathroom after flirting with Ernie. Soon the scumbags swipe the cop's firearm and have the trainload of passen-gers at their mercy, so who will survive until morning?

Released on DVD under its dual European titles of *La ragazza del vagone letto* and *Horror-Sex im Nachtexpress*, this utterly sleazy and entertaining slice of Italian trash from the country's seediest filmmaking period features a surprisingly low amount of onscreen carnage but makes up for it in sheer depravity, a constant atmosphere of menace, and loads of graphic sex scenes accompanied by a grinding, catchy synth score by the infamous Marcello Giombini, best known for several Joe D'Amato films and *The Beast in Space*. Speaking of D'Amato, his most famous leading man, George Eastman, was the screenwriter for this film and would have been perfect as one of the three villains based on his wide-eyed turn in *Rabid Dogs*; why he stayed behind the camera this time out is anyone's guess. Much more surprising is the film's director, Ferdinando Baldi, who's better known for a string of spaghetti westerns (*Blindman*, *Little Rita of the West*, etc.) which culminated in two of the best-remembered '80s 3-D films, *Comin' at Ya!* and *Treasure of the Four Crowns*. This one certainly feels nothing like the rest of his output (which might explain why he shies away from graphic violence), but his affinity for onscreen skin reveals some talents evident nowhere else. The cast is a weird hodgepodge of familiar faces, with onetime Ruggero Deodato girlfriend Silvia Dionisio (*Murder Obsession*, *Waves of Lust*) offering a somewhat chilly but attrac-tive centre for all the depraved activity. The three villains get to have most of the fun with the always unnerving Pochath (best known as the bloodsucking necrophile from *Mosquito*) adding another baddie to his roster.

Though it received no attention whatsoever in America, *Terror Express* became a VHS mainstay in Europe and became entangled with the U.K. video nasty craze in the '80s along with the similar *Night Train Murders*. The ridicu-lous English dub is nowhere to be found on the sole worldwide DVD release from Camera Obscura, but this is a rare film from the period to actually be shot in Italian so the omission isn't too damaging. The English subtitles are fine and definitely better than the dub (which may be good or bad depending on your viewpoint), with many character names also changing slightly in the translation (for example, "Peter" becomes "Pierre"). An option is also included with removable

T

German subs for the Italian track. The transfer is completely uncut and looks very good for about 95% of the running time, a handful of shots (including that very, very long exterior view of the train leaving the station and the first scene after the credits) look much dupier and, according to a note before the film, had to be sourced from an inferior print since they were missing from the negative. In any case, it easily blows away any version that's ever been available before. Also included are the Italian and English trailers (with the latter giving you an idea of what the bad dub sounded like), a photo gallery of stills from various countries, a solid liner notes booklet by Christian Kessler in German and English, and easily best of all, a lengthy new featurette called "Tales from the Rails" that's one of the most candid, fascinating overviews of an Italian sleaze production since Grindhouse's *Cannibal Ferox* and *Cannibal Holocaust*. Eastman, De Mejo, and Kerova all appear for new discussions in which they offer wildly diverging recollections about the production; Eastman has the most knowledge as he explains the genesis of the film (a train carriage set happened to be available and could be re-dressed to make it look like a much bigger train) and reveals the inspiration to be the American film *The Incident*, though one has to wonder whether *The Cassandra Crossing* played a hand as well given some of the similar passengers. De Mejo talks about his early career (including appearing in *Hair*) up to this film (though he doesn't discuss his very graphic sex scenes in much detail or his later multiple collaborations with Lucio Fulci), while Kerova lets loose talking about her displeasure with the film, her disappointment working with Baldi, and which actors she got along with and which ones she definitely didn't. Highly entertaining all around and worth the purchase as much as the main feature itself.

THAT KIND OF GIRL

B&W, 1963, 76m. / Directed by Gerry O'Hara / Starring Margaret Rose Keil, David Weston, Frank Jarvis, Linda Marlowe, Peter Burton / BFI (DVD & Blu-ray, UK R0 PAL/HD)

As you can probably deduce from the title, this story of a girl's plunge into disrepute is very much a product of its time. The girl of the title is Eva (Margaret Rose Keil), an Austrian tease who hits an early '60s London nightclub and has no problem using her charms to pry whatever she needs from any men in sight. She's really more clueless and impatient than malicious, though, and when a fellow club-goer named Max (Frank Jarvis) doesn't have the social status or cash to keep her interested, Eva flits like a butterfly from one prospect to the next including an older man, Elliott (Peter Burton), who turns out to be not quite what she expected.

Exactly the kind of film the BFI has made a specialty of salvaging with their essential Flipside line, *That Kind of Girl* is a fast-paced, pulpy pleasure from the jazzy opening frames to the harsh, somewhat twisted finale. The monochromatic photography looks terrific, delivering a pleasing succession of striking shots as Eva ambles her way through an urban wonderland that turns out to be fraught with peril.

The BFI release on DVD and Blu-ray transferred from the original negative is a real eye-popper and proof positive of how much a solid HD presentation can enhance the impact of a black-and-white film; in fact, the thought of one of its contemporaries like *Beat Girl* getting the same treatment is enough to make any cult film fan dizzy with delight. Some very minor hairline scratches pop up here and there, but

99% of the film looks terrific. The mono soundtrack is also clear and devoid of any noticeable faults. In the extras department, the theme of sin and punishment continues with "The People at No. 19" (an 18-minute short about the extreme consequences of infidelity), "No Place to Hide" (a documentary short about an anti-nuke rally similar to one seen in the main feature), and an additional half-hour ban the bomb rally documentary, "A Sunday in September", covering a real protest in London (including Vanessa Redgrave before she became the face of '60s London highbrow beauty in *Blow-Up* as well as Doris Lessing and John Osborne). More recent is a new 14-minute interview with producer Robert Hartford-Davis (future director of *Corruption*, *Gonks Go Beat* and *The Black Torment*), who talks about the film's relevance to a number of issues at the time and his memories of working with the cast and crew. The obligatory booklet contains notes by director Gerry O'Hara (this was his debut film before moving on to more sexy fare like *The Bitch* and another BFI title, *All the Right Noises*) and film writer Cathi Unsworth plus the usual helpful production and cast titbits of information.

THIRST

Colour, 1979, 93m. / Directed by Rod Hardy / Starring Chantal Contouri, Shirley Cameron, Henry Silva, David Hemmings / Synapse (US R0 NTSC), Elite (US R0 NTSC) Umbrella (Australia R0 PAL), BritFilms (UK R0 PAL) / WS (2.35:1) (16:9)

For some reason, 1979 was designated as the movie year of the vampire. Everything from the *Nosferatu* remake to *Love at First Bite* to Universal's big-budget *Dracula* had

blood spilling across movie screens, and even Aussie filmmakers got into the game with their own highly eccentric offering, which takes a very modern corporate spin on the bloodsucking myth. Our heroine, Kate (Chantal Contouri), is kidnapped by a sinister organisation of vampires who have created an industry of "blood cows", which are really people raised like cattle for their plasma supply. Turns out she's a descendant of the notorious blood bather Countess Bathory, and they want to reacquaint her with her family's nastier habits.

Though it isn't really terrifying, *Thirst* is just oddball enough to hold interest (the blood-filled milk cartons and chicken legs are hard to forget), and any movie with old pros David Hemmings and Henry Silva chomping at the scenery is obviously worth checking out. The DVD editions from Synapse and Elite are identical, offering a sterling scope transfer, an audio commentary with director Rod Hardy and producer Antony I. Ginnane, a trailer and TV spots, and an isolated music track for Brian May's creepy score. An Australian release on Umbrella dropped the isolated score but added a 13-minute interview with Ginnane entitled "*Thirst*: A Contemporary Blend". This later appeared on the BritFilms DVD without the commentary or the music track.

3 DEV ADAM

Colour, 1973, 80m. / Directed by T. Fikret Uçak / Starring Aytekin Akkaya, Yavuz Selekman, Dogan Tamer, Deniz Erkanat, Mine Sun / Onar (Greece R0 PAL)

One of the most outrageous Turkish superhero bashes imaginable, *3 Dev Adam* (*3 Mighty Men*, better known in grey market circles as *Captain America and Santo vs. Spider-Man*)

manages to throw no less than three well-known action figures into a mad stew of a plot that barely makes sense but delivers non-stop thrills all the same. However, this Spider-Man isn't the heroic webslinger most people know and love; here he's a crazy, misogynist bastard who cooks up wild criminal schemes when he isn't busy killing lovely women in the most gruesome manner possible. First seen driving a motorboat's rudder into the face of a woman buried up to the neck on a beach, he doesn't seem to have any particular superhero powers; instead he offs his opponents using any means available, whether it be stabbing, karate squads, strangulation with a showerhead hose, or in the funniest scene, pinning a big tube against a man's face and dumping a hungry guinea pig inside. Fortunately two leaders in the fight for truth and justice, Captain America (Aytekin Akkaya) and Santo (Yavuz Selekman), are hot on Spidey's trail with the aid of the police chief (Dogan Tamer), following both his penchant for using antiques for nefarious purposes and tailing his equally unscrupulous girlfriend, fashion model Nadia (Mine Sun). Much fighting ensues, with a mind-bending finale in which the arch-villain reveals a nasty trick up his sleeve that sends the blood flying wall-to-wall.

Whew! To say this movie is out of its mind really doesn't come close to conveying the sheer, giddy madness of watching Turkish actors in superhero outfits gouging people to death, swinging around in the air, and karate-chopping the supporting cast. Though it looks like it was shot for a bus fare, *3 Dev Adam* packs in non-stop entertainment during its compact running time, and Spidey makes a truly unique villain bordering on sheer blasphemy for American comic book fans. (His wild eyebrows are a nice touch, too.) Onar Films had a tough act to follow with its marvellous Kilink releases, but they've

certainly raised the bar with this one. A disclaimer at the beginning notes that the opening 16 seconds only survive courtesy of a dupey-looking Greek VHS tape, but otherwise the film is sourced from a superior tape source that looks a couple of generations ahead of the bootlegs floating around. It's nothing close to pristine, of course, but at least this puppy still survives in some sort of condition. Better yet, this marks the first official release with optional English subtitles! (Greek subs are included as well.) Now all the crazy plot twists at least come within the remote vicinity of making sense, though viewers may still want to switch 'em off and make up their own dialogue just for kicks.

As for extras, director T. Fikret Uçak (who bowed out after this film, understandably realising there was nowhere left to go) pops up for an entertaining half-hour video interview in which he talks about the making of the film and the '70s Turkish film industry. Then actors Akkaya and Tamer get their own chance to speak, in which they cover the basics of their careers and reflect on the golden age of copyright-puncturing Turkish cinema. Also included are some static extras, namely bios for Uçak and Akkaya and a stills gallery, but the real joy here is a batch of trailers; apart from two previously-released Kilink previews, you get the appetising Superman romp, *Demir Yumruk: Devler Geliyor*, and two staggering horror titles also available as an Onar double bill, the B&W gothic *Ölüler Konusmazki* and the Turkish *giallo* homage, *Aska Susayanlar Seks Ve Cinayet*.

THE THREE TRIALS

Colour, 2006, 100m. / Directed by Randy Greif / Starring Molinee Green, Max Herholz, Michael Q. Schmidt, Osa Wallander / Swinging Axe (US R0 NTSC) / WS (1.78:1) / DD2.0

Subtitled "Adventures in Psychotica", *The Three Trials* is a near-indescribable trip of a film revolving around the delirious misadventures of Catherine (Molinee Green), a former nun and housewife who experiences narcolepsy during moments of intense ecstasy. Her personal saviour and husband, a plastic surgeon, used to be a big hairy yeti, and members of the Church (including two priests, one of whom is a fat masochist and the other a giggling thug) as well as a mysterious meat cult keep trying to drag her back into their fold.

The very colourful and imaginative imagery is really this film's reason for existence; you literally have no idea what kind of eye-popping scenario will turn up next on the screen, and the grinding, atmospheric soundtrack (from groups with names like Nurse with Wound, Rapoon, Controlled Bleeding, and Lustmord!) is enough to approximate an acid trip in the safety of your own home. The film itself isn't really all that explicit, but the tone is extremely horrific and erotic throughout and director Randy Greif shows a sure hand at mixing avant garde sensibilities with baroque classicism, with a welcome dash of self-deprecating humour that automatically makes this more fun than your average cult item in the making. The film itself is presented widescreen (non-anamorphic) at 1.78:1 and looks very good considering the source; colours are punchy and vivid throughout, while the stereo audio works extremely well. Extras include three very abstract short films ("A Fist Full of Stars", "Paraliminal 2" and "Paraliminal 3"), all more or less adapted from footage shot for the main feature, as well as a reel of deleted scenes (the weirdest involving a screening of a vintage Popeye cartoon), and two different trailers.

TOKYO GORE POLICE

Colour, 2008, 110m. / Directed by Yoshihiro Nishimura / Starring Eihi Shiina, Itsuji Itao, Yukihide Benny / Tokyo Shock (US R1 NTSC), 4Digital (UK R2 PAL) / WS (1.85:1) (16:9) / DD5.1

When it comes to modern extreme exploitation, no one can outdo Japan. Case in point: *Tokyo Gore Police* (*Tôkyô zankoku keisatsu*), whose title alone should give you an idea of what to expect. This colourful, digitally-shot splatterfest lifts a few pages from the cyberpunk handbook crossed with some dashes of *Total Recall*, all mixed together for one seriously screwed-up stew.

In the future, rampaging crime has forced the corporate-owned police force to take aggressive action against the primary offenders, a strain of mutants called Engineers. A very disturbed scientist involved in the mutants' creation winds up tangling with Ruka (*Audition*'s Eihi Shiina), a beautiful police officer searching for the culprit who killed her cop father. Along the way, the red stuff spews, gushes, and eventually floods the camera with the ridiculous glee of *Shogun Assassin* and *The Evil Dead* combined.

Even with what appears to be a limited budget, director Yoshihiro Nishimura (the FX artist from films like *Suicide Club*) knows his way around a good gore gag and even throws in some fun TV spots that play like a cross between *Children of Men* and *RoboCop*. If you've been bemoaning the lack of decent bloodshed in the recent crop of movie offerings, look no further. Tokyo Shock's DVD features a very attractive transfer with eye-popping colours (often either neon-coloured or completely crimson), with Dolby Digital 5.1 and stereo options either in the original Japanese or an okay English dub. Stick with the former unless you're feeling too lazy to read. The only real extra is a very long Japanese theatrical trailer, along with promos for other extreme Asian titles like *Fudoh*, *Versus* and *Devilman*. A much more lavish 2-disc edition arrived later in the U.K. from 4Digital which, in addition to the same transfer, language options and extras, added on a bonus making-of featurette, video interviews with director Yoshihiro Nishimura and star Eihi Shiina, footage from the Japanese premiere, the original promo pitch reel and theatrical trailer, and the U.K. trailer.

A TOUCH OF GENIE

Colour, 1974, 89m. / Directed by Joe Sarno / Starring Doug Stone, Chris Jordan, Harding Harrison, Tina Russell, Ultramax, Harry Reems, Marc Stevens, Eric Edwards, Levi Richards / After Hours (US R0 NTSC)

Did you know there was an entire subgenre of genie smut in the 1970s? You're not the only one who missed out, but along comes this double-DVD set to prove it did indeed happen. The main attraction here is an obscure, presumed-lost oddity made by Joe Sarno during his brief goofball comedy period in the mid-'70s, and the end result mixing porno chic culture with rib-nudging Jewish humour resembles what might happen if some nutcase grabbed a colourised print of Roger Corman's *Little Shop of Horrors* and re-shot random scenes with actual sex. The performances and direction are all over the top, to say the least, and it's a grin-inducing reminder of a time when people treated this genre like any other.

To get away from his whiny mother (Ultramax), nerdy Melvin Finkelfarb (Doug Stone) whiles away his afternoons by hanging out at Times Square porn theatres in a pair of goofy fake glasses. One day with his buddy Irving (Harding Harrison) he stumbles upon a magic lamp containing a plucky genie (Sarno regular Chris Jordan, billed here as "Karen Craig") who offers to grant him his heart's desire. Naturally he wants to become his favourite adult movie studs so he can bed vixens like Tina Russell (whose nether regions are earlier given a queasy visual comparison to a certain delicatessen lunch specialty). The film then skips helter skelter as Melvin transforms into the likes of Harry Reems and Marc "10 1/2" Stevens by twirling around in a circle. Hey, nobody said this was hi-tech.

A perverse comedic deconstruction of the entire porn genre and the low-grade celebrity it inspired, *A Touch of Genie* is certainly unlike any other film. The humour goes way, way beyond broad, with the already hammy Reems going into overdrive and even the normally more restrained actors getting into the act with lots of goofy faces and eye-rolling. Somehow the extreme nature of the film manages to work, coming off more like a charming extended vaudeville sketch than a dirty movie. The sex isn't really hot in the traditional sense (thanks to some comical sound effects, for one thing), but it's a kick watching so many name faces appearing in a single movie, albeit one that hardly anyone seems to have viewed during its initial run. As this DVD is taken from the only print known to exist, evaluating the visual quality seems beside the point. That said, it's in pretty good shape overall; print damage is evident here and there but not really distracting, and colours seem to be in fine condition. The best extra here is a videotaped interview with Stone at a New York screening (questioned by Michael Bowen), and he seems accepting and good-natured about witnessing the film for the first time in decades. (Sarno also makes a quick cameo at the end, too.) The same screening also spawned another featurette, a "mini-doc" covering the event's reception with impromptu comments from various attendees, as well as "Memories from the Bottle", a 10-minute series of on-camera reminiscences from Sarno and Stone (with Marc Stevens the brunt of most of the jokes). The first disc also includes a slew of Sarno trailers and newly-created previews.

Then it's on to disc two, a celebration of genie smut beginning with "Swing Genie" (referred to as "The Swinging Genie" in the liner notes), a goofball one-hour storefront quickie about a tubby djinn in a turban who materialises out of bong smoke to grant wishes. The faces here are surprisingly high-profile (and don't miss the silly animated opening), with frequent soft-and-hardcore staples like Keith Erickson (*The Godson*), Sandy Carey (*The Devil's Garden*) and Ric Lutze among the writhing bodies. Then you get a female genie with "Genie's Magic Box", another semi-feature-length cheapie about a scientist whose Viagra-like potion falls into the hands of two numbskull assistants while he's off conjuring up a little sexy helper from a magic bottle. Suzanne Fields pops up in the penultimate sex scene to add some energy to the proceedings, while the scientist (a young guy in a terrible grey wig) finally gets his for the big finish. The disc is rounded out with another batch of After Hours promo trailers, and the package also comes with a set of liner notes by Michael Bowen and "The After Hours Collector". A watered-down soft version of this film was later tacked on as a bonus feature for the same label's *Deep Throat Sex Comedy Collection*, which is also reviewed here.

TRAPPED

Colour, 1982, 98m. / Directed by William Fruet / Starring Henry Silva, Nicholas Campbell, Barbara Gordon, Gina Dick, Allan Royal / Code Red (US R0 NTSC) / WS (1.85:1) (16:9)

After discussing the immorality of taking a human life, clean-cut college kid Roger (Nicholas Campbell) and three buddies decide to drive a jeep into the Tennessee woods for the afternoon. Unfortunately they decide to visit a town kept in a state of fear by Henry Chatwill (Henry Silva), a shotgun-toting brute who doesn't take too kindly to his pretty blonde wife diddling a stranger behind his back. Joined by his buddies, Henry punishes the other man with an old-fashioned tar and feathering with a fatal outcome, all witnessed by the four students who are then captured and chased by Henry and his goons before finally fighting back.

Made at the height of Canadian tax-shelter filmmaking which generated such filmmakers as David Cronenberg, *Trapped* (better known on VHS as *The Killer Instinct*) is another of the country's *Deliverance*-inspired revenge films after the excellent *Rituals*, albeit with a very different end result. While that 1976 outing was a moody and deliberately-paced creepfest, this one aims straight for the popcorn crowd with a string of rousing death scenes, car crashes, explosions and foot chases, including a crackerjack final half hour that should have made this an instant hit.

A reliable and intimidating character actor all the way back to *The Manchurian Candidate*, Silva gets a rare leading role here and makes the most of it as a truly loathsome villain. Along with this film, the '80s really turned out to be a strong decade for Silva as evidenced by his memorable work in *Alligator*, the absurd *Megaforce*, *Sharky's Machine*, *Chained Heat*, *Escape from the Bronx* and *Man Hunt*. Still a busy Canadian TV actor, Campbell is best remembered as the psycho who deep-throats a pair of scissors in *The Dead Zone* and handles his part well here, with the rest of the supporting cast adequate enough in their one-dimensional roles. If that pedigree isn't strong enough, it's worth noting that director William Fruet also helmed some of the more interesting Canadian exploitation films like *Death Weekend* and *Funeral Home*, while screenwriter John Beaird wrote the original *My Bloody Valentine*. Put 'em all together, and you've got quite a backwoods thriller on your hands.

Code Red's DVD features a fresh anamorphic transfer from film that's miles ahead of any other video editions; it really looks great all around. The wilderness scenes (which were shot in Georgia not far from the locations of *Deliverance*, not in Tennessee) look beautiful here, and the frequent crimson clothing never bleeds or causes distortion problems. The only extra is the very lively Canadian trailer, inexplicably dubbed in Spanish here but present in English on the company's other DVD releases.

TROMA'S WAR

Colour, 1988, 105m. / Directed by Lloyd Kaufman & Michael Herz / Starring Carolyn Beauchamp, Sean Bowen, Rick Washburn, Patrick Weathers, Jessica Dublin, Joe Fleishaker / Troma (US R0 NTSC)

After crashing on the beach of a remote, seemingly deserted tropical island (in a sequence bearing more than a passing resemblance to the pilot episode of a certain hit ABC series), the survivors able to crawl from the wreckage of their plane find an even worse threat awaiting them: a frenzied group of extremist terrorists who have banded together (for reasons not revealed until later) to train for a violent mission. Thinking the interlopers are mercenaries hired to take them out, the villains arm up and wage an attack involving countless gun battles, a rampaging AIDS-infected goon, an uppity preacher, a monstrous mutant hiding in the bad guy's camp, and hilarious hair-rock songs worthy of *South Park*.

At the time of its release in the late-'80s, *Troma's War* marked a turning point for the company whose name was actually embedded in the title (in what would soon become a tradition for many of its higher-tiered releases). The breakthrough success of *The Toxic Avenger* had given the scrappy New York-based purveyors of extreme exploitation primarily geared for the video market realisation they could set their sights higher for audience acceptance, blending squishy slapstick comedy seemingly ripped from an edition of *Truly Tasteless Jokes* with over-the-top, unrealistic gore – and lots and lots of loud overacting. This film boasted a higher budget than usual and was designed for theatrical cult status, though a not particularly receptive MPAA demanded so many cuts the film eventually lost nearly 20 minutes on its way to an R rating (and pretty much its entire reason for existence in the process). Fortunately most video audiences could sidestep this silliness due to the wide availability of the uncut version, though the film never came close to gaining the status of the Toxie series. Seen now, it's a flawed but fascinating time capsule of a dying indie theatrical wave and a peculiar political statement whose naïveté has somehow come back around to being alarmingly current again.

In what became something of a regular in films helmed or written by Troma honcho Lloyd Kaufman, *Troma's War* takes a quick time out to deliver an impassioned message about the evils of right-wing and terrorist extremism, which are lumped in together here as the same oppressive force, a before-its-time outlook later popularised in a number of George W. Bush-era books and films. Of course, it's a bit hard to take seriously when surrounded by a body count that goes into triple digits before the one-hour mark; mostly it's a big, dumb, fun *Rambo* parody that's way overlong but generally spirited all the way to the absurd ending. The cast does an efficient job delivering "Tromatic" performances, often with baffling make-up accessories like a bad guy sporting a pig snout.

Troma's initial DVD featured a dated transfer culled from the VHS era along with the usual clutch of "extras" primarily featuring Kaufman running around with goofballs in the office, though his intro at least provided some context. The belated "Tromasterpiece" edition of *Troma's War* is definitely a substantial upgrade in the extras department; not surprisingly, it still features the same recycled transfer (albeit with marginally better compression), but at least here the slew of bonus features shed a lot of light on how this film came to be and somehow slipped off the radar of its intended audience. Kaufman contributes an interesting commentary track that serves as a useful primer on how to make New York look like a Caribbean island (not too dissimilar from what *Combat Shock* did to create its Vietnam) and explains the distribution entanglements which led to the film's abortion of a theatrical release. Pretty much all of the available cast pop up for the short but substantial video extras including "Veteran's Day: A Post-Tromatic Reunion" ("terrorist" performer Joe Fleishaker interviewed by the film's FX artist and *Redneck Zombies* auteur Pericles Lewnes), "Rick Washburn Shoots the Shit" (self-explanatory), "Post-War Reflections" and "War Talk" (with leading man Sean Bowen and others offering some brief on-camera anecdotes), "Three Minutes with Rolfe" (a

chat with the film's P.A. and future *There's Nothing Out There* director Rolfe Kanefsky), "London's War" (a quick interview with cinematographer "James London" aka James Lebovitz), a couple of trailers, a very funny "Kill-o-Meter", and promos for other worthwhile "Tromasterpiece" releases. As Troma's last big theatrical hurrah before they went on to home video infamy with more audacious (and arguably more accomplished) fare, this one has finally been given its chance to shine and still holds up as one of the company's most ambitious, fascinating, and unapologetically violent offerings.

THE TRUE STORY OF THE NUN OF MONZA

Colour, 1980, 80m. / Directed by Bruno Mattei / Starring Zora Kerova, Mario Cutini, Paola Corazzi, Franco Garofalo / Exploitation Digital (US R1 NTSC) / WS (1.85:1) (16:9)

 At the height of Italian nunsploitation, aesthetically-challenged filmmaker Bruno Mattei churned out no less than two entries, *The True Story of the Nun of Monza* and *The Other Hell*, hiding out under the name "Stefan Oblowsky". This one's actually a bit more reputable than you might expect given the director; sure, there's plenty of nudity, lesbian groping and a guy in a shiny red devil outfit, but the 17th Century period settings are better handled than usual and it all looks a bit classier than the usual soft-focus nonsense. Zora Kerova, best known for her topless hook routine in *Cannibal Ferox*, headlines as a town official's young daughter cloistered away to purge her of impure thoughts and influences. Not such a hot idea, as it turns out, since she still

spends all day indulging in religious-themed sexual fantasies (one cribbed shamelessly from Ken Russell's *The Devils*) and attracting the interest of the other nuns, who spend their evenings groping each other under the covers. Then the local priest takes an interest as well and tries to jump her in the confessional booth, followed by a weird twist of fate that puts her in charge as the new Mother Superior with plenty of blackmail, a secret pregnancy, rape, murder, and an impromptu inquisition all soon to come.

Another obscure title rescued from oblivion, this film looks quite good in its anamorphic DVD presentation (and yes, the photography is supposed to be soft focus), with the original Italian audio track (with optional English subtitles) sounding just fine. Extras include a theatrical trailer and a pointless fake stills gallery, plus other trailers from the sleazy Media Blasters subdivision, Exploitation Digital.

THE UNSEEN

Colour, 1980, 89m. / Directed by Peter Foleg (Danny Steinmann) / Starring Barbara Bach, Sydney Lassick, Stephen Furst, Karen Lamm, Lelia Goldoni, Doug Barr / Code Red (US R0 NTSC) / WS (1.85:1) (16:9), Digital Entertainment (UK R2 PAL)

 The second-greatest horror film ever shot in the Danish-inspired California town of Solvang (right behind William Castle's *Homicidal*), this early '80s horror drive-in oddity has long been one of those films cult fans are passingly familiar with, having perhaps caught a few minutes here and there on TV. The film was barely released in theatres by the short-lived World Northal, who mainly promoted the presence of Bond girl/Beatle wife Barbara Bach after

her success in *The Spy Who Loved Me*. However, the wild departures from audience's slasher expectations and some truly demented plot elements ensured this would remain a word-of-mouth cult item rather than a bona fide hit.

Our story begins as TV reporter Bach leaves her apartment under cloudy circumstances with her injured athlete boyfriend (Doug Barr). Along with two perky blonde assistants, she drives to Solvang to cover their annual Danish celebration (whose bounciness leads one to expect Bill Murray and a groundhog to pop up any minute). However, their hotel accommodations turn out to be lost, so they find refuge instead at the home of jovial but very eccentric local museum owner Mr. Keller (*Carrie*'s Sydney Lassick), who lives in a nearby antiquated house with his mousy wife, Virginia (Lelia Goldoni). At night the husband experiences traumatic flashbacks involving his father and some hideous incestuous secret, while something monstrous and murderous lurks in the cellar below the young women's guest rooms...

Though audiences at the time most likely expected a monster-meets-slasher outing from *The Unseen*, the film draws far more inspiration from the string of perverse, Lovecraftian thrillers involving dark, nasty things tucked away in attics and basements (for example, *The Shuttered Room* and *The Beast in the Cellar*), albeit with a couple of murders involving more blood and T&A than censorship would previously allow. The film is still surprisingly non-explicit with its imagery but definitely unsettling in its implications, particularly in the final third when we finally meet the "unseen" of the title (played by an unrecognisable Stephen Furst shortly after *Animal House*) whose exact nature and appearance will remain unspoiled here. This revelation also opens up the story in some interesting directions with viewer sympathies swerving all over the place as the whole sick family drama plays out with more than a few shredded bodies in its wake. *The Unseen* features a few creepy moments, most memorably a bit involving one unfortunate character's scarf and a ventilation grate, but the real fascination lies with the actors; Bach makes a respectable scream queen after remaining largely passive and icy for the opening act of the story, but the true show here is Lassick and Furst, who carry the inherently ridiculous script to nearly operatic heights. Also worthy of a mention is the sterling music score by the criminally underrated Michael J. Lewis, who had already proven his horror mettle with *Theatre of Blood* and *The Legacy*. His moving main theme is surprisingly underused (grab the very scarce promo soundtrack CD if you can find it), but his evocative strings are perfectly used throughout to generate an air of classical unease.

Given this film's spotty distribution history, it's amazing that Code Red found enough elements and participants to assemble such a generous, two-disc DVD set. A murky, bare bones U.K. release preceded this (reviewed in *DVD Delirium Vol. 2*) but it in no way compares to the transfer here from the IP negative. Some of the interior night scenes were shot with low light and inherently look a bit grainy, but otherwise the progressive transfer is great, with solid flesh tones and bright, vivid colours throughout. Extras include a far-reaching and often hilarious audio commentary by Furst and producer Tony Unger (with moderator Lee Christian), who chart the film's difficult journey to the screen (with *Savage Streets* director Danny Steinmann yanking his name during post-production). Disc one also includes on-camera interviews with Furst and Barr, who talk for a few short minutes about how they became involved with the production, and both actors also contribute quick, funny video intros to the main feature (with Furst

calling it "really scary" because it's "the only film where you can see me wearing a diaper"). Other first-disc extras include the theatrical trailer, a lengthy stills gallery, and bonus Code Red trailers including a very tasty (but curiously time-coded) promo for *The Visitor*. If that's not enough *Unseen* for you, head on over to disc two where the film's effects are covered in detail with two featurettes, a 38-minute chat with future Hollywood make-up man Craig Reardon and a half-hour interview with writer Tom Burman, who also covers the effects as well as the reasons he wound up leaving the film before completion. For a troubled production, the surprisingly potent result is explained here in enough detail to answer anyone's questions. The final extra is a big batch of Reardon's test slides, sketches and production photos with a focus on the grisly effects and Furst's unforgettable climactic creation.

VAMPIRE STRANGLER

Colour, 1999, 92m. / Directed by William Hellfire / Starring Misty Mundae, William Hellfire, Joey Smack / After Hours (US R0 NTSC), Factory 2000 (US R0 NTSC)

 Once the most eagerly sought-after of the indie extreme titles on the market due to its status as Misty Mundae's only (sort of) hardcore film, *Vampire Strangler* has managed to earn a deluxe two-disc special edition after the initial DVD went out of print and started demanding absurd amounts of money. This was one of the very first films from Factory 2000, a homegrown sex-and-horror video outfit started by William Hellfire, often showcasing then-girlfriend Mundae. This release is something of a comprehensive survey of that DIY

company as well as an obvious "restored and newly edited" release geared to Mundae fans, who get to see her in her one and only "explicit" performance (which mainly consists of a few oral scenes with Hellfire). This new edition presents the aforementioned new cut of the film, which integrates the "ultra-naughty" outtakes of Mundae back into the main feature as well as a slew of other footage which was dropped (against the director's wishes) in order to turn in a one-hour final product during the initial release. Even now the plot's not much and basically a jabbering mess, but in summary it revolves around a Romanian girl moving in with her cousin Billy, who turns into a vampire when they're not busy fooling around in his bedroom.

The extras here are actually quite interesting, especially a head-scratching "lost" original prologue that finds one of Van Helsing's descendants having unsimulated sex in a basement with some girl, only to get attacked by vampires who turn them both into screaming bloody messes. It's even more technically crude and poorly-lit than the main feature, but is also probably the most extreme and baffling fusion of gore and sex in the entire Factory 2000 catalogue. Other extras include a really boring deleted scene at a dinner table, an option to watch all of the sex scenes isolated separately, and a batch of fetish Mundae shorts from 1998 to 2001 (apparently all helmed by Hellfire) including "My Property", "Vibrating Maid", and "My Date with Misty". While Mundae (now Erin Brown, since her original stage name is still owned by Seduction Cinema) has pretty much distanced herself from her softcore work and even more from her Factory days, the new DVD does what it can to explain how on earth this title came into existence. The surprisingly extensive insert booklet contains a long and detailed examination

of the origins of both Factory 2000 and this feature, written by Media Funhouse's Ed Grant, who does a solid job of covering the labyrinthine distribution, legal and personal entanglements involved over the years, interspersed with a few candid comments from Hellfire himself. Of course, the second disc is rounded out with a ton of Mundae trailers for her more polished efforts like *Flesh for Olivia* and *Sin Sisters*.

VANESSA

Colour, 1977, 91m. / Directed by Hubert Frank / Starring Olivia Pascal, Anton Diffring, Uschi Zech / Severin (US R0 NTSC, UK R0 NTSC) / WS (1.85:1) (16:9)

 As if the "exotic Orient" didn't host enough sexual awakenings with *Emmanuelle* and her imitators, *Vanessa* comes along to offer another take on this familiar scenario with *Bloody Moon*'s Olivia Pascal walking through her unclad paces as the title character. This one opens with Bach's "Toccata and Fugue", just like *Tales from the Crypt*, but that's pretty much where the similarities end as we follow convent-raised Vanessa going to Hong Kong to claim some inherited property – only to find that she's responsible for a bunch of brothels. As she comes to accept her new role, she also discovers her inner sexuality with both genders, meaning plentiful nudity everywhere from beaches to jacuzzis. It's all above-average TV-ready fare with lots of simulated moaning and groaning, naked lounging in wicker chairs, a laid-back vocal theme song, and that ever-present trash cinema veteran, Anton Diffring (*Faceless*, *Circus of Horrors*), popping up now and then to lend a bit of pseudo-class.

Once again Severin's featurettes are the real stars of the show, kicking off with "High Life in Hong Kong", in which director Hubert Frank (a German softcore regular) and cinematographer Franz X. Lederle have a genial on-camera chat for half an hour about the making of the film and the vagaries of Hong Kong shooting. Also worthwhile is "Vanessa Revealed", a 16-minute chunk of behind-the-scenes footage shot on Super 8, also packed with plenty of skin shots; the theatrical trailer is included as well. Severin later released an identical uncut version on DVD in the U.K. too.

VENGEANCE OF THE ZOMBIES

Colour, 1972, 87m. / Directed by León Klimovsky / Starring Paul Naschy, Romy, Mirta Miller, Vic Winner, Maria Kosty, Aurora de Alba, Pierre Besari / Victory Films, distributed by BCI Eclipse (DVD & Blu-ray, US R0 NTSC/HD) / DD5.1

Spanish horror staple Paul Naschy's fondness for playing multiple roles has given him plenty of room to flex his muscles (both literal and thespian) in several films, but one of the weirdest Paul-on-parade spectacles must certainly be *Vengeance of the Zombies*, which features the stocky leading man going through a variety of make-up permutations under the guidance of regular director León Klimovsky. Boasting a look and structure apparently inspired by viewings of *Curse of the Crimson Altar* and *Plague of the Zombies*, the film opens with a pair of grave robbers getting their just deserts when their quarry comes to life under the hand of a mysterious voodoo priest. Pretty soon London is turned upside down with zombie sightings, sprinkled with *giallo*-style murders by a masked maniac who likes slitting throats and planting hatchets in senior citizens' heads, hallucinatory visions of a horned demon (Naschy) surrounded by painted disciples, and rampant toplessness. Could the seemingly benevolent Eastern mystic Krisna (Naschy II) be involved in these ghastly shenanigans? Or what about his rather more sinister (and much uglier) brother, Kantaka (Naschy III)?

As with Naschy's other London-set monster outing, *Dr. Jekyll vs. the Werewolf*, he and Klimovsky strive to emulate the freewheeling early '70s ambience of drug-and-sex-sodden Old Blighty being similarly mined by Hammer films (see *Dracula A.D. 1972* for the most extreme example). However, the Spanish approach automatically gives the proceedings a flavour far different from its Hammer counterparts, with much looser plotting (you could barely even tell this film has a storyline per se) and plenty of enthusiastic skin and fake blood for the crowds outside of censor-happy Spain. Few of Naschy and Klimovsky's films could really be termed "scary" in the traditional sense, but the imagery here of undead, bug-eyed female corpses in flowing blue gowns is certainly some of the creepiest they ever concocted.

As with most of Naschy's other output from the '70s, this film was prepared in both clothed and "hot" versions depending upon territorial demands. BCI's much-needed official DVD release presents the main feature in the spicier cut, taken from the original negative and looking considerably fresher than past video versions, with dreary unofficial editions surfacing in the past from companies like Beverly Wilshire. The open matte 1.33:1 framing shown here is functional enough, though viewers with widescreen monitors may want to zoom it in to 1.78:1 for a far more interesting and aesthetically pleasing presentation. Colours look excellent, and black levels look dead on (though the original film stock makes

385

some shadowy scenes a bit murkier than might have been intended). Unlike some Naschy titles, the English dub works best here overall, giving the film at least a superficial fidelity to its Anglo setting. Purists can also enjoy the Spanish audio track either in the original mono or a newly tweaked 5.1 remix, though the latter is best avoided as it often diverges from the onscreen action and irritatingly channels much of the dialogue into the rear channels. Some brief footage present only in the Spanish version is presented in that language on all three tracks, so choose accordingly. The goofball music score sounds just fine in all three. Naschy presents the feature in a brief, newly-shot video intro, looking as genial as usual, while other extras include the alternative clothed scenes which plagued some unfortunate video releases, the original (similar) Spanish title sequences, a trailer playable in either English or Spanish, two hefty stills galleries packed with international art and photos, and the expected thorough and enlightened liner notes by Naschy expert Mirek Lipinski. Also available on Blu-ray as a double feature with *Night of the Werewolf.*

VIDEO VIOLENCE

Colour, 1987, 86m. / Directed by Gary P. Cohen / Starring Art Neill, Jackie Neill, Bart Sumner, David Christopher

VIDEO VIOLENCE 2

Colour, 1988, 82m. / Directed by Gary P. Cohen / Starring Art Neill, Jackie Neill / Camp (US R0 NTSC)

One of the most prevalent "big box" VHS titles on the indie horror market and a flagship title in Camp Video's Retro 80s Horror Collection on DVD, *Video Violence* (" when renting is not enough!") follows the mishaps of the Emorys, a couple from the Big Apple whose relocation to New Jersey and establishment of a video rental store puts their lives in peril. Several tapes fall into their hands depicting a series of gory snuff murders, and their sniffing around to discover the source of these literal video nasties pits them against the entire town, whose collusion with a pair of psychos, Howard and Eli, holds the key to these illicit home projects.

Carrying the theme to an absurd conclusion, *Video Violence 2* goes for flat-out gore comedy as Howard and Eli return as the hosts of a public access program packed with random murders and ghoulish humour. Mostly a series of *Laugh-In*-style sketches, the show trots out various tortures, executions, and other atrocities, executed with thankfully phoney effects and a minimum of genuine sadism. What's the story behind the show, and are the actors really being snuffed before a live studio audience?

Though both concepts sound like pretty good hooks for low-budget horror, be aware that the *Video Violence* films were shot on super-cheap consumer cameras from the '80s and certainly look it. The acting sticks to junior high mugging level for the most part, and the effects never come close to believable (which might be intentional). Still, there's a strange nostalgic kick if you're a seasoned horror fan who came of age in the '80s; the do-it-yourself oomph makes for compellingly cracked viewing if you're in the right frame of mind and willing to overlook tons of tracking problems, impenetrable lighting and lots of ketchup doused on unsuspecting actors. The director, Gary P. Cohen, contributes commentary tracks and an interview discussing the making of his, er, franchise, though he's not as energetic or charismatic as fellow Camp auteurs like *Cannibal Campout*'s Jon McBride.

VIOLENCE AND FLESH

Colour, 1981, 93m. / Directed by Alfredo Sternheim / Starring Helena Ramos, José Lucas, Nadia Destro / Impulse (US R0 NTSC)

Pornochanchada, or Brazilian sex flicks from the '70s and '80s, got their first English-aimed DVD release courtesy of the Impulse Pictures edition of *The Chick's Ability*. Their second release is another, even sleazier discovery, *Violence and Flesh* (*Violência na Carne*), starring that same film's voluptuous star, Helena Ramos, in what basically amounts to a skankier version of *Last House on the Beach*.

On the run from the law, three convicts pop a bullet in their getaway driver and torch the car for good measure (an opener that rivals *Pink Flamingos* for prolonged cinematic pyromania). Feigning a roadside injury, they carjack a passing motorist who happens to be a director en route to a weekend rehearsal with his cast at a beach cottage. Once there, they wait for all the thespians (a mixture of straight and gay characters) before unleashing a torrent of sexual abuse. However, one of the convicts winds up getting a little too close to one of his captives, setting the stage for a gruelling final showdown.

Filled with both elements found in the title, this isn't as explicit as some other *chada* titles (many of which verged on hardcore or just hopped right over that barrier completely); most of the carnal activity is confined to the second half and is basically lots of heaving bare breasts and butts, with some astoundingly nasty forced scenarios thrown in for good measure. Ramos gets a lot of screen time as one of the main actresses, showing off her dramatic assets as well as her more physical ones.

There's also a prolonged and pretty darn steamy encounter on the beach that's intercut with one of the most outrageous scenes in the film. Impulse's DVD appears to be a fine, fresh transfer from original film elements, presented full frame (with nothing noticeable missing as it's currently framed). The Portuguese mono audio sounds fine and comes with optional English subtitles. Deliciously decadent stuff, and proof positive that America and Europe weren't the only countries churning out great drive-in product back in 1981.

VIOLETTE

Colour, 1978, 124m. / Directed by Claude Chabrol / Starring Isabelle Huppert, Stéphane Audran, Jean Carmet, Lisa Langlois, Guy Hoffman / Koch Lorber (US R1 NTSC)

Immediately following her star-making turn in the 1977 international favourite *The Lacemaker*, rising young actress Isabelle Huppert reaffirmed her status as one of France's most valuable cinematic assets the following year with her next lead role as the titular *Violette Nozière* (known as *Violette* in the United States). This based-on-fact period crime thriller marked something of a return to form for director Claude Chabrol, whose career had flailed throughout the 1970s after the previous decade's impeccable run of groundbreaking thrillers. The teaming paid off more than anyone could have anticipated, with Huppert snagging a Best Actress Award at the Cannes Film Festival, co-star Stéphane Audran (the ex-Mrs. Chabrol) earning a César Award, and Chabrol going on to reunite with Huppert on numerous occasions for such high-profile titles as *Madame Bovary*, *Story of*

V

Women, *Merci pour le chocolat* and *La cérémonie*. Inexplicably, perhaps due to its indifferent domestic release from New Yorker, *Violette* vanished from view after its initial theatrical run, never earning a release on American home video until its much-belated DVD issue from Koch Lorber. Fortunately, the film still holds up rather well and maintains its status as a key entry in the careers of everyone involved; unfortunately, the presentation of the disc itself is not quite so stellar.

The spare, non-linear narrative charts the downward spiral of Violette, a 1930s Parisian teenager who draws inspiration from Hollywood glamour queens and finds little friendship or warmth in those around her, including her clueless parents, Germaine (a frumpy Audran) and Baptiste (busy character actor Jean Carmet). Violette spends her afternoon lolling around cafés, mocking the pretentious intelligentsia and, putting on her best fur-lined seductress vamp routine, attempting to seduce the callow young men around her. When she strikes up a relationship with a sleazy pimp, Violette realises she can turn her easy virtue into easy profit, but her parents prove to be an obstacle to realising her tawdry dreams.

A sharp contrast to Huppert's previous fresh-faced persona of open vulnerability, *Violette* is a fascinating departure from the usual Chabrol unfaithful heroine; here instead of the stifled suburban wife or schoolmarm, we have a teen whose budding sexuality manifests itself in a destructive fashion, though the woman herself is not specifically blamed. The first of Chabrol's thrillers to depart from a modern setting (not counting the weird, semi-comical *Bluebeard*), this film found the director scrambling to regain his foothold after the chilly reception to his excellent, woefully underrated 1977 horror-fantasy, *Alice*, and establishing a formula (biopic conventions plus period setting plus Huppert exploring the virgin/whore dynamic) he would later explore to greater effect with *Story of Women*, for which this film often resembles a rough draft. The period setting is lovingly rendered, with the burnished wood of the cafés, stifling claustrophobia of the urban dwellings, and dense textures of the post-flapper clothing all establishing a rich yet palpably decadent atmosphere.

Unfortunately, the director's accomplishment is difficult to appreciate in its DVD incarnation, which shockingly manages to surpass the disastrous late-'90s Fox Lorber disc of his *L'enfer* as the worst-looking Chabrol disc to date. The transfer is overly grainy, blown-out, riddled with print damage, and smothered with digital distortion and shimmering colour bleeding; furthermore, the 1.66:1 aspect ratio is awkwardly hacked to full frame after the letterboxed opening titles. At least the English subtitles are removable and easy to read, which is about the best that can be said. This release might have been passable at the dawn of the DVD era, but this late in the game, it's completely inexplicable; if this is the best video master of the film that currently exists, it's a sad state of affairs for French cinema indeed. Given that this is the only English-friendly commercial release of the film to date, Chabrol fans will no doubt want to snap it up just to watch the film (which at least looks maybe a notch better than the bootlegs floating around for years), but disappointment will be unavoidable. No extras are included apart from promos for other Koch Lorber releases, but perhaps that's all for the best.

VISIONS OF SUFFERING

Colour, 2006, 120m. / Directed by Andrey Iskanov / Starring Svyatoslav Iliyasov, Andrey Iskanov, Alexandra Batrumova, Igor Orlov / Unearthed (US R0 NTSC) / DD2.0

This berserk experimental horror film comes from Russian director Andrey Iskanov (*Nails*), who apparently locked himself in a room for a week with some hard chemical agents and a TV running a constant loop of *Tetsuo the Iron Man*. The packaging attempts to explain the plot as such: "Demons stalk a victim in his sleep. They appear whenever the rain falls and threaten to break free from the land of nightmares into his conscious world. A drug-induced vision allows the demons to finally tear apart the veil that separates him from their nightmare world, and the victim is dragged into their hellish realm." In other words, expect lots of strobe lighting, naked chicks in S&M gear rubbing on anything in sight, gruesome make-up effects, and loads of abrasive industrial-style sound effects. For two hours.

Fortunately most of the film looks gorgeous (the gothic landscape tableaux in particular are terrific), but this is far more easily digested in multiple sittings as a string of avant garde short films rather than a coherent whole. As usual Unearthed has done an extensive job of bringing this twisted puppy to DVD; the transfer looks vibrant and colourful despite the monetary limitations, and the aggressive soundtrack comes across nice, clear and loud. The biggest extra is a making-of documentary running nearly an hour, with the director and star rattling off influences, discussing the meaning of certain scenes, and breaking down some of the bizarre special effects. Another completely unrelated but very cool extra is "El Kuervo (The Crow)", an amusing goth-style short film adapting the famous Edgar Allan Poe poem into the story of a tormented musician. Also included are multiple image galleries (accompanied by the film's soundtrack), a trailer, and additional promos for *Nails* and other highly recommended Unearthed titles like *Frankenhooker* and *Rock & Rule*, which may not share much of an audience with the one for this film.

THE WARRIOR

Colour, 1981, 86m. / Directed by Sisworo Gautama Putra / Starring Barry Prima, Eva Arnaz, W.D. Mochtar, Dana Christina, S. Parya / Mondo Macabro (US R0 NTSC) / WS (2.35:1) (16:9)

Perhaps the most representative example of Indonesian exploitation, *The Warrior* made an instant local star out of Barry Prima (birth name: Bertus Knoch), a martial arts devotee who went on to star in a slew of action, fantasy and horror films, including two sequels to this film as well as the staggering *The Devil's Sword*. Here he teams up with his one-time wife, Eva Arnaz (right after the still seldom seen gem *Special Silencers*), for a rousing adaptation of an Indonesian comic about Jaka Sembung, a freedom fighter living in 19th Century Indonesia under Dutch colonial oppression. We first see our hero in a dirty labour camp where he leads his fellow prisoners in a small-scale uprising. Their keepers don't take kindly to this disobedience and quickly audition thugs to take out Jaka. The chosen one, big bald brute Kobar (played by *Satan's Slave*'s S. Parya), tracks down his prey for a showdown in the middle of a field but proves to be no match, leaving the Dutch baddies to call on an undead, rabbit-toothed black magician (*Mystics in Bali*'s W.D. Mochtar) to trap this troublesome pest. (The scene in which the magician is revived by hand-controlled bottle rockets which blow his coffin out of the ground is unlike anything else you've ever seen.) Soon Jaka's fallen into the clutches of his enemies and chained to a wall with his eyes gouged out, but even that can't stop our hero from staging a truly unique comeback with the aid of another wizard and lots of hard, fast-flying kicks and punches to his enemies' heads.

Loaded with absurd violence, bizarre plot twists, and frequent detours into the supernatural, *The Warrior* manages to somehow filter the more extreme elements of its horrific predecessors into an audience-friendly stew that made it an international favourite both in theatres and on home video. Prima's limited thespian skills are put to good use here as the stoic lead, while the villains all get to chew up the scenery with wild abandon. *The Warrior* is also significant in cult film history as the one that really solidified the standing of Rapi Films, one of Indonesia's steadiest drive-in purveyors, who recently staged a comeback with a string of new horror titles (more on that below). Some of the martial arts scenes appear to be influenced by earlier hits from companies like Shaw Brothers, but no other country could have come up with such sequences as the diabolical wizard being hacked to pieces and reattaching his limbs in one very memorable showdown. Prima is fairly inexpensive (except when he's getting his eyes popped out), paving the way for a subsequent decade of emotionless tough guys like Chuck Norris. Relentlessly entertaining, this is pure, mind-damaging cinematic junk food par excellence.

Fans of past Mondo Macabro Indonesian releases should have some familiarity with this title already thanks to the presence of its trailer (and those of its two official sequels, *The Warrior and the Blind Swordsman* and *The Warrior and the Ninja*) on their indispensable *Virgins from Hell* release, not to mention an interview with the cantankerous Prima on *The Devil's Sword*. Needless to say, they've really gone the extra mile here with a top-quality presentation. Ignore the opening disclaimer about imperfect source elements; the transfer looks spectacular with gloriously saturated colours and mint quality clarity. Some fleeting discolouration pops up in a few frames here and there, but it's so quick and minor you'd have to be a real grouch to be bothered. The English-dubbed track (the original audio prepared for the film) is magnificent goofiness as usual, in this case rendered even more surreal by the fact that all the Dutch and Indonesian characters look and speak exactly the same. Hmmm. The biggest extras here are two new video interviews, the first with writer Imam Tantowi, who talks about the various actors who brought his work to life, his intentions for bringing the classic Jaka Sembung character to the big screen, and of course, his brain-melting screenplay for *Queen of Black Magic*. Then Gope Samtani, the producer who established the Rapi Films legacy, talks for 11 minutes about his formula for commercial success, his move to more Westernised product, and the market demands which led Indonesian filmmakers to swerve over to TV work. The company's recent return to the big screen is also represented by three trailers for the recent *Ghost Train*, *40 Days – The Rise of Evil* and *Ghost with Hole*, all of which look atmospheric if a bit on the bland side. On top of that you get the usual extensive bios for Prima and Arnaz as well as an updated version of the lively Mondo Macabro promo reel, which contains "images of sex, violence and midget assassins".

THE WEEKEND MURDERS

Colour, 1970, 98m. / Directed by Michele Lupo / Starring Anna Moffo, Peter Baldwin, Evelyn Stewart (Ida Galli), Giacomo Rossi-Stuart, Lance Percival, Beryl Cunningham, Chris Chittel / Code Red (US R0 NTSC) / WS (2.35:1) (16:9)

Far better known for its outrageous theatrical trailer that's shown up on dozens of compilations over the years, *The Weekend Murders* was originally released to most English-speaking audiences courtesy of MGM as a double bill with the much more graphic *Black Belly of the Tarantula*, even though both films inexplicably share an R rating.

The plot is basically another rehash of *The Cat and the Canary* as a group of well-to-do malcontents get together for the weekend to hear the reading of the will of Sir Henry Carter, a recently deceased patriarch. The macabre opening certainly sets the tone as the guests witness the discovery of a corpse's hand beneath the soil of a golf course just as someone's teeing off, accompanied by violent zooms into each actor's face to the sound of Francesco De Masi's raucous Tchaikovsky-laced score. Among the possible suspects and victims are suave playboy Ted (*Kill Baby Kill*'s Giacomo Rossi-Stuart), wounded and estranged Isabelle (Evelyn Stewart) and her husband Anthony (*The Ghost*'s Peter Baldwin), and dedicated caregiver Barbara (Anna Moffo). The story constantly reverses the usual expectations of drawing-room mysteries as the butler winds up dead early on, a throat-slitting in a bathtub turns out to be something very different indeed, and the police prove to be more of a hindrance than a help.

Though ostensibly a *giallo* based on the fact that it's Italian and involves people being bumped off, *The Weekend Murders* has far more in common with the flamboyant and often jokey Edgar Wallace thrillers pouring out of Germany at the time, particularly with its string of knowing references to whodunit stories. Everyone seems to be in on the joke, and the very English setting and dialogue delivery actually comes off surprisingly well even if the costuming remains utterly Italian in its excessive details and colour schemes. Director Michele Lupo is far better known for comedic genre studies like *Seven Times Seven*, *Africa Express* and *Ben and Charlie*, and his sense of humour serves him well here along with his regular screenwriter, Sergio Donati (who also penned *The Big Gundown*, *Duck You Sucker* and Tinto Brass's *Deadly Sweet*).

The Weekend Murders languished for decades in the MGM vault without a legit video release, making it maddeningly difficult to see despite its wide theatrical release. Fortunately Code Red licensed the film from the original Italian owners and accessed MGM's original vault elements, which have held up extremely well. The image is colourful and looks authentically filmic throughout (understandably, the English opening titles are slightly drabber than the main body of the film), while the English audio track is looped as usual but matches the actors' lip movements far more often than it doesn't. Along with the obligatory trailer, the DVD also contains a trio of extras with Peter Baldwin, who abandoned acting shortly afterwards and became a prolific American TV director. He contributes a quick video intro as well as an interview in which he discusses his Italian and American acting career, working alongside performers like Barbara Steele and appearing in diverse projects like the woefully underrated *La donna del lago*. Then he contributes a lighthearted audio commentary track alongside regular Code Red moderator Lee Christian and *Intruder* director Scott Spiegel, reflecting on his memories of working with each of the actors such as Rossi-Stuart, with whom he appeared in two films. You also get a slew of additional trailers like *Stunt Rock*, *Dr. Death: Seeker of Souls*, *Sole Survivor*, *Devil's Express*, *Brute Corps*, *Trapped*, and *Night Warning*.

THE WEIRDOS AND THE ODDBALLS COLLECTION: MILLIE'S HOMECOMING

Colour, 1971, 65m. / Directed by Eduardo Cemano / Starring Fred J. Lincoln, Dolly Sharp, Tina Russell, Arlana Blue

THE WEIRDOS AND THE ODDBALLS

Colour, 1971, 60m. / Directed by Eduardo Cemano / Starring Dolly Sharp, Fred J. Lincoln, Betty Colman, Harry Reems / After Hours (US R0 NTSC) / WS (1.78:1) (16:9)

The first multiple-title entry in the "Grindhouse Directors Series" from After Hours is dedicated to the mysterious Eduardo Cemano, who appeared at the advent of XXX cinema and then disappeared. This set doesn't bear a consistent title on the packaging but has been promoted as *The Weirdos and the Oddballs Collection* on the promos and menu screens, so let's just settle for that. This one's fascinating for way more than its smut value, as both films are unusual, semi-experimental slices of New York exploitation featuring some prominent names in their salad days, and the extras contain some great interviews with the participants who place it all in context.

First up is *Millie's Homecoming*, a retitling of 1971's *Lady Zazu's Daughter*, a perverse little drawing room number about an upper crust New York couple, the Zazus, who take turns diddling their maid (played by Tina Russell) and eventually initiating their newly returned daughter, Millie (Arlana Blue, under the name "Angel Spirit"), into their bohemian lifestyle. The main couple is played by *Deep Throat*'s Dolly Sharp and, in a rare lead role, still-active hardcore director Fred Lincoln, best known as Weasel in Wes Craven's *The Last House on the Left*. Cemano shows a deft hand with both

dialogue and smut as well as an ability to come up with unique camerawork on a two-dollar budget, which serves him well in the superior follow-up film, *The Weirdos and the Oddballs*, a retitling of *Zora Knows Best.* A flat-out '30s-style screwball comedy, this one features most of the same cast with Reed and Lincoln returning as a kinky couple who sit around rubbing themselves while talking about this great new ad they took out for, ahem, couples therapy, with Harry Reems and his girlfriend turning up to participate. More unsuspecting innocents arrive and are promptly inducted into a world of naked dancing and wild partying as Reed spins everyone around in a carnal carousel. This one still predates *Deep Throat* by at least a year, but it's already a more accomplished and witty film than its famous successor.

Michael J. Bowen's informative liner notes explain that both films got considerable play on both coasts and were part of a deal with none other than drive-in legend Doris Wishman, who herself would go on to lens a couple of raincoaters under a pseudonym. The notes also reveal that, after a handful of additional films, Cemano bowed out of the industry and became a commercial illustrator, though he returns to the scene of the crime for this triple-disc set to talk about his work in no less than two new video interviews, plus an additional archival chat from the cable access show *Midnight Blue.* If that's not enough, you also get new video chats with Angel Spirit and Fred Lincoln (who's already familiar from his appearances on those special editions from *Last House*), who talk about their careers with a lot of enthusiasm and candour, plus a slew of bonus loops featuring Spirit, Reems, Russell, and Sharp. Disc three also includes a "sample West Coast one-day wonder", a far less artful, untitled quickie evidently included to beef up the extra interview footage. In any case, you get way more than your money's worth with this one.

WET WILDERNESS
Colour, 1975, 59m. / Directed by Lee Cooper / Starring Daymon Gerard, Alice Hammer, Raymond North, Faye Little

COME DEADLY
Colour, 1974, 60m. / Directed by Gil Kenston / Starring Kristine Heller, Kirt Jones, June Medusa / After Hours (US R0 NTSC)

Imagine what might happen if someone decided to remake Mario Bava's *Blood and Black Lace* for five dollars after hours in an abandoned New York theatre with a cast of non-actors. Same mask, convoluted *giallo* plot, etc. And then they decided to inject it with graphic sex. Sound weird? You have no idea, and the thing really exists as *Come Deadly*, one-half of this After Hours horror-smut double feature. The plot follows some aspiring actors getting ready to put on a show – in this case, Shakespeare's *The Taming of the Shrew* – while a mad stranger rapist dressed almost exactly like Bava's killer haunts the rafters and attacks the actresses. When a really homely cop decides to go undercover as one of the actors, he seems to spend most of his investigative time banging his shapely co-stars before finally figuring out a way to smoke out the psychopath. The sex scenes are pretty drab and off-putting, but the oddness of the whole enterprise makes it worth a peek. Besides, as far as slasher/porn hybrids go, it's certainly more digestible than, say, *Forced Entry.*

However, the same set's more famous and top-billed co-feature, *Wet Wilderness*, doesn't play nearly so nice. This is one seriously foul little puppy, especially for 1975 as it wedges some really gory slasher murders (machete, axe, etc.) into a "violation in the woods" scenario straight out of *The Last House on the Left.* Four shaggy-looking hippie leftovers are out camping in the woods and take time out to diddle each other, but a drawling loon wearing a yellow-and-black ski mask shows up in time to force two of the girls into some forced lesbianism before finishing one of them off. As the escapee tries to warn everyone in sight, the maniac tracks them all down and forces them into a series of increasingly degenerate compromising positions before the appropriately nasty finale. Lacking the outrageous chutzpah of truly out-there horror smut like *Widow Blue*, this one has little imagination and zero creative merit but might be worth a single look based on sheer geek factor alone. You have been warned. A note for die-hard collectors: *Wet Wilderness* was shown in theatres (and a briefly released VCA tape edition) with a soundtrack brazenly pilfered from studio films like *Psycho* and *Jaws*, a common practice at the time; to avoid getting their pants sued off in these clearance-happy times, the entire audio for the film had to be recreated, which also means new voice overdubs. There isn't much artistic violation going on here, but purists might want to know in advance. In any case, *Come Deadly* is certainly the film you'll feel far less guilty for watching the next morning.

WHITE SLAVE COLLECTION: NAKED AMAZON
B&W, 1954, 86m. / Directed by Zygmunt Sulistrowski / Starring Angela Maria, Jeffrey Mitchell, Andrea Bayard, Richard Olizar

WHITE SLAVE
Colour, 1985, 90m. / Directed by Mario Gariazzo / Starring Elvire Audray, Will Gonzales, Dick Campbell, Andrea Coppola

SACRIFICE OF THE WHITE GODDESS
Colour, 1995, 78m. / Directed by Louis Santana / Starring Lisa Beavers, Francine Chevalier, Steve McKinney / Camp (US R0 NTSC)

This trio of unwholesome, lower-tier jungle outings in the same vein as *Man from Deep River* and its successors contributes a few peculiar footnotes to the history of cannibal cinema. Actually the first film, Brazil's *Naked Amazon* (*Feitiço do Amazonas*), was made in 1954 and precedes all of those Italian films, with its combination of jackass white filmmakers and on-camera animal violence anticipating the likes of the mondo cycle and specifically *Cannibal Holocaust*. The unpleasant "story" concerns four incredibly callous explorers who head into the emerald inferno to find a remote tribe with strange, unexplored customs. Along the way they witness various animal atrocities and even participate in a few. Shot with zero artistry or social consciousness, it's a pretty tough wallow for casual moviegoers but does hold some fascination as a blueprint for the cinematic apocalypse soon to be unleashed in the following decade and a half. The full frame transfer looks like it's framed correctly and features a decent, clear picture despite some obvious film damage and blown-out brightness levels.

Up next is by far the most familiar title in this set, *White Slave*, whose VHS box cluttered up every video store during the 1980s. (Of course, the transfer here looks like it was taken directly from one of those tapes, which is at least good for some nostalgia value.) Undistinguished director Mario Gariazzo (best known for the trashy *Exorcist* rip-off, *The Eerie Midnight Horror Show*) isn't afraid to wallow in the muck here with a seedy story penned by mondo founder Franco Prosperi about Catherine Miles (*Ironmaster*'s Elvire Audray), a blonde vixen who winds up living with a tribe of natives responsible for lopping off her parents' heads. Soon she's bedding the most sensitive tribe member and enlisting his aid in getting back at the ones responsible for destroying her family. Lots of bloodshed and gratuitous nudity ensues. This one features a smattering of the usual animal violence but is considerably sillier than most, which is a welcome relief. The transfer's not so hot (a better anamorphic option is available from Shriek Show under the title *Amazonia: The Catherine Miles Story*, though some of the jungle stock footage still looks like it was shot on Super 8), but considering the bargain deal of this set, it's an okay option for casual viewers.

Last up and certainly least is a much newer amateur oddity entitled *Sacrifice of the White Goddess*, shot on someone's camcorder and, as the opening titles proudly proclaim, inspired by *The Treasure of the Sierra Madre*. Lots of voiceover, video dropouts, cheap tiki-style props, and bad costumes populate this endless trudge through the, ahem, "jungle" as a bespectacled college student named Holly goes to Mexico (represented by some shacks and a rail yard) to hang with the chain-smoking locals, endures some muddy-sounding local music, and finds a machete-wielding guide to take her wading (and wading and wading and wading) through waterfalls and undergrowth with another frequently topless female companion. They finally reach a tribe whose altar consists of some cardboard-looking steps, a fog machine and a big, ugly red chair swiped from a Chinese restaurant. To compensate there's a truly hilarious fantasy scene with a drugged Holly in a sparkly gold dress being served by a bunch of Chippendales dancers, so at least it's not a completely lost cause. A gory heart-ripping appears at the end, too, for anyone who's managed to stay awake that long. The disc also comes with a written appraisal of *Naked Amazon* by Justin Wingenfeld, who traces its roots all the way to our modern mondo-choked pop culture.

WHO CAN KILL A CHILD?

Colour, 1976, 111m. / Directed by Narciso Ibáñez Serrador / Starring Lewis Fiander, Prunella Ransome, Antonio Iranzo / Dark Sky (US R1 NTSC), Bildstörung (Germany R2 PAL), Manga (Spain R2 PAL), Stingray/Nippon (Japan R2 NTSC) / WS (1.85:1) (16:9)

 One-two punches in horror cinema are rare, and only two European directors pulled it off on the big screen perfectly without any other contributions to the genre before or since. In Italy the honour went to Pupi Avati (with *The House with Laughing Windows* and *Zeder*), while Spain's Narciso Ibáñez Serrador delivered a pair of remarkable, still-influential masterpieces, both released in edited versions by American-International Pictures in the 1970s: *The House That Screamed* and the film in question here, *Who Can Kill a Child?*, known in the U.S. (with a fantastic poster design) as *Island of the Damned*. Unfortunately both became extremely difficult to see in the home video era, at least until well into the age of DVD.

After an unsettling opening montage of real-life world atrocities against children (understandably excised from most export prints), the film focuses on the harrowing ordeal of English tourists Tom (musical stage actor Lewis Fiander) and Evelyn (British TV regular Prunella Ransome), who are celebrating the expected arrival of a new baby with a vacation in Spain at an oceanside festival. Despite the disruptive presence of freshly-murdered bodies turning up in the surf, they decide to charter a boat to visit Almanzora, a small nearby island Tom visited long before. Upon arrival they find the area strangely devoid of adults, while the local children prove uncooperative, sinister, and... threatening.

"Bad kid" horror films had certainly existed before, most notably with *The Bad Seed* and *Village of the Damned* (or on a much lower level, *Devil Times Five* and *Wild in the Streets*), but this film upped the ante considerably by depicting the entire child population as coldly homicidal, a terrifying concept American culture didn't adopt until well into the writings of Stephen King. Both of the leads handle their roles exceptionally well (try to watch the English language option on the DVD to fully appreciate them), while Serrador skilfully uses the island atmosphere and pitch-perfect pacing to deliver the shocks when they're most potent. The film follows its nasty thesis all the way to its logical conclusion (which parallels nicely with the almost simultaneous release of David Cronenberg's first feature film, *Shivers*), and along the way numerous indelible situations and images accumulate to provide a potent, gut-churning experience reliant more on mounting terror and suspense than buckets of blood. Underrated composer Waldo de los Ríos (who also contributed equally haunting melodies to *The House That Screamed* and *The Corruption of Chris Miller*) provides a wonderfully effective score using tender lullaby motifs to sparing but chilling effect; this is the only work of his to date fortunate enough to warrant a CD release, but hopefully more will surface in the future.

Dark Sky's DVD salvages this much-discussed but rarely-seen gem from the vaults of AIP, whose rights eventually expired. (Releases appeared on DVD from Japan, Spain and Germany, but they featured lesser transfers and no English-friendly options.) The anamorphic 1.85:1 transfer looks terrific, putting to shame the butchered U.S. prints. The film can be played either with its complete Spanish-language soundtrack (with optional English subtitles) or the preferable English version, which still segues into Spanish (also with subtitles) for a few brief bits never mixed into English, similar to the hybrid language presentations of such past essential DVD releases as *Deep Red* and *Castle of Blood*. Extras include a stills gallery, a newly-created trailer, and two excellent featurettes from Severin Films's David Gregory featuring interviews with Serrador and talented cinematographer José Luis Alcaine. They discuss the tricky location work needed to create the island, the uneven relationships with the actors, the origins of the script and related published novel, and their careers afterwards. Both featurettes preserve the talents of two men who, in a perfect world, would have delivered many more horror masterpieces.

WHO KILLED TEDDY BEAR

B&W, 1965, 94m. / Directed by Joseph Cates / Starring Sal Mineo, Juliet Prowse, Elaine Stritch, Jan Murray, Daniel J. Travanti / Network (UK R0 PAL)

 Brimming with twisted sexual subtext and urban nastiness, this cult item awaiting rediscovery stars Sal Mineo (*Rebel Without a Cause*) as Lawrence Sherman, a nightclub busboy who becomes obsessed with female DJ Norah (Juliet Prowse), so he spends his off hours making obscene phone calls to her while lounging around in his tighty whities. Oh, and he leaves decapitated stuffed teddy bears around for Norah to find too, which understandably creeps her out. Norah's butch boss Marian (played by Broadway legend Elaine Stritch) doesn't make things any easier, and by the time Lawrence manages to talk her out on a date, things go from queasy to downright disturbing.

Never officially released on video in any format before despite a limited theatrical reissue back in the '90s, *Who*

Killed Teddy Bear is one of the most deliciously seedy "mainstream" films made before the new age of late-'60s censorship overhaul. Shot in luminous black and white and loaded with amazing footage of New York's 42nd Street grindhouse scene, this is a real keeper and worth tracking down at any cost. Strand Releasing nabbed the rights for the U.S. but failed to get it out on video, which makes Network's region-free PAL edition the first legitimate version out of the gate. The open matte 1.33:1 transfer shows a few signs of damage here and there, but it's certainly better than the bootlegs that have been floating around. Plus it's completely uncut, containing Sal's eyebrow-raising workout and swimming scenes which were snipped from some prints. (Still, that's nothing compared to the climactic psycho dance routine!) A handful of scenes appear to be sourced in from a softer master, but for the most part it's quite crisp and watchable (and mattes off nicely on widescreen TV sets, too). Two Mineo-related extras are added as well, namely an episode of the '60s World War II program *Court Martial* entitled "The House Where He Lived" (with Sal guest starring) and the amusing anti(?)-drug short, "LSD: Insight or Insanity?", with Sal narrating about the dangers of teens dropping acid. You also get a newly created trailer (God knows if one ever circulated during the film's original brief run) and a pdf of the original press book. And be warned, you'll be humming the theme song for a very long time.

WHY DOES HERR R. RUN AMOK?

Colour, 1970, 88m. / Directed by Rainer Werner Fassbinder & Michael Fengler / Starring Kurt Raab, Lilith Ungerer, Irm Hermann, Lilo Pempeit, Hanna Schygulla / Fantoma (US R1 NTSC), Artificial Eye (UK R2 PAL)

The blackest of comedies and most despairing of dramas, *Why Does Herr R. Run Amok? (Warum läuft Herr R. Amok?)* is often cited as the first genuine Rainer Werner Fassbinder masterpiece. Essentially a slice of life portrayal of average family man Herr R. (Kurt Raab), the film walks the viewer through a succession of seemingly mundane events in which he lingers outside various social circles. First seen tagging with some joking co-workers, he never really connects with his wife (Lilith Ungerer) or child, while former school friends, neighbours, and colleagues go about their trivial business, leaving his inner compulsion for order and control increasingly irritated. Eventually his frustrations surface, calmly but horrifically, in a violent outburst that closes the film on a particularly grim note.

A relentless craftsman already fully in control of his cinematic voice, the 25-year-old Fassbinder etches the all-too-familiar events of Herr R. with a startling dramatic precision, captured with a casual, realistic filmic approach leagues away from the colourful, stylised melodramas which formed the latter stages of his career. An actor who manages to evoke uneasiness simply by sitting at a table, Raab is the perfect choice as the protagonist; interestingly, he would run amok far more dramatically six years later as the lead in Fassbinder's *Satan's Brew*, which is basically a sick-joke remake of this film. Future Fassbinder muse Hanna Schygulla also pops up in a nice supporting role as a school friend, and her warm, engaging presence is already a notable standout. Interestingly enough, Fassbinder chose to designate co-writing and co-directing credit to his friend, Michael Fengler,

a status also carried over to their TV movie collaboration the same year, *The Niklashausen Journey*. Most disturbingly, Fengler's son, Amadeus, plays Herr R.'s son without credit.

A key Fassbinder film held off long after the major flood of his masterworks onto DVD, *Herr R.* gets a welcome presentation with Fantoma's excellent new digital transfer maintaining the original 1.33:1 aspect ratio (apparently shot in 16mm) and looking much fresher than past video versions. The Dogme movement comparison on the sleeve is appropriate, as the film is flooded with bright, natural lighting and hard-edged exteriors that look especially crisp and striking here, coupled with Fassbinder's choice to shoot most of the feature in detached medium shots. Note that the opening credits run very tight against the edges of the frame, so some cropping may be visible depending on your monitor's settings. Audio is presented in sharp German mono with optional English subtitles.

The biggest extra is a 1992 video interview with regular Fassbinder cinematographer Dietrich Lohmann (later destined for such Hollywood fare as *Deep Impact* and *Color of Night*), who talks about his collaborations with the tempestuous but undeniably brilliant filmmaker during the early stages of their careers together. Fassbinder scholar James Clark also contributes a nice set of liner notes considering the various themes and questions explored by the film. (Too bad Fantoma couldn't also snag the wild, parodic 2004 short film, "Why Does Herr V. Run Amok?"; it would have made a great extra!)

The same transfer and trailer are available in the U.K. from Artificial Eye as part of their 4-disc "Rainer Werner Fassbinder Volume 1" box set, which also includes *Martha*, *Lola*, and the 1993 documentary about the director, *I Don't Just Want You to Love Me*.

WINSTANLEY

B&W, 1975, 96m. / Directed by Kevin Brownlow / Starring Miles Halliwell, Jerome Willis, Terry Higgins, Phil Oliver / BFI (DVD & Blu-ray, UK R2 PAL/HD), Image (US R1 NTSC)

In the 17th Century, optimistic and very enthusiastic Christian radical Gerrard Winstanley (played by Miles Halliwell) forms a group called the Diggers who establish a commune on public English land. However, the powers that be have already demonstrated in the opening scenes that they don't take kindly to people who veer from state doctrine and often haul the troublemakers off in wagons for a little forcible correction. Parked at Surrey's St. George Hill, the dwellers find their own principles challenged and in many cases completely undermined by what quickly turns into a localised civil war whose influence would linger for generations.

A film so defiantly anti-commercial one can only marvel that it managed to garner any release at all, this earthy, spare, and low-key historical drama existed for many years as a footnote as "that other film" by Kevin Brownlow and Andrew Mollo, the young duo who jolted 1960s audiences with their speculative "what if the Nazis successfully occupied England?" faux-documentary, *It Happened Here*. The same heightened realism carries over here, but otherwise the two films bear virtually nothing in common. However, the advent of home video has given *Winstanley* a second chance with viewers willing to accept the film on its own terms, and seen through contemporary eyes, it holds up quite well as a grit-covered, often stunning bit of cinematic time travel that would probably play well on a double bill with Michael Reeves's much more pessimistic but aesthetically similar *Witchfinder General*.

Featuring mostly amateur actors and shot for pocket change collected over a decade, *Winstanley* has a timeless appeal thanks to some incredibly powerful performances (especially Halliwell and, as the story's military antagonist, Jerome Willis) and notably convincing period detail, captured in beautiful monochrome. The film was initially released on DVD as part of the Milestone Collection through Image in the U.S., with a reasonably good transfer that won over many who had never been able to experience the film before. However, the BFI release on DVD and Blu-ray blows it out of the water with a fully restored HD transfer from the original negative source materials (a combination of 16mm and 35mm) that looks absolutely lustrous for much of the running time. The opening sequences depicting the final moments of the last Puritan civil war siege have a rough, documentary style that eventually segues to a much more polished, textured appearance, with some beautiful landscape compositions worthy of a classic painting. The audio is limited to the rough recording process at the time, but the disc preserves it as well as possible. Once again, the Blu-ray in particular is a shining example of how good B&W can look with additional resolution. Extras include a new Brownlow and Mollo interview clocking in a bit over half an hour (with some good info about the real-life activists and commune dwellers used in the film), an early 1962 Brownlow short called "9 Dalmuir West... a Record of the Last Weekend of the Glasgow Trams", a quick restoration demonstration, and an extensive 47-minute making-of documentary, "It Happened Here Again" (also on the prior American DVD), completed by director Eric Mival a year after *Winstanley* with extensive coverage of the film's genesis and budget-impaired production process, much of it captured in colour footage that will disorient anyone fresh off the main feature. The thick 32-page booklet features liner notes by Mival, Jonathan Rosenbaum, Tom Milne, Marina Lewycka, and David Robinson.

THE WITCHING HOUR

Colour, 2006, 106m. / Directed by Francois Merlin (Eric Anderson) / Starring Yann Joseph, Gilles Landucci, Ulrich Waselinck, Alexandre Guégan, Nicolas Tary, Nicolas Verdoux / Redemption (US R0 NTSC) / DD2.0

 If nothing else, *The Witching Hour* proves that desperate Quentin Tarantino knock-offs didn't die in the late '90s; they just migrated over to France. This particular 'homage' kicks off with a spastic fight sequence in front of a *Kill Bill* poster (really) and proceeds to ape the structure of *From Dusk Till Dawn* by setting up a crime thriller packed with stupid jokes and then morphing into a gory monster fest. Unfortunately it also proves once again that the true value of this type of film lies in the teller, not the tale. Setting the tone of what's the come, the opening of the film delivers about 3000 edits as it introduces a parade of unappealing, low-life thugs who spend their time hacking away at menial jobs and getting into trouble at night. Various text displays on the screen state random bios for each of them, but since the actors don't seem interested in creating actual characters and most of them die by the halfway point anyway, who cares? The point is, they all get called together by some gangster to go steal a rare jewel being held at a super-secure building. Unfortunately this jewel is the property of a powerful demon who, as some cartoon exposition explains, controls a bevy of nutso goth witches, each with a different superpower. Oh, and the building also houses a clan of cannibals who re-enact *Mother's Day* for about ten minutes for no discernible reason. Throats get slashed, chainsaws get pulled out, witches and Gen-X jerks fight it out for half an hour, and the viewer eventually contemplates suicide, or at least downing a dozen Tylenols.

Shot on video and relentlessly edited into a visual mush, *The Witching Hour* strives for an adrenaline-pumping pace akin to recent action and horror hits but comes off like a more splattery version of *Underworld* on a five dollar budget. The frenetic editing never achieves anything resembling a coherent rhythm, instead keeping each shot under two seconds lest anyone stop and think about the sheer incoherence of what they're watching. On the positive side, as mentioned before there's an avalanche of gore in the second half which might make this play adequately as video wallpaper at a party with the sound turned off. Unfortunately you'll have to turn off the subtitles, too, since the script tries to go for "hip" humour, most painfully with one jackass who views himself as a comedian and spouts jokes the film itself terms "unfunny". Of course, this doesn't stop the character from jabbering idiocy about underage Nazi concentration camp victims (how shocking! how trendy!) ad nauseam, which just makes you pray for his death even harder.

Redemption has certainly done God's work (or in their case, Satan's work) to enrich the lives of horror fans with hidden gems they might have otherwise missed; however, *The Witching Hour* won't win over many new fans for director Francois Merlin, who's outed on the packaging as Eric Anderson, director of the ridiculous French slasher film, *I Am the Ripper*. That said, Redemption's DVD does what it can, starting with the full frame transfer which varies wildly depending on the lighting conditions. The video used in its production never looks close to slick or glossy; most dark scenes are swarming with grain and extremely murky. Even those who can't speak a word of French beyond "merci" will be able to tell the acting makes the worst Jess Franco film seem like an Actor's Studio demonstration in comparison, and the optional, awkward English subtitles were written without much care or feeling for the translation. Extras include a French video trailer, a small photo gallery, 20 minutes of deleted and extended footage (yes, there's even more, despite the fact that the film already drags on for an unbelievable 106 minutes), plus the usual Redemption cross-promoting trailers and book promo.

WOMEN BEHIND BARS

Colour, 1975, 75m. / Directed by Jess Franco / Starring Lina Romay, Martine Stedil, Nathalie Chape, Roger Darton, Jess Franco / Blue Underground (US R0 NTSC), X-Rated Kult (Germany R2 PAL) / WS (2.35:1) (16:9)

Bound to surprise viewers expecting a typical Franco torture-fest like *Barbed Wire Dolls* or *Ilsa the Wicked Warden*, this mixture of crime film and prison ordeal has the director's regular muse Lina Romay doing something a bit different as Shirley, a voluptuous vixen caught in the middle of a diamond heist which culminates in the shooting of her boyfriend. When she winds up in the slammer, Shirley attracts the attention of various shady parties interested in locating the loot, and she's the only one alive who knows its location. Though Shirley goes through her share of trials behind bars, that's just the beginning as twist upon twist leads to the big double-cross finale.

Fast-paced, smartly plotted and sprinkled with just enough skin and violence to please the drive-in crowd, this is actually a good intro to Franco's prison style and holds up better than the soggy *99 Women*. Franco's scope framing really doesn't look like anyone else's, and once again his love for jungle settings pays off during the last third. Blue Underground's DVD sports a terrific 16x9 transfer, a decent enough English dub track (with another dreamy Daniel White score), a subtitled French trailer, and of course, another terrifically entertaining Franco interview in which he talks about his personal fondness for the film, working with Linda during that period, his own onscreen role as a pistol-wielding crook, and its place in his women-in-prison pantheon.

Franco completists with a working knowledge of French or German might also find some value in X-Rated Kult's Region 2 release, *Frauengefängnis 3*, which features a similar transfer (in English, French, or German with no subtitles) and different extras including the alternative French credits, a German trailer, photo and promo galleries, an additional trailer for *Angel of Death 2*, and a different Franco interview (in French language only) which finds him commenting about the film while watching it on a TV monitor.

WOMEN IN PRISON TRIPLE FEATURE:
THE HOT BOX

Colour, 1971, 85m. / Directed by Joe Viola / Starring Margaret Markov, Laurie Rose, Carmen Argenziano, Rickey Richardson / Retro Shock-O-Rama (US R0 NTSC)

WOMEN IN CELL BLOCK 7

Colour, 1973, 99m. / Directed by Rino Di Silvestro / Starring Anita Strindberg, Eva Czemerys, Jenny Tamburi, Umberto Raho / Retro Shock-O-Rama (US R0 NTSC)

ESCAPE FROM HELL

Colour, 1980, 93m. / Directed by Edoardo Mulargia / Starring Ajita Wilson, Anthony Steffen, Cristina Lay, Luciano Pigozzi / Retro Shock-O-Rama (US R0 NTSC), Troma (US R0 NTSC), X-Rated Kult (Germany R2 PAL) / WS (1.85:1)

Nothing personifies sleaze quite like a women-in-prison film, and newcomers and pros alike can rub their faces down in the muck with all three of the offerings in this Retro Shock-O-Rama set. The biggie here is definitely *The Hot Box*, a New World drive-in favourite (from back when Roger Corman was running the company). At the time, fledgling filmmaker Jonathan Demme was involved in several of Roger's offerings (and would go on to helm one of the best WIP films of all time, *Caged Heat*), but here you can see him building his chops as producer and co-writer for the tale of four sexy nurses just asking for trouble when they go abroad to a shady jungle nation where they wind up in "a tropical torture chamber where anything can happen." What that really means is they're enlisted into involuntary medical service by a bunch of revolutionaries and naturally wind up firing off a few rounds themselves before the last reel unspools, along with providing the obligatory topless shots when things threaten to slow down. The "prison" angle here is questionable to say the least, but it's nice to finally have this long-unavailable title back in circulation again.

Women in Cell Block 7 (not to be confused with Jess Franco's much nastier *Women in Cellblock 9* just around the corner) offers a more traditional take on babes behind bars, this time courtesy of director Rino Di Silvestro (best known for *Werewolf Woman*) who piles on the sleaze as busty Hilda (*giallo* and sexploitation vet Anita Strindberg) goes undercover in a prison to clear the name of her mobster father, who's actually an undercover agent. Or something like that; the muddled dubbing and parallel storylines never quite hash that whole angle out very clearly. Anyway, she soon discovers the joys of body searches, long hot showers, hairy prison guards and Sapphic experimentation. A frequent drive-in mainstay for years (under alternative titles like *Love and Death in a Women's Prison*, *Hell Prison*, and many more), this is presented here in its first-run U.S. version (running for 99 minutes as opposed to the truncated 81-minute second-bill version), which is obviously altered considerably from the Italian original with dubbed voiceovers patching up some of the storyline and library tracks filling in for the jettisoned original score by Franco Bixio. It's certainly an amusing and entertaining example of early '70s prison fare mixed with more gangster mayhem than usual, not to mention a really, really downbeat ending that cribs from the earlier *Cometogether* and *Oasis of Fear.*

Last up is *Escape from Hell*, a perplexing release that's earned a few fans in recent years after decades of theatrical anonymity. Previously available as a stand-alone DVD from Troma, it's an Amazon-set yarn with a mix of Italian and Spanish faces behind and in front of the camera (including spaghetti western director Eduardo Mulargia) churning out the degenerate story of a jungle prison camp where the women are relentlessly abused by their new warden, eventually enlisting the aid of the hard-drinking doctor (*The Night Evelyn Came Out of the Grave*'s Anthony Steffen) to help them overcome their captors. Yeah, that's pretty much it for story, but the curiosity factor here lies mainly in the cast, led by the infamous Ajita Wilson (whose gender history is already the stuff of legend), and Luciano Pigozzi, beloved everywhere as

Pag from *Yor, the Hunter from the Future*. Loads of nudity and abuse make this the most typical entry of the bunch, and even if you already have the Troma DVD version, the extra two films make it worth another peek. A letterboxed (1.85:1, non-anamorphic) but slightly shortened Region 2 German DVD was also released by X-Rated Kult as *Die Schwarze Nymphomanin 3. Teil*, which trims the original opening (added elsewhere as an extra) and features English and German audio options. Transfers for all three are unspectacular to say the least (*The Hot Box* fares best, relatively speaking, but it's not a huge leap over an old VHS tape); *Cell Block* is the weakest thanks to very obvious cropping and squeezing in the frame that make it a bit of an eyesore. Still, if you're in an undemanding mood and want hours and hours of pure, undiluted '70s female prison mayhem, this should be just the ticket.

WOODCHIPPER MASSACRE

Colour, 1989, 82m. / Directed by Jon McBride / Starring Jon McBride, Denice Edeal, Tom Casiello, Patricia McBride / Camp (US R0 NTSC)

Following the modest home video success of his incredibly gory debut *Cannibal Campout*, homegrown director Jon McBride returned the next year with a puzzling sophomore effort. Despite the title, *Woodchipper Massacre* avoids bloodshed in favour of attempted dark comedy. Yes, a couple of people do wind up in the titular machine, but it's all done offscreen and played for yucks, which probably isn't what the target audience expected. Basically it's another one of those kids-kill-and-no-one-believes-it stories as three siblings – Jon (McBride), Denise (Denice Edeal) and Tommy (Tom Casiello) – knock off their overbearing aunt (played by the director's mom), then are forced to slay again when their inventive body disposal sends more people sniffing around.

Rambling, goofy, and pretty inexplicable, *Woodchipper Massacre* would probably never be seen in today's video climate; angry renters would most likely start chucking copies at the windows of video stores if its show-no-gore stripes were exposed now. However, it somehow managed to become a mainstay on many shelves near the end of the '80s, and its portrait of bored Connecticut kids cutting up in front of the camera has a certain horrid fascination if you're in the right frame of mind. As with its companion film, this was actually shot on VHS and still looks it, with obvious dropouts and some tape wear visible at the bottom of the screen; however, the transfer is still crisper than the old tape version, and it's hard to imagine it looking much better. The low-fi audio is also about on par with what you'd expect from an '80s camcorder. Again McBride chips in with an ingratiating commentary track covering all the details ranging from the cast to the intentions behind the film, which helps explain why he took the approach he did. Also included are an on-camera interview with McBride and a new featurette with the various actors, all of which make you admire the chutzpah behind its creation even if the finished result can wear on the nerves pretty quickly. The usual trailers are included along with a gallery and an insert containing brief notes by McBride.

THE WORLD SINKS EXCEPT JAPAN

Colour, 2006, 98m. / Directed by Minoru Kawasaki / Starring Kenji Kohashi, Shuuji Kashiwabara, Masatoshi Matsuo, Takenori Murano / Synapse (US R1 NTSC) / WS (1.85:1) (16:9) / DD2.0

The most well-known title from prankster director Minoru Kawasaki (*Executive Koala*, *The Rug Cop*), *The World Sinks Except Japan* (*Nihon igai zenbu chinbotsu*) features a title which immediately gives away its intentions as a disaster movie spoof riffing on films like *The Submersion of Japan*, known to English-speaking audiences as *Tidal Wave*. Surprisingly ambitious and subversive, the film charts the aftermath which ensues when tectonic shifts result in one continent after another dropping into the ocean, with survivors flooding into the still-standing Japan.

Not surprisingly, the culture clash which ensues provides a lot of sharp-toothed humour, with Americans getting the lion's share of the ribbing (which is appropriate given how much filmmakers like Michael Bay and Roland Emmerich seem to think the U.S. is the only capable nation on the planet). The special effects themselves are fine, though certainly not up to the levels of a big-budget CGI fest, but that's hardly the issue considering the film's bigger satiric targets. Certainly not a movie for all tastes, it's nevertheless engaging and thought-provoking for viewers who are in the right frame of mind and worth a peek.

Along with the high-grade anamorphic transfer, Synapse's DVD is the most elaborate of their three Kawasaki releases as the extras consist of a director's commentary along with actor Takenori Murano, a 40-minute making-of featurette, a cast and crew intro, and a trailer and TV spot. It's fun seeing Kawasaki at work, and his restrained but impish personality only begins to indicate the wild visions which unfold in front of his camera with each project.

THE X-FILES: I WANT TO BELIEVE

Colour, 2008, 108m. / Directed by Chris Carter / Starring David Duchovny, Gillian Anderson, Amanda Peet, Billy Connolly, Xzibit, Mitch Pileggi / Fox (DVD & Blu-ray, UK R2 PAL/HD, US R1 NTSC/HD) / WS (2.35:1) (16:9) / DD5.1, DTS5.1

When an FBI agent goes missing in the snowy countryside after being abducted from her car, a former priest (Billy Connolly) who weeps tears of blood psychically leads the feds to a spot where they find what appears to be her severed arm. The mysterious trail of clues leads the FBI to approach Agent Scully (Gillian Anderson), a doctor now entangled in the ethically tricky terrain of using experimental medicine to treat afflicted children, and then her former partner, Mulder (David Duchovny), now a bearded recluse. The two re-team and investigate with the questionable assistance of the priest, a convicted paedophile now living in a complex consisting of sexual offenders. Multiple plot strands all point to medical supplies being bought by a mysterious enclave where various body parts are being assembled and replaced for a purpose only gradually revealed.

A lot of good ideas are rattling around inside this second feature successor to the popular television series, but that's the main problem. Any one of the plot threads would have made a perfectly good one-hour episode, but all smashed together, none of them quite resolve in a satisfactory manner. Questions of faith, altruism, penance, and devotion are bandied about by all the characters and even fuel the entire motivation of the main villains, but much of the film spins its wheels courtesy of charisma-free performances by Amanda

X

Peet and Xzibit, both cast as feds whose presence becomes an irritation after a few minutes. Duchovny and Anderson still reveal flickers of their old chemistry, but the script constantly conspires to separate them for the vast majority of the running time. On the positive side, the body part shenanigans yield some memorably creepy moments involving talking severed heads and snowy car wrecks resulting in limb amputations; also, a late-arriving appearance by Mitch Pileggi is surprisingly effective and will cause series fans to perk up with delight. Connolly also scores some affecting moments as the anguished man of the cloth whose heavily compromised morality raises some challenging questions the movie only halfway begins to answer, and it also pulls a few jolting surprises like a mid-film character demise obviously designed to throw off anyone who puts value in star billing.

Fox's DVD and Blu-ray editions contain an extended director's cut, which tacks on four additional minutes of exposition and grotesqueries as well as some ill-advised production shots over the end credits. Image and sound quality are both exceptional and virtually flawless, clearly designed for home theatre enthusiasts to show off their HD sets and sound systems. Extras include impassioned picture-in-picture and audio commentaries with director and series creator Chris Carter and Frank Spotnitz (who point out some ideas that fly by barely noticed in the actual feature), an excellent interactive timeline of the series studded with video clips illustrating the overarching structure of the narrative mythology, a dossier allowing users to create their own profile, a featurette on the (thankfully old school) special effects, an isolated score track, some deleted scenes and bloopers, a dispensable Xzibit music video for "Dying 2 Live", galleries of stills and production art, trailers, and a variety of alternative interactive commentary and image snippets on the Blu-ray edition only. Though the main feature itself may be obviously compromised, it's still a hefty package designed to leave fans satisfied nonetheless after suffering withdrawal from one of the most memorable sci-fi/horror franchises of the '90s.

ZOMBIE BLOODBATH

Colour, 1993, 70m. / Directed by Todd Sheets / Starring Chris Harris, Auggi Alvarez, Frank Dunlay

ZOMBIE BLOODBATH 2: RAGE OF THE UNDEAD

Colour, 1995, 98m. / Directed by Todd Sheets / Starring Dave Miller, Kathleen McSweeney, Gena Fischer

ZOMBIE BLOODBATH 3: ZOMBIE ARMAGEDDON

Colour, 2000, 90m. / Directed by Todd Sheets / Starring Abe Dyer, Curtis Spencer, Blake Washer / Camp (US R0 NTSC)

 Though it wasn't officially part of the '80s DIY shot-on-video horror cycle, Todd Sheets's "epic" *Zombie Bloodbath* series (made over the course of seven years) has the same look, feel and charm of those down-home gems all the same. Lots of mullets and bad facial hair star in these films, with the first instalment using that old standby, an ancient Indian burial ground which becomes desecrated by the construction of a nuclear power plant. Not surprisingly, the dead start popping up all over the place and adding to their legions, with lots of intestines and fake blood sloshing across the screen. Zesty, technically inept, poorly acted and very, very red, it's... well, you know, one of those movies you can't possibly defend, but it still satisfies much in the same way as a late night Big Mac.

Then it's more of the same with *Zombie Bloodbath 2: Rage of the Undead*, with a remote farmhouse containing a grisly secret – namely a cursed scarecrow capable of reviving the dead. Naturally, it does so after some criminals off the farmhouse's owner. Lots of people in the vicinity get mauled, and it's up to some local college kids to save the day. Finally, the most brain-dead instalment, *Zombie Bloodbath 3: Zombie Armageddon*, pits a bunch of high school kids against an army of undead flesh eaters being created in the basement(?) as part of a secret government plan. Oh, and everyone's named after a horror director (thanks so much, Joe Dante!). Super cheap, these films betray their public access-level origins at every turn in their digital incarnations courtesy of the fine folks at Camp Motion Pictures; don't expect much more than VHS quality here, but that's okay. The films and extras are spread out over two discs, with Sheets and his son adding commentaries for the first two films and some rambling making-of featurettes for each, an utterly perplexing Sheets bonus short called "Dead Things", and additional Camp trailers. You could probably make these exact same films with a bunch of butcher's scraps, Karo syrup and a few good buddies, but thanks to this set, now you don't have to.

Z

INDEX TO DVD DELIRIUM VOLUME 4

CONTENTS -
THE COMPLETE LIST OF FILMS REVIEWED IN DEPTH IN VOLUME 1:

E LIVING DEAD, HEMOGLOBIN (BLEEDERS), THE HITCHER, HOLLYWOOD CHAINSAW HOOKERS, HORROR EXPRESS, HORROR
OSPITAL, HORRORS OF SPIDER ISLAND, HOT SUMMER, HOUSE, HOUSE II: THE SECOND STORY, THE HOUSE BY THE CEMETERY,
OUSE OF GAMES, HOUSE OF WHIPCORD, HOUSE OF YES, HOUSE ON HAUNTED HILL, HOUSE ON HAUNTED HILL, THE HOUSE ON
ORORITY ROW, HOUSE ON THE EDGE OF THE PARK, THE HUMAN TORNADO, HUMANOIDS FROM THE DEEP, HYPNOSIS (THE
YPNOTIST), I, A WOMAN, I EAT YOUR SKIN, I KNOW WHERE I'M GOING!, I SAW WHAT YOU DID, I SPIT ON YOUR GRAVE, I STILL KNOW
HAT YOU DID LAST SUMMER, I, ZOMBIE, IDLE HANDS, IGUANA, ILSA, HAREM KEEPER OF THE OIL SHEIKS, ILSA, SHE WOLF OF THE
S, ILSA, THE WICKED WARDEN, IMMORAL TALES, IMMORTAL BELOVED, IMMORTALITY (THE WISDOM OF CROCODILES), IMPULSE,
IE IN CROWD, IN DREAMS, IN SEARCH OF DRACULA, IN THE MOOD FOR LOVE, IN THE MOUTH OF MADNESS, IN THE REALM OF
IE SENSES, IN THE WOODS, INCUBUS, THE INDIAN TOMB, INFERNO, L'INITIATION, INSEMINOID, INTRUDER, THE INTRUDER,
VASION OF THE BLOOD FARMERS, THE INVISIBLE MAN, THE IRREFUTABLE TRUTH ABOUT DEMONS, J.D.'S REVENGE, JACK BE
MBLE, JACK THE RIPPER, JACOB'S LADDER, JAIL BAIT, JAM—N JAM—N, JASON GOES TO HELL: THE FINAL FRIDAY, JAWBREAKER,
WEL OF THE NILE, THE JOHNSONS, JOSIE AND THE PUSSYCATS, JOY HOUSE, JOY RIDE, JURASSIC PARK III, JUST FOR THE HELL
F IT, THE KENTUCKY FRIED MOVIE, KILL, BABY... KILL!, KILLER KLOWNS FROM OUTER SPACE, KING KONG (1976), KISS ME DEADLY,
SS ME MONSTER, KNIGHTRIDERS, KNOCKING ON DEATH'S DOOR, KOLOBOS, KWAIDAN, LABYRINTH, LADY CHATTERLEY, LADY IN
HITE, LADY OF THE LAKE, LAIR OF THE WHITE WORM, LARA CROFT: TOMB RAIDER, THE LAST BROADCAST, THE LAST
EARFIGHTER, LAST TANGO IN PARIS, THE LAST WAVE, LAST YEAR AT MARIENBAD, THE LATHE OF HEAVEN, THE LEGEND OF HELL
OUSE, LET SLEEPING CORPSES LIE (THE LIVING DEAD AT MANCHESTER MORGUE), THE LIBERTINE, LICENCE TO KILL, THE
CKERISH QUARTET, LIFE OF BRIAN, LIPS OF BLOOD, LIQUID SKY, LISA AND THE DEVIL, A LITTLE BIT OF SOUL, LITTLE MOTHER, LIVE
ID LET DIE, LIVE FLESH, THE LIVING DAYLIGHTS, THE LIVING DEAD GIRL, LOLITA, LORD OF ILLUSIONS, LORD OF THE FLIES, THE
OST CONTINENT, LOST HORIZON, LOST IN SPACE, LUST FOR A VAMPIRE, LUST FOR FRANKENSTEIN, M, MABOROSI, MACABRE, THE
AD BUTCHER, MAHLER, THE MAN WITH THE GOLDEN GUN, THE MAN WITH TWO BRAINS, MANHATTAN BABY, MANIAC, MANJI,
ANTIS IN LACE, MARIHUANA, MARNIE, MARTIN, MAY MORNING, THE MEDUSA TOUCH, MEET THE FEEBLES, MEMENTO, MESA OF
OST WOMEN, THE MIGHTY PEKING MAN, MIRANDA, THE MIRROR CRACK'D, MISSISSIPPI MERMAID, MR. SARDONICUS, MR.
MPIRE, MODERN VAMPIRES, MON ONCLE D'AMERIQUE, MONA LISA, MONKEY SHINES, THE MONSTER OF CAMP SUNSHINE,
ONSTERS CRASH THE PAJAMA PARTY, MOONRAKER, THE MOST DANGEROUS GAME, MOTHER'S DAY, MOUNTAIN OF THE
ANNIBAL GOD, MS.45 (ANGEL OF VENGEANCE), THE MUMMY, THE MUMMY'S SHROUD, MUTANT, MY BEST FIEND, MYLENE FARMER:
USIC VIDEOS / MUSIC VIDEOS II & III, NADIE CONOCE A NADIE, THE NAMELESS (LOS SIN NOMBRE), NARCOTIC, NATIONAL
MPOON'S CHRISTMAS VACATION, NATIONAL LAMPOON'S VACATION, NATURAL BORN KILLERS, NEKROMANTIK, NEVER SAY NEVER
GAIN, NEW ROSE HOTEL, THE NEW YORK RIPPER, NIGHT CALLER FROM OUTER SPACE, NIGHT OF THE BLOODY APES, NIGHT OF
IE HUNTED, THE NIGHT OF THE HUNTER, NIGHT OF THE LIVING DEAD, NIGHT OF THE LIVING DEAD, NIGHT OF THE SEAGULLS,
IE NIGHT PORTER, NIGHT TIDE, A NIGHT TO DISMEMBER, NIGHTMARE CITY, NIGHTMARES, NIGHTS OF CABIRIA, NIGHTWATCH,
NTH GATE, NOSFERATU THE VAMPYRE, NOT OF THIS EARTH, NOTORIOUS, NUDE FOR SATAN, OASIS OF THE ZOMBIES,
CTOPUSSY, THE OLD DARK HOUSE, THE OMEN, OMEN IV: THE AWAKENING, ON HER MAJESTY'S SECRET SERVICE, 100 DAYS,
PEN YOUR EYES (ABRE LOS OJOS), THE OPENING OF MISTY BEETHOVEN, OPERA, ORCA THE KILLER WHALE, ORGAN, ORLOFF
ID THE INVISIBLE MAN, ORPHEUS, THE PASSENGER, THE PASSION OF JOAN OF ARC, PECKER, PEEPING TOM, THE PEOPLE THAT
ME FORGOT, PERCY, PERDITA DURANGO, PET SEMATARY, PETEY WHEATSTRAW: THE DEVIL'S SON-IN-LAW, PHANTASM, PHANTOM
THE OPERA, PHANTOM OF THE OPERA, PHANTOM OF THE OPERA, PHANTOM OF THE PARADISE, PHENOMENA, PICNIC AT
ANGING ROCK, PIECES, PIG, THE PILLOW BOOK, PINK FLOYD: THE WALL, PIONEERS IN INGOLSTADT, PIRANHA, PIRATES OF CAPRI,
T AND THE PENDULUM, THE PIT AND THE PENDULUM, PIT STOP, PITCH BLACK, THE PLAGUE OF THE ZOMBIES, PLAN 9 FROM
UTER SPACE, PLANET OF THE APES, PLANET OF THE VAMPIRES, THE PLAYGIRLS AND THE VAMPIRE, P.O. BOX TINTO BRASS,
ISON, POISON IVY, POLA X, PORTRAIT OF JENNIE, POSSESSION, PRACTICAL MAGIC, PREHISTORIC WOMEN, PRETTY AS A
CTURE: THE ART OF DAVID LYNCH, PRINCE OF DARKNESS, THE PRINCESS AND THE CALL GIRL, THE PRISONER, PROPHECY,
YCHIC KILLER, PSYCHO, PSYCHO III, PSYCHOMANIA, PUPPET MASTER, PUPPET MASTER II, PUPPET MASTER III: TOULON'S
VENGE, PUPPET MASTER 4, PUPPET MASTER 5, QUATERMASS AND THE PIT, QUATERMASS AND THE PIT, QUATERMASS II,
JERELLE, QUILLS, RABID, RABID DOGS, RABID GRANNIES, THE RAGE: CARRIE II, RAINBOW BRIDGE, RASPUTIN THE MAD MONK,
VENOUS, RAZOR BLADE SMILE, REBECCA, THE RED SHOES, THE RED VIOLIN, REEFER MADNESS (DOPED YOUTH), REPO MAN,
E REPTILE, REQUIEM FOR A VAMPIRE, RESURRECTION, RETRO PUPPET MASTER, RETURN OF THE EVIL DEAD, RETURN OF THE
DEADLY VENOMS, RETURN OF THE LIVING DEAD 3, RETURN TO OZ, RICHARD KERN: THE HARDCORE COLLECTION, RING, THE
OCKY HORROR PICTURE SHOW, ROLLERBALL, ROMANCE, ROMANCING THE STONE, ROSEMARY'S BABY, ROUGE, THE RULING
ASS, RUN LOLA RUN, RUNNING TIME, SACRED FLESH, SALEM'S LOT, SALOME'S LAST DANCE, SANJURO, SCARS OF DRACULA,
CHIZO, SCHRAMM, SCORE, SCREAM, SCREAM 2, SCREAM 3, THE SCREAMING SKULL, SCUM OF THE EARTH, SECOND SKIN
EGUNDA PIEL), SEE THE SEA, THE SENTINEL, 7 FACES OF DR. LAO, THE 7TH VOYAGE OF SINBAD, SEXTETTE, SHE FREAK, SHE
LLED IN ECSTASY, SHE-DEVILS ON WHEELS, SHEBA, BABY, THE SHINING, SHIVER OF THE VAMPIRES, SHIVERS, SHOCK, SHOCK
AVES, SHOGUN ASSASSIN, SHREK, SILENT NIGHT, BLOODY NIGHT, A SIMPLE PLAN, SINBAD AND THE EYE OF THE TIGER, SIRENS,
STERS, SIX DAYS IN ROSWELL, THE SIXTH SENSE, SKINNER, SLAVE GIRLS FROM BEYOND INFINITY, SLEEPY HOLLOW, THE
IPPER AND THE ROSE, SLUGS, THE SLUMBER PARTY MASSACRE, SMALL SOLDIERS, SOLARIS, SOMEONE TO WATCH OVER ME,
METHING WEIRD, SORORITY HOUSE MASSACRE, SORORITY HOUSE MASSACRE II, SOUTHERN COMFORT, SPACEWAYS,
ELLBOUND, SPIDER BABY, THE SPIRAL STAIRCASE, SPIRITISM, SPIRITS OF THE DEAD, SPLENDOR, THE SPY WHO LOVED ME,
AGEFRIGHT, STARMAN, THE STENDHAL SYNDROME, STOP MAKING SENSE, THE STORY OF O, THE STRAIGHT STORY, STRANGLER
THE SWAMP, STREET TRASH, THE STUFF, SUBCONSCIOUS CRUELTY, SUCCUBUS, SURRENDER DOROTHY, SUSPIRIA, SWAMP
ING, THE SWINGING CHEERLEADERS, SWITCHBLADE SISTERS, TALES OF ORDINARY MADNESS, TALES OF TERROR, A TASTE OF
OOD, TEENAGE MONSTER, THE TEMPEST, TENDER FLESH, TENDERNESS OF THE WOLVES, TENEBRE, THE 10TH VICTIM, TERROR
A MAN, TERROR OF FRANKENSTEIN, TERROR TRACT, TESS, THE TESTAMENT OF DR. MABUSE, THE TESTAMENT OF ORPHEUS,
E TEXAS CHAIN SAW MASSACRE, THE TEXAS CHAINSAW MASSACRE 2, THAT OBSCURE OBJECT OF DESIRE, THEATRE OF BLOOD,
EATRE OF DEATH, THERESE AND ISABELLE, THESIS (TESIS), THEY LIVE, THEY SAVED HITLER'S BRAIN, THE THING, THINGS TO
ME, THE THIRD MAN, 13 GHOSTS, THE 39 STEPS, THIS NIGHT I'LL POSSESS YOUR CORPSE, THE THOUSAND EYES OF DR.
BUSE, THUNDERBALL, TIE ME UP! TIE ME DOWN!, TIERRA, TIGER BAY, THE TIGER OF ESCHNAPUR, THE TIME MACHINE, THE
IGLER, TOKYO DECADENCE, TOKYO DRIFTER, TOMB OF TORTURE, TOMBS OF THE BLIND DEAD, TOMMY, TOMORROW NEVER
MES, TOMORROW NEVER DIES, TOO MUCH FLESH, TORSO, TOUCH OF EVIL, TOURIST TRAP, TOWER OF EVIL, TRADER HORNEE,
E TRIAL, TRILOGY OF TERROR, TURKISH DELIGHT, THE TWILIGHT PEOPLE, TWITCH OF THE DEATH NERVE, TWO DAYS IN THE
LLEY, TWO LANE BLACKTOP, 2001: A SPACE ODYSSEY, TWO THOUSAND MANIACS!, TWO UNDERCOVER ANGELS, THE UGLY, THE
BEARABLE LIGHTNESS OF BEING, UNBREAKABLE, THE UNDERTAKER AND HIS PALS, UP!, VALENTINE, VALERIE, VAMPIRES, THE
MPIRES' NIGHT ORGY, VAMPYRES, VAMPYROS LESBOS, THE VANISHING, VELVET GOLDMINE, VENGEANCE, THE VENGEANCE OF
E, VENUS IN FURS, VERTIGO, VERY BAD THINGS, VIBRATION, VIDEODROME, A VIEW TO A KILL, THE VIKING QUEEN, THE VIRGIN
ICIDES, VIY (THE VIJ), THE VOYEUR, WATER DROPS ON BURNING ROCKS, WHAT EVER HAPPENED TO AUNT ALICE?, WHAT HAVE
EY DONE TO YOUR DAUGHTERS?, WHEN A STRANGER CALLS, THE WHIP AND THE BODY, WHITE ZOMBIE, WHITY, THE WICKER
N, WILD THINGS, THE WITCHES, THE WIZARD OF GORE, THE WOLF MAN, THE WOLVES OF KROMER, THE WOMAN IN BLACK,
OMEN IN REVOLT, WONDERWALL, THE WORLD IS NOT ENOUGH, WOYZECK, X - THE MAN WITH THE X-RAY EYES, X THE UNKNOWN,
000: THE FILMS OF FRANÇOIS OZON, YELLOW SUBMARINE, YOJIMBO, YOU ONLY LIVE TWICE, YOUNG FRANKENSTEIN,
CHARIAH, A ZED AND TWO NOUGHTS, ZEDER, ZETA ONE, ZOMBIE FLESH-EATERS (ZOMBIE), ZOMBIE LAKE.

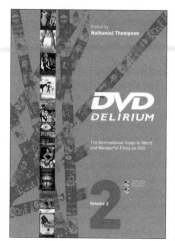

CONTENTS -

THE COMPLETE LIST OF FILMS REVIEWED IN DEPTH IN VOLUME 2

CONTENTS -

ALAXY, THE HORROR OF PARTY BEACH, THE HOUSE OF FEAR, HOUSE OF WAX, HOUSE ON BARE OUNTAIN, THE HOUSE WHERE EVIL DWELLS, HOW TO KILL A JUDGE, HULK, HUSTLE, I AM THE RIPPER, IF OU WERE YOUNG: RAGE, IMAGES IN A CONVENT, IN A YEAR WITH 13 MOONS, IN THE SOUP, THE HERITANCE, INSERTS, INUGAMI, INVASION OF THE BEE GIRLS, ISLAND OF THE FISHMEN, IT'S ALIVE, IT VES AGAIN, IT'S ALIVE III: ISLAND OF THE ALIVE, THE JACKET, JOE, KANTO WANDERER, KARATE FOR LIFE, ATIEBIRD* CERTIFIABLE CRAZY PERSON, KICHIKU, KILINK ISTANBUL'DA, KILINK STRIP & KILL, KILINK VS. UPERMAN, THE KILLER MUST KILL AGAIN, THE KILLING CLUB, THE KILLING OF A CHINESE BOOKIE, KING ONG (1933), KISS ME QUICK, LADY EMANUELLE, LADY SNOWBLOOD, LADY TERMINATOR, LARA CROFT: OMB RAIDER: THE CRADLE OF LIFE, THE LAS VEGAS SERIAL KILLER, THE LEAGUE OF EXTRAORDINARY ENTLEMEN, LEGEND OF THE EIGHT SAMURAI, LEMORA: A CHILD'S TALE OF THE SUPERNATURAL, LES CHIC 972), LES CHIC (2002), LET ME DIE A WOMAN, LIFEGUARD, LIFESPAN, THE LITTLE GIRL WHO LIVES DOWN HE LANE, LIVING DOLL, LONG WEEKEND, THE LOST BOYS, LOVE AT THE TOP, LOVE RITES, THE LOVELESS, HE LOWER DEPTHS (1936), THE LOWER DEPTHS (1957), MACHINE-GUN KELLY, MAD DOCTOR OF BLOOD LAND, MADE IN BRITAIN, MAGIC, MA"TRESSE, MAMMA ROMA, A MAN CALLED MAGNUM, THE MAN FROM EEP RIVER (DEEP RIVER SAVAGES), THE MAN WHO LAUGHS, MANIACAL, MANIACTS, THE MANITOU, THE ANSION OF MADNESS, THE MANSON FAMILY, MARK OF THE DEVIL, MATANGO, MIDNIGHT BLUE OLLECTION VOLUME 1: THE DEEP THROAT SPECIAL EDITION, MIDNIGHT BLUE COLLECTION VOLUME 2: ORN STARS OF THE 70'S, MIDNIGHT BLUE COLLECTION VOLUME 3: CELEBRITIES EDITION, MILL OF THE TONE WOMEN, MIRROR MIRROR, MIRROR MIRROR 2: RAVEN DANCE, MIRROR MIRROR 3: THE VOYEUR, IRROR MIRROR 4: REFLECTIONS, MOTORCYCLE GANG, THE MURDER IN THE RED BARN, MURDER SHE AID, MURDER AT THE GALLOP, MURDER MOST FOUL, MURDER AHOY, MY NAME IS NOBODY, MY OWN RIVATE IDAHO, THE MYSTERIANS, NAIL GUN MASSACRE, NEON NIGHTS, NIGHT AND THE CITY, THE NIGHT VELYN CAME OUT OF THE GRAVE, NIGHT TRAIN MURDERS, NIGHTMARES COME AT NIGHT, 9 SOULS, 99 OMEN, LE NOTTI BIANCHE, THE OBLONG BOX, THE OFFENCE, OLDBOY, OLGA'S GIRLS, THE OMEGA MAN, NE DEADLY SUMMER (L'ÉTÉ MEURTRIER), ONE FROM THE HEART, ONIBABA, OPEN WATER, OPENING GHT, THE ORACLE, THE OTHER, PANIC BEATS, THE PEARL OF DEATH, PENETRATION ANGST, PHONE OOTH, PHOTOGRAPHING FAIRIES, PICKUP ON SOUTH STREET, PINOCCHIO 964, PIRATES OF THE ARIBBEAN: THE CURSE OF THE BLACK PEARL, THE PLEASURE PARTY, THE POOL (SWIMMING POOL: DER OD FEIERT MIT), PRETTY POISON, PREY, PRIME CUT, PRISON HEAT, PROMISES! PROMISES!, PURSUIT TO GIERS, QUARTET, QUICKSAND, THE RAILROAD MAN, RED COCKROACHES, THE RED QUEEN KILLS SEVEN MES, RED SILK, REFORM SCHOOL GIRL, REFORM SCHOOL GIRLS, REVENGERS TRAGEDY, ROADRACERS, OBINSON CRUSOE, ROCK ALL NIGHT, ROCK & RULE, ROJO SANGRE, ROOTS OF EVIL, RUBBER'S LOVER, UDE BOY, RUN VIRGIN RUN, RUNAWAY DAUGHTERS, SALVATORE GIULIANO, SATANICO PANDEMONIUM, TAN'S BLACK WEDDING, SATAN'S BLOOD, SAW, THE SCARLET CLAW, SCHOOL OF THE HOLY BEAST, CISSORS, LA SCORTA, SCREAM AND SCREAM AGAIN, SCREAM QUEEN HOT TUB PARTY, SCUM (1977), SCUM 979), SEARCHING FOR THE WRONG-EYED JESUS, SECRETARY, SECRETS OF A CALL GIRL, SECRETS OF A NDMILL GIRL, THE SEDUCTION OF INGA, SEE NO EVIL, THE SENSUOUS NURSE, SEVEN DEATHS IN THE AT'S EYE, SEVEN WOMEN FOR SATAN, SEX AND LUCÍA, SEX NURSE, SHADOWS, SHERLOCK HOLMES AND HE SECRET WEAPON, SHERLOCK HOLMES AND THE VOICE OF TERROR, SHERLOCK HOLMES FACES EATH, SHERLOCK HOLMES IN WASHINGTON, THE SHINING, THE SIGN OF FOUR, SIN CITY, SINGAPORE LING, LA SIRÈNE ROUGE (RED SIREN), SISTER EMANUELLE, SIXTEEN TONGUES, SKY CAPTAIN AND THE ORLD OF TOMORROW, SLACKER, SMITHEREENS, A SNAKE OF JUNE, THE SOLDIER, SORORITY GIRL, PELLBOUND, THE SPIDER WOMAN, SPIDER-MAN 2, SQUIRM, SS CAMP: WOMEN'S HELL, SS EXPERIMENT OVE CAMP, SS GIRLS, THE STAND, STARCRASH, STARSTRUCK, STORY OF A LOVE AFFAIR, STRANGE DAYS, HE STRANGE VICE OF MRS. WARDH, STRAWBERRY ESTATES, STRAY CAT ROCK: SEX HUNTER, STREET W, STREET MOBSTER, STRIP NUDE FOR YOUR KILLER, THE STUDENT OF PRAGUE (1913), THE STUDENT ' PRAGUE (1926), SUGAR COOKIES, SUPERSTITION, SUSPICIOUS RIVER, SWAMP WOMEN, SWANN IN LOVE, VIMMING POOL, SWORD OF DOOM, SYMPATHY FOR MR. VENGEANCE, TAKING LIVES, THE TALENTED MR. PLEY, TALES FROM THE CRYPT: FROM COMIC BOOKS TO TELEVISION!, TARKAN VERSUS THE VIKINGS, STE THE BLOOD OF DRACULA, TEENAGE CAVE MAN, TEOREMA, TERROR AND BLACK LACE (TERROR Y CAJES NEGROS), TERROR BY NIGHT, TEXAS LIGHTNING, THE THREE LIVES OF THOMASINA, 3 NUTS IN ARCH OF A BOLT, THRILLER: A CRUEL PICTURE (THEY CALL HER ONE EYE), THUNDERBIRDS, TIGRERO, E TIN DRUM, TINTORERA, THE TIT AND THE MOON, TITANIC, TOMIE, TOMIE: REPLAY, TOMIE: REBIRTH, NY: ANOTHER DOUBLE GAME, TOOLBOX MURDERS, TOUCH OF DEATH, THE TOXIC AVENGER, TRAILER ASH, TRANCE (DER FAN), TROUBLE MAN, THE TULSE LUPER SUITCASES: THE MOAB STORY, TWIST AND OUT, 2069: A SEX ODYSSEY, THE UGLIEST WOMAN IN THE WORLD, UN DEUX TROIS SOLEIL, THE UNDEAD, E UNDERTOW, UNDERWORLD BEAUTY, UNKNOWN BEYOND, UNO BIANCA, UTOPIA, VALERIE AND HER EEK OF WONDERS, VAMPIRE JUNCTION, VENUS IN FURS, VERNON FLORIDA, VIKING WOMEN AND THE SEA RPENT, VIOLENT MIDNIGHT, THE VIRGIN SPRING, VIRGIN WITCH, VIRGINS FROM HELL, VIRIDIANA, VISITOR VOODOO WOMAN, WALKABOUT, WALLS IN THE CITY, WAR, WARLORDS OF ATLANTIS, WAXWORKS, ELCOME TO ARROW BEACH, WEREWOLVES ON WHEELS, WESTWORLD, A WHISPER IN THE DARK, WHO N KILL A CHILD?, WISCONSIN DEATH TRIP, THE WITCH WHO CAME FROM THE SEA, THE WOMAN IN GREEN, WOMAN UNDER THE INFLUENCE, WOMEN'S PRISON MASSACRE, X-312 FLIGHT TO HELL, YELLOW ANUELLE, YESTERDAY TODAY AND TOMORROW, YOUNG VIOLENT DANGEROUS, YOUR VICE IS A LOCKED OM AND ONLY I HAVE THE KEY, ZAPPA, ZERO FOCUS.

More Essential Cinema Books from FAB Press

Any Gun Can Play
The Essential Guide to
Euro-Westerns

ISBN 978-1-903254-61-5
UK £19.99 / US $34.95

320pp. 254mm x 192mm

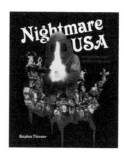

Nightmare USA
The Untold Story of the
Exploitation Independents

ISBN 978-1-903254-52-3
UK £29.99 / US $59.95

528pp. 289mm x 250mm

Blaxploitation Cinema
The Essential
Reference Guide

ISBN 978-1-903254-44-8
UK £14.99 / US $27.95

240pp. 254mm x 192mm

Book of the Dead
The Complete History
of Zombie Cinema

ISBN 978-1-903254-33-2
UK £19.99 / US $29.95

320pp. 254mm x 192mm

The Art of the Nasty

ISBN 978-1-903254-57-8
UK £19.99 / US $34.95

168pp. 295mm x 221mm

Behind the Pink Curtain
The Complete History
of Japanese Sex Cinema

ISBN 978-1-903254-54-7
UK £19.99 / US $34.95

416pp. 254mm x 192mm

For further information about these books visit our online store, where we also have a fine
selection of rare and collectable DVD and soundtrack CD titles from all over the world!

www.fabpress.com